THE WORLD IN FLAMES

A WORLD WAR II SOURCEBOOK

Frans Coetzee

Marilyn Shevin-Coetzee

NEW YORK   OXFORD

OXFORD UNIVERSITY PRESS

2011

Oxford University Press, Inc., publishes works that further Oxford University's
objective of excellence in research, scholarship, and education.

Oxford   New York
Auckland   Cape Town   Dar es Salaam   Hong Kong   Karachi
Kuala Lumpur   Madrid   Melbourne   Mexico City   Nairobi
New Delhi   Shanghai   Taipei   Toronto

With offices in
Argentina   Austria   Brazil   Chile   Czech Republic   France   Greece
Guatemala   Hungary   Italy   Japan   Poland   Portugal   Singapore
South Korea   Switzerland   Thailand   Turkey   Ukraine   Vietnam

Published by Oxford University Press, Inc.
198 Madison Avenue, New York, New York 10016
http://www.oup.com

Oxford is a registered trademark of Oxford University Press

Library of Congress Cataloging-in-Publication Data

The world in flames : a World War II Sourcebook / [edited by]
Frans Coetzee, Marilyn Shevin-Coetzee.—1st ed.
        p. cm.
    Includes bibliographical references and index.
    ISBN 978-0-19-517442-7 (pbk.)—ISBN 978-0-19-517441-0 (hardcover)
1. World War, 1939–1945—Sources.   I. Coetzee, Frans, [date.]   II. Coetzee,
Marilyn Shevin, [date.]
D735.W59   2010
940.53—dc22   2009039605

Printed in the United States of America
on acid-free paper

CONTENTS

INTRODUCTION

World War II was the costliest and most destructive war in history. Estimates of the number of people who died during it range as high as 60 million. Given the war's disruptive impact, those figures can only remain estimates, but the staggering totals conceal another grim fact: unlike previous conflicts, about two-thirds of the dead were not soldiers, but civilians. This reversal reflected the fact that between 1937 and 1945 the world witnessed a total war in which the line between combatants and noncombatants was erased by aerial bombing, artillery shelling, harsh occupation policies, and genocidal mass murder. Waged with an unremitting brutality fueled by racial prejudice, ideological polarization, justifiable outrage, and retributive vindictiveness, and abetted by technological innovation and unprecedented industrial mobilization, the war claimed lives from six continents and raged across the skies, the world's great oceans, and climes as diverse as arid deserts, steamy jungles, and frozen steppes.

Within these broad outlines, the war embodied a number of different stories. One was the massive and multifaceted change it stimulated. The conflict began with cavalry charges and biplanes and ended with jets, rockets, and nuclear weapons. It began with a powerful Germany the dominant power in central Europe and concluded with that state divided, its two halves grappling with what they had done together in a now discredited past and what they might do apart in an uncertain future. Some aspects of wartime change were more obviously beneficial, as in the new opportunities it brought to people formerly constrained by old assumptions and prejudices. Whether social and racial barriers were breached for good, or whether they were destined to reappear once peace returned and the atmosphere of national emergency faded, was a story whose conclusion was yet to be written by 1945. Another story involved the moral dimensions of a war that brought us both the term *genocide* and the clearest practical demonstration to date of its virulent impact, not to mention the wholesale slaughter of civilians, on the ground and from the air, as militaries sought to impose their will with greater force and over wider space than ever before. A third story, less dramatic, reflected continuity in the efforts of many people to preserve as familiar and normal a life under the circumstances as possible. Not even war-torn Russian towns or Pacific islands were the scenes of constant fighting, and seven European states, from Ireland to Vatican City, remained neutral. The continental United States, insulated in either direction from the fighting by two oceans, could maintain at least some of the rhythms of ordinary life. Many more such stories are embedded within the war, too many to allude to here, but can one identify a few guidelines as a realistic point of departure in the journey to comprehend what the war was all about?

"Of making many books there is no end," goes the biblical injunction (Ecclesiastes 12:12), and that certainly holds true for World War II. Despite that profusion of publications, no single one can hope to capture every aspect of the conflict, merely those themes that were most significant. This book is organized around a careful, representative selection of primary sources, whose proximity to the events they describe gives them a vividness and immediacy that only the best secondary accounts can match. They need to be read critically, of course, and understood in context, and the editorial introductions are intended to provide the necessary background and alert the reader to particular points of interest.

A good example of what the sources can yield is the pamphlet *Read This Alone and the War Can Be Won*, prepared by the Japanese Army's Headquarters Staff and distributed by the thousands to the troops. Intended to persuade soldiers of the necessity to fight, to uphold the expectations held by their countrymen, and to exploit the unfamiliarity of their "Western" opponents with a different and challenging environment, the pamphlet elucidated the Japanese leadership's strong sense of mission in 1941. It was a compound of specific economic grievances (Western imperialist exploitation, punitive trade embargoes) with a more generalized sense that the European powers had habitually acted toward Japan in a condescending or dismissive way that could no longer be tolerated. That very combination bred both a resentment and fatalism that leap from the pages of *Read This Alone* and enable one to appreciate how difficult it would have been to put aside such attitudes and work to avert the outbreak of war. Moreover, the pamphlet sharply contrasts the masculine, martial spirit of its Japanese audience with the effemininity of the Westerners, and suggests that the qualitative superiority of Japanese fighting men would enable them to triumph over a quantitatively superior enemy. Thus, this selection helps us to understand why the Pacific War spread to include the United States, why it was fought with such ferocity, and why the Japanese persisted in such dogged resistance after the eventual outcome was no longer in doubt.

It is especially important to grasp the war as a global phenomenon; American readers, for example, may not realize that the United States did not figure even in the top ten among countries' war dead. Leading that macabre roll call was the Soviet Union (roughly 25 million dead), China (11 million), Germany (7 million), Poland (6 million), and Japan (roughly 2 million). Some 295,000 Americans died in the war. In his *No Simple Victory*, the historian Norman Davies has devised a figure of "man-months" (one soldier employed in a campaign for one month) to measure and compare, however crudely, where the fighting was the heaviest. His calculations reinforce what serious students of the war have known: the struggle between Germany and the Soviet Union on the eastern front dwarfed all other campaigns (406 million man-months, with post–D-day operations registering the next highest total in Europe at 16.5 million). This book seeks to do justice to the geographic breadth and thematic scope of the war, to illustrate what it meant to be involved in it, whether you were a tank commander near Kursk, a partisan in Yugoslavia, a soldier in Burma, a marine on Peleliu, or a civilian in Hamburg or Long Beach. The war's impact did not cease when the guns fell silent, however, and the book concludes by exploring its legacy and the ways in which it has passed into popular memory.

In preparing this book, we have incurred a number of debts that is now our pleasure to repay. We would like to thank Peter Coveney, who had the foresight and courage to take on the earliest version of this project, Brian Wheel for his wise advice and good judgment in overseeing the successive versions, and Laura Lancaster and Thomas Pold for their skill in shepherding the book to its completion. Our gratitude also extends to the following reviewers whose comments and suggestions were extremely helpful: James C. Bradford, Texas A&M University; Michael Gannon, University of Florida; Allison Gilmore, Ohio State University; Mark P. Gingerich, Ohio Wesleyan University; Paul Jankowski, Brandeis University; John Long, Roanoke College; Mark Parillo, Kansas State University; Phillip Payne, St. Bonaventure University; Jeff Roberts, Tennessee Technological University; Adam Seipp, Texas A&M University; Leonard V. Smith, Oberlin College; and Jane Karoline Vieth, Michigan State University. Thanks go as well to our cousin Richard Becker for providing us with the picture of the World War II memorial. Although none of our parents lived to see this volume in print, their memories and experiences of the war helped to inspire us to prepare this book. Finally, our daughter Michelle always provided a shining light of compassion and optimism as we struggled to write about an era where all too often darkness prevailed.

CHAPTER 1

SEEDS OF TURMOIL

JAPAN'S ASSAULT ON CHINA   As their comrades look on, Japanese soldiers bayonet
Chinese prisoners in a trench.
Source: © Bettmann/CORBIS.

When, after World War I's conclusion in November 1918, the victorious Allies met
to discuss the outlines of formal peace treaties, the idealists among them hoped
that the massive conflict they had just fought would prove to be "the war to end all wars."
Surely no responsible statesman, after four years of unprecedented carnage, in which the
casualties and costs of the war mounted with appalling speed, would have risked another

war. Certainly, few civilians would have supported it. Little more than a decade later, however, Japan's 1931 incursion into Manchuria dimmed hopes for a lasting peace. They were dashed for good after hostilities erupted in Abyssinia (today's Ethiopia), China, Spain, and then Poland.

Why were the idealists so wrong, and why did the international situation remain so unsettled after 1918? A major reason is that the Great War (as awestruck contemporaries would dub it) disrupted much but settled little. The superiority of defensive firepower and mobilization of millions of conscripts had made it difficult for the generals to secure quick, overwhelming victories. It encouraged them to adopt strategies of attrition in which civilian production and morale were as crucial to victory or defeat in "total war" as events at the front. With the stakes thus raised, the consequences of defeat were all the greater. It is no accident that four defeated empires—the Austro-Hungarian, German, Ottoman, and Russian—ultimately crumbled in the face of military reversals and political revolution. A number of smaller successor states emerged, especially in eastern Europe, but the diplomatic stability and balance of power upon which nineteenth-century statesmen had depended could not be conjured anew from the wreckage of the old system. Political instability was compounded by economic instability, given the enormous costs of the war, the liquidation of many assets, and the post-1918 ravages of inflation and depression. Attempts to stabilize the situation by instituting a League of Nations and a policy of collective security foundered on the continued absence from the League of two indispensable great powers, the United States and (until 1934) the Soviet Union.

Although the end of the war brought an overwhelming sense of relief, few countries were satisfied with the eventual peace settlements. Italy and Japan both had ended World War I on the winning side, yet neither believed it was accorded the respect or awarded the territorial gains to which being a victor (in however limited a capacity) entitled it. In both cases, the countries sought to redress the situation by resorting to aggression in the 1930s. Italy's leader, Benito Mussolini, persistently recalled the glorious imperial heritage of ancient Rome and affirmed his intention to restore Italy to a position of comparable influence and grandeur. He began in northeastern Africa by attacking independent Abyssinia and thumbed his nose at the subsequent widespread international condemnation. Japan saw little reason why it, a latecomer to imperial expansion, could not act in the same imperious, self-interested way as older, established expansionist powers such as Britain and the United States had habitually done. Some of its leaders were determined to extend Japanese power, whether at the expense of the Chinese or at the cost of greater friction with the West. Only by tapping additional territory and resources in East Asia, the military and political elite believed, could the small Japanese islands compete with the other great powers. Because Burma, the Dutch East Indies, Indochina, Malaya, and the Philippines were the colonial preserves of European powers or the United States, the obvious first target was China.

Japanese expansionism within China was facilitated by several factors. Political authority in China was severely fragmented, for not only were there nationalist and communist factions at odds with each other, but the persistence of a number of influential but unpredictable warlords further complicated the situation. After its defeat of Russia in 1905, Japan exercised influence in Manchuria, to which it added additional privileges formerly held by Germany and relinquished after its defeat in 1918. Furthermore, political authority in Japan was also fragmented. Japan's Kwantung Army, which since 1906 had protected Japanese interests on China's Kwantung Peninsula, was staffed by zealously expansionist officers who were only loosely supervised by the civilian government in Tokyo. In practice, then, they enjoyed the latitude to stir things up on their own, and they could usually count on a sympathetic response from high-ranking military officials who were willing to condone local violations of existing treaties and other anti-Chinese initiatives. The most serious such violation occurred in September 1931 when Kwantung Army junior officers detonated explosives near a Japanese railway in Mukden, Manchuria, and blamed Chinese dissidents for the attack. The Japanese military claimed it needed to move in to restore order and undertook a full-scale occupation of Manchuria. A year later, in 1932, the Japanese set up the territory as the nominally sovereign but puppet state of Manchukuo, its resources and population to be exploited for the benefit of the Japanese military.

The "incident" at Mukden and subsequent creation of Manchukuo marked the beginning, rather than the end, of Sino-Japanese hostilities. Over the next six years, a fragmented China tried to organize regionally based military resistance to Japanese incursions and to secure diplomatic assistance from foreign powers to pressure the Japanese to withdraw. In 1937, tensions over another incident at the Marco Polo Bridge near Peking provided extremists within the Japanese military with the pretext they sought to escalate the situation into a full-fledged Sino-Japanese War. Others counseled caution: the Japanese navy opposed the allocation of scarce resources to an arduous land campaign (which would leave less money available for its own needs), and more cautious elements in the army worried that open war against China, with a size and population that dwarfed Japan's, would prove to be a mistake (one reason why the Japanese continued to refer to the war that erupted as the "China Incident"). In the end, cooler heads did not prevail. Although the League of Nations condemned Japanese actions, it never moved beyond a verbal response and refused to authorize sanctions or military retaliation. Of course, the League consistently failed to act in the face of provocation, no matter where the dispute, but its Eurocentric basis reinforced its members' conviction that tensions in the Pacific generally, and specifically where they involved China and Japan, were more a matter for the United States to police.

To the Europeans, the most dangerous of the revisionist powers seeking to undo what tenuous international stability had been achieved after 1918 was Germany. Because the war ended without invading armies having carried the fighting to German soil, unrepentant German ultranationalists peddled the notion that the armies had not actually been defeated, but that the country had been "stabbed in the back" by traitorous pacifists, communists, and Jewish interests. Moreover, this preposterous line of argument intersected with the superficially more tenable one that the Allies had dictated an illegitimate, unreasonably harsh peace settlement at Versailles that attributed to Germany the sole responsibility for the war's outbreak and burdened it with reparations payments as a result. This imaginatively reversed roles. Germany, whose bellicose militarism and fatalistic support for an aggressive solution to tensions in the summer of 1914 had been instrumental in provoking the war, was now cast as a victim. Such a stance appealed to disoriented

German civilians buffeted by political revolution, civil unrest in the streets, and economic dislocation.

More appealing still would be any individual who could erase the humiliation of a dictated peace and restore a sense of national pride in a rejuvenated Germany. Adolf Hitler rose to prominence by promising to do just that. He repudiated the provisions of Versailles that limited Germany's army (to a mere 100,000 men and denied it crucial weapons such as tanks or submarines), restored a military presence in sections of the Rhineland that had been demilitarized to provide a peaceful buffer zone along the border with France, and, most ominously, "purified" the German polity by purging it of allegedly non-patriotic and non-Aryan elements. In practice, this meant that Hitler and his Nazi Party espoused a vicious anti-Semitic, antisocialist, and anticommunist rhetoric that identified numerous internal enemies of the state, while the party's paramilitary wing (the Sturmabteilung, abbreviated *SA*) used violence to eliminate opponents and squelch dissent.

It is true that in the elections of the late 1920s and early 1930s, the Nazis failed to win a majority of the popular vote, but they succeeded in establishing themselves as the largest party and therefore indispensable in any solution to a political crisis deepened by the onset of the Great Depression. When Hitler was appointed chancellor in January 1933, other politicians hoped to manipulate him and use the votes he controlled to secure a traditionalist conservative regime. Within a few months, it would be painfully apparent how badly they had misjudged him. The ruthless Hitler, guided by a remorseless view of inevitable racial struggle, was in no mood to compromise or do someone else's bidding. He saw enemies everywhere and insisted that only a deadly combination of internal repression and foreign expansion could guarantee the long-term survival of a German empire (as a "thousand-year Reich").

The overall situation in the mid-1930s offered Hitler opportunities to pursue his revisionist agenda. The principal guarantors of the European status quo, Britain and France, had both suffered grievously during the First World War, and neither their statesmen nor their voters appeared ready to condone military action to preserve the Versailles settlement. Indeed, a decade or more after the treaties, opinion was more widespread that the provisions had been too harsh, and the Germans could count on a measure of sympathy for some limited modifications, thus affording Hitler some crucial initial leeway. In particular, the fact that the border configurations of the new states in eastern Europe had been drawn in ways that excluded numbers of ethnic Germans from their national homeland offered a tempting opportunity to argue that the borders must be redrawn in Germany's favor. Furthermore, given the Soviet Union's consolidation of the Bolshevik Revolution, Hitler's avowedly anti-Marxist regime took on an added luster as a possible bulwark against the westward spread of communism. It also inclined some otherwise percipient observers to overlook the fact that Hitler was not a traditional statesman seeking merely a more advantageous position for Germany within a continental balance-of-power.

After all, the interwar period was dominated by pervasive ideological polarization. The experience of the war had administered a sharp challenge to notions of individual responsibility (and political liberalism) while seemingly elevating attitudes of collective organization (state control) and group identities. Fascism and communism both extolled the importance of collective organization, and denied that there could be any role in between or outside these great blocs for isolated individuals. If any event symbolized to interwar Europeans this clash of ideologies, it was the Spanish Civil War in 1936–1937.

The conflict in Spain, between the coalition of labor and commercial interests that supported a fledgling republic and the military and conservative elites that sought to crush it, was rooted in domestic affairs, but it had international repercussions. Mussolini and Hitler both provided military equipment and support to fellow fascist General Franco, and Stalin reciprocated with Soviet assistance to the republicans. The conflict remained a brutal civil war, in which, for the most part, Spaniard fought Spaniard, but there was an emerging sense of indirect war, waged by proxy, in which states at the extremes of the political spectrum were willing to intervene in a weaker country's internal affairs, while those in the middle (notably Britain and France) chose not to get directly involved.

Certainly the conclusion Hitler drew from international affairs in the early 1930s is that the League of Nations would not stand in the way of his efforts to redraw the map of central Europe to Germany's advantage. His initial moves, to reintroduce conscription in 1935 and remilitarize the Rhineland in 1936, directly and provocatively repudiated the Versailles settlement, but could be excused as the legitimate actions of a sovereign nation state reclaiming its "normal" place among other states. Germany's subsequent ventures, however, clearly violated the sovereignty of other states: these actions included a union (*Anschluss*) with formerly independent Austria and demands that Czechoslovakia cede crucial territory to Germany. In each case, the justification was the right of ethnic Germans (and the territory they inhabited) to be incorporated within German borders. Although Europe teetered on the brink of war in September 1938 over the Czech crisis, Neville Chamberlain's conciliatory policy of appeasement acceded to German demands, averted an immediate conflict, and created, so Chamberlain thought and the otherwise reluctant French hoped, a permanent and final territorial settlement.

They were mistaken. In the spring of 1939, Hitler calculated—correctly—that he could overrun the remainder of Czechoslovakia without League interference. Britain and France responded to this egregious violation by guaranteeing the integrity of Germany's eastern neighbor, Poland, saying, in effect, that enough was enough. Hitler judged that if Britain and France had refused to stand by their previous obligations to the Czechs, who boasted a well-equipped army and formidable defenses, there was little reason to take the latest guarantees seriously, for Poland would be much harder to defend. A stunning nonaggression treaty negotiated with the Soviet Union in August 1939 (in which, secretly, the two countries agreed to divide Poland) neutralized the one power that could have helped Poland defend itself and opened the door to Germany's eastward expansion. On September 1, 1939, German troops crossed the Polish border, and two days later, Britain and France responded by declaring war. Two decades after the peacemakers had met, both Asia and Europe were now once again seared by conflict.

MUSSOLINI AND THE MASSES

With the March on Rome in 1922, Benito Mussolini and his Fascist Party rapidly rose to power in Italy. Although initially appointed by Italy's King Victor Emmanuel as prime minister to stem the tide of anarchism plaguing the country, Mussolini used both legitimate and other means to obtain dictatorial powers by 1925–1926. Mussolini's skillful manipulation of the media (press, radio, education, films) enabled him to consolidate his control over Italian society. Known as "Il Duce" (the leader), Mussolini was determined to restore Italy's prominence in world affairs. In 1932 the dictator published "What Is Fascism?" in which he sought to explain the meaning of his movement. In late March and early April of that same year, journalist and popular author Emil Ludwig interviewed the colorful dictator with the intention of creating a psychological portrait. Ludwig published his conversations in Italian and German only after Mussolini gave his approval. Born Emil Cohn in Breslau, Germany, in 1881, Emil Ludwig originally studied law but decided upon writing as his life profession. During the First World War, Ludwig worked as a journalist for a German newspaper and in the 1920s began writing popular, well-received biographies of famous historical and literary figures, including Goethe, Napoleon Bonaparte, Otto von Bismarck, German emperor Wilhelm II, Hitler, and Stalin. His conversations with Mussolini are revealing on the lesser importance accorded to race in Italian discussion and the emphasis on mass mobilization as a matter of faith that made fascist politics volatile. That volatility, the "enthusiasm for war" that a master politician could cultivate, would pose a challenge for the old elites who sought to contain these political upstarts and preserve peace by traditional diplomatic means.

But if nationalism be independent of forms of government, and also of questions of class, then it must also be independent of questions of race. Do you really believe, as some ethnologists contend, that there are still pure races in Europe? Do you believe that racial unity is a requisite guarantee for vigorous nationalist aspirations? Are you not exposed to the danger that the apologists of Fascism will...talk the same nonsense about the Latin races as northern pedants have talked about the "noble blonds," and thereby increase rival pugnacities?

Mussolini grew animated, for this is a matter upon, owing no doubt to the exaggeration of some of the Fascists, he feels he is likely to be misunderstood.

"Of course there are no pure races left; not even the Jews have kept their blood unmingled. Successful crossings have often promoted the energy and the beauty of a nation. Race! It is a feeling, not a reality; ninety-five per cent., at least, is feeling."...

"...[Y]ou have written harsh words about the masses; you have declared that His Holiness the People must be dragged down from His altar. There was another time, if I remember aright, when you said, 'We do not believe that the crowd can reveal any mystery to us.' But if the masses give you no revelation,

Emil Ludwig, *Talks with Mussolini* (Boston: Little, Brown & Company, 1933), 69, 119–123, 126–127. Used by permission.

how can they have any effect on you? Without mutuality, I cannot conceive of any exchange of influence between one man and twenty thousand. Fascism has been defined as an expansion and a tension. Can you expect these from the masses? And how long will such emotions last?"

Mussolini leaned back into the shadows; and, as the chains and the orders he wore ceased to glitter, I once more discerned the thinker of whom I was in search. The subdued ardour which radiates from him in his strong moments made itself felt. He seemed to be pondering some generalisation that would serve in place of a direct answer, for there was a pause before he slowly began to explain his thought.

"For the masses are nothing but a herd of sheep, so long as they are unorganised. I am nowise antagonistic to them. All that I deny is that they are capable of ruling themselves. But if you would lead them, you must guide them by two reins, enthusiasm and interest. He who uses one only of these reins is in grave danger. The mystical and the political factors condition each other reciprocally. Either without the other is arid, withered, and is stripped of its leaves by the wind. I cannot expect the masses to face the discomforts of life; that is only for the few. Therein will you find the mutuality to which you referred just now. Today I spoke only a few words to those in the Piazza. To-morrow millions will read them, but those who actually stood there have a livelier faith, in what they heard with their ears, and, if I may say so, heard with their eyes. Every speech made to the crowd has a twofold object, to clarify the situation and to suggest something to the masses. This is why speeches made to the people are essential to the arousing of enthusiasm for war."

"Perhaps you are the greatest living expert in this art of influencing the masses," said I. "But what about those who are not bound to the movement by any special interest?"

"They have hopes and the conviction that they are serving a great cause. I have known the masses for thirty years. In Milan I could empty the streets! There, they called me Barbarossa [twelfth-century German king and Holy Roman Emperor, one of the most powerful figures in medieval Europe]."

Never before had I heard Mussolini vaunt any of his achievements; but there was a proud ring in his voice when he spoke the words: "I could empty the streets."

"What part does music play in influencing the masses? What part do women play, and gestures, and emblems?"

"They are all spectacular elements," he replied in the same vibrant tone. "Music and women allure the crowd and make it more pliable. The Roman greeting, songs and formulas, anniversary commemorations, and the like—all are essential to fan the flames of enthusiasm that keeps a movement in being. It was just the same in ancient Rome." ...

"You have told me that you prepare your speeches months in advance. What difference does the sight of the masses make in them?"

"It is like the building of American houses," answered Mussolini. "First of all the skeleton is set up, the steel framework. Then, as circumstances may demand, the framework is filled in with concrete or with tiles or with some more costly material. I already have the girder skeleton ready for my speech at our next October festival. It will be the atmosphere of the Piazza, the eyes and the voices of the thousands who will be present to hear me, which will decide me whether to finish off the edifice with travertin or tiles or marble or concrete—or all of them together."

I was much impressed by this metaphor drawn from his sometime occupation as a mason. Lenin, I said, must have fashioned his speeches in much the same way; and Mussolini extolled Lenin's capacity for disciplining the masses.

"The Fascists," I went on, "talk a great deal about discipline. In Germany, we have had rather too much of it. We have been studying you Italians for the last thirty years and are afraid that your shoulders are not strong enough for the burden. Discipline may make you less happy and perhaps deprive you of your charm."

This pricked him and he turned vigorously from the defensive to the offensive.

"You may say that you have had too much discipline in your own land, but let me tell you, though we are not trying to transform Italy into a replica of pre-war Prussia, we want to make our country as strongly disciplined as was yours. Our conception of the nation is synthetic, not analytic. One who marches in step with others is not thereby diminished, as you and your friends are fond of saying; he is multiplied by all those who move shoulder to shoulder with him. Here, as in Russia, we are advocates of the collective significance of life and we wish to develop this at the cost of individualism....

"You wrote once that the masses ought not to know, but to believe. Do you still regard this principle of the Jesuits as practicable to-day, amid all the advances of modern technique?" He set his jaw resolutely as he answered:

"It is faith that moves mountains, not reason. Reason is a tool, but it can never be the motive force of the crowd. Today less than ever. To-day people have not so much time to think as they used to have. The capacity of the modern man for faith is illimitable. When the masses are like wax in my hands, when I stir their faith, or when I mingle with them and am almost crushed by them, I feel myself to be a part of them. All the same, there persists in me a certain feeling of aversion, like that which the modeller feels for the clay he is moulding. Does not the sculptor sometimes smash his block of marble into fragments because he cannot shape it to represent the vision he has conceived? Now and then this crude matter rebels against the creator!"

After a pause he went on:

"Everything turns upon one's ability to control the masses like an artist."

ABYSSINIA'S PLIGHT

In December 1934, eager to expand his colonial base and with it Italy's prominence, Benito Mussolini accused Abyssinia of aggression and used his troops in the Italian-occupied colony of neighboring Eritrea to provoke an incident with Abyssinia. Convinced of the League of Nations' inertia, and in abrogation of a twenty-year friendship treaty signed between Abyssinia and Italy in 1928, Mussolini ultimately ordered Italian troops to invade Abyssinia in October 1935. Haile Selassie (1891–1975), who acceded to Abyssinia's throne in 1930, realized that his poorly equipped army was no match for the Italian. A mere six months later in March 1936, Abyssinian troops were defeated and the emperor was forced into exile in the United Kingdom, where he remained until the British were able to reclaim Abyssinia in May 1941. Haile Selassie addressed the League of Nations (to which his nation had belonged since 1923) in Geneva on June 30, 1936. Although evoking sympathy from many countries, the emperor's speech failed to produce a political solution and demonstrated the League's ineffectiveness in the face of aggression.

Haile Selassie, Appeal to the League of Nations, www.mtholyoke.edu/acad/intrel/selassie.htm. Used by permission.

I, Haile Selassie I, Emperor of Ethiopia, am here today to claim that justice which is due to my people, and the assistance promised to it eight months ago, when fifty nations asserted that aggression had been committed in violation of international treaties.

There is no precedent for a Head of State himself speaking in this assembly. But there is also no precedent for a people being victim of such injustice and being at present threatened by abandonment to its aggressor. Also, there has never before been an example of any Government proceeding to the systematic extermination of a nation by barbarous means, in violation of the most solemn promises made by the nations of the earth that there should not be used against innocent human beings the terrible poison of harmful gases. It is to defend a people struggling for its age-old independence that the head of the Ethiopian Empire has come to Geneva to fulfil this supreme duty, after having himself fought at the head of his armies....

For 20 years past...I have never ceased to use all my efforts to bring my country the benefits of civilization, and in particular to establish relations of good neighbourliness with adjacent powers. In particular I succeeded in concluding with Italy the Treaty of Friendship of 1928, which absolutely prohibited the resort, under any pretext whatsoever, to force of arms, substituting for force and pressure the conciliation and arbitration on which civilized nations have based international order....

On October 3rd, 1935, the Italian troops invaded my territory. A few hours later only I decreed general mobilization. In my desire to maintain peace I had, following the example of a great country in Europe on the eve of the Great War, caused my troops to withdraw thirty kilometres so as to remove any pretext of provocation.

War then took place in the atrocious conditions which I have laid before the Assembly. In that unequal struggle between a Government commanding more than forty-two million inhabitants, having at its disposal financial, industrial and technical means which enabled it to create unlimited quantities of the most death-dealing weapons, and, on the other hand, a small people of twelve million inhabitants, without arms, without resources having on its side only the justice of its own cause and the promise of the League of Nations....

In December 1935, the Council made it quite clear that its feelings were in harmony with those of hundreds of millions of people who, in all parts of the world, had protested against the proposal to dismember Ethiopia. It was constantly repeated that there was not merely a conflict between the Italian Government and the League of Nations, and that is why I personally refused all proposals to my personal advantage made to me by the Italian Government, if only I would betray my people and the Covenant of the League of Nations. I was defending the cause of all small peoples who are threatened with aggression.

What have become of the promises made to me as long ago as October 1935? I noted with grief, but without surprise that three Powers considered their undertakings under the Covenant as absolutely of no value. Their connections with Italy impelled them to refuse to take any measures whatsoever in order to stop Italian aggression. On the contrary, it was a profound disappointment to me to learn the attitude of a certain Government which, whilst ever protesting its scrupulous attachment to the Covenant, has tirelessly used all its efforts to prevent its observance....

The Ethiopian Government never expected other Governments to shed their soldiers' blood to defend the Covenant when their own immediately personal interests were not at stake. Ethiopian warriors asked only for means to defend themselves. On many occasions I have asked for financial assistance for the purchase of arms. That assistance has been constantly refused me....

I assert that the problem submitted to the Assembly today...is not merely a question of the settlement of Italian aggression.

It is collective security: it is the very existence of the League of Nations. It is the confidence that each State is to place in international treaties. It is the value of promises made to small States that their integrity and their independence shall be respected and ensured. It is the principle of the equality of States on the one hand, or otherwise the obligation laid upon small Powers to accept the bonds of vassalship. In a word, it is international morality that is at stake. Have the signatures appended to a Treaty value only in so far as the signatory Powers have a personal, direct and immediate interest involved?

No subtlety can change the problem or shift the grounds of the discussion. It is in all sincerity that I submit these considerations to the Assembly. At a time when my people are threatened with extermination, when the support of the League may ward off the final blow, may I be allowed to speak with complete frankness, without reticence, in all directness such as is demanded by the rule of equality as between all States Members of the League? Apart from the kingdom of the Lord there is not on this earth any nation that is superior to any other. Should it happen that a strong Government finds it may with impunity destroy a weak people, then the hour strikes for that weak people to appeal to the League of Nations to give its judgment in all freedom. God and history will remember your judgment....

I ask the fifty-two nations, who have given the Ethiopian people a promise to help them in their resistance to the aggressor, what are they willing to do for Ethiopia? And the great Powers who have promised the guarantee of collective security to small States on whom weighs the threat that they may one day suffer the fate of Ethiopia, I ask what measures do you intend to take?

Representatives of the World I have come to Geneva to discharge in your midst the most painful of the duties of the head of a State. What reply shall I have to take back to my people?

SPAIN'S ANGUISH

Between 1936 and 1939, Spain endured a civil war that officially began on July 17–18, 1936. The coup, launched by members of the Spanish military, overthrew the Second Republic that had replaced the monarchy in 1931. The Republic's opponents included members of the military, aristocracy, conservatives, and the Catholic Church, who resented the government's reforms aimed at democratizing and secularizing Spanish society. Hitler's and Mussolini's decision to provide planes to the rebels, whose cause underscored their own antidemocratic and anticommunist thinking, prevented the coup from failing. In September 1936, Franz Borkenau, a sociologist and cultural historian, whose mixed Jewish heritage necessitated his leaving Nazi Germany, went to Spain as an international observer. Over the course of two months, he visited Barcelona, Valencia, Madrid, and other Republican-held areas and returned again in January 1937 for further observation. At that time he was arrested and tortured by Spanish communists before finally being released. Borkenau's eyewitness accounts of the Spanish Civil War were published as *The Spanish Cockpit*, an excerpt from which is reprinted here. It provides a vivid picture of several aspects of modern war, especially the use of airpower against civilians.

Franz Borkenau, *The Spanish Cockpit: An Eye-Witness Account of the Political and Social Conflicts of the Spanish Civil War* (London: Faber & Faber, 1937), 160–165, 216, 222, 225. Used by permission.

[5 September 1936]

...[C]ars and lorries were simply stormed by the inhabitants, a few of whom knew how to drive, and did drive the vehicles away, or if ignorant of driving, forced the drivers at the rifle point to disobey orders, leave the battlefield, and carry off the fugitives. All that naturally in a hullabaloo. Women carrying their babies in their arms, and their cattle at rope-ends; they sobbing, the babies crying; men trying to carry on their arms and backs what small portion of their movable property they could bear away in their haste....Wasn't it a shame that men armed with good rifles, and wearing the proud insignia of the CNT [National Confederation of Labor, an anarcho-syndicalist labor union founded in 1910], were running away like cowards? 'Rifles are no good against bombs and shells,' the fugitives shouted back....

It was only hours later that I found out exactly what had happened. The village had been bombarded throughout the whole morning from the air, and occasionally with artillery fire, too; then there had been the usual break in fighting during the siesta hours, from about one o'clock to half-past three, a ritual observed by both parties throughout the Spanish Civil War; and just when we arrived the bombardment of the village had reopened, and the strained nerves of the inhabitants could stand it no longer. When we entered the village, it offered a sorry sight; all houses deserted; most doors locked; cats, dogs, pigs wandering helplessly in the streets and yards. But the front line, in contrast to the village guard, stood unshattered. The village, in spite of the panic, had suffered very little; nothing was either destroyed or burning....

Suddenly there was a big crash, as near as could possibly be. A bomb had come down a few yards from the Red-Cross station, which was flying the Red-Cross flag in a way impossible to overlook....The enemy bomber, after launching a few bombs farther back in the village, went away, but returned after a few minutes. In the meantime I tried to get to the front line itself, but the fire was now too heavy to pass....It [machine-gun fire] took a nasty turn. First it had been ahead only, but it was clearly approaching from the left flank, across the railway line; a few Moorish [the Moors were Muslim peoples originally from North Africa] machine gunners had turned the flank of the government lines, unopposed. They might enter the village any minute.

Things gradually became unpleasant. If the Moors caught us in our shelter under the railway bank, there would be very little chance to explain that we were neutrals; they would kill us at once. Thus, dangerous as it might be, we had to leave cover, go into the open, and get out of the village as quickly as possible....We slipped from one house to the next during occasional breaks in the firing. Meantime, the bombing continued unchanged. There were two enemy planes now, alternately fetching bombs and bombing the village; they were completely unopposed. There had been talk during lunch of Government aircraft being ordered to come and take part in the fighting, but no Government plane appeared. The bombs were ridiculously inefficient; about 50 per cent. did not explode at all and the rest did very little damage; not a single one of the huts of which this miserable village consisted was burning when the bombardment stopped towards dusk. But the mere fact of standing in continual air bombardment for nearly three hours, unprotected and without aircraft to oppose the bombers, is nerve-shattering. Finally we got out of the village. A few hundred yards outside stood a number of cars and lorries, which, after having evacuated the village, had returned. But the scenes of flight of the afternoon were now repeated, only this time it was not the villagers but the militia from the front line, who went back, singly or in small groups, and forced the cars to drive them away. It was a scene of complete disorder. The officers, the men said, had run away first; why should they stay? One man got into our car, and when I asked him what business he had behind the lines he bluntly replied: "To escape."...

This experience of battle provided a few general observations. The enemy had not had to stand the ordeal of unopposed bombing and I have no means of judging how the Moors would behave in such circumstances. But there is no doubt that they are better soldiers than the militia; not only more courageous, but quicker in moving and seeing their advantage; this was evident in their flanking manoeuvre. Still, their capacities in this respect seemed to be very limited. There is no conceivable reason for their failure finally to attack and storm the village, where they would have found no resistance whatever. Such an attack would have brought them round to the rear of the Government line and would not only have won them the day, and led to the capture of the whole column, but would have meant a shattering blow to the whole Cordova front. Instead, they, and with them the planes, stopped their action at about half-past six; they probably thought that they had done a good day's work, that dusk was approaching, and that this was enough for this time. Moreover, the bombing was utterly incompetent....But it was worse on the Government side. It is difficult to find appropriate words to characterize the conduct of the staff. The officers in the front line lacked even ordinary courage. The village guards had run away, so had the militia, as soon as it found things really unpleasant. Some of the disastrous features of the combat witnessed were obviously due to the incompetence of the staff; and such a degree of incompetence and lack of responsibility must be exceptional. Still, there may be many staffs of inferior quality among the Government forces. And even where staff work is better than at Cerro Muriano, there remain certain disastrous peculiarities of the militia itself. It cannot stand the impact of modern arms, air-raids, and shelling, even from small guns. And it has no conception that a position must never be left without express orders from the command. When the militia runs away, the militiamen individually feel that fate has been against them; they do not feel guilty in the least. If this is not changed, the insurgents will certainly win the war. They have modern war material from abroad. It is neither copious nor good in quality, but it seems to be too much for the militia....

It is difficult to say which side displayed the greater destructive fury in Malaga [February 1937]. I entered through working-class suburbs. A few houses are destroyed by shells from the sea. My first idea was that this was much less terrible than what I had expected. I soon changed my mind. Next comes the fashionable Caleta district. It has been destroyed wholesale, burnt down in the first days by the crowd.

A few hotels are standing, the largest, the Miramar, requisitioned as a hospital; all the rich villas have only their walls left. It is impossible to describe the impression made by such a city of the dead....Ruins, ruins, ruins, some of them still smoking in the dreary rain...at half-past one in the afternoon, just at the closing hour of shops and offices, when large crowds were in the street, nine bombers swept down over the centre of the town; in a few minutes there were, I was told, 260 dead and over 1,000 wounded, men, women and children. At that time the military command in Malaga had not a single scout plane at its disposal. It was a massacre without resistance. The military command moved to a place somewhat out of town. The population never rid itself of the terror inspired by that slaughter....

Other attacks were made along the coast-line and were supported by heavy shelling from three insurgent cruisers. All reports agree that a German cruiser [actually a pocket battleship], the *Graf Spee*, followed the Spanish men-of-war closely in their movements, but the observers were not certain whether she had actually participated in the shelling....The tank attack presents a difficult problem to the student of the Spanish Civil War. How many tanks were there and of what origin? The republicans in a natural desire to explain their defeat by overwhelming forces of the adversary, spoke of about one hundred tanks. No means are available to check the figure, but I am not inclined to trust such figures on such occasions. Anyway, there were numerous tanks, but not concentrated on one sector, rather acting all along the front. One point seems to be well ascertained: they were all, or almost all of them, tanks of the smallest type, with only one machine gun and two men. Reports agree that the manning was German....

Considering the limitations of the type of tanks brought into action by the insurgents, probably the balance of arguments leads to the conclusion that Malaga need not have fallen. At the moment of the catastrophe the impression in the republican camp was that it had been taken by overwhelming forces. But later developments, notably the speedy stopping of the insurgents advance at Motril, proved that had only one of the many factors functioned a little better the disaster might have been avoided....

The militia had lost the habit of running before bombs, light shells, and machine-gun fire. It had stood firm as long as there were no tanks; it ran before this new unexpected arm, which it had not learnt how to oppose. It was a test from which they came out badly.... It was a sign of the inefficiency of the commands and of Spanish troops in general as compared with foreigners. Where the Spaniards had been unable to avert an utter rout, one small international contingent a few days later, at Motril, stopped the advance of the Franco troops swiftly and without much difficulty.

As to the local command, it has certainly not proved up to its task. The root of its inefficiency, in my opinion, lay in its incomprehension of the type of war it was directing.

JAPAN'S OUTLOOK

On December 22, 1938, Japan's prime minister, Prince Fumimaro Konoye (1891–1945), proclaimed the New Order in East Asia. The term itself is chillingly reminiscent of the Nazis' racial-imperialist ambitions in occupied Europe; here the Japanese leader employed it to justify his country's expansionist policies in China and the puppet state of Manchukuo as a legitimate defensive reaction to communist subversion emanating from the Soviet Union and external economic exploitation on the part of the Western powers. It encapsulated the thrust of Japanese policy over the past decade or so. As stated, Konoye's formulation did not explicitly predict further military or economic expansion, but the concept of a particular Japanese responsibility, willingly accepted, as a sort of senior partner for the oversight of China's welfare, would later be extended into the notion of a Greater East Asia Co-Prosperity Sphere to justify Japanese dominion over much of the continent.

The Japanese Government are resolved...to carry on the military operations for the complete extermination of the anti-Japanese Kuomintang Government [Chinese Nationalist Party led by Chiang Kai-shek beginning in 1925], and at the same time to proceed with the work of establishing a New Order in east Asia together with those far-sighted Chinese who share in our ideals and aspirations.

The spirit of renaissance is now sweeping over all parts of China and enthusiasm for reconstruction is mounting ever higher. The Japanese Government desire to make public their basic policy for adjusting the relations between Japan and China in order that their intentions may be thoroughly understood both at home and abroad.

Japan, China and Manchukuo will be united by the common aim of establishing the New Order in East Asia and of realizing the relationship of neighbourly amity, common defence against Communism, and economic cooperation. For that

"Konoye on the New Order in East Asia," in Joyce Lebra, ed., *Japan's Greater East Asia Co-Prosperity Sphere in World War II* (Kuala Lumpur: Oxford University Press, 1975), 68–70. Used by permission.

CHINA AND JAPAN IN THE 1930s

purpose it is necessary first of all that China should cast aside all narrow and prejudiced views belonging to the past and do away with the folly of anti-Japanism and resentment regarding Manchukuo. In other words, Japan frankly desires China to enter of her own will into complete diplomatic relations with Manchukuo.

The existence of the Comintern influence in East Asia cannot be tolerated.... Japan demands, in view of the actual circumstances prevailing in China, that Japanese troops be stationed, as an anti-Communist measure, at specified points...and also that the Inner Mongolian region be designated as a special anti-Communist area.

As regards economic relations between the two countries, Japan does not intend to exercise an economic monopoly in China. Nor does she intend to demand of China to limit the interests of third Powers who grasp the meaning of the New East Asia and are willing to act accordingly. Japan only seeks to render effective the cooperation and collaboration between the two countries. That is to say, Japan demands that China, in accordance with the principle of equality between the two countries, should recognize the freedom of residence and trade on the part of Japanese subjects in the interior of China, with a view to promoting the economic interests of both peoples; and that, in light of the historical and economic relations between the two nations, China should extend to Japan facilities for the development of China's natural resources, especially in the regions of North China and Inner Mongolia.

The above gives the general lines of what Japan demands of China. If the object of Japan in conducting the present vast military campaign be fully understood, it will be plain that what she seeks is neither territory nor indemnity for the costs of military operations. Japan demands only the minimum guarantee needed for the execution by China of her function as a participant in the establishment of the new order.

STATEMENT AT LUSHAN

Chiang Kai-shek (1887–1975), also known as Chiang Chung-cheng, led the Chinese Nationalist government between 1928 and 1949. Born in an eastern coastal province of China to a merchant family, Chiang Kai-shek entered a military training college in Japan at age eighteen and participated in the overthrow of the Chinese Qing dynasty in 1911 and establishment of a republic. Chiang joined the Chinese Nationalist Party (Kuomintang or KMT) founded by Sun Yat-sen, revamped the Chinese military and took over the leadership of the Nationalist Party upon Sun Yat-sen's death. In 1928 he became head of the Nationalist government in Nanjing. Unifying the new Chinese nation meant crushing the warlords in the northern provinces, but suppressing the communists, led by Mao Zedong, with whom he had cooperated until 1927, proved to be much more difficult. In September 1931, the Japanese, capitalizing on Chinese weakness, occupied the Chinese province of Manchuria, claiming it as an independent puppet state. This was the first step in Japan's plan to dominate its rival, China. In July 1937, the Japanese launched a full-scale invasion of China after claiming that Chinese troops at the Marco Polo Bridge near Beijing fired upon Japanese troops. Chiang Kai-shek, who was at the mountain resort of Lushan, popular as an escape from the summertime heat, responded with a defiant statement intended to rally Chinese opinion and elicit international pressure on Japan to cease its aggression and pursue a diplomatic settlement.

As the people of a weak country we have patiently endured a great deal for several years in our efforts to maintain peace. However, we are now faced with a critical situation wherein, in order to perpetuate our nation, we must resist aggression even at the cost of our lives. We cannot make any compromise at the last moment. All must fully recognize the meaning of what we call the critical situation. The Marco Polo Bridge Incident is clearly the result of international, provocative action on the part of the Japanese forces. Six years have passed since we lost our four northeastern provinces (Manchukuo)...and

Chiang Kai-shek, "Statement at Lushan," July 17, 1937, *Political Strategy Prior to Outbreak of War*, U.S. Army Japanese Monograph 144 Pt. 1 (September 1931–January 1940) (Washington, DC: Office of the Chief of Military History, 1952), Appendix 6. Used by permission.

now a clash between our forces and Japanese troops has taken place at the Marco Polo Bridge, which is a gateway to Peiping [the name for Beijing from 1928 to 1949]. Should it be occupied in force by the Japanese invaders, who could say definitely that our old capital, which has continued to thrive for 500 years as a political, cultural and military center in the north, would not become another Mukden [Manchurian incident of 1931 that allowed Japan to set up a puppet government in Manchuria under the name Manchukuo]? If the Peiping of today should become the Mukden of the old days, the China area would likewise follow the fate of the four northeastern provinces. Then who could be sure that Nanking would not become another Peiping? The development of the Marco Polo Bridge Incident is indeed of grave national concern, and whether this incident can be settled is a problem that may decide the fate of our people. Being a weak nation, we should make it a national policy to safeguard peace and not provoke war. However, should we be faced with a national crisis from foreign aggression, we must accept the challenge for the continuance of our national existence, for which we are responsible to our ancestors. Once a war is begun, there will be left no chance for compromise by this weak country of ours. In this eventuality, we should strive to gain a final victory even at the cost of our existence.

Whether the Marco Polo Bridge Incident will develop into an outright war between China and Japan depends entirely upon the attitude of the Japanese Government. Whether we can hope for peace hinges largely upon the action of Japanese troops. Even if the hope for peace lessens, we should still seek settlement of the incident through diplomatic negotiations. For the peaceful settlement of the incident, we must set forth the following four conditions which indicate the last line to be held in the diplomacy of the weaker nations:

1. A settlement must be achieved which does not violate the territorial right and sovereignty of China.
2. No illegal change in the administrative system of the Chicha area will be allowed.
3. Local government officials dispatched from the Central Government, such as Sung Cheyuan, Chairman of the Chicha Administration Committee, should not be replaced under pressure from outside.
4. No restriction can be placed on the present assignment area of the 29th Army.

In short, the Government has already formulated consistent policies and established irrevocable conditions for the settlement of the Marco Polo Bridge Incident, and intends to stand by these conditions. While hoping for peace, we do not seek momentary ease. While increasing preparations for a counteraction, we will never refuse to fight. Once a nationwide resistance is launched, the only way left for us will be its thorough execution at all cost. The Government should face this crisis with special prudence, while the people should prepare themselves resolutely and calmly for the defense of their own country, relying upon national unity and strictly observing discipline and public order at this time of crisis.

RAPE OF NANKING

The Marco Polo Bridge incident was the prelude to an all-out Japanese assault on China. Japanese troops took the crucial Chinese port of Shanghai in November 1937, and one month later made a final assault on Nanking (Nanjing), which had been declared the new capital after Beijing had been captured. By mid-December, Chinese troops could no longer stop the advancing enemy. Japanese soldiers showed no mercy to the city's inhabitants. Over a period of roughly six weeks, they ruthlessly butchered young (including babies) and old men and women and raped females of all ages as if they were engaged in sport. Reportedly 300,000 people were massacred. The savagery with which some Japanese soldiers committed these heinous crimes was a harbinger of the frequent brutality of the Pacific War. If few people anticipated the excesses of presumably well-disciplined Japanese, a group of about twenty Americans and Europeans living in Nanking realized the scope of the horrors being committed and established an "International Safety Zone by declaring a 2.5 square mile area of the city off-limits to the Japanese. Using Red Cross flags, these foreign men (including Germans) did their best to protect Chinese women and men from certain death by Japanese soldiers as the following excerpt demonstrates.

[Reports compiled December 19, 1937]

On December 15 a man came to the University Hospital with a bayonet wound and reported that six Chinese men were taken from the Safety Zone to carry ammunition to Hsiakwan and when they got there the Japanese soldiers bayonetted them all. He however survived....

On the night of December 15 a number of Japanese soldiers entered the University of Nanking buildings at Tao Yuen and raped 30 women on the spot, some by six men....

On the night of December 16 Japanese soldiers forced entrance to two University houses in which Americans are living, smashing the door in one case. Also several American-owned residences temporarily occupied by Chinese University staff frequently and irregularly entered....

Japanese soldiers were found in the house at Shing Yuan 11 of Mr. Borchardt and Mr. Poblo. The house was flying a German flag and had the certificate of the German Embassy. Everything was broken into. The soldiers tried to start the Borchardt's car but stopped when I arrived. However, they took it on December 17....

From a primary school at Wu Tai Shan many women were taken away and raped for the whole night and released the next morning, December 17....

December 18, 4 p.m.,...Japanese soldiers wanted a man's cigarette case and when he hesitated the soldier crashed in the side of his head with a bayonet. The man is now at the University Hospital and is not expected to live....

On December 17 Mr. Rabe reports his house was visited by about 15 Japanese soldiers. Some of them scaled the wall and came in with drawn bayonets,

Shushi Hsu, ed., *Documents of the Nanking Safety Zone* (Shanghai: Kelly & Walsh Ltd., 1939), 28–30, 32–34, 36–37, 40, 42–44. Used by permission.

robbing his sub-manager Mr. Han Siang-lin of his money and some business passports. The money was taken out of his inside pocket of his coat....In spite of Major Nagai's being kind enough to write a big poster forbidding Japanese soldiers to enter Mr. Rabe's house, which poster was stuck on the door of his house, and in spite of the fact that Mr. Rabe is a German subject and has four German Swastika flags flying on his property, two Japanese soldiers came in his at about six o'clock just when Mr. Rabe returned to his home. He found one of the soldiers partly undressed just about to rape a girl. Both these soldiers were ordered to get out and disappeared the same way they came over the wall. A motor car was removed from Mr. Rabe's house against a receipt reading as follows: "I thank you present, Japanese army, K. Sato." A proper receipt which was asked for was refused. Value of motor car $300....

There are about 540 refugees crowded in Nos. 83 and 85 on Canton Road....[T]hose houses have been searched and robbed many many times a day by Japanese soldiers in groups of three to five. Today the soldiers are looting the places mentioned above continually and all the jewelries, money, watches, clothes of any sort are taken away. At present, women of younger ages are forced to go with the soldiers every night who send motor trucks to take them and release them the next morning. More than 30 women and girls have been raped. The women and children are crying all night. Conditions inside the compound are worse than we can describe....

Yesterday it was reported to me that the residence of Mr. Douglas Jenkins, Jr. Third Secretary of Embassy of the U.S.A. had been looted and one of the servants on the place killed. Today at noon I inspected the place, which is at 29 Ma Tai Chieh, and found it as stated. The house was in utter confusion, and the corpse of the servant was in one of the servants' rooms. The other servants had fled, so there is no one on the place now....

[Reports filed December 20, 1937]

On the evening of December 19 about 4:45 p.m. Dr. Bates was called to the house at 16 Ping Tsang Hsiang where Japanese soldiers had a few days previously driven out refugees....They had just finished looting the place and started a fire on the third floor. Dr. Bates tried to put out the fire but it was too late and the whole house burned to the ground.

On December 19 about 6 p.m. in the dark, six Japanese soldiers scaled the garden wall of Mr. Rabe's compound at Siao Tao Yuen. When he pointed his flashlight on one of them, he (the soldier) laid his hand on his pistol, but he soon realized that it would be bad business to shoot a German subject. Mr. Rabe ordered all six of them to go over the top of the wall back to where they came from. They tried to make him open the door for them, but he strictly refused to do them the honor of passing out of the door, because they had come in without his permission....

December 20. Japanese soldiers came several times to Texaco Co. at 209 Chungshan Road and took away bedding, shoes, carpets, and some other furniture and broke a safe and many window glasses. Downstairs Japanese soldiers took away three motor cars from the Ginling Motor Car Co....

December 19, 12 p.m. two Japanese soldiers came to the Rural Leaders' Training School, Room No. 21 intending to rape a woman, but her husband could speak Japanese, so she was saved....

A man who was the owner of a hat store in South City was shot in the chest when Japanese soldiers asked him for money and he gave them all he had and they asked for more and he could not produce it. He came to the University Hospital today, December 20....

Five faculty residences clearly marked with an American flag and with the proclamations of the American Embassy have been entered and looted. One of these houses has been entered again and again and three doors have been smashed in....

HOSSBACH MEMORANDUM

Was the Hossbach Memorandum a blueprint for Hitler's intentions to wage war? The memorandum, actually a collection of notes taken by Hitler's adjutant, Colonel Friedrich Hossbach (1894–1980), during a top-secret meeting in Berlin at the Reich Chancellery on November 5, 1937, and written up five days later, remains a topic of intense debate. The fact is that on that November day, Hitler gathered his top military commanders and foreign minister to outline his sense of Germany's current situation and future direction. The memorandum was introduced at the Nuremberg Trials to substantiate the claim that Germany had premeditated the outbreak of war two years later.

The aim of German policy was to make secure and to preserve the racial community [*Volksmasse*] and to enlarge it. It was therefore a question of space.

The German racial community comprised over 85 million people and, by reason of their number and the narrow limits of habitable space in Europe, it constituted a tightly packed racial core such as was not to be found in any other country and such as implied the right to a greater living space than in the case of other peoples....Instead of increase, sterility was setting in, and in its train disorders of a social character must arise in course of time, since political and ideological ideas remain effective only so long as they furnish the basis for the realization of the essential vital demands of a people. Germany's future was therefore wholly conditional upon the solving of the need for space, and such a solution could be sought, of course, only for a foreseeable period of about one to three generations.

Before turning to the question of solving the need for space, it had to be considered whether a solution holding promise for the future was to be reached by means of autarky or by means of an increased participation in world economy.

AUTARKY

Achievement possible only under strict National Socialist leadership of the State, which is assumed...

A. In the field of raw materials only limited, not total autarky...
B. In the field of food the question of autarky was to be answered by a flat 'No.'...

PARTICIPATION IN WORLD ECONOMY

...The boom in world economy caused by the economic effects of rearmament could never form the basis of a sound economy over a long period, and the latter was impeded above all by the economic disturbances resulting from Bolshevism....The only remedy...lay in the acquisition of greater living space....If, then, we accept the security of our food situation as the principal point at issue, the space needed to ensure it can be sought only in Europe, not, as in the liberal-capitalist view, in the exploitation of colonies. It is not a matter of acquiring population but of gaining space for agricultural use. Moreover, areas producing raw materials can be more usefully sought in Europe, in immediate proximity to the Reich, than

"The Hossbach Memorandum," from J. Noakes and G. Pridham, eds., *Nazism, 1919–1945*, vol. 3 (Exeter: University of Exeter Publications, 2001), 535–536, 538–541, 617–618. Used by permission of University of Exeter Publications.

overseas; the solution thus obtained must suffice for one or two generations.…

Germany's problem could be solved only by the use of force, and this was never without attendant risk. The Silesian campaigns of Frederick the Great [the Prussian monarch attacked Austrian-held Silesia in 1740 in the First Silesian War], Bismarck's wars against Austria and France [campaigns in 1866 and 1870–1871 that had resulted in German unification], had involved unheard-of risk, and the swiftness of Prussian action in 1870 had kept Austria from entering the war. If the resort to force with its attendant risks is accepted as the basis of the following exposition, then there remain still to be answered the questions 'When?' and 'How?' In this matter there were three contingencies…to be dealt with:

CONTINGENCY I: PERIOD 1943–45

After this date only a change for the worse, from our point of view, could be expected.

The equipment of the Army, Navy and Luftwaffe [air force], as well as the formation of the officer corps, was nearly completed. Equipment and armament were modern; in further delay there lay the danger of their obsolescence. In particular, the secrecy of 'special weapons' could not be preserved forever. The recruiting of reserves was limited to current age groups; further drafts from older untrained age groups were no longer available.

Our relative strength would decrease in relation to the rearmament which would by then have been carried out by the rest of the world. If we did not act by 1943–45, any year could, owing to lack of reserves, produce the food crisis, to cope with which the necessary foreign exchange was not available, and this must be regarded as a 'waning point of the regime.' Besides, the world was expecting our attack and was increasing its counter-measures from year to year. It was while the rest of the world was still fencing itself off…that we were obliged to take the offensive.

Nobody knew today what the situation would be in the years 1943–1945. One thing was certain, that we could wait no longer.

On the one hand there was the great Wehrmacht [army], and the necessity of maintaining it at its present level, the ageing of the movement and its leaders;

and on the other, the prospect of a lowering of the standard of living and of a limitation of the birthrate, which left no choice but to act. If the Führer was still living, it was his unalterable determination to solve Germany's problem of space by 1943–45 at the latest. The necessity for action before 1943–45 would arise in contingencies 2 and 3.

CONTINGENCY 2

If internal strife in France should develop into such a domestic crisis as to absorb the French army completely and render it incapable of use for war against Germany, then the time for action against the Czechs would have come.

CONTINGENCY 3

If France should be so embroiled in war with another State that she could not 'proceed' against Germany.

For the improvement of our politico-military position our first objective, in the event of our being embroiled in war, must be to overthrow Czechoslovakia and Austria simultaneously in order to remove the threat to our flank in a possible operation against the West.

If the Czechs were overthrown and a common German-Hungarian frontier achieved, a neutral attitude on the part of Poland could be all the more surely counted upon, in the event of a Franco-German conflict. Our agreements with Poland only retained their force so long as Germany's strength remained unshaken. In the event of German setbacks, Polish action against East Prussia, and possibly against Pomerania and Silesia as well, had to be reckoned with.

Assuming a development of the situation, leading to action on our part as planned, in the years 1943–45, the attitude of France, Britain, Italy, Poland, and Russia could be conjectured as follows:

Actually, the Führer believed that almost certainly Britain, and probably France as well, had already tacitly written off the Czechs and were reconciled to the fact that this question would be cleared upon in due course by Germany. Difficulties connected with the Empire, and the prospect of being once more entangled in a protracted European war, were for Britain decisive reasons against taking part in a war against

Germany. France's attitude would certainly not be uninfluenced by that of Britain. An attack by France without British support, and with the prospect of the offensive being brought to a standstill on our western fortifications, was hardly probable. Nor was a French march through Belgium and Holland without British support to be expected: nor would this course be contemplated by us in the event of a conflict with France, because it would certainly entail the hostility of Britain. It would of course be necessary to maintain a strong defence... on our western frontier during the prosecution of our attack on the Czechs and Austria. And in this connexion it had to be remembered that the defence measures of the Czechs were growing year by year in strength, and that the actual quality of the Austrian army was also steadily increasing. Even though the populations concerned, especially that of Czechoslovakia, were not sparse, the annexation of Czechoslovakia and Austria would mean an acquisition of foodstuffs for 5–6 million people, on the assumption that the compulsory emigration of 2 million people from Czechoslovakia and a million people from Austria was practicable. The incorporation of these two States with Germany meant a substantial advantage from the political-military point of view, because it would mean shorter and better frontiers, the freeing of forces for other purposes, and the possibility of creating new units up to a level of about twelve divisions, that is, one new division per million inhabitants.

Italy was not expected to object to the elimination of the Czechs, but it was not possible at the moment to estimate what her attitude on the Austrian question would be; that depended essentially upon whether the Duce were still alive.

The degree of surprise and the swiftness of our action were decisive factors for Poland's attitude. Poland, with Russia at her rear, will have little inclination to engage in war against a victorious Germany.

Military intervention by Russia must be countered by the swiftness of our operations, but whether such intervention was a practical contingency at all was more than doubtful, in the attitude of Japan.

Should contingency 2, the crippling of France by civil war, occur, the situation thus created by the elimination of our most dangerous opponent must be seized upon, whenever it happened, even as early as 1938.

In the light of past experience, the Führer saw no early end to the hostilities in Spain. If one considered the length of time which Franco's offensives had taken up till now, it was entirely possible that the war would continue another three years. Neither, on the other hand, from the German point of view was a 100 per cent victory for Franco desirable; our interest lay rather in a continuance of the war and in the keeping up of the tension in the Mediterranean. Franco in undisputed possession of the Spanish Peninsula precluded the possibility of any further intervention on the part of the Italians or of their continued occupation of the Balearic Islands. As our interest lay rather on the prolongation of the war in Spain, it must be the immediate aim of our policy to strengthen Italy's rear with a view to her remaining in the Balearics. But the permanent establishment of the Italians on the Balearics would be intolerable both to France and Britain, and might lead to a war of France and England against Italy—a war in which Spain, should she be entirely in the hands of the Whites, might come out on the side of Italy's enemies. The probability of Italy's defeat in such a war was slight, for the road from Germany was open for the supplementing of her raw materials. The Führer pictured the military strategy for Italy thus: on her western frontier with France she would remain on the defensive, and carry on the war with France from Libya against the French North African colonial possessions.

As a landing by Franco-British troops on the coast of Italy could be ruled out, and a French offensive over the Alps against northern Italy would be very difficult and would probably come to a halt before the strong Italian fortifications, the crucial point... of the operations lay in North Africa. The threat to French lines of communication by the Italian Fleet would largely cripple the transportation of forces from North Africa to France, so that France would have only home forces at her disposal on her Italian and German frontiers.

If Germany made use of this war to settle the Czech and Austrian questions, it was to be assumed that Britain, herself at war with Italy, would decide not to act against Germany. Without British support, no warlike action by France against Germany was to be expected.

The time for our attack on the Czechs and Austria must be made dependent on the course of the Anglo-French-Italian war and would not necessarily coincide with the commencement of military operations by these three States. Nor had the Führer in mind military agreements with Italy; he wanted, while retaining his won independence of action, to exploit this favourable situation, which would not occur again, to begin and carry through the campaign against the Czechs. This descent upon the Czechs would have to be carried out with 'lightning speed.'

APPEASEMENT

When Neville Chamberlain (1869–1940) returned from Munich having concluded an agreement with Hitler, he insisted that he was the second British prime minister to return from Germany having secured "peace with honour" (the first being Lord Salisbury at the Congress of Berlin in 1878). In 1938 the word 'appeasement' did not carry the pejorative overtones it has today, and Chamberlain regarded his policy as an attempt by reasonable men to find reasonable solutions that would redress legitimate grievances. In his single-minded search for peace, the British prime minister was guided by his conviction that the British electorate, still seared by the horrors of the First World War, would repudiate any politician who dragged the nation into another war. Moreover, as he explained in a radio broadcast on the eve of Munich, he found it "horrible, fantastic, incredible" that British civilians could be "digging trenches and trying on gas-masks here because of a quarrel in a far-away country between people of whom we know nothing." He conveniently ignored the fact that as he spoke, Prague was hardly further from London than northern Scotland. Another deeper reason for Chamberlain's persistent inability or refusal to see through Hitler's promises may be that his father, the radical politician Joseph Chamberlain, had been despised as a destructive party wrecker (he split the Liberals over Ireland in 1886 and the Conservatives over tariff protection in 1903, earning him the epithet "Constipation Chamberlain," namely, "the big shit we can't get rid of"). Preserving peace in the 1930s, one might speculate, was attractive to Neville as a means of constructing a more positive, constructive legacy that would overshadow the bitter family disappointments of the preceding generation.

On October 3, 1938, the House of Commons met to debate appeasement in the light of the Munich agreement, a debate from which the following three selections are taken. Chamberlain recognized that the immediate threat of war had only subsided, not evaporated, but he defended his record as having laid the foundations for a secure peace. Criticism came both from within Chamberlain's own Conservative Party as well as the opposition Labour Party. Clement Attlee (1883–1967), the leader of the opposition, was frequently underestimated as "a modest man with much to be modest about," but he proved to be a shrewd, tenacious politician who worked effectively as part of a team. When Neville Chamberlain resigned in 1940, Attlee served as deputy prime minister in Winston Churchill's coalition government, and then as prime minister when Churchill's Conservatives were defeated by Labour in the general election of 1945.

Attlee's sharp criticism was echoed on this occasion by the supreme orator of the twentieth century, Winston Churchill (1874–1965). Churchill had been a persistent opponent of appeasement from the outset, and he was especially troubled by the fact that Neville Chamberlain's personal diplomacy with Hitler undermined Britain's efforts at collective security with France and its eastern European alliance partners. With the division of Czechoslovakia (which boasted a fine, well-equipped army), hopes for any meaningful deterrence through collective security lay in ruins. Despite Churchill's rhetorical brilliance and his accuracy in predicting that it was illusory to believe that one could deal with a "peaceable" Hitler, the great British statesman remained, even in the late 1930s, somewhat isolated. He had begun his political career as a Conservative, switched to the Liberals over Joseph Chamberlain's advocacy of tariff protectionism, and then later returned to the Conservative fold. He remained something of a voice in the wilderness: people questioned his loyalty, many remembered that his service during the First World War as First Lord of the Admiralty had been marred by the fiasco of a failed invasion at Gallipoli, and others recalled his extremism in defense of British imperial rule in India. His opportunity would finally come in May 1940 when Neville Chamberlain resigned as prime minister, discredited not just by the collapse of appeasement, but also by the failure of British forces to protect Norway as well. On May 10, 1940, Churchill became prime minister and so was finally positioned to provide Britain, and the free world, the inspirational leadership it would require.

I

Ever since I assumed my present office my main purpose has been to work for the pacification of Europe, for the removal of those suspicions and those animosities which have so long poisoned the air. The path which leads to appeasement is long and bristles with obstacles. The question of Czechoslovakia is the latest and perhaps the most dangerous. Now that we have got past it, I feel that it may be possible to make further progress along the road to sanity.…

In our relations with other countries everything depends upon there being sincerity and good will on both sides. I believe that there is sincerity and good will on both sides in this declaration. That is why to me its significance goes far beyond its actual words. If there is one lesson which we should learn from the events of these last weeks it is this, that lasting peace is not to be obtained by sitting still and waiting for it to come. It requires active, positive efforts to achieve it. No doubt I shall have plenty of critics who will say that I am guilty of facile optimism, and that I should disbelieve every word that is uttered by rulers of other great States in Europe. I am too much of a realist to believe that we are going to achieve our paradise in a day. We have only laid the foundations of peace. The superstructure is not even begun.

II

The events of these last few days constitute one of the greatest diplomatic defeats that this country and France have ever sustained. There can be no doubt that it is a tremendous victory for Herr Hitler. Without firing a shot, by the mere display of military force, he has achieved a dominating position in Europe which Germany failed to win after four years of war. He has overturned the balance of power in Europe. He has destroyed the last fortress of democracy in Eastern Europe which stood in the way of his

---

Neville Chamberlain, *Parliamentary Debates*, House of Commons, 5th series, vol. 339, October 3, 1938. Used by permission.

ambition. He has opened his way to the food, the oil, and the resources which he requires in order to consolidate his military power, and he has successfully defeated and reduced to impotence the forces that might have stood against the rule of violence.

The Prime Minister has given us an account of his actions. Everybody recognizes the great exertions he has made in the cause of peace. When the captain of a ship by disregarding all rules of navigation has gone right off his course and run the ship into great danger, watchers from the shore, naturally impressed with the captain's frantic efforts to try to save something from the shipwreck, cheer him when he comes ashore and even want to give him a testimonial, but there follows an inquiry, and inquest, on the victims, and the question will be asked how the vessel got so far off its course, how and why it was so hazarded. All the faults of seamanship and errors of judgment must be brought to light, and no amount of devotion at the eleventh hour will save that captain from the verdict that he has hazarded his ship through bad seamanship. Parliament is the grand inquest of the British nation, and it is our duty to inquire not alone into the actions of the Prime Minister during the last few days or the last few weeks, but into the whole course of policy which has brought this country into such great danger and such great anxiety.

III

If I do not begin this afternoon by paying the usual, and indeed almost inevitable, tributes to the Prime Minister for his handling of this crisis, it is certainly not from any lack of personal regard. We have always, over a great many years, had very pleasant relations, and I have deeply understood from personal experiences of my own in a similar crisis the stress and strain he has had to bear; but I am sure it is much better to say exactly what we think about public affairs, and this is certainly not the time when it is worth anyone's while to court political popularity....I will, therefore, begin by saying the most unpopular and

most unwelcome thing. I will begin by saying what everybody would like to ignore or forget but which must nevertheless be stated, namely, that we have sustained a total and unmitigated defeat, and that France has suffered even more than we have. The utmost my right hon. Friend the Prime Minister has been able to secure by all his immense exertions, by all the great efforts and mobilization which took place in this country, and by all the anguish and strain through which we have passed in this country, the utmost he has been able to gain for Czechoslovakia in the matters which were in dispute has been that the German dictator, instead of snatching the victuals from the table, has been content to have them served to him course by course.

The Chancellor of the Exchequer [Sir John Simon] said it was the first time Herr Hitler had been made to retract—I think that was the word—in any degree. We really must not waste time after all this long Debate upon the difference between the positions reached at Berchtesgaden [Hitler's Alpine retreat], at Godesberg and at Munich. They can be very simply epitomized, if the House will permit me to vary the metaphor. £1 was demanded at the pistol's point. When it was given, £2 were demanded at the pistol's point. Finally, the dictator consented to take £1 17s 6d and the rest in promises of goodwill for the future.

Now I come to the point, which was mentioned to me just now from some quarters of the House, about the saving of peace. No one has been a more resolute and uncompromising struggler for peace than the Prime Minister. Everyone knows that. Never has there been such intense and undaunted determination to maintain and secure peace. That is quite true. Nevertheless, I am not quite clear why there was so much danger of Great Britain or France being involved in a war with Germany at this juncture if, in fact, they were ready all along to sacrifice Czechoslovakia. The terms which the Prime Minister brought back with him could easily have been agreed, I believe, through the ordinary diplomatic channels at anytime during the summer. And I will say this, that I believe the Czechs, left to themselves and told they were going to get no help from the Western Powers, would have been able to make better terms than they got after all this tremendous perturbation; they could hardly have had worse....

Clement Attlee, *Parliamentary Debates*, House of Commons, 5th series, vol. 339, October 3, 1938. Used by permission.

I have always held the view that the maintenance of peace depends upon the accumulation of deterrents against the aggressor, coupled with a sincere effort to redress grievances. Herr Hitler's victory, like so many of the famous struggles that have governed the fate of the world, was one upon the narrowest of margins....France and Britain together, especially if they had maintained a close contact with Russia,...could have determined the attitude of Poland. Such a combination, prepared at a time when the German dictator was not deeply and irrevocably committed to his new adventure, would, I believe, have given strength to all those forces in Germany which resisted this departure, this new design. They were varying forces—those of a military character which declared that Germany was not ready to undertake a world war, and all that mass of moderate opinion and popular opinion which dreaded war, and some elements of which still have some influence upon the Government....All of these forces, added to the other deterrents which combinations of Powers, great and small, ready to stand firm upon the front of law and for the ordered remedy of grievances, would have formed, might well have been effective. Between submission and immediate war there was this third alternative, which gave a hope not only of peace but of justice. It is quite true that such a policy in order to succeed demanded that Britain should declare straight out and a long time beforehand that she would, with others, join to defend Czechoslovakia against an unprovoked aggression. His Majesty's Government refused to give that guarantee when it would have saved the situation, yet in the end they gave it when it was too late, and now, for the future, they renew it when they have not the slightest power to make it good.

All is over. Silent, mournful, abandoned, broken, Czechoslovakia recedes into the darkness....It is a tragedy which has occurred. There must always be the most profound regret and a sense of vexation in British hearts at the treatment and the misfortune which have overcome the Czechoslovakian Republic.

Winston Churchill, *Parliamentary Debates*, House of Commons, 5th series, vol. 339, October 3, 1938. Used by permission.

They have not ended here. At any moment there may be a hitch in the programme. At any moment there may be an order for Herr Goebbels [the Nazi propaganda minister] to start again his propaganda of calumny and lies; at any moment an incident may be provoked, and now that the fortress line is turned what is there to stop the will of the conqueror? Obviously, we are not in a position to give them the slightest help at the present time, except what everyone is glad to know has been done, the financial aid which the Government have promptly produced.

I venture to think that in future the Czechoslovak State cannot be maintained as an independent entity. I think you will find that in a period of time which may be measured by years, but may be measured only by months, Czechoslovakia will be engulfed in the Nazi regime. Perhaps they may join it in despair or in revenge. At any rate, that story is over and told. But we cannot consider the abandonment and ruin of Czechoslovakia in the light only of what happened only last month. It is the most grievous consequence of what we have done and what we have left undone in the last five years—five years of futile good intentions, five years of eager search for the line of least resistance, five years of uninterrupted retreat of British power, five years of neglect of our air defences. Those are the features which I stand here to expose and which marked an improvident stewardship for which Great Britain and France have dearly to pay....The responsibility must rest with those who have had the undisputed control of our political affairs. They neither prevented Germany from rearming, nor did they rearm ourselves in time. They quarreled with Italy without saving Ethiopia. They exploited and discredited the vast institution of the League of Nations and they neglected to make alliances and combinations which might have repaired previous errors, and thus they left us in the hour of trial without adequate national defence or effective international security....

But what will be the position, I want to know, of France and England this year and the year afterwards? What will be the position of that Western front of which we are in full authority the guarantors? The German army at the present time is more numerous than that of France, though not nearly so matured or perfected. Next year it will grow much larger, and its maturity will be more complete. Relieved from all anxiety in the East, and having secured resources which will greatly diminish, if not entirely remove, the deterrent of a naval blockade, the rulers of Nazi Germany will have a free choice open to them as to what direction they will turn their eyes. If the Nazi dictator should chose to look westward, as he may, bitterly will France and England regret the loss of that fine army of ancient Bohemia which was estimated last week to require not fewer than thirty German divisions for its destruction.

Can we blind ourselves to the great change which has taken place in the military situation, and to the dangers we have to meet?...Many people, no doubt, honestly believe that they are only giving away the interest of Czechoslovakia, whereas I fear we shall find that we have deeply compromised, and perhaps fatally endangered, the safety and even the independence of Great Britain and France....There can never be friendship between the British democracy and the Nazi power, that power which spurns Christian ethics, which cheers its onward course by a barbarous paganism, which vaunts the spirit of aggression and conquest, which derives strength and perverted pleasure from persecution, and uses, as we have seen, with pitiless brutality the threat of murderous force. That power cannot ever be the trusted friend of the British democracy.

I do not begrudge our loyal, brave people, who were ready to do their duty no matter what the cost, who never flinched under the strain of last week—I do not grudge them the natural, spontaneous outburst of joy and relief when they learned that the hard ordeal would no longer be required of them at the moment; but they should know the truth. They should know that there has been gross neglect and deficiency in our defences; they should know that we have sustained a defeat without a war, the consequence of which will travel far with us along our road; they should know that we have passed an awful milestone in our history, when the whole equilibrium of Europe has been deranged and that the terrible words have for the time being been pronounced against the Western democracies: "Thou art weighed in the balance and found wanting." And do not suppose that this is the end. This is only the beginning of the reckoning. This is only the first sip, the first foretaste of a bitter cup which will be proffered to us year by year unless by a supreme recovery of moral health and martial vigour, we arise again and take our stand for freedom as in the olden time.

FRANCE GOES TO WAR

Edouard Daladier (1884–1970) was a longtime radical socialist deputy, who, in the frequent upheaval of French ministerial politics, served three times as prime minister. He was in office during the Munich crisis and signed the fateful Munich Pact on September 30, 1938. Daladier harbored few illusions about France's inability to stand alone against German provocation without meaningful military allies. As the situation deteriorated, however, he recognized that France would have to fight to preserve its honor and territorial integrity. Upon France's fall to Germany in June 1940, Daladier escaped to French North Africa where he intended to establish a government-in-exile but was arrested in Morocco under orders from the Vichy government and brought back to France to stand trial. At his trial in 1942, Daladier accused General Philippe Pétain and his supporters of failing to prepare France for war and was incarcerated first by the Vichy government and then by the Nazis, whose prisoner he remained until 1945.

Gentlemen, these efforts towards peace, however powerless they were and still remain, will at least have shown where the responsibility lies. They insure for Poland, the victim, the effective co-operation and moral support of the nations and of free men of all lands.

What we did before the beginning of this war, we are ready to do once more. If renewed steps are taken towards conciliation, we are still ready to join in.

If the fighting were to stop, if the aggressor were to retreat within his own frontiers, if free negotiations could still be started..., Gentlemen, the French Government would spare no effort to ensure, even today, if it were possible, the success of these negotiations, in the interests of the peace of the world.

But the time is pressing; France and England cannot look on when a friendly nation is being destroyed, a foreboding of further onslaughts, eventually aimed at England and France.

Indeed, are we only dealing with the German-Polish conflict? We are not, Gentlemen; what we have to deal with is a new stage in the advance of the Hitler dictatorship towards the domination of Europe and the world. How, indeed, are we to forget that the German claim to the Polish territories had been long marked on the map of Greater Germany, and that it was only concealed for some years to facilitate other conquests? So long as the German-Polish Pact, which dates back only a few years, was profitable to Germany, Germany respected it; on the day when it became a hindrance to marching towards domination it was denounced unhesitatingly. Today we are told that, once the German claims against Poland were satisfied, Germany would pledge herself before the whole world for ten, for twenty, for twenty-five years, for all time, to restore or to respect peace. Unfortunately, we have heard such promises before!

On May 25, 1935, Chancellor Hitler pledged himself not to interfere in the international affairs of

Edouard Daladier, Speech to French Chamber of Deputies, September 2, 1939, www.yale.edu/lawweb/avalon/wwii/fr1.htm. Used by permission.

Austria and not to unite Austria to the Reich; and on March 11, 1938, the German army entered Vienna; [Austrian] Chancellor Schussnig was imprisoned for daring to defend his country's independence, and no one today can say what is his real fate after so many physical and moral sufferings. Now we are to believe that it was Dr. Schussnig's acts of provocation that brought about the invasion and enslavement of his country!

On September 12, 1938, Herr Hitler declared that the Sudeten problem was an internal matter which concerned only the German minority in Bohemia and the Czechoslovak Government. A few days later he maintained that the violent persecutions carried on by the Czechs were compelling him to change his policy.

On September 26 of the same year he declared that his claim on the Sudeten territory was the last territorial claim he had to make in Europe. On March 14, 1939, Herr Hacha [Benes' successor as president of Czechoslovakia] was summoned to Berlin; ordered under the most stringent pressure to accept an ultimatum. A few hours later Prague was being occupied in contempt of the signed pledges given to other countries in Western Europe. In this case also Herr Hitler endeavored to put on the victims the onus which in fact lies on the aggressor.

Finally, on January 30, 1939, Herr Hitler spoke in loud praise of the non-aggression pact which he had signed five years previously with Poland. He paid a tribute to this agreement as a common act of liberation, and solemnly confirmed his intention to respect its clauses.

But it is Herr Hitler's deeds that count, not his word.

What, then, is our duty? Poland is our ally. We entered into commitments with her in 1921 and 1925. These commitments were confirmed....

Since then we have never failed both in diplomatic negotiations and in public utterances, to prove faithful to it. Our Ambassador in Berlin has several times reminded Herr Hitler that, if a German aggression were to take place against Poland, we should fulfill our pledges....

Poland has been the object of the most unjust and brutal aggression. The nations who have guaranteed her independence are bound to intervene in her defense.

Great Britain and France are not Powers that can disown, or dream of disowning, their signatures....

[I]ndeed, Gentlemen, it is not only the honor of our country: it is also the protection of its vital interests that is at stake.

For a France which should allow this aggression to be carried out would very soon find itself a scorned, an isolated, a discredited France, without allies and without support, and doubtless, would soon herself be exposed to a formidable attack.

This is the question I lay before the French nation, and all nations. At the very moment of the aggression against Poland, what value has the guarantee, once more renewed, given for our eastern frontier, for our eastern frontier, for our Alsace, for our Lorraine, after repudiation of the guarantees given in turn to Austria, Czechoslovakia, and Poland? More powerful through their conquests, gorged with the plunder of Europe, the masters of inexhaustible natural wealth, the aggressors would soon turn against France with all their forces.

Thus, our honor is but the pledge of our own society. It is not that abstract and obsolete form of honor which conquerors speak to justify their deeds of violence; it is the dignity of a peaceful people which bears hatred toward no other people in the world and which never embarks upon a war save only for the sake of its freedom and of its life.

Forfeiting our honor would purchase nothing more than a precious peace liable to rescission, and when, tomorrow, we should have to fight after losing the respect of our allies and the other nations, we should no longer be anything more than a wretched people doomed to defeat and bondage.

CHAPTER 2

"ONLY MOVEMENT BRINGS VICTORY"

Blitzkrieg

THE FALL OF FRANCE Victorious German troops enter Paris in June 1940, having accomplished in less than two months what they had been unable to achieve in four years of battle during World War I. *Source:* © Hulton-Deutsch Collection/CORBIS.

As war broke out once again in 1939, Europeans wondered whether they would witness a replay of World War I, a lengthy stalemate that several years of futile, bloody offensives did little to dispel. Certainly the French High Command anticipated that the next war would look very much like the previous one and set about pouring money and concrete into a formidable defensive barrier, the Maginot Line, along the frontier with Germany. In fact, there were lessons to be drawn from the Great War that could be applied to make offensive operations more effective and decisive. In the war's latter stages, the Germans had developed tactics in which units probed for weak points in the lines, bypassed enemy strongholds, and sought to disrupt communications and the flow of supplies and reinforcements from the rear. Shock, surprise, and movement, rather than the sheer weight of a frontal assault, were the keys to success, and they nearly produced a breakthrough in Ludendorff's offensives in March 1918.

The First World War also witnessed the introduction of tanks and aircraft. Both weapons were in their infancy, and neither was available in numbers sufficient to overwhelm the enemy, but to innovative officers their potential value was clear. The proponents of airpower, such as Italy's General Giulio Douhet, argued that strategic bombing could devastate enemy cities, shatter civilian morale, and bring a country to its knees. Even politicians recognized the possibility, such as British prime minister Stanley Baldwin, who warned that "the bomber would always get through." Events in the Middle East, Africa, and Spain all confirmed the destructive potential of aerial warfare, even as many observers simultaneously drew the mistaken conclusion that armored warfare was less promising.

German theorists, however, realized that the two arms could work effectively in combination. Rather than dispersing tanks among infantry divisions and consigning them to a supporting role, they massed them together and employed armored formations as an offensive spearhead, with close tactical air support. Shock, surprise, and movement were emphasized, as the tanks would race ahead to exploit breakthroughs while leaving strongholds for the slower-moving infantry to clean up. This "lightning warfare," or Blitzkrieg, was unleashed on Poland in September 1939 under nearly ideal circumstances. Germany's air force (the Luftwaffe) maintained air superiority, and the Polish plain was ideally suited for motorized warfare. The Polish army fought bravely, but it was no match for the Germans in a war of movement, especially when it also had to rebuff a Soviet offensive from the rear. In addition to tactical air support and interdiction of Polish supply lines, the Luftwaffe unleashed terror bombing upon Warsaw shortly before the campaign ended. Within a month, it was all over.

What followed was a period of relative quiet, the so-called Sitzkrieg (sitting war). German and Anglo-French forces preferred not to undertake major operations during the winter, but the overconfident Soviet Red Army judged the moment auspicious to launch an offensive against Finland in December 1939. The Soviet campaign was intended to conquer Finnish territory to provide an additional territorial buffer that would facilitate defense of the approaches to Leningrad, but stout Finnish resistance stopped the Soviets in their tracks. Although the Soviets eventually compelled the outnumbered Finns to sue for peace, this "Winter War" appeared to confirm that the Red Army, shattered by Stalin's purges, was a mediocre fighting force, and that a spirited defense, conducted from behind entrenched positions, was still (as it had been in World War I) nearly impregnable.

Both of these propositions would be proven wrong. As the weather thawed, the war in western Europe heated up again. An April 1940 German thrust into Scandinavia, primarily to secure the Norwegian coastline and safeguard shipments of Swedish iron ore, was notable for the heavy damage absorbed by Germany's modest surface fleet (nearly half of its ships were sunk or put out of commission) and the political damage incurred by British prime minister Neville Chamberlain, whose administration appeared unable to conduct the war effectively. He would be replaced by Winston Churchill, who, with remarkable timing, came to power on May 10, 1940, just as German armies stormed across the Dutch, Belgian, and French frontiers.

During the First World War, the French had held out, despite heavy losses, for four years, until victory was secured. This time they lasted for barely six weeks, unable to respond to German attacks that outflanked the Maginot Line by boldly rushing through the allegedly impenetrable heavily forested region of the Ardennes. Nor did the French have an answer for the German combined arms Blitzkrieg operations. To hammer home the stunning reversal of fortunes, the French were compelled to sign an armistice on June 22, 1940, at Compiègne in the very same railway car where German generals had surrendered in 1918.

For their part, perhaps the greatest British achievement during the campaign was to extricate, miraculously it seemed, the bulk of their troops out from German clutches in a harrowing evacuation from the port of Dunkirk. They had been aided by a forty-eight-hour respite during which weary German armored formations had halted on Hitler's orders. Although they were forced to abandon their heavy equipment, the nearly 340,000 or so rescued soldiers were the irreplaceable nucleus of a force to defend Britain itself. Belgium and the Netherlands proved no match for German arms as well, and the Dutch experience was notable for the city of Rotterdam becoming the next great urban center to fall victim to terror bombing at the hands of the Luftwaffe. Belgium, like Poland before it, the Netherlands, and the Free French (who refused to concede the struggle against Germany), all maintained a government-in-exile in London, but would have to wait four years for liberation until Allied forces returned to the continent.

Britain now faced that "certain eventuality" (going it alone after the defeat of France), armed, it seemed, with little more than Winston Churchill's bulldog determination and mastery of the English language. Yet the English Channel insulated the country from another round of Blitzkrieg; German tanks and ground forces could not invade unless they could somehow protect the cross-channel invasion routes from attack by the powerful Royal Navy, and doing that would require maintaining aerial supremacy over the region. Thus the next stage of the conflict would be fought in the air. The Luftwaffe, whose priorities and experiences had lain with tactical air support, was less equipped to undertake the strategic bombing that must precede an invasion. The Royal Air Force (RAF), on the other hand, enjoyed a number of advantages: the radar which gave early warning of incoming German attacks, the proximity to bases which allowed British planes to operate for longer stretches in the air than their short-of-fuel opponents, and the nimble Spitfire fighter plane which outclassed the German Messerschmitt ME-109. As it was, when the German bombers concentrated on British air bases and aircraft factories, the Royal Air Force found itself perilously short of fighters to defend the skies, but when the Luftwaffe switched to targeting the cities to break civilian morale, it was able to recover. The "Battle of Britain" raged in the skies from mid-June to mid-September 1940, with heavy losses on both sides (some 800 British and 1,300 German planes), and indiscriminate destruction rained down upon many British urban centers, including London, Southampton, and, two months later, Coventry, which lost its famous medieval cathedral. The "Blitz" on Britain's capital strained the nerves of the city's population but failed to shake their resolve, and by October Hitler recognized that Britain would neither surrender nor collapse. Despite Germany's stunning early victories, the war would continue. Churchill paid eloquent tribute to the courage and skill of the RAF pilots, noting that never before had "so many owed so much to so few." German bombing would continue, and the British would begin to reciprocate, but both would be compelled to search for other ways to carry the war forward.

SOVIET-FINNISH WAR

Concerned about the vulnerability of Leningrad to an attack through the Karelian Isthmus that belonged to Finland, Josef Stalin hoped to acquire Finnish territory and push the Soviet Union's border farther west. His plan also included using communist exiles to foment pro-Soviet agitation among Finnish workers. Having procured German assurance of nonaggression and a secret protocol that allowed for Soviet influence in Finland via the German-Soviet Pact of August 19, 1939, Stalin ordered a full-scale invasion of Finland by Soviet Red Army troops on November 30, 1939. Things, however, did not go according to Stalin's plans. Instead, the Soviet-Finnish War revealed severe deficiencies in the Soviet military. Soviet military equipment was poorly designed for winter warfare, supplies (especially food) were scarce, young Soviet officers were insufficiently trained, and stout Finnish resistance in the fortified Mannerheim Line exacted a terrible toll in Soviet casualties. More than 126,000 Soviet soldiers were killed and 300,000 injured, while the Finns lost more than 48,000 soldiers and 43,000 were wounded. Although it first appeared that the Finns might defy the odds, eventually the Soviets' numerical superiority compelled the Finns to capitulate in March 1940. A month later, from April 14 to 17, 1940, Stalin convened a secret inquiry at the Kremlin with forty-six field commanders from the Finnish operation into why the Red Army had performed so poorly. Among the participants were generals Dmitry Kozlov (1896–1967) and Filipp Alabushev (1893–1941), who both led rifle units, as well as Kirill Meretskov (1897–1968), who as the commander of the Leningrad Military District had responsibility for the invasion's initial operations. Needless to say, in the otherwise remarkably frank discussions of the army's inquest, none of the participants mentioned that Stalin's purges had deprived it of its ablest leaders and contributed to the fiasco in the Winter War.

Kozlov: What has the infantry done? The infantry has demonstrated high heroism and devotion to the homeland and the cause of the party. But they carried out their tasks with difficulty. Why was this so? First, because the personnel in our units and formations were not appropriate for the given theatre of operations.

The personnel of motorized and non-motorised divisions were not suited to operations in the Finnish theatre of war. We must revise the manning tables right now.

The second question. Our men and commanders were not prepared adequately for the specific conditions of fighting on the Finnish front. This question should be given serious attention, too.

The third question. The reservists came practically untrained. They did not know how to handle grenades and mortars because they had not been

Stalin and the Soviet-Finnish War, 1939–1940, Harold Shukman, ed., 2002, Frank Cass, 34–36, 127–132. Reproduced by permission of Taylor & Francis Books UK.

taught to. As a result, infantry did not use or hardly used their weapons to battle. Merely 0.5 per cent grenades and 0.35 per cent rifle cartridges of the ammunition allocation were expended at Loimola, while the consumption of shells reached seven days of fire.

The last question. It is necessary to enhance the role and importance of army commanders. The authority of commanders who organize co-operation between arms, who direct the action and are responsible for the outcome of the battle must be strengthened radically. We do not have it now, particularly at the lower levels, at the levels of company, battery and even regiment. Frequently, a regimental commander would have to make a decision with a corps representative, a special administration representative and a political administration representative breathing down his neck....

Alabushev: The 123rd Division began to operate at the beginning of war with Finland, on 1 December 1939. The divisional units approached the front line of the fortified area, the so-called Mannerheim Line, on 12 December. On 17 December, without proper preparation for a breakthrough, the division mounted an attack. What I mean by unpreparedness is that we had not co-ordinated the actions of the arms. Each acted on its own. As a result, we lost many tanks, but could not pierce the front line of the fortified area.

The most diverse inferences were drawn from this attack. The tank troops blamed the infantrymen: 'If the infantry had been good, everything would have been done well.' Others even said: 'Tanks and a good infantry battalion would have done the job.' The case was somewhat different, however. We had fine infantrymen and they would have succeeded if the attack had been prepared adequately....

Meretskov: The high command and the participants in the meeting know about the progress of hostilities in detail. Therefore, I'll omit them and focus only on some questions that, in my opinion, have not yet been fully covered.

The first question: defence and offence.

1. DEFENCE

The events showed that we did not have a full idea of what we would encounter in the enemy's defences....

We conceived of a defence line prepared in advance as a totality of several (two or three) fortified lines, each with a prominent frontage, and with a zone of obstacles before the main resistance line, which we would approach closely after overcoming obstacles and making reconnaissance and which we would attack after artillery preparation.

What was the enemy defence line in reality?

First, it was not merely a zone of obstacles with local defence, but a foreground developed to a great depth, with eight lines of strong points connected by fire. All these lines were covered by strong anti-tank obstacles in the form of concrete and granite blocks, escarps of various kinds, and ditches, which were obstacles not only for tanks but also for infantry; various barbed-wire obstacles; and large areas of felled thick trees, obstructions and mine-fields. Moreover, some strong points had concrete structures.

In terms of its depth, degree of fortification, and the intensity of automatic fire, the foreground was in fact a separate defence line.

Second, the frontage of the main defence line was artfully camouflaged in keeping with the terrain and the arrangement of structures was camouflaged. Concrete works were sometimes covered with stone and log-and-dirt works, whose high resistance to 152- and even 203-mm shells made it difficult to distinguish them from concrete works.

Third, the entire 90-km-deep defences from the border to Vyborg inclusive were covered by wide minefields which protected the main directions over the entire defence depth.

We were not prepared for fighting against such large-scale minefields, which at first caused some confusion among the troops....

2. THE OFFENSIVE

The incorrect conception of the enemy's strength and defence system at first led to incorrect organization of the offensive battle. What were the shortcomings during the offensive and what should we amend in our manuals?

The first question: the use of second echelons.

The first period of the offensive in the foreground showed that we were prepared too sketchily for the offensive. When, in overcoming obstacles, the vanguard was delayed and the advance lost its pace, the main forces were immediately deployed and put fully into battle. As a result after breaking through one defence line, the troops approached the second line in unfavourable combat formations; a regrouping was required, taking extra time, owing to which the daily advance was limited to 5–7 km instead of ten.

During the battles we became convinced that it was the premature committal of the main forces into battle, due to the vanguard's delay in organizing the offensive, rather than its weakness, that was harmful. This happened because commanders had been taught to form the combat formation by the established rules, with the obligatory presence of the second echelon, which is used in the event of losing the pace of the offensive or for developing the breakthrough. Despite the fact that they encountered a defence that did not allow for any mechanical committal of second echelons into battle, they continued to advance according to the scheme laid down in the manuals.

All this disrupted the combat formation and led to an offensive without preliminary treatment of the enemy and detailed reconnaissance. The troops attacked *en masse* in line formation, for which Comrade Stalin repeatedly reproached us, but we, who had been trained to follow the fixed rules, could not rectify this error quickly, and it was only battle practice that gradually eliminated this shortcoming.

RETHINKING ARMORED WARFARE

Heinz Guderian (1888–1954) had the unusual distinction of being both dismissed by Hitler from command of an army and later reinstated by the German dictator who was loath ever to admit having made a mistake. Guderian hailed from a Prussian landowning family, but despite his traditionalist heritage, he featured as one of the most innovative and forward-looking officers in the German army. Service in the First World War persuaded him that Germany could not hope to fight and win another bloody stalemate, and he, like theorists such as J. F. C. Fuller and B. H. Liddell Hart, devoted the interwar period to rethinking the use of tanks, which had been introduced in the later stages of that conflict. Technological superiority could compensate for numerical inferiority (a necessity given that Germany's army had been limited in size by the Versailles Treaty), especially if the newer weapons were handled boldly and decisively. Guderian was appointed Commander of Mobile Troops in 1938, and the following excerpt suggests how he sought to hone his forces into a devastating offensive weapon.

Heinz Guderian, *Panzer Leader*, trans. by Constantine Fitzgibbon, © 1952 by Heinz Guderian. (London: M. Joseph, 1952), 39–44. Used by permission of Dutton, a division of Penguin Group (USA) Inc.

The layman, when thinking of a tank attack, tends to envisage the steel monsters of Cambrai and Amiens as pictured in the war reports of that period. He thinks of vast wire entanglements being crushed like so much straw; he remembers how the tanks crashed through dug-outs, smashing machine-guns to splinters beneath their weight; he recalls the terror that they inspired as they ploughed through the battlefield, flames darting from their exhaust pipes and how this "tank terror" was described as the cause of our collapse on the 8th of August, 1918. Such steam-roller tactics are one—though not the most important—of the things tanks can do; but the events of the last war have so impressed themselves on the minds of many critics, that they have built up an entirely fanciful idea of a tank attack in which vast numbers of tanks massed together roll steadily forward to crush the enemy beneath their tracks (thus providing a magnificent target for artillery and anti-tank fire) whenever and wherever ordered by the High Command, regardless of the nature of the ground. The firepower of the tanks is under-estimated: the tank is thought to be both blind and deaf; it is denied the ability to hold the ground that it has captured. On the other hand every advantage is ascribed to anti-tank defence: it is alleged that the defence will no longer be susceptible to surprise by tanks; anti-tank guns and artillery always find their mark regardless of their own casualties, of smoke, fog, trees or other obstacles and ground contours; the defence, too, is always located exactly where the tanks are going to attack; with their powerful binoculars they can easily see through smokescreens and darkness, and despite their steel helmets they can hear every word that is said.

As a result of this picture it follows that tank attacks have no future. Should tanks therefore be scrapped and—as one critic has suggested—the tank period be simply by-passed? If this were done all our worries about new tactics for old arms of the service could be scrapped at the same time and we could settle down comfortably once again to positional warfare as practiced in 1914–1915. Only it is not very sensible to leap into the dark if you have no idea where you are going to land. *It follows that until our critics can produce some new and better method of making a successful land attack other than self-massacre, we shall continue to maintain our belief that tanks—properly employed— needless to say—are today the best means available for a land attack....*

If an army can in the first wave commit to the attack tanks which are invulnerable to the mass of the enemy's defensive weapons, then those tanks will inevitably overcome this their most dangerous adversary....However, should the defence succeed in producing a defensive weapon which can penetrate the armour of all the attacker's available tanks, and should he manage to deploy such weapons at the right time and in the decisive place, then the tanks will have to pay heavily for their success or may even fail altogether if the defence is sufficiently concentrated and sufficiently deep. The struggle for mastery between missile and armour has been going on for thousands of years, and Panzer troops have to reckon with it even as do fortress troops, sailors and, recently, airmen. The fact that such a struggle exists, with results that continuously vary, is no reason for denigrating tanks as a land weapon; for if we do, we shall be reduced to sending men into the attack with no more protection than the woolen uniforms of the World War which, even then, were regarded as insufficient.

It has been said, "only movement brings victory." We agree with this proposition and wish to employ the technical means of our time to prove its truth....*Everything is therefore dependent on this: to be able to move faster than has hitherto been done; to keep moving despite the enemy's defensive fire and thus make it harder for him to build up fresh defensive positions; and finally to carry the attack deep into the enemy's defences.* The proponents of tank warfare believe that, in favourable circumstances, they possess the means for achieving this....We believe that movement can be kept up if certain conditions, on which the success of a tank attack today depend, exist; these include among others, concentration of force in suitable terrain, gaps in the enemy's defence, and an inferior enemy tank force....

Armour and movement are only two of the combat characteristics of the tank weapon; the third and the most important is fire-power....In land battles the tank possesses the unique quality of being able to bring its fire-power to bear while actually advancing against the enemy, and it can do this even though all the defence's guns and machine-guns have not been silenced....Now should a tank attack be envisaged simply as a means of steam-rolling a path through thick and deep defensive positions held by infantry and artillery fully equipped with anti-tank weapons, as was done during the battles of *materiel* of the last war? Certainly not. A man who would attempt this would be thinking purely in terms of the infantry tank, a weapon whose sole function was the closest cooperation with the infantry, a weapon adjusted to the foot-soldier's scale of time and space values. This was a concept which we hung onto for far too long....

What we want to do is, for a short period of time, to dominate the enemy's defence in all its depth....We want...reserves to be available in the form of Panzer Divisions, since we no longer believe that other formations have the fighting ability, the speed and the maneuverability necessary for full exploitation of the attack and breakthrough. In the tank we see the finest weapon for the attack now available; we will not change our minds until such time as the technicians can show us something better. We will in no circumstances agree to time-wasting artillery preparation and the consequent danger of losing the element of surprise, simply because the old maxim says that "only fire can open the way to movement." We believe, on the contrary, that the combination of the internal combustion engine and armour plate enable us to take our fire to the enemy without any artillery preparation, provided always that the important conditions for such an operation are fulfilled: suitable terrain, surprise and mass commitment.

ROTTERDAM IN FLAMES

On May 10, 1940, the Germans entered neutral Holland as a way to bypass the Maginot Line for reaching France. Initially, the Germans met little resistance from the Dutch, whose prime minister in 1937 had boasted that the Netherlands' best defense against invaders lay with the flooding of the dikes. While Dutch forces briefly managed to slow the German advance, they were no match for the Blitzkrieg. Impatient, though, with the resistance his troops met and eager to capture the port city of Rotterdam, the German commander threatened to bomb the city to force it to surrender on May 14. Although the Dutch finally acquiesced, the general's message to cancel the raid did not reach the German air force in time to prevent it. As a result of the raid, much of Rotterdam's historic city center was destroyed, and some 800 to 1,000 inhabitants were killed.

WITH THE GERMAN ARMY OF OCCUPATION, ROTTERDAM, MAY 23

This beautiful Netherland city, principal shipping center for a far flung Colonial empire, is today a sad skeleton of its former self. For on Tuesday, May 14, dive bombers of the German Air Force rained high explosives on approximately one square mile in the center of the city. The area bombed is a shambles with almost every single building so thoroughly razed that words cannot adequately describe the appearance of the wreckage.

Amazingly enough, the bombing occurred after the commanding Netherland general had capitulated. Negotiations had been in progress between the two commanders on surrender or evacuation of the city by Netherland troops. The defending general, it is said, after having broken off negotiations, reopened them but failed to inform the Germans in time, specifically the latters' commander.

Meantime, the Germans say, they instructed their air force to attack that part of the city allegedly occupied by troops immediately after expiration of the time limit. When they learned of the decision to surrender, the Germans declare, it was too late to recall all the dive bombers that had set out to eject the enemy.

How many German planes were recalled and how many attacked is not definitely known. It is suggested by German military officials that the havoc had been worked by 27 planes in nine and one half minutes. The dive bombers did a thorough, accurate job. For they devastated and reduced to ashes the wide area they attacked without damage at all points in most places outside.

The entire central section of the city situated on the north bank of the Maas was affected. All the buildings flanking the river on the north bank were destroyed. Today they are still smoldering in some places.

It is not known how many civilians lost their lives in the holocaust—perhaps it will never be known. A German officer estimated the number at probably several thousand while Netherland sources placed the figure between 10,000 and 15,000. Later German

figures given to us declared that 300 persons were killed and 365 wounded while 6,000 had been evacuated into the country before the attack began.

In modern warfare, a German officer explained, there are no longer open and fortified cities but merely defended and undefended cities. Rotterdam, he insisted, was defended and, he added, modern warfare demands that whenever there is resistance it must be broken by all means possible.

By taking up posts within the city, Germans declare, the defenders exposed themselves and their city to this fate.

We drove through ruins patrolled by armed Netherland police. The faces of pedestrians were sober, pensive, somber. Coolsingle Street, whose tall buildings mostly had housed banks and business concerns, was reduced to street level. The telegraph building, although damaged, and a new modern 12-story apartment house unscathed except for broken windows, were almost the only upright buildings in the vicinity. The clock in the telegraph building had stopped at 4:30.

Small canals in this sector were filled with debris, broken bits of furniture and household furnishings. In the sectors adjoining the immediate center of attack, weary civilians were salvaging what remained of their belongings....

Germans say the very speed of their invasion rendered it merciful to the human pawns who sought to obstruct their passage. For, they say, only 100 Netherland soldiers were killed and 850 wounded in the entire campaign.

Neutral observers of the invasion allege that the Fifth Column played an important role in the occupation, diverting the attention of the troops in The Hague and Rotterdam for some time. Ensconced in roof tops and windows, Netherland National Socialists fired on the Netherland defenders, who were obliged to divide their forces all over the interior towns in an effort to clean up this unlooked for enemy within....

Through the entire campaign, it is said, only 700 British soldiers were on Netherland soil, and 80 of them were sappers who blew up the huge oil tanks at Rotterdam.

FRANCE'S COLLAPSE

Captain D. Barlone served in France's Second North African Division and, by virtue of being posted to various sectors on the rapidly changing front lines, had the opportunity to observe the French army's inability to repel the German invasion. His account does not argue that the French lost because they were undermanned or poorly equipped, but rather that an unimaginative High Command failed to provide adequate leadership. Whereas German officers such as Guderian pioneered innovative tactics and implemented them with devastating effect, old and tired French officers thought in terms of the static defenses of the previous war, and, when the situation deteriorated, lacked the martial spirit to continue. Barlone himself made it to England during the Dunkirk evacuation and joined the Free French forces in the struggle to liberate his country.

1 June 1940...

All officers complain bitterly of the failure of the High Command after the first days of the battle to organize any traffic control. We are certain that with a little organization the heavy units of the army could have been freed much more quickly and so have embarked, with the aid of the great cranes of Dunkirk, which remained undamaged, precious war supplies, such as guns, tanks, anti-tank guns, anti-aircraft guns which would thus have been saved instead of being left in the hands of the enemy; they would have been damaged, of course, but not beyond repair.

A tremendous loss of money to be sure, but also an irreparable loss of enormous quantities of material which we shall miss sorely in the next Boche [derisive French slang for the Germans] offensive in which his army, released from Flanders, will be able to open out a gigantic offensive on the southern front. All those who fought in 1914–1918 say the High Command not only has not improved on the organization existing then, but has almost forgotten it. An impression that I have had a hundred times. Its [*sic*] heart-rending!

All the officers of the light-armoured divisions and the anti-tank units criticize the use made of them in placing them in small groups, useless for large-scale front line operations or in employing them for ridiculous jobs, such as guarding cross-roads. One feels that all are terribly uneasy on the issue of the war, after having been buoyed up with hope, just before entering Belgium. The poilus joined together in roundly cursing the total lack of aeroplanes; that strikes them most. The officers agree....

13 June 1940...

We listen to the wireless at 7:30 p.m., in which Paul Reynaud's message to Roosevelt is read, asking for the support, and the entry into the war, of America. We remain dumbfounded; this message is the cry of alarm and despair of the vanquished who foresee the fall of Paris; hence the Government's flight

D. Barlone, *A French Officer's Diary (23 August 1939–1 October 1940)* (New York: Macmillan Co., 1943), 64, 72–73, 77–84. Used by permission.

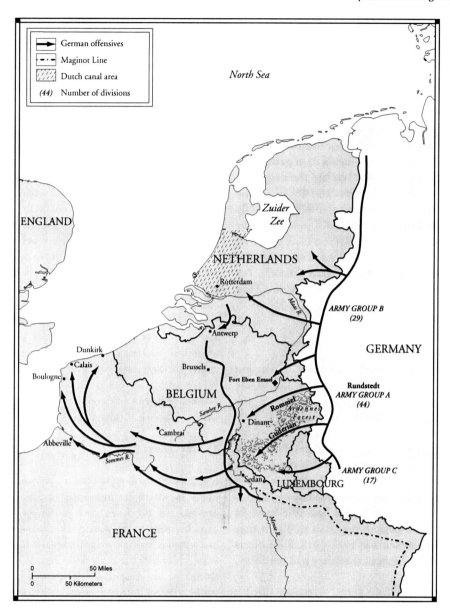

THE FALL OF FRANCE, 1940

to a province of France, thence to North Africa, and then if need be, to our possessions in America. I can understand his sending this message to Roosevelt with the intention of inducing the Americans to enter the war, but to broadcast it throughout France, to foreshadow endless withdrawals, that is defeat, the total loss of our soil. Is that the way to galvanize our troops, or to calm the fears of those behind the lines? Is it not rather the way to sow the seeds of panic? Was it necessary, or have we really reached the stage? The voting in the American Congress and Senate on the question of supplying arms and planes was pro-Ally with a large majority. Can this be a portent of the United State's entry into the war? If it is so, it will be a moral factor of the highest importance for us, and a cause for grave anxiety to the German people....But to-day, the Germans have advanced still farther. They are less than 20 miles from Paris....

14 June 1940...

The disastrous news is confirmed. The Government has declared Paris an open city and troops are retreating south of the capital. Everywhere the enemy advances; one feels that the Army is incapable of any further resistance. Probably it hasn't the means to continue fighting, for that was the case in Belgium. Never were the ranks broken there, never did men shrink from any sacrifice. They were crushed beneath the weight of metal, paralysed by new tactics of which our Staff and the British had little foresight and still less knowledge. It has been said that they were ready to go to war à la 1914–1918. But officers and men did their duty wherever they had the means of fighting....

15 June 1940...

The swiftness of defeat is so crushing that certain officers seem unsurprised. We were so accustomed to the idea of a continuous front-line, like that of the last war, that it seems difficult to conceive how to organize resistance without it. It is impossible to rebuild a new and impregnable front, one says; what can we do under the circumstances? A moral shock is necessary to restore confidence to these good people.

Everybody thinks of the U.S.A. But immediately the distress reappears: when will the men, the material, the planes arrive? How can we keep on until then? Has Weygand got a sufficient man-power—French and English to counter-attack and stop the Boches?...

18 June 1940.

We learn by wireless that Pétain and Weygand have asked for an armistice. Several officers weep bitterly. Others remain indifferent as if struck dumb by the disaster; we all discuss the news, which has not surprised us, for last night's wireless gave us to understand that Pétain would have to make a vital decision. Everyone tries to imagine what terms the enemy will impose; most of us are very pessimistic and expect atrocious conditions.

My mind is made up; I shall try to get to England and join up as a volunteer. Hardly had I said this when ten, fifteen, twenty of my friends decided to throw in their lot with me. I cannot believe that France, which has taken a thousand years to develop and has acquired a splendid colonial empire, will die within a month at the hands of a butcher....

21 June 1940...

It is incredible, despite Pétain's communiqué of last night in which he attempted to explain that our armies, cut off from each other, with enormous gaps between them were still continuing the fight, but without hope. We are under the impression that Pétain prevents his army from fighting; that he only thinks of his Armistice. Cherbourg is taken. How could a great military town, with forts and war-vessels lying in harbour, be taken without a fight? It bowls one over!...

Now we are trying to get used to the idea of seeing the Boches arrive, since Pétain has told them there was no longer any hope. Communiqués lose their interest; there have been no newspapers for three days; crushed by disaster, everyone lives just for the present trying to get something to eat in the early morning and to buy some food for the evening. The poor people of these parts try to persuade themselves that their lot may be less terrible than they thought at first; they will remain French, the Boches occupying the north and east of France. In order to break moral resistance the fifth column spreads reports that the Germans do not maltreat civilians....

The behaviour of civilians towards officers has already undergone a noticeable change. During the last few days they have been treated with a marked lack of respect. The people, embittered by defeat, do not distinguish between those officers who, on the whole, have fought admirably, sustaining grievous losses, and the High Command, which as I see it, has not been able to fulfil its task. Never have Frenchmen seen their country accept defeat after a month of battle: they do not understand and place the responsibility on the Command as a whole. If Great Britain should lose the war, if we should be unable to avenge our defeat, not only will it not be an asset to have been in command, but a liability "vae victis."...

In short, our High Command had learned nothing, understood nothing, and had no information about the preparations, the capacity and the tactics of the enemy; despite the campaigns in Poland and Norway. To be sure, the enemy had used motorized columns at great speed against the opposing force and behind the lines; but we could afford to smile.... I can see that we had an army, whose morale and courage were equal to that of the last war's army; save a restricted number of persons misled by hostile propaganda, everybody, workers and soldiers alike, animated by the traditional courage of Frenchmen, did his best. Two important breakdowns occurred: that of the political leadership and of the High Command. To be sure, we had not enough tanks

and planes—but according to all I have heard and seen, the High Command has used our armoured forces in an absurd manner, dispersing them in small units—three here, five others there—to guard the roads; the Boches arrived in great strength, crushing one small unit after the other, whereas tanks must be employed 'en masse,' to break through the enemy lines to surround the infantry, to cut adverse formations into several pieces; the tank is the modern cavalry; it is therefore necessary to use cavalry tactics: nobody would think of dispersing his cavalry into small units in order to achieve victory; it is necessary to keep great masses charging the enemy, swooping down on his rear, disorganizing his supply lines and so on. The tank, like the cavalry, is an offensive weapon; only under exceptional conditions should it be used in defence; and when used for defence purposes, it must still be employed in great quantity to counter-attack and by this means to delay the enemy's advance....

What purpose will be served by an armistice which will deliver us up bound and starving and at our enemy's mercy, forced to work for him against our ally, with whom we made a solemn pact not to make a separate peace? Once more we shall be perjured and forced to throw ourselves on the word of Hitler; the word that he gave to Austria, to Czecho-Slovakia, to Poland has meant nothing to our politicians....

In any case we regard Pétain and Weygand as two old men who serve as a screen for the clique of politicians who have seized power. One has always the right not to acquiesce in the murder of one's own country, and our desire is to regain our liberty.

STRANGE DEFEAT

The medievalist Marc Léopold Benjamin Bloch (1866–1944), one of France's greatest historians, stemmed from a family with its own long history of close identification with the French state. His great grandfather served in the revolutionary army in 1793, his father in the Franco-Prussian War of 1870, and Bloch himself in the French infantry in World War I, and again in 1940. Although Bloch achieved his reputation with studies of institutions from bygone centuries (notably medieval monarchy and feudalism), he was too ardent a French patriot and too dedicated a historian to let the collapse of his beloved France around him pass by without comment. His manuscript, based on his own military experience and written under difficult circumstances, was published posthumously as *Strange Defeat*, an excerpt from which follows. After the fall of France, Bloch, who was Jewish, tried unsuccessfully to get his family to safety in the United States, and joined the Resistance. Bloch was captured by the Nazis on June 16, 1944, and along with fellow resistance members was interrogated, tortured, and executed. In this passage, Bloch exposes the weaknesses within the French army that left it unable to duplicate its stout defense of France from 1914 to 1918. In 1940, in contrast, French forces crumbled with astonishing speed, suffering a truly "strange defeat" and ushering in a partial German occupation of the country.

We have just suffered such a defeat as no one would have believed possible. On whom or on what should the blame be laid? On the French system of parliamentary government, say our generals; on the rank and file of the fighting services, on the English, on the fifth column—in short, on any and everybody except themselves....Whatever the deep-seated causes of the disaster may have been, the immediate occasion...was the utter incompetence of the High Command....

Those who teach history should be continually concerned with the task of seeking the solid and the concrete behind the empty and the abstract. In other words, it is on men rather than functions that they should concentrate their attention. The errors of the High Command were, fundamentally, the errors of a specific group of human beings....

Misunderstandings are bound to occur at times in all armies, no matter what their nationality, between administrative and executive services. But it is not always the former who are responsible. Problems look different according to the angle from which they are observed, and those whose functions are not the same can hardly be expected to see eye to eye. The 'thinking oneself into the other fellow's shoes' is always a very difficult form of mental gymnastics, and it is not confined to men who occupy a special position in the military hierarchy. But it would be foolish to deny that staff officers as a whole have been a good deal to blame in this matter of sympathetic understanding. Their failure, when they did fail, was...due...not so much to contempt as to lack of imagination and a tendency to take refuge from the urgency of fact in abstractions. In the days before the real fighting had begun, we spent a lot of time working out troop movements on the map. But how many of us ever adequately realized what problems of detail, what frictions of psychology, are involved

Marc Bloch, *Strange Defeat* (Oxford: Oxford University Press, 1949), 25, 27, 34–41, 48–49. Used by permission.

when, in the depth of winter, men are asked to leave billets in which they have settled down and move somewhere else into what are, only too often, bad and unsuitable quarters? But that is not the worst of the staff's shortcomings. More than once during the First World War it was brought home to me how inefficient the High Command could be when it came to calculating accurately the length of time needed for an order, once issued from H.Q., to pass through its various recipients until finally it reached the formations who would have to act upon it. No amount of 'instructions' will ever succeed in convincing the unimaginative that a runner's pace is slow, and that he will often go wrong when roads and tracks have been turned into a sea of mud....I am not at all sure that the conduct of the Second World War was entirely free from similar mistakes. The blame for them falls, not on individuals, but on the whole method of training in vogue at the time....

What drove our armies to disaster was the cumulative effect of a great number of different mistakes. One glaring characteristic is, however, common to all of them. Our leaders, or those who acted for them, were incapable of thinking in terms of a *new* war. In other words, the German triumph was, essentially, a triumph of intellect—and it is that which makes it so peculiarly serious.

Let me be more precise. One fact, but that one of radical importance, differentiates our contemporary civilization from any of those that preceded it. Since the beginning of the twentieth century the whole idea of distance has changed. This alteration in its spatial values came about in little more than a single generation. But rapid though it was, it has become so much a part of our mental habit that we are inclined to forget how revolutionary its effects have been....The privations resulting from war and defeat have had upon Europe the repercussions of a Time Machine in reverse. We have been plunged suddenly into a way of life which, only quite recently, we thought had disappeared for ever....Now, when bicycles are the quickest means of transport available, and heavy loads have to be carried in donkey-wagons, every trip to market becomes a major expedition. We have gone back thirty or forty years! The ruling idea of the Germans in the conduct of this war was speed.

We, on the other hand, did our thinking in terms of yesterday or the day before. Worse still: faced by the undisputed evidence of Germany's new tactics, we ignored, or wholly failed to understand, the quickened rhythm of the times....We interpreted war in terms of assagai [spears of African Zulu tribesmen] *versus* rifle made familiar to us by long years of colonial expansion. But this time it was we who were cast for the role of the savage!...

The truth of the matter was that the Germans advanced a great deal faster than they should have done according to the old rules of the game. And so it went on. 'Niggling' was how I heard our strategic methods described by a colleague of mine, one of those younger men who did at least know how to think in contemporary terms, and suffered under a perpetual sense of frustration because of the way in which they were consistently ignored by their superiors....It was perfectly obvious that as soon as the Army of the Meuse had been broken, and the enemy began to show signs of becoming active on our front, the only hope of re-establishing the general situation lay in our 'disengaging,' and establishing a new defensive line sufficiently far back to ensure that it would not be overrun before it had been properly organized. But nothing of the sort was done. Instead, small groups of reinforcements were continually dribbled into every breach as it occurred, with the inevitable result that they were cut to pieces....

There can be no doubt that our whole plan of campaign was wrong. What *should* have been the reply of the Anglo-French forces to the German invasion of Belgium? The problem had been discussed all through the winter by the various 'G' staffs. Two solutions, among many others, found particular favor. One school of thought maintained that we ought to stand on a line in Belgium based at its northern end....The other school favoured immediate offensive action *across* the frontier....As everybody knows, it was this second plan that ultimately carried the day, and it seems fairly certain that General Billotte's personal influence was decisive in imposing this decision.

Not only were the German tanks a great deal more numerous than Intelligence had led us to suppose; some of them were quite unexpectedly powerful.

The extent to which our Air Force was outclassed was truly appalling....

There can be no doubt whatever that it was the collapse of the Armies of the Meuse and at Sedan which, by uncovering the rear of the troops engaged in Belgium, led to the complete failure of the entire scheme....

It can be seen from what I have said that the war was a constant succession of surprises. The effect of this on morale seems to have been very serious. And here I must touch on a delicate subject. I have no right to do more than record impressions which are those only of a looker-on. But there are some things that must be said, even at the risk of hurting a good many feelings. Men are so made that they will face expected dangers in expected places a great deal more easily than the sudden appearance of deadly peril from behind a turn in the road which they have been led to suppose is perfectly safe. Years ago, shortly after the Battle of the Marne [World War I French victory in September 1914 that halted the German drive toward Paris], I saw men who the day before had gone into the line under murderous fire without turning a hair, run like rabbits just because three shells fell quite harmlessly on a road where they had piled arms in order to furnish a water-fatigue. 'We cleared out because the Germans came.' Again and again I heard that said in the course of last May and June. Analysed, the words mean no more than this: 'Because the Germans turned up where we didn't expect them and where we had never been told we ought to expect them.' Consequently, certain breakdowns, which cannot, I fear, be denied, occurred mainly because men had been trained to use their brains too slowly. Our soldiers were defeated and, to some extent, let themselves be too easily defeated, principally because their minds functioned far too sluggishly.

Not only did we meet the enemy too often in unexpected places, but for the most part, especially, and with increasing frequency, *in a way* which neither the High Command nor, as a result, the rank and file had anticipated. We should have been perfectly prepared to spend whole days potting at one another from entrenched positions, even if the lines had been only a few yards apart as they were in the Argonne during the last war. It would have seemed to us the most natural thing in the world to carry out raids on occupied saps. It would have been well within our capacity to stand firm in face of an assault through a curtain of wire more or less cut by 'Minenwerfer' [mine-thrower], or to have gone over the top courageously in an attempt to rush a position that had already been flattened—though, as a rule, not very completely—by artillery fire. In short, we could have played our part without difficulty in operations beautifully planned by our own staff and the enemy's, if only they had been in accordance with the well-digested lessons learned at peace-time manoeuvres. It was much more terrifying to find ourselves suddenly at grips with a section of tanks in open country. The Germans took no account of roads. They were everywhere. They felt their way forward, stopping whenever they ran up against serious resistance. Where, however, the resistance was not serious and they could find a 'soft spot,' they drove ahead, exploiting their gains, and using them as a basis from which to develop the appropriate tactical movement or, rather, as it seemed, to take their choice of a number of alternative possibilities already envisaged in accordance with that methodical opportunism which was so characteristic of Hitler's methods. They relied on action and on improvisation. We, on the other hand, believed in doing nothing and in behaving as we always had behaved.

A CERTAIN EVENTUALITY

During the First World War, Britain and France had fought together against the German invader for four long years, so it was hard for the British to contemplate that they might have to fight on in a second conflict without French assistance. The rapid German gains, however, forced the British cabinet to reassess the situation and solicit this report from the Chiefs of Staff Committee. Prepared under the guidance of Admiral Dudley Pound, C. L. N. Newall for the Royal Air Force, and General Arthur E. Percival for the army (he would later surrender the British garrison at Singapore), this document provides an unflinching assessment of a worst-case scenario: could Britain reasonably expect to hold out against a seemingly unstoppable German military in the "certain eventuality" that France sued for peace? The Chiefs of Staff laid out a case for survival so long as certain conditions were met, including full American support short of military intervention, proper organization of the civilian population for total war, and maintenance of Britain's fighter defenses. It is important to recognize that at this point in the war, despite Churchill's stirring rhetoric, the British cabinet *was* considering various options, including an appeal to Italy as an intermediary to broker a negotiated settlement with Germany. In reviewing Britain's options, however, the Chiefs of Staff foresaw few prospects for offensive action to strike back at Germany. Bombing raids, commando actions, and fomenting discontent were the principal hopes in 1940–1941, accompanied by an overly optimistic evaluation of the economic shortages the German war machine might face in the near future.

MOST SECRET

C.O.S. (40) 390

MAY 25, 1940

TO BE KEPT UNDER LOCK AND KEY

It is requested that special care may be taken to ensure the secrecy of this document

The object of this paper is to investigate the means whereby we could continue to fight single-handed if French resistance were to collapse completely, involving in the loss of a substantial proportion of the British Expeditionary Force, and the French Government were to make terms with Germany. The [most important] assumptions we have made...are that:—

(i) United States of America is willing to give us full economic and financial support, *without which we do not think we could continue the war with any chance of success.*

(ii) Italy has intervened against us.

2. In particular we have asked ourselves two questions:—

(a) Could the United Kingdom hold out until assistance from the Empire and America made itself felt? And

---

"British Strategy in a Certain Eventuality," Report of Chiefs of Staff Committee, May 25, 1940, War Cabinet Papers CAB 80/11/58 (The National Archives, formerly Public Record Office, Kew). Used by permission.

(b) Could we ultimately bring sufficient economic pressure to bear on Germany to ensure her defeat?...

CONCLUSIONS

3. There are three ways in which Germany might break down the resistance of the United Kingdom—unrestricted air attack aimed at breaking public morale, starvation of the country by attack on shipping and ports, and occupation by invasion.

AIR FACTOR

4. The vital fact is that our ability to avoid defeat will depend on three factors:—
   (a) Whether the morale of our people will withstand the strain of air bombardment;
   (b) Whether it will be possible to import the absolute essential minimum of commodities necessary to sustain life and to keep our war industries in action;
   (c) Our capacity to resist invasion.

All of these depend primarily on whether our fighter defences will be able to reduce the scale of attack to reasonable bounds. This will necessarily mean the replacement of casualties in personnel and aircraft on a substantial scale. Our capacity to resist invasion may, however, depend also to a great extent on the maintenance of an effective air striking force.

These factors cannot be ascertained with certainty, and it is impossible to say whether or not the United Kingdom could hold out in all circumstances. We think there are good grounds for the belief that the British people will endure the greatest strain if they realize—as they are beginning to do—that the existence of the Empire is at stake. We must concentrate our energies primarily on the production of fighter aircraft and crews, and the defence of those factories essential to fighter production should have priority. At the same time it is clear that we cannot afford to neglect our bomber force or to expend it on operations that are not of first importance.

CIVIL DEFENCE

5. As long as the present quasi-peacetime organization continues, it is unlikely that this country can hold out. The present Home Security Organisation was constituted to deal with air attack only by aircraft operating from bases in Germany; it is not sufficient to grapple with the problems which would arise as a result of a combination of heavy air attack from bases on a semi-circle from Trondheim [Norway] to Brest [France], invasion, and internal attack by the "Fifth Column."

LAND FORCES

6. Germany has ample forces to invade and occupy this country. Should the enemy succeed in establishing a force, with its vehicles, firmly ashore—the Army in the United Kingdom, which is very short of equipment, has not got the offensive power to drive it out.

NAVAL FORCES

7. Our first naval task is to secure the United Kingdom and its seaborne supplies against naval attack. We have sufficient Naval forces to deal with those that the enemy can bring against us in Home Waters [i.e., around the British Isles] and we can provide naval security for our seaborne supplies. Our ability to defeat at sea a seaborne attack on this country is dependent on the extent to which our Naval forces can operate in the face of heavy air attack on both ships and bases, and it is of the greatest importance to strengthen our systems of intelligence and reconnaissance to ensure early and accurate warnings of enemy intentions is obtained.

SEABORNE SUPPLIES

8. We have adequate shipping to meet our requirements, but again the provision of air security is the main problem. We may have to abandon our ports on the South and East coasts for trade purposes, and our ability to carry on the war will then depend on West Coast ports entirely. These, therefore, must be adequately defended. All unimportant imports must be eliminated. If we

can maintain 60 per cent of our present imports we can obtain enough food for the population and raw materials to continue essential armament production.

OVERSEAS

9. On a long-term view, Germany, in concert with Italy, will strive to overthrow our position in Egypt and the Middle East.

10. The immediate effect of a French collapse would be the loss of naval control in the Western Mediterranean. Italy would be able to concentrate all her strength against Malta, Gibraltar and Egypt. Malta could probably withstand one serious assault. We could continue to use Gibraltar as a naval base until Spain became hostile. Even then Gibraltar should hold out for 60 days.

11. To contain the Italian Fleet and secure Egypt a capital ship fleet should be based on Alexandria. In due course a heavy scale of attack could be mounted on Egypt from Libya, and we might have to withdraw the Fleet through the Suez Canal to Aden and block the Canal. Preparations to do this should be undertaken as soon as the contingency considered in this paper arises.

12. The retention of Singapore is very important for economic control, particularly of rubber and tin. To counter Japanese action in the Far East, a fleet, adequately supported by air forces, is necessary at Singapore. It is most improbable that we could send any naval forces there, and reliance would have to be placed upon the United States to safeguard our interests.

13. We should endeavour to maintain our position in all our overseas possessions.

ABILITY TO DEFEAT GERMANY

14. Germany might still be defeated by economic pressure, by a combination of air attack on economic objectives in Germany and on German morale and the creation of widespread revolt in her conquered territories.

15. We are advised in the following sense by the Ministry of Economic Warfare. We cannot emphasize too strongly the importance of the substantial accuracy of this forecast, since upon the economic factor depends our only hope of bringing about the downfall of Germany.

16. In spite of immediate economic gains obtained from her conquests, Germany will still be very short of food, natural fibres, tin, rubber, nickel and cobalt. Above all, even with Roumanian supplies, she will still have insufficient oil.

17. Given full Pan-American co-operation, we should be able to control all deficiency commodities at source. There will be no neutrals except Japan and Russia.

18. The effect of a continued denial of overseas supplies to Germany will be:—

    (a) By the winter of 1940–41, widespread shortage of food in many European industrial areas, including parts of Germany.

    (b) By the winter of 1940–41, shortage of oil will force Germany to weaken her military control in Europe.

    (c) By the middle of 1941, Germany will have difficulty in replacing military equipments. A large part of the industrial plant of Europe will stand still, throwing upon the German administration an immense unemployment problem to handle.

19. Air attacks on Germany's oil centres will be an important contribution to the enemy's defeat and to the reduction of the intensity of his air offensive. The pressure we could exert by air action will be extremely limited for some time owing to the effects of the enemy's attacks and the need to conserve our striking power to deal with the contingency of invasion.

20. The territories occupied by Germany are likely to prove a fruitful ground for sowing the seeds of revolt, particularly when economic conditions deteriorate.

21. Finally, we emphasise once more that these conclusions as to our ability to bring the war to a successful conclusion depend entirely upon full Pan-American economic and financial co-operation.

22. In view of our terms of reference and the speculative nature of the problem, we have not considered whether the Empire can continue the war if the United Kingdom were defeated.

DE GAULLE'S APPEAL TO FRANCE

Refusing to recognize Pétain's collaborationist Vichy government, the forty-nine-year-old military leader and Undersecretary of State for War for Paul Reynaud (for all of twelve days between June 5 and 17, 1940), Charles de Gaulle fled to London on July 17 in the hope of establishing a French Resistance movement. Despite his relative obscurity, de Gaulle managed to win the support of the British prime minister, Winston Churchill, whom he had met on only four previous occasions. Against the wishes of British government officials, who worried about antagonizing the newly formed Vichy government, Churchill allowed de Gaulle to broadcast a speech on the British Broadcasting Company (BBC) radio on June 18, 1940. Although historic in content, the broadcast, a rallying cry for a free France, was heard by relatively few people. Nonetheless, on June 28, de Gaulle was recognized by the British government as "leader of all the Free French." What follows is the text of de Gaulle's speech.

The leaders who, for many years past, have been at the head of the French armed forces, have set up a government.

Alleging the defeat of our armies, this government has entered into negotiations with the enemy with a view to bringing about a cessation of hostilities. It is quite true that we were, and still are, overwhelmed by enemy mechanized forces, both on the ground and in the air. It was the tanks, the planes, and the tactics of the Germans, far more than the fact that we were outnumbered, that forced our armies to retreat. It was the German tanks, planes, and tactics that provided the element of surprise which brought our leaders to their present plight.

But has the last word been said? Must we abandon all hope? Is our defeat final and irremediable? To those questions I answer—No!

Speaking in full knowledge of the facts, I ask you to believe me when I say that the cause of France is not lost. The very factors that brought about our defeat may one day lead us to victory.

For, remember this, France does not stand alone. She is not isolated. Behind her is a vast Empire, and she can make common cause with the British Empire, which commands the seas and is continuing the struggle. Like England, she can draw unreservedly on the immense industrial resources of the United States.

This war is not limited to our unfortunate country. The outcome of the struggle has not been decided by the Battle of France. This is a world war. Mistakes have been made, there have been delays and untold suffering, but the fact remains that there still exists in the world everything we need to crush our enemies some day. Today we are crushed by the sheer weight of mechanized force hurled against us, but we can still look to a future in which even greater mechanized force will bring us victory. The destiny of the world is at stake.

I, General de Gaulle, now in London, call on all French officers and men who are at present on British soil, or may be in the future, with or without their arms; I call on all engineers and skilled workmen from the armaments factories who are at present on British soil, or may be in the future, to get in touch with me.

Whatever happens, the flame of French resistance must not and shall not die.

FRENCH COLLABORATION

Early in 1940, General Philippe Pétain (1856–1951) had anticipated living out his years in peaceful retirement, basking in the adulation of his countrymen after his distinguished military career during the First World War. He had been widely hailed for saving France during that conflict, having secured the front lines at Verdun in 1916 and restored the fighting capability of divisions wracked by mutiny in 1917. But as the situation deteriorated in May 1940, Reynaud, prime minister of France, appointed him to the government in the hope that the old soldier could rally the army—and the country—against the German invasion. Pétain, however, foresaw no prospect of success and, judging that the war was lost, was the key figure not only in securing an armistice but also in heading a French government that would work with the victorious Germans. Pétain's distaste for the French Third Republic with its liberal legislation and pronounced anticlericalism encouraged him to view France's defeat as an opportunity to create a more conservative political and social order, to "rebuild France on a heap of ruins." In his view, continuing to resist, as de Gaulle proposed, was an absurd refusal to recognize military reality and a misguided impediment to the regeneration of France. Pétain met with Hitler at Montoire in October 1940 and justified his policy of collaboration in the following radio address.

Such an interview was only possible, four months after our defeat, thanks to the dignity of the French in their trials, thanks to the immense effort of regeneration in which they had engaged themselves, thanks also to the heroism of our sailors, the energy of our colonial leaders, the loyalty of our native populations. France has pulled itself together. This first meeting between the victor and the vanquished marks the first recovery of our country.

It is freely that I accepted the *Führer's* invitation. I did not have to put up with any *'Diktat'* or pressure from him. A collaboration has been envisaged between our two countries. I have accepted the principle of it. The details will be discussed later. To all those who are today awaiting the salvation of France, I say that salvation is above all in our hands....

It is with honour, and in order to maintain French unity—which has lasted ten centuries—that

Philippe Pétain, "Speech of October 30, 1940," in Richard Griffiths, *Pétain* (Garden City, NY: Doubleday, 1972), 270–271. Used by permission.

in the framework of an activity which will create the European new order I today enter the road of collaboration.

Thus, in the near future, the weight of our country's sufferings may be lightened, the lot of our prisoners bettered, the charges of occupation lowered. Thus the line of demarcation may be made more supple, the administration and victualling of the territory facilitated. This collaboration must be sincere. It must exclude all idea of aggression. It must carry with it a patient and confident effort. The armistice, meanwhile, is not peace. France is bound by numerous obligations to the victor. At least she remains sovereign. This sovereignty imposes on her the duty to defend her soil, to extinguish divergences of opinion, to put down the dissidence in her colonies. This policy is mine. The ministers are solely responsible to me. It is I alone who will be judged by history.

OCCUPIED POLAND

Unlike the states of Western Europe, Poland initially endured occupation by *two* conquering powers, Germany and the Soviet Union, which had secretly agreed to carve up Poland prior to Germany's invasion. Soviet troops poured across Poland's eastern frontier on September 17, 1940, forcing the desperate Poles to fight on two fronts and precluding any hope that they might stave off yet another partition (the country had been successively dismantled by the Prussians and Russians in the eighteenth century). Germany annexed the area closest to its own border, incorporating that within the Reich, and established a huge 35,000 square mile swathe of central Poland as a labor colony/reservation, the so-called General Government, under German administration by Hans Frank. The Soviets set to work on the eastern half of the country. Both occupiers sought to eradicate Polish culture and with systematic brutality eliminated any of the officers, intellectuals, or politicians who might have led an independence movement. The Soviets, for example, massacred 4,400 Polish officers in the Katyn forest in April 1940 and, when the corpses were subsequently discovered, tried to pin the crime on the Nazis. Poland suffered terribly from both German and Soviet oppression until June 1941, when the Germans ousted the Soviet occupiers and proceeded to deal ferociously with the whole of Poland. Frank declared his intention to make the country "an intellectual desert," and the country was the central location of the Holocaust, and, unfortunately, the scene of a measure of vicious anti-Semitism as well. Some 6 million Polish civilians (about half of them Jews) died during the war. One of the most perceptive observers of the occupation was Zygmunt Klukowski (1885–1959), a physician and hospital director in the town of Szczrebrzeszyn. His reflections on the first anniversary of the German invasion provide insight into the occupiers' efforts to stamp out all aspects of Polish cultural life, as well as the people's quiet determination to preserve their heritage.

September 1

Today is the first anniversary of the war, so I am going back over the year's events to evaluate the situation. I am reading my diary to see if events have taken on a different meaning or significance. Looking at all the facts I am more and more convinced that short notes written under fresh impressions have more meaning as historical documents than elaborate writing done after a long time has passed. Time will change not only the details of the events but, most important, the feelings of the writer. In my half century of adult life this year has been the hardest one. So far I am alive and happy that, despite everything, I have survived. I am still in good psychological shape and hopefully my heart will allow me to withstand more blows.

From the intellectual point of view this year has been a complete disaster. I was unable to study, to perform any kind of scientific research about the history of medicine. My collection of books increased by only a few volumes. I was able to collect some documents regarding the German occupation and our fight against it. This is not satisfactory. Besides, I am still living with the fear that my collection can fall into German hands and be destroyed.

As of now we are stifled in our intellectual life. We know nothing about what is happening in the world concerning art, literature, or music. In Poland it looks like we are dead. During the past year not one new book was printed, with the exception of Polish-German dictionaries. No more Polish newspapers, weeklies, or magazines. Newspapers printed by the Germans in Polish in Warsaw, Cracow, or Lublin are even worse than the original German ones. No one buys them. Once in a while we find some illegal underground papers..., printed in a very primitive style, and the news they give is always old and not too reliable.

The same with radio information. People use their imagination. We are not being informed of any events around the world or how the war is progressing. But we are trying to learn anything that will keep our spirits higher and force us to believe in a good future and final victory. People live completely occupied by their own personal problems and the struggle for daily food. Some who are involved in the black market are doing well, but everyone is trying to survive until the end of the war, hoping that we will win. We must protect ourselves against the invasion of influence of not only the Germans but also the Ukrainians. The Ukrainians are beginning to invade our area with the blessing of the German administration....

We are exhausted. Life is nerve shattering. We are living in uncertainty about what will happen to us, not in a month or a week, but in one hour.

We live under the constant threat of search, arrest, beating, evacuation, and death, with the last one maybe not being the worst because of the treatment of prisoners in German prisons and camps. Slowly we become used to it. We are prepared for everything. We know that casualties are common in this type of fight and that we face even more terrible times. But we wait to be witnesses to the war's end and our final victory over this civil enemy.

From all sources of news, many times not reliable, we try to learn the real situation of the fighting nations. We are glad that in view of the fast fall of Holland, Belgium, Norway, and the final capitulation of France, our own fight in September 1939, particularly around Warsaw, showed Poland in a completely different light in the eyes of the world. Our involvement in the fight in Norway and France gives living proof of the worth of Polish soldiers.

Our position against German occupation is firm. The entire population, with minor exceptions, is showing pride in our national heritage. The efforts of the Germans to form a Polish government are completely fruitless.

Last September we suffered a terrible blow, but today it is clear that against German military might this was unavoidable, since we were the first to fight. The Germans have occupied Poland for a year. They have tried to destroy our Polish culture and everything that is Polish. Everywhere the Germans try to enforce the rules of German national-socialistic life, but we treat them as a temporary evil, hoping that soon they will be defeated and our revenge will come. We are glad that this gives us more strength to fight against the German occupation and that, in spite of our defeat, we believe in our final victory and our bright future.

AIR RAID ON SOUTHAMPTON

On September 7, 1940, with his plans for an invasion of Britain on hold, Hitler ordered the Luftwaffe to include bombing raids on civilian targets in London with the intent of demoralizing the population and bringing the island nation to its knees. So began the Blitz, a period of intense bombing of British cities, including London, Coventry, and Southampton, which lasted until May 1941. London suffered continuous bombing from September 7 until November 2, 1940. On November 30 and December 1, 1940, the British port city of Southampton became a target of the German Luftwaffe. Although the primary targets were its docks and factories, over 1,000 of the city's buildings were destroyed, leaving 137 civilians dead and 250 seriously injured by the Luftwaffe's incendiary bombs. The Mass-Observation project, from which the following material about the Southampton raids was taken, began in England in 1937 by three men (anthropologist Tom Harrisson, poet and journalist Charles Madge, and documentary filmmaker Humphrey Jennings) who recruited about 2,000 individuals, consisting of paid investigators and diarists from all over Britain, to study and document the lives of ordinary Britons—an "anthropology of ourselves"—in the twentieth century. In this instance, they confirmed that aerial bombing would neither terrify the population into submission nor bring the war effort to a halt.

Southampton is a town of some 183,000 people; it has a balloon barrage and a fairly large anti-aircraft barrage.

Periodically, the town has been raided, and these raids have been fairly heavy. The worst raids, however occurred on last Saturday and Sunday (Nov. 30 and Dec. 1), when 370 casualties were caused and very heavy damage was done. The central and dockyard portion of the town was, in particular, hit, and the High Street has hardly a building standing.

MORALE

People seemed stunned and quiet but, on the whole, not really depressed. One man...who had been in a shelter had been hit, and said to Inv. [Investigator] 'There's no interest left in anything now,' but most people seemed to have more hope than this. One woman, for instance, said in a depressed tone of voice, 'I dread the night coming on' and then almost immediately started singing 'Tipperary.'...

To strangers people were cheerful and civil. But in the hotel, where Inv. stayed and where the residents had spent the two nights of bombing in a shelter together, tempers were more frayed....

A...case of temper occurred later in the evening. A battery wireless set was working, but only faintly, and everybody was anxious to listen to the 9 o'clock news. At the crucial moment, when the announcer reached news of Southampton, one woman...rattled her beads loudly and prevented another...from hearing. Why she did this, Inv. has no idea, she seemed a little senile. At the end of the news, the other woman came up to her, said 'I'd like to murder you,' then

"Leonard England: File Report No. 517, Air Raid on Southampton, 4 December 1940," in Angus Calder and Dorothy Sheridan, eds., *Speak for Yourself: A Mass-Observation Anthology, 1937–49* (London: Jonathan Cape, 1984), 89–90, 92–96. Used by permission.

walked over to her husband and said 'That damned old woman.'

There was not a great deal of interest in bomb damage, except in one large crater near the Green, where a direct hit had been scored on a shelter. There was also some interest in the demolition work which was being undertaken by the army, and when one large wall was dynamited there were laughs and even some isolated cheering. Most interest in individual house damage was at a large departmental store, Jones, which was gutted; men and women were stopping and staring with such exclamations as 'shocking' and 'terrible.' There was very general comparison between damage here and at Coventry, and Inv. felt here a suppressed feeling of pride. On the Monday and early Tuesday people were saying that the damage was as bad as Coventry, but by late on Tuesday this was developing into 'worse than Coventry'; one man…said that it was worse than Pompeii. There was some annoyance at the papers because they had not made so much fuss about the Southampton raid as the Coventry one.

Interest in casualties was low. Inv. heard no talk about friends and relations who had been killed or injured, and round the casualty list, which was posted up outside the police station, there were very few people. Many people did not believe the official figures; they said that there must be many more still in shelters under wrecked buildings….

There was a fairly general feeling that Southampton was done for….

EVACUATION

It must be remembered that Southampton had had serious raids before those of the last week. Many women and children had already been evacuated, and more had probably made plans as to what they would do if the occasion arose.

Throughout Monday there was apparently a large unofficial evacuation. Two people…spontaneously compared the lines of people leaving the town with bedding and prams full of goods to the pictures they had seen of refugees in Holland and Poland….

On Monday evening from about 4:30 onwards a stream of people were leaving the town for the night. When Inv. left the train at the docks, he was impressed by the seeming deadness of the town; there were no cars, and hardly any people except those that had left the train with him. But farther out people were moving. The buses were full, men and women were walking with their baggage. Some were going to relations in outlying parts, some to shelters, preceded by their wives who had reserved them places, and some to sleep in the open….

FOOD, SHOPS, ETC

Outside the damaged area—the damage was confined mainly to the centre of the town and to the docks—shops were nearly all open. Inside the damaged area, a large proportion were still at work; very few shops, still whole, were closed. Nearly all the shops were well stocked, meat, fish, and vegetable shops being practically unvisited by the public. There seemed to be a rush on the bakeries, and, to a lesser extent, the general provision stores, and while there was plenty of bread in the morning this seemed to have run out by the afternoon (Tuesday). Two shops selling hot tea were packed….

There were no communal kitchens, and, though hot food was obtainable at the Rest Centres, there was very general complaint at the lack of hot food….Many people had apparently not had a hot meal for some days….

COMPLAINTS

There were very few complaints, beyond a general one at the discomfort caused by lack of services, and consequent inability to cook, shave, and so on. These complaints did not take the form of direct accusation of the borough or anybody, but were more general. The main point was the lack of hot food.

Other complaints:

The sanitary system
The ineffectiveness of the anti-barrage. (This is not a general complaint, held only by a few people.)
The fact that the papers were not making so much fuss over Southampton as they did over Coventry.
The fact that the papers were making too much of the endurance of Southampton. If the

Germans thought that the people were quite unaffected by the bombing, they would come over and give them another dose.

The lack of interest of railway officials, *not* the chaos of the services.

REPRISALS

There was very little reprisal talk, and even when Inv. asked people whether they wanted reprisals, the usual answer was 'What good would that do?' One woman…was heard to say 'We've got to do them as they do to us, that's the only thing to do'; a man…wanted drastic measures against the actual airmen who did the bombing, 'I'd like to tie them up and put one of their own time bombs round their necks.' On the other hand, a young soldier…said 'There must be thousands on the other side of the Channel feeling like we do every night.'

LONDON IS BURNING

Edward R. Murrow (1908–1965) rose to fame as a journalist during World War II. He was sent by CBS to Europe in 1937 to create a network of correspondents (the "Murrow Boys") who would report on the war that appeared imminent. Murrow himself reported from the midst of the London Blitz via the radio, introducing his segments with the trademark words, "This…is London." His descriptions of a London under siege from the Luftwaffe's incendiary bombs, the destruction of buildings, the resulting homelessness of helpless civilians, as well as scenes of resilient Londoners who sought refuge in bomb shelters but refused to be demoralized, brought home the war to millions of Americans who listened to his broadcasts and may have played a role in convincing Americans of the necessity to join the battle against Germany. Murrow published transcripts of his broadcasts during the Blitz in 1941 under the title *This Is London.*

September 9, 1940

I've spent the day visiting the bombed areas. The King did the same thing. These people may have been putting on a bold front for the King, but I saw them just as they were—men shoveling mounds of broken glass into trucks, hundreds of people being evacuated from the East End, all of them calm and quiet. In one street where eight or ten houses had been smashed a policeman stopped a motorist who had driven through a red light. The policeman's patience was obviously exhausted. As he made out the ticket and lectured the driver, everyone in the street gathered around to listen, paying no attention at all to the damaged houses; they were much more interested in the policeman.

These people are exceedingly brave, tough, and prudent. The East End, where disaster is always just around the corner, seems to take it better than the more fashionable districts in the West End.

Edward R. Murrow, *This Is London* (New York: Simon & Schuster, 1941), 160–161, 174–176. Used by permission.

The firemen have done magnificent work these last forty hours. Early this morning I watched them fighting a fire which was obviously being used as a beacon by the German bombers. The bombs came down only a few blocks away, but the firemen just kept their hoses playing steadily at the base of the flame.

The Germans dropped some very big stuff last night. One bomb, which fell about a quarter of a mile from where I was standing on a roof-top, made the largest crater I've ever seen, and I thought I'd seen some big ones. The blast traveled down near-by streets, smashing windows five or six blocks away.

The British shot down three of the night bombers last night. I said a moment ago that Londoners were both brave and prudent. Tonight many theaters are closed. The managers decided the crowds just wouldn't come. Tonight the queues were outside the air-raid shelters, not the theaters. In my district, people carrying blankets and mattresses began going to the shelters before the siren sounded.

This night bombing is serious and sensational. It makes headlines, kills people, and smashes property; but it doesn't win wars. It may be safely presumed that the Germans know that, know that several days of terror bombing will not cause this country to collapse. Where then does this new phase of the air war fit? What happens next? The future must be viewed in relation to previous objectives; those objectives were the western ports and convoys, the Midlands, and Welsh industrial areas, and the southern airfields. And now we have the bombing of London. If this is the prelude to invasion, we must expect much heavier raids against London. After all, they only used about a hundred planes last night. And we must expect a sudden renewal of the attacks against fighter dromes [airfields] near the coast, an effort to drive the fighters inland. If the Germans continue to hammer London for a few more nights and then sweep successfully to blasting airdromes with their dive bombers, it will probably be the signal for this invasion—and you will remember there have been others in the past—is sometime about September 18....

September 15, 1940

During the last week you have heard much of the bombing of Buckingham Palace and probably seen pictures of the damage. You have been told by certain editors and commentators who sit in New York that the bombing of the Palace, which has one of the best air-raid shelters in England, caused a great surge of determination—a feeling of unity—to sweep this island. The bombing was called a great psychological blunder. I do not find much support for that point of view amongst Londoners with whom I've talked. They don't like the idea of their King and Queen being bombed, but, remember, this is not the last war—people's reactions are different. Minds have become hardened and callused. It didn't require a bombing of Buckingham Palace to convince these people that they are all in this thing together. There is nothing exclusive about being bombed these days. When there are houses down in your street, when friends and relatives have been killed, when you've seen that red glow in the sky night after night, when you're tired and sleepy—there just isn't enough energy left to be outraged about the bombing of a palace.

The King and Queen have earned the respect and admiration of the nation, but so have tens of thousands of humble folk who are much less well protected. If the Palace had been the only place bombed the reaction might have been different. Maybe some of those German bomb aimers are working for Goebbels instead of Goering, but if the purpose of the bombings was to strike terror to the hearts of the Britishers then the bombs have been wasted. The fire bomb on the House of Lords passed almost unnoticed. I heard a parcel of people laughing about it when one man said: "That particular bomb wouldn't seriously have damaged the nation's war effort."

I'm talking about those things not because the bombing of the Palace appears to have affected America more than Britain, but in order that you may understand that this war has no relation with the last one, so far as symbols and civilians are concerned. You must understand that a world is dying, that old values, the old prejudices, and the old bases of power and prestige are going. In an army, if the morale is to be good, there must be equality in the ranks. The private with money must not be allowed to buy himself a shelter of steel and concrete in the front-line trench. One company can't be equipped with pitchforks and another with machine guns. London's civilian army doesn't have that essential equality—I mean equality of shelter. One borough before the war defied the authorities and built deep shelters. Now people arrive at those shelters from all over town and the people who paid for them are in danger of being crowded out. Some of those outsiders arrive in taxis, others by foot. Since it's a public shelter they can't be barred by the people whose money went into the digging. This is just one of the problems in equality that London is now facing.

CHAPTER 3

THE WIDENING WAR

AN EMPIRE MOBILIZED   As the conflict expanded, imperial nations mobilized native troops for the war effort, as reflected in this unit of cyclists from the Belgian Congo.
Source: © Bettmann/CORBIS.

In late 1940, World War II consisted of two still separate conflicts. In Asia, Japanese expansion into China had been under way for a decade already, with outright war having been waged since 1937. In Europe, Britain stood alone (though with increasing American aid) against a triumphant Germany, which, despite a respite from major land- or air-based combat operations, faced the dilemma of how to subdue its only remaining opponent. By the end of 1941, however, each conflict would have broadened significantly, and, with formal American entry, the two fused into the truly global event we know as the Second World War.

One reason for the war's breadth was the fact that several participants, most notably Britain, were imperial powers. Indeed, Britain did not really stand alone, for in 1939 it expected and received the support of the Dominions. Australians, Canadians, Indians, New Zealanders, and South Africans would all fight on Britain's behalf, although their contribution was often neglected because they were not in a position to contribute much to the direct defense of the British Isles. British statesmen took such support for granted, even to the lengths of committing India to the war without consulting the leaders of Indian opinion or addressing the incongruity of fighting a war to protect freedom while relying on mechanisms of imperial domination.

Many soldiers from the Dominions would distinguish themselves in campaigns in North Africa, part of the expansion of the war in the Mediterranean. Here the driving force was Italy's Mussolini, intent on re-creating the glories of the Roman Empire and demonstrating that he too was a dictator to be reckoned with. Diplomats in the nineteenth century had mocked Italy's expansionist ambitions, deriding it as a country with a large appetite but bad teeth, and so it proved in 1940. Mussolini's offensives in Libya (in September, to threaten British interests in Egypt and the Suez Canal) and Greece (October 1940) went so badly that German forces had to intervene to rescue the Italian armies from utter disaster. The British, who refused to cede naval control of the Mediterranean or abandon the Greeks, and certainly could not afford to lose Egypt and the direct route to India, matched the German escalation. In North Africa, fortunes swung back and forth as the German Afrika Korps, under the inspired leadership of Erwin Rommel, reclaimed lost ground but never had quite the strength or logistical support to effect a complete break-through. In Greece, however, the British were pushed out, leaving divided local resistance movements to face a brutal German occupation.

Hitler disdained operations in the Mediterranean as a sideshow that would divert German attention from the real tasks at hand, but he recognized the need to secure the Balkans to protect Germany's southern flank in a strike eastward against the Soviet Union. That ambitious goal—defeating Stalin, destroying Bolshevism, and conquering the massive swathe of territory he insisted was necessary to secure Germany's proper "living space"—was to Hitler the most significant legacy he could leave as a statesman. He viewed military operations against the Soviet Union not as a means to secure a traditional victory followed by a peace advantageous to Germany, but as an ideological war for survival in which it was necessary to extirpate a competing system. German officers were commanded (the so-called criminal orders) to execute communist functionaries attached to Soviet units, disregard the rights of prisoners or civilians, suppress resistance with disproportionate severity, and eliminate any Jewish influence (or presence) in captured territory. Some areas would be cleared for resettlement by ethnic Germans, other sections and their subject populations would exist only to serve German interests. Basic human rights were brushed aside in the belief that Slavic peoples were subhuman, best fitted for slavery. Hitler's obsession in early 1941 with invading the Soviet Union was reinforced by his conviction that Britain was continuing to hold out only because it counted upon eventual Soviet entry and a replay of the debilitating two-front war Germany had waged in 1914. If Germany could demolish the Red Army, Britain would finally recognize that further resistance was hopeless and seek an accommodation.

In preparation for an invasion of the Soviet Union (code-named Barbarossa), the Germans persuaded Bulgaria to permit them the right to bases in that country, and applied similar pressure on Yugoslavia. A coup in Belgrade by anti-Axis elements forced Hitler's hand, however, and in April 1941 German forces invaded. Although most of those troops were soon reallocated to Operation Barbarossa, Yugoslavia remained unsettled and the entire campaign delayed the invasion of the Soviet Union by several critical weeks. Not that most German officers were concerned about the delay, for they held a low opinion of the Red Army. Stalin's purges of the military in the 1930s had taken a terrible toll, with perhaps half of his officers being shot or imprisoned. Three of the five top commanders were killed, including the brightest single officer, Marshal M. N. Tuchachevsky, who could have done much to modernize Soviet military doctrine and improve the eventual response to the German invasion. The Red Army's disastrous showing in the opening stages of the Finnish campaign also encouraged a dangerous sense of overconfidence within the German military, which was riding high after its unbroken string of successes in Poland, France, and the Low Countries. No adequate preparations were made for wintertime combat on the assumption that the Red Army would have collapsed before the onset of winter weather.

Initially it appeared that the Germans' optimism was entirely justified. When Barbarossa began on June 22, 1941, the Soviets were caught unprepared. Stalin himself had dismissed credible warnings of the attack (from his own spies and from other countries) as misinformation spread by unscrupulous capitalist countries to embroil the Bolshevik nation in an unnecessary war that would destroy the great bastion of socialism. Soviet planners, whose job it was to anticipate a war with Germany, had expected a major thrust farther south than the blows German forces actually delivered, so poor preparation combined with an inadequate response to put the Red Army at a terrible disadvantage. Some 2.5 million German soldiers and their Axis allies punched huge holes in Soviet lines in which many troops were at the front, with too few held in strategic reserve. No match for their opponents' swiftly moving armored spearheads, Soviet armies were encircled, trapped, and mauled, one after the other. Within weeks the Germans had captured more than 3 million prisoners of war, most of whom died from intentional neglect or abuse. Because the Nazis had long preached that Slavic peoples were subhuman, the prisoners and Soviet civilians were treated with a brutality that provoked determined opposition even from regions that had suffered under Stalin (the Ukraine, for example) and might have been expected to greet the Germans as liberators, or at least to acquiesce in their conquest.

Despite the invaders' spectacular successes, including the destruction of many units and the occupation of 500,000 square miles of Soviet territory, the German armies found it impossible to maintain the initial blistering pace. They had seriously underestimated the numbers of troops opposing them, the quality of the best Soviet equipment (such as the T-34 tank which was superior to its German counterparts, the Panzers Mark III or IV), and the determination of these allegedly unmotivated, subhuman soldiers to resist. Although the Soviets were pushed back everywhere, they succeeded in exacting a terrible toll: by September 1941, German forces had suffered more than 400,000 casualties, and nearly half of their tanks were destroyed, damaged, or out of commission. Poor Russian roads, increasingly long supply lines, and the difference in gauges between the German and Soviet rail networks made logistics a nightmare. Moreover, although the prominence of the Panzer divisions might have misled observers into assuming that the German army was thoroughly mechanized, it certainly was not. It relied upon horse-drawn transport and a hodgepodge of trucks scrounged from every conquered country. More than once, even the hard-charging Panzers had to stop to refit, pause for supplies to catch up, or wait out torrential rains that turned barely passable roads into impassable quagmires.

Finally, the German drive eastward was interrupted by conflicting priorities. Despite the unprecedented buildup on the Soviet frontier, the simple fact was that the Germans did not have enough troops to advance simultaneously on all fronts and overwhelm Soviet opposition. About a month into the campaign, Hitler emphasized the northern thrust toward Leningrad, and a southern push through the Ukraine toward the oil-rich region of the Caucasus, but German forces could not then continue to apply full pressure on the center, in the direction of Moscow. Once units were redeployed in the fall and the sprint toward Moscow resumed, the Soviets were able to cobble together an adequate defense of the capital (including troops transferred from Siberia) and eventually slow the German advance to a crawl. Although German reconnaissance units could see the spires of the Kremlin through their binoculars, they would never get any closer. In December 1941 a fierce Soviet counteroffensive would push the weary, overextended invaders back, force them to regroup, and relieve the pressure on Moscow. Operation Barbarossa had dealt the Soviet Union a massive blow, but not the swift knockout its planners had envisioned.

Germany's invasion of the Soviet Union had profound consequences for the war in the Pacific as well. Tensions between the Japanese and the Soviets had persisted for some time, the result of Soviet patronage of the Chinese communists (who were instrumental in resisting Japanese aggression) and growing friction over borders in Manchuria, and fighting between Japan's Kwantung Army and Soviet troops erupted in August 1938 and again in May 1939. Any expansionist moves directed from Tokyo had to be tempered to avoid provoking Moscow. But after the German attack on June 22, 1941, it was clear that the Soviets had their hands full and could not take an aggressive line with Japan. Apart from spectacular (and infamous) successes in capturing cities like Nanking along the coast, operations in China did not hold the promise of quick victory or relief from Japan's dependence on vital imports. New targets beckoned. Nothing now stood in the way of the strategy to "hold north, go south," to expand into resource-rich Southeast Asia. Nothing, that is, except the opposition of the United States.

One of the intriguing questions about the origins of the Second World War is why the West was willing to appease Germany but not Japan. Certainly Japan's aggression in China seemed more blatant at the time than Germany's avowed efforts to reincorporate its ethnic compatriots. Given the precedent of World War I, many diplomats thought events in Asia were far less likely to precipitate another world war, and therefore conciliatory approaches were less urgent in the Pacific. Some presumed the threat of the Soviet Union would suffice to keep Japanese ambitions in check. And finally, the United States, which largely abstained from diplomacy in Europe, was more willing to get involved in Asia. For their part, the Japanese could not understand the Americans' moral outrage over their incursion in China, a country in which the United States did not exercise a decisive economic interest. They failed to appreciate the role of Christian missionaries, the respect for an ancient civilization, or the influence of the cultivated Madame Chiang (the Chinese leader's wife) and her Soong family, all of which cast China as an admirable underdog under assault from an upstart bully.

Japan's stated intention to create an area of exclusive influence, the "Greater East Asia Co-Prosperity Sphere," appeared to its authors as a defensible stratagem modeled on Western imperialism. It struck the United States as indefensible territorial aggrandizement by a power that had pledged, in the 1920s, to preserve the status quo and accept an important, though subordinate, position. Roosevelt's government initially turned to economic rather than military measures, such as abrogating commercial treaties and introducing embargoes on critical exports to Japan like aviation fuel and scrap iron. If these steps were intended to allow some latitude for the diplomats to reach a settlement, they only reinforced the conviction among Japanese militarists that they must seize by force what their armed services required, not depend upon the largesse of their rivals. When the United States took the precaution of basing the Pacific Fleet much closer to Japan, at Pearl Harbor in Hawaii instead of in California at San Diego, so that it could act as a deterrent, it was now in harm's way, within reach of an increasingly fatalistic Japanese government bent on expansion and willing to risk war to achieve it. A cabinet meeting on September 6, 1941, marked the final point at which preparations for an attack might have been averted, but the advocates for war argued strenuously that the odds against Japan were lengthening every month. If striking America now was a risky gamble, doing so later held an even slimmer prospect of success. On December 7, 1941, Japanese carrier-based planes swooping to attack Pearl Harbor confirmed that Tokyo had indeed chosen to throw the dice. Three days later, America found itself at hostilities, not just with Japan, but Germany as well, courtesy of Hitler's rash declaration of war. The Asian and European conflicts were now merged (at least insofar as the United States would be waging both of them), and the globe was now truly engulfed in a world war.

A WAR FOR FREEDOM?

As the conflict developed, it would have implications around the globe, even in areas that had yet to (or would never) hear the sound of gunfire. For example, the British government's chief administrator in India, the viceroy, Lord Linlithgow, took it for granted that he could commit India to the war against Germany without consulting any representatives of Indian opinion. This was despite the steady growth in Indian nationalist aspirations and the continuing prominence of the Indian National Congress (INC), the preeminent political party founded in 1885 to give voice to those aspirations. After the outbreak of the war and Linlithgow's declaration, the INC's Working Committee, an executive committee composed of senior Congress politicians, met to review the situation and issue a manifesto. That statement, released on September 14, 1939, indicated that most Indian politicians were sympathetic to the Allies, but wary that military conflict would only reaffirm British and French imperial rule.

The Congress has repeatedly declared its entire disapproval of the ideology and practice of Fascism and Nazism and their glorification of war and violence and the suppression of the human spirit. It has condemned the aggression in which they have repeatedly indulged and their sweeping away well established principles and recognized standards of civilized behaviour. It has been in fascism and Nazism the intensification of the principle of imperialism against which the Indian people have struggled for many years. The Working Committee must therefore unhesitatingly condemn the latest aggression of the Nazi government in Germany and Poland and sympathize with those who resist it.

The Congress has further laid down that the issue of war and peace for India must be decided by the Indian people, and no outside authority can impose this decision upon them, nor can the Indian people permit their resources to be exploited for imperialist ends. Any imposed decision, or attempt to use Indian resources for purposes not approved by them, will necessarily have to be opposed by them. If cooperation is desired in a worthy cause, this cannot be obtained by compulsion and imposition, and the Committee cannot agree to the carrying out by the Indian people of orders issued by external authority. Cooperation must be between equals by mutual consent for a cause which both consider to be worthy. The people of India have, in the recent past, faced great risks and willingly made great sacrifices to secure their own freedom and establish a free democratic State in India, and their sympathy is entirely on the side of democracy and freedom. But India cannot associate herself in a war said to be for democratic freedom when that very freedom is denied to her, and such limited freedom as she possesses taken away from her.

The Committee are aware that the governments of Great Britain and France have declared that they are fighting for democracy and freedom and to put an end to aggression. But the history of the recent past is full of examples showing the constant divergence between the spoken word, the ideals proclaimed, and the real motives and objectives. During

"Working Committee's Manifesto," in M. K. Gandhi, *Non-Violence in Peace and War*, 2 vols. (Ahmedabad: Navajivan Publishing House, n.d.), 1:218–223. Used by permission.

the War of 1914–18 the declared war aims were the preservation of democracy, self-determination, and the freedom of small nations, and yet the very governments which solemnly proclaimed these aims entered into secret treaties embodying imperialist designs for the carving up of the Ottoman Empire. While stating that they did not want any acquisition of territory, the victorious Powers added largely to their colonial domains....

If the war is to defend the *status quo*, imperialist possessions, colonies, vested interests and privileges, then India can have nothing to do with it. If, however, the issue is democracy and a world order based on democracy, then India is intensely interested in it. The Committee are convinced that the interests of Indian democracy do not conflict with the interests of British democracy or world democracy. But there is an inherent and ineradicable conflict between democracy for India or elsewhere and imperialism and fascism. If Great Britain fights for the maintenance and extension of democracy, then she must necessarily end imperialism in her own possessions, establish full democracy in India, and the Indian people must have the right of self-determination....

The crisis that has overtaken Europe is not of Europe only but of humanity and will not pass like other crisis [*sic*] or wars leaving the essential structure of the present-day world intact. It is likely to refashion the world for good or ill, politically, socially, and economically. This crisis is the inevitable consequence of the social and political conflicts and contradictions which have grown alarmingly since the last Great War [World War I], and it will not be finally resolved till these conflicts and contradictions are removed and a new equilibrium established. That equilibrium can only be based on the ending of the domination and exploitation of one country by another, and on a reorganization of economic relations on a juster basis for the common good of all.

WARNING SIGNS FROM JAPAN

Joseph Grew (1880–1965) reputedly got his first significant post in America's foreign service in 1904 because he shot a threatening tiger at close range in China, an act that persuaded then president Theodore Roosevelt that he was a man to be reckoned with. In any event, the diplomatic Grew habitually sought to contain trouble, not provoke it, and he rose rapidly from his initial post as a clerk to the consul general in Cairo to serve as American ambassador to Japan from 1932 until relations ceased with the Japanese attack on Pearl Harbor in December 1941. Grew warned his superiors in Washington DC that aggressive Japanese military leaders were bent on expansion, but he continued to hope that more reasonable civilian politicians might restrain them and preserve peace. Of particular note in this telegram (more than a year before Pearl Harbor) is Grew's warning that American embargoes or sanctions could provoke the Japanese military into an even more reckless posture, even to the point of a "sudden stroke" (i.e., a surprise attack). After war broke out, Grew was briefly interned by the Japanese, but then repatriated in 1942. He resumed his diplomatic career, serving as undersecretary of state, and, along with Henry Stimson, sought alternatives to the use of the atomic bomb in August 1945.

Whatever the intentions of the present Japanese Government may be there cannot be any doubt that the military and other elements in Japan see in the present world situation a "golden opportunity" to carry their dreams of expansion into effect; the German victories, like strong wine, have gone to their heads; they have believed implicitly until recently in Great Britain's defeat; they have argued that the war will probably be ended in a quick German victory and that Japan's position in Greater East Asia should be consolidated while Germany is still agreeable and before Japan might be robbed of her far-flung control in the Far East by the eventual hypothetical strengthening of the German naval power; although carefully watching the attitude of the United States they have discounted effective opposition on our part. It has been and is doubtful that the saner heads in and out of the government will be able to control these elements.

However, now a gradual change can be sensed.... It is beginning to be seen by the Japanese Government, the army, the navy, and the public, that Germany may not defeat Great Britain after all, a possibility which I have constantly emphasized in the plainest language to my Japanese contacts and now, in addition to that dawning realization, they see that Britain and the United States are steadily drawing closer together in mutual defense measures with the American support of the British fleet by the transfer of fifty destroyers and with our acquisition of naval bases in British Atlantic possessions. Reports are being heard of our rapid construction of a two-ocean Navy and of our consideration of strengthening our Pacific naval bases and they even hear rumors that we will eventually use Singapore. Japanese consciousness is logically being affected by these rumors and developments. They tend on the one hand to emphasize the potential danger facing

Joseph Grew to the Secretary of State, Telegram of September 12, 1940, U.S. Department of State, *Peace and War: United States Foreign Policy, 1931–1941* (Washington, DC: U.S. Government Printing Office, 1943), 569–571. Used by permission.

Japan from the United States and Great Britain eventually acting together in positive action...[and] furnish cogent arguments on the other hand for those Japanese elements who seek political and economic security by securing raw material sources and markets entirely within Japanese control....

I have expressed the opinion in previous communications that American-Japanese relations would be set on a downward curve if sanctions were applied by the United States. It is true that measures are now justified by our new program of national preparedness which need not fall within the category of outright sanctions. On the other hand, the probability must be contemplated that drastic embargoes on such important products as oil, of which a super-abundance is known to be possessed by the United States, would be interpreted by the people and government of Japan as actual sanctions and some form of retaliation might and probably would follow. The risks would depend not so much upon the careful calculations of the Japanese Government as upon the uncalculating "do or die" temper of the army and navy should they impute to the United States the responsibility for the failure of their plans for expansion. It may be that such retaliation would take the form of counter-measures by the government but it would be more likely that it would be some sudden stroke by the navy or army without the prior authorization or knowledge of the government.

JAPAN'S DECISION FOR WAR

Germany's invasion of the Soviet Union in June 1941 eliminated any possibility that Japan could persuade both of those countries to jointly apply diplomatic pressure on the United States to refrain from opposing Japanese expansion in French Indochina and toward the Dutch East Indies. Far from acquiescing, Roosevelt's government responded by freezing Japanese assets and imposing an oil embargo. Furthermore, the Anglo-American proclamation in August of the Atlantic Charter renewed in Japanese eyes the specter of Western imperialists who insisted in preserving a status quo favorable to them. Responding to the new situation, key Japanese policy makers had by the end of the month drafted a memorandum entitled "The Essentials for Carrying Out the Empire's Policies." At a crucial "Imperial Conference" in the presence of the emperor on September 6, 1941, the government met to ratify the future course of its military and foreign policy. The conference was marked by a curious compound of aggressive overconfidence and pessimistic fatalism, as evidenced by this statement by the navy's Chief of Staff, Admiral Osami Nagano. Although Hirohito was concerned by the bellicose attitude of the military advisors toward a looming war they admitted would be extremely difficult to win, in the end he did not oppose the meeting's overall conclusion: to make cursory diplomatic efforts (while rejecting the concessions that might have yielded some progress) and simultaneously prepare for a war that, if truly inevitable, should be waged sooner rather later, before Japan's comparative position deteriorated further.

As the Prime Minister has explained in general terms it is clear that our Empire must exert every effort to overcome the present difficult situation by peaceful means and must find a way to ensure her future prosperity and security. However, in the event that a peaceful solution is not attainable, and we have no alternative but to resort to war, the Supreme Command believes, from the standpoint of operations, that we cannot avoid being finally reduced to a crippled condition [if we delay for too long]. A number of vital military supplies, including oil, are dwindling day by day. This will cause a gradual weakening of our national defense, and lead to a situation in which, if we maintain the status quo, the capacity of our Empire to act will be reduced in the days to come. Meanwhile, the defenses of American, British, and other foreign military facilities and vital points in the Far East, and the military preparedness of these countries, particularly of the United States, are being strengthened with great speed. By the latter half of next year America's military preparedness will have made great progress, and it would be very dangerous for our Empire to remain idle and let the days go by.

Accordingly, if our minimum demands, which are necessary for the self-preservation and self-defense of our Empire, cannot be attained through diplomacy, and ultimately we cannot avoid war, we must first make all preparations, take advantage of our opportunities, undertake aggressive military operations with determination and a dauntless attitude, and find a way out of our difficulties.

As to our predictions of the way military operations are likely to go, the probability is very high that they [the United States] will from the outset plan on a prolonged war. Therefore, it will be necessary for us to be reconciled to this and to be prepared militarily for a long war. If they should aim for a quick war leading to an early decision, send their principal naval units, and challenge us to an immediate war, this would be the very thing we hope for. The naval units that Great Britain could send to the Far East would be rather limited because of the current war in Europe. Accordingly, if the combined American-British fleet should attack us in the areas of the ocean we have in mind, and when we take into consideration the role of aircraft and other elements, we can say with confidence that the probability of our victory is high. However, even if our Empire should win a decisive naval victory, we will not thereby be able to bring the war to a conclusion. We can anticipate that America will attempt to prolong the war, utilizing her impregnable position, her superior industrial power, and her abundant resources.

Our Empire does not have the means to take the offensive, overcome the enemy, and make them give up their will to fight. Moreover, we are short of resources at home, so we would very much like to avert a prolonged war. However, if we get into a prolonged war, the most important means of assuring that we will be able to bear this burden will be to seize the enemy's important military areas and sources of materials quickly at the beginning of the war, making our operational position tenable and at the same time obtaining vital materials from the areas now under hostile influence. If this first stage in our operations is carried out successfully, our Empire will have secured strategic areas in the Southwest Pacific, established an impregnable position, and laid the basis for a prolonged war, even if American military preparedness should proceed as scheduled. What happens thereafter will depend to a great extent on overall national power—including various elements, tangible and intangible—and on developments in the world situation.

Thus the outcome of a prolonged war is closely related to the success or failure of the first stage in our operations. The essential conditions that give a chance of success in the first stage of operations are: first, to decide quickly to commence hostilities in view of the realities of our fighting capacity and theirs; second, to take the initiative rather than to allow them to do so; third, to consider the meteorological conditions in the operational areas in order to make operations easier. It was in view of these considerations that the time when the crucial decision must be made, which is indicated in this proposal, was set. Of course we intend to proceed carefully with our war preparations, taking full account of the developments in diplomatic negotiations....

We must spare no efforts in seeking a way to settle the present difficult situation peacefully, and thus ensure the prosperity and security of our Empire. We must never fight a war that can be avoided. At the same time, I do not believe that a peace...in which we would be forced to fight again during the following summer under unfavorable conditions, would contribute to the long-term prosperity of our Empire.

AVENGING WESTERN IMPERIALISM

The Japanese military recognized that in any prolonged conflict against the Western powers, Japan would face a quantitative disadvantage in terms of population, military personnel, weapons, and other resources. But, Japanese officers believed, their army would prove qualitatively superior, fighting with a dedication, spirit, and adaptability to conditions that their enemies could never match. The following pamphlet was prepared to give Japanese soldiers a brief introduction to why their country called upon them to fight, what was expected of them, and how they could turn the abysmal conditions of tropical jungle warfare to their advantage. It stressed that soldiers were compelled to secure victory at any cost and avoid the stigma of dishonoring their ancestors through defeat, and, by linking such tenacity to codes of manliness which supposedly contrasted with the effeminate nature of Westerners, helps to explain why beaten Japanese units so often disdained surrender and fought to the death. Ironically, the author of the book in which the pamphlet was reprinted, Colonel Masanobu Tsuji, who was a chief of operations for the Twenty-fifth Army in Malaya, evaded capture or surrender, survived the war, and later served as a politician in Japan's House of Councillors of the National Diet.

The English, the French, the Americans, the Dutch, the Portuguese and others sailed into the Far East as if it were theirs by natural right, terrorized and subjugated the culturally backward natives, and colonized every country in the area. India and the Malay Peninsula were seized by the British, Annam by the French, Java and Sumatra by the Dutch, the Philippines by the Americans. These territories, the richest in natural resources in the Far East, were taken by a handful of white men, and their tens of millions of Asian inhabitants have for centuries, down to our own day, suffered constant exploitation and persecution at their hands.

We Japanese have been born in a country of no mean blessings, and thanks to the august power and influence of His Majesty the Emperor, our land has never once to this day, experienced invasion and occupation by a foreign power. The other peoples of the Far East look with envy upon Japan; they trust and honour the Japanese; and deep in their hearts they are hoping that, with the help of the Japanese people, they may themselves achieve national independence and happiness....

The reason why so many peoples of the Far East have been so completely crushed by so few white men is, fundamentally, that they have exhausted their strength in private quarrels, and that they are lacking in any awareness of themselves as a group, as peoples of Asia.

Without oil neither planes, warships nor cars can move. Britain and America, controlling the greater part of the world's oil and having far more than they can use for their own purposes, have nevertheless forbidden the export of oil to Japan, which is desperately short of it. More than that, they even obstruct Japan from buying oil in South Asia.

Read This Alone and the War Can Be Won, prepared by the Imperial Army Headquarters, 1941, as reprinted in Masanobu Tsuji, *Singapore: The Japanese Version* (New York: St. Martin's, 1960), 300–305, 307–308, 313, 330–331, 347–349. Used by permission.

Rubber and tin are likewise indispensable for military operations, and the countries of South Asia are the richest sources in the whole of the Far East for these valuable commodities too. Although our country has sought to purchase them by fair methods, the Anglo-Americans have interfered even in this. And in the unscrupulous behaviour of these two countries in these matters lies one of the reasons why the present campaign has been forced upon us....

This theatre of war knows no seasons. It is subject throughout the year to a heat comparable to that of mid-summer in Japan. Hence we call it a world of everlasting summer....Thunder and heavy rain is common after midday. These extremely violent cloudbursts, known as "squalls," are in quite a different class from the summer downpours we know in Japan. They are welcome in so far as they clear the oppressive atmosphere, but they also crumble roads, wash away bridges, and thus considerably hamper troop movements.

Again, because of the high humidity, gun powder becomes affected by damp; rifles, artillery and ammunition rust; spectacles mist over; and electric batteries run down quickly....The troublesome malarial mosquito is everywhere, harboring its grudge....

If the peoples of Asia, representing more than half of the world's population, were to make a united stand it would indeed be a sore blow to British, Americans, French and Dutch alike, who for centuries have battened and waxed fat on the blood of Asians.

Already Japan, the pioneer in this movement in the Far East, has rescued Manchuria from the ambition of the Soviets, and set China free from the extortions of the Anglo-Americans. Her next great mission is to assist towards the independence of the Thais, the Annamese [Vietnamese], and the Filipinos, and to bring the blessing of freedom to the natives of South Asia and the Indian people. In this we shall be fulfilling the essential spirit of 'one world to the eight corners of the earth.'

The aim of the present war is the realization, first in the Far East, of His Majesty's august will and ideal that the peoples of the world should each be granted possession of their rightful homelands....The significance of the present struggle, as we have shown, is immense, and the peril which Japan has drawn upon herself as the central and leading force in this movement is greater than anything she has ever faced since the foundation of the country....

In the Japan of recent years, where no one who cannot read English can proceed to higher education, and where English is widely used in all first-class hotels, trains and steamships, we have unthinkingly come to accept Europeans as superior and to despise the Chinese and the peoples of the South.

This is like spitting into our own eyes. Bearing in mind that we Japanese, as an Eastern people, have ourselves for long been classed alongside the Chinese and the Indians as an inferior race and treated as such, we must at the very least, here in Asia, beat these Westerners to submission, that they may change their arrogant and ill-mannered attitude.

The present war is a struggle between races, and we must achieve the satisfaction of our just demands with no thought of leniency to Europeans, unless they be the Germans and Italians. But pillaging, molesting women, and the heedless slaughter or maiming of people who offer no resistance, or any action which may sully the reputation of Japan as a country of moral rectitude, should be condemned by all in the strongest terms. You must do nothing to impair your dignity as soldiers of His Majesty the Emperor in His Majesty's Army. You must in particular show compassion towards the old and towards women and children....

Realizing that the war may well be a protracted affair you must carry forward preparations for a lengthy campaign, and as well as making the fullest use of the resources of the country, it will be important to take special care in the preservation of arms and clothing supplies. Since it is no small matter to transport supplies by sea all the way from Japan, you should fight and live on a bare minimum....

When you encounter the enemy...regard yourself as an avenger come at last face to face with his father's murderer. The discomforts of the long sea voyage and the rigours of the sweltering march have been but months of watching and waiting for the moment when you may slay this enemy. Here before you is the man whose death will lighten your heart of its burden of brooding anger. If you fail to destroy him utterly you can never rest at peace. And the first blow is the vital blow.

Westerners—being very superior people—very effeminate and very cowardly—have an intense dislike of fighting in the rain or the mist, or at night. Night, in particular (though it is excellent for dancing), they cannot conceive to be a proper time for war. In this, if we seize upon it, lies our great opportunity.

At stake in the present war, without a doubt, is the future prosperity or decline of the Empire. Slowly, little by little, like a man strangling his victim with a soft cord of silken floss, America has been prohibiting the export to Japan of oil and steel.... We embark now upon that great mission which calls upon Japan, as the representative of all the peoples of the Far East, to deal a resolute and final blow to centuries of European aggression in these lands....The final reckoning of our holy crusade will come on the battlefields ahead. Hundreds of thousands of the heroic dead will be watching over us. The supreme offering for which the souls of your departed comrades long is victory in this battle....Officers and men, the eyes of the whole world will be upon you in this campaign, and, working together in community of spirit, you must demonstrate to the world the true worth of Japanese manhood....

Corpses drifting swollen in the sea depths,
Corpses rotting in the mountain-grass—
We shall die, by the side of our lord we shall die.
We shall not look back.

YAMAMOTO'S STRATEGY

Admiral Isoroku Yamamoto (1884–1943) was widely regarded as Japan's supreme naval strategist and the brilliant architect of the surprise attack on Pearl Harbor. Unlike some of his bellicose colleagues in the Japanese fleet, Yamamoto did not favor Japan's aggressive imperialist expansion, and he regretted both the 1931 incursion into Manchuria and escalating tensions with the United States. In fact, his willingness to apologize to American ambassador Grew over a gunboat incident made him a target of Japanese right-wing assassins, who despised the admiral for the contacts he had made as a young man while studying at Harvard and serving as a naval attaché in Washington DC. Yamamoto's experience in the United States had given him a healthy respect for American industrial and military might, convincing him that, in the event of war, Japan's only hope lay in delivering a quick, knockout blow. As a result, he rejected the traditional Japanese naval strategy which had relied on luring the American fleet westward across the Pacific, whittling down its strength on the long voyage (through incessant small attacks by submarines and other vessels), and then annihilating the American battleships in a single decisive contest modeled on the crushing Japanese victory over the Russian navy at Tsushima in 1904. The following letter to Japan's naval minister makes clear Yamamoto's insistence that in a war with America, Japan must seize the initiative from the outset.

OPINIONS ON WAR PREPARATIONS

Although a precise outlook on the international situation is hard for anyone to make, it is needless to say that now the time has come for the Navy, especially the Combined Fleet, devote itself seriously to war preparations, training and operational plans with a firm determination that a conflict with the U.S. and Great Britain is inevitable....

The most important thing we have to do first of all in a war with the U.S., I firmly believe, is to fiercely attack and destroy the U.S. main fleet at the outset of the war, so that the morale of the U.S. Navy and her people goes down to such an extent that it cannot be recovered.

Only then shall we be able to secure an invincible stand in key positions in East Asia, thus being able to establish and keep the East Asia co-prosperity sphere....

[W]e should do our very best at the outset of a war with the U.S., and we should have a firm determination of deciding the fate of the war on its first day.

The outline of the operational plan is as follows:

a. In case of the majority of the enemy main force being in Pearl Harbor to attack it thoroughly with our air force, and to blockade the harbor.
b. In case they are staying outside of the harbor, too, to apply the same attack method as the above....

It is not easy to succeed in either case, but I believe we could be favored by God's blessing when all officers and men who take part in this operation have a

Letter of 7 January 1941 of Admiral Isoroku Yamamoto to Navy Minister Koshiro Oikawa in Donald M. Goldstein and Katherine V. Dillon eds., *The Pearl Harbor Papers* (Washington, D.C.: Brassey's, 1993), Potomac Books, Inc. (formerly Brassey's Inc.), 115–117. Used by permission of Potomac Books, Inc.

firm determination of devoting themselves to their task, even sacrificing themselves.

The above is an operation with the U.S. main force as a main target, and an operation of launching a forestalling and surprise attack on enemy air forces in the Philippines and Singapore should definitely be made almost at the same time of launching attacks on Hawaii. However, if and when the U.S. main force is destroyed, I think, those untrained forces deploying in those southern districts will lose morale to such an extent that they could hardly be of much use in actual bitter fighting.

On the other hand, when we take a defensive stand toward the east and await the enemy coming on out of fear that such an operation against Hawaii is too risky, we cannot rule out the possibility that the enemy would dare to launch an attack upon our homeland to burn our capital city and other cities.

If such happens, our Navy will be subject to fierce attacks by the public, even when we succeed in the southern operation. It is evidently clear that such a development will result in lowering the morale of the nation to such an extent that it cannot be recovered.

ATTACK ON PEARL HARBOR

Ryunosuke Kusaka (1893–1971) was Chief of Staff for the First Air Fleet, the experienced Japanese carrier pilots who would wreak such havoc at the end of 1941 and into early 1942. His account emphasizes some of the practical problems that faced Japanese military planners as they sought to find a way to deliver a knockout blow to unsuspecting American ships. Many naval experts had long assumed that capital ships anchored in a relatively shallow harbor were safe from torpedo attack because torpedoes ran too deep and would explode harmlessly on the harbor bottom. But the brilliantly successful British attack on the Italian fleet anchored at Taranto on the night of November 11-12, 1940, in which carrier-based aircraft carrying specially modified torpedoes sank one Italian battleship and seriously damaged two others, suggested to alert Japanese planners that an attack under similar circumstances against the American Pacific Fleet at Pearl Harbor might just work. It would require skilled aviators, strict radio silence, cooperative weather, refueling at sea, and sheer luck in avoiding neutral shipping or American patrols if it were to preserve the vital element of surprise and achieve its objectives. Kusaka himself thought that the entire operation was too risky, a reckless high-stakes throw of the dice. But Admiral Yamamoto foresaw no acceptable alternative and pressed ahead, with the all-too-infamous results.

Ryunosuke Kusaka, "Attack on Pearl Harbor," in Donald M. Goldstein and Katherine V. Dillon, eds., *The Pearl Harbor Papers: Inside the Japanese Plans* (Washington, DC: Brassey's, 1993), 159–161. Used by permission of Potomac Books, Inc.

At dawn, still so dark that black and white could barely be distinguished, planes lined up on the flight deck started the warming-up of engines before the sortie. There arose the roaring sound of propellers. Weaving through planes lined up wingtip to wingtip, maintenance crews were busy with their work. In the flying crew waiting room, already more than a dozen fliers were seen in complete flying kit with a map board hanging on their breasts. All of them seemed to be happy. On the bridge, two or three staff officers were seen busy making preparations before the take-off planes, checking the wind direction, consulting the wind meter or seeking the position of the ship on a chart.

The moon of 19 days' age was seen and disappeared in intermittent clouds which covered the whole sky. A considerable east wind blew in presenting an adequate condition for the take-off of planes. Due to the long swell peculiar to the south sea, the ship rolled and pitched a good deal; occasionally the ship listed to about 15 degrees to one side, which made us worry a bit. In peace-time training, it was considered pretty difficult for even trained fliers to take off loaded bombers from carriers when their rolling reached about 10 degrees to one side.

About the time day was ready to dawn and the horizon dimly seen, vessels of the Task Force were seen making way in a gorgeous formation. On the carrier flight decks planes were lined up in immediate ready for take-off. Signals of completing preparations successively came in from each carrier....

Then a flag signal "Take Off" was hoisted atop *Akagi*'s mast. All vessels of the force simultaneously turned their heads against the wind direction and increased their speed. First fighters, then dive bombers and other bombers in that order revved up engines and took off one after another. Even a good deal of rolling which occasionally reached 15 degrees could not be an obstacle to them. All the planes took off from their respective carriers without any fear at all in a short while....

As I sat in front of the maps in the operations room expecting to hear reconnaissance reports..., the first report...came in.... "the enemy fleet is in Pearl Harbor.... How pleased we were to receive this report! Instinctively Admiral Nagumo and all of his staff officers looked at each other and could not suppress their smiles. The only thing remaining was to await the result of the attack.

A pre-arranged word for a successful surprise attack made was a single word "Tora," the very word which all attention—not only of the Task Force but also the Malaya Invasion Force, the Philippine Force to the south, the flagship in Hiroshima Bay and the Imperial General Staff in Tokyo—were focused to catch.

Soon a telegram sent from the dive bomber leader to his planes just before the attack saying "wind direction, bearing 70, and wind strength, 10 meters" was intercepted. It was soon followed by a telegram order from the overall commander's plane notifying all planes "to launch attacks."

Sensing that they were now going to launch an attack at last, everyone in the operations room held their breath. At 0310 the long-awaited "tora" was received. At that moment, I was at the bridge with Admiral Nagumo directing actions of the force after launching all planes, and could not suppress tears coming down my cheeks. Without any words I firmly grasped Admiral Nagumo's hand.

Each plane which had kept radio silence by that time began to tap keys. An order of "charge" sent from each leader plane was successively intercepted. Then followed: "Torpedoed enemy battleships. Serious damage inflicted. 0335." "Bombed Hickam at Ford Island. 0340." "Bombed enemy battleships. Position, Pearl Harbor. 0340." "Torpedoed enemy heavy cruiser with serious damage inflicted. 0335." "3 hangars and 50 planes on the ground set on fire. 0345." "After torpedoing, counter fire was met. 0357."...

After a pause for a while, telegrams sent from planes of the second wave were received.... "Bombed an enemy heavy cruiser with serious damage inflicted." "Two enemy battleships left Pearl Harbor." "Bombed Kaneohe field with great damage inflicted. 0440."... "No enemy planes sighted in the air."...

PLAN DOG

Admiral Harold R. Stark (1880–1972), best known for incurring blame for American ill-preparedness at Pearl Harbor, was the Chief of Naval Operations for the U.S. Navy. His memorandum, reproduced in the following reading selection, was an effort to think through the implications for American military strategy of the threatening international situation in late 1940: the war that had already raged on the European continent and left Britain isolated following a series of German victories, and the conflict that seemed ever more likely to erupt with a Japan which had already conquered a swathe of Chinese territory and was bent on further expansion. Of the options Stark presented, that outlined in paragraph D (or dog) would form the basis of American planning, first as "Plan Dog" and subsequently as "Rainbow 5." Its "Germany first" orientation would survive unscathed through numerous reviews and attempted revisions as the cornerstone of Anglo-American grand strategy.

As I see affairs today, answers to the following broad questions will be most useful to the Navy:

(A) Shall our principal military effort be directed toward hemisphere defense, and include chiefly those activities within the Western Hemisphere which contribute directly to security against attack in either or both oceans? An affirmative answer would indicate that the United States, as seems now to be the hope of this country, would remain out of war unless pushed into it. If and when forced into war, the greater portion of our Fleet could remain for the time being in its threatening position in the Pacific, but no major effort would be exerted overseas either to the east or the west; the most that would be done for allies, besides providing material help, would be to send detachments to assist in their defense. It should be noted here that, were minor help to be given in one direction, public opinion might soon push us into giving it major support, as was the case in the World War.

Under this plan, our influence upon the outcome of the European War would be small.

(B) Shall we prepare for a full offensive against Japan, premised on assistance from the British and Dutch forces in the Far East, and remain on the strict defensive in the Atlantic? If this course is selected, we would be placing full trust in the British to hold their own indefinitely in the Atlantic, or, at least, until after we should have defeated Japan decisively, and thus had fully curbed her offensive power for the time being. Plans for augmenting the scale of our present material assistance to Great Britain would be adversely affected until Japan had been decisively defeated. The length of time required to defeat Japan would be very considerable.

If we enter the war against Japan and then if Great Britain loses, we probably would in any case have to reorient towards the Atlantic. There is no dissenting view on this point.

Admiral Harold Stark, "Memorandum for the Secretary of the Navy," November 12, 1940, in Steven T. Ross, ed., *American War Plans, 1919–1941* (New York: Garland, 1982), 5 vols., 3:245–248. Used by permission.

(C) Shall we plan for sending the strongest possible military assistance both to the British in Europe, and to the British, Dutch and Chinese in the Far East? The naval and air detachments we would send to the British Isles would possibly ensure their continued resistance, but would not increase British power to conduct a land offensive. The strength we could send to the Far East might be enough to check the southward spread of Japanese rule for the duration of the war. The strength of naval forces remaining in Hawaii for the defense of the Eastern Pacific, and the strength of the forces in the Western Atlantic for the defense of that area, would be reduced to that barely sufficient for executing their tasks. Should Great Britain finally lose, or should Malaysia fall to Japan, our naval strength might then be found to have been seriously reduced, relative to that of the Axis powers. It should be understood that, under this plan, we would be operating under the handicap of fighting major wars on two fronts.

Should we adopt Plan (C), we must face the consequences that would ensue were we to start a war with one plan, and then, after becoming heavily engaged, be forced greatly to modify it or discard it altogether, as, for example, in case of a British fold up. On neither of these distant fronts would it be possible to execute a really major offensive. Strategically, the situation might become disastrous should our effort on either front fail.

(D) Shall we direct our efforts toward an eventual strong offensive in the Atlantic as an ally of the British, and a defensive in the Pacific? Any strength that we might send to the Far East would, by just so much, reduce the force of our blows against Germany and Italy. About the least that we would do for our ally would be to send strong naval light forces and aircraft to Great Britain and the Mediterranean. Probably we could not stop with a purely naval effort. The plan might ultimately require capture of the Portuguese and Spanish Islands and military and naval bases in Africa and possible Europe; and thereafter even involve undertaking a full scale land offensive. In consideration of a course that would require landing large numbers of troops abroad, account must be taken of the possible unwillingness of the people of the United States to support land operations of this character, and to incur the risk of heavy loss should Great Britain collapse. Under Plan (D) we would be unable to exert strong pressure against Japan, and would necessarily gradually reorient our policy in the Far East. The full national offensive strength would be exerted in a single direction, rather than be expended in areas far distant from each other. At the conclusion of the war, even if Britain should finally collapse, we might still find ourselves possessed of bases in Africa suitable for assisting in the defense of South America.

FORGING ALLIED STRATEGY

Despite Winston Churchill's evocation of a "special relationship" between Britain and the United States, the overlap of language, culture, ancestry, and commitment to democracy did not always preclude suspicion and tension between the two nations. Americans suspected that Britain would conduct the war so as to preserve or extend its empire, even where this conflicted with the dictates of military logic, whereas Britain resented American moralistic condemnation of imperialist expansion and brash reliance on numerical and technological superiority whatever the cost, a commitment Britain could never afford to make. Churchill, who for once slept soundly the night he knew American entry into the war was assured, wasted no time in seeking to persuade American strategists that a "Germany first" orientation was the only logical policy. Two weeks after Pearl Harbor, he and an entourage of top military advisors traveled to Washington to meet with their American counterparts in the so-called ARCADIA conference. From this point onward, policy would be set and implemented by a Combined Chiefs of Staff Committee meeting in Washington; British interests, in particular, would be ably represented by Sir John Dill (1881–1944), the only foreigner to be buried in the Arlington National Cemetery. The key figure in directing American strategy was the army's Chief of Staff, General George C. Marshall (1880–1959), hailed by Churchill as "the organizer of victory." Indeed, so indispensable in Washington was Marshall that Roosevelt refused to spare him for assignments overseas such as the command of Operation Overlord (the D-day preparations, a responsibility that went to Eisenhower). On this occasion the Combined Chiefs gave the British delegation what it wanted. They agreed that operations against Japan would be limited to a holding pattern, that indirect operations against German forces would continue to feature prominently, and that they did not anticipate taking the war to Germany more directly with an invasion of continental Europe until 1943.

AMERICAN-BRITISH GRAND STRATEGY

Note: The circulation of this paper should be restricted to the United States and British Chiefs of Staff and their immediate subordinates.

I. Grand Strategy
  1. At the A-B [American-British] Staff conversations in February, 1941, it was agreed that Germany was the predominant member of the Axis Powers, and consequently the Atlantic and European area was considered to be the decisive theatre.

  Much has happened since February last, but notwithstanding the entry of Japan into the War, our view remains that Germany is still the prime enemy and her defeat is the key to victory. Once Germany is defeated, the collapse of Italy and the defeat of Japan must follow.

"Memorandum by the United States and British Chiefs of Staff, 31 December 1941," in *Foreign Relations of the United States: The Conferences at Washington, 1941–1942, and Casablanca 1943* (Washington, DC: United States Government Printing Office, 1968), 214–217. Used by permission.

2. In our considered opinion, therefore, it should be a cardinal principle of A-B strategy that only the minimum of force necessary for the safeguarding [*sic*] of vital interests in other theatres should be diverted from operations against Germany.

II. Essential Features of Our Strategy

The essential features of the above grand strategy are as follows....

a. The realization of the victory programme of armaments, which first and foremost requires the security of the main areas of war industry.

b. The maintenance of essential communications.

c. Closing and tightening the ring around Germany.

d. Wearing down and undermining German resistance by air bombardment, blockade, subversive activities and propaganda.

e. The continuous development of offensive action against Germany.

f. Maintaining only such positions in the Eastern theatre as will safeguard vital interests...and denying to Japan access to raw materials vital to her continuous war effort while we are concentrating on the defeat of Germany.

III. Steps To Be Taken In 1942 To Put Into Effect The Above General Policy...

THE SECURITY OF AREAS OF WAR PRODUCTION

5. In so far as these are likely to be attacked, the main areas of war industry are situated in:—

a. The United Kingdom.

b. Continental United States, particularly the West Coast.

c. Russia.

6. The United Kingdom. To safeguard the United Kingdom it will be necessary to maintain at all times the minimum forces required to defeat invasion.

7. The United States. The main centers of production on or near the West Coast of United States must be protected from Japanese sea-borne attack. This will be facilitated by holding Hawaii and Alaska. We consider that a Japanese invasion of the United States on a large scale is highly improbable, whether Hawaii or Alaska is held or not.

8. The probable scale of attack and the general nature of the forces required for the defense of the United States are matters for the United States Chiefs of Staff to assess.

9. Russia. It will be essential to afford the Russians assistance to enable them to maintain their hold on Leningrad, Moscow, and the oilfields of the Caucasus, and to continue their war effort.

MAINTENANCE OF COMMUNICATIONS

10. The main sea routes which must be secured are:—

a. From the United States to the United Kingdom.

b. From the United States and the United Kingdom to North Russia.

c. The various routes from the United Kingdom and the United States to Freetown, South America, and the Cape.

d. The routes in the Indian Ocean to the Red Sea and Persian Gulf, to India and Burma, to the East Indies, and to Australasia.

e. The route through the Panama Canal, and the United States coastal traffic.

f. The Pacific routes from the United States and the Panama Canal to Alaska, Hawaii, Australia, and the Far East.

In addition to the above routes, we shall do everything possible to open up and secure the Mediterranean route.

11. The main air routes which must be secured are:—

a. From the United States to South America, Ascension, Freetown, Takoradi, and Cairo.

b. From the United Kingdom to Gibraltar, Malta and Cairo.

c. From Cairo to Karachi, Calcutta, China, Malaya, Philippines, Australasia.

d. From the United States to Australia via Hawaii, Christmas Island, Canton, Palmyra, Samoa, Fiji, New Caledonia.

e. The routes from Australia to the Philippines and Malaya via the Netherlands East Indies.

f. From the United States to the United Kingdom via Newfoundland, Canada, Greenland and Iceland.

g. From the United States to the United Kingdom via the Azores.

h. From the United States to Vladivostok, via Alaska.

12. The security of these routes involves:—

a. Well-balanced A-B naval and air dispositions.

b. Holding and capturing essential sea and air bases.

CLOSING AND TIGHTENING THE RING AROUND GERMANY

13. This ring may be defined as a line running roughly as follows:

Archangel—Black Sea—Anatolia—The Northern Seaboard of the Mediterranean—The Western Seaboard of Europe.

The main object will be to strengthen this ring, and close the gaps in it, by sustaining the Russian front, by arming and supporting Turkey, by increasing our strength in the middle East, and by gaining possession of the whole North African coast.

14. If this ring can be closed, the blockade of Germany and Italy will be complete, and German eruptions, e.g. towards the Persian Gulf, or to the Atlantic seaboard of Africa, will be prevented. Furthermore, the seizing of the North African coast may open the Mediterranean to convoys, thus enormously shortening the route to the Middle East and saving considerable tonnage now employed in the long haul around the Cape.

THE UNDERMINING AND WEARING DOWN OF THE GERMAN RESISTANCE

15. In 1942 the main methods of wearing down Germany's resistance will be:

a. Ever-increasing air bombardment by British and American Forces.

b. Assistance to Russia's offensive by all available means.

c. The blockade.

d. The maintenance of the spirit of revolt in the occupied countries, and the organization of subversive movements.

DEVELOPMENT OF LAND OFFENSIVES ON THE CONTINENT

16. It does not seem likely that in 1942 any large scale land offensive against Germany except on the Russian front will be possible. We must, however, be ready to take advantage of any opening that may result from the wearing down process referred to in paragraph 15 to conduct limited land offensives.

17. In 1943 the way may be clear for a return to the Continent, across the Mediterranean, from Turkey into the Balkans, or by landings in Western Europe. Such operations will be the prelude to the final assault on Germany itself, and the scope of the victory program should be such as to provide means by which they can be carried out.

THE SAFEGUARDING OF VITAL INTERESTS IN THE EASTERN THEATRE

18. The security of Australia, New Zealand, and India must be maintained, and the Chinese war effort supported. Secondly, points of vantage from which an offensive against Japan can eventually be developed must be secured. Our immediate object must therefore be to hold:—

a. Hawaii and Alaska.

b. Singapore, the East Indies Barrier, and the Philippines.

c. Rangoon and the route to China.

d. The Maritime Provinces of Siberia.

The minimum forces required to hold the above will have to be a matter of mutual discussion.

ALLIED GRAND STRATEGY

One year after the ARCADIA meetings, and one year further into the challenges of coordinating a global strategy, agreement between the U.S. Joint Chiefs of Staff and their British counterparts on future operations was harder to secure. For one thing, the Soviet Union was absorbing tremendous punishment as it bore the brunt of the German war effort on the eastern front, and both America and Britain were under increasing pressure from Stalin to do something to lessen the Soviet burden and ease his suspicions that the two Western allies were prepared to watch from the sidelines as Germany and the Soviet Union bled each other white. For another, the astonishing Japanese advances in the Pacific had required a more comprehensive and costly response from the American military than either Stark's original Plan Dog or British strategists had anticipated. Moreover, American success at Midway ensured that Japan was now losing the initiative, and the "island-hopping" campaign of American amphibious landings was beginning to pay dividends, as with the capture of Guadalcanal. So the American commanders were not willing to write off the Pacific theater as a distraction. Nor were American politicians, who were necessarily responsive to an electorate that detested the Japanese as an enemy far more immediate and threatening than the distant German adversaries.

Accordingly, if the full weight of American military might would not be turned upon Japan until Germany had been defeated, there seemed every reason to press ahead with a strategy that would knock Germany out—sooner rather than later. American planners, who in the following memorandum took stock of the outlook for 1943, emphasized attacking Germany itself, not its satellite states like Italy, and supported the extensive buildup of Allied forces in Britain (code-named BOLERO, after Maurice Ravel's relentless orchestral piece made famous in the movie *Ten*) in preparation for a cross-channel invasion later in the year (ROUND-UP). The British response a week later reemphasized an indirect approach, a Mediterranean strategy, one that would knock Italy from the war, siphon German troops away from both the Russian front and the Belgian and French beaches, and build upon the successes already achieved in North Africa. At stake was a problem in perception: British commanders suspected that the cocky Americans, who had little experience fighting German units, vastly underestimated how difficult it would be to strike at the German homeland; for their part, many American officers perceived the British as worn-out and timid, lamentably (if understandably) overcautious after the slaughter of the First World War. A few weeks later, Roosevelt and Churchill would meet at Casablanca, where it was recognized that the Allies did not have the troops or the resources (especially shipping and landing craft) to conduct major offensive operations in the Mediterranean and a cross-channel invasion of north-western France at the same time. Eventually, by May 1943, the Americans would concede that ROUND-UP would have to be postponed until 1944. It would be renamed OVERLORD and enter American historical consciousness as "D-day."

"Memorandum by the United States Joint Chiefs of Staff," in *Foreign Relations of the United States: The Conferences at Washington, 1941–1942, and Casablanca 1943* (Washington, DC: United States Government Printing Office, 1968), 735–738. Used by permission.

December 26, 1942

SECRET

C.C.S. 135

BASIC STRATEGIC CONCEPT FOR 1943

3. ...In arriving at its recommendations the Joint Chiefs of Staff have taken note:
    (a) That Germany is our primary enemy;
    (b) That Russia is exerting great pressure on Germany is absorbing the major part of her war effort;
    (c) That Russia's continuance as a major factor in the war is of cardinal importance;
    (d) That timely and substantial support of Russia, directly by supplies and indirectly by offensive operations against Germany, must be a basic factor in our strategic policy.
    (e) That until such time as major offensive operations can be undertaken against Japan, we must prevent her from consolidating and exploiting her conquests by rendering all practicable support to China and by inflicting irreplaceable losses on Japanese naval, shipping, and air resources.
    (f) That a prerequisite to the successful accomplishment of the strategic concept for 1943 is an improvement in the present critical shipping situation by intensified and more effective anti-submarine warfare.

4. *Strategic objectives:*
    (a) *Western Hemisphere and United Kingdom.*
    Maintain the security, the productive capacity, and the essential communications of the Western Hemisphere and of the British Isles.
    (b) *Western Europe.*
    Insure that the primary effort of the United Nations [the Allies] is directed against Germany rather than against her satellite states by:
        (1) Conducting from bases in United Kingdom, Northern Africa, and as practicable from the Middle East, an integrated air offensive on the largest practicable scale against German production and resources, designed to achieve a progressive deterioration of her war effort.
        (2) Building up as rapidly as possible adequate balanced forces in the United Kingdom in preparation for a land offensive against Germany in 1943.
    (c) *North Africa.*
    Expel the Axis forces from North Africa, and thereafter:
        (1) Consolidate and hold that area with the forces adequate for its security, including the forces necessary to maintain our lines of communication through the Straits of Gibraltar against an Axis or Spanish effort;
        (2) Exploit the successes of the North African operations by establishing large scale air installations in North Africa and by conducting intensive air operations against Germany and against Italy with a view to destroying Italian resources and morale, and eliminating her from the war;
        (3) Transfer any excess forces from the North Africa to the U.K. for employment there as part of the build-up for the invasion of Western Europe in 1943.
    (d) *Russia.*
    Support Russia to the utmost, by supplying munitions, by rendering all practicable air assistance from the Middle East and by making the principal offensive effort of 1943 directly against Germany in Western Europe.
    (e) *Middle East*
        (1) Maintain Turkey in a state of neutrality favorable to the United Nations until such time as she can, aided by supplies and minimum specialized forces, insure the integrity of her territory and make it available for our use.
        (2) If Turkey can then be brought into the war, conduct offensive air operations from bases on her northern coast, in aid of Russia and against German controlled resources and transportation facilities in the Balkans.
    (f) *Pacific.*
    Conduct such offensive and defensive operations as are necessary to secure Alaska, Hawaii, New Zealand, Australia, and our lines of communication thereto, and to maintain the initiative in the Solomon-Bismarck-East New Guinea Area

with a view to controlling that area as a base for further offensive operations and involving Japan in costly counter operations.

(g) *Far East.*

Conduct offensive operations in Burma with a view to reopening the supply routes to China, thereby encouraging China, and supplying her with munitions to continue her war effort and maintain, available to us, bases essential for eventual offensive operations against Japan proper.

January 2, 1943

SECRET

C.C.S. 135/1

BASIC STRATEGIC CONCEPT FOR 1943—THE EUROPEAN THEATRE

1. We have considered the Memorandum of the Joint Chiefs of Staff and their recommendations for a Basic Strategic Concept for 1943 as set out in C.C.S. 135.... On most issues we are in agreement with the U.S. Chiefs of Staff. The main point of difference between us is that we advocate a policy of following up "TORCH" vigorously, accompanied by as large a "BOLERO" build-up as possible, while the U.S. Chiefs of Staff favor putting our main effort into "ROUND-UP" while adopting a holding policy in the Mediterranean, other than in the air.....

2. In support of our arguments we have divided our examination into two parts:

   (a) What is the largest Anglo-American Force that can be assembled in the United Kingdom by August 1943 for re-entering France, and what would be the effect of assembling this force on operations in other theaters.

   (b) What can we expect to achieve if we follow up "Torch" by offensive operations in the Mediterranean, and what forces can then

---

"Memorandum by the British Chiefs of Staff," in *Foreign Relations of the United States: The Conferences at Washington, 1941–1942, and Casablanca 1943* (Washington, DC: United States Government Printing Office, 1968), 738–741.

be assembled in the United Kingdom for re-entering France.

MAXIMUM "BOLERO"

3. If we go for the maximum "BOLERO" we calculate that the strongest land force, which we can assemble in the United Kingdom in August for an attack upon Northern France, will be—British 13 Divisions, United States 12 Divisions (at the very most).

4. Of the above, 6 divisions (4 British and 2 United States) is the maximum which could be organized as assault forces with the shipping and landing craft which can be made available, assuming that the highest priority is given to combined operational manning, training and repair requirements—possibly at the expense of the fleet....

6. We emphasize that even if we accepted the...curtailment of our activities in other theaters [the bombing offensive against Germany and amphibious operations in the Eastern Mediterranean and China], we should still be unable to stage an expedition on an adequate scale to overcome strong German resistance. The scale of "ROUND-UP" as originally planned was a total of 48 British and American Divisions. In the meanwhile the defenses on the French coast have been greatly strengthened. It is also to be noted that we cannot carry out even this reduced "ROUND-UP" until August. *In other words Russia would get no relief for another 7 or 8 months and the Axis would have a similar period to recuperate.*

THE "TORCH" FOLLOW-UP

7. If, on the other hand, we decide to exploit "Torch" during the spring of 1943 we consider that the effects would be as follows:—

ON THE AXIS

(a) We should have a good chance of knocking out Italy by a combination of amphibious operations (such as "Brimstone" and "Husky" and consequential assaults on the mainland of Italy), and an air offensive on the largest scale.

(b) We can ensure bringing the Axis air force to battle in the Mediterranean but, without surface operations, this cannot be guaranteed.

(c) We can greatly increase the number of Bombers arriving in the United Kingdom for offensive action against the Axis.

(d) German forces will be pinned in Northwest Europe by the build-up of the reduced "Bolero." ... Even though this build-up would be at a slower rate owing to other activities the enemy will not dare to relax their state of readiness to meet invasion....

CONCLUSIONS

12. To sum up we consider that our policy should be—

(a) To exploit "TORCH" as vigorously as possible with a view to

(1) Knocking Italy out of the war.

(2) Bringing Turkey into the war, and

(3) Giving the Axis no respite for recuperation.

(b) Increased bombing of Germany.

(c) Maintenance of supplies to Russia.

(d) The build-up of "BOLERO" on the greatest scale that the above operations permit in order that we may be ready to reenter the Continent with about 21 Divisions in August or September 1943, if the conditions are such that there is a good prospect of success. We believe that this policy will afford earlier and greater relief both direct and indirect to Russia than if we were to concentrate on "BOLERO" to the exclusion of all other operations, observing that at the best we could not put a force of more than 25 Divisions on to the Continent in late summer of 1943.

DESERT WAR

As in Greece, German intervention in North Africa was prompted by the need to come to Mussolini's aid after his Italian forces had been soundly defeated after an ill-judged invasion.

The forces involved on either side paled in comparison to those employed within Europe (to Hitler, the campaigns in North Africa were never anything more than a sideshow, a distraction from the "real" war against Bolshevism on the Russian front), but the events there attracted considerable attention for two reasons. First, the Axis advance on Egypt threatened the Suez Canal and Britain's direct lifeline to India, thereby placing the imperial war effort in jeopardy. Second, the campaigns in Libya and Egypt were viewed as unusually "clean," a "war without hate" that lacked the ideological edge and attendant atrocities that were found elsewhere. One of the most distinguished observers of the battles in North Africa was the Australian journalist Alan Moorehead (1910–1983). As foreign correspondent for London's *Daily Express*, he accompanied British troops throughout the region and displayed a sharp eye for how warfare in the desert differed from anything the infantry had expected or what their counterparts in other theaters had encountered.

More and more I began to see that desert warfare resembled war at sea. Men moved by compass. No position was static. There were few if any forts to be held. Each truck or tank was as individual as a destroyer, and each squadron of tanks or guns made great sweeps cross the desert as a battle-squadron at sea will vanish over the horizon. One did not occupy the desert any more than one occupied the sea. One simply took up a position for a day or a week, and patrolled about it with Bren-gun carriers and light armoured vehicles. When you made contact with the enemy you manoeuvred about him for a place to strike much as two fleets will steam into position for action. There were no trenches. There was no front line. We might patrol five hundred miles into Libya and call the country ours. The Italians might as easily have patrolled as far into the Egyptian desert without being seen. Actually these patrols in terms of territory conquered meant nothing. They were simply designed to obtain information from personal observation and the capture of prisoners. And they had a certain value in keeping the enemy nervous. But always the essential governing principle was that desert forces must be mobile: they were seeking not the conquest of territory or positions but combat with the enemy. We hunted men, not land, as a warship will hunt another warship, and care nothing for the sea on which the action is fought. And as a ship submits to the sea by the nature of its design and the way it sails, so these new mechanized soldiers were submitting to the desert. They found weaknesses in the ruthless hostility of the desert and ways to circumvent its worst moods. They used the desert. They never sought to control it. Always the desert offered colours in browns, yellows and greys. The army accordingly took these colours for its camouflage. There were practically no roads. The army shod its vehicles with huge balloon tyres and did

Alan Moorehead, *The March to Tunis: The North African War, 1940–1943* (New York: Harper & Row, 1965), 20–21. Used by permission.

without roads. Nothing except an occasional bird moved quickly in the desert. The army for ordinary purposes accepted a pace of five or six miles an hour. The desert gave water reluctantly, and often then it was brackish. The army cut its men—generals and privates—down to a gallon of water a day when they were in forward positions. There was no food in the desert. The soldier learned to exist almost entirely on tinned foods, and contrary to popular belief remained healthy on it. Mirages came that confused the gunner, and the gunner developed precision-firing to a finer art and learned new methods of establishing observation-posts close to targets. The sandstorm blew, and the tanks, profiting by it, went into action under the cover of the storm. We made no new roads. We built no houses. We did not try to make the desert liveable, nor did we seek to sub-due it. We found the life of the desert primitive and nomadic, and primitively and nomadically the army lived and went to war.

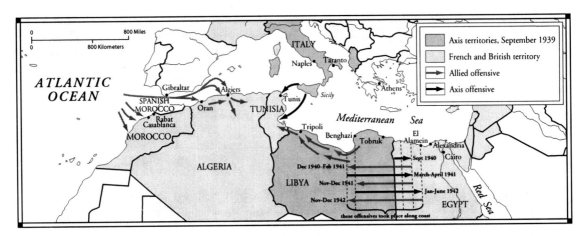

NORTH AFRICA

SURVIVAL IN NORTH AFRICA

As Alan Moorehead had observed, armies could not make the desert livable; life under the harsh conditions there forced soldiers to improvise and to develop certain routines merely to survive. In turn, those impositions, and the sense of sharing a struggle against the elements, united troops from the British Eighth Army and the German Afrika Korps in mutual respect and, at times, in a "live-and-let-live" attitude. Prisoners were treated well, and opposing forces bent simply on reconnaissance might cross paths without serious combat. But when major offensives came, the fighting would be intense, though difficult to sustain for too long, given the environment and the Germans' chronic logistical problems. A sense of what it was like in the intervals between combat is given by Major Hugh Peter de Lancy Samwell (1911–1945), the son of a Scottish clergyman, who was wounded twice in battle and decorated for bravery before dying in northern France.

Shortly after the failure of Rommel's attack we moved forward to an area behind the front on ground that had already been fought over in the recent battle. Here we practised day and night for what we now know was the Battle of El Alamein. It was a gruelling and testing time; we were suffering from all the usual diseases that afflict new troops when they first arrive in the Middle East—dysentery, "gyppy tummy," sand-fly fever, desert jaundice.

We lived in boxes, i.e., large areas capable of holding a complete brigade, boxed in on all sides by minefields, with two or three recognised exits. We were beginning to get used to the sun, but the flies were appalling; one couldn't raise a piece of bread and jam from plate to mouth without it becoming covered in flies. They buzzed round one's head, eyes, mouth, and ears. Every precaution was taken with food, latrines, &c., but it was difficult to stop men from throwing rubbish away or even not using the latrines during the night, when they had to go anything up to fifteen times, and at night it was quite possible to get lost by moving even fifty yards from one's "bivy," [bivouac, a temporary encampment] only to find oneself completely lost in another company area. Those of us who had compasses used to take a bearing on the latrines. This was a wretched time; the training was dreadfully hard and monotonous, and nearly all of us were feeling ill to varying degrees.

Some officers went up to the front during this time; they were attached to the Australians. Things were very quiet up there, and they came back with amazing stories of men strolling about in full view of the enemy, but they emphasised that the war was taken seriously at night and there was constant patrolling. As in other things military, the Australians were very unorthodox in their patrolling methods. They hardly bothered about compasses but went from point to point by means of battle landmarks, utilising everything from broken-down tanks to unburied corpses. One company had a skeleton whom they

Major H. P. Samwell, M.C., *An Infantry Officer with the Eighth Army: The Personal Experiences of an Infantry Officer during the Eighth Army's Campaign through Africa and Sicily* (Edinburgh: William Blackwood & Sons Ltd., 1945), 22–24. Used by permission.

affectionately called "Cuthbert," who was propped up with his arm pointing to the gap in our minefield. Coming back from patrols it was one of the most difficult things to find these gaps, and, as most patrols were timed to end just before dawn, one couldn't afford to waste time walking up and down trying to find the gap and thus risk being caught in the open during stand-to, thus inviting a burst of machine-gun fire....

Life at the front at this time was very quiet and rather unreal. We welcomed the rest from the gruelling training, and wished we could remain there indefinitely. Everything went according to a programme which was kept by both sides. Stand-to followed by another short sleep, then just before breakfast the enemy would put over a few shells which landed somewhere in the back area, occasionally frightening Battalion H.Q. but otherwise doing little harm. This was replied to by our own artillery, and then there was complete silence; gradually men emerged from the trenches and started brewing up and visiting each other. The enemy did the same; their advance posts were some three thousand yards away, but as the ground was completely flat, on a clear day one could quite easily see them. Neither side took the least notice of the other and went about their morning tasks....The trenches, old ones and very solid, had once been a Corps H.Q. when the front was on the Egyptian border; they were flea-ridden and even lice were evident. Jerry over the other side also went out for a swim, and sometimes we could spot them jumping about in the water. We had our big meal in the evening and then spent the rest of time preparing for patrols.

GERMANY STRIKES EAST

Franz Halder (1884–1972) was born into a distinguished military family that had produced soldiers for three centuries. Halder himself served as a general staff officer during the First World War and, by the outbreak of the second conflict, had risen to serve as Chief of the General Staff. In this position, he was intimately involved in planning the brilliantly successful attacks on Poland, France, the Low Countries, and eventually the Soviet Union. His wartime diary illustrates Hitler's almost messianic conviction that Soviet resistance would crumble in the face of the German attack launched with Operation Barbarossa on June 22, 1941, and the assumption just two weeks later, widely held and shared by Halder, that the campaign in the East was essentially won. Sooner than many of his contemporaries, however, Halder began to recognize that the invasion had been a mistake, and his diaries reveal increasingly frequent disagreements with Hitler's military decisions. By September 1942, relations between the two men had deteriorated to the point where Halder was dismissed. Suspicious that Halder might provide a focal point for resistance, Hitler had him arrested after the July 20, 1944, plot on the dictator's life, and Halder remained in custody throughout the remainder of the war. He later served as an advisor and war historian for the U.S. Army's Historical Division.

30 March 1941

1100. Meeting of generals at Führer office. Address lasting almost 2 ½ hours. Situation since 30 June. Mistake of British not to take advantage of chances for peace. Account of subsequent events. Italy's conduct of war and policies sharply criticized. Advantages for England resulting from Italian reverses.

England put her hope in the U.S., and Russia. Detailed review of U.S. capabilities. Maximum output not before end of four years; problem of shipping. Russia's role and capabilities. Reasons for necessity to settle the Russian situation. Only the final and drastic solution of all land problems will enable us to accomplish within two years our tasks in the air and on the oceans.

Our goals in Russia: Crush armed forces, break up state.—Comments on Russian tanks: Redoubtable; 4.7-cm gun (AT) a good medium strength weapon; bulk of tanks obsolete. Numerically Russia's tank strength is superior to that of any other nation, but they have only a small number of new giant types with long 10-cm guns (mammoth models, 42 to 45 tons). Air force very large in number, but mostly outmoded; only small number of modern models.

Problems of Russia's vastness: Enormous expanse requires concentration on critical points. Massed planes and tanks must be brought to bear on strategic points. Our air force cannot cover this entire huge area at one time; at the start of the campaign, it will be able to dominate only parts of the enormous front. Hence, air operations must be closely

Charles Burdick and Hans-Adolf Jacobsen, eds., *The Halder War Diary, 1939–1942.* Copyright © 1988 by Charles Burdick. (Novato, CA: Presidio, 1988), 345–346, 446–447, 505–506. Used by permission of Presidio Press, an imprint of the Ballantine Publishing Group, a division of Random House, Inc.

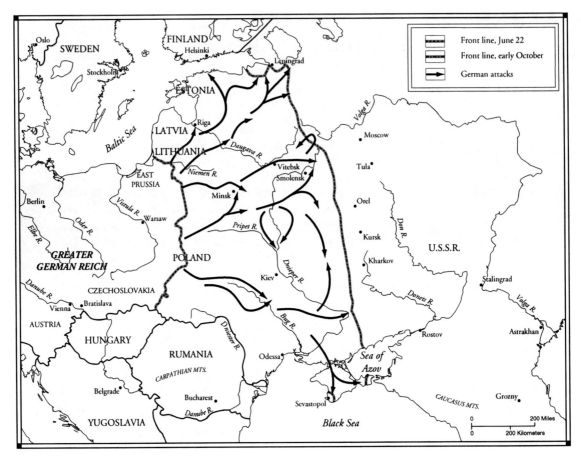

THE EASTERN FRONT, 1941

coordinated with ground operations. The Russians will crumple under the massive impact of our tanks and planes.

No illusions about our Allies! Finns will fight bravely, but they are small in number and have not yet recovered from their recent defeat. *Romanians* are no good at all. Perhaps they could be used as a security force in quiet sectors behind very strong natural obstacles (rivers). Antonescu [Romanian dictator and German ally Ion Antonescu] has enlarged his army instead of reducing and improving it. The fortunes of large German units must not be tied to the uncertain staying power of the Romanian forces....

Clash of two ideologies: Crushing denunciation of Bolshevism, identified with a social criminality.

Communism is an enormous danger for our future. We must forget the concept of comradeship between soldiers. A Communist is no comrade before or after the battle. This is a war of extermination. If we do not grasp this, we shall still beat the enemy, but thirty years later we shall again have to fight the Communist foe. We do not wage war to preserve the enemy.

Future political image Russia: Northern Russia goes to Finland. Protectorates: Baltic states, Ukraine, White Russia.

War against Russia: Extermination of the Bolshevist commissars and of the Communist intelligentsia. The new states must be Socialist, but without intellectual classes of their own. Formation of a new intellectual class must be prevented. A primitive Socialist intelligentsia is all that is needed. We must fight against the poison of disintegration. This is no job for military courts. The individual troop commanders must know the issues at stake. They must be leaders in this fight. The troops must fight back with the methods with which they are attacked. Commissars and GPU [Soviet Secret Police] men are criminals and must be dealt with as such. This need not mean that the troops should get out of hand. Rather, the commander must give orders which express the common feeling of his men....

This war will be very different from the war in the west. In the east, harshness today means lenience in the future. Commanders must make the sacrifice of overcoming their personal scruples....

3 July 1941

The enemy situation in the Pripet marshes remains obscure. We must not overrate the strength of this enemy. On the whole, with no more signs of enemy activity in the Novogrudok pocket, we may be fairly sure that the enemy in the Bialystok sector, who was estimated at fifteen to twenty divisions by a captured Russian corps CG, is annihilated except for some negligible remnants. On the front of AGp. [Army Group] North, we may also figure with twelve to fifteen divisions completely wiped out. On the front of AGp. South, the enemy's withdrawal and the crumbling of his front certainly cannot be interpreted as a disengaging movement planned by his command; it must be explained by the fact that his troops have been cut up and, for the most part, scattered by our unceasing, massive blows.

On the whole, then, it may be said even now that the objective to shatter the bulk of the Russian army this side of the Dvina and Dnieper [Russian rivers] has been accomplished. I do not doubt the statement of the captured Russian corps CG that east of the Dvina and Dnieper we would encounter nothing more than partial forces, not strong enough to hinder

realization of German operational plans. It is thus probably no overstatement to say that the Russian Campaign has been won in the space of two weeks. Of course, this does not yet mean that it is closed. The sheer geographical vastness of the country and the stubbornness of the resistance, which is carried on with all means, will claim our efforts for many more weeks to come....

11 August 1941

The results of the first day of the offensive in AGp North were very significant. On the fronts not involved in the offensive movement reigns the quiet of exhaustion. What we are now doing is the last desperate attempt to prevent our front line from becoming frozen in position warfare. The High Command is greatly handicapped in its capability for modifying the situation, as the army groups are separated by natural obstacles (marshes). Our last reserves have been committed. Any regrouping now is merely a shifting of forces on the baseline within individual army group sectors....

The whole situation makes it increasingly plain that we have underestimated the Russian colossus who consistently prepared for war with that utterly ruthless determination so characteristic of totalitarian states. This applies to organizational and economic resources, as well as the communications system and, most of all, to the strictly military potential. At the outset of the war, we reckoned with about 200 enemy divisions. Now we have already counted 360. These divisions indeed are not armed and equipped according to our standards, and their tactical leadership is often poor. But there they are, and if we smash a dozen of them, the Russians simply put up another dozen. The time factor favors them, as they are near their own resources, while we are moving farther and farther away from ours. And so our troops, sprawled over an immense front line, without any depth, are subjected to the incessant attacks of the enemy. Sometimes these are successful, because too many gaps must be left open in these enormous spaces.

"THE CRIMINAL ORDERS"

In the years immediately after 1945, the great majority of German historians and memoirists conceded that some atrocities had been committed on the Russian front, but blamed such lapses on the Waffen-SS (the combat arm of the SS). The atrocities could then be attributed to over-zealousness brought on by ideological indoctrination, or to an urge toward retribution for outrages committed by Soviet partisans or barbaric, "Asiatic" soldiers. The regular soldiers of the Wehrmacht, in contrast, were assumed to have had "clean hands," supposedly having fought professionally and honorably as their officers had directed them. In the wake of research by a younger generation of scholars, including Omer Bartov, Hannes Heer, Gerd Ueberschar, and Wolfram Wette, we now know this was not the case. Right from the outset, regular German army units were warned that they faced a brutal and bitterly ideological struggle to extirpate, root and branch, a hostile communist system that, left unchecked, threatened to infect the very roots of Western culture. German soldiers were given guidelines, the so-called criminal orders, on the ruthless treatment they were to mete out toward enemy civilians, prisoners of war, and especially political commissars (party officials who monitored the political reliability of Soviet units and were to be shot immediately). Although some German officers regarded the orders as a blot upon the army's honor, others willingly insisted on the strict application of such orders and welcomed the terror they anticipated would ensue.

13 May 1941

DECREE ON THE EXERCISE OF MARTIAL LAW IN DISTRICT BARBAROSSA AND SPECIAL MEASURES OF THE TROOPS*

I

Treatment of Criminal Offenses by Enemy Civilians

1. Until further notice criminal offenses by enemy civilians are removed from the competence of military courts and court martial.
2. Franctireurs [partisans], whether in battle or in flight, are to be disposed of ruthlessly by the troops.
3. Similarly, all other attacks against the military by enemy civilians, their members and followers, are to be suppressed immediately by extreme means until they are eliminated.
4. Where such measures are neglected or not possible initially, those suspected of criminal activity will be brought before an officer. He decides whether [the suspect] is to be shot. Upon the directive of an officer, villages from which the army is cunningly or maliciously attacked, will have punitive measures carried out against [them] in the case in which a speedy identification of individual offenders cannot be discerned....

Gerd R. Ueberschär and Wolfram Wette, eds., *"Unternehmen Barbarossa." Der deutsche Überfall auf die Sowjetunion 1941* (Paderborn: Ferdinand Schöningh, 1984), 306, 339–340. Used by permission.

*Translated by Marilyn Shevin-Coetzee

II

Treatment of Offences Committed by Members of the Military and its Retinue against the Resident Population

1. For cruelties committed by members of the military and their retinue against enemy civilians, there is no [threat of] prosecution; the same holds true if the offense is simultaneously a military crime or offense.

2. In the assessment of such acts, in each proceeding, it must be taken into consideration the collapse in 1918, the later period of suffering of the German nation and [that] the battle against National Socialism with [its] countless sacrifices of blood were crucial to reduce Bolshevism's influence, and that no German has forgotten this....

MILITARY ORDER OF GENERAL FIELD MARSHALL VON REICHENAU OF 10 OCTOBER 1941 CONCERNING THE BEHAVIOR OF THE TROOPS IN THE EASTERN SECTOR*

Concerning the behavior of the troops vis a vis the Bolshevik system, vague conceptions remain in many cases. The most essential goal of the campaign against the Jewish-Bolshevik system is the complete destruction of [their] means of power and the eradication of Asian influence upon European culture. Hereby tasks also arise for the soldiers that exceed the customary routine of the troops. In the Eastern territories the soldier is not only a combatant according to the rule of war but also a bearer of an inexorable national ideology and the avenger of bestialities that have been inflicted upon the German and racially-related nations.

Therefore, the soldier must have a complete understanding for the necessity of a severe yet just atonement against the Jewish subhumans. [The soldier] also has another purpose—to nip in the bud the revolts from the rear of the army that, from experience, have always been caused by Jews.

The struggle against the enemy behind front lines is still not being taken seriously enough. Malicious, cruel partisans and depraved women are still being made prisoners of war, and, moreover, partially-uniformed or civilian-clad snipers and vagabonds are being treated like respectable soldiers and marched off to prisoner of war camps. In fact, captured Russian officers speak sneeringly of Soviet agents moving openly about the streets and frequently eating at German field kitchens. Such conduct of the troops is only to be explained by complete thoughtlessness. Now is the time for the meaning of the present struggle to be instilled [among the troops].

In retreat, the Soviets frequently have set fire to buildings. The troops have an interest in extinguishing fires only if necessary billets must be secured. In general, the disappearance of symbols of the former Bolshevik government, also in the form of buildings, is part of the war of annihilation. Neither historic nor artistic [cultural] considerations play a role in the Eastern territories....

[In] the future the soldier has to fulfill two tasks:

1. The complete annihilation of the false Bolshevik doctrine, the Soviet state and its army.

2. The merciless eradication of foreign malice and cruelty and thereby the protection of lives of the German military in Russia.

Only in this way will we do justice to our historic task to liberate the German nation once and for all from the Asian-Jewish danger.

SAVING MOSCOW

As German forces advanced inexorably upon Moscow during the summer and fall of 1941, Stalin desperately searched among the depleted ranks of senior officers who had survived his military purges to find someone who could stem the German tide short of the Soviet capital. Stalin finally settled on General Georgi Zhukov (1896–1974), who had enjoyed success against the Japanese in Mongolia and the Germans at Leningrad. Zhukov proved an outstanding commander, one who could deal forthrightly with Stalin and retain his composure and judgment under dire circumstances. In the excerpt that follows, he explains how he cobbled together a defense of Moscow and then, drawing upon all available reserves, counterattacked against the overextended German lines. The attentive reader will note that Zhukov bristles somewhat at the notion that weather and distance defeated the Germans; while not dismissing their impact, Zhukov is careful to demonstrate that dedicated Soviet soldiers and civilians were due the credit for saving Moscow. Zhukov himself was promoted to marshal in January 1943 and oversaw the long campaigns that would conclude with the capture of Berlin in May 1945.

In the first days of October, the troops of our Western, Reserve, and Briansk Army Groups suffered reverses. The command of the Army Groups had obviously made serious miscalculations. The troops of the Western Army Group and the Reserve Group had been stationed in defensive positions for nearly a month and a half, and they had had enough time to prepare for the enemy attack. The necessary measures, however, had apparently not been taken. They failed to determine correctly with the help of their own intelligence the extent of the enemy force or the direction from which it was preparing the thrust, even though they had received a warning from Supreme Headquarters of very heavy fascist German troop concentrations against them. Consequently, despite the fact that the enemy lacked the advantage of surprise for the attack against our troops, he caught them unprepared. They had not built defenses in depth, and, moreover, our backbone—the antitank defenses—were not ready in time. Neither were the Army Group reserves brought up to help offset the attack. Artillery and air force counter-preparations against enemy concentrations in their initial attack positions were not organized. And when our defenses were penetrated in the region of Viaz'ma, the command failed to organize the withdrawal of troops, which resulted in the complete encirclement of the 16th, 19th, 20th, 24th, and 32nd Armies....

[Our] goal was to establish firm defenses along the line Volokolamsk-Mozhaisk-Maloiaroslavets-Kaluga [Soviet defensive line roughly fifty miles west of Moscow] as quickly as possible, to develop this defense in depth, and to create reserves for the Army Group.

Marshal G. K. Zhukov, "Battle," in Seweryan Bialer, ed., *Stalin and His Generals: Soviet Military Memoirs of World War II* (New York: Pegasus, 1969), 282, 285–288, 291–292. Used by permission.

The Mozhaisk line of defense had a number of clear advantages from the operational-tactical point of view. At its forward edge flowed the Lama, Moskva, Kolocha, Luzha, and Sukhodrev rivers. The high bluffs of these rivers constituted a serious obstacle for tanks. At the rear of the Mozhaisk line there was a developed system of roads and railways which provided maneuverability for troops in all directions. Here it was possible to establish a multiple-line defense system that would offer increasing resistance the deeper the enemy penetrated.

The trouble was, however, that by October 10 there were very few of our troops along the Mozhaisk line, which stretched for a distance of 220 km....To cover it we had a total of 45 battalions instead of the minimum of 150 required for any successful defensive action....This left the road to Moscow virtually unprotected.

Supreme Headquarters took drastic measures in order to avert the threat hanging over the capital....It dispatched five newly formed machine-gun battalions, ten antitank artillery regiments, and five tank brigades to this area....On this defensive perimeter the retreating units of the Western and Reserve Army Groups were concentrating; they were being joined by units transferred urgently from the right wing of the Western Army Group, by units from the Northwestern Army Group, by troops from the Southwest sector, as well as by reserves from the interior of the country...matériel and technical supplies were urgently brought in; medical and other rear-guard services were expanded. In this way a new Western Army Group, which was to repulse the attack on Moscow by the fascist German troops, was born....

The result of the October defense battles near Moscow is well known. In a month of fierce and bloody battles the fascist German troops succeeded in advancing 230–250 km. all told. But the plan of the Hitlerite command to capture Moscow was defeated; the enemy's forces were seriously drained; his assault groups became extended....

Much has been said in postwar years about the frequent complaints of Hitler's generals and bourgeois historians concerning the impassability of the Russian roads, the mud, Russia's frosts....Did the Hitlerite generals planning their Eastern campaign expect to roll along smooth, well-traveled roads straight into Moscow and farther?...In those days I saw with my own eyes how thousands upon thousands of Moscow women—city dwellers who were completely unaccustomed to heavy digging—left their city apartments in light dress, dug antitank ditches and trenches, set up obstacles, built barricades and tank barriers, dragged sacks of sand through the same mud and along the same impassable roads....I may add for those who are inclined to use mud to camouflage the real reasons for their defeat at Moscow that in October 1941 the period of impassable roads was comparatively short. At the beginning of November 'general offensive' of Hitler's troops the temperature in the battle area on the Moscow axis was 13–20 degrees Fahrenheit and at that temperature, as everyone knows, there isn't any mud....

In early December it became evident from the nature of the action and the force of the fascist German attacks that the enemy was becoming exhausted and no longer had the strength or the means to conduct serious offensive operations in this direction....Despite losses the enemy stopped for nothing; his tank wedges tried to break through to Moscow at any cost. But our deeply echeloned artillery and antitank defense withstood the savage onslaught thanks to well-organized interaction among formations and units of all branches and services of our armed forces. The Hitlerites covered the battlefield with many thousands of dead, but they did not succeed in breaking through to Moscow at any point. In the course of the battle Soviet troops would withdraw in good order to previously prepared positions held by the artillery and would continue to fight stubbornly, repulsing the furious attacks....

I have been asked many times since the end of the war how it was that Soviet troops managed to withstand the onslaught of the extremely strong fascist German groupings against Moscow....In planning a large-scale, complex strategic operation...Hitler's High Command seriously underestimated the strength, condition, and potential of the Soviet Army in the struggle for Moscow and greatly overestimated the potential of the troops it had concentrated for the purpose of piercing our defense line and capturing the capital of the Soviet Union.

Serious miscalculations were also made in the formation of assault groups in connection with the second stage....The flank assault groups of the enemy, especially those operating in the Tula area, were weak; they did not have a sufficient number of combined arms formations. Experience demonstrated the error of exclusive reliance upon armored formations in the given conditions. The tank units were exhausted; they suffered heavy losses and spent their breakthrough capacity.

The German command did not succeed in organizing a timely attack aimed at pinning down the center of our front, although it had sufficient forces to do so. In the absence of such an attack we were able freely to shift our reserves—including the divisional reserves—from the central sectors to the flanks where they opposed the enemy assault groups. Great losses, unpreparedness for combat in winter conditions, and the fierceness of Soviet resistance affected the enemy's combat capacity.

COMBAT ON THE RUSSIAN FRONT

Willy Peter Reese (1921–1944) began his adult life working in a bank, but was soon drafted into the German army and participated in the invasion of the Soviet Union. He was a keen and reflective observer who was determined to bear witness to the experience of war and its impact on human emotions and behavior. Reese's efforts to keep a diary on the eastern front reflected his own literary inclinations as well as the support of his mother, who sent him a steady stream of pencils and writing paper. When Reese was home on leave early in 1944, he typed many of his diary entries, and these, along with his letters, survived the war and were submitted for publication by a cousin nearly half a century later. Although Reese managed to return to action several times after being wounded, he did not survive the war (the Red Cross concluded that he died in action near Vitebsk in June 1944 at the age of twenty-three). Reese's diary provides a vivid account of what it meant to serve in the German army on the Russian front; it can be startlingly casual or matter-of-fact (about the murder of Soviet prisoners, for example), and it unflinchingly records his growing mental and physical exhaustion.

We took up a decoy position outside Volovo, while another section conducted the actual assault. We peppered the nests of resistance with all the light and heavy infantry weapons we had, but the Russians didn't give an inch. We knelt or lay in the snow; our knees froze fast to the ground; ice formed between our coats and our tunics. We stamped on the ground to get feeling back in our feet. The men's skin froze onto the metal of their rifles, because few had useable gloves; bleeding scraps were torn

Willy Peter Reese, *A Stranger to Myself. The Inhumanity of War: Russia, 1941–1944*, trans. by Michael Hofmann. Translation copyright © 2005 by Michael Hofmann. (New York: Farrar, Strauss & Giroux, 2005), 46–53. Used by permission of Farrar, Strauss & Giroux.

off their hands, which froze over before the blood could flow. Many froze to death, and many others ran off in despair. Even on our way here, there had been casualties, and now the numbers of dead and wounded climb.

Vainly we waited for the white flare that was the agreed signal that the others had fought their way into Volovo. Night came. We had waited seven hours. The last of us staggered to our feet under cover of darkness but promptly fell down, because our feet couldn't carry us. Some vomited. We crawled and staggered forward until the blood began to circulate again. Then we were ordered to retire, and under fire from Katyusha rockets, we made our way back....

Hand grenades went up in our midst. Several men fell, wallowed about on the snow with ripped-open bellies, got themselves tangled up in their own intestines. We broke up into smaller groups and laid into the drunken attackers with rifle butts; two of us were slit apart by bayonet thrusts. In pairs we stood by the corner of a barn, medic still with us, while ten feet in front of us, the Russians oozed up out of the night like phantoms of death. My comrade fell. I lay in the snow and didn't shoot. It wasn't that my rifle was jammed, but at that time I was unable to shoot at men who were trying to kill me; I would sooner have died. That was the only hour of trial by fire in that winter campaign. The doctor meanwhile was potting [shooting] attackers with his pistol.

The last of them melted away....We kept watch among the corpses. The fat face of the moon stared down on the corpses in the snow. Contorted features, calm faces, dull, staring eyes, smashed skulls, slit bellies, squirts of blood and brains came to light as day broke. We went around ashen-faced, like dead men.

Then, almost without a fight, we marched into Volovo, demanding food, warmth, sleep. The buildings were partly on fire; Katyusha rockets were being fired at us. But we found only a few isolated Red Army soldiers in the buildings. They were shot. An order had been given not to take any prisoners. In one house we came upon some hot noodle soup, which the Russians had simply left. We sat down on the benches, propped our freezing feet on the bodies, and ate hungrily, without thinking about death and danger. In the pockets of the dead, we found bread and sugar, and we ate our fill. We weren't fastidious anymore.

In the evening there was an agitated command to leave right away. We had to try to slit the noose that a vast preponderance of Russian forces had almost drawn around us....The retreat faltered. We had no maps and didn't know the roads and the terrain. We had intended to winter behind the line of the river Tim but we weren't there yet....We slept on hay spread over boxes of bullets and grenades. We had a stove for warmth and a rifle oil lamp for light. But that was pretty much all we had. We burned the fencing [of a nearby cottage] and finally the flooring. For twelve days we lived on potatoes, which we boiled with a little salt....We drank snowmelt. There was no soap, and each of us had just one thin blanket. Tangled hair and beards, black hands, and most of us either festering and frostbitten or eaten alive by lice, scabies, and the inflammations on our legs....

Advent for the doomed. We had to bear it; how we got through, no one bothered to ask. Our conversations revolved around relief—the perpetual delusion—and around home and flight. Bitterly we contemplated hunger, cold, need, and our disappearing position. We were all sick and irritable....There was nothing beyond the barest self-preservation. That was all that got us through so much cold and so many marches and sleepless nights. Never had I sensed and affirmed the will to live so strongly as now. Life was a balancing act, a rope suspended over death. Sometimes we were befallen by a kind of crying without tears.

HITLER'S OBSTINANCE

General Heinz Guderian (1888–1954) had made his reputation during the 1930s as a theorist for the flexible, innovative handling of Germany's armored forces in a style which, combined with close air support, would be labeled as lightning warfare or Blitzkrieg. When Guderian was given the opportunity to put his ideas into action, commanding Panzer units in Poland in 1939 and France in 1940, he succeeded brilliantly. In the invasion of the Soviet Union the following year, the charismatic Guderian's Second Panzer Group raged through the Ukraine and captured massive numbers of prisoners at Kiev. The German general was not one, however, to abstain from pointing out his superiors' mistakes, and this attitude, combined with his insistence that an overextended German advance must be pulled back, led to this unpleasant meeting with Hitler and his dismissal on December 20, 1941. Guderian would not receive another appointment until March 1943. Of course, like his fellow officers, he had a vested interest in sanitizing his wartime experience and playing up the degree to which he differed on most questions from more ardently Nazi soldiers, and the reader should approach all such memoirs from a critical perspective. Nonetheless, in this particular instance, Guderian's general point has been amply confirmed: Hitler thought he knew better than his generals how to conduct the war, with disastrous consequences.

"Little monk, little monk, you are taking a hard road!" These words of Frundsberg to Dr. Martin Luther before the Diet of Worms of 1521 were quoted to me by my comrades when they learned of my decision to fly to Hitler's headquarters. They were applicable enough. I was perfectly well aware that it would not be easy for me to bring Hitler over to my way of thinking. At that time, however, I still believed that our Supreme Command would listen to sensible propositions when they were laid before it by a general who knew the front....

The conference began with my description of the state of Second Panzer Army and Second Army. I then spoke of my intention of withdrawing both armies bit by bit to the Susha-Oka position, an intention which, as already stated, I had expressed to Field-Marshal von Brauchitsch [commander in chief of the invasion, dismissed five days after this meeting] on December 14th, in Roslavl, and which he had approved. I was convinced that Hitler must have been informed of this. I was, therefore, all the more taken aback when he shouted: "No! I forbid that!" I informed him that the withdrawal was already in progress and that there was no intermediate line at which it could be halted for any length of time before the rivers were reached. If he regarded it as important to preserve the lives of the troops and to hold a position throughout the winter he had no choice but to permit the withdrawal to be completed.

Heinz Guderian, *Panzer Leader*, trans. by Constantine Fitzgibbon, © 1952 by Heinz Guderian. (London: Michael Joseph, 1952), 264–266. Used by permission of Dutton, a division of Penguin Group (USA) Inc.

HITLER: "If that is the case they must dig into the ground where they are and hold every square yard of land!"

I: "Digging into the ground is no longer feasible in most cases, since it is frozen to a depth of five feet and our wretched entrenching tools won't go through it."

HITLER: "In that case they must blast craters with the heavy howitzers. We had to do that in the First World War in Flanders."

I: "If I use those shells to make craters I shall have 50 hollows in the ground, each about the width and depth of a washtub with a large black circle around it. I shall not have a crater position. In Flanders there was never such cold as we are now experiencing. And apart from that I need my ammunition to fire at the Russians. We can't even drive stakes into the ground for carrying our telephone wires; to make a hole for the stake we have to use high explosives. When are we to get sufficient explosives to blast out defensive positions on the scale you have in mind?

But Hitler insisted on his order that we remain where we were being carried out.

I: "Then this means taking up positional warfare in an unsuitable terrain, as happened on the Western Front during the First World War. In this case we shall have the same battles of material and the same enormous casualties as then without any hope of winning a decisive victory. If such tactics are adopted we shall, during the course of this coming winter, sacrifice the lives of our officers, our non-commissioned officers and of the men suitable to replace them, and this sacrifice will have been not only useless but also irreparable."

HITLER: "Do you think Frederick the Great's grenadiers were anxious to die? They wanted to live, too, but the King was right in asking them to sacrifice themselves. I believe that I, too, am entitled to ask any German soldier to lay down his life."

I: "Every German soldier knows that in wartime he must risk his life for his country and our soldiers have certainly proved up to now that they are prepared to do so. But such a sacrifice may only be asked of a man if the results to be obtained from it are worth having. The intentions I have heard expressed will lead to losses that are utterly disproportionate to the results that will be achieved. My soldiers will not have protection against the weather and the Russians until they reach the Susha-Oka line and the fortified positions that were built there during the autumn. I beg you to remember that it is not the enemy who is causing us our bloody losses; we are suffering twice as many casualties from the cold as from the fire of the Russians. Any man who has seen the hospitals filled with frost-bite cases must realize what that means."

HITLER: "I know that you have not spared yourself and that you have spent a great deal of time with the troops. I grant you that. But you are seeing events at too close a range. You have been too deeply impressed by the suffering of the soldiers. You feel too much pity for them. You should stand back more. Believe me, things appear clearer when examined at longer range."

CHAPTER 4

MOBILIZING FOR WAR

WOMEN DOING WAR WORK   Women workers, pressed into factory work for wartime production, assemble nose cones for American bombers in a Douglas Aircraft facility in Long Beach, California.
Source: © CORBIS.

"Workers by hand and by brain" was how Britain's Labour Party in 1918 had described the civilian labor force whose contributions underlay the nation's ultimately successful effort in World War I. In World War II the basic challenge the combatant nations faced was similar: how to mobilize brawn and intellect, how to develop and maintain the workforce required to keep factories producing weapons and munitions, how to harness the best minds to refine existing weapons and design new ones, and how to apply experience and expertise to the issue of military intelligence, to reveal the enemy's intentions and troop dispositions while concealing one's own. The tasks, while familiar, were all the more complex in the Second World War, however. Technology was more sophisticated, weapons more destructive, and the demands from the various services more voluminous. Aircraft production, for example, dwarfed what had been done in World War I in numbers and complexity and, except for in the United States, had to be carried on in the face of aerial bombing or advancing troops. Over the course of the war, it would be the Allies who responded best to these challenges, and their relative success in doing so would underpin their eventual victory over the Axis powers.

Maintaining mass production meant in the first place managing the workforce. Government intrusion into the workplace was essential to ensure the most efficient use of manpower and to avoid losing to the front lines workers whose skills were truly irreplaceable. Factory managers and labor administrators had to free up enough men to satisfy the voracious demands of the military and find satisfactory substitutes for workers who could be spared. Often "manpower" would be insufficient, and women would be drawn into the workforce to fill the gap. At the two ends of the spectrum here were the Soviet Union, in which the shift was relatively easy because the reality of female wage labor was already well established, and Germany, where even the prospect, let alone the presence, of too many women in the workplace was abhorrent. Labor substitution, in which new workers unfamiliar with or suspicious of each other were now expected to operate side by side, contributed to social mixing and challenged conventional social boundaries. Nowhere was this more pronounced than in the United States. American factories were safely insulated by distance from any attack or war-related disruption of production, but they drew upon a far more ethnically diverse population whose mobilization carried its own challenges. In a war Americans fought to preserve democracy, prejudice remained one distinguishing feature. In some areas it was overcome, but its persistence in others arguably diminished the magnitude of the overall achievement.

Mass production geared to military ends meant the conversion of major civilian peacetime industries. Chief among these was the car industry, and it was no accident that in the United States the massive task of assembling B-24 Liberator bombers was entrusted to the Ford Motor Company. Likewise, in Germany, the famous Tiger tanks were turned out by Porsche, better known for its high-performance sports cars than the ponderous fifty-five-ton tracked leviathans. In general, American and Soviet industry did a much better job of turning out massive quantities of fairly basic designs, while German industry was frequently sidetracked by demands from its military to produce limited numbers of more complex designs, or variants to existing models in which the modest improvements in performance were not commensurate with the difficulties and delays involved in production. Nobody doubted that the Germans designed exceptionally innovative weapons (jet fighter planes, rockets, sophisticated tanks), but they only became available in limited quantities, could prove difficult to maintain or employ, and never threatened to change the course of the war. The most innovative and destructive weapon of all, the atomic bomb, was, fortunately, the one weapon only the United States had the financial and scientific resources to pursue.

In addition to doing a better job of mobilizing labor and standardizing production, the Allies handily won the information war. The full extent of their advantage only became public in the 1970s, when it was revealed that code-breakers, many working in seclusion in Bletchley Park northwest of London, had been reading supposedly unbreakable coded German messages encrypted by the infernally complex Enigma machines. Thanks to the assistance of Polish cryptologists who provided their British counterparts with a working model, British (and later American) leaders gained invaluable insight from this intelligence (labeled "Ultra") into the intentions and dispositions of German military commanders. Allied cryptologists could not break every code or read every message, and the Germans periodically changed codes, nor could the Allies act on every intelligence success, but Ultra decrypts significantly affected the battle of the Atlantic and enabled the Allies to monitor the effectiveness of their attempts at deception before Operation Overlord in 1944. American code-breakers were successful at breaking some Japanese codes as well, with momentous consequences at the battle of Midway in 1942. Signals intelligence was the most intricate aspect of the information war, but human intelligence had a role to play. Both sides derived some useful material from individual spies, but with mixed results: the Soviets dismissed some of the most valuable tips (the updates on German plans for Barbarossa passed along by Tokyo-based Richard Sorge) but effectively penetrated the British Secret Service (the notorious five Englishmen recruited at Cambridge, including Donald Maclean and Kim Philby). Human intelligence went beyond cloak-and-dagger intrigues or systematic observations by strategically placed operatives to include more mundane activities. Interpretation of photo intelligence—that is, analysis of pictures taken by reconnaissance aircraft flying over enemy territory—was another Allied specialty, which led both to a more realistic evaluation of the impact of strategic bombing (the Butt Report) and to the discovery of otherwise secret German weapons programs (the V-1 flying bombs). In short, in each of these varied but crucial aspects of modern warfare, the Allied edge would be increasingly apparent.

ARSENAL OF DEMOCRACY

In 1940 President Franklin D. Roosevelt found himself in a quandary. He recognized the threat to democracy from Hitler's Third Reich and was sympathetic to Britain as it battled alone against the German dictator's forces after the fall of France. He was constrained, however, by domestic political realities and specific legislation in how much more than moral support he could offer. Isolationism was a strong and pervasive theme in American political life, and with an election looming in November 1940, Roosevelt could ill afford to alienate voters who had no wish to see America embroiled in a war thousands of miles away. Moreover, he was bound by the Neutrality Act of 1937's prohibition on American banks from lending belligerent countries the money to buy American arms (a reaction to the experience of World War I, when only Finland had settled its war debt with the United States). Britain, which had liquidated large sterling reserves overseas between 1914 and 1918, was in no position to take advantage of America's best offer: "cash and carry," whereby foreign countries paid cash for materials and transported them in their own ships. Moreover, American industry was not geared to the demands of war, part of the country's broader lack of preparation for a major conflict (its professional army, for example, was smaller than Poland's had been a year earlier). Roosevelt's response was the policy of "lend lease," in which British demand would stimulate American production, and the settling of accounts would be postponed. Already in September 1939, while insisting on the country's neutrality, the American president had admitted that "even a neutral cannot be asked to close his mind or his conscience." Lend lease would open America's factories to the British without exposing the fact that any checks Britain wrote to cover the expenses would have bounced. One of the first initiatives was to resort to barter, to trade fifty aging World War I–vintage destroyers to the British (for convoy escort duty) in exchange for bases in the Bermudas and elsewhere. By December 1940, having been reelected to an unprecedented third term, Roosevelt could safely reveal to the American people the very fine line he had drawn between isolationism and intervention. A shrewd politician, he made effective use of radio addresses, his so-called fireside chats. In the famous address that follows, delivered on December 29, 1940, he memorably defined his vision of America's new role as "the arsenal of democracy." He likened America's position to that of a homeowner whose neighbor's house (Britain) had gone up in flames. Under the circumstances, it was only prudent to lend the neighbor one's own garden hose, so that he could fight the flames himself. Only once the fire was out would the two gentlemen quibble over the condition of the hose. Roosevelt thus appealed to isolationists with the argument that America's best hope of avoiding war lay, paradoxically, in providing Britain (and later the Soviet Union) with the assistance to fight off Germany by itself. Within a year, of course, the semantic distinctions would fade into insignificance, but the introduction of lend lease would prove critical, both for providing America's battered future allies with essential assistance and for prompting the American economy to take the first halting steps toward thorough mobilization.

President Franklin Delano Roosevelt, "Arsenal of Democracy," from http://www.fdrlibrary.marist.edu/122940.html. Used by permission.

December 29, 1940

Thinking in terms of today and tomorrow, I make the direct statement to the American people that there is far less chance of the United States getting into war if we do all we can now to support the nations defending themselves against attack by the Axis than if we acquiesce in their defeat, submit tamely to an Axis victory, and wait our turn to be the object of attack in another war later on....

The people of Europe who are defending themselves do not ask us to do their fighting. They ask us for the implements of war, the planes, the tanks, the guns, the freighters [cargo ships] which will enable them to fight for their liberty and for our security. Emphatically we must get these weapons to them, get them to them in sufficient volume and quickly enough, so that we and our children will be saved the agony and suffering of war which others have had to endure....

In a military sense Great Britain and the British Empire are today the spearhead of resistance to world conquest. And they are putting up a fight which will live forever in the story of human gallantry.

There is no demand for sending an American Expeditionary Force outside our own borders. There is no intention by any member of your government to send such a force. You can, therefore, nail, nail any talk about sending armies to Europe as deliberate untruth.

Our national policy is not directed toward war. Its sole purpose is to keep war away from our country and away from our people.

Democracy's fight against world conquest is being greatly aided, and must be more greatly aided, by the rearmament of the United States and by sending every ounce and every ton of munitions and supplies that we can possibly spare to help the defenders who are in the front lines. And it is no more unneutral for us to do that than it is for Sweden, Russia, and other nations near Germany, to send steel and ore and oil and other war materials into Germany every day in the week.

We are planning our own defense with the utmost urgency and in its vast scale we must integrate the war needs of Britain and the other free nations which are resisting aggression.

This is not a matter of sentiment or of controversial personal opinion. It is a matter of realistic, practical military policy, based on the advice of our military experts who are in close touch with existing warfare. These military and naval experts and the members of the Congress and the administration have a single-minded purpose—the defense of the United States.

This nation is making a great effort to produce everything that is necessary in this emergency—and with all possible speed. And this great effort requires great sacrifice....

If our capacity to produce is limited by machines, it must ever be remembered that these machines are operated by the skill and the stamina of the worker. As the government is determined to protect the rights of the workers, so the nation has a right to expect that the men who man the machines will discharge their full responsibilities to the urgent needs of defense.

The worker possesses the same human dignity and is entitled to the same security of position as the engineer or the manager or the owner. For the workers provide the human power that turns out the destroyers, and the planes and the tanks.

The nation expects our defense industries to continue operation without interruption by strikes or lockouts. It expects and insists that management and workers will reconcile their differences by voluntary or legal means, to continue to produce the supplies that are so sorely needed.

And on the economic side of our great defense program, we are, as you know, bending every effort to maintain stability of prices and with that the stability of the cost of living....

The appropriation of vast sums of money and a well-coordinated executive direction of our defense efforts are not in themselves enough. Guns, planes, ships, and many other things have to be built in the factories and the arsenals of America. They have to be produced by workers and managers and engineers with the aid of machines which in turn have to be built by hundreds of thousands of workers throughout the land....

American industrial genius, unmatched throughout the world in the solution of production problems, has been called upon to bring its resources and its talents into action. Manufacturers of watches, of farm implements, of linotypes and cash registers and automobiles and sewing machines and lawn mowers and locomotives are now making fuses and bomb packing crates and telescope mounts and shells and pistols and tanks.

But all of our present efforts are not enough. We must have more ships, more guns, more planes— more of everything. And this can be accomplished only if we discard the notion of "business as usual." This job cannot be done merely by superimposing on the existing productive facilities the added requirements of the nation for defense....

I want to make it clear that it is the purpose of the nation to build now with all possible speed every machine, every arsenal, every factory that we need to manufacture our defense material. We have the men, the skill, the wealth, and above all, the will.

I am confident that if and when production of consumer or luxury goods in certain industries requires the use of machines and raw materials that are essential for defense purposes, then such production must yield, and will gladly yield, to our primary and compelling purpose.

So I appeal to the owners of plants—to the managers, to the workers, to our own government employees—to put every ounce of effort into producing these munitions swiftly and without stint. With this appeal I give you the pledge that all of us who are officers of your government will devote ourselves to the same wholehearted extent to the great task that lies ahead.

As planes and ships and guns and shells are produced, your government, with its defense experts, can then determine how best to use them to defend this hemisphere. The decision as to how much shall be sent abroad and how much shall remain at home must be made on the basis of our overall military necessities.

We must be the great arsenal of democracy. For us this is an emergency as serious as war itself. We must apply ourselves to our task with the same resolution, the same sense of urgency, the same spirit of patriotism and sacrifice as we would show were we at war.

We have furnished the British great material support and we will furnish far more in the future.

There will be no bottlenecks in our determination to aid Great Britain. No dictator, no combination of dictators, will weaken that determination by threats of how they will construe that determination.

MEXICAN-AMERICAN DISCRIMINATION

As assistant to the chairman of the President's Committee on Fair Employment Practice, Dr. Carlos E. Castañeda, professor of history at the University of Texas, investigated cases of labor discrimination against Mexican-Americans throughout the United States during the war. Not until 1943, as Dr. Castañeda testified, did factories even consider hiring Mexicans—this despite the fact that many industries were desperate for additional labor so they could meet the expanding needs of the military. Some of the opportunities that presented themselves included construction jobs for the building of training camps, air bases, and prisoner of war camps, while the aircraft and shipbuilding industries employed a few. Employment in industry for the fortunate few Mexican Americans who found positions posed a number of challenges, including confronting bigoted coworkers and adjusting to an urban environment. Reproduced here is a portion of Dr. Castañeda's testimony regarding the employment practices of industry toward Mexican-Americans.

Eighteen months of investigation in connection with complaints filed with the President's Committee on Fair Employment Practice involving Mexican-Americans in Texas, New Mexico, Colorado, Arizona, and California, shows that in spite of the constantly increasing demand for manpower for the successful prosecution of the war, the Mexican-American reservoir of available labor has been neither exhausted nor fully utilized at the highest skill of the individual worker.

In the oil industry, basic and essential to the war effort, Mexican-Americans have been refused employment in other than common labor, yardman, and janitor classifications regardless of qualifications or training in higher skills. The practice is so firmly entrenched that it has been reduced to the blueprint stage. Employment charts in general used throughout the oil industry restrict the employment of Mexican-Americans to the three positions mentioned.

The railroads and the brotherhoods and railways unions have likewise generally restricted the utilization of available Mexican labor supply. By Mexican, no distinction is made between Mexican nationals and American citizens of Mexican extraction, who are restricted in general to common labor, trackmen, general maintenance labor, and car droppers, regardless of previous training, time of service, or other qualifications.

The mining industry in the Southwest with very few exceptions employs Mexicans only in common and semiskilled jobs. In many instances they are restricted from underground work, where wages are higher and the danger is less. Mexicans can be oiler-helpers, crane operators helpers, and helpers to most skilled jobs and positions and machine operators, but they can never be employed or classed as master craftsmen or machine operators.

In military installations throughout the Southwest, where large numbers of civilians are

"Statement of Dr. Carlos E. Castañeda, Regional Director, Fair Employment Practice Committee, Region 10, San Antonio, Texas," in Alonso S. Perales, *Are We Good Neighbors?* (San Antonio, TX: Artes Graficas, 1948), 99–101. Used by permission.

employed, Mexicans are hired but not always on a level of equality, be they of American citizenship or not. Frequently they are found in jobs that do not utilize their highest skill. They have been promoted slowly and with evident reluctance. Public utility companies and telephone and telegraph companies throughout the Southwest have failed to utilize the available Mexican labor supply in other than common-labor jobs, with rare exceptions here and there.

The aircraft and shipbuilding industries, be it said in all justice, have given the Mexican worker practically equal opportunities to develop his various skills and to attain promotion in accord with his qualifications. This is true also of munitions and arms factories. But since these are essentially war industries that on VE- and VJ-day will not be readily reconverted to civilian goods production, their workers will be the first to seek employment in the newly acquired industrial skills.

Wives, sisters, and other women relatives of men in the armed forces have been refused employment in war and essential industries because of their Mexican origin. One Maria Garcia, of Clifton, Arizona, declared that her son was in the Army; that he had previously worked in the mines and had been the chief support of the family; and that when she learned that women were being employed by the mining company, she applied for a job, but was told that no Mexican women could be hired.

Another complainant, one Cleo M. Garcia, speaking for herself and seven others, said, "We applied at an ordnance plant in north Texas. Here is what was told me: "We cannot hire you because the Latin-American people, men and women, are not capable of doing war work." When I asked him why, and how did he know that we were not capable of doing work if he did not give us a chance to prove we could, and that it is our right as much as anybody else to work in this kind of work, he very rudely disregarded my question and told me that there was a lot of janitor work that had to be done, and that was the only place where they could place us or any other Mexicans. We feel this is an injustice to our boys by holding up production when there's a lot of people that is willing to work to speed victory." ...

Increasing shortage of labor has forced industry to give the Mexican-American a try, but not without the greatest reluctance and misgiving. Employers agree generally that they produce with the same efficiency as members of any other group. The Fair Employment Practice Committee, set up by Executive Order 9346, has helped to overcome the reluctance of employers to utilize more fully and effectively this remaining pool of available labor.

FACTORIES ON RAILS

Alexander S. Yakovlev (1906–1989), not to be confused with Mikhail Gorbachev's prominent advisor of the same name who died in 2005, was the Soviet Union's most famous aircraft designer. He made a reputation during the interwar period designing gliders and sporting aircraft, but quickly established himself thereafter producing military planes. His rugged, dependable, and effective fighter planes, especially the YAK-1, YAK-3, and YAK-9, produced in huge numbers (over 36,000), eventually enabled the Soviets to wrest aerial supremacy from the Germans. The great challenge Yakovlev and fellow designers faced, however, was not just to match German technical standards on the drawing board, but also to put designs into production when Soviet industrial areas were being overrun by rapid German advances. The solution, detailed in Yakovlev's memoirs, was to dismantle entire factories, transport them eastward by train to safety across the Ural Mountains, and then reassemble them and resume production. In this way, the Soviets shrugged off enormous losses of territory and war material without undermining their war effort.

The production of new types of airplanes was enormously complicated by the necessity of evacuating these plants east to quieter and less vulnerable areas.

Thousands of trainloads of aircraft-plant equipment were sent beyond the Volga to the Urals and Siberia. Tank, artillery, moto-car and small arms factories and plants were evacuated together with them....

Many trainloads of equipment were already on their way to Siberia while the assembly shop was finishing planes which were turned over to front-line pilots right there in the yard of the plant. They were fueled with petrol and very often the pilots would take their machines up into the air and fly off on a combat sortie straight away. Thus the planes often had their first tests in encounters with enemy fighters.

Rolling up their sleeves, designers loaded the train side-by-side with workers and employees. The work went on round the clock. Special care was taken to make sure that the expensive and fragile equipment of the designing bureau and laboratories arrived at our place of destination safely. Each foreman, worker and engineer made sure everything needed for the speedy organization of production was taken to the new site....

I decided to ride down to Khimka and see for myself how the loading and expedition of trains was preceding. The car sped along the Leningradsky Prospekt, past the Dynamo Stadium, across the bridge over the canal and finally turned off the highway and drove up to the railway siding belonging to the plant. Hundreds of people were bustling about near the train standing at the wooden platform to which a continuous string of trucks was bringing machines. I made my way towards the train through the noisy bustle. The train was already loaded and final preparations were being made before it pulled out.

Workers looked out of the box-cars, jumped down and gathered round me. Everyone was excited but I could not spot a single gloomy or sorrowful face.

Alexander Yakovlev, *Notes of an Aircraft Designer* (Moscow: Foreign Languages Publishing House, n.d.), 144–149. Used by permission.

"Come to our house-warming." It was an invitation to one of the box-cars. Double tier bunks with mattresses and rugs thrown over them, an iron stove in the middle, a table and chairs and a paraffin lamp dangling from the ceiling. Inquisitive children's eyes peered at me from the bunks. Women were already busy with their cooking.

"We are comfortable enough. If only we get there before the frosts," said Mikhail Glazkov who was in charge of the loading.

"You'll get there before the frosts," I replied. "What about the food?"

"We've managed that, we've organized a special canteen car in every train and put our people to work there. We have enough food to last us for the journey, and we have arranged for hot water to be available throughout the day."

"And who's to maintain order on route?"

"Each train has its commandant, usually one of the shop superintendents. They'll manage."...

Fresh trains of box-and-flat-cars loaded with workers, machines and materials set out every eight or ten hours from this platform for Siberia. Hard as we tried to make things for our people as comfortable as possible, we realized that it was still very difficult for the thousands of them who were burdened with small children to move to Siberia in cramped box-cars.

It took the trains weeks to complete their journey. Winter came and frosts set in. There were food difficulties. But everyone realized that the country was living through hard times, they realized the significance of events and knew that they must weather all the hardships and privations.

Great was the heroism of people who, exhausted by a long weary journey, arrived in far Siberia in winter and started to turn out airplanes in an incredibly short space of time.

While trains were still being loaded in Moscow, in Siberia preparations were made to receive workers and staffs and equipment. Shops were arranged, production plans were drawn up, electric power, compressed air, steam and water mains were laid on to put the machines into operation immediately on arrival.Barracks were put up for the workers in which each family was given a room. On arrival it took two or three days for people to establish their new homes, unload the trains and arrange the equipment in the shops. Six days later the plant began to operate.

I had no idea myself that it would be possible to organize the evacuation so efficiently and with so little time lost for the production of aircraft. It makes me proud to recall that only three weeks later, the production of planes started to pile up every day and even every hour. In three months we not only caught up with our Moscow output level but considerably outstripped it. Eleven months later we were turning out seven and a half times more aircraft than in the pre-war period.

If, before the war, we had been told that thousands of plants could be moved elsewhere in the country and put into operation in such a short time many of us would have laughed. But what yesterday seemed impossible today became the reality.

PRODUCING FOR VICTORY

Alexander Werth (1901–1969) did as much as anyone to bring home to English-speaking readers the events on the Russian front. Russian-born and English-educated, Werth was equally fluent in both languages and, as a wartime BBC correspondent, enjoyed a degree of access and sensitivity of observation that his colleagues could only envy. Here Werth's emphasis on the obstacles the Soviets faced in achieving full-fledged industrial production and technological parity with Germany is a necessary antidote to simplistic views that the Soviet Union could rest content and rely upon its harsh climate, vast distances, and manpower advantage to secure victory without bothering to mobilize for all-out war.

Soviet armaments production did not reach a satisfactory level until the autumn of 1942. The evacuation of hundreds of plants from west to east in the autumn and winter of 1941 had resulted in an almost catastrophic drop in arms production, which largely accounted for the disappointing results of the Russian Moscow counter-offensive in the winter of 1941–2 and for the disasters of the summer of 1942.

[T]here was a serious shortage in the east (where most of the armaments industry was now concentrated) of both power and metals. The total fuel resources were only half of what they had been before the war. The engineering works of Siberia and the Urals could not work at full capacity, and during most of 1942 the output of tanks, planes, guns and ammunition was well below the Red Army's requirements. Draconian measures had to be taken to increase output. New coal mines had to be speedily sunk; new power-plants had to be built; the People's Commissariat for Coal had some 200,000 more or less "improvised" new miners placed at its disposal, and a special food reserve had to be constituted to keep them going. Tens of thousands of new miners were sent from various parts of the country to the Karaganda coal area in Kazakhstan—nearly all of them women and very young people, who had to be trained in the shortest possible time. The morale of the Russian women, conscious of working for their husbands or sons or brothers in the Army was particularly admirable....[T]he stupendous mass-effort made by the women of Russia during the war, whether in industry or agriculture, had nothing to equal it....

In 1943 oil resources were very low, too; Maikop had been put out of action by the retreating Russians; Grozny, with its refineries, had suffered severely from German bombing; and during the temporary breakdown of communications, in the Stalingrad period, many of the Baku wells had to be temporarily closed down. Instead, a special effort was made to develop the "Second Baku" in the east at top speed....

New industrial "giants" had to be speedily built— thus an enormous new power station was built in 1942...to supply dozens of armaments works over a large area, and a gigantic new blast furnace...was completed during the year....Altogether, although the Soviet engineering industry had lost half its potential through the German occupation of the Ukraine and other areas, it had, in the main, overcome its difficulties by 1943.

Alexander Werth, *Russia at War, 1941–1945* (New York: Dutton, 1964), 620–623. Used by permission of Dutton, a division of Penguin Group (USA) Inc.

All this had a decisive effect on Soviet arms production. A tremendous effort was put into creating an air force superior to the Luftwaffe; gone were the grim days of 1941 when most of the Russian planes were suicidally obsolete. The principal planes that began to be produced in quantity in 1942 were the Il-2 stormovik (low-flying attack plane), and the Pe-2 operational dive-bomber; and the La-5 fighter, which was better than the Messerschmitt 109, but not as good as the Messerschmitt 109F or 109G. In 1943 the La-5-FN, which proved better than any German fighter, including the Fokke-Wulf 190, went into mass-production, and, in May, so did the Yak-9, with a 37 mm. gun, which was superior to German fighters with their 20 mm. guns....The average monthly production of planes rose from 2,100 in 1942 to 2,900 in 1943, of which 2,500 were combat planes. Altogether, in 1943, 35,000 planes were produced, thirty-seven per cent more than in 1942, and including eighty-six per cent of combat planes....

[G]reat progress was made in tank construction throughout 1942....Some spectacular improvements were made in 1942 for speeding up the production of tanks; thus the turrets of the T-34 medium tank were stamped instead of being cast. The T-34 was, altogether the best medium tank of World War II....

Altogether, in 1943, 16,000 heavy and medium tanks were made; 4,000 mobile guns and 3,500 light tanks. This total was eight-and-a-half times more than in 1940 and nearly four times more than in 1941.

FORD'S WILLOW RUN

Following Pearl Harbor, the United States raced to increase its industrial output. Henry Ford, whose adoption of Taylorism in his Ford Automobile Company made him a wealthy man, applied the process for first time ever to the production of military planes at his Willow Run plant in the early 1940s. Taylorism, the idea of scientific management used in the early twentieth century, was a process whereby the control traditionally accorded to skilled laborers over their working conditions was replaced by methods that increased mechanization, coordination, and intensity of work on an assembly line. Although more goods could be produced as a result, the end result was a decline in the workers' bargaining position (salary) coupled with rising profits for the industrialist. Upon its completion in the late autumn of 1941, Ford's Willow Run plant, located in Ypsilanti, Michigan (about thirty miles west of Detroit), became the world's largest factory under a single roof. Inside the massive structure, the long-range B-24 bomber (the first delivered in September 1942, followed by over 8,600 by June 1945) was built. Workers, who poured into Willow Run from all parts of the country, especially from the South, hoping for jobs found a woeful lack of housing (many were forced to commute from towns miles away from Ypsilanti or lived in tents and trailers often lacking toilets and running water) and encountered racism from local inhabitants, who resented the incursion of "hillbillies" and "southern blacks." Many disgruntled workers referred to their plant as "Will it Run?" and wondered if Detroit, home to a large number of military industries, should be nicknamed the "arsehole of democracy" rather than the "arsenal of democracy." By June 1943 tensions ran so high that race riots broke out in Detroit. Two sociologists from the University of Michigan, Lowell Carr and James Stermer, wrote a damning monograph about the failings of Willow Run and the Ford Motor Company's callous attitudes toward its workers.

Who was going to pay the privation costs of social change at Willow Run—the settled folks in possession or the uprooted bomber workers?

The folks in possession from the thrifty householders of Ypsilanti to the hard-driving Ford Motor Company executives never had any doubts about the answer; let the "outsiders" look after themselves! *Our* little areas of security, *our* privileges, *our* settled ways of life aren't going to be changed, not if *we* can help it! This is *our* home, *our* town, *our* company, *our* way of life—and we mean to keep it *ours!*

All over the United States, folks in possession felt and acted in the same way. All over the United States, war-production workers moving in to make the guns, the shells, the tanks, and the airplanes needed to beat Hitler and Hirohito met the same reception. They were intruders, outsiders, interlopers. All over the United States the home folks treated incoming war workers as "foreigners."

At Willow Run from the modest homes of local paper-mill operatives to the busy offices of realtors and building contractors, from the prosperous counters of Ypsilanti merchants to the smoke-filled chamber of the supervisors in Ann Arbor, from the clangor of the local foundry to the sumptuous quiet of the Ford Motor Company's high command at Dearborn—everywhere everyone not specifically charged with helping the newcomers and their families make a go of it did his level best to contribute *as little as possible* to their making a go of it.

Of course, nobody did this to hinder the war effort....As they saw it, all they were doing was to resist the "socialistic" ideas of those bureaucrats in Washington and to defend the community against the "dangerous" aggressiveness of the U.A.W.–C.I.O. [labor organization, United Auto Workers–Congress of Industrial Organizations, despised and obstructed by Henry Ford]....

But the net result was inescapable. Inadequate housing, inadequate community services, inadequate everything threw the major burdens of the bomber upheaval squarely on the shoulders of the men and women needed so desperately to get the bombers rolling. In absenteeism, in turnover, in the energy-consuming, morale-wrecking struggles of workers...all this high-minded obstructionism of the folks in possession took its toll of the war effort....

How, then, did we achieve the world-smashing production miracle that broke the Axis?

Not by increased individual productivity. And not by any rise in the life efficiency of our industrial communities. We got it by lengthening the working day and by pulling into the factories 3 million teenagers, nearly 7 million unemployed, and more than 5 million women and oldsters. We got it by manning more factories and more jobs more hours a day more days a week....We did it by working 63 million workers 46.7 hours a week for a total of 2,021.0 million man hours per week in 1940—a 45.5 per cent increase in total man hours per week. And we did it in war-production areas like Willow Run and Newport News [Virginia] and San Diego, choked with newcomers living like peons. We did *not* do it by any all-out increase in individual or community efficiency, mark that. Factory efficiency, perhaps; community, no....

The Ford Motor Company actively recruited hillbillies to overcome the desperate labor shortage at the bomber plant. Most Washtenaw county businessmen, civic leaders, and government officials, on the other hand, heartily detested hillbillies....

For there were still plenty of influential citizens in Washtenaw county who regarded the National Labor Relations Act of 1935 [the "Wagner Act" guaranteeing workers' rights to organize unions and engage in collective bargaining or strike action] as the passing vagary of a "radical" administration, temporarily protected by the urgencies of wartime....

This local power struggle among interest groups during the war passed through three major phases. First, came the struggle over shelter, the Ford Company and local groups holding the line, the U.A.W. plunging for government housing. Then came a phase in which, with the delayed arrival of a bare minimum of government housing in 1943— the issue shifted sharply to the bomber plant itself. Industrial relations instead of shelter became the hot spot, the area of insecurity....

Finally, with the success of the European invasion in 1944, everybody at Willow Run with the possible exception of the Ford management itself suddenly began to worry about the future of the bomber plant and of Willow Village. What was going to happen to the plant? And what were the hillbillies going to do after it closed?

In the first phase, the struggle over housing,...the cautious tenderness of the Washington government toward vested interests in war-production areas in general; and second, in Washtenaw county in particular, the smugness and negativism that marked the whole approach of most of the folks in possession....[N]early everybody in and around Willow Run seemed to regard the whole business not only as a problem for Washington or Henry Ford but more especially as a problem that must not be allowed to disturb Washtenaw county.

Undoubtedly a good deal of this stemmed straight from the high degree of specialization inherent in modern industrial culture. Everybody has his own little special niche, his own little area of responsibility, and very few people indeed have any conception of what to do and fewer still have any competence to do anything specific when a problem arises that existing agencies are unprepared to meet. At Willow Run the housing needs of tens of thousands of incoming bomber workers constituted a problem exactly of this kind; existing local agencies were totally unprepared to meet them. In 1940 in all Washtenaw county there had been only 1,425 males and 31 females employed in the construction industry. At the most liberal estimate, 1,400 construction workers in 1941 and 1942 could have built only some odd hundreds of small houses each year. But the need had to be measured in thousands, not hundred, and it was to develop in months, not years....Who, in short, could possibly have seen the picture whole, or have had a reasonable basis for estimating the future? Obviously, only the Ford Motor Company or the United States government.

But both were integral parts of a culture that provided no clear-cut patterns for dealing with that crisis situation as it was to develop at Willow Run. For Ford, the industrialist, the industrial culture told him that *in ordinary situations* he could get more profit by using his capital for manufacture than for housing his workers. It told him that *in ordinary* situations the smart thing for him to do, as for thousands of other employers, was to rely on the community, i.e., on the capital of *other* businessmen and of *local taxpayers*, to provide the protections and the commercial services needed by his workers. *But it did not tell him precisely when an ordinary situation ceases to be ordinary....*

The industrial culture gives no answers.... Just as the automobile companies of Michigan spent millions on product research every year, experimenting with this and experimenting with that, but spent hardly one red penny on research in human relations, so when the Ford Motor Company built its gigantic new factory at Willow Run it spent no time and no money whatever trying to find out what pattern of settlement a prospective work force might *prefer* to follow. It never occurred to anybody, apparently, to survey the job-nearness distribution of Detroit automobile workers or to ask any of them how near to their jobs they would *like* to live. So the Ford Motor Company put $90 million of taxpayers' money into a plant that would concentrate 42,000 men and women six days a week in the middle of an ex-soybean field 3 miles away from a little town of 12,000, already "full up" and 27 miles from the nearest adequate shopping center. True to the dominant patterns of the industrial culture *in ordinary situations,* the Ford Motor Company thus relied on those distant communities....

Even Pearl Harbor and the resultant tire and gas rationing failed to change that policy. Let 42,000 men and women drive 2 million miles a day—500,000 car miles—so what? *In ordinary situations no employer has any responsibility for his workers off the job....*

Why should Ford have been willing to rely on the businessmen of communities to house his workers, even though they couldn't, and have been so unwilling to let the government do it for him at Willow Run adequately and in time? The answer to that takes us into the whole question of how the government itself dawdled and bungled here, as in every other congested war-production area, and never anywhere handled war-production areas with the firmness, overall vision, and competent certainty that it applied to its own military communities.

The building of the war cantonments can hardly be cited as the ideal way in which to build "model towns." But at least each cantonment was planned; it was planned as a unit; and it was planned *and organized* to subordinate everything to just one job—the job of turning out trained soldiers.

By way of contrast, no ordinary civilian war-production area, and least of all Willow Run, was ever planned at all. No attempt was ever made to handle all the problems of any civilian area as a unitary whole. And no attempt was ever made to organize any civilian war-production area—certainly not Willow Run—to subordinate every conflicting interest to the one overriding purpose that had made it a war-production area in the first place—the production of war materials. *For reasons inherent in our culture...civilian war-production areas were permitted to "organize" themselves.* In other words, they were permitted to subordinate war production to local interests, as they did at Willow Run. They were permitted to throw the major inconveniences, deprivations, and health risks on the incoming war workers. And they were permitted to do all this—to allocate the social costs of the local war effort—not in terms of maximizing technological efficiency or of meeting military need but purely in terms of the age-old political power struggle, the folks in possession vs. the folks who needed jobs.

GERMANY'S DELAYED MOBILIZATION

Hitler fancied himself a great war leader, and although he regularly astonished visitors and even his own advisors with specific details of weaponry, he had little interest in, or appreciation for, the varied measures necessary to put Germany's economy on a true war footing. Furthermore, he recalled from bitter experience that the German home front had collapsed near the end of World War I from hunger and war-weariness, and from that memory drew the conclusion that the civilians should be insulated, as far as possible, from the sacrifices and production demands dictated by total war. His preference was also for quick campaigns that did not require enormous stockpiles of material, and that enabled German troops to capture or plunder much of what they needed. Accordingly, for much of the conflict, Germany's economy was not fully mobilized for war, despite the popular image of a country having for years armed itself to the teeth in preparation for battle. Confirmation of the disparity between appearance and reality came from the Strategic Bombing Survey, an initiative begun by the American government in November 1944 to review the actual impact of bombing on the German economy, to draw lessons from that experience to suggest ways in which the bombing of Japan might be made more effective, and to predict the likely implications for the use of airpower in the postwar era. The survey of the European theater was completed in September 1945; its participants (both military and civilian officials, including the famous economist John Kenneth Galbraith) had personally surveyed bomb damage, questioned German political and business leaders, and pored over captured official documents (some tracked to such unlikely hiding places as coffins and a henhouse).

The outstanding feature of the German war effort is the surprisingly low output of armaments in the first three years of the war.... In aircraft, trucks, tanks, self-propelled guns, and several other types of armaments, British production was greater than Germany's in 1940, 1941, and 1942.

For these early years the conclusion is inescapable that Germany's war production was not limited by her war potential—by the resources at her disposal—but by demand; in other words, by the notions of the German war leaders as to what was required for achieving their aim. The Germans did not plan for a long war, nor were they prepared for it. Hitler's strategy contemplated a series of separate thrusts and quick victories over enemies that were even less prepared than Germany; he did not expect to fight a prolonged war against a combination of major world powers.... Eventual intervention by the United States was not taken seriously. The attack on Russia was started in the confident expectation that the experience of the earlier campaigns was to be repeated; Russia was to be completely subjugated in three to four months.

The underestimation of Russia's strength was the major miscalculation in this strategy....

The Effects of Strategic Bombing on the German War Economy (Washington, DC: U.S. Government Printing Office, 1945), 6–9, 11–13. Used by permission.

While the German economy was approaching its basic limitations in mid-1944, it never attained its full war potential. Production capacity, except in a few special cases, of which oil was the most notable, was never really short; machinery capacity was never fully utilized. Manpower—particularly woman power—was never fully mobilized. Raw material stocks of the most important categories, such as steel, were rising up to mid-1944. The output of civilian consumption goods, after the restriction of the first two years of the war…was maintained virtually stable until the second quarter of 1944.

Yet, at least from the end of 1942 onwards, the Germans were arming as fast as they could. If they did not reach their full war potential before the end of the war, this was due to limitations on the speed with which they were able to convert and expand. Expansion was held up by temporary shortages of components and parts and by the introduction of new types of armaments. Air raids and the dispersal of industry also played their part in slowing down expansion.…

The German economy does not appear to have suffered from shortages of machine tools, general machinery, or plant facilities—except temporarily in a few isolated cases. On the contrary, machine tool and machinery capacity was generally in excess of needs.…Furthermore, the German machine tool industry hardly expanded during the war, worked on a single shift basis throughout, and converted almost 30 percent of its capacity to direct munitions production.

Germany's easy machine tool position is in striking contrast with the experience of the United States and Great Britain, where machine tools were kept working 24 hours a day seven days a week, and the machine tool industry was very much expanded and strained to the utmost to supply requirements. One reason for Germany's strong position was her large machine tool industry which, being an important exporter, had a capacity greatly in excess of Germany's domestic peace time requirements. Secondly, Germany started the war well stocked with machine tools which, unlike the American inventory, consisted mainly of universal machines and could therefore easily be converted to war production.…

Germany's experience was fundamentally different from that of the Anglo-American Allies also as far as the manpower problem is concerned. While England and America both entered the war with substantial unemployment, Germany's labor force was fully employed already in 1939. Total employment increased by 8 million, or 30 percent, between 1933 and 1939. Industrial employment nearly doubled, with most of the increase concentrated on the heavy goods industries.…

Germany entered the war with a "guns and butter" philosophy which was continued well after the initial defeats in Russia.

With the progress of the war, the mobilization of manpower increased both in Great Britain and in the United States; but not so in Germany, where the total employment of Germans…remained practically unchanged throughout the war and reductions in the civilian labor force due to military draft were not completely offset by the employment of foreigners.

The increase, from September 1939 to September 1944, in the number of German men and women employed (including the armed forces) was less than one million, and it fell short of the natural growth of the working age population over the period. Her armed forces mobilized 11 ½ million men from the outbreak of the war up to September 1944; and their place in the civilian labor force was but partially filled by 7 million foreign workers and prisoners of war and the 1 million newly mobilized Germans, resulting in a net loss of 3 ½ million (10 percent) to the civilian labor force.

This decline in civilian manpower is the more remarkable, because Germany did not exhaust her reserves of manpower in the course of the war. She began the war with about the same proportion of occupied women (outside agriculture) as Britain. But while in Britain the number of women in full- or part-time work increased 45 percent in the course of the war, the number of German women mobilized remained practically unchanged.…

There is no doubt that manpower for the armed forces was short, in the sense that after the Russian defeats, Germany would have liked to put a larger army in the field. Even here, however, there remained some reserve which could have been mobilized for the Wehrmacht.…

Prior to the summer of 1943, air raids had no appreciable effect either on German munitions production or on the national output in general. The area attacks of the RAF did considerable damage to buildings and caused local delays in production by diverting labor to repair work and debris clearance, and by causing absenteeism and local disorganization.... But considering the nature of the German economy during this period, it is impossible to conclude that either submarine production or munitions output as a whole was any smaller as a result of air raids than it would have been otherwise....

The effects of air raids became more noticeable from the summer of 1943 onward. This was partly due to the heavier weight of the RAF attacks and partly to the appearance of the AAF in major strength....

The attack on transportation beginning in September 1944 was the most important single cause of Germany's ultimate economic collapse.... The effects of the attack are best seen, however, in the figures of coal transport, which normally constituted 40 percent of rail traffic.... The operation of Germany's raw material industries, her manufacturing industries, and her power supply were all dependent on coal. By January their stocks were becoming exhausted and collapse was inevitable.

The index of total munitions output reached its peak in July 1944 and fell thereafter. By December it had declined to 80 percent of the July peak, and even this level was attained only by using up stocks of components and raw materials. Air raids were the main factor in reducing output....

By the third quarter of 1944 bombing had succeeded in tying down a substantial portion of the labor force....

As to the effects of bomb damage on the civilian economy, there is no evidence that shortages of civilian goods ever reached a point where the German authorities were forced to transfer resources from war production in order to prevent disintegration on the home front. It was not until the end of 1943 that the area raids of the RAF had caused important shortages in certain segments of the civilian economy; and even for the whole of 1944, the output of manufactured consumer goods was only slightly below that of 1943. The most that can be said is that bombing destroyed a substantial part of the consumer goods cushion and thereby prevented the further conversion of the civilian economy to war production in 1944.

From December 1944 onwards, all sectors of the German economy were in rapid decline. This collapse was due to the results of air raids working in combination with other causes....

GERMAN FORCED LABOR

Although Germany had not undertaken a comprehensive mobilization for the war that broke out in 1939, its leaders remained reluctant to rectify their mistakes as the conflict proceeded. Rapid victories in the war's early stages facilitated an economy of plunder that enabled the Germans to maintain an effective war machine. But from June 1941 onward, when the German military faced a Soviet foe with access to enormous economic and demographic resources, Hitler's regime would have to confront an inescapable dilemma: how could it deploy the maximum number of German men in uniform in the field and yet simultaneously produce the maximum of weapons and munitions to equip them properly? Resorting to female labor on the home front was an option Hitler had already ruled out, for it violated the Nazi emphasis on women's reproductive rather than productive role. Another alternative, to import male laborers from outside Germany to do the necessary work, was distasteful to many Nazis, for it seemed to threaten the primacy of racial purity by permitting the mixing of German citizens with their ethnic or racial inferiors. The demands of the war, however, continued to escalate. Early attempts to put Polish prisoners of war (from the September 1939 campaign) to work met with some success, but really continued an older tradition of migrant Polish workers who had come to work temporarily in German agriculture. More innovative (if that is the right word) and draconian measures awaited the ascendancy of the former architect Albert Speer (1905–1981) over the war economy from late 1942. From that point on, the Nazis increasingly relied upon forced labor from outside Germany's borders to keep their production going. The new "Plenipotentiary for Employment," Fritz Sauckel (1894–1946), set to work with a vengeance, and by August 1944, some 7.1 million foreign civilians and prisoners of war were registered for work (the majority from the Soviet Union). Foreign civilians were paid modest wages but poorly housed and fed in separate camps, while prisoners of war were deemed expendable and worked remorselessly, despite the fact that such treatment violated basic ethical standards and accepted provisions of international law. These horrors were compounded by the resort to concentration camp inmates to perform particularly onerous war work, often underground, in conditions which limited the average life span of those engaged on some projects (such as flying bomb/rocket production) to a mere three weeks. The issue of forced labor figured at the Nuremberg Trials, from which the following excerpt is taken, and resulted in the execution of Sauckel.

"Report on Forced Labor in Germany," in Office of U.S. Chief of Counsel for Prosecution of Axis Criminality, *Nazi Conspiracy and Aggression* (Washington, DC: U.S. Government Printing Office, 1946), 8 vols., 2:792–799. Used by permission.

...(2) The prisoners of war and foreign workers at the Krupp factories did not voluntarily engage in the manufacture of arms and ammunitions; they were forced to do so....

   (a) Workers were brought to Essen from Poland and Russia in grossly overcrowded, unheated, and unsanitary cattle cars and upon debarking, were beaten, kicked, and otherwise inhumanely treated....

   (b) Foreign workers were compelled to go to work under guard and were closely watched....

   (c) After working hours, foreign workers were confined in camps under barbed wire enclosures and were carefully guarded....

CONTRARY TO ARTICLES 4, 6, 7, AND 46 OF THE HAGUE REGULATIONS, 1907, ARTICLES 2 AND 3 OF THE PRISONERS OF WAR CONVENTION (GENEVA, 1929), THE LAWAS AND CUSTOMS OF WAR, AND ARTICLES 6 (b) AND 6 (c) OF THE CHARTER, KRUPP, AS HEAD OF THE KRUPP CONCERN, WAS RESPONSIBLE FOR DENYING ADEQUATE FOOD, SHELTER, CLOTHING, AND MEDICAL CARE AND ATTENTION TO PRISONERS OF WAR AND WORKERS FORCIBLY DEPORTED FROM OCCUPIED COUNTRIES, FOR FORCING THEM TO WORK UNDER INHUMANE CONDITIONS, AND FOR TORTURING THEM AND SUBJECTING THEM TO INDIGNITIES.

(1) The prisoners of war and foreign laborers at the Krupp works were undernourished and forced to work on a virtual starvation diet.

   (a) In a memorandum upon Krupp stationery to Mr. Hupe, Director of the Krupp locomotive factory in Essen, dated 14 March 1942 and entitled "Employment of Russians," it was said:

"During the last few days we have established that the food for the Russians employed here is so miserable, that the people are getting weaker from day to day."

Investigations showed that single Russians are not able to place a piece of metal for turning into position for instance, because of lack of physical strength. The same conditions exist at all places of work where Russians are employed."...

   (f) Dr. Jaeger, senior camp doctor in the Krupps' workers' camps, has stated under oath that not only did the plan for food distribution to foreign workers call for a very small quantity of meat every week, but also that they received only contaminated meats rejected by the health authorities, such as horse or tuberculin infested meat.

(2) The prisoners of war and foreign workers at the Krupp factories were forced to live in grossly overcrowded hutted camps and otherwise were denied adequate shelter....

"Sanitary conditions were exceedingly bad. At Kramerplatz, where approximately 1,200 eastern workers were crowded into the rooms of an old school, the sanitary conditions were atrocious in the extreme. Only 10 children's toilets were available for the 1,200 inhabitants. At Dechenschule, 15 children's toilets were available for the 400–500 eastern workers. Excretion contaminated the entire floors of these lavatories. There were also very few facilities for washing."...

(3) The prisoners of war and foreign workers at the Krupp factories were denied adequate clothing....

"They worked and slept in the same clothing in which they had arrived from the east. Virtually all of them had no overcoats and were compelled, therefore, to use their blankets as coats in cold and rainy weather. In view of the shortage of shoes, many workers were forced to go to work in their bare feet, even in the winter. Wooden shoes were given to some of the workers, but their quality was such as to give the workers sore feet...."

(4) Prisoners of war and foreign laborers at the Krupp works were denied adequate medical and treatment, and as a consequence, suffered severely from a multitude of diseases and ailments....

"The percentage of eastern workers who were ill was twice as great as among the Germans. Tuberculosis was particularly widespread among the eastern workers. The T.B. rate among them was 4 times the normal rate (2% eastern workers, Germans .5%)...."

(5) Russian juveniles were compelled to work at the Krupp factories, and prisoners of war and foreign workers were generally forced to work long hours, to and beyond the point of exhaustion....

(6) The prisoners of war and foreign laborers used at the Krupp works were beaten, tortured, and subjected to inhuman indignities.

CHICANAS IN THE FACTORY

For many American women, like Beatrice Morales Clifton, exchanging traditional domestic routines for work in wartime factories was a new, initially frightening, but ultimately liberating experience. Those women who entered the workplace for the first time in their lives often encountered gender and racial prejudice by male coworkers and supervisors who belittled them for their inexperience and skin color. Aware of the challenges to women in their new role, President Roosevelt warned in his Columbus Day speech of 1942 that Americans could no longer afford to perpetuate gender or racial prejudice because winning the war demanded unity of purpose as well as domestic harmony. Beatrice Morales Clifton, a first generation Mexican-American in Southern California, married at age fifteen, mother of two and a divorcée before age twenty, and shortly thereafter remarried to a man thirty years her senior, entered the workforce as an unskilled laborer after Pearl Harbor. The following excerpt from her reminiscences provides the reader with a poignant picture of her experiences working in a Lockheed aircraft factory in the early 1940s.

I filled out the papers and everything and I got the job. Why I took Lockheed, I don't know, but I just liked the name....

To me, everything was new. They were doing the P-38s [fighter planes] at that time. I was at Plant 2, on Seventh and Santa Fe. It was on the fifth floor. I went up there and saw the place, and I said, "Gee ——," See, so many parts and things that you've never seen. Me, I'd never seen anything in my whole life. It was exciting and scary at the same time.

They put me way up in the back, putting little plate nuts and drilling holes. They put me with some guy—he was kind of a stinker, real mean. A lot of them guys at the time resented women coming into jobs, and they let you know about it. He says, "Well, have you ever done any work like this?" I said, "No." I was feeling just horrible. Horrible. Because I never worked with men, to be with men alone other than my husband. So then he says "you know what you've got in your hand? That's a rivet gun." I said, "Oh." What could I answer? I was terrified. So then time

---

Beatrice Morales Clifton, "Should your wife take a war job?" in Sherna Berger Gluck, ed., *Rosie the Riveter Revisited: Women, the War, and Social Change* (Boston: Twayne, 1987), 209–212.

went on and I made a mistake. I messed up something, made a ding. He got so irritable with me, he says, "You're not worth the money Lockheed pays you."

He couldn't have hurt me more if he would have slapped me. When he said that, I dropped the gun and I went running downstairs to the restroom, with tears coming down. This girl from Texas saw me and she followed me. She was real good. She was one of these "toughies"; dressed up and walked like she was kind of tough. She asked me what was wrong. I told her what I had done and I was crying. She says, "Don't worry." She started cussing him. We came back up and she told them all off.

I was very scared because, like I say, I had never been away like that and I had never been among a lot of men. Actually, I had never been out on my own. Whenever I had gone anyplace, it was with my husband. It was all building up inside of me, so when that guy told me that I wasn't worth the money Lockheed paid me, it just came out in tears.

At the end of that first day, I was so tired. I was riding the streetcar and I had to stand all the way from Los Angeles clear to Pasadena....My husband, he didn't have very much to say, 'cause he didn't approve from the beginning. As time went on, his attitude changed a little, but I don't think he ever really, really got used to the idea of me working....

They had a union, but it wasn't very strong then. It wasn't like it is now. But I joined. I joined everything. And they gave me a list of the stuff that I would be needing. At that time they used to sell you your tools and your toolboxes through Lockheed. So I bought a box. I bought the clothing at Sears. It was just a pair of pants and a blouse. To tell you the truth, I felt kind of funny wearing pants. Then at the same time, I said, "Oh, what the heck." And those shoes! I wasn't used to low shoes. Even in the house, I always wore high heels....

As time went on, I started getting a little bit better. I just made up my mind that I was going to do it. I learned my job so well that then they put me on the next operation. At the very first, I just began putting little plate nuts and stuff like that. Then afterwards I learned how to drill the skins and burr them. Later,

as I got going, I learned to rivet and buck. I got to the point where I was very good.

I had a Mexican girl, Irene Herrera, and she was as good a bucker as I was a riveter. She would be facing me and we'd just go right on through. We'd go one side and then we'd get up to the corner and I'd hand her the gun or the bucking bar or whatever and then we'd come back. Her and I, we used to have a lot of fun. They would want maybe six or five elevators a day. I'd say, "let's get with it." We worked pretty hard all day until about 2:00. Then we would slack down.

I had a lot of friends there. We all spoke to each other. Most of them smoked, and we'd sit in the smoking areas out there in the aisle. Then, some of the girls—on the next corner there was a drugstore that served lunches. There was a white lady, she used to go, and Irene would go. We'd talk about our families and stuff like that.

Irene stayed on that same operation. I don't know why I got a chance to learn all the other jobs, but I learned the whole operation until I got up to the front, the last step. They used to put this little flap with a wire, with a hinge. I had to have that flap just right so that it would swing easy without no rubbing anywhere. I used to go with a little hammer and a screwdriver and knock those little deals down so that it would be just right. That guy that I used to work with helped me, teached me how to do it, and I could do it just like him.

New people would come in, and they would say, "You teach them the job. You know all the jobs." Sometimes it would make me mad. I'd tell them, "What the heck, you get paid for it. You show them the job." But I would still show them.

Then, like the lead person, they'd say, "Look at her now. You should have seen her a year ago when she first came in. You'd go boo and she'd start crying. Now she can't keep her mouth shut." I figured this is the only way you're going to survive, so I'm going to do it.

I was just a mother of four kids, that's all. But I felt proud of myself and felt good being that I had never done anything like that. I felt good that I could do something, and being that it was war, I felt that I was doing my part.

I went from 65 cents to $1.05. That was top pay. It felt good and, besides, it was my own money. I could do whatever I wanted with it because my husband, whatever he was giving to the house, he kept on paying it. I used to buy clothes for the kids; buy little things that they needed. I had a bank account and I had a little saving at home where I could get ahold of the money right away if I needed it….My money, I did what I wanted.

I started feeling a little more independent. Just a little, not too much, because I was still not on my own that I could do this and do that. I didn't until after. Then I got really independent.

NAVAJO CODE TALKERS

Of crucial importance to Allied victory was finding an encrypted code that would defy deciphering by the Axis powers. Philip Johnston, the son of a missionary to native American Navajo tribes who spoke the Navajo language fluently (having been raised on a reservation), realized that the complexities of Navajo, which belongs to the Athapaskan language branch of the Na-Dene language family, would make it a logical choice for safely transmitting messages via phone and radio. The language was unwritten, had no alphabet or symbols, and was spoken only on Navajo lands in the southwestern United States. Aware that the Americans had used another native American language (Choctaw) to encode messages during the First World War, Johnston met with Major General Clayton B. Vogel, commanding general of the Amphibious Corps, Pacific Fleet, and conducted tests under simulated combat conditions. These tests convinced the general of the language's usefulness, and he recommended that the marines recruit 200 Navajos for code training. In the spring of 1942 at Camp Pendleton, Oceanside, California, the first group of twenty-nine Navajos developed a dictionary and words for military terms. Upon completion of their training, they were sent to a Marine unit in the Pacific and employed as transmitters of critical battlefield information, including tactics and troop movements.

HEADQUARTERS
AMPHIBIOUS FORCE, PACIFIC
CAMP ELLIOTT, SAN DIEGO,
CALIFORNIA

March 6, 1942

From: The Commanding General
To: The Commandant, U.S. Marine Corps

Subject: Enlistment of Navaho Indians…

1. Mr. Philip Johnston of Los Angeles recently offered his services to this force to demonstrate

Major General Clayton Vogel, "Navajo Code Talkers," Letter of March 6, 1942, National Archives and Records Administration, Records of the United States Marine Corps, Record Group 127. Used by permission.

the use of Indians for the transmission of messages by telephone and voice- radio. His offer was accepted and the demonstration was held for the Commanding General and his staff.

2. The demonstration was interesting and successful. Messages were transmitted and received almost verbatim. In conducting the demonstration messages were written by a member of the staff and handed to the Indian; he would transmit the messages in his tribal dialect and the Indian on the other end would write them down in English.... The Indians do not have many military terms in their dialect so it was necessary to give them a few minutes, before the demonstration, to improvise words for dive-bombing, anti-tank gun, etc.

3. Mr. Johnston stated that the Navaho is the only tribe in the United States that has not been infested with German students during the past twenty years. These Germans, studying the various tribal dialects under the guise of art students, anthropologists, etc., have undoubtedly obtained good working knowledge of all tribal dialects except Navaho. For this reason the Navaho is the only tribe available offering complete security for the type of work under consideration. It is noted in Mr. Johnston's article (enclosed) that the Navaho is the largest tribe but the lowest in literacy. He stated, however, that 1,000—if that many were needed—could be found with the necessary qualifications. It should also be noted that the Navaho tribal dialect is completely unintelligible to all other tribes and all other people, with the possible exception of as many as 28 Americans who have made a study of the dialect. This dialect is thus equivalent to a secret code to the enemy, and admirably suited for rapid, secure communication.

4. It is therefore recommended that an effort be made to enlist 200 Navaho Indians for this force. In addition to linguistic qualifications in English and their tribal dialect they should have the physical qualifications necessary for messengers.

AN ANTHROPOLOGIST GATHERS INTELLIGENCE

Carleton Stevens Coon (1904–1981), a Harvard-educated anthropologist whose knowledge of the North African Arab-speaking Muslim Riffians (or Rif Berbers) of Northern Morocco and of other Near Eastern "tribes," led to his recruitment in 1941 by what would become the Office of Strategic Services (OSS). The OSS, looking for agents to help guide the Allied landings (Operation Torch, November 1942), enlisted the multilingual Coon to sway the Riffians in the Spanish-controlled regions of North Africa to rebel against Spain should Franco decide to join the Axis powers. Coon assisted in a number of covert assignments, often posing as a British army officer, and is credited with inventing an explosive mixed with mule dung ("Coon-Browne explosive turds") used by the Allies to disable German tanks in the desert. After the war, Coon was awarded the Legion of Merit for his war service. Coon's recollections of North Africa, dictated in early 1943 but not published until 1980, provide insight into the cloak-and-dagger operations in the early years of the war.

When I arrived in Tangier I did not, of course, know that American troops were going to land in North Africa. I did not know that for several months, and I did not know the exact date until D-14 [two weeks before], when I was told by a British colleague. But I know that I was there to prepare for military eventualities and that my probably job was to make things hot for the Germans if and when they should move westward from Egypt and Tripoli.

In the meantime it was my duty to pretend to be a member of the State Department and to ally the curiosity of the legitimate or career personnel, who from the beginning viewed us irregulars with suspicion. I was supposed to serve as special assistant to the Legation, and no one knew exactly what that meant. Therefore I had to whittle out a cover job under that title....

Browne and I made ample use of the profound knowledge of Morocco of Mr. Randolph Mohammed Gusus.... Gusus, fifty-three, was born in Manchester,

England, of a Moorish father and an English mother. He came back to Fez, his father's home as a child, and was brought up an Arab. Later he went to the States where he sold Moroccan leather goods, with an office in Boston, and he lived during this period next door to me and across the street from Browne, in Cambridge....Before he went to Morocco in 1942, he was working for the British SIS [the Secret Intelligence Service now known as MI6], but they considered him of little worth and gladly relinquished him to us....We later found that Gusus was a priceless agent, and that the SIS objected to him merely because he could not spell English properly in his written reports....

Mr. Childs asked me to take over the Arabic news bulletin..., and later he wanted me to take charge of the distribution of all bulleting other than through the mail. That is, I was to distribute all the Arabic bulletins, and to distribute the European-language ones, through all channels except the mail....

Carleton Stevens Coon, *A North Africa Story: The Anthropologist as OSS Agent, 1941–1943* (Ipswich, MA: Gambit, 1980), 10–21. Used by permission.

We were to distribute nothing in the French Zone, and our distribution in Tangier and the Spanish Zone was alternately forbidden and permitted...as the Spaniards let the Germans get away with something....

Mr. Childs set me the task of finding out how influential our propaganda was in Tangier. Browne and I spent two days going from shop to shop visiting native friends and acquaintances, and discovered that none of them had ever seen or heard of the bulletin. We asked how it was being distributed, and Geier said that he gave several hundred copies a week to Mohammed, the head Shaoush, who slipped them under doorsills and in mailboxes, in the dark of the night.

I said that Mohammed could not have been doing this since none had read by a fair sample of the shopkeepers. Mr. Childs then said, "We will get to the bottom of this; send Mohammed...in." Mohammed came in, and Mr. Childs said "Dr. Coon says that you have not been distributing your bulletins at all, and that no one has heard of them. How do you account for this?" Mohammed put on a toothy grin, and replied, "Well, Dr. Coon is new here and knows nothing about the natives; of course they would not admit to him that they had seen them." "So you see," said Mr. Childs to me, and dismissed Mohammed. That settled it as far as Mr. Childs was concerned.

A few minutes later I got Mohammed in a quiet place and gave him a hearty sock on the jaw. I should not, in theory, have done this, but from then on he did not interfere with my affairs. He was either destroying the bulletins, or turning them over to the Germans. We know that he saw the Germans frequently, but whether or not he gave them the bulletins we could not determine. We never found out what he did with them.

One of the few useful things we did in this cover job was to translate the President's Flag Day speech into Arabic. Browne and I would reword the English in a more Arabic-sounding way, and Gusus would sing out an Arabic poetical version and then write it down. Every time Mr. Roosevelt mentioned God once, we named Him six times; and the result was a piece of poetry that might have come out of the Koran. It was a free translation, but it caught Mr. Roosevelt's

sense perfectly, and the original English lent itself well to this treatment. Finally we had it checked by the British Arabic expert at their Legation, and gave it to Geier to have several thousand copies printed. We mailed it all over the Spanish Zone, and some copies got (by mistake) into the French Zone. There the French announced that any native found with it in his possession would receive three months imprisonment.

Since the landing, this document has been read several times over the Rabat radio. More than anything else it gave the natives the idea that we would come across the sea to set them free; this influenced many of them in our favor, particularly those who had been wavering in an Axis direction, and it was very hard to explain to these natives, after the landing, why their condition had not immediately changed for the better.

Gusus, Browne, and I also supplied the Legation once or twice a week with translations of leading or significant articles from the Arabic press....We also handed in a periodical scandal sheet of rumors from...[the] rumor center of North Africa. Any other intelligence we received from our undercover sources and considered safe for State Department consumption was submitted in the same manner....

In general the British found that their printed propaganda was as useless as ours. They had bales of funny books and cartoons that the Arabs either could not understand or did not consider funny. Just as we had one successful issue, the President's speech, so they had one, a beautifully printed Ramadan greeting card made up in London, with red and gold and green Moorish designs. They gave us hundred of these to distribute, as we gave them hundreds of copies of the President's speech.

We had one stroke of luck which Mr. Childs was quick to appreciate....It seems that the most powerful religious brotherhood in Northern Morocco, which we will call the Strings organization, has its seat in Tangier....The divine leader we will call Mr. Strings. He is a living God, and tens of thousands of fighting men all over the Spanish zone and in parts of the French Zone will obey his orders blindly to the death. It is as formidable an organization as the medieval Assassins.

Now Mr. Strings wanted cash to build a new wing on his Mother Mosque. The Spanish government had promised it several times, but never produced the money. So Mr. Strings sent a circular letter to the heads of all legations asking for contributions, and Mr. Childs sent me his copy of the letter. I told Mr. Childs that this seemed a priceless opportunity, and that I would like to go as his representative. I went, and Mr. Strings received me graciously. After a little sparring he said that he had been accused by the Spaniards and Germans of working with us, and that put the idea into his head. By this circular letter he could get me to visit him openly and we could talk. I agreed to give him 50,000 francs, and he agreed to put his organization at the service of the United States government, for intelligence, for propaganda, and for armed revolt among all the tribes of the Ghomara confederacy, and many of those of the Jebala.

I went back to Mr. Childs and said that Mr. Strings needed money, and that a gift of this nature would create much good will for America among the tribes of Northern Morocco; that it would be our prime coup in the propaganda field. Mr. Childs, who accepted this idea enthusiastically, gave me 20,000 francs of State Department money. I took 30,000 more out of the naval attaché's safe...since Mr. Strings had said that he needed 50,000. From that time on Mr. Strings was our man....

Our purpose in organizing subversive groups in Spanish Morocco was to prevent the Germans from taking this country in the event that they (a) moved west from Tripoli or (b) moved south through Spain. Later on we added to this the purpose of facilitating the success of American and British arms in case the United States should make a landing in International or Spanish territory, or both, or in case the Spaniards should try to close the Straits of Gibraltar. The British SOE [Special Operations Executive for covert operations, a counterpart to the American OSS] had much the same idea, but early in the game we agreed on a division of labor whereby the British would handle Christians in Tangier and Spaniard I Morocco, and we Moslems. Their plans with Gibraltareans, Spanish Reds, and dissident Hungarians and Yugoslavs were well laid, and still are. It was up to us to do equally well with the Moslems.

Our first fruitful contact in this field was with Tassels. He was a general, in charge of recruitment and supplies, in Abd el Krim's army, and is still one of the most influential leaders, undercover, in the Rif. He came to Tangier periodically to compare notes about business with Gusus, since he had established himself as a wealthy and prominent merchant in Tetuan....

It was not easy to arrange meetings with Tassels, since he is a well-known man and if he should be seen with us by the Spanish or anyone in contact with the Spanish, he would be shot. He was well aware of this and did his best to keep these meetings secret. The usual system was for Gusus to see him by coincidence in the Tingis café, where both habitually sat at noontime, to eat lunch and drink coffee. There Gusus would slip him the details of the rendezvous. These were always nocturnal. Browne and I would get out of the car, or if possible borrow some other car for variety. We would be at a prearranged place on a lonely street at a prearranged hour, and would see Tassels walking along. If no one was about, we would stop and get him quickly into the back seat; if there were too many people around, we would come back and pick him up a few minutes later.

Once in the car we would transform him. Sometimes we would turn him into a Fatma, or Arab woman, with a veil. Other times we would turn him into a shaush, with a tall fez on his head garnished with the US seal in gold metal, or the naval attaché's seal—thus we were merely taking one of our servants to a villa to wait on a cocktail party. Later we would shift him to a Spaniard, putting a European hat on his head, and a European coat over him. We never were able to eliminate the baggy trousers, but when we got out of the car we would walk beside him so that these would not be visible....

During these meetings we laid our plans for the revolt of the Riffians if needed, and plotted the landing of troops, the dropping of parachutists, the delivery of guns, the cutting off of roads and garrisons, etc. We laid on a system of signals by which the Riffians were to assemble and seize various key positions, and to await our arrival....After the landing,...I consulted with Tassels...[and] laid on a new scheme by which we were to enter the Rif from the South overland in case the Germans should come through Spain. Only after the fall of Tunis did these plans become obsolete.

Our other subversive planning was with the Strings group, who were to do for the western Spanish Zone what Tassels and his gang were to do for the Rif. These plans were equally elaborate and also took many meetings. Sometimes we talked with Strings himself, and he arranged our meetings in his holy of holies with great secrecy; the streets were cleared by his henchmen, who silently handed us

on from corner to corner, and did the same on the way out....

With Strings as with Tassels, we devised alternate plans for the period from November 8, 1942, to May 8, 1943. Strings even more than Tassels furnished us with intelligence, and laid on alternate plans—he was prepared to hide us out in case the Germans surprised us in Tangier, to hide other Europeans for us, and to engineer the escape of American parachutists from concentration in Sheshawen. Fortunately we did not have to make use of any of these services.

PHOTO INTELLIGENCE

Constance Babington-Smith (1912–2000) was a pioneer in Britain's interpretation of aerial photographs. She began her work in aerial intelligence in 1940 as a trainee surveillance interpreter and by 1943 headed her own section. Thanks to her hard work and expertise, Babington-Smith's discovery of an unidentified pilotless aircraft at Peenemunde on the Baltic coast in 1943, coupled with intelligence from the Polish underground, enabled the Allies to disrupt German plans to deploy and launch V-1 and V-2 rockets. Photographic interpretation proved to be a crucial tool of military intelligence in the search for enemy troop formations, military camps and barracks, and weaponry.

Photographic intelligence was...only one of many complementary sources of information. The agents who risked their lives in German and the occupied countries, the interrogators who questioned the prisoners of war, the men and women who combed through trade magazines and monitored German broadcasts, the technical experts who examined V-weapon fragments; these were only a few of the vast incongruous team that supplied the raw material of the investigation. Finally,

at the top, there were the intelligence experts who weighed all the varied evidence, and upon whose judgment depended what action was likely to be taken....

On May 15, 1942, Flight Lieutenant D. W. Steventon flew in his Spitfire high above the western shores of the Baltic....He happened to notice that there was an airfield at the northern tip of the island, with quite a lot of new development nearby, and he switched on his cameras for a short run....

Constance Babington-Smith, *Air Spy: The Story of Photo Intelligence in World War II* (New York: Harper & Brothers, 1957), 203–207, 210–213, 215–217, 219, 223–224, 229. Used by permission.

I remember flipping through the stack of photographs and deciding the scale was too small to make it worthwhile looking at the aircraft. Then something unusual caught my eye, and I stopped, to take a good look at some extraordinary circular embankments. I glanced quickly at the plot to see where it was, and noticed the name Peenemuende. Then I looked at the prints again. "No," I thought to myself, "those don't belong to me. I wonder what on earth they are. Somebody must know all about them, I suppose."... But when the sortie finished its rounds, no one had staked a claim for the mysterious "rings" at Peenemuende, and the cardboard boxes full of photographs were set in place on a shelf in the print library, for future reference. There the matter rested...for the next seven months.

Meantime, as we now know, General Dornberger and Wernher [sic] von Braun were working day and night at their rockets, and the first fully successful launching of an A-4 rocket—later known as the V-2—took place at the experimental station in the woods on October 3, 1942; while in December an early version of the flying bomb, the V-1, was launched from below a large aircraft over Peenemuende.

In that same December reports of "secret weapon trials" in this area began reaching London, and began to cause concern. The fact that the Germans were developing long-range weapons was already known to British intelligence, for a communication known as the "Oslo Report," giving advance information on plans for new weapons, including rockets, had reached London via Oslo as early as the autumn of 1939. But like those first photographs of Peenemuende that Steventon took by chance in 1942, the "Oslo Report" had been filed away—for future reference when required....

[T]he photographic search for secret weapons began in earnest in April 1943. No one really quite knew what they were looking for, although the Air Ministry did suggest that the interpreters should be on the lookout for three things: a long-range gun, a remotely controlled rocket aircraft, and "some sort of tube located in a disused mine out of which a rocket could be squirted."...

It was at this point, in June 1943, that I myself was first able to say something positive about the experimental work at Peenemuende, for on the same sortie that showed those first rockets there were several runs over the airfield. My brief was to watch for "anything queer," and the four little tailless airplanes that I found taking the air on June 23 looked queer enough to satisfy anybody. This was the first time I was able to analyze and measure the Messerschmitt liquid-rocket fighter, the Me163....

The photographs taken on June 23 also showed the first "jet marks" I had ever recognized—single, dark, fan-shaped marks, from which dark streaks led out across the airfield....

Meanwhile, the photographs of northern France were providing ominous evidence. Early in July a ground report had reached London linking secret weapon activity with a village named Watten near Calais....Work was well ahead on what was clearly going to be some gigantic concrete structure. Suspicious-looking preliminaries were also going ahead at two other places in the rocket-range area, and all three sites were rail-served from main lines—a fact to which many of the British rocket experts attached great importance. For by this time they were talking of forty-ton or forty-five ton rockets....

[I]t was a time of frustrating confusion in the secret weapon investigation, which by now had been given the code name *Bodyline*—a time of groping in the dark, of trying to lay foundations in a swamp....

In spite of the conflicting views about rockets...the decision was made to attack Peenemuende. On the night of August 17, 1943, when Bomber Command made their famous raid, forty aircraft were lost, but considerable destruction was caused. We know now that it seriously delayed the whole V-2 program, though estimates of just how long a delay it caused vary from four weeks to six months.

Then ten days later, on August 27, the U.S. Eighth Air Force attacked Watten. The attack on the "launching shelter" for V-2s...could not possibly have been better timed, for a huge mass of concrete was in process of hardening when the bombs came down, and within a day or two a chaotic jumble of steel, props, and planking was utterly rigid and immovable....

Into this rocket-conscious atmosphere there came suddenly, on November 4, 1943, a major new discovery....A few days earlier, a report had reached London from an agent in France, telling that the construction firm he worked for was engaged in building eight "sites" in the Pas-de-Calais, not far from Abbeville....On November 3 the eight places in question were photographed....

There was something "starting" all right at each of the eight pinpoints, and it was evidently the same "something" in each case. But there were no railway anywhere near, let alone new rail spurs leading to the sites....

"Skis," he [a photo interpreter] thought aloud. "That's what they look like—skis." Two of them seemed to be identical, and the third was shorter; and each, in plain view, had one gently curving end. They were like a giant's skis laid down on their sides.

Through the early hours of the morning the *Bodyline* interpreters measured and checked, compared and discussed. Each clearing and each pit, each dump of building materials, each semicomplete building, each road and path, was analyzed from the viewpoint of the overriding question of the day: "What is the connection with the rockets?" But at the end of it all the answer was inconclusive. These new sites might be for launching projectiles of some sort, but they bore no relation to anything else that had been found so far....

A meeting was called for the morning of November 8, 1943, at which the primary evidence was to be examined....

The opening stages of the meeting can, indeed, be compared to the opening stages of the meeting which once took place in ancient Babylon [the famous episode which lent the phrase "the writing on the wall"], in the days of Beshazzar the king:

Then came in all the king's wise men: but they could not read the writing, nor make known to the king the interpretation thereof....

By the time the meeting reassembled on November 10 a total of twenty-six "ski sites" had been found. But no clues had yet been discovered to show what sort of missile they were meant for. In the report which Sir Stafford Cripps submitted to the War Cabinet a few days later, however, he judged that pilotless aircraft were a more immediate danger than long-range rockets. He also advised that photographic cover of Peenemuende and of the danger area in France should be kept up....

On November 13, however [Douglas] Kendall [wing commander, in charge of topographical reporting] came and asked me to search afresh at Peendemuende for an aircraft which might be pilotless....

Something smaller than a fighter would only show up on good photographs, so I went to the print library and fetched the famous set of photographs on which I had earlier found the "Peenemuende 30s." It was by far the best of the early covers, and, sure enough, I did find a midget aircraft on those splendid photographs. The absurd little object was not on the airfield, but sitting in a corner of a small enclosure some way behind the hangars, immediately adjoining a building which I suspected, from its design, was used for testing jet engines....I named it "Peenemuende 20," as its span was about twenty feet....

I pondered over the photographs and reviewed what I had found. There were four of these strange structures. Three of them looked very much like the sort of cranes that have a box for the operator and a long movable arm. But the fourth seemed different, and it was the one that drew my attention most....

Late through the night I worked feverishly with Kendall to trace back the history of the "Peendemuende Airfield Site." We found that the first experimental ramp had been built late in 1942....

But the ramp near the airfield was not the only one on the Baltic coast that was reported...on December 1, 1943....And almost at the same moment that I was looking at the earlier cover, and asking myself what on earth the ramp near the airfield could be, they had found, between Zinnowitz and the village of Kempin, eight miles away down the coast of Usedom, a launching site with firing points aiming out to sea, which also matched up with the foundations for ramps at the ski sites. It was, in fact, a Luftwaffe center for training the personnel who were going to operate the launching sites in France.

Before daylight next morning, Kendall's report on both Peenemuende and Zinnowitz was on its way to London, with the news that the nature of the most imminent cross-Channel threat was at last established beyond doubt. It was going to be a flying bomb.

THE ROLE OF SCIENCE

An engineer whose scientific inventions had important implications for both civilians and the military, Vannevar Bush (1890–1974) enjoyed professional success at MIT and the Carnegie Institution. In June 1940 he was appointed by President Roosevelt to chair the National Defense Research Committee that would promote government sponsorship of private scientific research with military applications. That organization was soon superseded by the new Office of Scientific Research and Development, which Bush would head from 1941 until 1947. In that position, Bush argued that the thoughtful and thorough mobilization of the nation's scientific resources was as imperative to the war effort as the organization and expansion of its armed services. Moreover, a national scientific policy, one sustained by the government's financial support of the private sector, was essential to America's continued progress and security in the postwar world. His efforts helped lead to the creation of the National Science Foundation in 1950.

One of our hopes is that after the war there will be full employment. To reach that goal the full creative and productive energies of the American people must be released. To create more jobs we must make new and better and cheaper products. We want plenty of new, vigorous enterprises. But new products and processes are not born full-grown. They are founded on new principles and new conceptions which in turn result from basic scientific research....

We all know how much the new drug, penicillin, has meant to our grievously wounded men on the grim battlefronts of this war—the countless lives it has saved—the incalculable suffering which its use has prevented. Science and the great practical genius of this nation made this achievement possible.

Some of us know the vital role which radar has played in bringing the United Nations to victory over Nazi Germany and in driving the Japanese steadily back from their island bastions. Again it was painstaking scientific research over many years that made radar possible.

What we often forget are the millions of pay envelopes on a peacetime Saturday night which are filled because new products and new industries have

Vannevar Bush, *Science: The Endless Frontier* (Washington, DC: U.S. Government Printing Office, 1945), 6, 9–10, 21–24, 26–27, 35. Used by permission.

provided jobs for countless Americans. Science made that possible too.

Advances in science when put to practical use mean more jobs, higher wages, shorter hours, more abundant crops, more leisure for recreation, for study, for learning how to live without the deadening drudgery which has been the burden of the common man for ages past. Advances in science will also bring higher standards of living, will lead to the prevention or cure of diseases, will promote conservation of our limited natural resources, and will assure means of defense against aggression. But to achieve these objectives—to secure a high level of employment, to maintain a position of world leadership—the flow of new scientific knowledge must be both continuous and substantial.... [W]ithout scientific progress no amount of achievement in other directions can insure our health, prosperity, and security as a nation in the modern world....

We have no national policy for science. The Government has only begun to utilize science in the nation's welfare. There is no body within the government charged with formulating or executing a national science policy. There are no standing committees of the Congress devoted to this important subject. Science has been in the wings. It should be brought to the center of the stage—for in it lies much of our hope for the future....

Two great principles have guided us in this country as we have turned our full efforts to war. First, the sound democratic principle that there should be no favored classes or special privilege in a time of peril, that all should be ready to sacrifice equally; second, the tenet that every man should serve in the capacity in which his talents and experience can best be applied for the prosecution of the war effort. In general we have held these principles well in balance.

In my opinion, however, we have drawn too heavily for nonscientific purposes upon the great natural resource which resides in our trained young scientists and engineers. For the general good of the country too many such men have gone into uniform, and their talents have not always been fully utilized. With the exception of those men engaged in war research, all physically fit students at graduate level have been taken into the armed forces. Those ready

for college training in the sciences have not been permitted to enter upon that training....

Higher education in this country is largely for those who have the means. If those who have the means coincided entirely with those persons who have the talent we should not be squandering a part of our higher education on those undeserving of it, nor neglecting great talent among those who fail to attend college for economic reasons. There are talented individuals in every segment of the population, but with few exceptions those without the means of buying higher education go without it. Here is a tremendous waste of the greatest resource of a nation— the intelligence of its citizens.

If ability, and not the circumstance of family fortune, is made to determine who shall receive higher education in science, then we shall be assured of constantly improving quality at every level of scientific activity....

We have been living on our fat. For more than five years many of our scientists have been fighting the war in the laboratories, in the factories and shops, and at the front. We have been directing the energies of our scientists to the development of weapons and materials and methods...but they have been diverted to a greater extent than is generally appreciated from the search for answers to the fundamental problems—from the search on which human welfare and progress depends. This is not a complaint—it is a fact. The mobilization of science behind the lines is aiding the fighting men at the front to win the war and to shorten it; and it has resulted incidentally in the accumulation of a vast amount of experience and knowledge of the application of science to particular problems, much of which can be put to use when the war is over. Fortunately, this country had the scientists—and the time—to make this contribution and thus to advance the date of victory....

One lesson is clear...the Federal Government should accept new responsibilities for promoting the creation of new scientific knowledge and the development of scientific talent in our youth....It is clear that the effective discharge of these responsibilities will require the full attention of some over-all agency devoted to that purpose....

But nowhere in the governmental structure receiving its funds from Congress is there an agency adapted to supplementing the support of basic research in the universities, both in medicine and the natural sciences; adapted to supporting research on new weapons for both Services; or adapted to administering a program of science scholarships and fellowships....

Legislation is necessary. It should be drafted with great care. Early action is imperative, however, if this nation is to meet the challenge of science and fully utilize the potentialities of science. On the wisdom with which we bring science to bear against the problems of the coming years depends in large measure our future as a nation.

CHAPTER 5

THE TIDE TURNS

June–December 1942

RUINS OF STALINGRAD This stark scene of refugees surveying the rubble of Stalingrad conveys the destructive impact of intense combat under harsh conditions on the eastern front.
Source: © Hulton-Deutsch Collection/CORBIS.

Although the surprise Japanese attack on Pearl Harbor caught the United States unprepared, American military planners had already anticipated the challenge of fighting in two separate theaters simultaneously against both Germany and Japan. Their reviews of possible strategies had concluded, though not without dissent, that the best course of action was to concentrate upon Germany first, a decision obviously advocated by Britain as well and reaffirmed by both nations by the end of 1941. That decision, about who to fight, had obvious consequences for how to fight. Because Germany had virtually no surface fleet to speak of, the naval war in that theater would be an anti-submarine campaign, freeing the battleships and aircraft carriers for service in the Pacific. And because defeating Germany meant coming to grips with the Wehrmacht, its army, on land, in continental Europe, it would be some time before the United States could bring its full weight to bear. Not only would American forces have to be transported across the Atlantic Ocean, they would then have to conduct an amphibious assault against coastlines well defended by enemy troops. The military and logistical challenges involved (especially the chronic shortage of landing craft) would delay a cross-channel assault until June 1944, nourishing Stalin's suspicion that Britain and the United States were waiting until the Germans and Soviets exhausted each other on the eastern front. The delay also meant searching for less costly or risky substitutes to an invasion of fortified Europe, and so prompted combined Anglo-American operations in North Africa.

In the back-and-forth war of movement that was possible in the thinly inhabited Libyan desert, Rommel's Axis forces had driven eastward into Egypt but ground to a halt in August 1942 at El Alamein. Outnumbered and short of supplies, the Afrika Korps could not penetrate the defensive positions of Britain's Eighth Army, now led by General Bernard Montgomery, who only got the job because the initial choice, General William "Strafer" Gott, was killed when his plane was shot down by German fighters. Montgomery was convinced that he was the right man all along, and he methodically set about raising the army's morale and building a 2:1 superiority in men and tanks. The front was relatively short (perhaps forty miles), limited by the impassable Qattara Depression to the south and the Mediterranean to the north, which precluded Rommel from employing his customarily devastating flanking maneuvers. After cleverly disguising the timing and focal point of their attack, Montgomery's troops smashed into the German and Italian lines on October 23, 1942. The outcome hung in doubt for nearly two weeks of fierce fighting, but in early November, British troops achieved a decisive breakthrough and forced Rommel's remaining units into a general retreat.

They would chase the remnants of the Afrika Korps all the way westward to Tunisia, where they would link up with American forces, which in Operation Torch had stormed ashore in Morocco and Algeria, swept aside any resistance from Vichy French forces, and gained valuable combat experience against tenacious German resistance in the Tunisian mountains. Success in North Africa would lay the groundwork for a methodical but slow campaign up through Sicily and Italy. Although it was hardly a route to Berlin, the Italian campaign precipitated the collapse of Mussolini's regime and drew off German units that otherwise would have fought in Russia. It also enabled the Allies to claim they were doing at least something to relieve the pressure on Stalin's armies. In orders of magnitude, the numbers of soldiers involved at El Alamein paled in comparison to the eastern front (the Axis suffered some 37,000 casualties, the Eighth Army 14,000). But the events there in November 1942 marked the first victory of British troops over German ones and suggested that the tide was beginning to turn. Winston Churchill accepted that it was not the end, nor even the beginning of the end, but predicted that El Alamein marked "the end of the beginning." After so disastrous a beginning to the war, that was grounds enough for celebration.

November 1942 was, in retrospect, no less symbolic on the eastern front. After stabilizing their front during the winter of 1941–1942, the Germans resumed the offensive as soon as weather and road conditions would permit. This time the focus of their thrust (code-named Operation Blue) would be to the south, toward the industrial city of Stalingrad, a key transportation hub on the Volga River, the gateway to the oil-rich Caucasus region, and the namesake of the Soviet leader. Losing the city would deal the Soviets a severe economic and military blow, not to mention a major propaganda embarrassment. The German Sixth Army under General Friedrich Paulus was charged with taking the city itself, which was now commanded by General Vasily Chuikov, who had been ordered by Stalin to hold on at all costs. Aerial bombardment by the Luftwaffe turned most of the buildings into rubble and, far from destroying the defenders, gave Soviet troops ideal positions from which to slow the German advance. Stalin's infamous July 27, 1942, Order 227, popularly known as "not a step back," prescribed lethal penalties for commanders who conducted unauthorized retreats, and further stiffened the resolve of the defenders. Chuikov's tactic of not yielding ground, of keeping his troops as close to the German attackers as possible ("hugging" them), within a combat environment of rubble, neutralized Germany's advantages in mobility, firepower, and aerial support. Worn down by these tactics, German soldiers reached the Volga, but were unable either to consolidate their gains or to control the entire city.

More ominously, the advancing Sixth Army was unable to secure its flanks, the defense of which was entrusted to less reliable or motivated Hungarians and Romanians. The Soviets steadily built up strong forces to both the north and south of the city and on November 19, 1942, unleashed Operation Uranus, a devastating envelopment of the Sixth Army. The northern and southern Soviet armies met to the west of Stalingrad, sealing off the city and the German forces within it in two concentric rings of Red Army troops (the inner one to keep Paulus' army trapped, the outer one to ward off German efforts to rescue their beleaguered compatriots). More than 200,000 German troops were encircled, but Hitler ordered them to hold their ground rather than attempt to break out. He insisted that they not surrender, but wait to be resupplied from the air by the Luftwaffe. In any event, the German air force's motley collection of planes was not up to the task, which was nearly insurmountable given the horrible weather and dense Soviet antiaircraft fire. Paulus' troops were now starving and running low on ammunition, and though he was promoted by Hitler to the rank of field marshal (not one had ever been taken prisoner), he surrendered what was left of his army (91,000 men) on January 31, 1943. The result was an undeniable and decisive Soviet victory. It had been achieved at tremendous cost: estimates of the total number of casualties on both sides range from 1.5 to 2 million. But once again, in yet another region, in November 1942 it appeared that the tide was finally beginning to turn.

In the Pacific, the American strategy of "Germany first" obviously did not preclude major battles, in part because the Japanese were determined to press home their initial advantage. But the environment was significantly different from that in Europe; rather than huge armies facing each other on land, the adversaries dueled over thousands of square miles of the Pacific Ocean. Even where troops did campaign for prolonged stretches on land, as in Burma or China, the inhospitable terrain and climate and logistical deficiencies limited the sheer numbers involved. Likewise, the way to measure progress in the struggle between Japan and the United States was not in the number of historic cities conquered or defended, but in aerial supremacy, whether from carrier-based aircraft or airstrips on the various island chains that dotted the vast expanses of water. For several years Tokyo would be too remote from American bases to be directly touched by war, save for daring raids like that by Jimmy Doolittle's carrier-launched bombers or the persistent predations of American submarines prowling around Japan's home islands (though their effectiveness was initially marred by unreliable torpedoes).

After incurring serious losses in the naval battles of the Coral Sea and Midway (May and June 1942, respectively), the Japanese navy relinquished the initiative to its American counterparts. Destruction of three Japanese carriers within a matter of minutes near Midway (followed by the sinking of a fourth a day later), in particular, was the turning point in the Pacific War, after which American forces would inexorably assume the offensive. The Japanese remained confident, however, that even if they could not further expand their empire, they could protect their core home islands by maintaining an effective defensive perimeter on the varied islands and atolls great distances from Tokyo. If the Americans incurred heavy enough casualties on the periphery, this strategy entailed, public enthusiasm for the war in the United States would wane and a peace settlement could be reached that would recognize many of Japan's territorial gains. The Japanese seriously underestimated the doggedness and valor of the American military and the determination of an aggrieved nation as a whole (fueled by outrage at Japanese atrocities, the desire to avenge a "cowardly" sneak attack, and more than a dose of racialist prejudice) to settle for nothing less than total victory.

A key early step on the road to Tokyo was the campaign for the island of Guadalcanal in the Solomons. Cursed with a horrible climate and terrain, and infested with a sickening array of deadly insects, Guadalcanal had little to recommend it but a patch of land flat enough to sustain an airstrip. Admiral Ernest King, the U.S. commander-in-chief, had little patience for concentrating on Germany and was determined to carry the war to Japan as swiftly and comprehensively as possible. Control of Guadalcanal would threaten the major Japanese base at Rabaul (New Britain) and facilitate operations against New Guinea. American Marines stormed ashore in August 1942, and although their initial landings were largely unopposed, the next few months featured constant fighting as the Japanese poured soldiers, planes, and warships into the fray to dislodge the United States from the vital Henderson Field, as the airstrip was known. The contest over the island turned into a battle of attrition which, by November 1942, the Americans were clearly winning. By maintaining naval and aerial supremacy, and restricting the Japanese to desperate nighttime operations to reinforce and resupply their troops, the Americans established a vital position in the southern Pacific. In February 1943, the Japanese conceded defeat and evacuated their remaining forces, confirming that, after early catastrophes, the American military could take on and beat the Japanese in their own environment. Once again, November 1942 proved to be a pivotal month, another indication that the tide was turning in favor of the Allies.

THE MOOD IN AMERICA

Despite the commonly held view (from the perspective of the early twenty-first century) that American society was solidly united in a single-minded determination to wage war to the utmost, the conflict did provoke controversy about the most appropriate or effective ways of achieving victory. The British government, in particular, was worried that America's tradition of isolationism, its long-standing suspicion of British imperialist aims, and its persistent partisan rivalries and disputes over the power of organized labor might all prevent Britain from reaping the maximum advantage from its new ally's entry into the war. Accordingly, the British embassy in Washington provided weekly summaries of the American political scene for policy makers in London. The majority of these dispatches, avidly read by Winston Churchill, were written by the Russian-born British philosopher and historian of ideas Isaiah Berlin (1909–1997). Berlin, a shrewd observer and brilliant writer, met frequently with members of America's cultural and intellectual elite, and in so doing he helped to shape American attitudes to Britain as much as he reported upon them. The following selections are valuable for their insight into the varied attitudes to the war in the United States, as well as the sense that the Torch landings and El Alamein together marked a milestone in the Allies' cooperative struggle against Germany.

8 August 1942

A large section of the public is becoming more and more bewildered by the war. There is no call for action, no outlet for enthusiasm, no glimmer of success. These people do not understand what is happening in the distant war theatres nor why the United States Forces are inactive. Hence a kind of puzzled boredom about the war in general. At the same time the war effort is constantly hampered by the party struggle which runs along in a subdued form on the stage of Congress and more merrily behind the scenes.

The opening of a Second Front in Europe is a major subject of both private and public discussion. Any public speaker who raises the subject is assured of press attention and as the autumnal conventions increase in number it may be expected to be thrashed

out before influential audiences in the weeks to come. The two opposing points of view have been expressed this week by, amongst others,

(1) Senator Pepper [Democrat from Florida] who pointed out that the instincts of peoples were better than the bound minds of discipline-nurtured men;
(2) the more cautious CIO leader, Reuther [Walter Reuther, head of the United Auto Workers], who stated before the Resolutions Committee of the War Convention of the UAW-CIO, one of the largest unions in America, that the timing of the offensive cannot be based on emotion but must be determined by the military leaders of the various nations.

The division for and against does not follow party lines or the usual classifications of opinion although

H. G. Nicholas, ed., *Washington Despatches, 1941–1945* (Chicago: University of Chicago Press, 1981), 67–68, 108. Used by permission.

the arguments for and against are slanted by preconceived likes and dislikes. Former isolationists express their anti-British bias in criticizing the British for not opening such a front and for waiting for the Americans. There has been some suggestion in left-wing circles that influential Americans and Britons of the 'Cliveden' [reference to Lady Astor's country house in Buckinghamshire where she hosted upper-class parties for those who sympathized with Germany; used as a synonym for appeasers] German way of thought are holding back the project of a Second Front simply because Russia is Russia, and Lady Astor's speech has provided ammunition to this school of thought. So far as the press is concerned, the most militant demands for opening a Second Front come from the West and Middle West. The Southern and Eastern papers tend to be more cautious. Reports from the country districts and small towns in the Middle West show that there is greater enthusiasm for the war than in the larger towns or in the East.

The cognate subject of a generalissimo of the Allied forces in the European theatre and whether this should be a British, American or Canadian general has not yet become a subject of widespread discussion despite the stimulation given by London dispatches on the subject. The demand that an American be appointed is by no means confined to former isolationist and anti-British circles and one of the arguments advanced is that American generals are more used than the British to handling the vast problems of supply involved in a Second Front....

15 November 1942

Developments in North Africa and France have given rise to an emotional response comparable, although in reverse, to the German *Blitzkrieg* in Western Europe in the spring of 1940. The news of the landing of United States forces in Africa was like cool water to a parched throat. It was badly needed to counteract the feeling of frustration and meaninglessness which has been a depressing feature in recent months. As the days passed with the impetus provided by streamer headlines and special broadcasts and a welter of sensational and often conflicting rumours and speculation, public opinion took a turn towards over-optimism in the same way as after the fall of France it had turned to over-pessimism. On the Stock Exchange 'War' stocks fell and 'Peace' securities such as the bonds of occupied countries had a noticeable rise. Daily one hears talk of the war being over in six months. The Administration is making obvious endeavours to check these unhealthy tendencies. The President at his press conference recalled an earlier warning by himself against giving way to peaks of overconfidence and valleys of depression. The situation in the Solomon Islands is still giving rise to considerable public anxiety....

The mobilization of an enthusiastic public opinion behind the war effort has been greatly assisted by the realization that the North African campaign is not limited to one single objective but appears to be a carefully devised plan of strategy which it is thought will prove to be the turning-point of the war....

These developments, happily preceded by the enthusiastic reception of the British victory in the Battle of Egypt combined with the continued British success, have caused a notable improvement in sentiment towards us and it is likely that the general attitude of American opinion towards the British war effort will show continued improvement in the next few weeks, not only because Americans themselves are no longer in that mood of irritated frustration in which a scapegoat is eagerly sought.

ROMMEL REFLECTS ON THE DESERT WAR

Erwin Rommel (1891–1944) was easily the most famous German general of the war, one whose reputation stood so high among his American and British opponents that Winston Churchill paid tribute to his gifts in the House of Commons (though some of his German colleagues did not rate him as highly). Even as a junior infantry officer in the First World War, Rommel displayed the daring and flair for leadership that would mark his career, though it would be to the command of armored forces that he was most suited. His inspirational leadership of the Seventh Panzer Division during the French campaign of May 1940 and relentless exploitation of the possibilities of mobile warfare contributed to the French collapse and marked him as a rising star. He felt, however, that his assignment to lead German troops in North Africa (the famous Afrika Korps) did not afford him the chance to shine, for Hitler regarded the Mediterranean as a marginal theater, a mere sideshow to the momentous events in Russia. Rommel complained bitterly that he was never given the forces or supplies he needed to match British resources and that, as a result, Hitler squandered an opportunity to capture Egypt and control much of the Middle East. The German general kept notes during his campaigns and wrote them up during his frequent periods of convalescence back in Germany; in the following extract, Rommel reflects on some of the reasons he was driven back from El Alamein.

The first essential condition for an army to be able to stand the strain of battle is an adequate stock of weapons, petrol and ammunition. In fact, the battle is fought and decided by the Quartermasters before the shooting begins. The bravest men can do nothing without guns, the guns nothing without plenty of ammunition, and neither guns nor ammunition are of much use in mobile warfare unless there are vehicles with sufficient petrol to haul them around. Maintenance must also approximate, both in quantity and quality, to that available to the enemy.

A second essential condition for an army to be able to stand in battle is parity or at least something approaching parity in the air. If the enemy has air supremacy and makes full use of it, then one's own command is forced to suffer the following limitations and disadvantages:

> By using his strategic air force, the enemy can strangle one's supplies, especially if they have to be carried across the sea.
> The enemy can wage the battle of attrition from the air.
> Intensive exploitation by the enemy of his air superiority gives rise to far-reaching tactical limitations...for one's own command.

In future the battle on the ground will be preceded by the battle in the air. This will determine which of the contestants has to suffer the operational and tactical disadvantages detailed above, and thus be forced, throughout the battle, into adopting compromise solutions.

Excerpts from pp. 328–331 of *The Rommel Papers*, copyright 1953 by B. H. Liddell-Hart and renewed 1981 by Lady Kathleen Liddell-Hart, Fritz Bayerlein-Dittmar, and Manfred Rommel, reprinted by permission of Houghton Mifflin Harcourt Publishing Company.

In our case, neither the conditions I have described were in the slightest degree fulfilled and we had to suffer the consequences.

As a result of British command of the air in the Central Mediterranean, and of other reasons I have already given, the army's supplies were barely sufficient to keep life going, even on quiet days. A build-up for a defensive battle was out of the question. The quantity of material available to the British, on the other hand, far exceeded our worst fears....

The methods which the British employed for the destruction of my force were conditioned by their overwhelming material superiority. They were based on:

Extreme concentrations of artillery fire.

Continuous air attacks by powerful waves of bombers.

Locally limited attacks, executed with lavish use of material and manifesting an extremely high state of training, fully in line with previous experience and the conditions under which the battle was fought....

In the training of their armoured and infantry formations the British command had made excellent use of the experience they had gained in previous actions with the Axis forces—although, of course, the new methods they used were only made possible by their vast stocks of ammunition, material and new equipment....

TANK TACTICS

Here the new British methods were made possible by the use of new tanks, more heavily gunned and armoured than ours (including the Grant, Lee and Sherman); the heavy Churchill is also said to have put in an appearance, and their inexhaustible supplies of ammunition.

With the light tanks sent out in advance, the heavier, gun-carrying tanks remained more and more in the rear. The task of the light tanks was to draw the fire of our anti-tank and anti-aircraft guns and armour. British tanks opened a destructive fire on all the targets they had located, from a range of up to 2,700 yards and, if possible, from the rear slope of a hill. Their fire seemed always to be directed by the commander of the squadron. The vast quantities of ammunition which this system needed were continually fed forward in armoured machine-gun carriers. By this means the British shot up our tanks, machine-gun nests and anti-aircraft and anti-tank gun positions at a range at which our own guns were completely incapable of penetrating their heavier tanks and could not, in any case, have afforded the ammunition they would have needed to shoot themselves in.

ARTILLERY TACTICS

The British artillery once again demonstrated its well-known excellence. A particular feature was its great mobility and tremendous speed of reaction to the needs of the assault troops. The British armoured units obviously carried artillery observers to transmit the needs of the front back to the artillery in the shortest possible time. In addition to the advantage given by their abundant supplies of ammunition, the British benefited greatly from the long range of their guns, which enabled them to take the Italian artillery positions under fire at a range at which the Italian guns, most of which were limited to 6,000 yards, were completely unable to hit back. As by far the greater part of our artillery was made up of these obsolete Italian guns, this was a particularly distressing circumstance for us.

INFANTRY TACTICS

When our defence had been shattered by artillery, tanks and air force, the British infantry attacked.

With our outposts pinned down by British artillery fire—their positions had been located long before by air reconnaissance—highly-trained British sappers, working under cover of smoke, cleared mines and cut broad lanes through our minefields. Then the tanks attacked, followed closely by infantry. With the tanks acting as artillery, British storming parties worked their way up to our defence posts, suddenly to force their way into our trenches and positions at the point of bayonet. Everything went methodically and according to a drill. Each separate action was executed with a concentration of superior strength. The artillery followed up close behind the infantry in order to crush any last flickers of resistance. Success was not usually exploited in any depth but was confined to occupation of the conquered positions, into which reinforcements and artillery were then brought up and disposed for defence. Night attacks continued to be a particular speciality of the British..

BREAKTHROUGH AT EL ALAMEIN

In October–November 1942, the British victory at the Egyptian railway station of El Alamein, some sixty miles west of Alexandria, marked the last time Rommel and his Afrika Korps would threaten the Suez Canal or Anglo-French authority in the Middle East. It also marked the first major triumph for British land forces against German troops. When Alan Moorehead, the journalist who accompanied Britain's Eighth Army in the desert campaign, looked back on El Alamein, he did not dismiss the importance of Britain's superiority in men and weapons (to which Rommel attributed his loss), but he particularly emphasized the leadership of the Eighth Army's new commander, Bernard Montgomery, as the most significant factor.

Within four months—from October to January—the British Eighth Army had done amazing things in the desert. It had advanced fifteen hundred miles across some of the most inhospitable country in the world. It had smashed the Italian Fascist Empire in Africa. It had fought one major action at Alamein in Egypt and two minor ones at El Agheila and Zem-Zem in Tripolitania.

It had captured 30,000 prisoners including a dozen important generals and killed and wounded something like 40,000 men. In their retreat the Axis lost perhaps 500 tanks, 1000 aircraft, 1500 vehicles and stores worth many millions of pounds. Three vital ports, Tobruk, Beghazi and Tripoli, were in our hands and in operation. We had failed to catch Rommel, but the power of his Afrika Korps was at least halved. Incontestably the Eighth Army was the finest fighting machine in the Anglo-American forces and the name of its general stood higher than that of any other. Probably it is still too soon to assess this extraordinary crusade across the desert; but at least now we can make a selection of the most vital events and lay them out for analysis.

If you put the story through a critical sieve a whole mass of things that looked important at the time fall through and you are left with half a dozen hard lumps of military discovery.

First, there was the personality of the new general. Bernard Montgomery, as we saw him when he first arrived in the desert, was a slightly built man with a thin nervous face, an ascetic who neither drank nor smoked. He was a military scholar who had cut away from himself most of the normal diversions of life, and this left him with a fund of restless energy, part of which he expended in a religious faith in himself and his God and part in a ruthless determination to make battle. Like most missionaries he was flamboyant, and there was in him an almost messianic desire to make converts and to prove his doctrines were the right ones. An unusual man, not an easy companion.

General Montgomery represented central control in the British Army as against the democratic ways of most of the other generals—Wavell and Alexander, for example. These last preferred to accept the army and its system as they found it. They tried nothing revolutionary but endeavoured to improve on the existing state of things. They moved on the principle that there is *some* good in every man and every weapon if they were used in the right way. They

Alan Moorehead , *The March to Tunis: The North African War, 1940–1943* (New York: Harper & Row, 1965), 476–482. Used by permission.

consulted their subordinates and left a good deal of the actual control to them. They commanded by a system of compromises and makeshifts which were adjusted to meet each emergency that came up. England and the British Empire had been governed on these lines for several hundreds of years and so the system seemed natural enough.

Now Montgomery was just the reverse. He believed in surgery, not homoeopathy. If a thing was not going right or only partially right, then cut it out altogether; don't try makeshifts and slow drugs; sack the man to blame outright. His ideas were a logical extension of the Bedaux efficiency system in America and the Stakhanov system in the Soviet factories [efforts to apply techniques of scientific management to rationalize factory work and maximize production]. By the Montgomery method the whole art of war was reducible to a pattern and a series of numbers; it was all based on units of man-power and fire-power and so forth. He by no means rubbed out the human element; he simply believed that a correct system and good leadership would inspire the troops and draw out hitherto wasted resources of energy.

Montgomery had this system and this faith, and he believed in them passionately. He was itching to put his ideas into practice. Suddenly Churchill gave him the chance.

When the General arrived in the Middle East in August 1942 he had the great good fortune to find a ready-made and experienced army waiting for him. Two years' fighting and training had made many of them wonderful troops and there were plenty of them. The three armoured divisions—the First, Seventh and Tenth—were English, and there were in addition two English foot divisions, the Fiftieth and the Forty-Fourth. The Empire had provided five more infantry divisions—two South African, one Indian, one New Zealand and one Australian. There was also the Highland Division. A total of eleven divisions, all ready to go into battle. Moreover, the equipment was pouring in at a rate never approached in the Middle East before—British guns, American tanks and aircraft from both countries.

In itself this huge instrument of nearly two hundred thousand men was ready for anything. But the things it lacked badly were a clearly defined purpose and a leader. They got both in Montgomery. "Follow me," he cried, "and we will smash Rommel." Since the General believed this himself, it was not long before the troops began to believe it too. Before their own eyes great squadrons of tanks and guns were pouring into the desert and naturally the new General was given the credit for it. From now on the subordinates took a very subordinate position indeed. Everything came straight from the General. Moreover, the new General was a man the troops could understand. He was very much one of the boys. He painted Monty on his tank and he went round wearing a most stimulating array of hats and badges. He harangued the army like a prophet. All this might seem like bad form to the officers of the old school, but the troops loved it. Monty had won them over before the battle started. His shrewdest move of all was to spread the idea that the Eighth Army was an independent striking force, taking its orders from no one. He was their General and he was going to lead them on their own private crusade across Africa....

I personally was not at the battle of Alamein, but Lieutenant Colonel J. O. Ewart, one of Montgomery's intelligence officers, has supplied me with this compact and lucid account:

"The twenty-third of October 1942 was a still and moonlight night in the desert. At 9:40 the roar of 800 guns broke the silence and marked the start of the battle of Alamein. Twenty minutes of flashing, deafening chaos, interrupted by a nervous silence while the barrage lifted from the enemy's forward positions to his gun line. For these twenty minutes the sky was lit by the winking flashes along the horizon, then a quiet, broken by the sound of tank tracks and the rattle of small arms. The Eighth Army was unleashed. Since Rommel had left his hopes of taking Egypt with forty blackened tanks south of Alem Halfa ridge late in August, the army had been waiting and building. There had been endless activity round the back areas and in the workshops of the Delta. More tanks, new tanks—the Shermans—more guns, new guns— the Priests—more and more six-pounders, more men had been pouring up the switchback road. Tracks had been constructed leading up to the assembly area carefully camouflaged, and behind the lines there were as many dummy tanks as real ones, to mislead the enemy as to the point of our attack.

"The German, too, had been busy. Rommel had fenced himself in behind barriers of mines and wire, sandwiching Italian battalions between German battalions. It was the deepest defence that either side had constructed in Africa, and there was no possibility of outflanking it....

General Montgomery had decided to make a break-in in the north,...because a break-through in the north threatened the coastal road, the enemy's life, and imperiled the security of all his forces on the southern part of the line....

"By first light on the 24th the greater part of the objectives had been gained, and we had bitten deep into the enemy's main defences. Gaps had been made in the minefields and the armour of the 10th Corps had started to move up. We had broken in, but not through. On the enemy side there was confusion. Rommel's deputy, Stumme, had been killed by a stray shot in the first moments of the battle. The Axis command was taken over by von Thoma, who was comparatively new to the desert. His handling of the situation was indecisive....

"The first phase of the battle continued until the 26th. While our infantry ground down the enemy defences slowly and steadily and beat off the counter-attacks of the 15th Panzer Division, the sappers were making corridors for the armour behind. The second phase began on the 27th. A purposefulness appeared in the enemy's movements. We guessed that Rommel was back. Subsequent evidence proved we were right. He took an immediate grip on the situation, and concentrated all his reserves in the north....

"Montgomery was making his plan for the break-through....The plan had the simplicity of genius. It was to persuade the Germans that we were going one way, and then to go the other. It worked perfectly. On the 29th the 9th Australian Division after bitter fighting, advanced due north across the coast road almost cutting off an enemy force...[that] looked just like a thumb stretched up toward the sea. The Australians were exposed in this precarious salient, but they were told to stay there. Rommel was drawn. All day on the 30th and the 31st the enemy dashed himself against the Thumb. Gradually the whole of the enemy reserve, including the 21st Panzer and the 90th Light was concentrated astride the road, right in the north. It was tired and battle worn. The Australians had not yielded an inch.

"It was the moment Montgomery was waiting for. After a night attack by the Highlanders and the New Zealanders, gaps were made farther south, and on November 2nd the whole weight of the Eighth Army's armour poured west straight out of the bulge. The Germans were caught off balance. Their attention was toward the north and the Thumb had become an obsession to Rommel. Before he could re-concentrate to meet the threat from a new direction, the 1st and 10th Armoured Divisions were among him....By night fall the enemy had cracked, and was starting to disengage....

"There was no longer a line with two firm flanks. The southern desert flank was open and the 7th Armoured Division was round it before Rommel could call a halt. The Afrika Korps commander, von Thoma, was in the bag [captured] and the retreat for the moment became a rout....The Axis had suffered its first great defeat of the war, and the tide had turned.

EISENHOWER REFLECTS ON OPERATION TORCH

The North African campaign marked the first major commitment of American forces in the European theater during World War II and, inevitably, there were numerous problems to be worked out by the inexperienced forces before things began to flow more smoothly. Matters were complicated by the status of Vichy France and whether French armed forces were duty bound to resist an invasion, to observe strict neutrality, or to join with their Free French countrymen in inflicting a blow (albeit a peripheral one) on a German war machine which occupied their homeland. The entire Torch operation required someone of tact, sensitivity, and organizational ability to manage it, and the Allies found the right person in General Dwight Eisenhower (1890–1969). It was a mystery to some observers how Eisenhower rose to command so rapidly despite not having fought in battle himself, but the following extract from his own diary provides a partial answer, illustrating Eisenhower's cool, methodical analysis of the situation and his unflinching self-criticism.

December 10, 1942

This operation has been in progress just slightly over a month.

To compare the picture as it exists today with what was anticipated before we came in here, it is necessary to recall the differing assumptions upon which our calculations were made. These assumptions were three. *First*, that there might be definite opposition from the French, continuing as long as their forces were capable of fighting. *Second*, that we might from the outset obtain active and effective cooperation from the French all the way from Casablanca to Tunis, and especially in Algiers and Tunis. *Third*, that opposition from the French might not be severe but that we would get little in the way of effective help from them.

Under the first conception, we figured that it would be at least two months after D-day [the landing date for North Africa, not to be confused with the more famous Normandy D-day of 1944] before

we could move much to the eastward of Bougie and that thereafter we would have a rather laborious campaign, with a great number of troops actually immobilized on our lines of communication. Under the second assumption, we felt we might, even with a few parachute forces and some light ground troops, be in Tunis and Bizerte in a matter of ten days or so after landing at Algiers. Under the third assumption, we felt that the going would be pretty slow and that we would meet German resistance in western Tunisia. It was felt that within thirty days our general battle line might be along the western boundary of that province.

Actually, the situation we have encountered contained elements of all three of these basic assumptions. We had some pretty tough fighting against the French in the west and some of shorter duration in the center, and this reacted to make our eastward advance somewhat less strong. Moreover, after our landings were firmly established, some days elapsed before we could get any active help from the French.

Robert H. Ferrell, ed., *The Eisenhower Diaries* (New York: Norton, 1981), 82–85. Used by permission of John S.D. Eisenhower.

Within the last two weeks, this help has been of inestimable value to us but, even so, is no longer decisive because the enemy was allowed by the French forces in Tunis and Bizerte to enter the country in considerable force. The French under the control of Giraud seem to be perfectly willing to fight, but their forces are very light and lacking in the special equipment necessary to modern warfare.

In any event, we started for Tunis, pell mell, as soon as we got our leading troops ashore at Algiers.... Enemy opposition, particularly by air, became more effective from the beginning, and as the rains came on and made our mud fields unusable, and as our ground troops pushed well ahead of the most advanced landing fields we could employ, the situation gradually became such as to compel a halt. Conditions were aggravated by the impossibility of getting up supplies. It takes time to organize a line of communications extending through four or five hundred miles of mountainous country, and time was something we did not have....

Through all this, I am learning many things: (1) that waiting for other people to produce is one of the hardest things a commander has to do; (2) that in the higher positions of a modern army, navy, and air force, rich organizational experience and an orderly, logical mind are absolutely essential to success. The flashy, publicity-seeking type of adventurer can grab the headlines and be a hero in the eyes of the public, but he simply can't deliver the goods in high command. On the other hand, the slow, methodical, ritualistic person is absolutely valueless in a key position. There must be a fine balance—that is exceedingly difficult to find. In addition to the above, a person in such a position must have an inexhaustible fund of nervous energy. He is called upon day and night to absorb the disappointments, the discouragements, and the doubts of his subordinates and to force them on to accomplishments, which they regard as impossible. The odd thing about it is that most of these subordinates don't even realize that they are simply pouring their burdens upon the next superior and that when they receive orders to do something, they themselves have been relieved of a great load of moral responsibility. To find a few persons of the kind that I have roughly described above is the real job of the commander....

All in all, I would rate our prospects for the present as good. We are having our troubles; so is the enemy. If we can make up our minds to endure more and go farther and work harder than he does, and provided only that the comparative logistics of the situation does not favor him too much, we can certainly win.

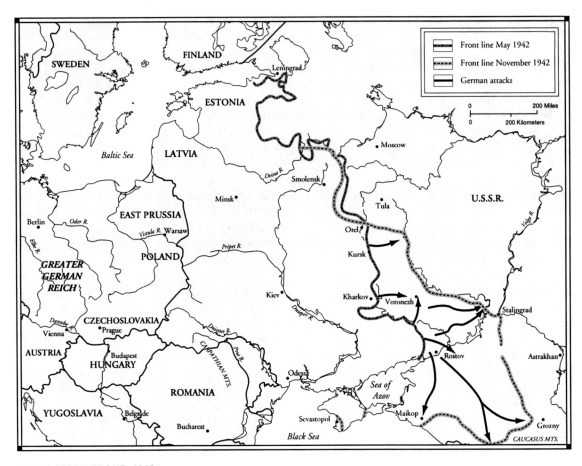

THE EASTERN FRONT, 1942

STALINGRAD: THE RATS' WAR

Even Joseph Goebbels (1897–1945), the Nazi Party's formidable propaganda chief, found his talents challenged in trying to distill the meaning of defeat at Stalingrad for his German audience. In a famous speech of February 18, 1943, at the Berlin Sportpalast, he admitted there was "no point in disputing the seriousness of the situation" and warned that the stark alternatives facing the country were ruthless domestic mobilization for victory in a total war or defeat and absolute destruction. He urged listeners to "look the facts in the face, however hard and dreadful they may be," leaving them in no doubt that a possible turning point had been reached. But what about the facts of the campaign itself? During the battle of Stalingrad, the open country in which the mechanized German forces had enjoyed an initial advantage was but a distant memory. The battle for the city was a horrific, house-by-house struggle under appalling conditions, prompting German soldiers to dub it the "rats' war." Any journalist who hoped to report accurately on the battle, therefore, had to stay in the lines of fire with the troops, as did the Soviet writer Vasily Grossman (1905–1964). A gifted novelist and experienced reporter, Grossman wrote for the *Red Star*, a Soviet army paper. His candor and willingness to share hardships was appreciated by the troops, who in turn confided in him, and the result was, as here, a compelling description of the war from the perspective of the individual soldier.

Stalingrad is the glory of the Russian infantry. Our infantry has taken and made use of German weapons and ammunition....A soldier who'd spent three days here considered himself an old-timer. Here, people only lived for one day....Weapons for close-quarter combat have never been used as they have in Stalingrad...[and our men] didn't fear tanks any longer. Our soldiers have become so resourceful. Even professors wouldn't be able to think up their tricks. They can build trenches that are so good you wouldn't notice soldiers in them even if you step on their heads. Our soldiers were on an upper floor [in a building]. Some Germans below them wound up a gramophone. Our men made a hole in the floor and fired [through it] with a flame thrower....

Sometimes, the trenches dug by the battalion are twenty meters from the enemy. The sentry can hear soldiers walking in the German trench, and arguments when Germans divide up the food. He can hear all night the tap dance of a German sentry in his torn boots. Everything is a marker here, every stone is a landmark....

All those who, for a hundred days, held on to the Volga crossing and crossed the dark grey icy river, looked into the eyes of a quick, pitiless death. One day someone will sing a song about those who are now asleep on the Volga's bed....

At night, we could walk upon the Volga. The ice was two days old and did not bend any longer beneath our feet. The moon lit the network of paths, uncountable tracks of sledges. A liaison soldier was

Antony Beevor and Luba Vinogradova, eds., *A Writer at War: Vasily Grossman with the Red Army, 1941–1945*, trans. by Antony Beevor, copyright © 2005 by Ekaterina Vasilievna Korotkova-Grossman and Elena Fedorovna Kozhichkina. (New York: Pantheon, 2005), 154–155, 199. Used by permission of Pantheon Books, a division of Random House, Inc.

walking in front of us, quickly and confidently as if he'd spent half of his life walking on these intermingling paths. Suddenly the ice started cracking. The liaison soldier came to a wide ice clearing, stopped and said: 'Aha! We must have taken the wrong path. We should have stayed to the right.' Liaison men always utter this sort of consoling phrase, no matter where they take you.

Barges smashed by shells have frozen into the ice. There's a bluish glistening of ice-covered hawsers [mooring lines]. Sterns rise steeply up, so do the bows of sunken motor boats.

Fighting is still going on in the factories...Guns fire with hollow bangs, rumblings, and the explosions of shells resound drily and clearly. Often, bursts of machine-gun and sub-machine-gun fire can be heard distinctly. This music is fearfully similar to the peaceful work of the plant, like riveting or steam hammers beating steel bars, and flattening them. It is as if liquid steel and slag pouring into a mould are lighting the fresh ice on the Volga with a pink, quick glow.

The sun rises and illuminates the edges of large holes made by heavy bombs. The depths of these frightening holes are always in a gloomy penumbra. The sun is afraid to touch them....

The sun shines over hundreds of railway tracks where tanker wagons are lying like killed horses, with their bellies torn open; where hundreds of freight carriages are jammed one on top of another, blasted there by the force of an explosion, and crowded around cold locomotives like a panic-stricken herd huddling around its leaders.

ADMIRAL UGAKI REFLECTS ON MIDWAY

Japan's surprise attack on Pearl Harbor had either sunk or neutralized the battleships of America's Pacific Fleet, but the crucial aircraft carriers had been out of port and so escaped the disaster. Yet for all the initial success Japanese forces enjoyed as they rampaged throughout Southeast Asia and the western Pacific, Japanese leaders like Admiral Yamamoto recognized they could not conduct fleet operations with impunity unless the American carriers were destroyed. Accordingly, Yamamoto devised a plan to lure them to their destruction, in which he would dispatch an invasion force to the island of Midway (about two-thirds of the distance from Tokyo to Hawaii), while keeping his own carrier forces hidden farther behind the invasion fleet. When the American carriers sallied forth to protect Midway, presumably unaware of the proximity of the other Japanese units, he would destroy the American ships with devastating air strikes from the Japanese carriers. Midway would provide a useful staging point for a future invasion of Hawaii. But Yamamoto's plan was handicapped by two major flaws: in its complexity and emphasis on diversionary action (including an attack on the Aleutian Islands near Alaska), it weakened Japanese forces, and in its unwillingness to consider that American cryptologists had broken Japanese codes, it relinquished the element of surprise to the Americans. The American Pacific Fleet's commander-in-chief, Admiral Chester Nimitz (1885–1966), thus knew what to expect and deployed his forces accordingly. Japanese carrier-based planes bombed Midway as they had planned, but were then horrified to learn that American ships were much closer than they had anticipated, indeed were lying in wait. Confusion over whether to arm their planes with weapons appropriate to launching a second attack on a target on land (Midway Island) or at sea (American ships) left the Japanese carriers vulnerable to attack. That attack came on June 4, 1942. Slow American torpedo planes flying near the surface were butchered by Japanese fighter escorts, but their sacrifice allowed American dive-bombers to attack from above unimpeded, exactly at the point when the decks of the Japanese carriers were crammed with refueling and rearming planes. In just five minutes, the course of the war in the Pacific would change decisively. Three Japanese carriers were destroyed, and a fourth would join them on the ocean bottom the next day. Lost too were the veteran flight crews who had taken such a toll at Pearl Harbor, and whose skill and experience was irreplaceable. The Americans lost only one carrier, and the Japanese were compelled to withdraw. In retrospect, now that the United States had decisively blunted the Japanese thrust, it could now assume the initiative and begin a strategy of "island-hopping." Perhaps the long-range implications were not immediately crystal clear, and the war would continue for another three years, but Japanese commanders sensed they had squandered a precious opportunity. Vice-Admiral Matome Ugaki (1890–1945) served as Yamamoto's Chief of Staff and earned a reputation for courage and dedication. Here he reflects in his diary upon the battle of Midway; his dates are a day ahead of the American calendar because of Japan's position relative to the international date line.

Selections from pp. 138–140, 142, 152 from Chapter 4 entitled "Don't Let Another Day Like This Come" from *Fading Victory: The Diary of Admiral Matome Ugaki, 1941–1945*, translated by Masataka Chihaya with Donald M. Goldstein and Katherine V. Dillon, © 1991. Reprinted by permission of the University of Pittsburgh Press.

Friday, 5 June 1942.

Thick fog. Since operations on the 5th, 6th, and 7th were so urgent, I couldn't find time to put the daily account in this war diary. I feel like a week or ten days have elapsed since then. As I have some time today...I'm going to write down first the main problems in my head.

Main causes for the failure of this operation:

1. There are questions as to whether the enemy knew our plan, apart from its extent. These doubts are endorsed by the fact that the enemy defense in this district has been intensified of late, in addition to brisk submarine activities and their concentration of forces. Whether the enemy discovered our plan by their subs sighting our invasion force leaving Saipan on the 28th or the sortie of our Main Body and others from the Inland Sea, whether the enemy suspected a reinforcement movement of our northern force through information from Russian ships, or whether the enemy found out, either based upon security leakage from messages sent from our army forces in the homeland, or based upon judgment of general radio intelligence—all these can't be ascertained. But much suspicion about these questions is not lacking.

The enemy couldn't possibly have advanced its task force from Hawaii to the north of Midway Island by merely discovering our invasion force on the 4th. The possibility that the enemy's powerful task force left Hawaii on 30 May can be confirmed by increased flights of the many planes in that district since that day.

It's impossible to judge that the enemy just happened to meet us on its way westward with an offensive intention (for instance, an air-raid on our capital). This can be reasoned by the fact that the enemy strength included not only all the remaining three carriers (*Yorktown, Enterprise,* and *Hornet*) but two converted carriers [these reports were erroneous because the last two ships were also cruisers] with several powerful cruisers and more than a dozen destroyers....

2. Our reconnaissance of the enemy was insufficient. An advance attempt to reconnoiter the Hawaii district by Type Two flying boats couldn't be carried out, as two enemy vessels were in French Frigate Shoals. In addition, Wake Island couldn't afford enough sea area for them to take off. So our operation had to be made without any information on the enemy force and activities in Pearl Harbor....

Unlike the Pearl Harbor operation, in which the surprise element could be expected, the Midway operation lacked such an element. Nevertheless, we admittedly didn't sufficiently consider searching the sea area by submarines and other means. That is, only *I-68* was positioned around Midway and the other fifteen subs of the Third Submarine Squadron, the Fifth Submarine Squadron, and the Thirteenth Submarine Division were positioned on the north-south line six hundred miles west of Hawaii to meet an enemy force expected to come from Pearl Harbor as reinforcements.

Even if we didn't consider the enemy had suspected our intention, at least we should have either positioned an element of our force at an expected enemy attack area to meet a powerful strike, or made a sweeping search from midway toward Hawaii. Either one of these steps would have served, for one thing, as a means to obtain information about the enemy and at the same time a measure for protecting the flank of our task force. I seriously feel it to be a grave responsibility of our headquarters that we failed to take these steps.

3. An unexpectedly large enemy force attacked our task force at its most vulnerable moment.

The enemy had only two carriers in operational condition and contact with them had been entirely lost since they were seen east of Tulagi for a while on 15 May, after having come down from Hawaii for the Coral Sea battle. Although they were estimated to have returned to Hawaii, we never expected them, even including another one and two converted carriers, to ambush our force near Midway Island.

A carrier force has a vulnerable point when the enemy forestalls it, especially so when it's concentrating its attack upon another target, because it not only lacks a sufficient defensive force, namely interceptors, but it isn't in a position immediately to switch its attack upon the new enemy carrier. In all sea battles since the outbreak of the war—namely, the Pearl Harbor attack, the attack upon Port Darwin or the attack upon Ceylon—we achieved brilliant success under circumstances where no powerful enemy air force was in the operational area. It was just like striking a sitting enemy....

4. To the enemy's advantage, they attacked our force while our carriers were concentrated in one group, offering many eggs in one basket....

Don't let another day like this come to us during the course of this war! Let this day be the only one of the greatest failure of my life!

THE STRAIN OF JUNGLE WARFARE

Battle under the tropical conditions on Guadalcanal was a trying experience for American soldiers fresh from training camps back home. The exotic locations, the stifling heat and humidity, the almost impenetrable vegetation, and an enemy whose tactics sometimes seemed more reminiscent of the eighteenth-century French and Indian Wars than modern combat, all combined to disorient American forces and challenge them to adapt quickly to these unfamiliar conditions. One of the best accounts of the struggle for Guadalcanal was by Robert Leckie (1920–2001), a young scout and machine-gunner in the First Marine Division. Leckie had begun his career as a sportswriter and newspaper reporter, but enlisted in the marines immediately after Pearl Harbor. He went on to become one of America's most prolific and influential popular military historians.

Our entrenching tools made muffled noises while we scooped foxholes out of the jungle floor. It was like digging into a compost heap ten thousand years old. Beneath this perfection of corruption lay a dark rich loam. We had barely finished when night fell, abruptly, blackly, like a shade drawn swiftly from jungle roof to jungle floor. We slipped into the foxholes. We lay down and waited.

It was a darkness without time. It was an impenetrable darkness. To the right and the left of me rose up those terrible formless things of my imagination, which I could not see because there was no light. I could not see, but I dared not close my eyes lest the darkness crawl beneath my eyelids and suffocate me. I could only hear. My ears became my being and I could hear the specks of life that crawled beneath my clothing, the rotting of the great tree which rose from its three-cornered trunk above me. I could hear the darkness gathering against me and the silences that lay between the moving things.

I could hear the enemy everywhere about me, whispering to each other and calling my name. I lay open-mouthed and half-mad beneath that giant tree. I had not looked into its foliage before

Excerpts from pp. 68–70, 80–81, 224–225 from *Helmet for My Pillow* by Robert Leckie, copyright © 1957 by Robert Hugh Leckie Illus. © 1979 by Bantam Books, Inc. Used by permission of Bantam Books, a division of Random House, Inc.

the darkness and now I fancied it infested with Japanese. Everything and all the world became my enemy, and soon my very body betrayed me and became my foe. My leg became a creeping Japanese, and then the other leg....I now know why men light fires....

The Tenaru River lay green and evil, like a serpent across the palmy coastal plain. It was called a river, but it was not a river; like most of the streams of Oceania, it was a creek—not thirty yards wide.

Perhaps it was not even a creek, for it did not always flow and it seldom reached its destination, the sea. Where it might have emptied into Iron Bottom Bay, a spit of sand, some forty-feet wide, penned it up....As we dug, we had it [the sandspit] partially in view; that is, what would be called the enemy side of the sandspit....

The Japanese would have to force the river to our front; or come over the narrow sandspit to our left, which was well defended by riflemen and a number of machine gun posts and barbed wire; or else try our right flank....No one went to bed. The stars were out, and this was enough to keep everyone up, unwilling to waste a bright night.

Suddenly in the river, upstream to our right, there appeared a widening, rippling V. It seemed to be moving steadily downstream. At the point of the V were two greenish lights, small, round, close together.

Jawgia wooped and fired his rifle at it. To our right came a fusillade of shots. It was from G Company rifleman, shooting also at the V. More bullets hit the water. The V disappeared.

Lights—swinging, bumping lights, like lanterns or headlights—glittered across the river in the grove....This was too much. Everyone was awake. The mysterious V in the river and now these ghostly lights—it was too much! We jabbered excitedly and once again warmed our souls in the heat of our voices.

Shattering machine gun fire broke out far to the left. As far down as the sandspit, perhaps. There came another burst....The conflagration was sweeping towards us up the river, like a train of powder....

A man says of the eruption of battle: "All hell broke loose." The first time he says it, it is true—wonderfully descriptive. The millionth time it is said, it has been worn into meaninglessness: it has gone the way of all good phrasing, it has become cliché.

But within five minutes of that first machine gun burst, of the appearance of that first enemy flare that suffused the battlefield in unearthly greenish light—and by its dying accentuated the reenveloping night—within five minutes of this, all hell broke loose. Everyone was firing, every weapon was sounding voice; but this was no orchestration, no terribly beautiful symphony of death, as decadent rear-echelon observers write. Here was cacophony; here was dissonance; here was wildness; here was the absence of rhythm, the loss of limit, for everyone fires what, when and where he chooses; here was booming, sounding, shrieking, wailing, hissing, crashing, shaking, gibbering, noise. Here was hell.

Yet each weapon has its own sound, and it is odd with what clarity the trained ear distinguishes each one and catalogues it, plucks it out of the general din....The plop of the outgoing mortar with the crunch of its fall, the clatter of the machine guns and the lighter, faster, rasp of the Browning Automatic Rifles, the hammering of fifty-caliber machine guns, the crackling of rifle fire, the *wham* of thirty-seven millimeter anti-tank guns firing point-blank caliber at the charging enemy—each of these conveys a definite message, and sometimes meaning, to the understanding ear, even though that ear be filled with a total wail of battle....

Our regiment had killed something like nine hundred of them [Japanese]. Most of them lay in clusters or heaps before the gun pits commanding the sandspit, as though they had not died singly but in groups. Moving among them were the souvenir hunters, picking their way delicately as though fearful of booby traps, while stripping the bodies of their possessions....One of the marines went methodically among the dead armed with a pair of pliers. He had observed that the Japanese have a penchant for gold fillings in their teeth, often with solid gold teeth. He was looting their very mouths. He would kick their jaws agape, peer into the mouth with all the solicitude of a Park Avenue dentist—careful, always careful not to contaminate himself by touch—and yank out all that glittered. He kept the gold teeth in an empty Bull Durham tobacco sack, which he wore around his neck in the manner of an amulet. Souvenirs, we called him....

Our victory in the fight which we called "the Battle of Hell's Point" was not so great as we had imagined it to be. It was to be but one of many fights for Guadalcanal, and in the end, not the foremost of them. But being the first in our experience, we took it for total triumph; like those who take the present for the best of all worlds, having no reference to the past nor regard for the future.

From the high plateau of triumph we were about to descend to the depths of trial and tedium. The Japanese attack was to be redoubled and prolonged and varied. It would come from the sky, the sea and the land. In between every trial there would stretch out the tedium that sucks a man dry, drying off the juice from body and soul as a native removes the contents of a stick of sugar cane, leaving it spent, cracked, good for nothing but the flames....

Their [Japanese soldiers] passage had been through near impenetrable jungle and they had not arrived on the scene until two days after our own coming. Nevertheless, they attacked us. They attacked us, some one hundred of them against our force of some twelve hundred, and, but for the [five] prisoners, we had annihilated them.

Were they brave or fanatical? What had they hoped to gain? Had their commander really believed that a company of Japanese soldiers could conquer a battalion of American marines, experienced, confident, better armed, emplaced on higher ground? Why had he not turned around and marched his men home again? Was it because no Japanese soldier can report failure, cannot "lose face"?

I cannot answer. I can only wonder about this fierce mysterious enemy—so cruel and yet so courageous—a foe who could make me in his utmost futility, fanaticism, if you will, call upon the best of myself to defend against him....

The Japanese dead lay in heaps on the hillside, and they filled the trench....The souvenir-hunters were prowling among them, carefully ripping insignia off tunics, slipping rings off fingers or pistols off belts. There was Souvenirs himself, stepping gingerly from corpse to corpse, armed with his pliers and a dentist flashlight....

I stood among the heaps of dead. They lay crumpled, useless, defunct. The vital force was fled. A bullet or a mortar fragment had torn a hole in these frail vessels and the substance had leaked out. The mystery of the universe had once inhabited these lolling lumps, had given each an identity, a way of walking, perhaps a special habit of address or way with words or a knack of putting color on canvas. They had been so different then. Now they were nothing, heaps of nothing. Can a bullet or a mortar fragment do this? Does this force, this mystery, I mean this soul—does this spill out on the ground along with the blood?

WINNING THE SOLOMONS

Like Robert Leckie, Ira Wolfert (1908–1997) came to the Solomon Islands with experience as a sports reporter, which enabled him (more so than his previous work as a New York drama critic) to establish a good relationship with the marines whose exploits he would cover. Wolfert had a sharp eye for the big picture, and his success in conveying the broader significance of the American victory on Guadalcanal helped to earn him a Pulitzer Prize in 1943. Here he explains just why the capture of a small island so far from Japan or the United States could be so important to the war effort.

GUADALCANAL, SOLOMON ISLANDS

This is no banana war going on in the Solomons, involving potting hopped-up Japanese killers from trees, but the fightingest engagement involving American troops since Bataan.

The reason for the necessity of victory after victory for the Americans holding a spot of land on one-hundred-mile long Guadalcanal is that the Japs keep on sneaking men and guns into remote places, accumulate a striking force in the jungles, and then hit with it.

The Japs were pretty well convinced by their parade down the Pacific that islands were impossible militarily to hold. Our strategists, trying a stepping-stone route to Tokyo, are out to convince the Japanese that islands are impossible militarily to hold only for them.

The prolonged Japanese effort to break off our toehold in the Solomons is continuing today in a now tragically familiar tempo. The Japs are paying dearly for their sudden access of ambition, but presenting a bill and collecting it is no picnic....

If the nature of the war here has been puzzling you, then you have plenty of company, but it seems primarily to be a naval free-for-all in which every weapon known to man, from the most primitive to the most modern, plays a part. This is probably the most extraordinary naval war in history. Admirals not only have to use carriers, battleships, and submarines, but also field artillery, machine guns, rifles with telescopic sights, machetes, and even bows and arrows. Our troops do not carry bows but the natives do, and their jungle tactics will form A.E.F. [Allied Expeditionary Force] legends of the immediate future just as the tactics of the giant Senegalese in France formed A.E.F. legends of the past....

The reason for the profusion and confusion of weapons in this naval war is the fact mentioned previously—that this sector of the war is being fought primarily for islands to be used as unsinkable aircraft carriers. Not only must the jungle-covered land be held and made useful by the Navy's construction battalions and the Army's engineers, who labor like ancient Romans—under such long-range fire as the Romans never knew—to stamp permanently the imprint of civilization upon a primeval wilderness, but the waters around the islands must be held and the lines of communications must be batted through and preserved over areas of thousands of square miles. Water and over-water communications is Navy business, and they attend to

Ira Wolfert, *Battle for the Solomons* (Boston: Houghton Mifflin, 1943), 45–46, 60–61, 101–102. Used by permission.

it with a hard-hitting vigor which is earning the respect of all the navies of the world, including the Japanese....

It must be remembered that the fight for Guadalcanal is not for the hundred-mile island, but for the air facilities on the one tip of it and the sea roads leading there. Those air facilities are useful to the Jap as a base for operations southward and to us as a base for operations northward.

We hold the ground and continue to hold it against ceaseless pressure by the Japs. In the sense that the Jap has not pushed us back and that we have denied the Jap a base there, we have won a whole series of battle for Guadalcanal thus far. But we have not yet won a victory there. For, while the Jap no longer has a base there, neither have we been able to make a base out of it. Guadalcanal is not a base at all, but a battlefield.

We are winning in the Solomons in another sense too. The Guadalcanal area has become a kind of Verdun, a maw into which the Jap is pouring his power and giving us a chance to blunt it. This is not a nickel-and-dime operation for the Jap. In the last five days here, he has lost somewhere about three hundred planes. That's not a filibustering expedition. That's a battle.

WHY JAPAN LOST GUADALCANAL

Raizo Tanaka (1892–1969) was perhaps Japan's foremost destroyer squadron commander and rose to the rank of vice-admiral. In August 1942 he was ordered to assume command of relief operations to bring supplies and reinforcements to beleaguered Japanese troops on Guadalcanal. These usually took the form of swift nighttime sorties at which the Japanese navy had excelled, but despite their frequency (leading the weary Americans to dub them the "Tokyo Express"), they were unable to dislodge the tenacious marines. In this essay, originally published in 1956, Tanaka reviews the Japanese mistakes that led to defeat.

A simple statement of the facts makes it clear that the Japanese attempt to reinforce Guadalcanal ended in failure. The causes of this failure, however, are probably as diverse as the people who may offer them. From my position as commander of the reinforcement force, I submit that our efforts were unsuccessful because of the following factors:

Command complications

At one and the same time I was subject to orders from the Combined Fleet, the Eleventh Air Fleet, and the Eighth Fleet. This was confusing at best; and when their orders were conflicting and incompatible, it was embarrassing at least, and utterly confounding at worst.

Raizo Tanaka, "The Struggle for Guadalcanal," in David C. Evans, ed., *The Japanese Navy in World War II: In the Words of Former Japanese Naval Officers* (Annapolis: Naval Institute Press, 1986), 209–211. Used by permission.

Force composition

In almost every instance the reinforcement of Guadalcanal was attempted by forces hastily thrown together, without specially trained crews, and without previous opportunity to practice or operate together. Various types of ships of widely varying capabilities were placed under my command one after the other, creating unimaginable difficulties and foreordaining the failure of their effort.

Inconsistent operation plans

There never was any consistent operation plan. Vessels, troops, and supplies were assembled piecemeal to suit the occasion of the moment without overall long-range plan or purpose. This was a frailty our army and navy should have recognized soon after the outbreak of the China Incident. It was a fatal Japanese weakness that continued through the attempts to reinforce Guadalcanal and even after.

Communication failures

Our communication system was seldom good, and during the fall and winter of 1942 it was almost consistently terrible. In wide theaters of operations and under difficult battle situations it is indispensable for a tactical commander to have perfect communication with his headquarters and with his subordinate units. The consequence of poor communications is failure.

Army-navy coordination

This situation was generally unendurable. It did little good for the army or the navy to work out their own plans independently, no matter how well founded, if they were not coordinated. Time and time again in these operations their coordination left much to be desired.

Underestimation of the enemy

Belittling the fighting power of the enemy was a basic cause of Japan's setback and defeat in every operation of the Pacific War. Enemy successes were deprecated and alibied in every instance. It was standard practice to inflate our own capabilities to the consequent underestimation of the enemy's. This was fine for the ego but poor for winning victories.

Inferiority in the air

Our ships, without strong air support, were employed in an attempt to recapture a tactical area where the enemy had aerial superiority. This recklessness resulted only in adding to our loss of ships and personnel.

The greatest pity was that every Japanese commander was aware of all these factors, yet no one seemed to do anything about any of them. Our first fruitless attempt to recapture Guadalcanal was made with a lightly equipped infantry regiment. The key points of the island had already been strongly fortified by the U.S. Marines under cover of a strong naval force. The next Japanese general offensive was made with one lightly equipped brigade against the same points, and it also failed. Meanwhile the enemy had increased and strengthened his defenses by bringing up more sea and land fighting units. Japan's only response was to bring forward a full division in a direct landing operation. Ignoring the tremendous difference in air strength between ourselves and the enemy, this landing operation was attempted directly in front of the enemy-held airfield. As a result, officers and men were able to disembark, but there was no chance to unload our heavy guns and ammunition. We stumbled along from one error to another while the enemy grew wise, profited by his wisdom, and advanced until our efforts at Guadalcanal reached their unquestionable and inevitable end—in failure....

Operations to reinforce Guadalcanal extended over a period of more than five months. They amounted to a losing war of attrition in which Japan suffered heavily in and around that island. The losses of our navy alone amounted to two battleships, three cruisers, twelve destroyers, sixteen transports, well over one hundred planes, thousands of officers and men, and prodigious amounts of munitions and supplies. There is no question that Japan's doom was sealed with the closing of the struggle for Guadalcanal. Just as it betokened the military character and strength of her opponent, so it presaged Japan's weakness and lack of planning that would spell her defeat.

CHAPTER 6

THE EUROPEAN THEATER

D-DAY INVASION   American troops storm ashore the Normandy coastline on June 6, 1944 (D-day), in the largest amphibious assault to date.
Source: © AP images.

If one wants to appreciate the scale of World War II, one need only recall that it was fought on, or involved participants from, six of the world's continents, sparing only Antarctica. Neither the skies nor the seas around the globe escaped untouched from the conflict's impact. Even if for the moment one ignores the Pacific War, the struggle to subdue Germany involved a massive expenditure of men, weapons, and resources: a campaign of aerial bombing by night and day, a bitter contest under harsh conditions between German sub-marines and Allied shipping for supremacy in the North Atlantic, a truly titanic struggle on the eastern front with the Red Army that dwarfed previous conflicts between nations, and, last and to some degree least, the efforts of British and American forces to defeat Italy and to return to the European continent and apply direct pressure on ground forces defending the German homeland.

Between the evacuation of British troops from Dunkirk in June 1940 and the German invasion of the Soviet Union a year later, the only way to carry the war to Germany was through aerial bombing. The bombers with which the Royal Air Force began the war, how-ever, were virtually obsolete due to their slow speeds, poor protection, and modest bomb loads. In daylight they would be easy prey for German fighters, so the British chose to confine themselves to nighttime bombing, even though it was much harder to locate and damage tar-gets in the dark. Indeed, internal evaluations, such as the Butt Report in the summer of 1941, confirmed that a majority of bombs were missing the mark. But the RAF's Bomber Command could not discontinue operations for both psychological and strategic reasons. Bombing, however ineffective in the beginning, at least reassured the British public that something was being done to retaliate for the Blitz and make Germany pay, and offered some assurance to a skeptical Stalin that the Allies were committed to a "second front" (even if for the time being it was an aerial one) to relieve some of the massive pressure upon the Red Army.

One way to compensate for inaccuracy was to increase the number of planes and ton-nage of bombs dropped, and by 1943 Bomber Command had at its disposal many more heavy aircraft, of much higher quality, notably the Avro Lancasters, and an air marshal, Arthur Harris, committed to using them en masse. By that point, units of the United States Army Air Forces (USAAF) under generals Henry "Hap" Arnold and Ira Eaker were also operating from bases in Britain, committed to the daylight precision bombing they believed was possible from rugged, heavily armed Boeing B-17s. In July 1943, massed Lancasters devastated Hamburg, creating a massive firestorm and incinerating the city cen-ter and some 40,000 residents. Harris then turned his attention to Berlin, launching waves of raids, but the greater distances and ferocious German defenses (a combination of radar detection, coordinated direction from the ground, fighter interception, and lethal antiair-craft fire or "flak") took a dreadful toll on British planes and aircrews. The U.S. Eighth Air Force attempted to disable German fighter-plane and ball bearing production in daylight raids on Regensburg (August) and Schweinfurt (August and October 1943). Conducted deep into German territory, beyond the protective range of fighter escorts, the American bombers were slaughtered. Of 291 planes involved in the second Schweinfurt attack, 60 were destroyed and another 140 or so damaged. No military force, even with the produc-tive might of American industry behind it, could continue to sustain such losses of aircraft and trained men. No branch of any of the British and American services suffered such a high proportion of casualties as the bomber crews, even if exposure to risk was capped at twenty or twenty-five missions. Moreover, much of the damage inflicted was made good in a relatively short time, and overall German production continued to increase. If the tide of war seemingly had changed on land in November 1942, there was no indication yet which way fortunes would go in the skies over central Europe.

The solutions the Allies devised were both simple and ingenious. The American P-51 Mustang, for example, was, when first delivered, an undistinguished fighter plane. When someone had the bright idea to equip it with a British-built Merlin engine, the P-51 was transformed into one of the outstanding aircraft of the war. When Allied engineers devised additional external fuel tanks which the Mustangs could jettison before combat, they now had the range to escort B-17s across Germany and take on an increasingly overmatched Luftwaffe. For their part, the British developed a number of navigating devices (intersecting radio beams and so forth) to improve location and recognition of targets, and utilized "pathfinder" planes equipped with flares to illuminate the bomb-drop sites. Within months aerial supremacy was achieved, and Allied bombers, though battered by flak, could reach their targets otherwise unimpeded. One after another of Germany's cities was flattened. In preparation for the D-day landings in June 1944, Allied planes systematically pulverized transportation lines and rail marshaling yards, and then destroyed the synthetic oil industry. By 1945 the German war economy had been driven underground, for anything in the open had virtually ground to a standstill.

In the final analysis, the Allied bombing campaign never delivered the full results its most enthusiastic proponents had anticipated. It did not break German morale (as indeed the Germans had not broken that of Britain) or precipitate the collapse of the German state. The human cost, in bomber crews (100,000 airmen lost) and civilians (perhaps 400,000 killed) was appalling and belied the aura of sterile technological efficiency that antedated the war. Horrific firestorms in Hamburg and Dresden, to name but two cities whose historic old buildings and many of whose residents were burned beyond recognition, raised disturbing ethical questions of whether some bombing missions were more vindictive than militarily effective. But bombing did cause widespread disruption and absenteeism. It forced the Germans to transfer home aircraft and weaponry (the deadly 88 mm gun) badly needed on the eastern front. By forcing the production of more fighter planes for home defense, it denuded the Luftwaffe of new bombers that might have supported operations against the Red Army. And eventually, by paralyzing German transport and oil, it made a significant contribution to eventual Allied victory.

Without aerial supremacy, Allied troops could never have invaded Normandy, liberated France and the Low Countries, and pushed forward into Germany. Nor could they have done so without naval supremacy as well. Indeed, the British Isles, from which the invasion was launched, could not have survived if Germany had been able to cut its seaborne lifelines. Britain relied upon imports for everything crucial to maintaining both the war effort and the welfare of its civilian population. To interrupt the flow of supplies, Germany could employ a handful of surface raiders (the most notable was the battleship *Bismarck*, which was hunted down and sunk in May 1941 after the loss of the battle cruiser HMS *Hood*), but the principal threat lay beneath the surface in its formidable submarine fleet. Moreover, if left unchecked, the U-boats would wreak havoc with Britain's efforts to transport troops and equipment to and from North Africa, India, and the Pacific, as well as to deliver crucial convoys of war material to the embattled Russians via the Arctic port of Murmansk. Despite their significant advantages in manpower and productive capacity, the Allies could not bring their full economic or military weight to bear unless they could guarantee the safety of the sea lanes.

The situation was precarious for several years, and never more so (ironically) than in 1942 *after* American entry, when the U-boats found bountiful targets of an opponent inexperienced and unprepared in the ways of submarine warfare. But American, British, and Canadian cooperation, the introduction of long-range aircraft, and more numerous escort vessels all helped to stem the losses. Of particular value was Britain's ability to frequently (though not continually) intercept and decode the coded transmissions between German submarines and their commander at the U-boat bases in occupied France, Admiral Karl Dönitz. These ULTRA intelligence decrypts enabled the Allies to shift convoy routes away from massing groups of submarines (the deadly "wolfpacks") and to identify the location of individual boats or rendezvous points for refueling at which the boats would be vulnerable to attack. As the war progressed, Germany slowly introduced technological upgrades (bigger and faster vessels, *schnorkel* tubes to allow them to run longer under water, and so forth), but it could not compensate for the incredible upsurge in Allied shipbuilding capacity (the United States, in particular, launched ships much faster than the U-boats could sink them) and the increasing sophistication of Allied sub-killing techniques. As a result, the nightmare scenario of a Britain starved and strangled into submission was averted; the nightmare was to be experienced by German submariners, for their chances of surviving the war were lower than that of any other branch within the German military.

Bombed from the air, blockaded by sea, German forces would eventually be squeezed from all directions on land. Allied troops moving from North Africa through Sicily and up the Italian boot would find their progress slowed by tenacious German units that made effective use of terrain well suited to defense, but they succeeded in toppling Hitler's ally, Mussolini. In mountainous areas such as Greece and Yugoslavia, the Germans had experienced initial success, but found their strength sapped by persistent resistance. Indeed, throughout eastern Europe and the Balkans, German aggression was significant for smashing existing state structures, unleashing lethal ethnic hostilities, and exposing divisions within those populations so deep that some resistance factions seemed as hostile to each other as to the occupying Germans. German policy was to stimulate multiple ethnic identities within conquered populations (to make unified opposition less likely), which resulted, after the Nazi defeat, in fertile soil for postwar communist agitation and political turmoil (as in the Greek civil war).

Even in western Europe, fractures within the resistance movements would reshape the political landscape. In France, for example, socialists or communists only rose to prominence within the resistance after the Soviet Union was attacked, and after which, therefore, capitalism and socialism were clearly—if temporarily—on the same side. Those Frenchmen who had chosen to support the Vichy government, a client regime that administered the unoccupied inner half of the country, found those loyalties tested when Hitler ordered the occupation of the whole of France in November 1942. France would again become a battleground: not just between competing visions of who had saved it (Free French, *Maquis*, or Vichy) but between those Allied invaders who would finally return to the continent intent on its liberation and German occupiers who would fight a rearguard action all the way eastward until they were backed up against the advancing Red Army.

The delay until mid-1944 in launching D-day reflected the complexity of a multinational amphibious assault against entrenched defenders and the logistical challenges of mounting such an operation, especially the shortages of landing craft. Once the Allies secured a foothold on the Normandy coast, they could pour massive reinforcements ashore, widen the beachhead, and, with aerial supremacy, deny the enemy the ability to deploy his reserves. The Germans could hope to exploit natural barriers (the tangled, almost impenetrable French hedges or "hedgerows," the Rhine River) but these were overcome (the first by the welding or bolting of iron teeth to the front of tanks, which could then uproot them; the second by the seizure, intact, of a bridge at Remagen). The Germans could also try to regain the initiative by counterattacking when prolonged bad weather neutralized Allied airpower (as in the Battle of the Bulge in December 1944), but the preponderance of American and British planes, tanks, and soldiers would reassert itself, and by the spring of 1945 German towns and cities were falling, one after another, to their Allied captors.

Nonetheless, in the final reckoning it was the Soviet Union that destroyed German military power. In Normandy some fifteen divisions on either side fought for advantage, but on the Russian front each side fielded upwards of 400 divisions (anywhere from 5 to 6 million men) in a desperate life-or-death struggle for survival. The eventual Soviet quantitative edge in manpower and weapons helps to explain the inexorable advance of the Red Army in the war's later stages, but does not adequately account for its survival or revival when the opposing forces were more evenly balanced. Stalin's nation triumphed in part because it mobilized Soviet society more thoroughly and effectively than anyone (least of all the Germans) had expected, and deployed a citizenry already familiar with being directed by the state. The Red Army itself learned from experience, adjusted its tactics, developed the defenses in depth that made "deep war" so effective against the invaders, and identified commanders who in skill and sophistication could match their German counterparts. Even Stalin, whose paranoia and interference had done so much to hobble Soviet conduct of the war, learned not to meddle, to project a reassuring image of unwavering defiance, and to trust the instincts and analysis of his senior commanders. Obscure individuals of all ranks performed miracles in dismantling crucial industries and relocating them beyond the reach of German troops, ensuring that the Soviet Union could continue to wage total war despite losses of men, material, and territory that would have crippled another combatant. So in a sense it was poetic justice that the Red Army conquered Berlin, though as the course of future events would reveal, it was anything but a liberation.

BOMBING PLOESTI

A lawyer who gave up his practice in Frankfort, Kentucky, to enlist in the air corps, Philip Ardery (1914–) wrote about his experiences in combat with the Eighth Air Force in Europe and North Africa in *Bomber Pilot*. His most memorable experience was the daring August 1943 raid on the Romanian oil refineries at Ploesti. Because up to 60 percent of Germany's crude oil supplies were refined there, Ploesti was an obvious target and very heavily defended. Moreover, to inflict appreciable damage required flying extremely low, further exposing the B-24 Liberator bombers (the ones built at Willow Run) to ferocious antiaircraft fire, and 54 of the 178 planes participating were lost. Ardery's account is a vivid reminder that for all the talk of precision bombing and clinical technological efficiency, flesh-and-blood bomber crews suffered horribly in their attempt to cripple the German war machine from the air.

When we left England for Africa we heard rumors about a great raid we were to run. The stories hinted at a maximum-range mission to be flown at low altitude. The first one I heard...was that we were going on a raid which could almost be characterized as a suicide mission. As the tale went, anyone who participated could be sure he would get at least the Silver Star [decoration for gallantry in action]. It was funny how great the percentage of truth in that one turned out to be....

By this time we were sure we were really going to make a long, low-level raid on the oil fields of Ploesti, Romania. We hadn't been told officially, but the strength of the rumors made the matter almost incontrovertible....

Finally, we turned down a valley between two steep ridges of mountains. We were supposed to make a run down a valley to the little town of Campina, north of the town of Ploesti. Steaua Romana, the most modern refinery in all Romania, lay on the edge of Campina in the Ploesti region. As soon as we turned down the valley I got a call from Lieutenant Solomon, the navigator. Sollie's voice was the voice of calm as he said over the interphone, "They've turned too soon. We are not in the right valley." He was an excellent navigator and his calmness on that harrowing day is something I'll never forget.

Sure enough, after we had flown about twenty minutes on the wrong heading we got a call from the lead ship indicating they had located their error and were turning north again to resume the proper course. One of the factors that we were briefed on as a most hopeful aspect of the mission was that we might take the enemy defenses of the oil fields by surprise. Now we realized that asset was spent. We must have been picked up by enemy radar, and we knew that after all this milling around we would meet enemy defenses fully alerted to our presence.

We turned south again. This time we were going down the right valley. My squadron was to be the second over the target. Ahead of the lead element of my squadron—that is, the three ships in my immediate formation—were six airplanes. We saw them spacing themselves the way they had been briefed. We slowed up. The first three ships headed straight down the valley, letting down fast to hit the deck as quickly

Philip Ardery, *Bomber Pilot: A Memoir of World War II* (Lexington, KY: The University Press of Kentucky, 1978), 96, 102–107. Used by permission.

as possible. The second element of three turned to the left for a few seconds and then turned back to the right to come in from the briefed angle. We spaced ourselves for a straight-on run over the same course as the first three ships. The bombs we carried were fused to allow sufficient delay so that all our ships could get over the target before the first bombs began blowing up. They were also fused so that if any rescue crews tried to enter the refinery after they were dropped and remove the fuses, they would blow up at once. This would, of course, prevent successful rescue work.

We were very close behind the second flight of three ships. As their bombs were dropping we were on our run in. There in the center of the target was the big boiler house, just as in the pictures we had seen. As the first ships approached the target we could see them flying through a mass of ground fire. It was mostly coming from ground-placed 20 mm. automatic weapons, and it was as thick as hail. The first ships dropped their bombs squarely on the boiler house and immediately a series of explosions took place. They weren't the explosions of thousand pound bombs, but of boilers blowing up and fires of split-open firebanks touching off the volatile gases of the cracking plant. Bits of the roof of the house blew up, lifting to a level above the height of the chimneys, and the flames leaped high after the debris. The second three ships went over coming in from the left, and dropped partly on the boiler house and partly on the cracking plant beyond. More explosions and higher flames. Already the fires were leaping higher than the level of our approach. We had gauged ourselves to clear the tallest chimney in the plant by a few feet. Now there was a mass of flame and black smoke reaching much higher, and there were intermittent explosions lighting up the black pall....

We found ourselves at the moment running a gauntlet of tracers and cannon fire of all types that made me despair of ever covering those last few hundred yards to the point where we could let the bombs go. The antiaircraft defenses were literally throwing up a curtain of steel. From the target grew the column of flames, smoke, and explosions, and we were headed straight into it....

As we were going into the furnace, I said a quick prayer. During those moments I didn't think that I could possibly come out alive....Bombs were away. Everything was black for a few seconds. We must have cleared the chimneys by inches. We must have, for we kept flying—and as we passed over the boiler house another explosion kicked our tail high and our nose down. Fowble pulled back on the wheel and the Lib leveled out, almost clipping the tops off houses. We were through the impenetrable wall....

My attention was drawn back to the task of self-preservation. We flew over part of the town of Campina after bombing. We could feel the heat inside the ship that resulted from flying over that furnace-like target with bomb bays open. The engineer in the top turret said he saw flames blown up into the bomb bay by the explosion that occurred as we went over, but we were not on fire. At that time there was no visible evidence of damage to our ship at all....

After we left the little town we passed over grain fields. The top of a big straw stack in front of us slid back and two Nazi gunners appeared there firing 20 mm. machine guns at us. I switched on my remote control guns and watcher their tracers spray out. The boys in the nose were firing their flexible guns, too, but I could see my fire going over the target. "Shove the nose down a little, Ed," I shouted. Just at that moment he saw what I was yelling about. He pushed forward on the wheel and kicked a little rudder back and forth and we saw a mass of tracers of all our forward firing guns splitting into the gun emplacement. The Jerries [Germans] stopped firing and fell beside their guns. Maybe they were dead; I hoped so. The brutality of heavy bombardment is highly impersonal. I was used to carrying out my mission four miles above the point of impact. It is difficult under those circumstances to get any feeling of injuring the enemy at all. But here I got the satisfying sensation of thinking I had stopped at least two of the maggots corrupting the body of Europe....

The sky was a bedlam of bombers flying in all directions, some actually on fire, many with smoking engines, some with great gaping holes in them or huge chunks of wing or rudder gone. Many were so riddled it was obvious their insides must have presented starkly tragic pictures of dead and dying, of men grievously wounded who would bleed to death before they could be brought any aid; pilots facing the horrible decision about what to do—whether to make a quick sacrifice of the unhurt in order to save the life of a dying man, or to fly a ship home and let some crew member pay with his life for the freedom of the rest.

By this time, with my mission accomplished, I had at last come to the point of being frightened for my own safety. Earlier I had reconciled myself to the probability that I would not return, and I was willing to stick by that decision. Funny, but when it seemed to me there was slight hope of my returning from a mission—as there had been in the beginning of this one—I didn't worry much. But when it appeared I had passed the point of greatest danger and thereafter stood a good chance to make it, I began to sweat it out in earnest.

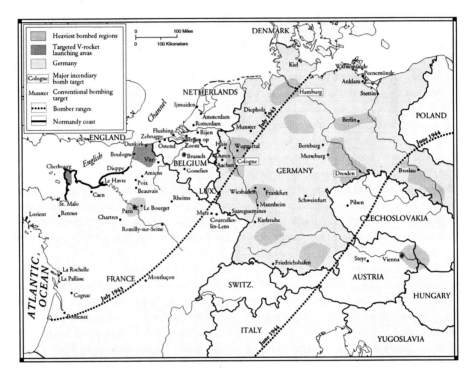

WESTERN EUROPE; STRATEGIC BOMBING

FLYING A B-17

Among the other vital targets American bombers sought to destroy were the massive concrete submarine pens in which U-boats took refuge upon their return from missions in the North Atlantic. Elmer Bendiner (1916–2001), a writer and journalist who served as a navigator, describes a typical mission to bomb the northern German port city of Wilhelmshaven. Although the rugged B-17 bombers in which he flew were heavily armed and well armored, they lacked fighter escorts on longer missions and had to struggle to their targets through heavy antiaircraft gunfire ("flak") and persistent attacks from faster, more mobile German fighter planes. Identifying and reaching the target under such conditions was difficult enough (especially if it was obscured by clouds or smoke), but then the planes had to deliver their payloads accurately and survive the long flight home.

The cold at 25,000 feet, our bombing altitude, penetrated through the fleece and wool to the toes. A chill crept up my sleeves and fastened icy fingers around my ribs. I checked and rechecked the course I would take if we had to fly home. When I felt secure in my mind that at that particular moment I knew precisely where we were and could get from there to anywhere else, I turned to scraping frost from my window....

I recall that not the hazard of fighters but only the penetrating cold seemed real to me.... I warned the cockpit several minutes ahead, of the time and degree of our turn. When I saw the lead group bank and swing from shadow into sun I scribbled the second into the log. On the horizon in the milky haze of morning fog I saw a shape materialize out of the water. It was Wanderooge. If we went over it there would be flak, according to the notes I had made at our morning lecture....

The interphone crackled: "Flak at six o'clock." I noted it and unslung my gun so that it hung free in my hand. Little black clouds materialized up ahead and tore themselves into ugly tatters. I felt the whoosh and, as *Tondelayo* reeled and plunged, I heard the *ping, ping, ping* like pebbles on a metal roof. I realized with a sense of shock that these were shrapnel fragments beating at the shell that held us 25,000 feet above the flatlands of Germany. The flak was coming from Cuxhaven, I thought, and I noted that as absolute fact. We were perhaps a little off course. I could see the Weser as it wound south of Bremerhaven, off the starboard wing, guiding us to Bremen.

A squawk from someone: "Fighters at nine o'clock." I rested my gun on the desk to note developments and saw that the gun was making a grease puddle on the log and the maps. The word "fighters" scrawled its way through the stain.

The convulsion of the turret gun blasting over my head filled the nose. I stopped writing and picked up my gun. The fighters coming in were each an inch of silver against the blue. They came in three abreast at eleven o'clock above the frosty patterns on the portside windows. The wings grew to two or three inches

---

Elmer Bendiner, *The Fall of Fortresses: A Personal Account of the Most Daring, and Deadly, American Air Battles of World War II* (New York: Putnam, 1980), 98–105. Used by permission.

and touched off little sparklers. Then they were no longer inches but massive aircraft, flipping over, spitting, and sliding down out of my gunsights, like gulls gliding down currents of air to the dull metallic sheen of the distant earth.

I pulled the trigger and sent a long burst into space. *Tondelayo*, in evasive action, seemed to jump and fall so that much of the time I was standing in air seeking to steady myself on the handlebars of my gun.

My charts were on the floor along with the dividers, the plotters and the other paraphernalia. I noted that we were flying straight on course. I noted the time that had elapsed from the turn into Germany. Cartridge shells littered the nose, and when I moved my feet I slipped on them. When I slipped I swore. When I swore I could feel the sweat on my forehead and marveled that a man could sweat and freeze simultaneously. In the close quarters of our plexiglass cabin, the sting of gunpowder and perhaps the smell of a fart mingled in my nostrils. . . .

Karlshofen was our initial point from which we would begin our straight-and-level bomb run to Bremen perhaps six minutes away. At Karlshofen it was quite obvious that we would not see Bremen that day. A bank of thick clouds, rising like mountains out of snowy plains, stretched before us. The armada wheeled and headed westward. Bremen would be spared.

Those unreal fighters, beautiful as swift arrows, came at us again in twos and threes. When a gunner called out from the waist or the tail or the belly turret that he had got one, I logged it for his record, but I couldn't say that I saw an enemy actually downed. From my vantage point I saw them only when they came head on, flashing, turning and exiting in marvelous choreography. The impersonal quality of the menace was eerie. It was as if I were in battle with beautiful birds of prey. I fired my gun and saw the tracers arch toward them inflicting no damage, causing no pain.

I saw death long before I saw pain. . . . There was a yellow flare on the outboard engine nearest me. The great silver ship banked sharply and turned its belly to the sun, which paled the yellow flames. There were no screams. The plane lost speed, slipped back and spiraled gently down. I saw a piece of wing shatter

and fly off like a target in a skeet shooting. The broken wing was jagged and flaming. The plane turned tail up, plummeted past my gun port and was no more.

A jangling splutter on my head set: "Plane going down." I acknowledged the report and noted it. I observed the time, place and altitude of each event in an indecipherable scrawl stained with grease and powder marks.

Silently planes were peeling out of that German sky and twisting past my window. I stood on tiptoe to follow them down. In the arctic chill my forehead dripped sweat onto my brows and my nose. I had just pulled aside the elephantine hose of my oxygen mask to tally the dimly seen curves of the Weser with those on my map when I heard an unfamiliar noise like the crunch of metal. Simultaneously I felt that someone had brushed against my helmet, knocking it slightly awry.

White fleecy cotton padding was fluttering around me as if a playful cat had ripped a pillow. Bob turned to me, and his eyes above his mask were clouded with concern. I waved cheerily, then followed his eyes to a jagged hole in the metal frame beneath my window. There *Tondelayo*'s skin had curled inward. I looked behind me to where the cat had ripped the pillow and followed the bullet's course to where it exited above and behind me into the wadding that cushioned the bulkhead. . . .

The shell that creased my helmet went on to pass through Johnny's rudder pedal, missing his foot narrowly as it had missed my head. . . . Holes were opening in the group's formation, but there was still a semblance of order in the ranks as we started our run to Wilhelmshaven. . . .

We saw only that Colonel Mo's ship was swooping to left and right, describing S turns in the sky, and that the 379th, in trying to follow him, was falling into a formless rout. We did not know that the lead plane of the group ahead of us had two of its engines blasted by flak and had slowed to a crawl over that landscape from which came bomb bursts and legions of Focke-Wulfs and Messerschmitts.

Mo was trying to avoid overrunning the group ahead of him. We were trying to avoid overrunning Mo, and so the group disintegrated. Battles had not been fought in tidy formations since the Crimean

War [Anglo-French vs. Russian conflict, 1853–1856, notable for the gallant but ill-fated charge of British cavalry, the Light Brigade], but we had been taught that strict formation flying was as vital to us as the British square had once been to the infantry. Not for us the anarchic whooping attack en masse. To be uncovered by a formation's friendly fire was to be naked and next to dead.

Seeing our ragged line zigzagging on a bomb run, the enemy came at us like wolves after straggling sheep. We had moved in so close to Colonel Mo that our wing tip was almost within reach of his waist gunner....

Bohn's tactic was to follow Mo as a chick follows its mother. We were tucked in so tight that our spent shells bounced off the wings of a B-17 beneath us. We could see that in the low group there was not a single plane that did not have at least one feathered prop.

When we came to the wide bay we saw the German smoke pots cloaking our target, Wilhelmshaven. Out of the smoke rose a storm of flak, rocking *Tondelayo*,

sending fragments through its metal skin, biting into her delicate electric nerves....

We could not bomb as a group but only in train, following the plane ahead, hoping to hit the submarine pens we could not see. The explosions billowed up above the veil of smoke, but we could not be sure of whether we were plastering the shipping, the bay, the harbor or the bistros, whorehouses, shops and homes of Wilhelmshaveners.

I had worked out a course for home, straight across the Helgoland Bight to the open sea and then on a dogleg to England.

Once we got past the archipelago that guarded Germany's North Sea coast, the fighters left us. We drew together in formation as geese do. No one on *Tondelayo* was wounded. But the plane itself had been riddled, and the hydraulic line was cut so that we had only mechanical brakes....

Even though *Tondelayo's* crew had lost no blood there was a silent, invisible hemorrhage that was beyond the healing power of our flight surgeon....

AREA BOMBING

How accurate was high-altitude bombing? The so-called Butt Report, an analysis of photographs of bomb damage taken after a series of British raids in the summer of 1941, suggested that it was not very accurate at all, that perhaps only about one-sixth of aircraft managed to drop their bombs within five miles of their intended target. Therefore, was the bombing campaign, the only significant way in which the British could strike at the German homeland, of any real use? Churchill's scientific advisor, Frederick Lindemann (1866–1957), ennobled as Lord Cherwell but widely known as "The Prof.," calculated that even if bombers rarely hit their exact and specific target (a factory or a refinery, for example), their bombs were not wasted so long as they fell in urban areas, destroying cities and demolishing homes. This "de-housing" effect was cited by proponents of "area bombing" who accepted the disruption of civilian life (and heavy casualties on the ground, including women and children) as a legitimate, indeed essential, military objective.

Min. Cherwell to Churchill, 30 March 1942. Circulated by the Prime Minister to Defence Committee on 9 April 1942 in Sir Charles Webster and Noble Frankland, *The Strategic Air Offensive against Germany, 1939–1943*, vol.1 (London: HMSO, 1961), 331–332. Crown copyright materials is reproduced with the permission of the Controller of HMSO and Queen's Printer for Scotland.

The following seems a simple method of estimating what we could do by bombing Germany:

Careful analysis of the effects of raids on Birmingham, Hull and elsewhere have shown that, on the average, 1 ton bombs dropped on a built-up area demolishes 20–40 dwellings and turns 100–200 people out of house and home.

We know from our experience that we can count on nearly 14 operational sorties per bomber produced. The average lift of the bombers we are going to produce over the next 15 months will be about 3 tons. It follows that each of these bombers will in its lifetime drop about 40 tons of bombs. If these are dropped on built-up areas they will make 4,000–8,000 people homeless.

In 1938 over 22 million Germans lived in 58 towns of over 100,000 inhabitants, which, with modern equipment, should be easy to find and hit. Our forecast output of heavy bombers (including Wellingtons) between now and the middle of 1943 is about 10,000. If even half the total load of 10,000 bombers were dropped on the built-up areas of these 58 German towns the great majority of their inhabitants (about one-third of the German population) would be turned out of house and home.

Investigation seems to show that having one's house demolished is most damaging to morale. People seem to mind it more than having their friends or even relatives killed. At Hull signs of strain were evident, though only one-tenth of the homes were demolished. On the above figures we should be able to do ten times as much harm to each of the 58 principal German towns. There seems little doubt that this would break the spirit of the people.

Our calculation assumes, of course, that we really get one-half of our bombs into built-up areas. On the other hand, no account is taken of the large promised American production (6,000 heavy bombers in the period in question). Nor has regard been paid to the inevitable damage to factories, communications etc. in these towns and the damage by fire, probably accentuated by breakdown of public services.

MASSACRE BY BOMBING

Oxford-educated writer, pacifist, and feminist Vera Brittain (1893–1970) was born in Newcastle-upon-Tyne, England. Although her wealthy paper manufacturer father disapproved of public roles for women, Brittain managed to persuade him to allow her to pursue a higher education at Oxford. Her learning, however, was briefly interrupted when she volunteered as a nurse during World War I. That experience and the increasing threat in the 1930s of another war left her a convinced pacifist. While Brittain, perhaps, is best known for her well-received three-volume autobiography, *Testament of Youth* (1933), *Testament of Friendship* (1940) and *Testament of Experience* (1957), it was *Seeds of Chaos*, a reprint of her vigorous rebuke of wartime civilian bombing published in 1944, that made her a controversial figure. Brittain steadfastly argued that the adoption of "saturation bombing" or "area bombing" by the British military in its war against Germany was tantamount to senseless slaughter and would not achieve the military's objective of ending

Vera Brittain, "Massacre by Bombing," *Fellowship*, pt. 2, vol. 10, no. 3 (March 1944), 50–51. Used by permission of Mark Bostridge and Timothy Brittain-Catlin, Literary Executors of the Vera Brittain Estate 1970.

the war. Her criticisms would take on added weight after the February 1945 incendiary bombing of Dresden, whose splendid baroque architecture and exquisite porcelain had been prized across Europe. Some 90 percent of the city center was burned in the firestorm and tens of thousands of civilians, including many hapless refugees who had fled there in the belief that the city's historic importance guaranteed that it would not be targeted. Harris and other Allied air commanders insisted on the city's military significance, given its various factories, command sites, and rail yards, and were determined to show the advancing Red Army what their bombers could do. Many observers, however, felt that the casualties and damage inflicted were disproportionate to the military results achieved, and, on viewing the incinerated corpses of victims, were moved to ask, as did Red Cross assistant Margaret Wolf after a similar raid on Chemnitz a month later, "if this is a man" (a reference to Primo Levi's book of the same title).

How much do the American and British people understand and approve of the policy of "obliteration bombing" now being inflicted by us upon the civilians of enemy and enemy-occupied countries, including numbers of young children born since the outbreak of war? The propagandist paragraphs in the press which describe this bombing and its results skillfully conceal their real meaning from the normally unimaginative reader by such carefully chosen phrases as *softening up an area, neutralizing the target, area bombing, saturating the defenses, and blanketing an industrial district.*

It is only when the facts are collected, and the terrible sum of suffering which they describe estimated as a whole, that we realize that, owing to our air raids, hundreds of thousands of helpless and innocent people in German, Italian, and German-occupied cities are being subjected to agonizing forms of death and injury comparable to the worst tortures of the Middle Ages.

From the extreme discomfort of this realization, the average citizen seeks to escape by two principal arguments.

BOMBING TO SHORTEN THE WAR

In the first place he maintains that mass bombing will "shorten the war," a contention now much favored by government officials and some leading churchmen.

To this there are several replies.

First, there is no *certainty* that such a shortening of the war will result, and nothing less than absolute certainty entitles even the most ardent of the war's supporters to use these dreadful expedients. Mr. Churchill himself has described the mass bombing of German cities as an "experiment." What does appear certain is the downward spiral in moral values, ending in deepest abysses of the human spirit, to which this argument leads. Those who remember the First World War will recall that precisely the same excuse—that it would "shorten" the period of hostilities—was given by the Germans for their policy of *Schrecklichkeit* (terror), and was used in connection with their submarine campaign. We refused to accept the argument as valid then or when the Nazis revived it in this war to justify the bombing of Warsaw, Rotterdam, Belgrade, London and Coventry.

Second, when the word "shorten" is used, it is generally meant to imply the limiting or reduction of the total amount of human suffering and destruction. Such a time test is misleading. In a vast, concentrated raid, lasting a few minutes, more persons may be killed or injured than in a modern major battle lasting two or three weeks, in addition to the destruction of an irreplaceable material heritage of buildings, art treasures and documents, representing centuries of man's creative endeavor. In fact, mass bombing of great centers of population represents a speedup of human slaughter, misery and material destruction superimposed on that of the military fighting fronts.

Third, the "experiment" has demonstrated, so far, that mass bombing does not induce revolt or break morale. Victims are stunned, exhausted, apathetic, absorbed in the immediate tasks of finding food and shelter. But as they recover who can doubt that there will be, among the majority at any rate, the desire for revenge and a hardening process, even if, for a time, it may be subdued by fear? Thus we are steadily creating in Europe the psychological foundations for a Third World War.

BOMBING FOR REVENGE

The second main argument brought forward to excuse our present policy of obliteration bombing is that we too have suffered—as indeed we have—and that therefore we are *fully entitled to pay back what we have endured.*

With this double contention George Bernard Shaw [prominent British literary figure] dealt characteristically in a letter to the *Sunday Express* (November 28, 1943): "The blitzing of the cities has carried war this time to such a climax of infernal atrocity that all recriminations on that score are ridiculous. The Germans will have as big a bill of atrocities against us as we against them if we take them into an impartial international court."

There are three further replies that should also be considered carefully by all rational people.

First, investigations into the origins of civilian bombing (as distinct from the bombing that forms part of a military campaign) make clear the difficulty of justly assessing with whom lay the fault of starting it. The cumulative growth of civilian bombing to its present nightmare stage seems, on present information, to be an outstanding instance of the tragic fashion in which wartime cruelty grows like a snowball by its own momentum once the power of Juggernaut has taken control. Some accidental violation of international law, assumed to be deliberate, is repaid by a reprisal "in kind." The enemy "hits back"; we retaliate harder still; in each case the accidental consequences (such as the bombing of a church in mistake for a factory) are advertised by the victim as intentional, for propaganda purposes. So the grim competition goes on until the mass murder of civilians becomes part of our policy, a descent into barbarism that we should have contemplated with horror in 1939.

Second, though parts of Britain suffered cruelly in the "Blitz," some of the terrible inventions and tactics now being used were not known or practiced at that stage of the war. Even in those early days the

knowledge of our distress and confusion was limited to the areas that endured them, and particularly to the surviving victims and to Civil Defense and rescue workers who actually had to deal with the shambles to which German bombs reduced many humble homes. It is, I believe, the comparative rarity of firsthand experience among the majority of the British and American people which accounts for the supine acquiescence in obliteration bombing....

Third, retaliation in kind and worse means the reduction of ourselves to the level of our opponents whose perverted values have persuaded us to fight. However anxious we may be to win the war, the *way* in which we win it will also determine our future standing as nations. If we imitate and intensify the enemy's methods, we shall actually have been defeated by the very evils which we believe ourselves to be fighting!

It is to the credit of some of the worst-bombed areas of England that many of their inhabitants have recognized this vital truth. In April, 1941, when the British Institute of Public Opinion carried out a survey of the whole country's response to the question: "Would you approve or disapprove if the RAF adopted a policy of bombing the civilian population in Germany?" it was noticeable that *the people of the heavily bombed areas were less in favour of reprisal bombing than those who had escaped the raid.* The largest vote in favour of reprisals (76 per cent of the population) came from the safe areas of Cumberland, Westmorland, and the North Riding. In the bombed areas of London, which had then endured eight months of heavy and continuous raids, 47 per cent disapproved of reprisals, 45 per cent approved, and the rest were undecided....

"I wouldn't wish this trouble on any other woman!" cries the young mother in A. Burton Cooper's Lancashire play, *We are the People,* after her small boy has been blown to pieces by a daylight bomb on a local playground. And that, I believe, is the normal reaction of every decent person, once real knowledge has come to him or her through individual suffering....

Only when you know these facts are you in a position to say whether or not you approve. If you do not approve, it is for you to make known your objection, *remembering always that it is the infliction of suffering far more than its endurance, which morally damages the soul of the nation....*

The adoption of area bombing has been marked by many new developments that have increased the terror and torture of our raids....

The destruction of Hamburg, between July 24 and August 2, 1943, like the later mass attacks on Berlin may testify to our capacity to win the war, but it also provides irrefutable evidence of the moral and spiritual abyss into which we have descended.

In eight heavy raids during ten days and nights, a total of about 10,000 tons of high explosives and incendiaries was dropped on this city of 1,800,000 inhabitants, completely destroying nine square miles or 77 per cent of the built-up area (*Daily Telegraph*, Sept. 20, 1943)....

A Danish consular official, interviewed by the Stockholm newspaper *Aftonbladet* after he had escaped from the blitzed city, said:

"Hamburg has ceased to exist. I can only tell you what I saw with my own eyes—district after district razed to the ground. When you drive through Hamburg you drive through corpses. They are all over the streets, and even in tree-tops."...

Other reports stated that owing to the great heat of the fires, people died from suffocation in shelters, and on September 20 this was confirmed in the following (translated) article by the editor of the *Baseler Nachrichten* (Basle News).

This article describes how, as a result of a physical phenomenon produced by a mass fire during one of the Hamburg raids, many more persons perished in a few hours than the total of air raid victims in London since the beginning of the war:

It must be emphasized that the effect was one which can only be achieved when bombing densely populated residential districts....[E]very open fire sucks in the oxygen it needs from the surrounding atmosphere, and that large fires, unless there is a strong wind, will lead to the creation of so-called air chimneys up which the flames will rush with ever-increasing force. If the area of the fire covers several square kilometres, then the flames licking out of individual rows and blocks of houses will combine into one big blanket of fire, covering the entire area and rushing up to ever greater heights. According to English reports, the Hamburg fire reached a height of six kilometres, that is, up to that height the heat rose in one compact body....The streets serve as channels through which the air passes toward the center and at the same time the air rushing through the streets sucks the flames from the burning houses horizontally into the streets. Thus, human beings and flames will compete for the available oxygen and, naturally, a fire of this size will get the better of it. The flames suck the last remains of oxygen from all rooms, shelters and cellars, and at the same time devour all the oxygen in the streets....

The condition of the cellar shelters, which have meanwhile been opened, give some indication of the temperature which must have prevailed in the streets. The people who remained in these rooms were not only suffocated and charred but reduced to ashes.... It appears, therefore, that the air war in this form can indeed turn entire districts of a large city, and, above all, the residential quarter of workers and employees, into a fiery grave which no one can escape who has not the courage to flee in the early stages through the rain of phosphorous, high explosive and incendiary bombs.

U-BOAT PERIL

"The only thing that really frightened me during the war," recalled Winston Churchill, "was the U-boat peril." Britain had faced the threat of German submarines to its seaborne lifelines during World War I and managed to survive, in part because the individual primitive vessels proved no match for the introduction of the convoy system, whereby massed merchant ships sailed together with an escort of warships. In World War II, however, the German U-boats were more sophisticated and were employed more effectively, grouped together in "wolfpacks" with sufficient strength to chase, attack, and disrupt British convoys. In the "happy days" early in the war, German submarines seemed set to solve the basic equation of Britain's survival: could they sink more merchant tonnage than Britain could launch itself or procure elsewhere, and thereby steadily starve Britain into submission? Churchill had every right to be frightened. But by May 1943, Allied countermeasures turned the tide in their favor. U-boats had earlier sought refuge in the central North Atlantic's "air gap," an area beyond the range of any Allied land-based planes where submarines could surface to recharge their batteries and refresh their stale air without fear of aerial attack. It was no longer a safe haven. Longer ranged planes, light escort carriers, effective hunter-killer tactics, and broken German naval codes all enabled British, Canadian, and American forces to hunt and kill the German wolfpacks. In the end, more German submarines were sunk from the air than by naval vessels, and nine of every ten U-boats never returned to port. Herbert Werner was among the minority of submariners who did survive; he joined the service at age nineteen and served upon five different boats, making several harrowing escapes from near certain destruction. His account here details the point at which the fortunes of the submarine war shifted decisively in favor of the Allies.

May 12. 0716: I swung into the seat. Seven miles on port I saw an amazing panorama. The entire horizon as far as I could see was covered with vessels, their funnels and masts as thick as a forest. At least a dozen fast destroyers cut the choppy green sea with elegance. As many as two dozen corvettes flitted around the edges of the convoy....

0915: U-230 surfaced. Mounting the bridge while the deck was still awash, I took a hurried look in a circle. Far to the northeast, mastheads and funnels moved along the sharp line which divided the ocean from the sky. U-230 forged through the sea, parallel to the convoy's track, in an attempt to reach a forward position before dusk. Riedel flashed the message of our contact to Headquarters and the other wolves in the ambush: CONVOY BD 92 COURSE NORTHEAST ELEVEN KNOTS. STRONG DEFENSE. REMAIN SURFACED FOR ATTACK. U-230.

0955: A startled cry at my back, *"Flugzeug!!"* [airplane]

I saw a twin-engined plane dropping out of the sun. The moment of surprise was total.

"Ala rrr mmm!" We plunged head over heels into the conning tower. The boat reacted at once and shot

Herbert A. Werner, *Iron Coffins: A Personal Account of the German U-Boat Battles of World War II* (New York: Holt, Reinhart & Winston, 1969), 119–126. Used by permission.

below surface. At this moment of our maximum danger and minimum ability to act, our lives depended upon a miracle, an accident, or the good luck that had so far saved us from extinction.

Four short, ferocious explosions shattered the water above and around us. The boat trembled and fell at a 60-degree angle. Water splashed, steel shrieked, ribs moaned, valves blew, deck-plates jumped, and the boat was thrown into darkness. As the lights flickered on, I saw astonishment in the round eyes of the men. They had every right to be astounded: the attack out of the sun was a complete mystery. Where had the small plane come from? It did not have the range to fly a round-trip between the nearest point of land and the middle of the Atlantic. The conclusion was inescapable that the convoy launched its own airplanes. It seemed highly likely, though we did not want to believe it, that the planes returned to convoy and landed on an aircraft carrier. The idea of a convoy with its own air defense smashed our basic concept of U-Boat warfare. No longer could we mount a surprise attack or escape without meeting savage counterattacks.

1035: U-230 came up to periscope depth. A careful check with our "skyscope," an instrument similar to the periscope, revealed no aircraft. We surfaced at high speed.

The hunt went on. We pressed forward obstinately, with that terrible constriction in the stomach....

1110: I detected a glint of metal between the clouds. It was a small aircraft, and it was diving into the attack. "Alarrmmm!"

Fifty seconds later, four explosions nearby taught us that the pilot was a well-trained bombardier. Shock waves rocked boat and crew. Friedrich, struggling to prevent the boat from sinking, caught her at 180 meters, balanced her out, and brought her up to periscope depth....

1208: A call from below reached us on the bridge: "Message for Captain, signal just received: ATTACKED BY AIRCRAFT. SINKING. U-89." Again we were stunned. With a shudder, I pictured what would happen to us, once our own hull was cracked....

1638: Up periscope. Then: "Tubes one to five stand ready." "Tubes one to five are ready," I answered quickly, then held my breath.

Siegmann swiveled around to check the opposite side. Suddenly he cried, "Down with the boat, Chief, take her down for God sake, destroyer in ramming position! Down to two hundred meters!

I fully expected the bow of a destroyer to cut into the conning tower momentarily. As the boat swiftly descended, the harrowing sound of the destroyer's engines and propellers hit the steel of our hull. It grew so fast, and echoed so deafeningly, that we were all unable to move. Only our boat was moving, and she went downward much too slowly to escape the blow.

An earshattering boom ruptured the sea. A spread of six depth charges lifted the boat, tossed her out of the water, and left her on the surface at the mercy of four British destroyers. The screws of U-230 rotated in highest revolutions, driving us ahead. For seconds there was silence. For seconds the British were baffled and stunned. After a whole eternity, our bow dipped and the boat sank—and sank.

A new series of exploding charges lifted our stern with a mighty force. Our boat, entirely out of control, was catapulted toward the bottom five miles below. Tilted at an angle of 60 degrees, U-230 tumbled to 250 meters before Friedrich was able to reverse her fall. Floating level at a depth of 230 meters, we thought we were well below the range of the enemy's depth charges. U-230 was speedily rigged to withstand pursuit. Once again we were condemned to sit it out in crushing depths....

1716: A new spread deafened us and took our breath away. The boat listed sharply under the shattering blow. The steel knocked and shrieked and valves were thrown into open position. The shaft packings leaked, and a constant stream of water soon filled the aft bilge. Pumps spouted, the periscope packings loosened, and water trickled into the cylinders. Water everywhere. Its weight forced the boat deeper into the depths. In the meantime, the convoy crawled in a thunderous procession over our boat....

2000: The new group launched its first attack, then another, and another. We sat helpless 265 meters below. Our nerves trembled. Our bodies were stiff from cold, stress, and fear. The mind-searing agony of waiting made us lose any sense of time and any desire for food. The bilges were flooded with water, oil, and urine. Our washrooms were under lock and key; to use them then could have meant instant death, for the tremendous outside pressure would have acted in reverse of the expected flow. Cans were circulated for the men to use to relieve themselves. Added to the stench of waste, sweat and oil was the stink of the battery gases. The increasing humidity condensed on the cold steel, dropped into the bilges, dripped from pipes, and soaked our clothes. By midnight, the Captain realized that the British would not let up in their bombardment, and he ordered the distribution of potash cartridges to supplement breathing. Soon every man was equipped with a large metal box attached to his chest, a rubber hose leading to his mouth, and a clamp on his nose. And still we waited....

May 13. 0400: The boat has fallen to 275 meters. We had been under assault for 12 hours and there was no sign of relief. This day was my birthday and I wondered whether it would be my last. How many chances could one ask for?...

2000: The air was thick and even more so as we breathed it through the hot cartridges. The devil seemed to be knocking on our steel hull as it creaked and contracted under the enormous pressure.

2200: The barrage increased in violence as dust closed in on surface. Wild attacks at shorter intervals indicated that the enemy had lost his patience.

May 14. By midnight, we had approached the limit for boat and crew. We had reached a depth of 280 meters and the boat was still sinking. I dragged myself through the isle, pushing and tossing men around, forcing them to stay awake. Whoever fell asleep might never be awakened.

0310: A thunderous spread rattled down, but without effect. We were closer to being crushed by the mounting pressure than by the exploding canisters. As the echo of the last blast slowly subsided, something else attracted our attention. It was the thrashing of retreating propellers. For a long time we listened to the fading sound, unable to believe that the Tommys had given up the hunt.

0430: For over an hour there was silence....Using the last of our compressed air and battery power, the Chief managed to lift the overloaded boat meter by meter....U-230 broke through to air and light. We pushed ourselves up to the bridge. Around us spread the infinite beauty of night, sky, and ocean. Stars glittered brilliantly and the sea breathed gently. The moment of rebirth was overwhelming. A minute ago, we could not believe that we were alive; now we could not believe that death had kept his finger on us for 35 gruesome hours.

GERMANY'S U-BOAT STRATEGY

In the two decades before World War I, Germany under Admiral Tirpitz had embarked on building a massive surface fleet to challenge Britain's Royal Navy for naval supremacy. For most of the war, however, the German battleships remained bottled up in port, and the one major but inconclusive surface battle (Jutland in May 1916) did not break the British blockade. That mediocre record, coupled with Germany's geographic position, meant that when Germany rearmed in the 1930s, the fleet came a distant third in the competition for resources with the army and air force. A grandiose naval building program (Plan Z) resulted in the construction of a few fine capital ships (including the famous battleships *Bismarck* and *Tirpitz*) and a number of submarines, but had been predicated on war breaking out several years later. As a result, the German navy was not well prepared for war. Its commanders continuously pleaded for a bigger share of the military budget, and at this conference with Hitler, Admiral Karl Dönitz (the fleet's commander-in-chief) outlined the strategy that, if supported by massive new submarine construction, he believed Germany could win the war in the West. But the focus of the German war effort lay elsewhere— against Russia to the east, and on land no less—and the navy would never get U-boats in the decisive numbers they demanded.

1. The C.-in-C., Navy, reports.—The submarine losses in February amounted to 19. In March 15 and, so far, in April 16 ships were sunk. These losses are high. Submarine warfare is difficult. However, it is obvious, that the aim of sinking merchant ships must be to sink more than the enemy can build. If we do not reach this objective, the enemy would continue to suffer severely through loss of his material substance, but we would not be successful in bleeding him to death due to diminution of his tonnage. I therefore fear that the submarine war will be a failure if we do not sink more ships than the enemy is able to build. I believe that the enemy could not stand an overall loss of 100,000–200,000 tons per month for any length of time. Both Germany, with her submarines, E-boats, and Air Force, and her allies, Japan and Italy, must exert every possible effort to achieve this objective.

A situation must not be allowed to arise where we must blame ourselves for not having defeated the enemy because we did not put forth a little more effort and press home the attack against merchant shipping. In this course, many more submarines are required today to achieve what one U-boat could accomplish in 1940. We must therefore increase our submarine building programme as much as our shipyard capacity permits, so that the proportion between losses and new ships does not become too unfavorable. The C.-in-C., Navy, herewith submits the proposed plan for the increase in our submarine building programme. *The Fuehrer* fully agrees with the C.-in-C., Navy. An increase in the submarine building programme must be made possible.

2. Supporting his contentions with maps, the C.-in-C., Navy, explains that it is a matter of life and

"Minutes of the Conference between the C.-in-C., Navy, and the Führer on April 11, 1943, at the Berghof," in J. P. Showell, ed., *Führer Conferences on Naval Affairs, 1934–1945* (Annapolis: Naval Institute Press, 1990), 316–318. Used by permission.

death for us to maintain our supply lines and our foreign trade. The protection of this ocean traffic is very much endangered because it has to be accomplished with comparatively small forces. The available protection is definitely not able to cope with the increasing attacks of the enemy. These attacks, however, must be anticipated, because the enemy's material is constantly increasing. Besides, some day we will have to expect a stronger attack against our shipping lanes by forces which will be released from some other theatre. When that happens we will no longer be in a position to give this protection with our meager forces. We cannot permit our lines of communication to be broken. Tunis should be a warning to us. Anticipating this danger, we should do everything possible at this time to speed up the building programme of our defence forces, because the realization of such a plan will take a long time. Besides, any extension of our sphere of influence in Europe...will certainly increase our supply problem.

The C.,-in-C., Navy presented a chart, to explain the proposed increase in the building programme....The

problem remains: Where can the steel be obtained? To be sure, in a totalitarian state he could order that the required amount be made available, but that would mean exacting it from some other arm. The pressing needs of the Army for tanks and anti-tank guns, and of the Air Force for A.A. [antiaircraft] guns, etc., would not permit this over a period of time. He feels that the Army should be equipped with the newest type of weapons in sufficient quantities to prevent excessive loss of life. In order not to lose the war in the air, the material of our Air Force should be increased enormously. Finally, the Navy must receive sufficient material not only to prevent the submarine warfare from falling off, but rather to increase its effectiveness. Something also must be done for the Merchant Marine in order to help solve the supply problem. To this end Minister Speer and Messrs. Roechling and Duisberg were ordered to take part in a conference with him during the next few days to discuss the question of increasing the steel production from 2.6 to 4 million tons per month.

THE FALL OF MUSSOLINI

Writer Iris Origo, neé Cutting, was born in 1902 to a wealthy American father and English mother. In accordance with her dying father's wishes, her mother raised her in Italy where they lived in a Renaissance villa near Florence. Iris later married Antonio Origo, an aristocratic cavalry officer and artist, the illegitimate son of a marquis, and settled down with him on a rural estate called La Foce, where they worked the land. During World War II she not only attended to the needs of her agricultural workers and their families but also helped to save individuals who were fleeing Italian fascism. Mussolini's government collapsed in July 1943, he himself was dismissed by the monarch, Victor Emmanuel III, and then arrested. His successor, Marshal Badoglio, publicly reiterated Italy's commitment to fight as an ally of Germany, but he secretly concluded an armistice with the Allies in September 1943. The first Axis power had fallen. The following excerpt, taken from Origo's memoirs, reveals the euphoria but also the confusion and trepidation that Italians felt upon Mussolini's fall from power on July 23, 1943.

July 24th

[T]he city is full of rumours: the coup d'état is at last about to take place. It is said that at Mussolini's recent interview with Hitler, the latter demanded, as the condition of his sending reinforcements, that the conduct of the war in Italy should be handed over entirely to the German Command, and the whole of Southern Italy (including Rome) abandoned; the first line of defence to be on the Apennines [mountain range along the 'spine' of Italy], and the second on the Po [river in northern Italy].

July 26th

The long-expected news has come at last: Mussolini has fallen. The news was given by radio last night, but we did not hear it until this morning. Mussolini has resigned, the King has appointed Marshal Badoglio [field marshal who led Italian attack on Abyssinia, and as prime minister after Mussolini, accepted an armistice with the Allies] in his place and has himself taken over the command of the Army. A proclamation of Badoglio's announces: "Italy will keep her pledge; the war continues."...

'Have you heard: After twenty years—after twenty years....' We all have a lump in our throat. Hope—perplexity—anxiety—doubt—then hope again—infinite relief. A weight has been lifted, a door opened; but where does it lead? We spend the day in speculation, fed by driblets of news. First a proclamation of martial law, with the institution of a curfew at sunset and a prohibition of any public meetings: moreover, it is forbidden to carry firearms or to circulate in any private vehicle; a few hours later we hear with delight of the disbanding of the Fascist militia: its members are to be incorporated in the regular Army. In the evening comes the list of the new Cabinet; mostly permanent officials or under-secretaries. It is clearly to be a moderate, traditional government of administrators, not of 'great men.' Italy has had enough heroes. But still innumerable questions are unanswered. What has happened to Mussolini and his satellites? And above all—increasingly with every hour—what about Germany?

July 27th

Slowly, some of these questions are answered—though not the most important. To-day's papers publish, without comment, the motion…that brought about the end of Fascism.…[I]t is a more complete and ignominious recantation of the Fascist doctrine than any that could have been composed by its enemies. In it the Fascist leaders recognize that in order to obtain 'the moral and political unity of all Italians in this grave and decisive hour' it is necessary to proceed to an immediate restoration of all the functions of the State, 'restoring to the Crown, the Grand Council, the Government, the Parliament and the Corporations all the duties and responsibilities by our constitutional laws.'

In consequence the Council moved that the Prime Minister, Mussolini, should hand over the military command to the King. With this motion—affirming, as it does, the necessity, in a time of crisis, of returning to constitutional government—the Fascist doctrine stands condemned by its own adherents. Mussolini, like all other dictators, is betrayed by his own men.

July 28th

To-day fuller details reach us. It appears that when Grandi (of whom Mussolini had been jealous and suspicious for a long time) presented his motion to the assembled Grand Council, Mussolini drew forth a voluminous dossier of the error and misdeeds of his lieutenants during the past twenty years. These, he stated, he had suppressed until now, but would now make public. A 'discussion' took place which lasted ten hours and ended with a vote of nineteen to seven, in favour of Grandi's motion. Meanwhile, all over the city the news had spread that something was afoot. At three a.m. on Sunday morning the long black police cars which had brought the Fascists to Palazzo Venezia drove away again, and the anxious satellites (industrial magnates, financiers, politicians, diplomats, and smart young women) who had been waiting anxiously all night in the hall of the Excelsior, were called

to the telephone or to the houses of their friends. By dawn, the news began to spread all over the city; in the afternoon, Mussolini went to Villa Savoia, and before evening he and his friends were under arrest, while the broadcast at ten-forty-five announced his fall and the King's proclamation. The next morning a great crowd of working people from all the outlying quarters surged into the centre of the city and made its way to the Quirinal, singing.…They broke into all the offices and club-rooms of the Fascio; destroyed every bust and statue of Mussolini, set fire to the offices of the Messagero and the Tever and carried in triumph on their shoulders any officers of the regular Army that they encountered. The only bloodshed was at the Viminale, where some of the militia fired into the crowd—whereupon the Carabiniere fired back, killing several Blackshirts. Similar demonstrations took place in Milan, Turin, Bologna, Florence—with the result that by eleven o'clock on Monday morning a special broadcast issued a firm order of Badoglio's, that all public meetings and processions would be dispersed by the police. 'This is no moment to give way to impulsive demonstrations. The gravity of the hour requires from each one of us discipline and patriotism, dedicated to the supreme interests of the nation."

Meanwhile we listen-in eagerly to the foreign broadcasts, for comments from abroad. The first statement of the news from Germany affirms that Mussolini has resigned 'on account of his health' and subsequent statements refrain from any comment whatever, merely emphasizing Badoglio's affirmation: 'The war goes on." What lies beneath this restraint?…

July 30th

Yesterday, at the first meeting of the new Cabinet, the *Camera dei Fasci e delle Corporazioni* was officially dissolved. No political parties may be formed and no political activities are to be permitted, until four months after the end of the war, when a constitutional parliament will again be elected. For the present, Italy remains under martial law.

Simultaneously comes the news that the liberation of political prisoners has begun.…

V., arriving from Ferrara, brings tales of rioting in some of the northern cities. In Milan, he says, many

Fascists have been killed or beaten up by their old enemies; there is still shooting in the streets.... There have been similar incidents in Turin, Bologna, Genoa and Florence—and numerous strikes in factories, where the workmen refuse to go on working under Fascist foremen. The Fascist Party secretaries throughout Italy have been arrested—partly for their own protection—and the prefects are under temporary arrest in their own homes.

A broadcast this morning warns the Italian people to mistrust 'false and unfounded rumours of sensational events, which are evidently being spread by irresponsible and unpatriotic individuals, who wish to create a disturbance of the peace.' These rumours—as they have reached us here—include the suicide of Hitler and the desertion to the Russians of the thirty Italian divisions in the Balkans....

July 31st

The papers announce that all railway and post-office employees are to be 'militarized.' All Fascist provincial secretaries, vice-secretaries and *squadristi* are to be called to the colours—this last a most popular measure.

Demonstrations in the various towns continue, and to-day the B.B.C. [British Broadcasting Corporation] (quoting the Swiss papers as its authority) affirms that they are not only against Fascism, but for peace....

Undoubtedly the majority of the Italian people *do* want peace, but how many, in order to obtain it, are prepared to break with Germany and to submit passively to Allied occupation I have no idea.

August 1st

To-day the B.B.C. announces that the lull which has lasted since July 25th is over: the bombing of Italy will begin again. Throughout the night Radio Algiers has broadcast this news to the Italian people, warning them to keep away from factories producing war material, and from airports, railways, etc. So now we are once again expectant....

THE POLISH RESISTANCE

Resistance within Poland was among the most effective and sophisticated in occupied Europe, and was lent a particular urgency by the brutality of the German occupiers and their undisguised contempt for the Polish civilians they felt to be an inferior species. A well-developed Polish resistance network scored a number of major successes and provided the Allies with important information on the development of the Holocaust and of the V-2 rocket program (the first of which the Allies ignored, the second to which they responded by bombing rocket installations at Peenemünde on the Baltic). Much vital information was transmitted by courageous couriers such as Jan Nowak (1913–2001), who traveled at great personal risk both within Poland and to London to keep the Polish government-in-exile and British officials informed. Nowak himself had been born Zdzislaw Jezioranski, been captured by the Germans, escaped, and adopted a pseudonym to avoid subsequent detection. The Action N he refers to (N for *Niemcy*, the Polish word for Germany) was a clever counterfeiting operation whereby the Polish resistance prepared leaflets written and printed in German, ostensibly by disaffected German soldiers, predicting the defeat of the Nazis. These would be left in trains and waiting rooms frequented by the German military to sow distrust and lower morale.

...Action N was in the development stage. For the moment there was quite an efficient distribution network in Warsaw and in the *General Gouvernement*. The Germans, having occupied Poland, had incorporated all the western provinces into the Reich. In the center they created a state that they called the *General Gouvernement*, which was like a vast cage for about 12 million Polish people, completely surrounded by closed and well-guarded frontiers. Poles had no right to cross the frontiers, and crossing permits were issued only those special cases in which the journey of a Pole was in the German interest. Although the leaflets were dropped in trains going to Germany and back or were sent by mail, the lack of distribution outside the *General Gouvernement* area would sooner or later lead to the exposure of the scheme. Action N foresaw an extension of its activities both to the west (the lands which had been incorporated into the Reich itself) and to the east, the area which included the Eastern Front....

Action N must remain unknown not only to the Germans but also to the Polish community and even...[the] intelligence service.

The next meeting was held in my room on the top floor of 6 Krolewska Street....That time Leszek brought with him a girl known as "Black Janka," a short, shapely brunette, who was to maintain contact between him and me. From then on each day Janka would appear and produce the secret mail from a capacious bag. She was highly intelligent and consistently cheerful but, alas, hopelessly unpunctual—always late and on each occasion shamelessly blaming someone else for it. She was Jewish, so being on the Warsaw streets from morning till night with compromising documents required special courage.

Jan Nowak, *Courier from Warsaw* (Detroit: Wayne State University Press, 1982), 69–71. Used by permission.

I started work with great enthusiasm. What was required was not the dropping of Action N literature at random or through friends: a troop of couriers had to be found and conditions created for safe and frequent crossing of the frontier in both directions. It was also necessary to build up, in the western territories, a network of safe people who could handle distribution in their areas or pass material into the Reich. This effort necessitated frequent journeys.

I began by meeting a representative of "The Dairy," a cell that supplied people with false documents. I needed a certain number of frontier permits called *Durchlaßscheine* empowering the bearer to cross the frontier between the *General Gouvernement* and the Reich. At the outset I suffered a disappointment. The real documents, produced in Germany, had watermarks which could not be counterfeited. The false papers produced by the Dairy were such bad forgeries that they gained the nickname "passes to a better world." As for military documents, they obviously could only be used by people who spoke fluent German.

"What documents are used by the intelligence?" I asked.

"That you will never learn. Everybody guards his own secrets. Otherwise one piece of bad luck could start a chain reaction."

I knew that hundreds of smugglers were crossing the frontier daily in both directions, and I decided to find out for myself how they did it. It was not too difficult to establish contact with the smugglers. To mask my real intentions I provided myself with several cartons of cigarettes. If I were caught, the Germans would think that they had a smuggler.

My guide across the frontier was a young girl. In order to make a crossing to the nearest village beyond the frontier one had to wait until the German patrols changed at lunchtime. Our expedition took place in a group quite widely spread out but maintaining visual contact. At a given signal my companion rose from the ground and, although burdened by a rucksack full of goods, started running through a wood with the speed of an Olympic champion. Following her, and completely winded, I reached the appointed hut on the other side. Hardly had I caught my breath than the owner of the hut rushed in shouting "Raid in the village—get out into the potatoes!"

In one jump I was outside. From the threshold he added a warning: "Crawl, don't run! The bastards have field glasses!" Luckily the potato field came right up to the walls of the hut. I crawled slowly on my belly as far into it as I could. I had been told not to move until I heard that the raid was over.

I stayed there until darkness fell. During the night, again with the smuggler's help, I returned in the same way safely to the other side of the frontier. There was no question of penetrating deeper into the Reich. The "game" for which the Germans were hunting was myself. It was quite simple. Through their field glasses the Germans had noticed somebody in city clothes, while most smugglers were peasants or workers from the suburbs of Warsaw and wore quite different things.

GREECE AT WAR

Greece entered the war when it was invaded by Italian forces in October 1940. The Italian dictator, Mussolini, had, with a characteristic lack of foresight, impulsively decided to attack in the mistaken belief that Greece would fall easily to his troops and that the ensuing glorious victory would confirm him as a man to be reckoned with on the international scene. In fact, the poorly prepared Italians were decisively repulsed by the Greek army, forcing Hitler to send German divisions to the aid of his fascist ally and postpone Operation Barbarossa against the Soviet Union (indeed, some historians have suggested that the delay made all the difference, assuming that the Germans could have captured Moscow before the onset of winter weather). The German invasion of April 1941 succeeded where the Italians had failed, breaching the Greek defenses and forcing the king, George II, into exile. In the resulting political vacuum, the invaders imposed a brutal occupation over parts of the country, while the local economy virtually collapsed in the face of shortages and astronomical price inflation. Resistance was widespread, though it was divided between the communist National Liberation Front (EAM and its military wing, ELAS) and the non-communist National Republican Greek League (EDES). In each case, it was armed guerilla bands which harried German forces, disrupted communications, and mobilized Greek civilians against the occupation. Faced with all they could handle against Rommel in North Africa, the British government would not commit an army to liberate Greece, but sent small teams to help organize the anti-Nazi resistance. They were dispatched with the aim of not only arming and encouraging the guerillas, but also of ensuring that in the political chaos that would likely follow the war's end, it would not be the communists who rode to power. J. M. Stevens (1913–1973), a British commando, parachuted into Greece in March 1943 in order to review the situation and report back to his government. What follows is taken from his report on conditions in central Greece, prepared in June 1943.

The most striking feature of Free Greece to-day is its safety. It is perfectly safe to move about alone and unarmed in practically all of Free Greece, except in north West Macedonia where Comitajis wander at night shooting up Antartes, and in Western Epirus where the Chams indulge in the same sport....

Travel is normally on foot or by mule or donkey and is painfully slow, especially as changing animals involves regularly a delay of two to four hours....The ELAS have several cars and motor cycles which are in constant use. There appears to be no great difficulty in obtaining petrol.

The Postal services no longer function except through the organizations. Each has its couriers who are intercepted where possible by the rival organizations. Most letters are read en route. The telephone system works in many areas but is not continuous throughout Free Greece....

The villages cannot differ much in appearance from peacetime. The war has deprived them of

Lars Bærentzen, ed., *British Reports on Greece 1943–44*, by J.M. Stevens, C.M. Woodhouse and D.J. Wallace, (Museum Tusculanum Press, University of Copenhagen, 1982), 28–33. Used by permission.

remarkably little. The small towns such as Karpenisi and Grevena, have a very dilapidated untidy appearance due to difficulty in obtaining paint and glass and the fatalistic attitude of the population that it is not worth while repairing places which will be bombed or burnt on the morrow.

The countryside bears many scars of war in the villages burnt or smashed by the Axis. Some have been completely razed to the ground, others partially. In every case, great hardship has been caused and the population have either fled to the mountains or else built themselves shacks in near-by woods. This systematic policy of burning houses, coupled with the seizure of hostages if found, has caused the whole-sale burying of valuables and furniture. In villages near the Axis troops, the villagers spend every night outside their village so as not to be caught by surprise during the night.

Shops still exist, except in small towns, have little to sell and what they have is practically all from peace-time stocks. Besides shops, there are many itinerant black-marketeers and weekly markets at which these congregate....Much comes from the Axis, who will sell most things in return for food.

All major business is at a standstill. Banks are closed. Most were looted by EAM who also emptied the Post Office Savings Bank.

The food situation is not wholly bad. For the rich man it is possible to live quite sufficiently. Meat, bread, butter, cheese, eggs, milk, honey, dried and fresh fruit, and vegetables, are all procurable at present but prices are very high and it requires much coming and going of black-marketeers to fill one's larder. The chief deficiencies are sugar, coffee, and oil.

The civilian population are content with much less and, provided they have enough bread, they seem satisfied....

The civil population are adequately clad except those villages whose belongings have been looted and burnt by the Axis. These conditions are pitiful to see, with almost everyone in rags. However, the relief scheme for these villages is now under way....

Whereas foreign news is given wide circulation, international news travels very slowly....

As a result, there is a wide gulf between Athens and Salonika on the one hand and the mountains on the other. There is also wonderful scope for rumour. Turkey enters the war once a week and the Antartes perform the most ludicrous feats of daring....

The Church has to a certain extent maintained an independent attitude in all these convulsions. It is not attacked by the EAM as a body, though certain Bishops are accused of collaborating with the Axis. It is generally admitted the Church has stood out during the occupation in condemning the Axis and in supporting the freedom movements. This is especially true of the Archbishop of Athens and the Bishops of Kyme and Kozani. The latter resides permanently in Free Greece and supports EAM wholeheartedly, not without an eye to future promotion....

Of the occupation forces, the Italians are the most hated. This is not surprising as after the Albanian war there is no Greek who does not profoundly despise them and regard their participation in the occupation as an insult. But what has really intensified this present hatred was their behaviour in the early stages of the occupation. A village to village search for arms was carried out in conditions of extreme brutality. In this the Italians were assisted by Greek informers but especially by Vlachs and Roumanians. Not only in their searches for arms but also in the casual visits by Italian soldiery to villages for food, they showed an infinite capacity for barbarity and looting. Thus the famous Meteora monasteries near Kalambaka were stripped of their treasures "by Christians after the Turks had left them for centuries," so the Greeks remarked.

The Italians did their best to provoke Antartes and in the end succeeded. The second phase of the Italian treatment of the civil population proved more savage than the first. When they suffered various defeats at the hands of the Antartes, they behaved like children possessed with impotent rage. They burnt villages, smashed up others and removed the contents for sale by auction in the nearest town. In Siatista, they made the population empty their food and drink into the streets and mix it with mud and broken glass. As recruiting propaganda for the Antartes, this could not be bettered.

Now a third phase has been reached. The Italians are almost everywhere on the defensive, wired in the towns they still occupy. When they move, it is by convoy often accompanied by aeroplanes. When they wish to take reprisals, they bomb villages from three to five thousand feet. They still terrorise the civilian population areas and take and shoot hostages. They are short of food, so now they take hostages and offer to release them for food and drink.

The German occupation, whilst rigorous, has exasperated the Greeks less. The change when passing into the German from the Italian zone is very noticeable. The Germans forfeited their considerable popularity by their callous behavior during the famine and their wanton looting of public and private property. The removal of art treasures to Berlin and the flagrant commandeering of luxury goods and furniture, which could have no military justification, disillusioned the Greeks. Lastly, they showed that they were the Herrenvolk [master race] in many infuriating ways, by knocking Greeks off trams, by hitting them in the streets.

But latterly the Germans have only behaved harshly when they had some pretext. German troops have been instructed to behave properly to the civilian population and they seem to have fraternized with the Greeks. It is possible for 20 Germans to visit a village in circumstances in which the Italians would only go 1,000 strong.

The ignorance of the Germans about the Antartes is most extraordinary. They had heard vague rumours of British and American parachutists in the mountains but did not believe them. They had no idea the Antartes were formed bodies of troops with military organization.

Until recent actions, the Antartes and the Greek civil population were frightened of them. Now that they have several successful skirmishes and captured prisoners, they are no longer afraid and the Antartes talk about them as boastfully as they do the Italians.

YUGOSLAVIA'S PARTISANS

Yugoslavia, of strategic value to a Germany bent on invading both Greece and then the Soviet Union, was also attacked by Nazi troops in April 1941. Furthermore, also like Greece, wartime Yugoslavia offered a political vacuum, though one riven by greater ethnic divisions and rivalries than Greece (especially between Serbs and Croats, whose mutual antipathy was still evident a half century later). Accordingly, the Yugoslav resistance was also badly fractured. Partisans, or armed irregular forces, harried the Germans (or each other) and looked to outside governments for assistance. The American Office of Strategic Services (OSS for short, a predecessor of the Central Intelligence Agency), in conjunction with Britain's Special Operations Executive (or SOE, which had sent Stevens and others into Greece), sought to provide arms, explosives, and political and military direction to Yugoslav partisans. The OSS dispatched a resourceful recent Stanford graduate, Franklin Lindsay (1916–), to orchestrate American assistance; he met up with Britain's Fitzroy MacLean (1911–1996), a debonair daredevil Scotsman (and possible inspiration for Ian Fleming's James Bond) who had been instructed "to find out who was killing the most Germans and suggest means by which we could help them to kill more." Appalled by the murderously anti-Serbian Croatian *Ustashi,* and disappointed by a somewhat ineffective Serbian movement led by Colonel Mihailovic, the Allies' men on the ground cast their lot with the faction most likely to disrupt the German occupation, communist partisans led by Josip Broz (1892–1980), known as Tito. After the war, it was Tito who led Yugoslavia and succeeded in keeping it from falling under the Soviet domination that held sway over the rest of eastern and southern Europe. Lindsay's memoirs provide a vivid account of how Tito's partisans managed to disrupt communications, fulfill the task of killing Germans, and tie down divisions that Hitler badly needed to repel advancing Soviet troops.

The [Partisan unit] was well armed and appeared to be well disciplined. The majority of men appeared to be in their teens and early twenties, with a few in their thirties. Officers were all in their twenties, most in their early twenties. They looked healthy and fit.

For the most part the Partisan rank and file wore German uniforms and boots. Officers were in brown British battle dress with Partisan insignia of rank, or in Partisan-designed high-collared tunics cut from British blankets that had been dropped with the loads of guns and explosives. Uniforms and boots, especially in winter, were among the highest priority needs for supplies to be parachuted by the Allies. The brigade commander told us that since they had no uniform factories they had to capture German and collaborationist soldiers for their clothing. Captured, they would be stripped to their underwear and sent back to their units, where they would be reoutfitted. The Partisans then would capture them again and the cycle would be repeated. This, equipped, was the way the Partisans manufactured their uniforms. It

Franklin Lindsay, *Beacons in the Night: With the OSS and Tito's Partisans in Wartime Yugoslavia* (Stanford: Stanford University Press, 1993), 41–42, 75–76, 79–83. Used by permission.

must have been a popular joke. I later heard Tito had told MacLean the same story.

The troops were armed with German rifles, some of which they had captured, and some of which had come from German stocks captured by the Allies in North Africa and Italy and subsequently dropped to the Partisans. In order to minimize difference in ammunition some units were equipped with Italian weapons and others, as was this brigade, with German guns....

The several talks with the Partisan officers gave me an appreciation of the fighting that had taken place since the German and Italian occupation of Slovenia. The Partisans' armed organization had grown from a few isolated units of 50–100 men each in 1941 to a few thousand men in 1942, organized into brigades of 200–500 men each. By launching attacks against isolated Italian garrisons in Dolenjska southeast of Ljubljana they had forced the withdrawal of the Italians from an area around the town of Kocevje, which became the first liberated territory under Partisan control. That same year the first Partisan units were sent across the Reich frontier to Stajerska to pick up recruits who were evading German mobilization....

The morning of our arrival at Fourth Zone headquarters the Partisan leaders and I went to work on our plan of attack....Maps were spread out on the ground and we all poured over them, looking at likely places to cut the railroads....I was tremendously impressed by the eagerness of these Partisans to attack this main rail net across the Alps—so important to the Germans as they tried to stem the advance of the Allied armies....

The three lines that came together at Zidani Most provided the German high command with the ability to shift its divisions quickly between Germany, the Balkans, and the Eastern and Italian fronts; to supply weapons and fuel to the Italian front; and to bring raw materials from the Balkans, chiefly oil, bauxite, copper, zinc, lead, and chrome, to German war industry—and to transport the slave labor to work in German factories. After our first strikes we would also operate against the Balkan and Italian segments of the line. If we could cut these lines and keep them closed for a good part of the time we could deal a strategic blow to Hitler's ability to fight.

In those days aerial bombardment was the only way to reach almost all German targets. It was also the least efficient because of its inaccuracy—a large number of bombs had to be delivered to ensure that one or two hit the target....But if one could get next to the target and plant the explosives by hand right on the most vulnerable parts of, for example, a bridge, the probability of its destruction could be increased greatly and the explosives used would be a tiny fraction of that used in aerial bombardment....

As we conferred on the Pohorje mountain, we concluded that our strategy should be to take the fullest advantage of surprise. Up to now the Partisans, for lack of explosives, had made no major attacks on the German railroads. Bridges and tunnels were reported to be lightly guarded....We quickly settled on our initial targets: a 350–foot stone viaduct [and a 700–foot tunnel]....

The Partisan position in the Pohorje, besides its access to our targets, was ideal for supply. Rogla, the summit of the Pohorje, was perfect for receiving parachute drops. The very top was a flat grassy meadow of several acres completely surrounded by forest. It was the highest point for several miles around. Even on a dark night supply aircraft could fly a few hundred feet above the meadow without danger of hitting a higher mountain nearby. If the pilots came in low the parachutes would not be carried laterally by wind before touching ground, thus simplifying the collection of the containers, and preventing them from drifting into German hands. Finally, the ring of forest around the drop area shielded us and our fire signals from any German observation except from the air.

Since one of our chosen targets was a multiple-arch stone viaduct and the other a tunnel and masonry bridge, the explosives required would amount to several thousand pounds....Later that morning I enciphered and sent out a message by radio giving our location in latitude and longitude, the fire pattern and the recognition signal, and asked for a drop of guns, ammunition, and explosives....

The night after the successful airdrop to us we attacked the granite masonry viaduct on the rail line at the foot of the Pohorje to the west....Our column halted just before reaching the viaduct. Three Partisans went ahead to scout the track for German guards and to remove them quietly before we arrived. There was the German garrison of 350 men less than a mile from the viaduct and we fully expected that it would be well guarded....To our great surprise, the patrol on returning reported that there were no guards at all on the viaduct. Our column immediately formed, and we moved to the viaduct to place the explosives. It quickly became apparent to all of us that the 1,000 kilos of plastic [explosives] the Partisans had brought were inadequate to blow up all six of the columns. I later learned that neither the demolition unit nor the brigade intelligence officer had made a reconnaissance in advance. The individual columns were much larger than we had expected.

Three of the seven massive columns which supported the four center spans were selected to be blown....The next step was to dig holes for the explosives in the rocky soil next to the columns on the uphill side. The more confined the explosive when it is detonated the more efficient it is in its destructive effect....More than an hour was spent digging these holes. The almost continuous thunder of the mountain storm fortunately masked the sounds of digging. The center columns were massive—12 feet by 20 feet—and it would take a lot of plastic to knock them down. In each of two of the holes were put 250 kilos, and 150 kilos went in the third, for a side column....When all was ready the explosives chief pushed down the plunger with great verve. The noise of the explosion seemed of an order of magnitude greater than any thunder clap I had ever heard. It reverberated up and down the mountain valley for several seconds.

To cover our withdrawal, the brigade commander had placed Partisans with Bren [machine] guns on a ridge overlooking the nearby German garrison. Immediately after the blast the Brens opened up on the garrison. The Germans were completely surprised—and at least as scared as we were. The sound of the explosion, immediately followed by machine-gun fire directed at them, must have totally confused them about what was happening. Fortunately, they did not leave the garrison to investigate, but instead defended themselves against what they thought was an attack on the garrison itself.

Meanwhile, as soon as the rocks thrown into the air by the explosion stopped falling, we went forward to see what damage we had done. The charges had not been enough to completely topple the three columns and the four arches they supported, but had only blown away a large part of the base of each of the columns. In this condition, the columns could be shored up with concrete or masonry in a relatively short time and the bridge made usable again. Fortunately, we still had about 250 kilos of plastic and the Partisans now proceeded to load it into the cavities.

The night air was now crisscrossed with tracer bullets. The Germans continued to defend themselves in their bunkers rather than coming out after us. The reloading of explosives took another hour. Then the new charges were detonated. When the echo of the explosion died away I was sure I heard another quite distinct crash. The columns of the bridge had shuddered for a few seconds, then disintegrated.

Again, we went back to the site. This time the columns and the arches they supported were completely destroyed. Broken stone masonry was scattered on the ground below. I suspected that the plastic we had kept back was the precise amount necessary to finish the job. In any case, there was a gap of more than 150 feet in the viaduct, and the reconstruction would take weeks if not months....When I left Stajerska six months later the line was still closed to through traffic. It is probable that the viaduct was not rebuilt until well after the war ended.

SIEGE OF LENINGRAD

However much civilians in occupied western Europe might struggle to adjust to the deprivations and arbitrary cruelty of German rule, their situation never approached the misery and horrors endured by the populations on the eastern front. One of the worst episodes was the so-called 900 Days of Leningrad. When German forces invaded the Soviet Union in June 1941, Army Group North under Field Marshal von Leeb drove northeastward toward the elegant and historic city of Leningrad, which had served as Russia's capital under the Romanov dynasty until it was toppled by revolution in 1917. Home to some 3 million people, it had been its very vulnerability in part that had prompted Stalin to invade Finland and secure a larger territorial buffer for protection. Although no defenses seemed secure against the German onslaught, Hitler forbade a direct assault on the city, preferring to see it destroyed through artillery bombardment, aerial bombing, and starvation. The German siege, or blockade, began in September 1941, and the encircled city depended on a slender lifeline across Lake Ladoga to the east. An ice road across the frozen lake enabled some supplies to be transported in winter, while in summer barges attempted the trip, though at fearful risk. Leningrad thus became a symbol of the Soviet Union's will to resist Nazi aggression, no matter how bleak the circumstances. Even the most stringent rationing and creative efforts at vegetable gardening could not produce enough food to go around; when coupled with harsh winter weather and German shelling or bombing, the human toll was horrendous. Only about 700,000 starving people remained when the siege was finally broken in January 1944. A fair number of Leningraders had been evacuated, and others simply disappeared, but the best current estimate is that more than 700,000, and perhaps more than 1 million, Soviet citizens perished in the city.

In December [1941] 52,000 people died, as many as normally died in a year; while in January 1942, between 3,500 and 4,000 people died every day; in December and January 200,000 people died. Although, by January, the rations had been somewhat increased, the after-effects of the famine were to be felt for many months after; altogether...632,000 people died in Leningrad as a direct result of the Blockade—a figure which is undoubtedly an under-estimate....

Apart from hunger, people also suffered acutely from cold in their unheated houses. People would burn their furniture and books—but these did not last long.

To fill their empty stomachs, to reduce the intense sufferings caused by hunger, people would look for incredible substitutes: they would try to catch crows or rooks, or any cat or dog that had still somehow survived; they would go through medicine chests in search of castor oil, hair oil, Vaseline or glycerine; they would make soup or jelly out of carpenter's glue (scraped off wallpaper or broken-up furniture). But not all people in the enormous city had such supplementary sources of "food."

Alexander Werth, *Russia at War, 1941–1945.* Copyright 1964 by Alexander Werth. (New York: E. P. Dutton, 1964), 324–325. Used by permission of Dutton, a division of Penguin Group (USA) Inc.

Death would overtake people in all kinds of circumstances; while they were in the streets, they would fall down and never rise again; or in their houses where they would fall asleep and never awake; in factories, where they would collapse while doing a job of work. There was no transport, and the dead body would usually be put on a hand-sleigh drawn by two or three members of the dead man's family; often wholly exhausted during the long trek to the cemetery, they would abandon the body half-way, leaving it to the authorities to deal with it.

According to another witness:

> It was almost impossible to get a coffin. Hundreds of corpses would be abandoned in cemeteries or in their neighbourhood, usually merely wrapped in a sheet.... The authorities would bury all these abandoned corpses in common graves; these were made by the civil defence teams with the use of explosives. People did not have the strength to dig ordinary graves in the frozen earth.... On January 7, 1942 the Executive Committee of the Leningrad City Soviet

noted that corpses were scattered all over the place, and were filling up morgues and cemetery areas; some were being buried any old way, without any regard for the elementary rules of hygiene.

Later, in April, during the general clean-up of the city—which was absolutely essential to prevent epidemics, once spring had come—thousands of corpses were discovered in shelters, trenches and under the melting snow, where they had been lying for months....

Hospitals were of very little help to the starving. Not only were the doctors and nurses half-dead with hunger themselves, but what the patients needed was not medicine, but food, and there was none.

In December and January the frost froze water mains and sewers, and the burst pipes all over the city added to the danger of epidemics. Water had to be brought in pails from the Neva or the numerous Leningrad canals. This water was, moreover, dirty and unsafe to drink, and in February, about one and a half million people were given anti-typhoid injections....

PANZER WARFARE IN THE EAST

The debilitating effect of brutal Russian winters upon invaders, as both Napoleon and Hitler discovered, was real enough (sufficient to persuade British general Montgomery to list never invading Russia as one of his two cardinal rules of warfare; the second was never to invade China). But it was not just the penetrating cold that brought attacking armies to a standstill, as this questionnaire by the German High Command makes clear. German armored (or Panzer) divisions, which achieved such spectacular results in France and the initial stages of Barbarossa, fell victim to the suffocating dust of summer and the impenetrable mud of autumn. The sheer distance German units were required to travel in vast flanking or encircling operations took a further toll, so that after extended campaigning, divisions that appeared strong on paper were down to a fraction of their original effective strength. It is easier to appreciate, then, how German offensives that began promisingly would bog down, even without taking into account the increasing sophistication and tenacity of Soviet defenses. This particular survey is also instructive for revealing that terror tactics, such as destroying entire villages, were regarded as militarily useful.

1. *Command and Training*

Question I: Influence of Russian Terrain:

a) Shortage of roads often forced whole divisions onto a dirt road mostly consisting of bad patches. Thus the march was delayed, the column had to stop time after time, and thus the unit lost the calm vital to the operation.

Delayed mission.

Supply support problems (especially when there were several motorized divisions on one road).

Little opportunity to deploy the motorized divisions. Anti-aircraft guns inadequate, since one march route especially under threat.

At defiles a small enemy force was enough to hold up the march. Only in exceptional cases was it possible to chase and encircle the enemy.

Fighting on and close to the road on both sides. Enemy in the intermediate area not completely neutralized and later posed a threat to the flanks and supply support.

The Division's sectors of combat were often too large because another advance route for the adjacent divisions was a greater distance away.

High degree of wear and tear of machinery. Time was needed for repairs and maintenance work. Since there was no time allowed for this, the result was a fall in the number of tanks still operational in the panzer regiments to a fraction of their marching-out strength, as well as a partial collapse of matériel strength in the other motorized arms.

Question 2: Experiences concerning the operation of larger units:

a) Panzer divisions are units which rely on the weather not being too bad. Where there are more than 15 degrees of frost or rainstorms

---

"Answers to Questionnaire OKH Concerning Experiences Eastern Campaign in Command, Training and Organisation," from Fourth Panzer Division War Diary, March 12, 1942, in Rudolf Steiger, *Armour Tactics in the Second World War: Panzer Army Campaigns of 1939–41 in German War Diaries*, trans. Martin Fry (New York/Oxford: Berg, 1991), 136–137. Used by permission.

which turn roads into quagmires, technical breakdowns occur which far outstrip any small achievements made in spite of this. If the unit is forced to retreat under such circumstances, there will be possibly catastrophic losses of matériel. In order to avoid this, the higher command echelons should think in a more technical way. For example, they should consider carefully whether it is worthwhile committing armoured divisions in bad weather, or else take them out well before the bad weather starts.

b) Attack is the nature of the Panzer Division. If there is a standstill and the enemy has time to ascertain the positions of individual fighting units, there will be problems. Therefore there should only be a deep forward thrust if it is certain that further forces can be brought through the gap breached by the Panzer Division. Here one must also take road and weather conditions into account.

After the enemy has been encircled the PZ. Div. should be pulled out as soon as possible and made available for other tasks.

As long as the tanks are moving forward, breakdowns can be tolerated, because then immobilized vehicles can be taken in for repair.

Every backward movement, however, causes extremely high losses in vehicles and weapons, thus strengthening enemy morale.

It should be up to the commanders to avoid putting the Panzer Division through such difficult withdrawals.

The higher command echelons became used to acknowledging cries for help from the units concerning spare parts and so on without taking steps to help, because our luck continued to hold regardless and the Division achieved what was thought to be impossible.

This led to the fact that on 5 December 1941 (the day before the start of the withdrawal) the Division had at its disposal only: 15% of its tanks, 30% of its personnel carriers; 34% of its trucks; 10% of its motorcycles....

Question 5: Experience in fighting under special conditions:

b) Combat in towns and villages:

The best means of combat—shoot the village into flames. In the warmer months the Russians are mostly dug in in front of or to the side of the village. Even then the burning village is almost always valuable to the attacker (dazzling effect, destruction of vehicles, effect on morale).

SOVIET TACTICAL DOCTRINE

Ill-prepared, poorly led, and caught by surprise despite advance warnings, Soviet forces were initially overwhelmed by the German attack, and even into 1942 German forces continued to score major successes. One way the Soviets redressed the situation was to introduce improved weapons (such as the excellent T-34 tank) in great numbers, achieving qualitative parity and quantitative superiority. A second way was to recognize that, however they had been or would be equipped, Soviet forces had been handled poorly in the field. Order 325 from the Soviet High Command was issued after chastened leaders had absorbed the lessons of defeat, observed the methods their German counterparts employed in victory, and formulated responses that would offer a better prospect of success. In particular, Soviet commanders would eventually demonstrate a better grasp of using combined arms, namely coordinating different units more flexibly and effectively. Infantry, artillery, and antitank units would now support armor, so that vulnerable tanks could not be picked off in isolation, or unprotected infantry easily encircled. As a result, Soviet military performance improved significantly, and before long it would be the Soviet armies, not the German units, which held the military initiative.

ORDER OF THE PEOPLE'S COMMISSAR OF DEFENSE NO. 325 16 OCTOBER 1942

The practical experience of the war against the German fascists has shown that in the matter of using tank units we have, up to now, great shortcomings. The main shortcomings can be summarized as follows:

1. During an attack of the enemy defense our tanks are cut off from the infantry and relinquish their interaction with it. The infantry, being cut off from the tanks by enemy fire, does not support our tanks with its artillery fire. The tanks, being cut off from the infantry, find themselves alone in battle against enemy artillery, tanks, and infantry, and suffer heavy losses.

2. Tanks are thrown against an enemy defense without the necessary artillery support. Before the commencement of the tank attack the artillery has not suppressed the antitank means on the forward edge of the enemy defense, and tank support guns are not always used. With the approach to the enemy's forward edge, tanks encounter enemy antitank artillery fire and suffer heavy losses....

3. Tanks are pressed into battle quickly, without reconnoitering the terrain adjacent to the forward edge of the enemy defense, without studying the terrain in the depth of the enemy deployment, and without the tankers' carefully studying the enemy's system of fire....

Combined arms commanders do not allot the time necessary for the technical preparation of tanks in battle, and do not prepare the terrain in an engineer respect on the direction of tank action. Mine fields are poorly reconnoitered and are not cleared. Passages are not made in antitank obstacles and the assistance necessary to overcome terrain sectors which are difficult to negotiate is not rendered.

David M. Glantz, ed., *Soviet Documents on the Use of War Experience: The Winter Campaign, 1941–1942* (London: Frank Cass & Co., 1991), 233–235. Used by permission.

Sappers are not always designated to accompany tanks.

This leads to tanks being blown up on mines, getting stuck in bogs and on antitank obstacles, and not participating in the battle.

4. Tanks do not carry out their primary mission of destroying enemy infantry and are diverted to fighting against enemy tanks and artillery. The established practice of opposing our tanks against enemy tank attacks and engaging them in tank battles is incorrect and harmful.

5. Tank combat actions are not provided with sufficient aviation cover, aerial reconnaissance, or air guidance. As a rule, aviation does not accompany tank formations in the depth of the enemy defense, and aviation combat actions are not coordinated with tank attacks.

6. Control of tanks on the battlefield is poorly organized. Radio is insufficiently used as a control means. Commanders of tank units and formations located at command posts are cut off from the battle formations, do not observe tank actions in battle, and do not influence the course of the tank battle....

I order the following instructions to be observed in the combat use of tank and mechanized units and formations.

1. Individual tank regiments and brigades are designated to reinforce the infantry on the main direction and operate in close interaction with it as direct infantry support tanks.

2. Tanks operating jointly with infantry have as their primary mission the destructions of enemy infantry, and should not be separated from their own infantry by more than 200–400 meters....

3. To support tank actions, the infantry should suppress enemy antitank means using all the power of its fire and the fire of accompanying guns, reconnoiter and clear mine fields, assist tanks in overcoming antitank obstacles and boggy sectors of terrain, fight against German destroyer tanks, decisively follow the tanks into the attack, rapidly fortify the lines captured by them, cover the delivery of ammunition and fuel to the tanks, and assist in the evacuation of damaged tanks from the battlefield.

4. Before the entry of the tanks into the attack, artillery should destroy antitank means of the enemy defense. During the attack of the forward edge and battle in the depth of the enemy defense it should suppress on the signals of the tank commanders the fire means hindering the advance of the tanks, for which the artillery commanders are obliged to control artillery fire from mobile forward observation posts for radio-equipped tanks. Artillery and tank commanders jointly establish signals for calling and ceasing artillery fire.

5. With the appearance of enemy tanks on the battlefield, artillery conducts the primary fight against them. Tanks conduct battle against enemy tanks only in the case of a clear superiority of forces and an advantageous position.

6. Our aviation, by means of its actions, fires on the enemy antitank defense, prevents the approach of his tanks to the battlefield, covers the battle formations of tank units from enemy aviation actions, and provides the combat actions of the tank units with constant, uninterrupted aerial reconnaissance.

7. Tanks crews conduct the attack at maximum speeds, suppress enemy gun, mortar, and machine gun teams and infantry from the march, and capably maneuver on the battlefield, using the terrain profile to arrive at the flank and rear of enemy fire means and infantry. Tanks do not conduct frontal attacks.

BATTLE OF KURSK

During the spring and summer of 1943, a focal point for both German and Soviet planners was the "salient" near Kursk, some 500 miles south of Moscow, where the front lines suddenly shifted in a westward bulge about 100 miles wide and 75 miles deep. To the Soviets this salient presented an opportunity to strike deeper behind German lines, while to the Germans it afforded the chance to strike simultaneously from the north and south to pinch off the bulge and surround the Soviet troops within. Both sides reinforced their positions, and in early July 1943 the Germans mounted a massive offensive spearheaded by Panzer divisions newly equipped with Panther and Tiger tanks against carefully prepared Soviet positions. All told, some 2 million men and 6,000 tanks and assault guns were involved, resulting in the largest tank battle of the war. Nikolai Litvin (1922–), originally trained as airborne paratrooper but deployed as a Soviet antitank gunner, was one participant in the heavy fighting. He composed his memoirs in 1962 during the brief thaw in intellectual life under Khrushchev, but before he could publish them, the authorities again imposed heavy censorship. In any event, they were in no mood to allow realistic depictions to tarnish the image of an infallible Soviet army and the "Great Patriotic War." More than half a century would pass until Litvin's memoirs could be published. The extract that follows confirms the effect of the tactics prescribed by Order 325; the emphasis on combinations of arms and defense in depth (what the Soviets called "deep operations") effectively blunted the German attack. After Kursk, German operations on the eastern front would focus on fighting a tenacious defensive campaign, for the days of surrounding enormous numbers of Soviet prisoners and capturing huge chunks of territory were long gone.

In preparation for the German offensive, the Stavka [Soviet High Command] gave the order to create an extensive, multilayered system of defensive fieldworks. Five such bands of fortifications were built, the strongest of which were the first, second, and third belts. Each belt consisted of entrenchments, rifle pits, fire positions for antitank artillery, and in the forward zone there were antitank batteries, antitank rifles, and a heavily mined no-man's-land. Communication trenches connected the defensive belts, and in addition shelters and dugouts for the infantry had been built. The basic plan was that when the German tanks advanced, only the antitank guns and their crews would remain above ground, while the infantry and *avtomatchiki* [submachine gunners] would remain concealed and under cover. When the tank battle concluded, our infantry and *avtomatchiki* would emerge.

The task of the five belts of defense was to destroy the maximum number of enemy tanks, self-propelled guns, and infantry. We wanted to bleed the attacking German armies dry. Once the enemy had spent itself and lost the capability to conduct an offensive, then we would go on the counterattack....

We prepared intensively for the German offensive. Whenever there was a lull, our gun crews

Nikolai Litvin, *800 Days on the Eastern Front: A Russian Soldier Remembers World War II* (Lawrence: University of Kansas Press, 2007), 10, 12–13, 17–18. Used by permission.

trained. In the eight-man gun crew, each member had his own role. The weapon commander selects the target, the type of shell, the number of rounds, and gives the order to open fire. The gunner aims the gun and fires the weapon. The breech operator opens and closes the gun's breech in case the automatic device fails. The loader loads the shell into the gun and removes the spent shell casings after firing. The *snari-adny* [literally, the "shell man"] prepares the shells for firing and hands them to the loader. What does it mean, to "prepare" the shell? He sets the distance that a shrapnel shell will travel before it explodes. The *iashchechny* [literally, the "case man"] opens the caissons, wipes the dust from the shells, and so forth. The ammunition carrier carries the shells from the caisson to the gun. The eighth member of the crew is either a driver for horse-drawn guns or the chief mechanic for mechanized towed guns. I was the gunner on my gun crew....

We particularly prepared psychologically to confront German tanks. Once we were marched to a special training ground, with entrenchments facing an open field. In the distance, tanks began rolling toward us. We quickly took shelter in the trenches, and the tanks continued to advance closer and closer. Some comrades became frightened, leaped out of the trenches, and began to run away. The commander saw who was running and quickly forced them back into the trenches, making it clear they had to stay put. The tanks reached the trench line and, with a terrible roar, passed overhead. Here and there, someone might get covered with dirt, or might receive a bruise, but we quickly grasped the idea: it was possible to conceal oneself in a trench from a tank, let it pass right over you, and remain alive. Lie down and press yourself to the bottom of the trench, and shut your eyes. As soon the tank passes, jump up and toss an antitank mine at its weakly armored rear facing. Those who tried to run away the first time were forced to repeat the exercise until they became accustomed to the noise and sensations of a roaring metal monster passing just overhead....

The morning of 6 July dawned cloudy, with a low overcast sky that hindered the operations of our force. Around 6:00 a.m., our position was attacked head-on by a group of approximately 200 sub-machine gunners and four German tanks, most likely PzKw IVs. The tanks led the way, followed closely by the infantry. The Germans were attempting to find a weak spot in our lines.

The Germans advanced across the uncut rye field directly toward our firing positions, but they didn't seem to see us. We felt a gnawing fear in the pit of our bellies as the German tanks rumbled toward us, stopping every fifty to seventy meters to scan our lines and fire a round. In the general din of battle, we practically could not hear the German shells exploding, but we could see the shells streaking through the air in the direction of our positions. The shells flew harmlessly over our heads; as the Germans hadn't yet spotted us and were targeting likely positions behind us. My knees and legs began to tremble wildly, until we received the command to swing into action and prepared to fire. The shaking stopped, and we became possessed by the overriding desire not to miss our targets.

When the Germans had reached within approximately 300 meters of us, we opened fire at the tanks. Our Number One gun set a tank ablaze with its first shot, and then managed to knock out a second tank. The combined fire of our Number Three and Number Four guns knocked out a third German tank. The fourth tank managed to escape. Since my gun had no tanks in its zone of fire, we opened up on the advancing infantry with fragmentation shells. The German submachine gunners stubbornly continued to push forward. As they drew closer, we switched to shrapnel shells and resumed fire on them. Not less than half the Germans fell to the ground, and the remaining drew back to their line of departure. As we watched the Germans fall back and the one German tank continued to burn, we wanted to leap for joy and shout "Urrah!" at the top of our lungs; such was our happiness at our success.

EISENHOWER AND OVERLORD

Critics who belittled General Dwight Eisenhower for having risen to supreme command of the Allied invasion of western Europe (Operation Overlord), despite not having had major combat experience, neglected the specific demands of Eisenhower's assignment and the particular skills he brought to that task. As planned, the invasion was an immensely complex operation that would require the coordination of varied services (ground troops, naval units, air force, and airborne formations) from four countries (the United States, Britain, Canada, and the Free French) and the cooperation of fractious or hypersensitive fellow officers (such as Montgomery and Patton) or politicians (notably Churchill). The eventual landing site (the Normandy beaches) had to be selected and kept secret, diversions introduced (such as the campaign of misinformation to persuade the Germans that the assault would fall farther east, near Pas-de-Calais, where crossing the English Channel would be quicker and easier), and the whole business matched to the appropriate weather and tidal conditions. The ultimate responsibility was Eisenhower's alone, and he could not betray whatever anguish or uncertainty he may have felt when so many troops looked to him for leadership. Eisenhower could confide his inner thoughts to his diary, as he did on the eve of the D-day landings, providing us with insight into his difficult (but correct) decision to proceed with the invasion and send soldiers ashore on June 6, 1944.

June 3, 1944

The matter of coordination with the French has been highly complicated because of lack of crystallization in ideas involving both the political and military fields. Specifically, the president desires that coordination be effected with the French on the basis of dealing with any group or groups that can effectively fight the Germans. His directive apparently recognized the influence of the National Committee of Liberation in France but he is unwilling to promise any exclusive dealing with the group since that, he apparently believes, would be tantamount to recognizing the committee as a provisional government, set up from outside.

We have our direct means of communication with the resistance groups on France but all of our information leads us to believe that the only authority these resistance groups desire to recognize is that of De Gaulle and his committee. However, since De Gaulle is apparently willing to cooperate only on the basis of our dealing with him exclusively, the whole thing falls into a rather sorry mess. De Gaulle is, of course, now controlling the only French military forces that can take part in this operation. Consequently, from the purely military viewpoint, we must at least until the time that other French forces might conceivably be organized completely independent of his movement, deal with him alone. He, however, takes the attitude that military and political matters go hand in hand and will not cooperate militarily unless political recognition of some kind is accorded him. We do not seem to be able, in advance of D-day, to straighten the matter at all. I have just

Robert H. Ferrell, ed., *The Eisenhower Diaries* (New York: W. W. Norton & Co., 1981), 118–121. Used by permission of John S.D. Eisenhower.

learned that De Gaulle has failed to accept the prime minister's invitation to come to England, saying that he would make his decision this afternoon. The rapid sorting out of all the conflicting ideas is quite necessary if we are to secure the maximum help from the French both inside and outside the country.

The weather in this country is practically unpredictable. For some days our experts have been meeting almost hourly, and I have been holding commander-in-chief meetings once or twice a day to consider the reports and tentative predictions. While at this moment, the morning of June 3, it appears that the weather will not be so bad as to preclude landings and will possibly even permit reasonably effective gunfire support from the navy, the picture from the air viewpoint is not so good.

Probably no one who does not have to bear the specific and direct responsibility of making the final decision as to what to do can understand the intensity of these burdens. The supreme commander, much more than any of his subordinates, is kept informed of the political issues involved, particularly the anticipated effect of delay upon the Russians. He, likewise, is in close touch with all the advice from his military subordinates and must face the issue even when technical advice as to weather is not unanimous from the several experts. Success or failure might easily hinge upon the effectiveness, for example, of airborne operations, the question becomes whether to risk the airborne movement anyway or to defer the whole affair in the hopes of getting weather that is a bit better.

My tentative thought is that the desirability for getting started on the next favorable tide is so great and the uncertainty of the weather is such that we could never anticipate really perfect weather coincident with proper tidal conditions, that we must go unless there is a real and very serious deterioration in the weather.

Since last February the enemy has been consistently busy in placing obstacles of various types on all European beaches suitable for landing operations. Most of these are also mined. Under ordinary circumstances of land attack these would not be particularly serious but because they must be handled quickly and effectively before the major portion of our troops can begin unloading, they present a hazard that is a very considerable one. It is because of their existence that we must land earlier on the tide than we had originally intended. This gives us a chance to go after them while they are still on dry land, because if their bases were under water, they would be practically impossible to handle. If our gun support of the operation and the DD [duplex-drive] tanks during this period are both highly effective, we should be all right.

The underwater obstacles, that is, the sea mines, force us to sweep every foot over which we operate, and this adds immeasurably to the difficulties in restricted waters in which we are operating. The combination of undersea and beach obstacles is serious, but we believe we have it whipped.

Because the enemy in great strength is occupying a country that is interlaced with a fine communication system, our attack can be looked upon as reasonable only if our tremendous air force is able to impede his concentrations against us and to help destroy the effectiveness of any of his counterattacks. Weather again comes into this problem, because it is my own belief that with reasonably good weather during the first two weeks of the operation our air superiority and domination will see us through to success.

D-DAY

For British and Canadian troops who came ashore at beaches code-named Gold, Juno, and Sword, as well as the Americans at Utah Beach, the Normandy landings went more smoothly and faced lighter opposition than they had anticipated. The opposite was true of Omaha Beach, a site dominated by well-entrenched veteran German soldiers on bluffs overlooking a thin gravelly strip of land littered with dangerous obstacles and dreadful mines. The preliminary naval bombardment, hampered by poor visibility and the clever concealment of many German positions by the terrain, left the defenders largely intact. The murderous hail of gunfire, the toll it took and the terror it could inspire, figured unforgettably in the opening minutes of the movie *Saving Private Ryan,* but emerge with equal clarity in this account by Thomas Valence [A Company, 116th] of the much-decorated First Infantry Division (nicknamed the "Big Red One" for its conspicuous shoulder patch). The sheer heroism demonstrated by so many otherwise seemingly ordinary individuals to wrest the gain of a mere few hundred yards at horrific cost (2,000 casualties on the first day) remains as compelling today as it did to observers more than sixty years ago.

[THOMAS VALENCE, COMPANY A] THE 116TH AT OMAHA BEACH

We proceeded toward the beach, and many of the fellows got sick. The water was quite rough. It was a choppy ride in, and we received a lot of spray.

Our boat was one of six of A Company in the first wave, and when we got to the beach, or close to it, the obstacles erected by the Germans to prevent the landing were fully in view, as we were told they would be, which meant the tide was low.

I was the rifle sergeant and followed Lieutenant Anderson off the boat, and we did what we could rather than what we had practiced doing for so many months in England. There was a rather wide expanse of beach, and the Germans were not to be seen at all, but they were firing at us, rapidly, with a great deal of small-arm fire.

As we came down the ramp, we were in water about knee high, and we started to do what we were trained to do—move forward, and then crouch and fire. One of the problems was we didn't quite know what to fire at. I saw some tracers coming from a concrete emplacement which to me looked mammoth. I never anticipated any gun emplacements being that big. I attempted to fire back at that, but I had no concept of what was going on behind me. There was not much to see in front of me except a few houses, and the water kept coming in so rapidly, and the fellows I was with were being hit and put out of action so quickly that it became a struggle to stay on one's feet. I abandoned my equipment, which was very heavy.

I floundered in the water and had my hand up in the air, trying to get my balance, when I was first shot. I was shot through the left hand, which broke a knuckle, and then through the palm of the hand. I felt nothing but a little sting at the time, but I was aware that I was shot. Next to me in the water, Private Henry C. Witt was rolling over towards me. 'Sergeant, they're leaving us here to die like rats. Just to die like rats.' I certainly wasn't thinking the same thing, nor did I share that opinion. I didn't know whether we were being left or not.

I made my way forward as best I could. My rifle jammed, so I picked up a carbine and got off a couple of rounds. We were shooting at something that seemed inconsequential. There was no way I was going to knock out a German concrete emplacement with a .30 caliber rifle. I was hit again, once in the left thigh, which broke my hip bone, and a couple of times in my pack, and then my chin strap on my helmet was severed by a bullet. I worked my way up onto the beach, and staggered up against a wall, and collapsed there. The bodies of the other guys washed ashore, and I was one live body amongst many of my friends who were dead and, in many cases, blown to pieces.

ERNIE PYLE'S WAR

Ernest (Ernie) Taylor Pyle, an Indiana native born in 1900, was a Pulitzer Prize–winning journalist who covered the military campaigns of North Africa, the Mediterranean, Europe, and the Pacific. After attending Indiana University, Pyle became a reporter with a local Indiana newspaper and later joined the staff of the Washington DC *Daily News*. Pyle's World War II reporting began in 1940 with the Battle of Britain, and a year later he covered Allied operations in North Africa, Sicily, Italy, and France. His success as a journalist lay with his "foxhole" view of the conflict and his ability to convey to the American home front the daily realities of the average soldier. *Time* magazine once referred to him as "America's most widely read war correspondent." In 1945, while accompanying American forces in the Pacific, Pyle was killed on the island of Ie Shima by a Japanese sniper's bullet. The following is an excerpt from his report from the D-day invasion at Omaha Beach, France, in June 1944.

A PURE MIRACLE

NORMANDY BEACHHEAD, JUNE 12, 1944

Now that it is over it seems to me a pure miracle that we ever took the beach at all. For some of our units it was easy, but in this special sector where I am now our troops faced such odds that our getting ashore was like my whipping Joe Louis down to a pulp.

In this column I want to tell you what the opening of the second front in one sector entailed, so that you can know and appreciate and forever be humbly grateful to those both dead and alive who did it for you.

Ashore, facing us, were more enemy troops than we had in our assault waves. The advantages were all theirs, the disadvantages all ours. The Germans were dug into positions that they had been working

David Nichols, ed., *Ernie's War: The Best of Ernie Pyle's World War II Dispatches*. Copyright © 1986 by David Nichols. (New York: Random House, 1986), 278–279, 282–283. Used by permission of Random House, Inc.

on for months, although these were not yet all complete. A one-hundred-foot bluff a couple of hundred yards back from the beach had great concrete gun emplacements built right into the hilltop. These opened to the sides instead of to the front, thus making it very hard for naval fire from the sea to reach them. They could shoot parallel with the beach and cover every foot of it for miles with artillery fire.

Then they had hidden machine-gun nests on the forward slopes, with crossfire taking in every inch of the beach. These nests were connected by networks of trenches, so that the German gunners could move about without exposing themselves.

Throughout the length of the beach, running zigzag a couple of hundred yards back from the shoreline, was an immense V-shaped ditch fifteen feet deep. Nothing could cross it, not even men on foot, until fills had been made. And in other places at the far end of the beach, where the ground is flatter, they had great concrete walls. These were blasted by our naval gunfire or by explosives set by hand after we got ashore.

Our only exits from the beach were several swales or valleys, each about one hundred yards wide. The Germans made the most of these funnel-like traps, sowing them with buried mines. They contained, also, barbed-wire entanglements with mines attached, hidden ditches, and machine guns firing from the slopes.

This is what was on the shore. But our men had to go through a maze nearly as deadly as this before they even got ashore. Underwater obstacles were terrific. The Germans had whole fields of evil devices under the water to catch our boats. Even now, several days after the landing, we have cleared only channels through them and cannot yet approach the whole length of the beach with our ships. Even now some ship or boat hits one of these mines every day and is knocked out of commission....

In addition to these obstacles they had floating mines offshore, land mines buried in the sand of the beach, and more mines in checkerboard rows in the tall grass beyond the sand. And the enemy had four men on shore for every three men we had approaching the shore.

And yet we got on....

A LONG THIN LINE OF PERSONAL ANGUISH

NORMANDY BEACHHEAD, JUNE 17, 1944

It extends in a thin little line, just like a high-water mark, for miles along the beach. This is the strewn personal gear, personal gear that will never be needed again, of those who fought and died to give us our entrance into Europe.

Here in a jumbled row for mile on mile are soldiers' packs. Here are socks and shoe polish, sewing kits, diaries, Bibles and hand grenades. Here are the latest letters from home, with the address on each one neatly razored out—one of the security precautions enforced before the boys embarked.

Here are toothbrushes and razors, and snapshots of families back home staring up at you from the sand. Here are pocketbooks, metal mirrors, extra trousers, and bloody, abandoned shoes. Here are broken-handled shovels, and portable radios smashed almost beyond recognition, and mine detectors twisted and ruined.

Here are torn pistol belts and canvas water buckets, first-aid kits and jumbled heaps of lifebelts. I picked up a pocket Bible with a soldier's name in it, and put it in my jacket. I carried it half a mile or so and then put it back down on the beach. I don't know why I picked it up, or why I put it back down....

Two of the most dominant items in the beach refuse are cigarets and writing paper. Each soldier was issued a carton of cigarets just before he started. Today these cartons by the thousand, water-soaked and spilled out, mark the line of our first savage blow.

Writing paper and air-mail envelopes come second. The boys had intended to do a lot of writing in France. Letters that would have filled those blank, abandoned pages.

Always there are dogs in every invasion. There is a dog still on the beach today, still pitifully looking for his masters.

He stays at the water's edge, near a boat that lies twisted and half sunk at the water line. He barks appealingly to every soldier who approaches, trots eagerly along with him for a few feet, and then, sensing himself unwanted in all this haste, runs back to wait in vain for his own people at his own empty boat.

CHAPTER 7

THE ASIAN THEATER

THE TOLL OF WAR This photo, taken during the February 1943 invasion of New Guinea, was the first to be published in the United States that showed American war dead where they fell in combat.
Source: © Getty Images.

If the war in the Pacific never had an apocalyptic land battle on the scale of Kursk or Stalingrad, its struggles more than matched those in Europe in intensity, ferocity, and variety. From 1942 until 1943, the Pacific theater witnessed at least three major campaigns occurring simultaneously: in China, Burma/India, and in the central Pacific. At times, the first of these, the Sino-Japanese War, appeared as a three-way contest, with Chinese nationalists and communists eyeing each other warily while trying to keep the Japanese invaders at bay. The battles were different from those in Europe where large motorized formations faced each other; in China, neither side fielded many mechanized forces, and the Chinese, isolated from the factories and ports along the coastline, were perennially short of weapons and munitions. Only the heroic efforts of Allied pilots to fly supplies over rugged mountainous terrain ("the hump") improved the situation, but until later in the war Chinese forces were still unable or (according to Western observers critical of the cautious Chinese Nationalist leader Chiang Kai-shek) unwilling to mount sustained offensive operations. American leaders hoped that the fighting in China would tie down substantial numbers of Japanese troops and yield air bases from which American planes could bomb Japan, but only the first of these objectives was realized to any degree. The Japanese never realized an adequate return on their own imperialist venture in China, and found themselves embroiled ever deeper in a war they could not win. Meanwhile, the real beneficiaries were the Chinese communists, who demonstrated greater flexibility in mobilizing popular resistance and articulating a seductive vision of a postwar future, and, once the Japanese were gone, would wield an advantage in securing power and seeking to purge the country of foreign influence.

The second campaigns, in Burma and toward India, were intended by the Japanese partly to cover their operations in Malaya and the Dutch East Indies (which provided oil and rubber crucial to the war effort), and partly to secure resources (such as Burmese rice) and threaten India, upon whose military participation Britain depended. All of these areas had been controlled by Europe's colonial powers, so the Allies could not be certain whether the local populations would resist the Japanese as invaders or welcome them as anti-imperialist liberators. In this uncertain environment, Japanese forces possessed an initial advantage, given their familiarity with jungle warfare and ability to elicit intelligence and compliance from local groups. European leadership in the region was badly shaken, with the "Quit India" movement threatening British control there, and a nominally independent regime in Burma under Ba Maw following Japan's eviction of British troops there. British forces (primarily units composed of Indian soldiers), supplemented by Chinese divisions, only stemmed the onslaught because of the inspirational leadership of General William Slim and the eventual achievement of aerial superiority, which allowed Slim to reinforce and resupply his troops more effectively than the Japanese, who struggled to use overland routes. Key victories at Kohima in April 1944 and Imphal in June marked the farthest point of the Japanese advance, after which a relentless Allied counteroffensive would relieve pressure upon India and clear Burma and Siam of Japanese troops. But it was one thing to evict the invader; after the upheaval of war, with old structures of authority destroyed and political consciousness stirred, it would be quite impossible to restore the region to the way it had been before 1941.

American strategy, especially as directed by Admiral Ernest King, the navy's chief of operations, was to concentrate on defeating Japan by the most direct means possible. To reach that country's home islands, however, would mean puncturing the outer Japanese defensive perimeter of various island groups in the Pacific and then, step by step, closing in on Tokyo itself. America's war in Asia then would be an amphibious one, conducted by marine or army divisions which would invade crucial islands, and a naval one, conducted by U.S. fleets under whose protective guns and carrier aircraft the attacks could be undertaken. This was a formidable task: the distances across a trackless ocean were great, the logistical challenges immense, the entrenched Japanese defenders determined, and the Japanese navy itself still an extremely skilled, experienced, and dangerous foe. The main American thrust would be through the central Pacific, encompassing the Solomons, Gilbert, and Marianas island chains and specific locales—Guadalcanal, Tarawa, Saipan, and Peleliu—whose names would reverberate in the nation's historical memory.

The key in this vast enterprise was to destroy the fighting power of the Imperial Japanese Navy, for without sea power the Japanese could not reinforce or supply their island garrisons or, ultimately, protect their home shores. In a battle of attrition, America's industrial strength and productive might was important, because the United States could replace sunken or badly damaged ships much more quickly (especially in carrier construction). But after an initial period of adjustment, in head-to-head combat the U.S. Navy systematically outfought its Japanese counterparts. By 1944 the battles were startlingly one-sided. In the so-called Marianas turkey shoot in the Battle of the Philippine Sea (June 19, 1944), American pilots downed 243 Japanese planes while losing just 20 of their own. After that debacle, whatever Japanese carriers remained had hardly any pilots left to repeat the exploits of the skilled aviators who had attacked Pearl Harbor. The Japanese surface fleet, which contained some of the most powerful ships afloat, met its end a few months later at Leyte Gulf (October 24–26) off the Philippines. Starved of fuel oil by the depredations of American submarines whose blockade destroyed the Japanese merchant marine, these grand capital ships sallied forth on what amounted to suicide missions. In fact, as the war wound down, that seemed to be a disturbing trend, namely that the closer the Americans got to Japan itself, the more desperate and suicidal the Japanese defense. Pilots willingly sacrificed their lives to crash their planes into American ships, while on island after island the defenders fought virtually to the last man. Or, on the island of Saipan, it was to the last civilian as well. Horrified American soldiers watched as women, children, and elderly men were herded to cliffs, where they either jumped to their death or were pushed or shot. It was a grim harbinger of what could be expected on a massive scale in Japan's home islands. Deliverance for the American troops slated to make the amphibious landings on the Japanese homeland came in the form of two atomic bombs in August 1945, though at a cost and in a way that horrified the world as well.

BATAAN DEATH MARCH

Fascinated by flying since his childhood days, Texas-born William E. Dyess (1916–1943) enlisted in the Army Air Corps in 1938. In 1941 he became the commander of the Twenty-first Pursuit Squadron in the Philippines where he led many successful aerial attacks against the Japanese. With supplies and equipment to fight the Japanese dwindling in 1942, Dyess and his men were captured on April 8, 1942, at Bataan. They were then subjected to a brutal sixty-five-mile march across the Bataan Peninsula to prisoner of war camps. The environment was difficult enough, but what made the march particularly lethal was the atrocious behavior of the Japanese soldiers guarding the American prisoners who, under accepted laws of warfare, were entitled to humane treatment.

The first thing I heard after our arrival was an urgent whispering which came to us from all sides. "Get rid of your Jap stuff, quick!"

"What Jap stuff?" we whispered back.

"Everything: money, souvenirs. Get rid of it!" We did so without delay—and just in time. Jap non-commissioned officers and three-star privates were moving among us ordering that packs be opened and spread out. They searched our persons, then went through the other stuff, confiscating personal articles now and then.

I noticed that the Japs, who up to now had treated us with an air of cool suspicion, were beginning to get rough. I saw men shoved, cuffed, and boxed. This angered and mystified us. It was uncalled for. We were not resisting. A few ranks away a Jap jumped up from a pack he had been inspecting. In his hand was a small shaving mirror.

"Nippon?" he asked the owner. The glass was stamped: "Made in Japan." The solder nodded. The Jap stepped back, then lunged, driving his rifle butt into the American's face. "Yaah!" he yelled, and lunged again. The Yank went down. The raging Jap stood over him, driving crushing blows to the face until the prisoner lay insensible.

A little way off a Jap was smashing his fists into the face of another American soldier who went to his knees and received a thudding kick in his groin. He, too, it seemed, had been caught with some Japanese trifle.

We were shocked. This treatment of war prisoners was beyond our understanding. I still didn't get it, even after someone explained to me that the Japs assumed the contraband articles had been taken from the bodies of their dead. I was totally unprepared for the appalling deed that came next....

The victim, an air force captain, was being searched by a three-star private. Standing by him was a Jap commissioned officer, hand on sword hilt. These men were nothing like the toothy, bespectacled runts whose photographs are familiar to most newspaper readers. They were cruel of face, stalwart, and tall.

"This officer looked like a giant beside the Jap private," said my informant, who must be nameless because he still is a prisoner of war. "The big man's

Charles Leavelle, ed., Lt. Col. William E. Dyess, *Bataan Death March: A Survivor's Account* (Lincoln: University of Nebraska Press, 2002), 69–71, 73, 76–77. Used by permission.

face was as black as mahogany. He didn't seem to be paying much attention. There was no expression in his eyes, only a sort of unseeing glare.

"The private, a little squirt, was going through the captain's pockets. All at once he stopped and sucked in his breath with a hissing sound. He had found some Jap yen.

"He held these out, ducking his head and sucking in his breath to attract notice. The big Jap looked at the money. Without a word he grabbed the captain by the shoulder and shoved him down to his knees. He pulled the sword out of the scabbard and raised it high over his head, holding it with both hands....

"Before we could grasp what was happening, the black-faced giant had swung his sword. I remember how the sun flashed on it. There was a swish and a kind of chopping thud, like a cleaver going through beef.

"The captain's head seemed to jump off his shoulders. It hit the ground in front of him and went rolling crazily from side to side between the lines of prisoners.

"The body fell forward. I have seen wounds, but never such a gush of blood as this. The heart continued to pump for a few seconds and at each beat there was another great spurt of blood. The white dust around our feet was turned into crimson mud....

"When I looked again the big Jap had put up his sword and was strolling off. The runt who had found the yen was putting them into his pocket. He helped himself to the captain's possessions."

This was the first murder. In the year to come there would be enough killing of American and Filipino soldier prisoners to rear a mountain of dead.

Our Jap guards now threw off all restraint. They beat and slugged prisoners, robbing them of watches, fountain pens, money, and toiletry articles. Now, as never before, I wanted to kill Japs for the pleasure of it.

The thing that almost drove me crazy was the certainty that the officer who had just been murdered couldn't have taken those yen from a dead Jap. He had been in charge of an observation post far behind the lines. I doubt that he ever had seen a dead Jap.

Gradually I got control of myself. By going berserk now I would only lose my own life without hope of ever helping to even the score.

The score just now was far from being in our favor. The 160 officers and men who remained of the 21st Pursuit Squadron were assembled with about 500 other American and Filipino soldiers of all grades and ranks. They were dirty, ragged, unshaven, and exhausted. Many were half starved....

We stood for more than an hour in the scalding heat while the search, with its beating and sluggings, was completed. Then the Jap guards began pulling some of the huskiest of our number out of line. These were assembled into labor gangs, to remain in the area....

The Japs made no move to feed us. Few of us had had anything to eat since the morning of April 9. Many had tasted no food in four days. We had a little tepid water in our canteens, but nothing else....

When I thought I could stand the penetrating heat no longer, I was determined to have a sip of the tepid water in my canteen. I had no more than unscrewed the top when the aluminum flask was snatched from my hands. The Jap who had crept up behind me poured the water into a horse's nosebag, then threw down the canteen. He walked on among the prisoners, taking away their water and pouring it into the bag. When he had enough he gave it to his horse.

Whether by accident or design we had been put just across the road from a pile of canned and boxed food. We were famished, but it seemed worse than useless to ask the Japs for anything. An elderly American colonel did, however. He crossed the road and after pointing to the food and to the drooping prisoners, he went through the motions of eating.

A squat Jap officer grinned at him and picked up a can of salmon. Then he smashed it against the colonel's head, opening the American's cheek from eye to jawbone. The officer staggered and turned back toward us, wiping the blood off.

It seemed as though the Japs had been waiting for just such a brutal display to end the scene. They ordered us to our feet and herded us back into the road.

We knew now that Japs would respect neither age nor rank. Their ferocity grew as we marched on into the afternoon. They no longer were content with mauling stragglers or pricking them with bayonet points. The thrusts were intended to kill.

"VINEGAR JOE" AND CHINA

General Joseph Stilwell (1883–1946) was the American officer dispatched to head American interests in China and serve as Allied Chief of Staff to General Chiang Kai-shek. Stilwell himself, having previously served in China and mastered the language, was a vigorous proponent of substantial American military support to the embattled Chinese, who had been fighting the Japanese for a decade before Pearl Harbor. Most American military leaders, however, considered China a sideshow, either a distraction from more direct action against the German and Japanese homelands, or a potential quagmire complicated by the division of the Chinese resistance into nationalist and communist factions. Moreover, they doubted that Chinese troops would fight very effectively, even if "stiffened" with American units, and searched for other ways to provide aid. For example, the American Claire Chennault, famous for leading a volunteer group of American pilots, the "Flying Tigers," to fly missions over China, was convinced that American airpower could by itself liberate China. Stilwell, on the other hand, believed that without ground forces, airfields would be vulnerable to capture, and in any event he was optimistic that Chinese soldiers, properly trained and equipped, could acquit themselves well against the Japanese. He expected no real support from the British, who he felt were only interested in preserving their empire and viewed Burma and China as buffer zones to protect India. The following notes by Stilwell from a May 1943 conference in Washington reflect his frustration with the situation and are expressed with his characteristic abrasiveness and acerbity (not for nothing was the tart-tongued Stilwell known as "Vinegar Joe").

Continual concessions have confirmed Chiang K'ai-shek in the opinion that all he needs to do is yell and we'll cave in. As we are doing, F.D.R. had decided on an air effort in China before we reached Washington. This suited the British, who want no part of a fight for Burma. Why should they fight to build up China, if we can be euchered into bearing the brunt of the war against Japan? They'll get Burma back at the peace table anyway.

Nobody was interested in the humdrum work of building a ground force but me. Chennault promised to drive the Japs right out of China in six months, so why not give him the stuff to do it? It was the short cut to victory.

My point was that China was on the verge of collapse economically. That we could not afford to wait another year. That Yunnan [province in southwestern China] was indispensable and that a force had to be built up to hold it. That if the Japs took Yunnan, the recapture of Burma would be meaningless. That any increased air offensive that stung the Japs enough would bring a strong reaction that would wreck everything and put China out of the war....That the first essential step was to get

Joseph W. Stilwell, *The Stilwell Papers* (New York: W. Sloane, 1948), 204–206. Used by permission.

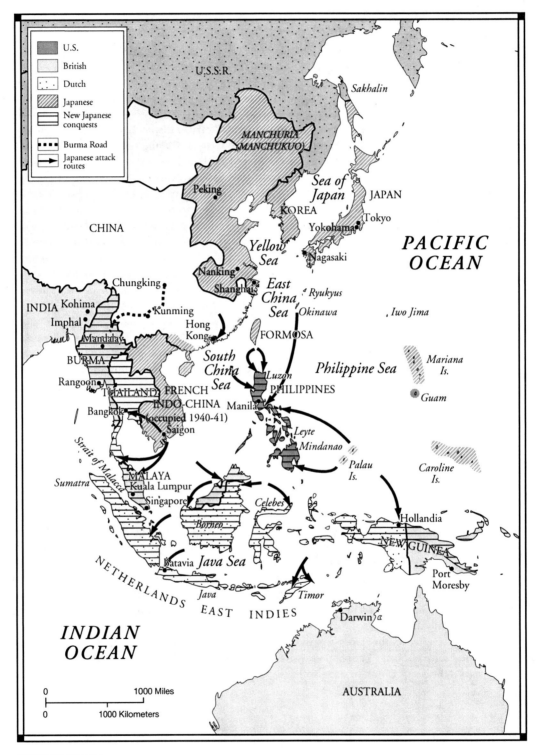

U.S.

British

Dutch

Japanese

New Japanese conquests

Burma Road

Japanese attack routes

U.S.S.R.

Sakhalin

MANCHURIA (MANCHUKUO)

CHINA

Peking

Sea of Japan

KOREA

JAPAN

Yokohama

Tokyo

Yellow Sea

Nanking

Shanghai

East China Sea

Nagasaki

PACIFIC OCEAN

Chungking

INDIA   Kohima

Imphal

Kunming

Hong Kong

Ryukyus

Okinawa

Iwo Jima

Mandalay

South China Sea

FORMOSA

Philippine Sea

Mariana Is.

BURMA

Rangoon

THAILAND   FRENCH INDO-CHINA (occupied 1940-41)

Bangkok

Saigon

Luzon

PHILIPPINES

Manila

Guam

Strait of Malacca

MALAYA

Kuala Lumpur

Singapore

Sumatra

Celebes

Borneo

Leyte

Mindanao

Palau Is.

Caroline Is.

NETHERLANDS

Batavia

Java Sea

Hollandia

NEW GUINEA

Java

EAST   INDIES

Timor

Port Moresby

Darwin

INDIAN OCEAN

0   1000 Miles

0   1000 Kilometers

AUSTRALIA

SOUTHEAST ASIA

a ground force capable of seizing and holding air-bases, and opening communications to China from the outside world. Overruled. Churchill's idea was, so he said, that China must be helped, and the only way to do it within the next few months was by air.

At the same time they decided on Saucy [code name for a Burma offensive in the fall] they made it practically impossible for me to prepare the Y force, and then ordered it used in an offensive. But the British reluctance caused the wording of the directive to be so loose that it would be up to the commander as to what he could do. He could go the limit or he could quit at any time. With Wavell in command, failure was inevitable; he had nothing to offer at any meeting except protestations that the thing was impossible. The Limeys [the British] all wanted to wait another year....

The inevitable conclusion was that Churchill has Roosevelt in his pocket. That they are looking for an easy way, a short cut for England, and no attention must be diverted from the Continent at any cost. The Limeys are not interested in the war in the Pacific, and with the President hypnotized they are sitting pretty.

Roosevelt wouldn't let me speak my piece. I interrupted twice, but Churchill kept pulling away from the subject, and it was impossible.

So everything was thrown to the air offensive. F.D.R. pulled 7,000 tons...out of the air when told that 10,000 was impossible, and ordered that tonnage for July. First 4,750 [tons] for air [Fourteenth Air Force], then 2,250 for ground. They will do the Japs some damage but at the same time will so weaken the ground effort that it may fail. Then what the hell use is it to knock down a few Jap planes?

Farewell lunch. Mr. Churchill: "Mr. President, I cannot but believe that an all-wise Providence has draped these great events, at this critical period of the world's history, about your personality and your high office." And Frank lapped it up.

Henry Stimson and George Marshall were understanding. The War Department was O.K. Even the air was a bit fed up on Chennault. But what's the use when the World's Greatest Strategist is against you.

THE BRITISH ARMY IN BURMA

Japanese divisions poured into Burma in January 1942 to sever supply routes to China and to cover of the flank of their ultimately successful assault on the British fortress of Singapore. At first, the Burmese attack went equally well and the British feared that Burma would be used as a staging ground for a thrust on India, the crown jewel of their empire. Ill-prepared and poorly led, the British forces (primarily Indian units) showed few signs of being able to stop the Japanese onslaught. Matters began to change, however, with the appointment of General Sir William Slim (1891–1970) to command of the Fourteenth Army. An imposing man physically, Slim radiated a bulldog-like determination which, coupled with a lack of pretension and a shrewd military mind, endeared him to his men and dramatically improved their performance. In particular, his men proved themselves in exceptionally bitter fighting during 1944 around Kohima and Imphal in western Burma, blunting a major Japanese offensive and regaining the initiative. He made effective use of airpower to reinforce isolated positions and move men and supplies more quickly than the Japanese. Slim's memoirs of the Burmese campaigns provide an exceptionally clear and refreshingly candid perspective on the reasons for Britain's initial difficulties and also for her eventual success.

In Burma we ought, whatever our strength, to have had one great advantage over the Japanese—we should have been fighting in a friendly country. The inhabitants should have been not only on our side, but organized and trained to help us. They were not. It is easy to say the Burmans disliked British rule and were therefore hostile to us, but I do not think that was actually so. A very small minority was actively and violently hostile. I should estimate it as certainly not more than five per cent....A larger section of the Burmese population was actively loyal as long as it seemed we should hold their native districts, while many of the hill tribes remained faithful to the British at great cost to themselves even during the Japanese occupation. The fact was that to the main mass of the peasant population the invasion was an inexplicable and sudden calamity; their only interest was, if possible not become involved in it and to avoid the soldiers of both sides.

Up to December 1941, even the military regarded the likelihood of invasion as remote, so it was not surprising that the civil government did not take comprehensive measures to educate and prepare the population for it. When it became evident that war was imminent, the civilian authorities were reluctant to organize evacuation schemes, refugee control, intelligence machinery, the militarization of railways, or anything in the nature of a Home Guard. There was a fear...that if the people were told unpleasant things about an unpleasant situation they might become depressed and panic. As a result, no one was prepared for war and the series of British reverses was a stunning surprise.

Viscount William Slim, *Defeat into Victory: Battling Japan in Britain and India, 1942–1945* (London: Cassell, 1956), 116–121, 181–189. Reprinted by permission of Harold Ober Associates Incorporated. Copyright © 1956 by Viscount William Slim.

The Burmese fighting forces themselves were affected in much the same way as their civilian brethren. They were hurriedly expanded with raw recruits who had no military tradition, and had incorporated in them civil armed corps such as the Burma Frontier Force and the Burma Military Police who were neither equipped nor trained for full-scale war. The position of their families was what really undermined the reliability of the Burmese soldiers, the police, and the lower grades of all the civil services. As we retreated their homes were left in the dangerous no-man's-land between the lines or in the crudely and brutally administered Japanese-occupied territory. Small wonder that many Burmans deserted to protect their families. Indians in the Burmese services, and there were many, were in an even worse plight, for their families not only suffered all the dangers that the Burmese did, but in addition were liable, without British protection to the savage hostility of Burmans, only too ready to seize an opportunity to vent their hatred. If the families of Indians, Anglo-Indians, and Anglo-Burmese in government employ could have been evacuated to India at the start of the campaign it might have caused some despondency among the local population, but it would have increased the reliability of the Burmese military and civil services considerably.

In spite of all these disadvantages we could have, if not defeated the Japanese, at least made a much better fight of it with even the small force of reliable troops we possessed, had they been properly trained. To our men, British or Indian, the jungle was a strange, fearsome place; moving and fighting in it was a nightmare. We were too ready to classify jungle as 'impenetrable,' as indeed it was to us with our motor transport, bulky supplies, and inexperience. To us it appeared only as an obstacle to movement and to vision; to the Japanese it was a welcome means of concealed manoeuvre and surprise. The Japanese used formations specially trained and equipped for a country of jungle and rivers, while we used troops whose training and equipment, as far as they had been completed, were for the open desert. The Japanese reaped the deserved reward for their foresight and thorough preparation; we paid the penalty for our lack of both.

To me, thinking it all over, the most distressing aspect of the whole disastrous campaign, had been the contrast between our generalship and the enemy's. The Japanese leadership was confident, bold to the point of foolhardiness, and so aggressive that never for one day did they lose the initiative. True, they had a perfect instrument for the type of operation they intended, but their use of it was unhesitating and accurate. Their object, clear and definite, was the destruction of our forces; ours a rather nebulous idea of retaining territory. This led to the initial dispersion of our forces over wide areas, an error which we continued to commit, and worse still it led to a defensive attitude of mind.

General Alexander had been confronted with a task beyond his means. He had been sent to Burma with orders to hold Rangoon, presumably because it was obvious that, if Rangoon fell, it was almost inevitable that all Burma would be lost. On his arrival he found the decisive battle of the campaign, the Sittang Bridge, had already been lost, and with it the fate of Rangoon sealed. The advent of the Chinese may have roused a flicker of hope that its recovery was possible, but the loss of Toungoo and the state of the Chinese armies soon quenched even that glimmer. It was then that we needed from the highest national authority a clear directive of what was to be our purpose in Burma. Were we to risk all in a desperate attempt to destroy the Japanese Army and recover all that had been lost? Ought we to fight to the end on some line to retain at least part of Burma? Or was our task to withdraw slowly, keeping our forces intact, while the defence of India was prepared? Had we been given any one of these as our great overall object it would have had an effect, not only on the major tactics of the campaign, but on the morale of the troops. No such directive was ever received. In the comparatively subordinate position of a corps commander, immersed in the hour-to-hour business of a fluctuating battle, I could not know what pressures were being exerted on the local higher command, but it was painfully obvious that the lack of a definite, realistic directive from above made it impossible for our immediate commanders to define our object with the clarity essential. Whoever was responsible, there was no doubt that we had been weakened basically by this lack of a clear object.

Tactically we had been completely outclassed. The Japanese could—and did—do many things that we could not. The chief of these and the tactical method on which all their successes were based was the 'hook.' Their standard action was, while holding us in front, to send a mobile force, mainly infantry, on a wide turning movement round our flank though the jungle to come in on our line of communications. Here, on the single road, up which all our supplies, ammunition, and reinforcements must come, they would establish a 'road-block,' sometimes with a battalion, sometimes with a regiment. We had few if any reserves in depth—all our troops were in the front line—and we had, therefore, when this happened, to turn about forces from the forward positions to clear the road-block. At this moment the enemy increased his pressure on our weakened front until it crumbled. Time and again the Japanese used these tactics, more often than not successfully, until our troops and commanders began to acquire a road-block mentality which often developed into an inferiority complex.

There was, of course, nothing new in this idea of moving round a flank; it is one of the oldest of stratagems, and there were many answers to it. The best answer would have been to do the same to the Japanese before they did it to us, but we, by reason of our complete dependence on motor transport and the unhandiness of our troops in the jungle, could not carry out these hooks successfully in any strength. They were only possible for forces trained and equipped for them. Another counter would have been to have put in the strongest possible frontal assault on the enemy while the flanking force was still distant in the jungle and he was divided. Japanese tenacity in defence and our lack of artillery, however, was such that before our assault had made much progress the flank blow was likely to be delivered. If we could have arranged our forces in more depth we might have held off the hook when it approached the road, but we never had enough troops to allow this. In any case, if we had, we could have employed them more profitably offensively. Lastly, there was at least a partial answer in supply by air, which would, temporarily at any rate, have removed our dependence on the road, but that needed aircraft and we had

literally none. Equipped and trained as we were in 1942, we had no satisfactory answer to the Japanese road-block....

In preparation, in execution, in strategy, and in tactics we had been worsted, and we had paid the penalty—defeat. Defeat is bitter. Bitter to the common soldier, but trebly bitter to his general. The soldier may comfort himself with the thought that, whatever the result, he has done his duty faithfully and steadfastly, but the commander has failed in *his* duty if he has not won victory—for that *is* his duty. He has no other comparable to it. He will go over in his mind the events of the campaign. 'Here,' he will think, 'I went wrong; here I took counsel of my fears when I should have been bold; there I should have waited to gather strength, not struck piecemeal; at such a moment I failed to grasp opportunity when it was presented to me.' He will remember the soldiers whom he sent into the attack that failed and who did not come back. He will recall the look in the eyes of men who trusted him. 'I have failed them,' he will say to himself, 'and failed my country!' He will see himself for what he is—a defeated general. In a dark hour he will turn in upon himself and question the very foundations of his leadership and his manhood.

And then he must stop! For, if he is ever to command in battle again, he must shake off these regrets, and stamp on them, as they claw at his will and his self-confidence. He must beat off these attacks he delivers against himself, and cast out the doubts born of failure. Forget them, and remember only the lessons to be learnt from defeat—they are more than from victory....

The men were calling themselves a 'Forgotten Army' long before some newspaper correspondent seized on the phrase. It was an understandable one. After all, the people of Britain had perils and excitements enough on their own doorsteps and Burma was far away. Its place in the general strategy was not clear, nor did what happened there seem vital. Much more stirring news was coming out of Africa. It was no use belly-aching because the Fourteenth Army was not in the headlines of the home papers; so far, we had not done anything to put us there. When we had won a victory or two we should be in a better position to complain. All the same, this feeling of neglect, of being at the bottom of all priority lists, had sunk deep. There was a good deal of bitterness in the army, and much too much being sorry for ourselves.

So when I took command, I sat quietly down to work out this business of morale, I came to certain conclusions, based not on any theory that I had studied, but on some experience and a good deal of hard thinking. It was on these conclusions that I set out consciously to raise the fighting spirit of my army.

Morale is a state of mind. It is that intangible force which will move a whole group of men to give their last ounce to achieve something, without counting the cost to themselves; that makes them feel they are part of something greater than themselves. If they are to feel that, their morale must, if it is to endure—and the essence of morale is that it should endure—have certain foundations. These foundations are spiritual, intellectual, and material, and that is the order of their importance. Spiritual first, because only spiritual foundations can stand real strain. Next intellectual, because men are swayed by reason as well as feeling. Material last—important, but last—because the very highest kinds of morale are often met when material conditions are lowest....

It was one thing thus neatly to marshal my principles but quite another to develop them, apply them, and get them recognized by the whole army.

At any rate our spiritual foundation was a firm one. I use the word spiritual, not in its strictly religious meaning, but as belief in a cause. Religion has always been and still is one of the greatest foundations of morale, especially of military morale. Saints and soldiers have much in common.... Yet religion, as we understand it, is not essential to high morale. Anyone who has fought with or against Nazi paratroops, Japanese suicide squads or Russian

Commissars, will have found this; but a spiritual foundation, belief in a cause, there must be.

We had this; and we had the advantage over our enemies that ours was based on real, not false, spiritual values. If ever an army fought in a just cause we did....It must be positive, aggressive, not a mere passive, defensive, anti-something feeling. So our object became not to defend India, to stop the Japanese advance, or even to occupy Burma, but to destroy the Japanese army, to smash it as an evil thing....

Now these things, while the very basis of morale, were the most difficult to put over, especially to the British portion of the army. The problem was how to instill or revive their beliefs in the men of many races who made up the Fourteenth Army. I felt there was only one way to do it, by a direct approach to the individual men themselves. Not by written exhortations, by wireless speeches, but by informal talks and contacts between troops and commanders....

It was in these ways we laid the spiritual foundations, but that was not enough; they would have crumbled without the others, the intellectual and the material. Here we had first to convince the doubters that our object, the destruction of the Japanese Army in battle was practicable....A victory in a large-scale battle was, in our present state of training, organization, and confidence, not to be attempted. We had first to get the feel through the army that it was we who were hunting the Jap, not he us....

This was done in a series of carefully planned minor offensive operations, carried out as the weather improved, against enemy advanced detachments. These were carefully staged, ably led and, as I was always careful to ensure, in greatly preponderating strength....We laid the first of our intellectual foundations of morale; everyone knew we could defeat the Japanese, our object *was* attainable.

JAPANESE OPERATIONS IN BURMA

General Slim had worked hard to restore the morale and military efficiency of his forces as a prelude to repulsing attacks and then seizing the initiative and driving the Japanese out of Burma. The following selection by a Japanese officer relates how their offensive was blunted by logistical difficulties in supplying a campaign in inhospitable terrain, the greater firepower of the Allied troops than of the Chinese forces this particular Japanese unit had previously faced, and a lack of intelligence about their adversaries' strength and intentions. In the midst of the tenacious combat, Captain Kameyama specifically notes that his unit was ordered *not* to execute prisoners or neglect enemy wounded as had apparently been common in previous actions. His account also evokes the courage as well as the close personal bonds and mutual respect that kept his unit functioning under harrowing circumstances.

I took part in 'Operation Imphal' as we called it: the Japanese official name was 'Operation U-Go,' which we were told a necessity was for the defence of Burma. However, we thought that it would not be easy to win, as we had to cross the rugged Arakan mountain range for about 200 kilometres from east to west. As the supply of food, ammunitions and many others was crucial, we had to carry by ourselves two weeks' rations, ammunition, shovels and clothes; a total weight of 40 to 50 kilograms. This was so heavy that once we sat down to rest we could not stand up by ourselves; we had to be pulled up by someone....

In the evening of 21 March, we occupied the village of Sangshak and found that it was not the main position of the enemy, so we then attacked a hill north-west of the village and occupied the enemy's south front position. The enemy mounted a heavy counterattack on us after sunrise. This was the first time we had fought with the British-Indian forces, which was very different from our experience of fighting the Chinese army which had inferior weapons to ours.... From our experience in China we were

confident of the success of the night attack, but we had to expect that a mass of bullets from the overwhelming enemy automatic weapons would result in much greater casualties....

As the grenades we threw into the enemy position exploded continuously with much noise, some of the enemy seemed to be getting rattled. Taking this opportunity, the battalion commander stood up crying excitedly, 'Charge! Charge!' and took the lead in dashing at the enemy position. We secured the position and 6th Company took up formation to prepare for the counterattack. After a while, when the situation seemed settled, I ventured an opinion to the commander. 'On the next charge, please follow the company commander and platoon leader. Your presence is the basis for morale of all soldiers of the battalion.' He thought for a while and then looked up at me gently: 'I understand your opinion. I do hate the need to urge soldiers to fight more vigorously. But I must respect the pride of my commanders.'...

We attacked every night from the 22nd to 25th and every night many soldiers were killed. Despite

Captain Shosaku Kameyama, Third Battalion, Fifty-eight Infantry Regiment, Thirty-one Division, "Operation Imphal," in Kazuo Tamayama and John Nunneley, *Tales by Japanese Soldiers of the Burma Campaign, 1942–1945* (London: Cassell & Co., 2000), 157–159, 161–163, 167–171. Used by permission.

that, we went forward. In war it is hard to comprehend the real situation. We felt that we were badly off as we knew our situation well, while we did not know the state of the enemy. But it happened that the enemy at Sangshak escaped. As we attacked on five consecutive nights, the enemy could not sleep and their nerve must have broken down. That's why they retreated....

I was very much impressed to see that the corpse and sword of LT [Lieutenant] Ban had been buried neatly packed in a blanket. Our men were all moved by this. As the enemy treated our company commander respectfully, our regimental commander ordered that enemy wounded should be treated and prisoners of war (those captured) should not be killed. After fierce battles when many comrades were killed, men were excited and felt strong hatred against the enemy soldiers and were provoked to kill even helpless prisoners. At that time our commanders had a conscience and controlled our men. The badly wounded enemy soldiers were sent to a Japanese field hospital.

Eight hundred and fifty men of our battalion crossed the River Chindwin, but now after twelve days, active men were reduced to half, 425 men. It was very heavy damage and in a normal situation the fighting power of the battalion would be regarded as almost lost....

Although my commander was shot through his neck he did not agree to be hospitalized. I wished to treat my own wound [fragments in the face from a mortar shell] as I could hardly open my mouth and eyes. But as the wounded commander said he would proceed to the next battlefield and asked me, 'How about you?' I had to say, 'I will accompany you,' against my personal inclination. So both the commander and I were bandaged like monsters and went to Kohima [a village of 4,000 people and important road junction]. Because of my wound I could not chew, so my only food was milk poured into my mouth as I looked upward....

On the evening of 6th April Captain Nagaya went ahead to scout the enemy positions and happened to come out in front of one. Being in imminent danger, the commander and his men rushed the position and captured it, but a grenade struck his head and he was killed. At that time I remained in the rear to organise arriving units for the attack. When I ran to him, he was dead, lying on makeshift stretcher, a tent sheet tied between two poles. A small bundle of white wild chamomile was laid near his nose, which was the only offering to him. As we were to charge the enemy that evening, I could do nothing for him as my duty came first. I asked someone to take care of the corpse; to bury him in earth and cut off his finger and cremate it. The finger bone would be sent to his home....

I still told the men that we would keep fighting, but in order to lessen our load we should first send back the wounded and then the bodies of the dead soldiers for their bones to be sent home. On the battlefield if a man feels 'I should do this' or 'I should defend here,' he thinks of nothing other than his mission. If he is told to retreat, he feels that he is saved and wants to stay alive and loses his courage. When about half of the dead were carried down, I told the men regretfully that we should not try again as we would not win even if we charged the enemy. So we went down with machine guns and the remaining corpses. I carried on my back a dead soldier. A dead man is heavy, in the same way as a sleeping baby is heavier. When I carried him on the back, his head bumped against my neck. When I changed his position, his cold head stuck to the other side of my neck. Painful feeling of sorrow....

From the bitter experience of the last attack, we realised that we could not win against the strong enemy, who had many automatic weapons, by surprise night attack as we had done successfully in China. So we laid out all available anti-tank guns, medium machine guns, light machine guns and grenade launchers (2-inch mortars), and assigned each gun a specific target....After breaking through several defence lines we finally captured the hilltop by noon of 9 April. But our strength had been exhausted....

After the attack our rifle companies which originally had 180 men each were reduced to four in the 5th, four in the 6th, sixteen in the 7th and none in the 8th. Machine Gun Company had thirty-five and Battalion Gun Platoon fifteen. With such small numbers of men we were not able to attack any more. As our mission was to prevent the enemy reaching Imphal as long as we could, we went on the defence....

Although we kept fighting it was very lonely and miserable to stay isolated in a foxhole on the mountain in the situation when a chance of winning seemed too remote. We ran out of ammunition and food, so sometimes we went out to attack an enemy position at night, and when the enemy ran away after firing several rounds, we collected rations, bullets and grenades, and used them the next day. In this way we held out stoutly day by day, but inevitably someone got hurt or killed, so only a few,

maximum seven to eight, men defended a position. It was heartbreaking that even if one did his best, nothing could help....

We were short of food, but most distressing was that we did not have bullets. Still we did not give up and never thought of running away. In fact, our unit was not beaten off in the fighting, but by the bold strategic decision of Lt General Kotoku Sato, Commander 31 Division, we turned back towards Burma. We walked over the muddy mountains, drenched in rain, exhausted and hungry, and got back to our base on the River Chindwin in the latter part of July 1944.

MARXISM AND BURMESE RESISTANCE

World War II sounded the death knell of European colonialism. Traditional systems of European domination simply crumbled in the face of Japanese attacks, and with that, the deferential respect Asian or African subjugated populations had been accustomed to grant their colonial masters. Many independence-minded politicians were prepared to work with the Japanese conquerors, therefore, and to turn the anti-imperialist rhetoric of Japan's much-hyped "Greater East Asia Co-Prosperity Sphere" to their own ends. Burma, for example, was declared independent from British rule in 1942. To their dismay, however, many Asian nationalists discovered that with the arrival of Japanese armies they had merely exchanged one imperial master for another. "Co-Prosperity" meant Japan's prosperity, and all forms of political expression or economic activity were subjugated to the Japanese military's overriding concern with its own security. Thein Pe Myint (1914–1978) was a leading Burmese Marxist intellectual who differed from his colleagues in refusing to work with the "Japanese fascists" from the outset. He had become involved in anticolonial politics as a university student in Rangoon (the capital of Burma) in the 1930s, and served during the war as an effective liaison between independence-minded Burmese officers and British special forces. He was also keenly interested in the war's impact on India, and whether Indian nationalists could work together toward independence as well. The well-traveled Thein Pe Myint's wartime memoirs offer both a summary of the obstacles the Japanese faced in conquering Burma, and the challenges the Allies would face, once the Japanese were defeated, in dealing with the new political realities of the postwar era.

Excerpts from pp.172–174, 270–272 from *Marxism and Resistance in Burma, 1942–1954: Thein Pe Myint's Wartime Traveler*, edited by Robert H. Taylor. Reprinted with permission of Ohio University Press, Athens, Ohio, 1984, (www.ohioswallow.com).

We wanted to go to Bombay because the situation between the National Congress and the government of India was growing tense. We would arrive on August 9. An All India Congress Committee meeting was arranged for that day. At this meeting the so-called Struggle Resolution to resist the authorities and boycott the government, the call of the "Quit India" movement, was to be passed. The Muslim League, headed by Mr. Jinnah [Muslim India-born politician who first sought to secure rights of Muslim minority within India and later viewed partition as the only solution], was repeatedly demanding to be given a separate Pakistan. In fierce opposition to the Congress, the League insisted that the British could not quit India without separating Pakistan. But the Congress would not agree to a separate Pakistan. They would not recognize a Muslim people.

The conflict between the National Congress and the Muslim League was an elixir that strengthened the continued rule of the British. The British even encouraged general unrest and emphasized these differences.

At this time the Communist Party was still in the Congress. The proposals of the Party included demands, first, that India move against the chief enemy, fascist Japan: second, that accord be established between the National Congress and the Muslim League; and third, that the British hand over power while remaining basically united with India in the anti-Japanese resistance battle....

This whole situation was very good for the Japanese....If India fell under the hand of the Japanese fascists, then fascist domination of the whole world would be inevitable. Great peril was about to befall all peoples—the human race would be without freedom for years to come.

At this time there were many reports of the battle of Stalingrad, which, when we heard them, rekindled and fanned our fervor....[I]f Stalingrad were taken, then the Caucasus could be crossed and the Germans would thrust down into the Middle East. Once they succeeded in dominating the Middle East, they would enter India from the west. The Germans and the Japanese would then join hands in India. This was the fascists' grand strategy.

However, the Germans were facing the fiercest resistance yet at Stalingrad, suffering great casualties at the hands of the Soviet Red Army. For us, the antifascist workers of Burma and India, the battle of Stalingrad was a ray of hope in a night of darkness....

August 9 arrived. Before dawn the police arrested at their homes the leaders of the Congress including Mr. Gandhi, Pandit Nehru, and Sardar Patel. Then turbulence descended on the country. In Delhi many mass demonstrations erupted though there was no planning or special calls for meetings. The masses demonstrated of their own accord. The streets were filled almost everywhere. Demonstrations continued for four days. The masses surrounded and destroyed trams, gas stations, offices, and jails, and arsonists set fires. These, after all, were the symbols of English capitalism and the English bureaucracy.

Needless to say, our sentiments were on the side of the Congress. However, we were not pleased with the destruction. It could produce good only for the fascist Japanese.

The Communist Party joined the demonstrations of the masses, but it attempted to keep law and order as much as possible. The Party members argued with the demonstrators not to allow their hatred of the English to improve the fortunes of the Japanese. Shouting the slogan "Hindu-Muslim bai bai," they checked the anti-imperialist spirit so that it would not turn into a race riot....

The Japanese front-line forces in Burma were reckoned to have at least 130,000 men. With reinforcements there was probably a total of about 200,000 Japanese. In terms of quantity, victory could be secured only if the Chiang Kai-shek Chinese were included. However, Chiang Kai-shek was not reliable and was used to bargaining for advantages. If he could not get the right price, not only would he not send more troops but he would even withdraw those troops already sent. Therefore, the Allied side did not underestimate the Japanese....

On the Lushai-Chin war front, on the Manipur-Chin state war front, and on the Arakan war front, the battles were fierce. They estimated that thirty thousand Japanese perished. In 1942 and 1943 not one Japanese prisoner of war was taken; now in the present battles the Allies took special pride in the fact that they captured about one hundred Japanese prisoners of war during a single week. The Japanese had to withdraw from these battle zones.

The Allies thought the Japanese would regroup and mass their forces on the Shwebo-Sagaing plain. A Japanese counterattack from this plain would cause enormous battles. From the Allies' point of view the plain ordinarily was preferable as a site for battle because they used large weapons that were better on the plains than in hilly areas, jungles, and forested regions. They would even be able to use artillery and the famous Sherman tank and therefore would be able to destroy the Japanese by force of arms. Despite the obvious advantages, the plain had one major drawback since the Chittagong and Manipur bases of the Allies were far away and communications were difficult; there were large rivers and jungled mountains between. The roads, which were specially cut, were not good. As a result, they would have to rely primarily on air to convey all their arms and supplies. In this respect the Japanese, who would be able to use the land and water routes easily, had the advantage because they would also be able to bring in reinforcements rapidly.

Thus our antifascist resistance soldiers inside the country had a role of great importance. They could strike the Japanese from behind and inflict serious injury. They could break their communication lines....

In addition, in planning strategy and tactics, the two aims—the Allies' imperialist aims and our people's aims—began to appear quite different. The imperialists' aim was to rule as firmly as before as soon as the Japanese were defeated and Burma reconfiscated. To the fulfillment of this aim the solidly united armed Burmese resistance forces would provide an impediment. Therefore, the Allies did not wish all of the Burmese resistance forces to rise together. The Allies wished only that groups in the Burmese resistance forces would rise, revolt, and fight in separate sections just in front of the Allied troops, close to the battle line immediately behind the Japanese front line....

Our people's aim was to win complete independence from the British imperialists after defeating the Japanese fascists. To satisfy an aim like this, the armed forces had to be solidly united under the control of the Burmese independence forces. Therefore, it was important to have nationwide armed resistance against the Japanese. Only through nationwide resistance would it be possible to organise by proper stages to enter into battle for complete liberation of the whole country. Relying primarily on ourselves, all of the Burmese masses would enter into the struggle of the great antifascist resistance people's war. Only then would a military victory be a people's victory.

THE INDIAN SITUATION

Viscount, later Earl, Archibald Wavell (1883–1950) was a very capable officer who had a knack for being in the wrong place at the wrong time. As British commander in the Middle East in 1941, he oversaw the rout of Italian troops in North Africa with numerically inferior forces, only to be stripped of some of his best units (which were sent to aid Greece) and driven back toward Egypt by Rommel's Afrika Korps. In July 1941, he was given command in India and expected to mastermind the defense of Burma, only to find his army overmatched against the Japanese (for the reasons already analyzed by General Slim) and forced to retreat. Two years later, in October 1943, Wavell was appointed as viceroy (the British Crown's administrative head) of India, in what was assumed would be a less challenging post than military command. Yet Wavell was confronted by a myriad of difficulties: Indians were largely united in their conviction that Britain could no longer continue to govern them in a paternalistic and colonialist manner, yet they were deeply divided over what shape a postwar India might take, given the deep rifts over religion and caste. Moreover, although many Indian nationalists were willing to support the British war effort against Japan in anticipation of postwar self-government (as had been offered by British emissary Stafford Cripps in March 1942) or outright independence, others felt that no imperialist power merited their assistance and called either for passive resistance (as championed by Gandhi) or rebellion to force Britain to "quit India." The British government responded by breaking up the main institution voicing Indian nationalist aspirations (the Indian National Congress) and arresting many of its members. No sooner had Wavell arrived into this highly charged atmosphere than he was forced to deal with ruinous inflation and a catastrophic famine in Bengal, the result of harvest failure and the disruption of rice imports from Burma. Despite his best efforts to divert food shipments for the starving (British bureaucrats emphasized that the necessary shipping was required for military purposes), perhaps 3 million Indians died. By the time Wavell had served a year as viceroy, he recognized that the political landscape in India had changed forever as a result of the war, and he urged Churchill and the British cabinet to adopt a more flexible and sympathetic approach to India than they had demonstrated in the past.

24th October 1944

My dear Prime Minister [Winston Churchill],

I will begin by saying that my primary reason for writing is that I feel very strongly that the future of India is the problem on which the British Commonwealth and the British reputation will stand or fall in the post-war period. To my mind, our strategic security, our name in the world for statesmanship and fairdealing and much of our economic well-being will depend on the settlement we make in India. Our prestige and prospects in Burma, Malaya, China and the Far East generally are entirely subject to what happens in India. If we can secure India as a friendly

Penderel Moon, ed., *Wavell: The Viceroy's Journal* (London: Oxford University Press, 1973), 94–99. Used by permission.

partner in the British commonwealth our predominant influence in these countries will, I think, be assured; with a lost and hostile India, we are likely to be reduced in the East to the position of commercial bag-men.

And yet I am bound to say that after a year's experience in my present office I feel that the vital problems of India are being treated by His Majesty's Government with neglect, even sometimes with hostility and contempt. I entirely admit the difficulty of the problems, I know the vital preoccupations of the European war. I agree in the main with what I think is your conviction, that in a mistaken view of Indian conditions and in an entirely misplaced sentimental liberalism we took the wrong turn with India 25 or 30 years ago; but we cannot put back the clock and must deal with existing conditions and pledges; and I am clear that our present attitude is aggravating the mischief.

May I give you a few instances of what seem to me a neglectful or unfriendly attitude to India and her problems.

I read the proceedings of the meetings of the Dominion Premiers. India, one of the most vital problems of the Commonwealth, was hardly mentioned, either from the strategic or political point of view.

At the last big debate on India in the House of Commons, I am told that there were hardly ever more than 40 members present.

In spite of the lesson of the Bengal famine, I have had during the last nine months literally to fight with all the words I could command, sometimes almost intemperate, to secure food imports; without which we should undoubtedly be in the throes of another famine, and probably of uncontrolled inflation, since without these imports I could hardly have held food prices from soaring as they did last year.

The recent increase of soldiers' pay, which have added some £50,000,000 to our inflationary position, already precarious, and a considerable part of this sum to the Indian tax-payer's burden, were introduced without any consultation of India at all, or even warning; though we could have suggested means of easing the burden both for the British and Indian tax-payer; and Indian Members of Council

would have felt no resentment if they had been consulted in advance.

The obloquy now being heaped on India for the lack of amenities for soldiers is mainly due to disregard of repeated requests during the past three years or more for doctors, nurses, medical comforts, and goods of all kinds....

Apart from the food problem, I have endeavoured to stimulate planning for post-war development over the whole administrative field, both in industry and agriculture, so as to secure a better standard of living for the Indian people; and I have appointed a special additional Member of Council to deal with the problem. This is an immense task, perhaps impossible under the present Government of India....

When we started, 20 or 30 years again, on the political reform of India, we laid down a course from which we cannot now withdraw. It may have been a mistaken course, and it would probably have been better to have prescribed economic development first; but I am afraid it is too late to reverse the policy now. And the general policy, of giving India self-government at an early date, was confirmed not long ago in the Cripps offer.

Nor do I think that in any case we can hold India down by force. Indians are a docile people, and a comparatively small amount of force ruthlessly used might be sufficient; but it seems to me clear that the British people will not consent to be associated with a policy of repression, nor will world opinion approve it, nor will British soldiers wish to stay here in large numbers after the war to hold the country down. There must be acquiescence in the British connection if we are to continue to keep India within the Commonwealth.

India will never, within any time that we can foresee, be an efficient country, organised and governed on western lines. In her development to self-government we have got to be prepared to accept a degree of inefficiency comparable to that in China, Iraq, or Egypt. We must do our best to maintain the standards of efficiency we have tried to inculcate, but we cannot continue to resist reform because it will make the administration less efficient.

The present Government of India cannot continue indefinitely, or even for long. Though ultimate responsibility still rests with His Majesty's Government, His Majesty's Government has no longer the power to take effective action. We shall drift increasingly into situations—financial, economic, or political—for which India herself will be responsible but for which His Majesty's Government will get the discredit....

If our aim is to retain India as a willing member of the British Commonwealth, we must make some imaginative and constructive move without delay. We have every reason to mistrust and dislike Gandhi and Jinnah, and their followers. But the Congress and the League are the dominant parties in Hindu and Muslim India, and will remain so. They control the Press, the electoral machine, the money bags; and have the prestige of established parties. Even if Gandhi and Jinnah disappeared tomorrow...I can see no prospect of our having more reasonable people to deal with....

When we should make any fresh move is a difficult problem. I am quite clear that it should be made some considerable time before the end of the Japanese war. When the Japanese war ends, we shall have to release our political prisoners. They will find India unsettled and discontented. Food will still be short; demobilization and the closing down of the war factories, and overgrown clerical establishments, will throw many people out of employment. They will find fertile field for agitation, unless we have previously diverted their energies into some more profitable channel, i.e., into dealing with the administrative problems of India and into trying to solve the constitutional problem. We cannot move without taking serious risks; but the most serious risk of all is that India after the war will become a running sore which will sap the strength of the British Empire. I think it is still possible to keep India within the Commonwealth, though I do not think it will be easy to do so. If we fail to make any effort now we may hold India down uneasily for some years, but in the end she will pass into chaos and probably into other hands.

To be effective any move we make must be such as to capture the Indian imagination. If India is not to be ruled by force, it must be ruled by the heart rather than by the head. Our move must be sincere and friendly, and our outlook towards India must change accordingly. I am prepared to put proposals for a move, which will involve risks, but which I think constitute the best chance of making progress.

What I have in mind is a provisional political Government, of the type suggested in the Cripps declaration, within the present constitution, coupled with an earnest but not necessarily simultaneous attempt to devise means to reach a constitutional settlement....But the real essential is a change of spirit, a change which will convince the average educated Indian that the British Government is sincere in its intentions and is friendly towards India. It will not be easy to do, there is very deep-rooted feeling of suspicion to overcome, but certain steps could be taken which would help to reduce the mistrust and enmity now generally felt. In fact, if we want India as a Dominion after the war, we must begin treating her much more like a Dominion now. If certain measures, which I would suggest, were taken by His Majesty's Government, and I were permitted within a policy approved by His Majesty's Government to try and convince India of British sympathy, I believe it would be possible to effect a considerable improvement.

MARINES ON PELELIU

Eugene Sledge's *With the Old Breed,* his recollection of his service in the Pacific with the First Marine Division, is widely regarded as one of the finest memoirs of not just World War II, but of any war. Sledge (1923–2001), from Mobile, Alabama, initially wrote his account just for his family, so they could understand what he went through, and it was his wife who brought the manuscript to the attention of a publisher. Sledge served in some of the bloodiest campaigns of the war, though none worse than the invasion of the tiny island of Peleliu in September 1944. A six-square-mile dot of land with an airstrip, it was defended by some 11,000 Japanese soldiers. The campaign, which was expected to take a few days, lasted some two months. When it was over, all but 200 of the Japanese defenders had died, and the marines had absorbed some 10,000 casualties (dead and wounded) themselves. Eight congressional Medals of Honor (the nation's highest distinction for bravery) were awarded. Here Sledge provides an extraordinarily vivid and candid account of that fighting, and of its impact upon him. Miraculously, Sledge survived the war unhurt and went on to become a biology professor, though he would be haunted by nightmares of his wartime experiences.

As we jumped into the crater, three Japanese soldiers ran out of the pillbox door past the sand bank and headed for a thicket. Each carried his bayoneted rifle in his right hand and held up his pants with his left hand. This action so amazed me that I stared in disbelief and didn't fire my carbine. I wasn't afraid, as I had been under shell fire, just filled with wild excitement. My buddies were more effective than I and cut down the enemy with a hail of bullets. They congratulated each other while I chided myself for being more curious about strange Japanese customs than with being combat effective.

The amtrac [an armed amphibious tractor] rattling toward us by this time was certainly a welcome sight. As it pulled into position, several more Japanese raced from the pillbox in a tight group. Some held their bayoneted rifles in both hands, but some of them carried their rifles in one hand and held up their pants with the other. I had overcome my initial surprise and joined the others and the amtrac machine gun in firing away at them. They tumbled onto the hot coral in a forlorn tangle of bare legs, falling rifles, and rolling helmets. We felt no pity for them but exulted over their fate. We had been shot at and shelled too much and had lost too many friends to have compassion for the enemy when we had him cornered.

The amtrac took up a position on a line even with us. Its commander, a sergeant, consulted Burgin. Then the turret gunner fired three armor-piercing 75mm shells at the side of the pillbox. Each time our ears rang with the familiar *wham-bam* as the report of the gun was followed quickly by the explosion of the shell on a target at close range. The third shell tore a hole entirely through the pillbox. Fragments kicked up dust around our abandoned packs and mortars on the other side. On the side nearest us, the hole was about four feet in diameter. Burgin yelled to the tankers to cease firing lest our equipment be damaged.

Someone remarked that if fragments hadn't killed those inside, the concussion surely had. But even before the dust settled, I saw a Japanese soldier appear at the blasted opening. He was grim determination

Eugene Sledge, *With the Old Breed* (New York: Oxford University Press, 1990), 116–117, 156–157. Used by permission.

personified as he drew back his arm to throw a grenade at us.

My carbine was already up. When he appeared, I lined up my sights on his chest and began squeezing off shots. As the first bullet hit him, his face contorted in agony. His knees buckled. The grenade slipped from his grasp. All the men near me, including the amtrac machine gunner, had seen him and began firing. The soldier collapsed in the fusillade, and the grenade went off at his feet.

Even in the midst of these fast-moving events, I looked down at my carbine with sober reflection. I had just killed a man at close range. That I had seen clearly the pain on his face when my bullets hit him came as a jolt. It suddenly made the war a very personal affair. The expression on that man's face filled me with shame and then disgust for the war and all the misery it was causing.

My combat experience thus far made me realize that such sentiments for an enemy soldier were the maudlin meditations of a fool. Look at me, a member of the 5th Marine Regiment—one of the oldest, finest, and toughest regiments in the Marine Corps—feeling

ashamed because I had shot a damned foe before he could throw a grenade at me! I felt like a fool and was thankful my buddies couldn't read my thoughts....

None of us would ever be the same after what we had endured. To some degree that is true, of course, of all human experience. But something in me died at Peleliu. Perhaps it was a childish innocence that accepted as faith the claim that man is basically good. Possibly I lost faith that politicians in high places who do not have to endure war's savagery will ever stop blundering and sending others to endure it.

But I also learned important things on Peleliu. A man's ability to depend on his comrades and immediate leadership is absolutely necessary. I'm convinced that our discipline, espirit de corps, and tough training were the ingredients that equipped me to survive the ordeal physically and mentally—given a lot of good luck, of course. I learned realism, too. To defeat an enemy as tough and dedicated as the Japanese, we had to be just as tough. We had to be just as dedicated to America as they were to their Emperor. I think this was the essence of Marine Corps doctrine in World War II, and that history vindicates that doctrine.

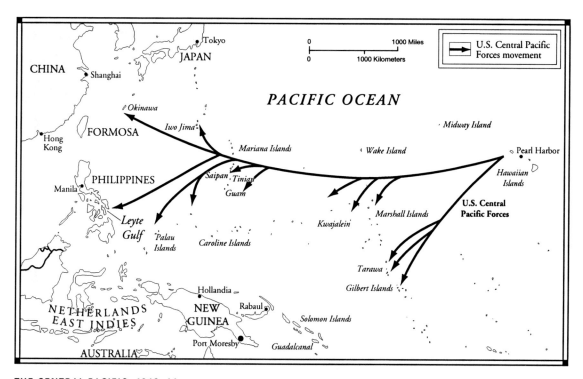

THE CENTRAL PACIFIC, 1942–44

KAMIKAZE ATTACK

One of the most stressful aspects of the Pacific War, and what differentiated it from the European theater, was the willingness, indeed the determination, of the Japanese to fight to the death, even when it served no rational military purpose. American sailors had to endure suicide bombing runs on their ships by kamikazes, planes whose pilots would not seek to drop a bomb and return to base to fly another mission, but rather would attempt to crash their planes into American ships, detonating the bombs and killing themselves in the process. The term *kamikaze* (divine wind) evoked the miraculous survival of Japan against numerically superior forces centuries earlier when a threatening enemy fleet was dispersed by a timely typhoon. Seaman James Fahey (1918–1991) was a resourceful Manhattan-born (from the section known as "Hell's Kitchen") antiaircraft gunner who served about the light cruiser USS *Montpelier*. He scribbled diary entries whenever he had sufficient paper and free time, though in November 1944, when his ship was participating in action in Leyte Gulf, there was little opportunity for relaxation or reflection.

Monday, November 27, 1944

Jap planes were coming at us from all directions. Before the attack started we did not know that they were suicide planes, with no intention of returning to their base. They had one thing in mind and that was to crash into our ships, bombs and all. You have to blow them up, to damage them doesn't mean much. Right off the bat a Jap plane made a suicide dive at the cruiser *St. Louis*, there was a big explosion and flames were seen shortly from the stern. Another one tried to do the same thing but he was shot down. A Jap plane came in on a battleship with its guns blazing away. Other Jap planes came in strafing one ship, dropping their bombs on another and crashing into another ship. The Jap planes were falling all around us, the air was full of Jap machine gun bullets. Jap planes and bombs were hitting all around us. Some of our ships were being hit by suicide planes, bombs and machine gun fire. It was a fight to the finish. While all this was taking place our ship had its hands full with Jap planes. We knocked our share of planes down but we also got hit by 3 suicide planes, but lucky for us they dropped their bombs before they crashed into us. In the meantime exploding planes overhead were showering us with their parts. It looked like it was raining plane parts. They were falling all over the ship. Quite a few of the men were hit by big pieces of Jap planes.... One suicide dive bomber was heading right for us while we were firing at other attacking planes and if the 40 mm. mount behind us on the port side did not blow the Jap wing off it would have killed all of us.... Another suicide plane crashed into one of the 5 inch mounts, pushing the side of the mount in and injuring some of the men inside.... A Jap dive bomber crashed into one of the 40 mm. mounts but lucky for them it dropped its bombs on another ship before crashing....

Another suicide plane just overshot us. It grazed the 6 inch [gun] turret. It crashed into Leyte Gulf.

There was a terrific explosion as the bombs exploded, about 20 ft. away. If we were going a little faster we would have been hit. The Jap planes that were not destroyed with our shells crashed into the water close by or hit our ships. It is a tough job to hold back this tidal wave of suicide planes. They come at you from all directions and also straight down at us at a very fast pace but some of the men have time for a few fast jokes, "This would be a great time to run out of ammunition." "This is mass suicide at its best." Another suicide plane came down at us in a very steep dive. It was a near miss, it just missed the 5 inch mount. The starboard side of the ship was showered with water and fragments. How long will our luck hold out? The Good Lord is really watching over us. This was very close to my 40 mm. mount and we were showered with debris. If the suicide plane exploded on the 5 inch mount, the ammunition would have gone up, after that anything could happen.

Planes were falling all around us, bombs were coming too close for comfort. The Jap planes were cutting up the water with machine gun fire. All the guns on the ship were blazing away, talk about action, never a dull moment. The fellows were passing ammunition like lightning as the guns were turning in all directions spitting out hot steel.

Parts of destroyed suicide planes were scattered all over the ship. During a little lull in the action the men would look around for Jap souvenirs and what souvenirs they were. I got part of the plane. The deck near my mount was covered with blood, guts, brains, tongues, scalps, hearts, arms etc. from the Jap pilots.... The Japs were spattered all over the place....

These suicide or kamikaze pilots wanted to destroy us, our ships and themselves. This gives you an idea what kind of an enemy we were fighting. The air attacks in Europe are tame compared to what you run up against out here against the Japs. The Germans will come in so far, do their job and take off but not the Japs.... You do not discourage the Japs, they never give up, you have to kill them. It is an honor to die for the Emperor. We do not know how many Jap planes were shot down or the total of planes that attacked us during all the action but they threw plenty of them at us.... The attack lasted for 2 hours, we went to battle stations at 10:50 a.m. in the morning and secured at 2:10 p.m. in the afternoon. The action took place not too far from Leyte. Every ship had its hands full with the Jap planes during those 2 hours. The Japs started the attack with 30 planes but after that more planes kept joining them.

THE DECISION TO USE THE BOMB

After scientists recognized the destructive potential of weapons harnessing the principle of nuclear fission, and strategists began to ponder the tremendous military advantage that possession of such weapons would confer, halting efforts began in several countries toward the production of atomic bombs. But the practical and financial obstacles to be overcome were tremendous, and Germany, Japan, and the Soviet Union were unable to make significant progress toward building a workable bomb. The United States, however, possessed the necessary critical mass of political will, scientific talent, money, and undisturbed research facilities, all brought together in the Manhattan Project (named for the initial headquarters of the program), to turn scientific theory into military reality. Directed from the summer of 1942 onward by General Leslie Groves, under the aegis of the Secretary of War, Henry Stimson, the Manhattan Project required the then staggering sum of $2 billion, and was conducted in secrecy around the country in Los Alamos (New Mexico), Oakridge (Tennessee), and Hanford (Washington). In its early stages, Manhattan Project scientists were apprehensive that Germany would beat them to the finish line and produce a bomb first, but by the spring of 1945 it was clear that the European war would end with no recourse to nuclear weapons. But their use on Japan remained a possibility, and by mid-July 1945, Dr. Robert Oppenheimer (the scientific director of the project) and his fellow researchers had overcome the myriad obstacles and were ready to test a prototype. That test, at the remote Alamogordo Reservation, New Mexico, was successful. An atomic bomb detonating enriched uranium (the "Little Boy") was dropped on the Japanese city of Hiroshima on August 6, 1945, and a second bomb, utilizing plutonium (the "Fat Man"), leveled Nagasaki three days later. Historians may debate whether the course of the war was truly affected, but there was little doubt among thoughtful observers that the existence of such awesomely destructive and environmentally catastrophic weapons had changed the world itself forever. Henry Stimson (1867–1950) grasped some of the implications of atomic weaponry even as the Manhattan Project progressed, and he was a deeply principled man who strenuously (and successfully) objected to the identification of the historic city Kyoto as a target, opposed the introduction of the Morgenthau Plan (see chapter 11) to dismantle postwar Germany, and forcefully advocated bringing German war criminals to justice. Once Harry S. Truman had become president upon the death of Franklin D. Roosevelt, and while others pondered where and how the bomb might be used, Stimson felt duty-bound to discuss with Truman the wider ramifications of a new nuclear age.

1. Within four months we shall in all probability have completed the most terrible weapon ever known in human history, one bomb of which could destroy a whole city.

2. Although we have shared its development with the UK, physically the US is at present in the position of controlling the resources with which to construct and use it and no other nation could reach this position for some years.

3. Nevertheless it is practically certain that we could not remain in this position indefinitely. a. Various segments of its discovery and production are widely known among many scientists in many countries, although few scientists are now acquainted with the whole process which we have developed.

b. Although its construction under present methods requires great scientific and industrial effort and raw materials, which are temporarily mainly within the possession and knowledge of US and UK, it is extremely probable that much easier and cheaper methods of production will be discovered by scientists in the future, together with the use of materials of much wider distribution. As a result, it is extremely probable that the future will make it possible to be constructed by smaller nations or even groups, or at least by a large nation in a much shorter time.

4. As a result, it is indicated that the future may see a time when such a weapon may be constructed in secret and used suddenly and effectively with devastating power by a wilful [sic] nation or group against an unsuspecting nation or group of much greater size and material power. With its aid even a very powerful unsuspecting nation might be conquered within a very few days by a very much smaller one, although probably the only nation which could enter into production within the next few years is Russia.

5. The world in its present state of moral advancement compared with its technical development would be eventually at the mercy of such a weapon. In other words, modern civilization might be completely destroyed.

6. To approach any world peace organization of any pattern now likely to be considered, without an appreciation by the leaders of our country of the power of this new weapon, would seem to be unrealistic. No system of control heretofore considered would be adequate to control this menace. Both inside any particular country and between the nations of the world, the control of this weapon will undoubtedly be a matter of the greatest difficulty and would involve such thorough-going rights of inspection and internal controls as we have never heretofore contemplated.

7. Furthermore, in light of our present position with reference to this weapon, the question of sharing it with other nations and, if so shared, upon what terms, becomes a primary question of our foreign relations. Also our leadership in the war and in the development of this weapon has placed a certain moral responsibility upon us which we cannot shirk without very serious responsibility for any disaster to civilization which it would further.

8. On the other hand, if the problem of the proper use of this weapon can be solved, we would have the opportunity to bring the world into a pattern in which the peace of the world and our civilization can be saved.

9. ...[S]teps are under way looking towards the establishment of a select committee of particular qualifications for recommending action to the Executive and legislative branches of our government when secrecy is no longer in full effect. The committee would also recommend the actions to be taken by the War Department prior to that time in anticipation of the postwar problems. All recommendations would of course be first submitted to the President.

PREPARING TO INVADE JAPAN

As American units completed the costly invasion of the island of Okinawa, the final stepping stone to Japan, planning shifted to work out the details for the Pacific War's final phase. There was no doubt that the Japanese war effort was tottering toward utter defeat. At sea, the U.S. Navy, in particular its submarine force, had subjected the Japanese home islands to a devastating blockade. From the air, powerful B-29 bombers were raining down destruction on one Japanese city after another, especially after General Curtis LeMay switched from high-altitude precision bombing to lower-level incendiary raids that burned urban areas to the ground and killed tens of thousands of Japanese civilians at a time. But most American leaders, as well as the soldiers who had witnessed the tenacity of Japanese defenders up close, shared the conviction that only the direct invasion of Japan itself could bring the war to an end. Therefore, the next obvious target was the southernmost home island of Kyushu, from which, once it had been subdued, the neighboring island of Honshu could be invaded and Tokyo finally captured. On June 18, 1945, the U.S. Joint Chiefs of Staff and other key advisors met with President Truman to brief him on invasion plans (known as "Operation Olympic") and obtain his authorization to proceed with preparations for the first phase of the operation. To go ahead with the invasion plans, Truman had to be convinced on several points: that a combination of naval blockade and aerial bombing would not by themselves force the Japanese to surrender without the need to resort to an invasion; that diplomatic initiatives combined with the shock of Soviet entry into the war against Japan also would not elicit a surrender; that if an invasion of Honshu went ahead, the cost in casualties would not be too much for the military or the American public to bear. These points are important not just because they affected Truman's decision in June 1945 to proceed with an invasion of Kyushu (which, because of weather conditions would have to begin no later than November 1), but also because they formed the context in which the decision to drop the atomic bomb would be taken in early August. Unfortunately for Truman, as he struggled with a decision, there was no unambiguous consensus on how many American soldiers would be killed, wounded, or missing in an attack on Kyushu. Estimates varied according to whether they were based on a straight percentage of the attacking force likely to become casualties or on a ratio of American casualties to Japanese losses, which would then depend on an accurate estimate of the number of Japanese defenders. Many estimates only covered the troops wading ashore and omitted U.S. Navy personnel, even though the fleet was sure to incur heavy losses from persistent kamikaze attacks. There was every reason to believe that Japanese soldiers would behave even more fanatically when defending one of their home islands, so it was not clear that any preceding action was an accurate guide to predicting future losses. Moreover, over the next month intercepts from radio intelligence would confirm that the Japanese were reinforcing Kyushu's defenses far more heavily than anticipated, and stockpiling more suicide aircraft as well. Nonetheless, on the basis of the briefing that follows, Truman saw no alternative but to go ahead with an invasion.

"Minutes of Meeting Held at the White House, Monday, 18 June 1945," Records of the Joint Chiefs of Staff, RG218, Box 198 334 JCS, National Archival and Records Administration.

General Marshall:

Our air and sea power has already greatly reduced movement of Jap shipping south of Korea and should in the next few months cut it to a trickle if not choke it off entirely. Hence, there is no need for seizing further positions in order to block Japanese communications south of Korea.

General Mac Arthur and Admiral Nimitz are in agreement with the Chiefs of Staff in selecting 1 November as the target date to go into Kyushu because by that time:

a. If we press preparations we can be ready.
b. Our estimates are that our air action will have smashed practically every industrial target worth hitting in Japan as well as destroying huge areas in the Jap cities.
c. The Japanese Navy, if any still exists, will be completely powerless.
d. Our sea action and air power will have cut Jap reinforcement capabilities from the mainland to negligible proportions....

The Kyushu operation is essential to a strategy of strangulation and appears to be the least costly worth-while operation following Okinawa. The basic point is that a lodgement in Kyushu is essential both to tightening our strangle hold of blockade and bombardment on Japan, and to forcing capitulation by invasion of the Tokyo Plain.

We are bringing to bear against the Japanese every weapon and all the force we can employ and there is no reduction in our maximum possible application of bombardment and blockade, while at the same time we are pressing invasion preparations. It seems that if the Japanese are ever willing to capitulate short of complete military defeat in the field they will do it when faced by the completely hopeless prospect occasioned by (1) destruction already wrought by air bombardment and sea blockade, coupled with (2) a landing on Japan indicating the firmness of our resolution, and also perhaps coupled with (3) the entry or threat of entry of Russia into the war....

Casualties

Our experience in the Pacific war is so diverse as to casualties that it is considered wrong to give any estimate in numbers. Using various combinations of Pacific experience, the War Department staff reaches the conclusion that the cost of securing a worthwhile position in Korea would almost certainly be greater than the cost of the Kyushu operation. Points on the optimistic side of the Kyushu operation are that: General MacArthur has not yet accepted responsibility for going ashore where there would be disproportionate casualties. The nature of the objective area gives room for maneuver, both on the land and by sea. As to any discussion of specific operations, the following data are pertinent:

The record of General MacArthur's operations from 1 March 1944 through 1 May 1945 shows 13,742 U.S. killed compared to 310,165 Japanese killed, or a ratio of 22 to 1.

There is reason to believe that the first 30 days in Kyushu should not exceed the price we have paid for Luzon. It is a grim fact that there is not any easy, bloodless way to victory in war and it is the thankless task of the leaders to maintain their firm outward front which holds the resolution of their subordinates....

Campaign	U.S. Casualties Killed, wounded, missing	Jap Casualties Killed and Prisoners (Not including wounded)	Ratio U.S. to Jap
Leyte	17,000	78,000	1:4.6
Luzon	31,000	156,000	1:5.0
Iwo Jima	20,000	25,000	1:1.25
Okinawa	34,000 (Ground) 7,700 (Navy)	81,000 (not a complete count)	1:2
Normandy (1st 30 days)	42,000	—	—

General Marshall said that it was his personal view that the operation against Kyushu was the only course to pursue. He felt that air power alone was not sufficient to put the Japanese out of the war. It was unable alone to put the Germans out. General Eaker [deputy commander of the Army Air Forces] and General Eisenhower both agreed to this. Against the Japanese, scattered through mountainous country, the problem would be much more difficult than it had been in Germany. He felt that this plan offered the only way the Japanese could be forced into a feeling of utter helplessness. The operation would be difficult but not more so than the assault in Normandy. He was convinced that every individual moving to the Pacific should be indoctrinated with a firm determination to see it through....

ADMIRAL LEAHY recalled that the President had been interested in knowing what the price in casualties for Kyushu would be and whether or not that price could be paid. He pointed out that the troops on Okinawa had lost 35 percent in casualties. If this percentage were applied to the number of troops to be employed in Kyushu, he thought from the similarity of the fighting to be expected that this would give a good estimate of the casualties to be expected. He was interested therefore in finding out how many troops are to be used in Kyushu.

ADMIRAL KING called attention to what he considered an important difference in Okinawa and Kyushu. There had been only one way to go on Okinawa. This meant a straight frontal attack against a highly fortified position. On Kyushu, however, landings would be made on three fronts simultaneously and there would be much more room for maneuver. It was his opinion that a realistic casualty figure for Kyushu would lie somewhere between the number experienced by General MacArthur in the operations on Luzon and the Okinawa casualties.

GENERAL MARSHALL pointed out that the total assault troops for the Kyushu campaign were shown in the memorandum prepared for the President as 766,700. He said, in answer to the President's question as to what opposition could be expected on Kyushu, that it was estimated at eight Japanese divisions or about 350,000 troops. He said that divisions were still being raised in Japan and that reinforcement from other areas was possible but it was becoming increasingly difficult and painful....

THE PRESIDENT stated that one of his objectives in connection with the coming conference would be to get from Russia all the assistance in the war that was possible. To this end he wanted to know all the decisions that he would have to make in advance in order to occupy the strongest possible position in the discussions.

ADMIRAL LEAHY said that he could not agree with those who said to him that unless we obtain the unconditional surrender of the Japanese that we will have lost the war. He feared no menace from Japan in the foreseeable future, even if we were unsuccessful in forcing unconditional surrender. What he did fear was that our insistence on unconditional surrender would result only in making the Japanese desperate and thereby increase our casualty lists. He did not think that this was at all necessary.

THE PRESIDENT stated that it was with that thought in mind that he had left the door open for Congress to take appropriate action with reference to unconditional surrender. However, he did not feel that he could take any action at this time to change public opinion on the matter.

THE PRESIDENT said he considered the Kyushu plan all right from the military standpoint and, so far as he was concerned, the Joint Chiefs of Staff could go ahead with it; that we can do this operation and then decide as to the final action later.

HIROSHIMA

By late July 1945, two facts were clear to American planners: one, after the successful Alamogordo test, atomic bombs (albeit in very limited numbers) would be available for use against Japan; two, at the same time that America's arsenal was strengthened, Japan was rapidly augmenting its own defenses on Kyushu. The buildup, the result of troops having been transferred from Manchuria and elsewhere, a renewed draft to scrape the bottom of the manpower barrel, and frightening efforts to conscript ordinary Japanese civilians armed with anything from sharpened bamboo stakes to garden implements into plans for suicide attacks, all called into question the assumptions underlying Operation Olympic. Instead of the 3:1 numerical superiority assumed necessary to assure the success of a seaborne invasion, it now appeared that American invaders would be met by an equal number of Japanese soldiers. Moreover, the loss of civilian life on Saipan and Okinawa, and the degree to which Japanese civilians willingly accepted that death would be preferable to the brutal or dishonorable treatment they expected from American soldiers, did not bode well for future operations on the Japanese homeland. The Japanese plan to defend Kyushu (*Ketsu-Go*, or Operation Code-Name Decision) was not simply the fantasy of intransigent army officers who were determined to protect the honor of a doomed nation by killing as many Americans as possible on the path to ultimate defeat; although there certainly were such fanatics, *Ketsu-Go* was embraced by military advisors who hoped that they could exact such a toll on an invasion force that the American public would protest at what it repudiated as an unacceptable level of casualties and force American leaders to offer peace terms to conclude the war on a basis more favorable to Japan than she could expect without so ferocious a defense.

Publicly, the only peace terms on offer were unconditional surrender. They had been first enunciated in 1943 at Casablanca (partly to prevent Germany and Russia from arranging a separate peace) and reiterated in July 1945 when the "Big Three" (the Americans, British, and Soviets) met at Potsdam. The so-called Potsdam Declaration, made public on July 26, reaffirmed that Japan's military and political elites must be broken, war criminals brought to justice, the country disarmed and occupied, and conditions laid for the emergence of a democratic system that would embody freedom of speech, thought, and religion. It did not specify whether Japan could retain its emperor, a point of cardinal importance, but it did warn of "prompt and utter devastation" if the country did not accept. The Japanese government chose not respond, preferring to "kill with silence" the Allied ultimatum.

At this point, the die was cast. The Manhattan Project had proceeded on the assumption that atomic weapons would be used if they could be developed successfully, and so it was up to the opponents of the bomb to persuade President Truman and his advisors that it *should not* be used, rather than the proponents to make the case that it *should*. Some historians have argued that the prospect of a postwar cold war was the paramount consideration and that the real reason why the bomb was dropped was to impress and intimidate the Soviet Union. But American planners were frustrated with the unwillingness of the Japanese to surrender when it was clear enough that by any conventional measure they were militarily beaten (something the Japanese leadership did not accept, but that is precisely the point). Tightening the blockade and increasing the bombing had so far failed to budge the Japanese from their intransigent position. An invasion of Kyushu, presumably followed by an attack on Honshu in the spring of 1946, would prolong the killing on both sides, not to mention continue the conflict in China and elsewhere in the Pacific. As rail and road transport ground to a halt, Japan faced the prospect of a famine as devastating as the one in Bengal. One did not need mathematical calculations or projections to recognize that the number of casualties would be enormous.

In this context, the one way to slice the Gordian knot of Japanese resistance would be to administer some shock spectacular enough to end the war quickly. The entry of the Soviet Union into the war would certainly surprise the Japanese, and Soviet forces would quickly come to grips with Japanese troops in Manchuria, but it would be some time before the weight of Soviet power could be applied against the home islands. The atomic bomb offered the prospect of a quicker solution, and considerable thought went into where it would be used for the first time. The American military desired a "clean" target (one that had not already been damaged) to demonstrate the new weapon's destructive power, and preferably one with some military implications (because Japanese factory production often tended to be decentralized into small workshops and home-based work, it was often hard to draw a clear demarcation between residential and factory areas). Fortunately, Henry Stimson (who knew the country from personal experience) was able to remove the ancient city of Kyoto with its historic buildings and irreplaceable artifacts from the target list, and so the initial site would be Hiroshima. It was the headquarters of Field Marshal Hata's Second Army and housed some 43,000 soldiers and another 280,000–290,000 civilians. A special bombing squadron (the 509th Composite Group) commanded by Colonel Paul Tibbets Jr. practiced the dangerous evasive maneuvers necessary if a crew were to deliver the bomb and avoid the blast. On August 6, 1945, Tibbets flew the B-29 bomber *Enola Gay* (named for his mother) and dropped the first atomic bomb, which detonated at an altitude of 1,900 feet at 8:16 a.m. local time.

Fewer than 10 percent of the city's buildings survived the blast undamaged. The human toll was staggering and, although in absolute terms the initial number of people killed had been surpassed by the losses in the Tokyo incendiary raids (with conventional weapons) on the night of March 9–10, one particular horror of a nuclear blast was the radiation sickness that would continue to claim victims for years to come. One of the first clear accounts for Western readers of what had happened came from the American journalist John Hersey (1914–1993). Born in China, the son of American missionaries, Hersey worked for *Time* magazine and reported on events in the Pacific. He went to Hiroshima in June 1946 on behalf of the *New Yorker* magazine to produce something for the first anniversary of the bombing and interviewed some of the survivors. His report, first published in the *New Yorker's* August 31, 1946, issue and immediately reprinted as a book, vividly conveyed just how shocking the effects of this new weapon were, even as, in conjunction with a second atomic bomb dropped three days later on Nagasaki, they prompted a stunned but divided Japanese government to finally sue for peace.

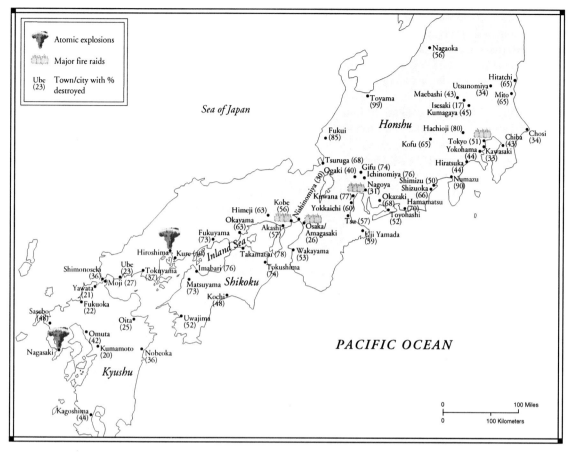

Atomic explosions

Major fire raids

Ube
(23)   Town/city with %
destroyed

Sea of Japan

Nagaoka
(56)

Hitatchi
(65)

Utsunomiya
(34)   Mito
(65)

Maebashi (43)

Toyama
(99)

Isesaki (17)
Kumagaya (45)

Honshu

Fukui
(85)   Hachioji (80)

Kofu (65)   Tokyo (51)   Chiba
(43)   Chosi
(34)

Yokohama
(44)   Kawasaki
(33)

Tsuruga (68)

Ogaki (40)   Gifu (74)

Ichinomiya (76)   Hiratsuka
(44)

Nagoya
(31)   Shimizu (50)

Shizuoka
(66)   Numazu
(90)

Kuwana (77)   Okazaki
(68)   Hamamatsu
(70)

Kobe
(56)

Himeji (63)   Yokkaichi (60)   Toyohashi
(52)

Okayama
(63)   Akashi
(57)   Tsu (57)

Fukuyama
(73)   Osaka/
Amagasaki
(26)   Uji Yamada
(39)

Hiroshima   Kure (40)   Wakayama
(53)

Inland Sea

Takamatsu (78)

Shimonoseki
(36)   Ube
(23)   Tokuyama
(37)   Imabari (76)   Tokushima
(74)

Yawata
(21)   Moji (27)   *Shikoku*

Matsuyama
(73)   Kochi
(48)

Fukuoka
(22)

Sasebo
(48)   Oita
(25)   Uwajima
(52)   *PACIFIC OCEAN*

Omuta
(42)

Nagasaki   Kumamoto
(20)   Nobeoka
(36)

Kyushu

Kagoshima
(44)

Nishinomiya (30)

0   100 Miles

0   100 Kilometers

THE BOMBING OF JAPAN

The Reverend Mr. Tanimoto got up at five o'clock that morning. He was alone in the parsonage, because for some time his wife had been commuting with their year-old baby to spend nights with a friend in Ushida, a suburb to the north. Of all the important cities of Japan, only two, Kyoto and Hiroshima, had not been visited in strength by *B-san*, or Mr. B, as the Japanese, with a mixture of respect and unhappy familiarity, called the B-29; and Mr. Tanimoto, like all his neighbors and friends, was almost sick with anxiety. He had heard uncomfortably detailed accounts of mass raids on Kure, Iwakuni, Tokuyama, and other nearby towns; he was sure Hiroshima's turn would come soon....[A] rumor was going around that the Americans were saving something special for the city....

Besides having his wife spend the nights in Ushida, Mr. Tanimoto had been carrying all the portable things from his church, in the close-packed residential district called Nagaragawa, to a house that belonged to a rayon manufacturer in Koi, two miles from the center of town....A friend of his named Matsuo had, the day before, helped him get the piano out to Koi; in return, he had promised this day to assist Mr. Matsuo in hauling out a daughter's belongings. That is why he had risen so early....

Before six o'clock that morning...the two men set out....The two men pulled and pushed the handcart through the city streets....The morning was still; the place was cool and pleasant.

Then a tremendous flash of light cut across the sky. Mr. Tanimoto has a distinct recollection that it travelled from east to west from the city toward the hills. It seemed a sheet of sun. Both he and Mr. Matsuo reacted in terror—and both had time to react (for they were 3,500 yards, or two miles, from the center of the explosion). Mr. Matsuo dashed up the front steps into the [rayon man's] house and dived among the bedrolls and buried himself there. Mr. Tanimoto took four or five steps and threw himself between two big rocks in the garden....He felt a sudden pressure, and then splinters and pieces of board and fragments of tile fell on him. He heard no roar....

When he dared, Mr. Tanimoto raised his head and saw that the rayon man's house had collapsed. He thought a bomb had fallen directly on it. Such clouds of dust had risen that there was a sort of twilight around....In the streets, the first thing he saw was a squad of soldiers who had been burrowing into the hillside opposite, making one of the thousands of dugouts in which the Japanese apparently intended to resist invasion, hill by hill, life for life; the soldiers were coming out of the hole, where they should have been safe, and blood was running from their heads, chests and backs....

Mr. Tanimoto, fearful for his family and church, at first ran toward them by the shortest route, along Koi Highway. He was the only person making his way into the city; he met hundreds and hundreds who were fleeing, and everyone of them seemed to be hurt in some way. The eyebrows of some were burned off and skin hung from their faces and hands. Others, because of pain, held their arms up as if carrying something in both hands. Some were vomiting as they walked. Many were naked or in shreds of clothing. On some undressed bodies, the burns had made patterns—of undershirt straps and suspenders, and on the skin of some women (since white repelled the heat from the bomb and dark clothes absorbed it and conducted it to the skin), the shapes of flowers they had had on their kimonos....

On his back with a fever of 104, Mr. Tanimoto worried about all the funerals he ought to be conducting for the deceased of his church. He thought he was just overtired from the hard work he had done since the bombing, but after the fever had persisted for a few days, he sent for a doctor. The doctor was too busy to visit him in Ushida, but he dispatched a nurse, who recognized his symptoms as those of mild radiation disease....[The disease had] three stages. The first stage had been all over before the doctors even knew they were dealing with a new sickness; it was the direct reaction to the bombardment of the body, at the moment when the bomb went off, by neutrons, beta particles, and gamma rays. The apparently uninjured people who had died so mysteriously in the first few hours or days had succumbed in this first stage. It killed ninety-five per cent of the people within a half mile of the center and many thousands who were farther away....The second stage set in ten or fifteen days after the bombing. Its first symptom was falling hair. Diarrhea and fever, which in some cases went as high as 106, came next. Twenty-five to thirty days after the explosion, blood disorders appeared....The drop in the number of white blood corpuscles reduced the patient's capacity to resist infection....If fever remained steady and high, the patient's chances for survival were poor....The third stage was the reaction that came when the body struggled to compensate for its ills....In this stage, many patients died of complications....

Statistical workers gathered what figures they could on the effects of the bomb. They reported that 78,150 people had been killed, 13,983 were missing and 37,425 had been injured. No one in the city government pretended that these figures were accurate—though the Americans accepted them as official—and as the months went by and more and more hundreds of corpses were dug up from the ruins, and as the number of unclaimed urns of ashes at the Zempoji Temple in Koi rose into the thousands, the statisticians began to say that at least a hundred thousand people had lost their lives in the bombing....The statisticians' figures on property damage were more reliable: sixty-two thousand out of ninety thousand buildings destroyed, and six thousand more damaged beyond repair. In the heart of the city, they found only five modern buildings that could be used again without major repairs.

CHAPTER 8

THE WAR AT HOME IN AMERICA

ON THE HOMEFRONT "Help bring them back to you! Make yours a victory home!"
Source: Courtesy Northwestern University Library.

"This war will not only be a long war, it will be a hard war," President Roosevelt warned the American public in his December 9, 1941, "fireside chat" radio address. Sacrifices would be expected in view of Japan's surprise attack on Pearl Harbor and America's entry into World War II. He continued: "That is the basis on which we now lay all our plans. That is the yardstick by which we measure what we shall need and demand; money, materials, doubled and quadrupled production—ever-increasing." Soldiering, purchasing bonds, paying more taxes, foregoing profits, working longer hours, and doing without basic commodities were all privileges, the president explained, not sacrifices, for a nation whose democratic values and way of life were under attack. Roosevelt put the American public on notice that national consensus on the home front would ensure American victory on the battlefield.

The president's plea for a united American home front conjured up the powerful image of America as a "Melting Pot," an idea promoted by the east European–born Jewish immigrant playwright Israel Zangwill in his 1908 production by the same name. Zangwill believed that the homogenizing pressures of assimilation would melt away distinctive immigrant cultures and social divisions. Divisiveness would not persist in a nation built upon democratic ideals of religious and political freedom. Not everyone, however, believed in the idea of the melting pot, and some critics called the playwright's optimism "symbolic" as opposed to "practical." The xenophobia that swept the United States after World War I—in part a result of the nation's isolationist urge, nativist impulses, and economic uncertainty—lent credence to these critics' claims. The Emergency Quota Act of 1921 that limited Jewish immigration and the McCarren Walter Act of 1924 that prohibited all Asian immigration had given legal expression to the distrust harbored by many Americans against immigrants as well as the so-called hyphenated Americans of Asian, African, Hispanic, and European descent. If Zangwill's "melting pot" ever really existed, it clearly revealed fissures during the Second World War.

Not all was quiet on the American home front. The swift transition from a peace to a wartime footing produced a number of significant changes as well as daunting challenges for women as well as minorities. The prevailing isolationist sentiment meant that before 1939 relatively few steps had been taken to ensure successful mobilization and coordinate both the military and civilian spheres. The military was woefully undermanned and ill-equipped. Not only were fewer than 200,000 men in the army, 125,000 in the navy, and perhaps 20,000 in the marines, but new recruits, lacking rifles and tanks for training, were forced to make do with broomsticks and trucks as substitutes. Not until September 1940 did Congress pass the first peacetime draft requiring all men between the ages of eighteen and forty-five (nearly 50 million individuals) to register for military service.

After war was declared in December 1941, 10 million men would infuse new life into the military, but with their absence America's labor force began to hemorrhage from the military drain. Yet the loss of so many able-bodied male workers presented an opportunity (if only a temporary one in the government's view) for American women—married as well as single, white as well as African- and Hispanic-American, poor as well as middle-class—in the workplace. Roughly 19 million American women participated in the labor market during World War II. Norman Rockwell's iconic Rosie the Riveter—lips pursed with determination, knotted bandana taut across her head, attired in factory blue with sleeves rolled up to reveal a muscular forearm—was one of the most successful and best-known symbols created by American war propaganda. Women workers, however, did more than simply rivet. For example, they entered the workforce as streetcar conductors, taxi drivers, telephone and large crane operators, volunteered for noncombative positions in the Women's Army Auxiliary Corps (WAAC), the navy's Women Accepted for Voluntary Emergency Service (WAVES), the Women Airforce Service Pilots (WASP), and the Coast Guards' SPAR (an acronym taken from the Coast Guard's motto, *Semper paratus*, meaning "Always ready"), and served as journalists and photographers. While many women found work economically and socially emancipating, often they were unable to eliminate the gender bias that male factory workers and administrators harbored against them. Women spent long hours toiling alongside their male counterparts, but when the factory whistle blew to acknowledge the end of their day or night shift, they returned home to their second yet unsalaried job as mainstays of the household. As mothers and wives, working women endured the same routine as those women who chose not to work outside the home for a variety of reasons. Whether or not her husband was in the military or working as well, the working woman continued to be responsible for cooking, cleaning, and raising children. In 1945 the stress of this doubled responsibility, coupled with the negative reaction of their returning husbands toward their workplace participation, forced millions of women to return to domestic life.

The stress and strains of war were also evident in American's attitudes toward and treatment of minorities. In a war overshadowed by religious and racial prejudice in Europe, Americans, too, found themselves grappling with their own homegrown biases toward the "hyphenated" Americans: Japanese-Americans, African-Americans, Hispanic-Americans, German-Americans, and Italian-Americans. Motivated by the Japanese attack on Pearl Harbor and the fear of Japanese spies on American territory, President Roosevelt signed in February 1942 Executive Order 9066, incarcerating over 100,000 Japanese immigrants (Issei) and native American-Japanese (Nissei) in "relocation centers" scattered throughout the western United States until January 1945 when they were permitted to return to their homes. Yet, prejudices continued to prevail against Japanese-Americans now cleared of "subversive activities." In February 1945, a nineteen-year-old American-born female patient of Japanese heritage was denied access as a patient to a Chicago hospital emergency room because some of its patients, as a hospital administrator explained, objected to coming in contact with a Japanese person. That Japanese-American's physician, Dr. Selig A. Shevin, himself an immigrant from Europe, fumed at the hospital's decision, calling it "un-American, unpatriotic, and inhuman," and resigned in protest from the hospital's medical staff. Italian- and German-Americans, too, were viewed with great suspicion, given that their homelands were America's enemies. Although far fewer of them were confined to internment camps, they nevertheless were hounded and spied upon by local police agencies to prevent the possibility of espionage. The fact remains that from each of these so-called hyphenated American groups came soldiers who served their country in various theaters of the world war.

Discrimination continued to overshadow the lives of African- and Hispanic-Americans in the service as well as on the home front. Despite the fact that roughly 1 million African-American men served largely in segregated army units, the majority in military support groups or labor battalions, African-Americans stateside continued to find barriers erected in their paths. In April 1944, Corporal Rupert Trimmingham complained in *Yank Magazine* about an incident whereby he and fellow African-American soldiers witnessed German prisoners of war receiving better treatment than themselves. "I stood on the outside looking on," he wrote, "and I could not help but ask myself...are we not American soldiers, sworn to fight for and die if need be for this country? Then why are they treated better than we are? Why does the Government allow such things to go on?" The migration of more African-Americans to northern cities in search of better-paying jobs (the first major migration having taken place from the South to the North during World War I) led to further discrimination and racial tension. In cities like Detroit, where housing and educational facilities were considerably strained by the influx, but also in New York City (Harlem), Mobile, Baltimore, and Indianapolis, violent race riots erupted. The Detroit Riot (June 1943), a particularly ugly display of racism in which hundreds of people were injured, thirty-four killed, and property destroyed, was exploited by Axis powers as proof of America's weakness. In Los Angeles in June 1943, anti-Hispanic-American sentiment exploded in the so-called Zoot Suit riots. Young Hispanic males, wearing flashy suits (known as zoot suits), were accosted by white sailors who accused them of being unpatriotic. The assaults quickly spilled over to attacks on African-Americans and Filipinos.

Anti-Semitism did not vanish in the United States despite the situation in Nazi Germany. The anti-Semitic hyperbole of the 1930s as espoused by Henry Ford, Charles Lindbergh, and Father Charles Coughlin, a Catholic priest, whose praise for both Mussolini and Hitler and denunciations of President Roosevelt were broadcast in his radio addresses, continued to be promoted by groups like America First and the right-wing women's National Legion of Mothers of America, which openly sympathized with the Nazis. Anti-Semitism was present in the military as well, where, according to historian Deborah Dash Moore, about 550,000 Jewish men and women served.

While racism and xenophobia persisted on the home front, neither completely overshadowed Americans' positive response to the president's call for assisting their country in time of crisis. Both home front adults and children supported the war effort through conservation, rationing, recycling, planting of "victory gardens," and buying bonds. Some efforts were also made by educators to defuse prejudice and hate by reminding schoolchildren of the common values they shared as members of a democratic society and de-emphasizing ethnic, racial, and religious identities. Yet, as powerful a tool as education was, it ultimately paled against the usefulness of xenophobia in rallying the nation against its external (and imagined internal) enemies. Xenophobia begat fear and fear begat xenophobia. Few Americans it seemed gave credence to President Roosevelt's warning in March 1933 that the "only thing we have to fear is fear itself."

THE RABBIS MARCH ON WASHINGTON

On October 6, 1943, 400 rabbis arrived by train in Washington, DC, three days before the holiest day in the Jewish calendar, the fast day of Yom Kippur, to implore the American government to take action to save Europe's Jews from destruction by the Nazis. The protest was organized by Hillel Kook (alias Peter Bergson from Jerusalem), the nephew of the chief rabbi of Palestine and a founder of the Irgun Zeva'i Le'umi (National Military Organization), which engaged in a military campaign against the British in Palestine. The rabbis, accompanied by some Jewish war veterans, marched solemnly from Union Station to the Capitol, where they were met by Vice President Henry Wallace and several members of Congress, including both the Senate majority and minority leaders and the Speaker of the House. Two of the march's leaders read in English and Hebrew the group's petition to the president to request that he create a special agency with the task of rescuing the remaining European Jews. Later the rabbis proceeded to the gates of the White House in the hope that they would meet with Roosevelt to discuss the matter at greater length. That meeting, however, was not to happen. Presidential secretary Marvin McIntyre claimed that the president's schedule was too crowded with other business. In reality, Roosevelt could have met with the group, but he was advised against the meeting by his Jewish speechwriter, Samuel Rosenman, and prominent reform rabbi Dr. Stephen Wise, who feared that the public protest in general might provoke anti-Semitism. In the following letter, Eri Jabotinsky (son of Zev Jabotinsky, a founder of the Irgun) reports on the march to Dr. Altman, the director of the Washington office of the Emergency Committee to Save the Jewish People of Europe.

Dear Dr. Altman,

On Wednesday, October 6th, the march on Washington of the Orthodox Rabbis of the U.S. was a great success. It was organized by the Emergency Committee to Save the Jewish People of Europe [founded in July 1943 in New York City to assist Jews in occupied Europe]....

There were 400 Rabbis and about 100 reporters and friends who participated in the march. The main body of the delegation arrived at Union Station at 12:35. They were met by some forty Rabbis who had assembled in the station earlier, coming from the South and the West. Also some five or six local Washingtonian Rabbis were present. The main part of the participants arrived, however, from New York, Philadelphia, and Baltimore....[T]hey represented two organizations:—The Union of the Orthodox Rabbis (Misnagdin) and the Union of the Grand Rabbis of the U.S. and Canada (Hasidim).

They marched from the station to the Capitol and up the steps to the Senate. A delegation of five Rabbis was taken by Peter Bergson into the office of the Vice President of the United States, Mr. Wallace (who is the president of the Senate). In that office they were received by the Vice-President in the presence of all the Jewish members of the House of Representatives, including even Mr. Sol Bloom of Bermuda. It is of interest to note that these Congressmen had done all

Letter of Eri Jabotinsky to Dr. Altman, October 12, 1943, from www.wymaninstitute.org. Used by permission.

they could to dissuade the Rabbis from making their bearded appearances in Washington....At a certain moment they almost succeeded but Mr. Bloom spoiled the soup by telling one of the Rabbis, as an additional inducement for not going, that it would be very undignified for a group of such un-American looking people to appear in Washington. This created a lot of resentment and in the end instead of 250 Rabbis on whom we counted, we had to cope with 400. Even Rabbi Levinthal who is considered as the Dean of the Orthodox Rabbis of America...aged 77 participated. A day before the march Congressman Cellar of New York told us that the Jewish Congressmen had held a meeting and decided that we had licked them and that they would appear in a body to greet the Rabbis.

The 3 Rabbis who were received by the Vice President, handed over to him a petition and then, accompanied by him and the Jewish Congressmen, they joined the main group on the steps of the Senate. There they were joined by the group of Senators and Representatives, including the majority and minority leaders of both Houses and Mr. Rayburn, Speaker of the House of Representatives.

Rabbi Eliezer Silver, a two-fisted, red faced rabbi of Cincinnati, Ohio, read the petition in Hebrew and then in English. Vice President Wallace answered by reading a prepared statement in which he said that "the Jewish problem is a part of the general problem."

From the Capitol the Rabbis proceeded to the Lincoln Memorial on the steps of which a prayer was offered. From there they marched to the White House where, again, a delegation was received. Instead of the President, however, they were received by one of the President's secretaries, Mr. Mc Intyre. The main body of the Rabbis proceeded meanwhile to the Ohev Sholom synagogue where some food had been prepared for them. The delegation, returned from the White House, caused a storm by their reporting that the President had not received them. One of the leading Rabbis from Brooklyn said that this was a slap in the face not only to the delegation but to American Jewry. From the synagogue the Rabbis returned to the station and left to report to their various congregations....

The general press reported the march extensively, including photographs. It was also photographed by 3 of the leading newsreels. The Jewish press of New York carried laudatory articles on the front page. In some of the Jewish papers the march was featured in the main headlines....

TO UNDO A MISTAKE

As First Lady, Eleanor Roosevelt (1884–1962) was a tireless advocate for the cause of democracy and human rights. Roosevelt remained a vocal critic of restrictive American visa policies and worked to assist refugees fleeing Nazi Germany and Franco's Spain. She supported working women in war industry by advocating the idea of equal pay for equal work and lobbying for the establishment of day care centers for their children. Her opposition to racial discrimination led her to call for equal treatment of African-Americans in the military and to promote the creation of the Fair Employment Practices Commission to prevent industries receiving federal contracts from discriminating against African-American employees. She was, however, less successful in convincing her husband against signing Executive Order 9066 of February 1942, requiring the internment of Japanese-Americans in relocation centers. In April 1943, Mrs. Roosevelt toured the Gila internment camp near Phoenix, Arizona, observing the physical surroundings and talking to some of the interned Japanese. "To Undo a Mistake," written by Mrs. Roosevelt about her visit, presents an interesting dilemma in its simultaneous justification of, and apology for, Executive Order 9066.

Now we come to Pearl Harbor, December 7, 1941. We see the problems which faced the Pacific coast from this date on. There was no time to investigate families, or to adhere to the American rule that a man is innocent until he is proven guilty. These people were not convicted of any crime, but emotions ran too high, too many people wanted to wreak vengeance on Oriental-looking people. Even the Chinese, our Allies, were not always safe on the streets....

In an effort to live up to the American idea of justice as far as possible, the Army laid down the rules for what they considered the safest of our West Coast. They demanded and they supervised the evacuation. A civil authority was set up, the War Relocation Authority, to establish permanent camps and take over the custody and maintenance of these people, both for their own safety and for the safety of the country.

To many young people this must have seemed strange treatment of American citizens, and one cannot be surprised at the reaction which manifests itself not only in young Japanese Americans, but in others who had known them well and been educated with them, and who bitterly ask: "What price American citizenship?"

Nevertheless most of them recognized the fact that this was a safety measure....The early situation in the camps was difficult. They were not ready for occupation. Sufficient water was not available, food was slow in arriving. The setting up of large communities meant an amount of organization which takes time, but the Japanese proved to be patient, adaptable and courageous for the most part....

Eleanor Roosevelt, "To Undo a Mistake," originally published in *Collier Magazine* (October 10, 1943) and reprinted here in original draft form from J. Burton, M. Farrell, F. Lord, and R. Lord, eds., *Confinement and Ethnicity: An Overview of World War II. Japanese American Relocation Sites* (Tucson: Western Archeological and Conservation Center, 1999). Used by permission.

In reading the various accounts which have been written it struck me that practically no one has recognized what a tremendous variety of things the War Relocation Authority [agency established in March 1942 with authority to relocate civilians in the interest of national security] has had to develop to meet the innumerable problems created by the removal of a great group of people from one small section of the country and their temporary location in other parts of the country. When I read the accusations against the Authority for acquiring quantities of canned goods, and laying in stocks of food, I realized there was a lack of understanding of one basic fact, namely, that government authorities such as this have to live up to the law, and if it is the law of the land that we are rationed, we are rationed everywhere—in prisons, in hospitals, in camps, wherever we may be, individuals are rationed—even the War Relocation Authority cannot buy more than is allowed for the number of people they have to feed....

In these transplanted communities, schools have had to be established, hospitals have had to be equipped and manned. At Gila [located about fifty miles from Phoenix, Arizona], the land is rented from the Indian Reservation and no special buildings could be erected to accommodate either schools or hospitals. The buildings are just barrack buildings, adapted as well as human ingenuity can do it, to the needs for which they are used. Those of us who are familiar with the type of migratory labor camp which was gradually developed in different parts of the country during the past few years will understand what these relocation camps are like. They have certain familiar arrangements, such as a central washing unit for laundry and for personal cleanliness, and a central mess hall where the people gather for their meals. These are located in every barrack block containing about two hundred and fifty people.

The day I was at Gila there was no butter and no sugar on the tables. The food was rice and fish and greens. There was some milk for the children and some kind of pudding on the table. Neither in the stock-rooms, or on the tables did I notice any kind of extravagance.

Except for the head doctor in the hospital who was an American, the other doctors are Japanese. One had been a surgeon and had had a large Caucasian practice, he is now earning $19.00 a month, the standard pay for all work except for those who are working under Army or Navy contracts.

Ingenuity has been used in the schools. The class in typing only had two typewriters, so they worked out a keyboard of cardboard with holes for the keys and on this the class practiced. The typewriters were rationed, ten minutes use a day to each member of the class.

In the nursery school the toys were quite obviously homemade, and the children stretched out on the floor for their midday rest, with little makeshift covers under them which they folded up when the rest period was over....

The desert has few trees, but the scrub growth which usually holds down the land to a certain extent is completely removed around the camps I have seen. This makes a high wind a pretty disagreeable experience as you are enveloped in dust. It chokes you and brings about irritations of the nose and throat and here in this climate where people go to recover from respiratory ailments, you will find quite a number of hospitals around the camps, both military and non-military, with patients suffering from the irritations that the swirling dust cannot fail to bring....

At Gila there is a big farm where the Japanese who worked on the land, but perhaps grew only one type of vegetable, are now learning to cultivate as a complete farm enterprise and they care for cattle, chickens and grow a variety of foodstuffs. If some are never able to go back to the West Coast, they will be better able to learn a living on a general farm. Others work in various activities necessary to the life of the community. Since the formation of a Japanese division in the Army, it has been possible for Japanese American young men who have been checked and found loyal to the United States to volunteer for this division, and many of the Japanese American girls asked me if they would have an opportunity to serve in the same way in the Auxiliary Military Services.

Under the living conditions which exist in these camps it is natural that some of the most difficult problems faced are problems of morality. This is neither strange nor new, since overcrowding and restraint of free and normal living always bring up such problems, but crimes of violence or of theft have been remarkably low. A small force of Japanese policemen does the policing of the camps and has apparently few difficulties with which to contend....

There is perhaps a higher percentage of people with college degrees here than in the average community of the same size. They are taken from every background and yet must work in unfamiliar occupations, and one can realize that the close living quarters must create great problems.

I can well understand the bitterness of people who have lost loved ones at the hands of the Japanese military authorities, and we know that the totalitarian philosophy, whether it is in Nazi Germany or Fascist Italy or in Japan, is one of cruelty and brutality. It is not hard to understand why people living here in hourly anxiety for those they love have difficulty in viewing this problem objectively, but for the honor of our country the rest of us must do so. These understandable feelings are aggravated by the old time economic fear on the West Coast and the unreasoning racial feeling which certain people, through ignorance, have always had wherever they came in contact with people who are different from themselves. This is one reason why many people believe that we should have directed our original immigration more intelligently. We needed people to develop our country, but we should never have allowed any groups to settle as groups where they created a little German or Japanese or Scandinavian island and did not melt into our general community pattern....

To undo a mistake is always harder than not to create one originally but we seldom have the foresight. Therefore we have no choice but to try to correct our past mistakes and I hope that the recommendations of the staff of the War Relocation Authority, who have come to know individually most of the Japanese Americans in these various camps, will be accepted. Little by little as they are checked, Japanese Americans are being allowed on request to leave the camps and start independent lives again. Whether you are a taxpayer in California or in Maine, it is to our advantage, if you find one of two Japanese American families settled in your neighborhood, to try to regard them as individuals and not to condemn them before they are given a fair chance to prove themselves in the community.

"A Japanese is always a Japanese" is an easily accepted phrase and it has taken hold quite naturally on the West Coast because of fear, but it leads nowhere and solves nothing. A Japanese American may be no more Japanese than a German-American is German, or an Italian-American is Italian, or of any other national background. All of these people, including the Japanese Americans, have men who are fighting today for the preservation of the democratic way of life and the ideas around which our nation was built.

We have no common race in this country, but we have an ideal to which all of us are loyal: we cannot progress if we look down upon any group of people amongst us because of race or religion. Every citizen in this country has a right to our basic freedoms, to justice and to equality of opportunity. We retain the right to lead our individual lives as we please, but we can only do so if we grant to others the freedoms that we wish for ourselves.

THE INTERNMENT OF GERMAN-AMERICANS

In 1940 the American government passed the Alien Registration Act that required all aliens fourteen years and older living in the United States to register with the government and restricted their movements within the United States. In 1942 Japanese-Americans as members of an "enemy nationality" were rounded up and sent off to internment camps. Some German- and Italian-Americans, too, were incarcerated in camps scattered across the United States—especially in the southern states—but their numbers (in the thousands) paled in comparison with the Japanese internees. Those held prisoners were not simply Nazi soldiers or Italian fascists captured in Europe and brought back for internment in the United States; rather they consisted mainly of German and Italian aliens living in the United States, suspected of being Nazi Party members, spies, or fascist sympathizers, as well as some American citizens of German and Italian heritage. Surprisingly, even some German Jews were reportedly sent to these prison camps, the largest of which were located in Crystal City and Seagoville, Texas, and Ft. Lincoln, North Dakota. The incarcerated were treated according to international rules of conduct in the hope that the Germans would accord American prisoners of war similar treatment. The United States actually hired neutral Swiss inspectors to visit the camp sites and to report on the conditions inside to the Germans. Armed guards with dogs controlled the camps' perimeters. Prisoners' mail was censored, and many innocent never learned why they had been incarcerated in the first place. Although many internees were released from these camps following Japan's surrender in August 1945, still others remained until late 1947 and early 1948. Reportedly, none of the internees was ever convicted of a war-related crime against the United States. The following excerpt from a Swiss questionnaire provides a glimpse of life for those German-Americans interned in American camps.

1. Address of Station:
   Seagoville, Texas
2. Situation in what environment:
   Rural
3. U.S. Department in charge of prisoners:
   Immigration and Naturalization Service

4. Officer in Charge of Station:
   Amy N. Stannard, M.D.
   William S. Southerland (Assistant Officer in Charge)

Questionnaire of the Swiss Legation for War Prisoners, Visit to Seagoville, Texas, Internment Camp, August 22, 1944, in Don Heinrich Tolzmann, ed., *German-Americans in the World Wars*, vol. 4, sec. 1, pt. 2: *The World War II Experience: The Internment of German-Americans* (Munich: K. G. Saur, 1995), 1–11. Used by permission.

5. Number and description of prisoners at time of visit: Total 381

Nationality	Men	Women	Juv.	Category
				Internees
German	132	*136	—	(Continental US)
Hungarian	—	1	—	" "
American	—	29	7	" "

*being voluntary

				Non
German	32	36	1	(Continental US)
Italian	2	3	1	" "
Czecho-Slovakian	—	1	—	" "
	166	206	9	(infants to 14 years of age)

— — —

6. Departures from this Station since January 1, 1944:
   <u>Repatriation</u> 59 to Germany
   2 to Panama
   <u>Interim Parole</u> 35 individuals—22 family units
   <u>Internment at Large</u> 21 " "—7 " "

II. SPOKESMEN FOR PRISONERS

1. METHOD OF ELECTION OF SPOKESMEN

The Administration has endeavored to develop self-government in the internee population in all possible fields. As an outgrowth of this policy the Family Camp Committee has come into being. Each building elects from among its inhabitants a spokesman to represent its interests and the Committee is composed of these 7 spokesmen. This body elects from its members a chairman, whose current title is "Speaker."...
   Speaker:...

   Full name: Stangl, Fritz
   Education: 13 years Public School, Germany
   Former occupation: Printer
   Former residence: 546 East 146th Street, (Bronx), New York, N.Y....

2. NUMBER, NATIONALITY AND CATEGORY OF PRISONERS REPRESENTED BY SPOKESMEN

Interned in this camp are male and female adults (exception, 9 children), who are predominantly German by birth or derivation. The non-German internees are: 6 Italians, 1 Hungarian, 1 Czechoslovakian. Among the adults there are 78 voluntary Internees, of whom 29 are U.S. citizens....

VIII. THE EDUCATION & RECREATION OF PRISONERS

1. NUMBER AND TYPES OF BOOKS IN THE LIBRARY . . .

<u>English:</u> Books—fiction, 871; nonfiction, 2096. <u>Total—2967.</u>
<u>German:</u> Books—fiction, 728; nonfiction 802....

2. IS TEXT OF GENEVA CONVENTION IN LIBRARY OR OTHERWISE PUBLICLY ACCESSIBLE

yes.

3. ORGANIZATION OF LECTURES

Several concerts and one lecture have been sponsored by the American Friends Services Committee [Quaker relief organization founded in 1917]. Three lectures on Texas and historical subjects are scheduled by the organization for the autumn. Lectures are given weekly by internees on a variety of subjects, such as China and porcelain, astronomy, Simon Bolivar, etc.....

5. IS RADIO PERMITTED

Yes. Internees may have radios in their own rooms, and the Government furnishes radios in the living rooms of each housing unit....

6. MUSICAL AND THEATRICAL ACTIVITIES

The Government supplies 8 upright pianos, 1 grand piano, 1 Hammond electric organ, 9 combination radio-phonographs. A 7-piece internee orchestra performs at all entertainments. The internees stage musical programs and variety shows....

7. WHAT FACILITIES EXIST FOR SPECIAL INSTRUCTION IN LANGUAGES, HANDICRAFTS, ETC.

School Committee consists of 3 members, elected by school faculty from own personnel. <u>School Building</u>: Houses a library, 10 classrooms, 2 conference rooms, Beauty Shop, and Auditorium seating 400 persons. Last year classes sponsored by the School Committee were held in English, German, French, Italian, Spanish, portrait painting, oil painting, wood burning, technical drawing, mathematics, bookkeeping, beauty-shop technique—Total enrollment, 158....

IX. RELIGIOUS SERVICES FOR PRISONERS

1. WHAT ARE THE RELIGIONS OF THE PRISONERS

1. Protestant
2. Catholic

2. ARE THERE ANY MINISTERS OR PRIESTS AMONG THE PRISONERS

None.

X. CONTACT OF PRISONERS WITH OUTSIDE WORLD

1. How many visits are allowed: no limit has become necessary as yet.
2. Can prisoners receive any visitor he desires to see (family, counsel, business partner, etc.): any visitor approved by the Officer in Charge may be received by the internees. The visits are held in the Visiting Room, in the presence of one of the official staff.
3. Is incoming mail restricted: no limit has become necessary as yet.
4. How many outgoing letters are permitted and of what length: Three outgoing letters per person per week are permitted, with no designated length except in the case of those directed outside the continental United States....
8. Are telephone messages permitted and in what cases: telephone messages have been permitted with administrative officer listening in on the call. Permission has been granted only in cases of emergency.
9. Who censors the communications: Mail Censors all incoming and outgoing letters and cards. That officer has three regular assistants, and other interpreters from the official staff as needed.

WHY SHOULD WE MARCH?

The expansion of America's war industry required the hiring of additional labor. The influx of a large number of African-Americans into northern and western states in search of skilled work in defense industries often met with active resistance from employers. In September 1940, African-American labor activist and head of the Brotherhood of Sleeping Car Porters, Asa Philip Randolph (1889–1979), addressing a porters' convention, stressed the need for an end to discrimination in the defense industry. In the audience that night was First Lady Eleanor Roosevelt, whose own address to the convention the following evening advocated making America a place in which every minority could reside in equality and opportunity. In a private letter, Roosevelt urged her husband to meet with Randolph to discuss these pressing issues. On September 27, 1940, Randolph, accompanied by the president of the National Association for the Advancement of Colored People (NAACP), Walter White, met with President Roosevelt. When, following the meeting, hope for decisive action by the president to combat racism faded rapidly, Randolph called for a march on Washington, DC (set for July 1, 1941) by thousands of African-Americans down Pennsylvania Avenue in view of White House. Fearful of the repercussions of the march in wartime, Roosevelt finally signed Executive Order 8802 on June 25, 1941. The order rejected the policy of discrimination in the workplace because of race, creed, color, or national origin and established a Fair Employment Practices Committee to investigate companies that refused to comply. Randolph's success as a labor and civil rights leader led one congressman to call him "the most dangerous Negro in America."

We have met an hour when the sinister shadows of war are lengthening and becoming more threatening. As one of the sections of the oppressed darker races, and representing a part of the exploited millions of the workers of the world, we are deeply concerned that the totalitarian legions of Hitler, Hirohito, and Mussolini do not batter the bastions of democracy. We know that our fate is tied up with the fate of the democratic way of life. And so, out of the depth of our hearts, a cry goes up for the triumph of the United Nations. But we would not be honest with ourselves were we to stop for a victory of arms alone. We know this is not enough. We fight that the democratic faiths, values, heritages and ideals may prevail....

Our aim then must not only be to defeat Nazism, fascism, and militarism on the battlefield but to win the peace, for democracy, for freedom and the Brotherhood of Man without regard to his pigmentation, land of his birth or the God of his fathers.

We therefore sharply score the Atlantic Charter as expressing a vile and hateful racism and a manifestation of the tragic and utter collapse of an old, decadent democratic political liberalism which worshipped at the shrine of a world-conquering monopoly-capitalism. This system grew fat and

A. Philip Randolph, "Why Should We March?" *Survey Graphic*, vol. 31 (November 1942): 488–489. Used by permission.

waxed powerful off the sweat and tears of the tireless toilers of the human race and the sons and daughters of color in the underdeveloped lands of the world.

When this war ends, the people want something more than the dispersal of equality and power among individual citizens in a liberal, political democratic system. They demand with striking comparability the dispersal of equality and power among the citizen-workers in an economic-democracy that will make certain the assurance of the good life—the more abundant-life—in a warless world....

Thus our feet are set in the path toward equality—economic, political and social and racial. Equality is the heart and, essence of democracy, freedom and justice. Without equality of opportunity in industry, in labor unions, schools and colleges, government, politics and before the law, without equality in social relations and in all phases of human endeavor, the Negro is certain to be consigned to an inferior status. There must be no dual standards of justice, no dual rights, privileges, duties or responsibilities of citizenship. No dual forms of freedom....

But our nearer goals include the abolition of discrimination, segregation, and Jim Crow [reference to segregationist and racist legislation from 1876 onward that discriminated against African-Americans] in the Government, the Army, Navy, Air Corps, U.S. Marine, Coast Guard, Women's Auxiliary Army Corps and the Wave, and defense industries; the elimination of discriminations in hotels, restaurants, on public transportation conveyances, in educational, recreational, cultural, and amusement and entertainment places such as theatres, beaches, and so forth.

We want the full works of citizenship with no reservations. We will accept nothing less....

Therefore, if Negroes secure their goals, immediate and remote, they must win them and to win them they must fight, sacrifice, suffer, go to jail, and if need be die for them. These rights will not be given. They must be taken....

As to the compositions of our movement. Our policy is that it be all-Negro, and pro-Negro but not anti-white, or anti-Semitic or anti-labor or anti-Catholic. The reason for this policy is that all oppressed people must assume the responsibility

and take the initiative to free themselves. Jews must wage their battle to abolish anti-semitism. Catholics must wage their battle to abolish anti-catholicism. The workers must wage their battle to advance and protect their interests and rights.

But this does not mean that because Jews must take the responsibility and initiatives to solve their own problems that they should not seek the cooperation and support of Gentiles, or that Catholics should not seek the support of Negroes, or that the workers should not attempt to enlist the backing of Jews, Catholics, and Negroes in their fight to win a strike; but the main reliance must be upon the workers themselves. By the same token because Negroes build an all-Negro movement such as the March, it does not follow that our movement should not call for the collaboration of Jews, Catholics, trade unions and white liberals to help restore the President's Fair Employment Practice Committee to its original status of independence, with responsibility to the President....

The essential value of an all-Negro movement such as the March on Washington is that it helps to create faith by Negroes in Negroes. It develops a sense of self-reliance with Negroes depending on Negroes in vital matters. It helps to break down the slave psychology and inferiority complex in Negroes which comes and is nourished with Negroes relying on white people for direction and support. This inevitably happens in mixed organizations that are supposed to be in the Negro....

Now, the question of which I have been discussing involves, for example, the March on Washington Movement's position on the war. We say the Negro must fight for his democratic rights now for after the war it may be too late. This is our policy on the Negro and the war. But this policy raises the question of method, programs, strategy, and tactics; namely, how is this to be done. It is sufficient to say that Negroes must fight for their rights now, during the war....

Hence, it is apparent that the Negro needs more than organization. He needs mass organization with an action program, aggressive, bold and challenging in spirit. Such a movement is our March on Washington.

Our first job then is to actually organize millions of Negroes, and build them into block systems with captains so that they may be summoned into physical motion. Without this type of organization, Negroes will never develop mass power which is the most effective weapon a minority people can wield. Witness the strategy and maneuver of the people of India with mass civil disobedience and non-cooperation and the marches to the sea to make salt. It may be said that the Indian people have not won their freedom. This is so, but they will win it....

We must develop huge demonstrations because the world is used to big dramatic affairs. They think in terms of hundreds of thousands and millions and billions. Millions of Germans and Russians clash on the Eastern front. Billions of dollars are appropriated at the twinkling of an eye. Nothing little counts.

Besides, the unusual attracts. We must develop a series of marches of Negroes at a given time in a hundred or more cities throughout the country, or stage a big march of a hundred thousand Negroes on Washington to put our cause into the main stream of public opinion and focus the attention of world interests....

Therefore, our program is in part as follows:

1. A national conference for, the integration and expression of the collective mind and will of the Negro masses.
2. The mobilization and proclamation of a nationwide series of mass marches on the City Halls and City Councils to awaken the Negro masses and center attention upon the grievances and goals of the Negro people and to serve as training and discipline for the Negro masses for the more strenuous struggle of a March on Washington, if, as and when an affirmative decision is made thereon by the Negro masses of the country through our national conference.
3. A march on Washington as evidence to white America that black America is on a march for its rights and means business.
4. The picketing of the White House following the March on Washington and maintain the said picket line until the country and the world recognize the Negro has come of age and will sacrifice his all to be counted as men, free men....

PROGRAM OF THE MARCH ON WASHINGTON MOVEMENT

1. We demand, in the interest of national unity, the abrogation of every law which makes a distinction in treatment between citizens based on religion, creed, color, or national origin. This means an end to Jim Crow in education, in housing, in transportation and in every other social, economic, and political privilege. Especially, we demand, in the capital of the nation, an end to all segregation in public places and in public institutions.

2. We demand legislation to enforce the Fifth and Fourteenth Amendments guaranteeing that no person shall be deprived of life, liberty or property without due process of law, so that the full weight of the national government may be used for the protection of life and thereby may end the disgrace of lynching.

3. We demand the enforcement of the Fourteenth and Fifteenth Amendments and the enactment of the Pepper Poll Tax bill [finally enacted in 1964 to outlaw local laws limiting the vote to certain taxpayers and effectively disenfranchising African-American or poor white voters] so that all barriers in the exercise of suffrage are eliminated.

4. We demand the abolition of segregation and discrimination in the army, navy, marine corps, air corps, and all other branches of national defense....

NEW WORLD A-COMING

Vincent Lushington "Roi" Ottley (1906–1960) was the first African-American war correspondent to write for major American newspapers. A first generation American, his parents having emigrated to the United States from Granada, Ottley grew up in New York City and for a time attended St. Bonaventure University, where he was an accomplished athlete and student. He went on to briefly study journalism at the University of Michigan, but left after experiencing racism. Upon his return to New York, Ottley took a job with the *Amsterdam News*, a Harlem-based newspaper established in 1909 to serve the African-American community. Ottley wrote about what it was like to be an African-American in his *New World A-Coming*, for which he won three major literary awards. In 1944, as a war correspondent, Ottley described racial relations within the American military as well as the impact of racism in Europe. In 1945 he became the first African-American journalist to meet with Pope Pius XII, then head of the Catholic Church. After the war, and until his death from a heart attack in 1960, Ottley continued his work as a journalist with the *Chicago Tribune*, writing about both the accomplishments of and obstacles remaining for African-Americans in the United States.

Six months before the Japanese attack on Pearl Harbor, Negro communities in the urban areas were seething with resentment. This was reflected by the outspoken utterances of ordinarily conservative Negro leaders, by the pointed editorialized reporting in the Negro press, and, as well, by the inflammatory letters-to-the-editor. Responsible observers were manifestly worried, fearing that the resentment would burst into a social holocaust, perhaps to rival anything the nation had known. Harlem's *Amsterdam-Star News* described the situation in this language:

'Where there was once tolerance and acceptance of a position believed to be gradually changing for the better, now the Negro is showing a democratic upsurge of rebellion,' bordering on open hostility.

Among other things, this unrest had been brought to a head by the frustration Negroes were experiencing at being barred from jobs in the defense industries. One million and more Negroes were unemployed—but no longer did the Negro have the cold comfort of the Depression when white men too were unemployed. His had become a black fate. According to the 1940 census, there were 5,389,000 Negroes in the labor force, 3,582,000 of which were men. A government survey found that, of 29,215 employees in ten war plants in the New York area, only 142 were Negroes. In fifty-six war-contract factories in St. Louis, each employed an average of three Negroes. Outside the N.Y.A. and W.P.A. [the National Youth Administration and Works Progress Administration, agencies under Roosevelt's New Deal program to reduce unemployment], there were practically no provisions for Negroes in the program of defense-employment training, despite the need for manpower and the increasing number of Negroes on the W.P.A. rolls. The United States Employment Service sent out an inquiry to a selected number of defense industries as to the number of job openings

Roi Ottley, *New World A-Coming* (New York: Houghton Mifflin, 1943), 289–305. Used by permission.

and whether they would employ Negroes. More than fifty per cent stated flatly that they would not. In Texas, of 17,435 defense jobs, 9117 were barred to Negroes—and in Michigan, the figure was 22,042 of our 26,904. Moreover, contrary to the assumption that Negroes are barred only when they seek skilled work, no less than 35,000 out of 83,000 unskilled jobs were declared closed to Negro applicants....

A great Negro push was mobilized to dramatize the situation. Early in 1941, A. Philip Randolph, president of the Brotherhood of Sleeping Car Porters, called for a 'Negro March on Washington!' In the midst of the mobilization campaign, he told me, 'The administration leaders in Washington will never give the Negro justice until they see masses— ten, twenty, fifty thousand Negroes on the White House lawn!'...In short order, buses were hired, special trains chartered, and a demonstration of upwards of fifty thousand Negroes was planned to take place on July 1, 1941....Both the N.A.A.C.P. and the National Negro Congress supported the march actively....Thousands of dollars were spent. Press and pulpit played decisive roles in whipping up sentiment....

The prospect of thousands of determined Negroes in the nation's capital alarmed white Washington, a city with a Negro population of two-hundred-odd thousand restive Negroes. Some people recalled the race riot which occurred in the capital following the last war. When it became apparent...that the number of marchers was likely to be very large, Fiorello La Guardia, mayor of New York and then boss of the Office of Civilian Defense, pleaded with them to abandon it. Mr. Roosevelt journeyed to New York and personally asked that the march be called off, and was politely refused....

Four days before the critical day—with the nation rapidly approaching war—Randolph...and others were called to Washington. They went demanding the issuance of an executive order forbidding discrimination. Sitting with the President were ranking members of his cabinet and representatives of the Office of Production Management, predecessor of the War Production Board. The conversations took place at a time when the government could ill afford to risk a demonstration which might further crystallize

the antagonism of Negroes. The Negro leaders were shown a first draft of an order which outlawed discrimination in industry, but said nothing about government. They rejected it. Finally, Mr. Roosevelt wrote his famous Executive Order 8802, and the march was canceled. But the masses of Negroes were bewildered. Even Randolph's colleagues were disappointed by the easy conclusion of the affair.

As it turned out, Randolph and White displayed considerable statesmanship, for the President's proclamation—the first presidential order affecting Negroes directly since Lincoln's day—created the Committee on Fair Employment Practices, an agency which may very well prove to be the opening wedge to the economic equality that Negroes seek. Certainly it commits the government to opposing racial discrimination in jobs. Moreover, its broad democratic implications affected, as well, five million Jews, five million aliens, six million foreign-born citizens, one million Orientals and American Indians, and five million Spanish-speaking peoples. The order declared:...

> the policy of the United States [is] to encourage full participation in the national defense program by all citizens of the United States, regardless of race, creed, color, or national origin, in the firm belief that the democratic way of life within the Nation can be defended successfully only with the help and support of all groups within its borders....

To the South, Executive Order 8802 is—in the words of Governor Dixon of Alabama, who refused to accept on behalf of his state an Army contract for tent cloth because there was a clause in the contract against race discrimination—'meddling with the racial policies of the South' and 'a crackpot reform.' Other Southerners talk in stronger language. Horace C. Wilkinson, a Birmingham lawyer and politician with a reputation for race-baiting,...viewed with alarm Negroes working alongside of white workers in offices and factories. The Alabama politician had a solution for all this. He proposed the organization of a 'state-wise, South-wide, nation-wide League for White Supremacy.'...

The grim truth is, the South has thrown down the challenge to the federal government. It regards

Executive Order 8802 as the initial assault on its way of life....Apparently, they don't believe with Mrs. Roosevelt that 'We have probably come to a point where we have to make up our minds either to live in a democracy and make it a reality or to accept the fact that we are not capable of meeting the challenge.'

Executive Order 8802 may or may not be a social document of tremendous import, but it certainly is a significant stride in the Negro's advance....

THE ZOOT SUITERS

In the early twentieth century with the expansion of the railroad and industry in Southern California, Los Angeles underwent a significant population explosion. Migrants from other parts of the United States as well as Mexico arrived in Los Angeles in the hope of securing work in area aircraft and military-related industries. Increasingly, many of these migrants, often ethnic minorities, encountered discrimination in the workplace and on the streets throughout the city. Tensions were especially high between authorities and Latino youth, who expressed themselves by wearing oversized, high-waisted suits with wide-legged pants and a long coat (first associated with African-American jazz culture). With parents either at work in industry or in the army, more youth were able to congregate late at night to socialize, sometimes leading to fights and violence. The Zoot Suit riots, which began during the first few days of June 1943, eventually spread to other cities like Detroit, Michigan. Agnes Ernst Meyer (1887–1970), the daughter of German Lutheran immigrants and a prominent journalist, philanthropist, and educational activist, wrote an anthropological study, *Journey Through Chaos* (1944), in which she examined the war's impact on the American home front, criticizing the government's inability to deal with important domestic issues—the needs of its veterans, the problems facing education (she was a member of President Roosevelt's Commission on Higher Education), and racial unrest. The following is an excerpt from Meyer's impression of the Zoot Suit riots of Los Angeles, involving members of the military and the local Chicano and African-American communities.

June 13, 1943

It took the Navy to put zoot-suiters on the front pages, but this particular manifestation of the rebellious spirit that is prevalent among American adolescent groups has long been troubling thoughtful students of our social scene. Let it be said at once that gangsterism of our sailors in the Los Angeles area is no less alarming than the violent reaction of the zoot-suiters....

Excerpts from pp. 245–251 from *Journey Through Chaos*, copyright © 1944 by Agnes E. Meyer and renewed 1970 by Eugene Meyer and Katherine Graham, reprinted by permission of Houghton Mifflin Harcourt Publishing Company.

On the whole, the street brawls between sailors and zoot-suiters which took place in Los Angeles throughout the last week are more of an indictment of Navy discipline than of the zoot-suit movement. But the lawless behavior of both groups is more than an accidental occurrence.

It is a symptom of profound weakness in our American civilization....

Zoot-suiters can be found in most of the larger American cities; our own city of Washington has its share of them; New York has a great many; but they seem to be most numerous and most annoying to the authorities in Los Angeles and Detroit. The movement is not new. It has developed out of groups whose main objective was enjoyment of expressional orgies in the jitterbug dance, and for a large number of participants it still retains this meaning.

In some places this orgiastic tendency increased in vehemence and intensity. The original enjoyment of the dance was replaced by an interest in tough-guy behavior, in alcoholic excesses, in uninhibited and ostentatious sex behavior....

The uniform of this movement is fascinating. The baggy trousers that narrow around the ankles give freedom of movement for jitterbugging and the tails of the long coat swirl like the girls' skirts during a pirouette. The outfit is very expensive, costing $100 or more, has pronounced swank and goes into infinite details.

Chief features are the broad felt hat, the long key chain, the pocket knife of certain size and shape, worn in the vest pocket by boys, in the stocking by girls; the whisky flask of peculiar shape to fit into the girl's bosom; the men's haircut of increasing density and length at the neck—all of which paraphernalia has symbolic and secret meanings for the initiates....

The uniform seems to replace the formal dress of conventional society, and to some students of tribal mores, the zoot-suiter's costume seems a willful distortion or parody of the dress suit.

The behavior patterns have a loose uniformity and are a definite part of the movement. Special skill in jitterbugging is a source of status in the group; ardent kissing of partners on the dance floor is often the cause of offense to other jitterbug dancers, and

the cause of trouble when this freedom of behavior is practiced toward some girl not a member of the group or gang....

In the East the movement is divided fairly evenly into white and colored groups, whereas in Los Angeles the Mexican racial situation has become involved in this curious phenomenon. Everywhere the zoot-suiters are composed of underprivileged youngsters, or those who feel themselves to be such—a fact that must always be remembered in any attempt to deal with them constructively.

The movement leapt over the country like a forest fire without any acknowledged leadership. Nobody has been able to discover any planned organization of the membership. Officially there is none. Originally membership was gained by expert performance in the dance ritual, and though the recent outbursts of gang warfare among themselves and of depredations against outsiders seems to indicate a new type of leadership, so far it cannot be defined.

The fluid nature of such a group makes it all the more difficult to understand and to handle. Some authorities feel that the only thing to do is to let the whole mysterious business wear itself out and disappear through inner exhaustion of its possibilities.

But growing manifestations of destructive impulses make this a difficult attitude to maintain. Social workers complain that the presence of even a few uniformed jitterbugs exposes their recreational activities to sudden scandals and disturbances, and, therefore, try to exclude them from their entertainments. This treatment only increases the zoot-suiter's feeling of inferiority, and intensifies his belligerency....

The City Council of Los Angeles, in an attempt to stop open warfare between servicemen and the teen-aged rebels, has resorted to a desperate ordinance which provided a 30-day jail sentence for the wearing of the zoot-suit within the city limits....The very helplessness of welfare workers and of the highest officials should indicate that the problem of the zoot-suit movement is social and economic and can, therefore, only be solved by a slow and patient understanding of its nature and origin.

In addition to asking what ails the zoot-suiters, we should have the courage to ask—what ails America?

For the activities of these groups are not criminal. They provoke quarrels, cut up plush chairs, break windows, or crash parties where they swoop down like the hero in a Western movie and try to win admiration by starting ructions. Even their secret jargon which only the initiated can understand, is a commonplace manifestation of adolescent solidarity against the grown-up world. Likewise the costume gives them the childish pleasure of shocking respectable people and affronting established conventions. These are all typical symptoms of the neglected child who compensates for a feeling of insecurity by anti-social behavior.

But its origin in the dance suggests that the zoot-suit movement is something more. It is the expression of an unconscious desire to escape from our hard, purposeful, rational life into an atmosphere where the only competition is for artistic prestige. It has kinship with the Dionysian cult and like its Greek original, is a protest against the cruel and dusty realities of everyday life. The tensions of war have exaggerated this impulse into outbreaks of the roughest gangsterism, but even now the fantastic costume and the love of dance must be viewed as a romantic substitute for the humdrum uniformity and the sordid aspect of life in our city slums.

To anyone who has encountered as many unhappy, maladjusted youngsters as I have during my tour of the war areas, the zoot-suiters are only an extreme and articulate expression of the cynicism and rebellion which characterize many of our adolescents in all walks of life.

Most of them have absorbed for years a materialistic pacifism, at school, from the magazines, in the very air. Now they find our material comforts disappearing one after the other, and the whole adult world engaged in another life-and-death struggle.

The battlefields are remote; the issues involved even more so. They cannot cope with our war-converted society....Too young to go into the Army, made old beyond their years by the wartime collapse of social standards, these adolescents are getting on as best they can in a moral vacuum. The schoolroom is a bore in comparison with the excitements of the boom-towns in which they live; and yet there is nothing else to do except to get into mischief of one sort or another....

What then is the answer to a frightening phenomenon such as the zoot-suiters? If they are merely one manifestation of our failure toward the youth of the Nation, what are we going to do about them? Obviously letting the Navy beat them up is only going to increase the solidarity of this spontaneous if perverted youth movement. On the West Coast the rioting between sailors and the zoot-suiters is spreading from city to city.

There is a real danger that it will leap to other war centers where the costumed jitterbugs are numerous, unless the naval commanders realize at once that the reckless behavior of their servicemen is on a par with that of the zoot-suiters, and put an end to it.

But that still leaves us confronted with a serious national manifestation that should be carefully and sympathetically studied with a view to guiding this unwholesome and pathetic youth movement into more constructive channels. The mere fact that these young people have given a positive expression to their dissatisfaction indicates qualities of character and imagination that should be utilized for better purposes than street brawls and dancing.

DISCRIMINATION AGAINST MEXICAN-AMERICANS

Despite having endured ridicule and mistreatment during basic training in the First World War, Mexican-Americans continued to enlist in the military during the Second World War, more than 350,000 of them having served in both the Pacific and European theaters. Praising the 158th Regimental Combat Team (the Bushmasters), an Arizona National Guard unit with a large number of Hispanic soldiers, for its valor, General MacArthur reportedly referred to that unit as "the greatest fighting combat team ever deployed for battle." Members of an entire Spanish-speaking American unit, Company E of the 141st Regiment of the 36th Texas Infantry Division, serving in Europe, received recognition for its service with Distinguished Service Crosses among other medals. But, as the following excerpt demonstrates, bravery on the battlefield did not always translate to acceptance on the home front where discrimination against Mexican-American soldiers (as well as citizens) prevailed.

VALLEY EVENING MONITOR, THURSDAY, MARCH 30, 1944

On a warm summer evening last July in Mission, a thousand or more citizens gathered at an open-air meeting to greet and acclaim a young soldier who had just returned from England.

This young soldier had been a turret gunner in a B-17 bomber crew. His squadron had participated in the first aerial raids on Germany.

On his first raid, this young gunner had been wounded. But the wound was slight and after a short stay in a hospital the gunner went back to his turret. Twenty-four more times he rode through the deadly air over Europe on bombing raids.

The boy wasn't any more of a hero than thousands of his fellow soldiers who are fighting for democracy and against the "super race" which preaches and practices with the sword that false and hateful doctrine holding some races of men superior to others. This boy wasn't a hero. He was just doing his part

as decent people everywhere in the world today are doing theirs—and dying.

After his twenty-fifth bombing mission, this young gunner from Mission was sent back to the United States to train other gunners. While he wasn't any special hero, they did pin a few medals on his chest before he sailed for home. He brought back the Air Medal with three oak leaf clusters and the Distinguished Flying Cross and the Purple Heart.

At the open-air meeting in Mission, this young gunner was lauded for his exploits by fellow citizens, and presented with a fine watch. The visit had a very special purpose. Then he went off to Sioux City, Ia. to be a gunnery instructor.

Last week the young gunner from Mission came back for another visit. This visit had a very special purpose. He came back to claim himself a bride.

Turret gunners and their brides, like any newly married couple, are happy people and like to kick up

Alonso S. Perales, *Are We Good Neighbors?* (San Antonio, TX: Artes Graficas, 1948), 267–269. Used by permission.

their heels on a well-polished floor to the strains of good music. So the gunner and his bride, together with two other young couples, betook themselves down to the Blue Moon between Pharr and San Juan, thinking to enjoy an evening of dancing which is one of the many privileges enjoyed by citizens of this enlightened and democratic nation.

The Blue Moon, it might be pointed out, is not exactly comparable with the Rainbow Room in Rockefeller Center nor do its patrons expect their social pedigrees to be enhanced by being seen there, but as Valley night spots go it is a fair average.

Anyhow, the young gunner and his wife and the two other young couples entered the Blue Moon and proffered their money for admission to the dance floor.

The place was not crowded and the money they proffered was not counterfeit. But the young gunner and his wife were not admitted. They could not qualify, the doorman, explained, because "we do not permit Mexicans in here."

The gunner and his wife, of course, are not Mexicans. They are citizens of the United States—much better citizens, it might be added, than the doorman of the Blue Moon. But they were turned away because the Blue Moon is operated on the same despicable racial policies that have made Nazi Germany the scourge of the civilized world. It so happens that one of the three couples in the young gunner's party belonged to the group commonly referred to as Anglo-American, but naturally the entire party departed after learning the club's policy, as any self-respecting American citizen would....

But as long as this is the United States of America and as long as the Constitution sets forth its declarations of equality among all citizens, to say nothing of the instincts of common decency and reason which govern the behavior of all good men, it is not possible to keep silent in the face of such bigoted behavior....

If there is any place in the nation where two so-called races (actually both Latin and Anglo-Americans are of the same race) of people should live in harmony and understanding and mutual appreciation it is here in the Valley. If there is any ethnological basis for showing preference to any group herein in the Valley, that preference lies in the favor of our Latin-American people whose ancestors rightfully called this soil home centuries before the paleface knew of its existence....

While we are engaged in fighting to the death against similar hostile influences abroad, how can we tolerate them right under our noses here at home?

THE STOCKING PANIC

DuPont chemical company's Wallace Hume Carothers invented Fiber 66, or nylon, as an alternative to women's traditional silk stockings. The new product was unveiled to the public in 1939 at the World's Fair, worn by a young lady known as "Miss Chemistry," but was not sold commercially until May 1940. On the first day alone, DuPont reportedly sold 64 million pairs of its nylon stockings. The new rage, however, was temporarily disrupted when the production of nylon was redirected away from commercial to military use (nylon was crucial for parachutes and airplane accessories) and resulted in a stocking shortage. Stockings that had cost $1 per pair before were now selling for upwards of $20 on the black market. In August 1945 DuPont announced resumption of nylon stocking production, ending the dearth of stockings but creating a renewed demand for nylon so great that even DuPont was unable to replenish quickly enough. The so-called Stocking Panic was representative of the difficulties consumers experienced in adjusting to wartime shortages and rationing.

In most countries, silk stockings are a luxury pretty much restricted to a few fortunate women in the upper income brackets. But to the average U.S. female over the age of 12, they are one of the basic necessities. The United States imports almost its entire supply of raw silk from Japan, and 90% of this goes into stockings, mostly women's. Last week, women took one quick look at the headlines announcing the new crisis in Japanese-American relations, grabbed their pocketbooks, and dived headlong for the nearest stocking counter.

The result was a rush of business practically unparalleled in retail history. In one New York specialty shop, an imperious customer said, "I use four pairs a month, give me enough to last two years." In Denver, one woman put three $100 bills on the counter and ordered, "That many stockings, size 9 1/2—I don't care what color." Stores everywhere added extra sales help, in many cases taking on inexperienced girls. The plea...that women avoid piggishness and buy only for their immediate needs did not even check the tide.

CHRISTMAS IN JULY

—*Women's Wear Daily*, in a quick survey of the situation, reported sales in individual cities up 100% to 300%, with the heaviest buying on the East and West Coasts. Total volume was estimated as better than double that of the big Christmas season, which ordinarily accounts for between 17% and 18% of annual stocking sales.

By the beginning of this week, following OPM's [the Office of Production Management, a government agency] order of last Saturday halting processing of raw silk and announcing that the government would take over all stocks on hand for the production of parachutes and silk bags for explosives, the run on the market had reached such proportions that most stores were limiting customers to two or three pairs apiece. Even rationing, however, did not prevent a virtual sell-out of almost all popular brands, lines and sizes by the end of this week....

ALL SILK SALES UP

—There were substantial sales increases in other silk items, mostly women's lingerie and piece goods, but nothing to touch the stocking boom.

While retailers struggled with mobs of stocking mad women, representatives of the industry spent last week in Washington, petitioning the government for help. The 175,000 silk workers, 110,000 of them in hosiery, were the most immediate concerns of both government and industry....

FORM RAYON POOL

—The workers' plight was what chiefly motivated the Office of Price Administration and Civilian Supply in announcing an emergency rayon allocation program for August and September. This obliges all rayon yarn producers to turn 10% of their daily output and 10% of their stocks on hand into government pool. The hosiery industry will get 70% of the pooled yarn, with the remaining 30% going to other silk users and to present rayon customers on whom the order may work undue hardship.

PRAYER AT IWO JIMA

The first Jewish chaplain ever appointed by the Marine Corps, Roland B. Gittelsohn (1910–1995), was ordained as a rabbi of Reform Judaism at Hebrew Union College in Cincinnati in 1936 and served congregations in New York State and in Boston. While active in many Jewish organizations, he devoted himself as well to broader political causes, promoting civil rights and the protection of the laboring poor and opposing the death penalty. Although he thought of himself as a pacifist, he considered World War II as a "just war" and thus justified his participation in it. Assigned to the Fifth Marine Division that fought at Iwo Jima, Gittelsohn ministered to the nearly 1,500 Jewish marines in the division as well as to those of all faiths. When the fierce fighting had finished, a Protestant minister, Division Chaplain Warren Cuthriell, asked Gittelsohn to deliver a nondenominational memorial sermon to dedicate the Marine Cemetery in honor of the fallen from all racial, social, and religious backgrounds. Cuthriell's request met with stiff opposition from other chaplains (Catholic as well as Protestant), who rejected the idea of having a Jew preach over Christian graves. Cuthriell, however, stood his ground, but Gittelsohn, not wishing Cuthriell to endure further criticism, acquiesced to the dissenters, preaching the original sermon meant for a nondenominational group to seventy Jewish participants and three Protestant chaplains who supported Cuthriell and Gittelsohn.

Rabbi/Lt. Roland Gittelsohn, "Prayer at the Fifth Marine Division Cemetery Iwo Jima," March 26, 1945, as cited in www.jwv-md.us. Used by permission.

This is perhaps the grimmest, and surely the holiest task we have faced since D-Day. Here before us lie the bodies of comrades and friends. Men who until yesterday or last week laughed with us, joked with us, trained with us. Men who were on the same ships with us, and went over the sides with us as we prepared to hit the beaches of this island. Men who fought with us and feared with us.

Somewhere in this plot of ground there may lie the man who could have discovered the cure for cancer. Under one of these Christian crosses, or beneath a Jewish Star of David, there may rest now a man who was destined to be a great prophet…to find the way, perhaps, for all to live in plenty, with poverty and hardship for none. Now they lie here silently in this sacred soil, and we gather to consecrate this earth in their memory. It is not easy to do so. Some of us have buried our closest friends here. We saw these men killed before our very eyes. Any one of us might have died in their places. Indeed, some of us are alive and breathing at this very moment only because men who lie here beneath us had the courage and strength to give their lives for ours. To speak in memory of such men as these is not easy. Of them, too, can it be said with utter truth: "The world will little note nor long remember what we say here. It can never forget what they did here." No, our poor power of speech can add nothing to what these men and the other dead of our division who are not here have already done. All that we can even hope to do is follow their example. To that, by the grace of God and the stubborn strength and power of human will, their sons and ours shall never suffer these pains again. These men have done their job well. They have paid the ghastly price of freedom. If that freedom be once again lost, as it was after the last war, the unforgivable blame will be ours, not theirs. So it is we, the living, who are here to be dedicated and consecrated.

We dedicate ourselves, first to live together in peace the way they fought and are buried here in war. Here lie men who loved America because their ancestors generations ago helped in her founding, and other men who loved here with equal passion because they themselves or their own fathers escaped from oppression to her blessed shores. Here lie officers and men, Negroes and whites, rich men and poor…together. Here are Protestants, Catholics, and Jews…together. Here no man prefers another because of his faith or despises him because of his color. Here there are no quotas of how many from each group are admitted or allowed. Among these men is no discrimination. No prejudice. No hatred. Theirs is the highest and purest democracy. Any man among us, the living, who fails to understand that will thereby betray those who lie here dead. Whoever of us lifts his hand in hate against a brother, or thinks himself superior to those who happen to be in the minority, makes of this ceremony and of the bloody sacrifice it commemorates, an empty, hollow mockery. To this, then, as our solemn, sacred duty, do we the living now dedicate ourselves; to the right of Protestant, Catholics, and Jews, of white men and Negroes alike, to enjoy the democracy for which all of them have here paid the price.

To one thing more do we consecrate ourselves in memory of those who sleep beneath these crosses and stars. We shall not foolishly suppose, as did the last generation of America's fighting men, that victory on the battlefield will automatically guarantee the triumph of democracy at home. This war, with all its frightful heartache and suffering, is but the beginning of our generation's struggle for democracy. When the last battle has been won, there will be those at home, as there were last time, who will want us to turn our backs in selfish isolation on the rest of organized humanity, and thus to sabotage the very peace for which we fight. We promise you who lie here: we will not do that! We will join hands with Britain, China, Russia in peace, even as we have in war to build the kind of world for which you died. When the last shot has been fired, there will still be those whose eyes are turned backward, not forward, who will be satisfied with those wide extremes of poverty and wealth in which the seeds of another war can breed. We promise you, our departed comrades: This too we will not permit. This war has been fought by the common man; its fruits of peace must be enjoyed by the common man! We promise, by all that is sacred and holy, that your sons—the sons of miners and millers, the sons of farmers and workers, will inherit from your death the right to a living that is decent and secure.

When the final cross has been placed in the last cemetery, once again there will be those to whom profit is more important than peace, who will insist with the voice of sweet reasonableness and appeasement that it is better to trade with the enemies of mankind than, by crushing them, to lose their profit. To you who sleep here silently, we give our promise: We will not listen! We will not forget that some of you were burnt with oil that came from American wells, that many of you were killed by shells fashioned from American steel. We promise that when once again men seek profit at your expense, we shall remember how you looked when we placed you reverently, lovingly, in the ground. Thus do we memorialize those who, having ceased living with us, now live within us. Thus do we consecrate ourselves, the living, to carry on the struggle they began. Too much blood has gone into this soil for us to let it lie barren. Too much pain and heartache have fertilized the earth on which we stand. We here solemnly swear: this shall not be in vain! Out of this, and from the suffering and sorrow of those who mourn this, will come we promise the birth of a new freedom for the sons of men everywhere. Amen.

READJUSTING TO FAMILY LIFE

On June 22, 1944, President Roosevelt signed the Servicemen's Readjustment Act (better known as the GI Bill), which provided assistance to veterans for college education, unemployment insurance, and housing in the postwar era. The bill, whose provisions were discussed already in 1942–1943, was designed by the American Legion to facilitate the transition for servicemen (and women) from military to civilian life and to reduce the likelihood of widespread depression that could result from the readjustment to family life. Although well intentioned, the framers of the bill could not calculate the degree to which soldiers suffering from combat-related post-traumatic stress disorders would be able to deal with the new public roles their wives, girlfriends, or mothers had taken on. Would the soldiers willingly concede to some women's preference to continue working outside the private sphere? Would they recognize the broader responsibilities women accepted in the domestic sphere? And, in turn, would the "emancipated" women be able to reestablish their relationships with the men whose lives were changed by the war? This article, published in a popular women's magazine, offers insight into the problem.

Mona Gardner, "Has Your Husband Come Home to the Right Woman?" *Ladies Home Journal*, vol. 62, no. 12 (December 1945), 41, 72. Used by permission.

The Army is discharging husbands right now at the rate of more than 5000 a day. This means each day 5000 more wives are experiencing varying degrees of the same emotional impact—welcoming a man whose dear face is familiar, yet whose mind and emotions are liable to be bewilderingly different. But it also means the contrary. Those 5000 husbands are gathering in their arms a woman who may be as much a stranger as her hair-do.

Home-coming isn't as simple as a homesick man getting off a train, hanging his hat in the hall, and eating all the shortcake and devil's food his wife can wring out of her sugar allowance. Human relations are never static. Living with other men, crossing oceans, experiencing fear and destruction have engendered many deep and ineradicable changes in him. Working at a drill press, living with in-laws, making her own decisions have certainly remolded her. After the first glad flush of reunion, these differences work their way to the surface, disturbingly, delightfully, hatefully, unpredictably.

The tension inherent in making radical changes in a pattern of living is tremendous—far, far greater than many individuals realize. Just as it takes six months to make a husband into a soldier, so it takes six months to unmake that soldier and turn him back into a family man again. Psychologists and medical men say women require the same amount of time to fit back fully in to the wife mold again.

Four years of war have stamped Mrs. G.I. into one of four general wife types. A—she has tried on the family pants, become a competently functioning individual and loves it; B—she has reluctantly worn the pants and can hardly wait to get them off; C—she has never acquired maturity because she has continued to live a little-girl relationship with parents; D—she is exaggeratedly feminine because she has been living a purely feminine routine with three or four other women....

For instance, one of the A type: while her husband has been in the Army this Mrs. A has made herself into another woman—a more interesting, resourceful and acute woman....At twenty-six she started in a routine office job, showed ingenuity and solid dependability, and by appreciable jumps became manager of an important department in a sizable business. Now at thirty she is making good money, her contacts are stimulating; furthermore, she likes the feel of independence and of managing her own affairs. Her feelings about her husband's return are bound to be mixed. She knows she doesn't need him back for security. But she does need *and want him* for companionship, for love, for fulfillment.

Churning around in her emotions are such questions as: Will he resent her working afterward? Her outside contacts: Her independence? And if he does, what will her reaction be? A blowup? Insistence that she has a right to be a person? Or submission and retirement, for the sake of his feelings, with cankerous enmity just slightly below the surface?...

[R]econverting to a domestic pattern is a major step in which they feel they are doing all the giving. Trading eight hours of clean methodical work at a factory to go back to a sixteen-hour day of mopping floors, washing dishes and cooking, with no pay check at the end of the week, strikes them as an unfair and unattractive exchange. Some of them reject any thought of reconverting themselves to this with such vigorous words as: "Why should we go back again to being economic drudges and slaves, just to keep a man's ego happy? The man who feels he's less a man just because his wife works and contributes to the family income is outmoded and medieval. It's time for those men to redo their egos!"

If returning G.I's come home with the same definition of a wife they went away with, and all indications confirm that they will, then there are rocks ahead for a vast number of marriages. According to a recent survey made by the Women's Bureau of the United States Department of Labor, 50 per cent have indicated their desire to work after the war. In some communities the percentage runs as high as 70 per cent of those now working. All together this adds up to more than 2,000,000 women in industry alone who have made up their minds to go on working after husband G. I. takes off his uniform. Yet husbands are so opposed to it that the congressman of a New England state has already expressed the fear that returning veterans will organize against women in industry as they have against labor unions....

CHAPTER 9

THE CULTURE AND
PSYCHOLOGY OF WAR

ENDURING THE BLITZ Weary Londoners sought refuge from German air raids during the "Blitz" any-where they could, including in underground railway (commonly known as the "tube") stations. This photo of Aldwych Station on the night of October 8, 1940, vividly illustrates the strain and lack of comfort or pri-vacy that the city's civilian residents were forced to endure.
Source: © Imperial War Museum, London.

Napoleon Bonaparte's oft-quoted dictum that in war, "the moral is to the physical as three is to one," was as true during the Second World War as it had been when he said it nearly a century and a half earlier. As a war of mobilized nations, in which the participa-tion of civilians and soldiers alike was crucial in an all-encompassing "total war," World War II forced its participants to attend to its moral dimensions and to the maintenance of morale. More specifically, the strain and duration of the conflict raised fundamental questions such as: What was the war about? Why would nations fight it, and what did they hope to achieve? How did the experience of fighting it affect the participants, and could nations frame the struggle in ways that encouraged people to continue to believe that their massive exertions or sacrifices were justified? Within the context of a culture of war, states were challenged to justify the morality of their causes and to find ways of maintaining morale and continuing to command the loyalty of their populations.

At first glance, there were obvious differences between the two sides. The Axis powers were the aggressors, while the Allies, having been attacked, fought in terms of justifiable self-defense. Nor, from the outset, did the Allies wage war with so wanton a disregard for the rights of prisoners or civilians, or display the murderously repellent attitudes characteristic of German and Japanese perpetrators who denied human attributes at all in the victims they methodically butchered (as in the Jews or Chinese, for example). As aggressors, the Nazis rarely spelled out a positive vision of what they were fighting for; rather it was to undo the restrictions of Versailles, restore Germany's rightful place in the world, and then to forestall the threat of Judeo-Bolshevism, as they often put it, to the very survival of Germany's people and culture. In a Manichean world, the argument ran, Germany launched a preemptive strike and its violation of treaties, customary diplomatic practice, and even the established rules of war were but simply harbingers of sheer ruthlessness in service of the nationalist interest. One of the rare instances in which officials revealed their conception of Europe's future after a Nazi victory painted a bleak picture of a garrison state, a "continent behind barbed wire." Japan's leaders, too, rarely condescended to explain to the population what they hoped to achieve through an aggressive war; justifications couched in vaguely defensive terms (responses to imperialist pressure) and exhorting absolute fidelity to the emperor radiated a rather macabre emphasis on self-sacrifice.

In sharp contrast stood the democracies' commitment to freedom. The Allies could hardly claim to be conducting a crusade against dictatorship, given that one partner, the Soviet Union, had an unsurpassed record of opposition to individual liberties. All were agreed on the need to smash "Hitlerism" because the cost of failure to do so would be impossible to bear. Contemporaries grasped that Hitler's war transcended the traditional conflicts in which adversaries merely sought to secure more advantageous positions but leave the international system intact. He obviously represented an altogether more radical, ambitious, and evil threat, but opinions were divided over whether ordinary Germans should be spared as coerced and manipulated accessories or crushed as the latest representatives of a long line of aggressors including the Huns, Bismarck, and the Kaiser. This demonization of the enemy provided a satisfying focal point for pent-up frustration and disgust, but both Britain and the United States were able to articulate a more positive vision of the precious heritage the Allies were fighting to protect, of how victory would underwrite further improvement in their citizens' lives (even if this committed them to postwar educational and social reforms).

With the very survival of societies at stake, it is no surprise that governments used any means at their disposal to ensure the discipline and morale of soldiers and the compliance and support of civilians in the pursuit of victory. The war witnessed a major expansion in the responsibilities and intrusive capabilities of governmental power (it is no accident that

George Orwell would be compelled to write his famous *1984* on this theme), and nowhere more so than in the cultural sphere. They battled for the hearts, minds, and even souls of their people through propaganda, education, and organized religion. By dint of their state systems and ideologies, the Axis powers aspired to exercise strict and total control over the formation of public attitudes. In Germany, the Ministry for Public Enlightenment and Propaganda, created shortly after Hitler's accession to power in 1933 and led by Joseph Goebbels, centralized control over all media—newspapers, magazines, books, movies, radio, and art. Japan had its corresponding Government Information Bureau to ensure conformity and uniformity in public attitudes to the war, and, though less draconian, a similar organization, the Ministry of Popular Culture, existed in Italy. Britain's Ministry of Information and the United States Office of War Information (OWI) relied as much on persuasion as prohibition to police the media, while in the Soviet Union the need to suppress bad news or contradictory reports and to stifle dissent was a task all too familiar to a Communist Party apparatus deeply suspicious of popular attitudes and the free exchange of information.

Despite all these intensive efforts, there were limits to what governments could impose from above. A famous study by sociologists Morris Janowitz and Edward Shils based on interrogations of prisoners of war concluded that German soldiers fought effectively because of primary group loyalties (the wish not to let their "buddies" down) rather than ideological indoctrination. It should be noted, however, that these arguments applied to soldiers captured in western Europe; it has been argued equally persuasively that many in the Wehrmacht on the eastern front subscribed to the Nazi worldview of an inferior Slavic population and accepted that pitiless behavior toward such subhumans was appropriate. American soldiers often seemed to have only a hazy idea of what they were fighting for, and they readily defined their participation in terms of protecting home and family, and staying true to their comrades.

Even if soldiers could not always articulate clearly their war aims in terms that meshed with the politicians' and propagandists' evocation of cosmic struggle and a clash of civilizations, they knew that the hopes of those on the home fronts rested on their shoulders. That pressure, in addition to the undeniable risks and burdens of modern combat, placed the troops under severe strain. One way of coping was by recourse to the consolation of religion, and indeed religious observance flowered in the most unlikely places, such as the avowedly atheistic Soviet Union. Or, perhaps more accurately, the Soviet system had failed to eradicate popular religiosity and was forced to accommodate it amid the strains of total war. But religion did more than console, or even provide attitudes governments might be tempted to exploit to their own ends (which is why Stalin was willing to condone it). Religious ethics as easily underlay criticism of the war, or sought to hold the participants morally accountable for the ways they conducted it. An obvious case was aerial bombing and the loss of civilian life, and courageous churchmen spoke eloquently of the moral consequences. For some, the taking of human life under any circumstances was too repugnant, and they refused to participate on the grounds of conscientious objection. This option was only available in the democracies, where objectors might choose alternatives to military service such as ambulance work, fire fighting, or road construction. Those who refused any form of alternative service might expect a prison sentence, while in Germany and the Soviet Union, imprisonment was not the last resort but merely the best alternative to execution.

For those who fought but could not easily cope, there was psychiatric help. The First World War had already proven combat veterans' susceptibility to psychoses like shell shock and combat fatigue, and the inability or unwillingness of many military and medical personnel to accept them as legitimate illnesses rather than thinly disguised efforts to escape service in the front lines. In World War II, though, the situation differed, and in the U.S. Army, for example, by 1943 psychiatrists were attached to every division. The Red Army was ever alert to soldiers who experienced difficulties in doing their duties, though its approach smacked more of the stick than the carrot: those deemed slackers would be the first to be thrown against German lines, with correspondingly high casualties, while the NKVD (People's Commissariat for Internal Affairs) lay in wait behind the lines to shoot deserters.

Psychology and psychiatry were no less a part of life behind the lines. The idea of psychological warfare (or so-called black propaganda) took hold whereby the target audience was not one's own soldiers or workers, but the enemy's, who were to be demoralized by leaflets dropped from the air or scattered by hand (as in the Polish resistance) or radio broadcasts (the infamous Lord Haw Haw and Tokyo Rose spring to mind). Sometimes these efforts involved deliberate deception and misinformation, and sometimes they were merely programs designed to appeal to homesick soldiers or forced laborers far from home. Psychologists were enlisted to assess foreign leaders and predict their likely actions in the future (both the United States and Soviet Union, for example, commissioned studies of Hitler). The mass media, especially the medium of radio with its vast potential audiences and opportunities for clandestine listening, offered the prospect of shaping mass behavior, and sociologists, too, were quick to identify its potential for mass persuasion. But creating a community of consent, whereby peer pressure reinforced individual loyalty toward the war effort, really only worked effectively when governments preserved a sense of legitimacy. Education could promote a certain consensus, or disposition among the citizens to disregard the inevitable war weariness, and reinforce their willingness to accept that loved ones in uniform might not return. But in the long run, the sacrifices that governments demanded and the reports about the progress of the war they rationed out, had to make some sense, had to honor those who had already given their lives, but had to promise that future casualties would not be in vain. When it no longer seemed worthwhile, no longer made sense, the war effort would lose its moral bearings and morale would collapse. And in a total war, that collapse would ensure defeat.

THE NAZI NEW ORDER

Hans Fritzsche's contemptuous tone in his speech to the Berlin Foreign Press Association reflected the confident mood of many within the German government in the autumn of 1941 before the initially spectacular invasion of the Soviet Union lost momentum and, within two months, was frozen in its tracks. Fritzsche (1900–1953) pursued a career in print journalism and radio before joining the Nazi Party in 1933. By 1941 he was entrenched in Goebbels' Propaganda Ministry with responsibility for overseeing whatever news German newspapers saw fit to print. His address on this occasion is noteworthy for its reminder that the controlled dissemination of information was crucial to the survival of a dictatorship, but also for its forecast of the world the Nazis were fighting to create, and of the "responsibility" of compliant journalists to educate the German public about their expectations as the war, already presumed to be won, slowly wound down.

Militarily this war has already been decided. All that remains to be done is of predominantly political character both at home and abroad. The German armies in the East will come to a halt at some point, and we shall draw up a frontier there which will act as a bulwark against the East for Europe and for the European power bloc under German leadership. It is possible that military tensions and perhaps even small-scale military conflicts may continue for eight or ten years, but such a situation—and this is the will of the German leadership—will not prevent the reconstruction and organization of the European continent along the lines laid down by Germany. Certainly this will be a 'Europe behind barbed wire,' but this Europe will be entirely self-sufficient economically, industrially and agriculturally, and it will be basically *unassailable* militarily.

The German state leadership has no intention of pursuing Britain and America into the wilderness in order to engage them in battle. This would be of no profit to Europe, and the expenditure in men and material would be out of proportion to the advantage to be derived. Things are different with regard to the island territory of Britain....It is out of the question that, after the outcome in the East, we should approach Britain over any negotiation of terms—it is most conceivable that Britain, at the moment of her total military defeat, should approach us with a view to receiving a place assigned to her by us as an outer island within the framework of the new Europe. In this connexion it is irrelevant whether Britain is to be attacked and occupied very shortly—or in the spring of next year, or in the summer, or whenever. Such a military operation would be carried out and completed by only a small portion of our total Wehrmacht. Germany will now lead a well-protected and secure European continent towards reconstruction, even though behind barbed wire and ever ready to defend herself. We do not desire to conquer boundless distances but instead to concentrate on the vast European tasks of the future. Should we be disturbed in this by enemy bombing or by attacks on the eastern frontier, or in some other frontier regions, then retribution will inevitably be frightful—until such actions by the enemy are stopped. As for the nations dominated by us, our language to them will become very much freer and colder. There will, of course, be no question of some crummy little state obstructing European peace by some special requests or special demands—in such an event it would get a sharp reminder of its task in Europe. In consequence, whenever the status of a peaceful Europe is proclaimed in future, the German press will be able to be very much freer in its treatment of the European nations and small countries. No censorship will then be necessary any longer since the imperial instinct will probably be sufficient to assert the German point of view at every opportunity.

Once the German people have in their own minds reconciled themselves to the fact that a war of this nature, naturally on a smaller scale than the present one, will persist for ten years, then nine of those years will virtually have been mastered. It is now the task of the German press to pursue this enlightenment during the coming winter, following up certain cues—and for psychological reasons this is, needless to say, a *highly political task*. The German people's *staying power* must be strengthened; when that is done the rest will follow of its own accord, so that within a very short space of time, no one will notice that no peace has been concluded at all. This may sound odd at first sight, but it must be remembered that very considerable relaxations will be introduced in the near future as indeed they must

as part of our European task; moreover, in extensive regions of the Reich, above all in the east, the south and the centre, the blackout will be partially lifted so that the entire labour effort of the people will now concentrate on production targets more in line with peacetime; also, within a foreseeable time, foodstuff supplies from the east, etc., will begin to function again—in short, the hardships of war will disappear. Perhaps not at one blow but by and by, an enormous working rhythm will begin, with earnings and land gain and big transactions. Bombing raids...will also gradually lessen, simply because the subsequent German reprisals will make it seem inadvisable to the enemy to intimidate the German people in *this* way. The press will become much more flexible, it will be able to touch on much wider issues, and it will be able to operate politically in a sovereign manner where in the past it was tied to the most petty directives. For this purpose, of course, newsprint will be necessary, and during the course of this winter allocations of newsprint will become available in ever more generous quantities, since this is a decision by the Fuehrer....

The outcome of this war has been decided. After so many years of hardships and of discipline German journalism will soon have a chance of collecting its reward. It will continue to be *the* instrument of guidance, before which the radio, the People's Assembly and every Gauleiter and Reichskommissar have to fall silent.

THE FOUR FREEDOMS

On January 6, 1941, President Franklin D. Roosevelt went before Congress, like his predecessors in the White House, to give an address on the state of the union. But if the responsibility to inform the nation was depressingly familiar, both the circumstances and Roosevelt's speech itself were anything but pedestrian. Given that the United States was already involved in an undeclared war to assist Britain to hold out against German military pressure, the American president was required to enunciate just what fundamental issues were at stake. He chose to emphasize the disparity between democracy and tyranny, and in effect provided a ringing affirmation of what America would be fighting for—and against—in the coming years. It is striking, though, that Roosevelt went beyond emphasizing the freedom of speech, expression, and religion traditionally protected by the Constitution, and also committed the government to ensuring economic security and working to promote these values, prosperity, and American influence abroad, an altogether more ambitious agenda. The implication was that an eventual victory overseas would necessarily be accompanied by a healthy dose of peaceful revolution at home. And it also suggested that America could not retreat into an era of isolation as it had sought to do after the previous world war.

January 6, 1941

The Nation takes great satisfaction and much strength from the things which have been done to make its people conscious of their individual stake in the preservation of democratic life in America.

Those things have toughened the fibre of our people, have renewed their faith and strengthened their devotion to the institutions we make ready to protect.

Certainly this is no time for any of us to stop thinking about the social and economic problems which are the root cause of the social revolution which is today a supreme factor in the world.

For there is nothing mysterious about the foundations of a healthy and strong democracy. The basic things expected by our people of their political and economic systems are simple. They are:

Equality of opportunity for youth and for others.
Jobs for those who can work.
Security for those who need it.
The ending of special privilege for the few.
The preservation of civil liberties for all.
The enjoyment of the fruits of scientific progress in a wider and constantly rising standard of living.

These are the simple, basic things that must never be lost sight of in the turmoil and unbelievable complexity of our modern world. The inner and abiding strength of our economic and political systems is dependent upon the degree to which they fulfill these expectations....

"Four Freedoms Speech," in United States, 77th Congress [Senate], Document no. 188, *Development of United States Foreign Policy: Addresses and Messages of Franklin D. Roosevelt* (Washington, DC: United States Government Printing Office, 1942). Used by permission.

In the future days, which we seek to make secure, we look forward to a world founded upon four essential human freedoms.

The first is freedom of speech and expression—everywhere in the world.

The second is freedom of every person to worship God in his own way—everywhere in the world.

The third is freedom from want—which, translated into world terms, means economic understandings which will secure to every nation a healthy peacetime life for its inhabitants—everywhere in the world.

The fourth is freedom from fear—which, translated into world terms, means a world-wide reduction of armaments to such a point and in such a thorough fashion that no nation will be in a position to commit an act of physical aggression against any neighbor—anywhere in the world.

That is no vision of a distant millennium. It is a definite basis for a kind of world attainable in our own time and generation. That kind of world is the very antithesis of the so-called new order of tyranny which the dictators seek to create with the crash of a bomb.

To that new order we oppose the greater conception—the moral order. A good society is able to face schemes of world domination and foreign revolutions alike without fear.

Since the beginning of our American history, we have been engaged in change—in a perpetual peaceful revolution—a revolution which goes on steadily, quietly adjusting itself to changing conditions—without the concentration camp or the quick-lime in the ditch. The world order which we seek is the cooperation of free countries, working together in a friendly, civilized society.

This nation has placed its destiny in the hands and heads and hearts of its millions of free men and women; and its faith in freedom under the guidance of God. Freedom means the supremacy of human rights everywhere. Our support goes to those who struggle to gain those rights or keep them. Our strength is our unity of purpose.

To that high concept there can be no end save victory.

THE ATLANTIC CHARTER

In August 1941, aboard the U.S. cruiser *Augusta* and the British battleship *Prince of Wales* anchored off the coast of Newfoundland, President Roosevelt and British Prime Minister Winston Churchill met over the course of several days, subsequently issuing a joint statement on August 14 regarding their principles for a post–World War II world. The document was drawn up at a time when the United States, unlike Britain, had not yet entered the war. Although a separate note was drafted that threatened Japan with joint action if it continued its menacing actions, its tone was substantially weakened by the time it reached Japanese officials. In Washington DC in January 1942, these basic principles were agreed upon by the remaining Allied governments, creating the Atlantic Charter and forming the basis for the United Nations charter in 1945.

The President of the United States of America and the Prime Minister, Mr. Churchill, representing His Majesty's Government in the United Kingdom, being met together, deem it right to make known certain common principles in the national policies of their respective countries on which they base their hopes for a better future for the world.

First, their countries seek no aggrandizement, territorial or other;

Second, they desire to see no territorial changes that do not accord with the freely expressed wishes of the peoples concerned;

Third, they respect the right of all peoples to choose the form of government under which they will live; and they wish to see sovereign rights and self government restored to those who have been forcibly deprived of them;

Fourth, they will endeavor, with due respect for their existing obligations, to further the enjoyment by all States, great and small, victor or vanquished, of access, on equal terms, to the trade and to the raw materials of the world which are needed for their economic prosperity;

Fifth, they desire to bring about the fullest collaboration between all nations in the economic field with the object of securing, for all, improved labor standards, economic advancement and social security;

Sixth, after the final destruction of the Nazi tyranny, they hope to see established a peace which will afford to all nations the means of dwelling in safety within their own boundaries, and which will afford assurance that all the men in all lands may live out their lives in freedom from fear and want;

Seventh, such a peace should enable all men to traverse the high seas and oceans without hindrance;

Eighth, they believe that all of the nations of the world, for realistic as well as spiritual reasons must come to the abandonment of the use of force. Since no future peace can be maintained if land, sea or air armaments continue to be employed by nations which threaten, or may threaten aggression outside of their frontiers, they believe, pending the establishment of a wider and permanent system of general security, that measure which will lighten for peace-loving peoples the crushing burden of armaments.

THE GI'S PERSPECTIVE

A social scientist who helped develop the field of quantitative social research methodology, Shirley A. Star (1918–1976) worked in the Research Branch of the Information and Education Division of the War Department, which carried out research on the attitudes of soldiers during World War II. Her contribution to *The American Soldier*, published in 1949, helped examine the motives behind why soldiers continued to fight. The book has been hailed as one of the most influential social science studies and an impetus for the development of empirical studies in military sociology.

Shirley A. Star, "The Orientation of Soldiers toward the War," in Samuel Stouffer, Edward Suchman, Leland C. DeVinney, Shirley A. Star & Robin M. Williams Jr., *The American Soldier: Adjustment during Army Life* vol. 1 (Princeton: Princeton University Press, 1949), 431–451. Used by permission of Princeton University Press.

I f we seek to define the area of consensus with regard to the war among Americans, both in and out of the Army, it lies simply in the undebatable assumptions that the Japanese attack on Pearl Harbor meant war, and that once in the war the United States had to win....

After complete agreement on the war as a matter of defensive necessity, the men went on to apparent disagreement on questions of the idealism of American motives in the war.... [A]bout two thirds of the men either accepted or were undecided about at least one of the three rather critical views of how the war came about ("Big business," "the British Empire," "Imperialism in Asia")....

[B]eyond acceptance of the war as a necessity forced upon the United States by the aggressor, there was little support of attempts to give the war meaning in terms of principles and causes involved, and little apparent desire for such formulations. For example, in the summer of 1943, at a time when government information agencies had been trying to popularize the "Four Freedoms" concept of war aims which had been stated in the Atlantic Charter, over a third of a sample of 3,139 men in the Continental United States admitted that they had never even heard of the Four Freedoms, and actually only 13 per cent could name three or four of them....

At the same time, men were asked to write freely, in their own words, what it was they personally thought the United States was fighting for.... [A] large number of the men made no attempt to answer, a fact which may be variously interpreted as inarticulateness or lack of interest. Another group replied only with one-word, slogan-like concepts—"Freedom," "Peace" and the like—from which, again, it is impossible to conclude what lay behind them, that is whether they were used to conceal a lack of thought or to summarize a real orientation with respect to the war. But together these two groups account for over half of the men, which itself suggests that sheer inarticulateness alone is an inadequate explanation. Another quarter of the men answered in the pragmatic terms of defense against attack and national survival, 5 per cent expressed negative attitudes about the war, and 2 per cent admitted to confusion and concern, leaving about 15 per cent who attempted to define the war for themselves in terms of the moral principles involved....

While none of these data is conclusive, they are consistent with...what other observers have reported to have been the attitudes of Americans toward the war. Certainly, in the light of the divided attitudes of the American people toward entry into the war up to the Pearl Harbor attack, it was not to be expected that there would be consensus about the war on any level other than that of a patriotic rallying to the country when it was attacked....

It was no doubt, psychologically important to men in the Army to feel that they did understand why they were there.... [T]here is as well a tendency for a somewhat higher proportion of men familiar with the Four Freedoms concept to feel that they were clear about the meaning of the war....

It seems reasonable to conclude that, when men talked of understanding the war, they were not so much concerned with explanations of this order, but rather were satisfied to regard the war as an unavoidable fact—a fact because it was presented to them as *fait accompli,* and unavoidable because their love of country required that foreign aggression be opposed....

[T]he more closely men approached the real business of war, the more likely they were to question its worthwhileness. There was a certain amount of revulsion to war as men were more and more forced to look upon it. A revulsion to war also followed upon its ending, as indicated by an upswing after VJ-Day ["Victory over Japan Day," on which the Japanese surrender was announced, August 15, 1945 in Tokyo, August 14 in the United States] in the proportion questioning the value of the war. An intensive study of...overseas veterans medically discharged during the war showed that one of the major reservations they had about the war was its cost in human lives and resources. Apart from the feeling of some men that nothing could justify the expenditure of human lives involved, those veterans who had reservations about the war were plagued by a "backward look" which concluded that, although the war was in an immediate sense necessary, it was a high price to pay for what could from a long run point of view have been prevented. And, finally, the sense of futility about the war rested, for some of these veterans, on a conviction that, though winning the war saved the United States from a worse evil, there would be little in the way of positive gains and, especially, there would be other wars....

Particularly, this would be expected with respect to the concept of a "war to end war." Such a war had been fought once within recent memory; there was no magic in a slogan like this in World War II. Not only was there the most painful past evidence of the potential deceptiveness of such an idea; in addition there was another concrete reason, not present in World War I, for skepticism. When the First World War ended, there was no possible enemy whose power the democracies of America, Britain, and France need fear—unless it might be Japan, which hardly could be expected to challenge all mankind. Germany was defeated; Russia was in turmoil of the early years of her revolution. But soldiers well knew that victory in World War II would mean not only victory for countries like America and Britain but also victory for a country whose ways of life differed greatly from ours and whose power might be tremendous—namely, Russia....

Evidence is unmistakable that the belief that World War II would not put an end to wars for even a quarter of a century reflected largely a distrust of America's major Allies. When the men who believed there would be another war were asked to name the probable antagonists, over 80 per cent replied. Less than 1 per cent outlined a war which did not involve any of the Big Three—the United States, Great Britain, and Russia—and only another 14 per cent visualized wars in which members of the Big Three would participate without fighting each other. Eighty-five per cent, then, expected trouble between Allies, among whom the most frequent expectation...was that the United States with or without Great Britain's help would fight Russia....

In their discussions of these future wars, men of all classes were practically unanimous in locating responsibility for them away from the United States. Less than 5 per cent felt that the United States would be to blame for any war in which she was involved; the majority felt these wars would be Russia's fault, with England placing a low second....

Though the war was accepted by American soldiers, there were...reservations. In addition, their acceptance of the war was a rather passive one. Since the only universally agreed-upon war aim was to put an end to the threat to American existence, it would follow that the more vivid the threat appeared, the more deeply people would be stirred to action on its behalf. And, while the Pearl Harbor attack did kindle this kind of rallying, the shock, indignation, and real sense of national danger soon faded. By early 1943...over 90 per cent of a cross section of troops in the United States felt sure that the United States would win the war and only 1 per cent conceded the other side a chance of winning. Accompanying and reinforcing this attitude was a complete confidence, at least among troops in training in the United States, in American superiority in material and fighting ability....

Over-optimism about the duration of the war was a continuing phenomenon, not confined to the early phases....

This translation of the goal from preventing conquest of the nation to getting the war over with so that normal life could resume implies...that...the war was simply a vast detour made from the main course of life in order to get back to that main (civilian) course again....

Certainly, the concept of "total war" so effectively propagated stressed the doctrine that each person in his niche, whatever it was, was making a contribution to victory. Undoubtedly many of the men who said they could do more for the war effort in war jobs than in the Army were sincerely convinced that they could make a greater contribution in a civilian capacity and the "soldier-war worker" question cannot be taken simply as a measure of the extent of personal zeal for the war....

Fundamentally, however, the feeling that one has done one's share and ought not be sent into combat again, or kept overseas any longer, or even retained in military service...can only imply that the desire to be safe, or to be home, or to be free to pursue civilian concerns, was stronger than any motivation to make a further personal contribution to winning the war....

Of course, this attitude of limited commitment was also often rationalized in terms of the "total war" doctrine...but the evidence...indicates that soldiers did not really believe that the home front's contribution compared with theirs, except when they were so rationalizing their desires to be civilians....

JAPAN AND GREATER EAST ASIA

Japanese leaders poured scorn on the idea that the Allied powers were animated by a commitment to liberty and justice in their war against Axis aggression. Instead, they presented Japan's war aims as the necessary defensive response to years of Allied imperialism, and justified the enormous wartime expansion of the Japanese empire as a political and economic union of willing Asian partners that would ultimately result in greater freedom and prosperity for the newly conquered states. This formulation underlay the proclamation of the Orwellian-sounding Greater East Asia Co-Prosperity Sphere by Japanese Foreign Minister Matsuoka in August 1940. When Japan's premier, General Hideki Tojo (1884–1948), faced the challenge of making this case persuasively before invited delegates in Tokyo two months later, he devoted as much time to the negative aspects of Allied prewar policy as to the supposed positive attributes of Japan's wartime new order. He declined to mention the horrendous impact on subjugated peoples of Japanese occupation. Nonetheless, his address affords insight into the ways in which the Japanese might conceptualize their conduct of the war, contrast it with that of their opponents, and rally support for that effort.

Some time ago, the Japanese Government proposed the convening of an Assembly of the Greater East-Asiatic Nations for the purpose of holding frank deliberations on policies relative to bringing the War of Greater East Asia to a successful conclusion and to constructing a New Order in Greater East Asia....

During the past centuries, the British Empire, through fraud and aggression, acquired vast territories throughout the world and maintained its domination over other nations and peoples in the various regions by keeping them pitted and engaged in conflict against one another. On the other hand, the United States which, by taking advantage of the disorder and confusion in Europe, had established its supremacy over the American continents, spread its tentacles to the Pacific and to East Asia following its war with Spain. Then, with the opportunities afforded by the First World War, the United States began to pursue its ambition for world hegemony. More recently, with the outbreak of the present war,

"Address of Prime Minister Hideki Tojo before the Assembly of Greater East-Asiatic Nations," in Joyce Lebra, ed., *Japan's Greater East Asia Co-Prosperity Sphere in World War II* (Kuala Lumpur: Oxford University Press, 1975), 88–92. Used by permission.

the United States has further intensified its imperialistic activities, making fresh inroads into North Africa, West Africa, the Atlantic Ocean, Australia, the Near East and even into India, apparently in an attempt to usurp the place of the British Empire.

The need of upholding international justice and of guaranteeing world peace is habitually stressed by America and Britain. They mean thereby no more and no less than the preservation of a world order of their own, based upon division and conflict in Europe and upon the perpetuation of their colonial exploitation of Asia. They sought to realize their inordinate ambitions in Asia, through political aggression and economic exploitation; they brought on conflict among the various peoples; they tried to destroy their racial integrity under the fair name of education and culture. Thus, they have to this day threatened constantly the existence of the nations and peoples of Asia, disturbed their stability, and suppressed their natural and proper development. It is because of their notion to regard East Asia as a colony that they harp upon the principles of the open door and equal opportunity simply as a convenient means of pursuing their sinister designs of aggression. While constantly keeping their own territories closed to us, the peoples of Asia, denying us the equality of opportunities and impeding our trade, they sought solely their own prosperity....

Next, it is my desire to express to you the fundamental views of the Japanese Government regarding the construction of Greater East Asia....

It is an incontrovertible fact that the nations of Greater East Asia are bound, in every respect, by the ties of an inseparable relationship. I firmly believe that such being the case, it is their common mission to secure the stability of Greater East Asia and to construct a new order of common prosperity and well-being. This new order of Greater East Asia is to rest upon the spirit of justice that is inherent in Greater East Asia. In this respect it is fundamentally different from the old order designed to serve the interests of the United States and Britain who do not hesitate to practice injustice, deception and exploitation in order to promote their own prosperity.

The nations of Greater East Asia, while mutually recognizing their autonomy and independence, must, as a whole, establish among themselves relations of brotherly amity....

A superior order of culture has existed in Greater East Asia from its very beginning. Especially the spiritual essence of the culture of Greater East Asia is the most sublime in the world. It is my belief that in the wide diffusion throughout the world of this culture of Greater East Asia by its further cultivation and refinement lies the salvation of mankind from the curse of materialistic civilization and our contribution to the welfare of all humanity. It is incumbent upon us all mutually to respect one another's glorious traditions and to develop the creative spirit and genius of our peoples and thereby to enhance even more the culture of Greater East Asia.

Furthermore, I believe that in order to promote the welfare of the people and to replenish the national power, the nations of Greater East Asia must carry on close economic collaboration on the basis of reciprocity and jointly promote the prosperity of Greater East Asia. Hitherto, Greater East Asia has been for many years the object of Anglo-American exploitation, but henceforth we must also be autonomous and independent in the economic field to gain prosperity, by mutually depending on and helping each other....

The construction of Greater East Asia is being realized with a grim steadiness in the midst of war.... Japan is determined to follow, together with the other nations of Greater East Asia, the path of justice, to deliver Greater East Asia from the fetters of America and Britain and, in conjunction with her neighboring nations, to strive toward the reconstruction and development of Greater East Asia.

THE ANTHROPOLOGY OF JAPANESE CONDUCT

Ruth Fulton Benedict (1887–1948) was an anthropologist whose research on Native American Indians and on Japan helped shape the field of cultural anthropology. During World War II, she worked for the Office of War Information where she applied anthropological methods to the study of contemporary cultures. The government was interested in obtaining studies of national character like that of the Japanese that might explain their actions in war and how the United States could best deal with them. Benedict's own research into the interaction between individuals and their own cultures led her to undertake an examination of the Japanese based upon classified documents culled by the U.S. government rather than upon an actual field study in Japan. Benedict was one of the few analysts to take seriously the reverential attachment of most Japanese to their emperor (a remote and mystical figure dismissed as inconsequential by many American experts) and was influential in securing his retention after the war's end.

In every cultural tradition there are orthodoxies of war and certain of these are shared in all Western nations, no matter what the specific differences. There are certain clarion calls to all-out war effort, certain forms of reassurance in case of local defeats, certain regularities in the proportion of fatalities to surrenders, and certain rules of behavior for prisoners of war which are predictable in wars between Western nations just because they have a great shared cultural tradition which covers even warfare.

All the ways in which the Japanese departed from Western conventions of war were data on their view of life and on their convictions of the whole duty of man. For the purposes of a systematic study of Japanese culture and behavior it did not matter whether or not their deviations from our orthodoxies were crucial in a military sense; any of them might be important because they raised questions about the character of the Japanese to which we needed answers.

The very premises which Japan used to justify her war were the opposite of America's. She defined the international situation differently. America laid the war to the aggressions of the Axis. Japan, Italy, and Germany had unrighteously offended against international peace by their acts of conquest. Whether the Axis had seized power in Manchukuo or in Ethiopia or in Poland, it proved that they had embarked on an evil course of oppressing weak peoples. They had sinned against an international code of 'live and let live' or at least of 'open doors' for free enterprise. Japan saw the cause of the war in another light. There was anarchy in the world as long as every nation had absolute sovereignty; it was necessary for her to fight to establish a hierarchy—under Japan, of course, since she alone represented a nation truly hierarchal from top to bottom and hence understood the necessity of taking 'one's proper place.' . . .

Japan put her hopes of victory on a different basis from that prevalent in the United States. She would win, she cried, a victory of spirit over matter. America was big, her armaments were superior, but what did that matter? All this, they said, had been foreseen and discounted. 'If we had been afraid of mathematical figures,' the Japanese read in their great newspaper, the *Mainichi Shimbun*, 'the war would not have started. The enemy's great resources were not created by this war.'...

The furthest extreme to which this Japanese theory [the necessity of hierarchy, the supremacy of spirit, and the expendability of individuals]...could be pushed was their no-surrender policy. Any Occidental army which has done its best and finds itself facing hopeless odds surrenders to the enemy. They still regard themselves as honorable soldiers and by international agreement their names are sent back to their countries so that their families may know that they are alive. They are not disgraced either as soldiers or as citizens or in their own families. But the Japanese define the situation differently. Honor was bound up with fighting to the death. In a hopeless situation a Japanese soldier should kill himself with his last hand grenade or charge weaponless against the enemy in a mass suicide attack. But he should not surrender. Even if he were taken prisoner when he was wounded and unconscious, he 'could not hold up his head in Japan' again; he was disgraced; he was 'dead' to his former life....

The shame of surrender was burned deeply into the consciousness of the Japanese. They accepted as a matter of course a behavior which was alien to our conventions of warfare. And ours was just as alien to them....

The emphasis falls in Japan...on the importance of shame rather than on the importance of guilt.

In anthropological studies of different cultures the distinction between those which rely heavily on shame and those that rely heavily on guilt is an important one. A society that inculcates absolute standards of morality and relies on men developing a conscience is a guilt culture by definition, but a man in such a society may, as in the United States, suffer in addition from shame when he accuses himself of gaucheries which are in no way sins.... In a culture where shame is a major sanction, people are chagrined about acts which we expect people to feel guilty about. This chagrin can be very intense and it cannot be relieved, as guilt can be, by confession and atonement. A man who has sinned can get relief by unburdening himself. This device of confession is used in our secular therapy and by many religious groups which have otherwise little in common. We know it brings relief. Where shame is the major sanction, a man does not experience relief when he makes his fault public even to a confessor. So long as his bad behavior does not 'get out into the world' he need not be troubled and confession appears to him merely a way of courting trouble. Shame cultures therefore do not provide for confessions, even to the gods. They have ceremonies for good luck rather than for expiation.

True shame cultures rely on external sanctions for good behavior, not, as true guilt cultures do, on an internalized conviction of sin. Shame is a reaction to other people's criticism. A man is shamed either by being openly ridiculed and rejected or by fantasying to himself that he has been made ridiculous. In either case it is a potent sanction.

SOLDIERS UNDER STRESS

World War II accelerated the growth of psychosomatic medicine. While shell shock and similar psychoses were evident during World War I, during the Second World War the army mobilized psychiatrists and other individuals in psychosomatic medicine to assist it in dealing with these issues. Air force medical officers, Roy R. Grinker (1900–1994), the director of the Institute for Psychosomatic and Psychiatric Research and Training and chairman of the Psychiatry Department of Michael Reese Hospital in Chicago, and John P. Spiegel (1911–1991), Department of Neuropsychiatry at Michael Reese Hospital, were two of these professionals who observed and chronicled the impact of the strain of modern warfare upon combatants in their book, *Men Under Stress*.

Some soldiers of this war have little hatred toward the Germans, although in many instances it may be directed against the ideology of fascism, the Nazi activities or some other abstraction and it often is directed against the Jap soldier. In our culture the most efficient fighting man is not one consumed by a self-destructive emotion like hate. Once the enemy has given up the fight, he is treated like a human being, given food, water and cigarettes and prompt, efficient medical care. Hatred could not be turned off like a tap on surrender, but our soldiers take the respected enemy as prisoners rather than vent revengeful hostility on them.

This is all the more true of our flying personnel, who fight machine against machine, gun against gun. They become greatly disturbed when the pilot of an enemy plane comes close enough for them to see his destruction; they are uneasy when strafing transport vehicles containing personnel, or troops on the road. For the same reason many gunners are not anxious to press their claims to have shot down enemy ships, as if lack of official credit creates less guilt than a recorded positive score. In one squadron a Greek-American gunner strafed a parachuting German pilot and was ostracized by his fellows for two weeks as punishment.

It is true that in battle the enemy is soundly cursed with numerous derogatory adjectives and dire threats of revenge, all made after the death or injury of a comrade. However, psychiatrists overseas who listen to the war-weary soldier speak under pentothal hear little in the war of enemy-directed hostility. Watch and listen to the soldier relieved from battle and you do not observe a tough, fighting, aggressive fellow. In attempting to contrast the normal soldier, unscathed psychologically from his battle experiences, with the psychiatric casualty, we saw no greater quantity of overt expressions of aggression in the former. The happy, high-spirited veteran filled with liquor caroused a bit, broke a few windows and violated a few regulations but only as an expression of a general ebullient spirit.

Why is this? Have we not heard that war creates a new type of superego that permits and condones release of aggression and facilitates abandonment of old repressions? Was not one of the major sociological problems after the war supposed to be concerned with the animal-like warriors whose unleashed

Roy R. Grinker and John P. Spiegel, *Men Under Stress* (Philadelphia: Blakiston, 1945), 307–308, 362–363. Used by permission.

hostilities, no longer directed against the enemy, would be directed against society? It has become quite obvious that for the majority of men, removal of external prohibitions against killing and even encouragement of human destruction do not develop a killer....

However, the returned soldiers and particularly those suffering from war neuroses show much more aggressiveness and hostility in their verbalizations and behavior than was characteristic of their pre-combat personalities. They are resentful and openly angry at civilians and toward soldiers who have not been overseas, and are freely and destructively critical of what they see and hear at home. Many get into difficulties with civil and military law. Their favorite word of depreciation is "chicken s...t," which is used to describe the morally soft, selfish attitudes of people who think only of their own interests, and not of those of the soldier. It is our conviction that the apparently normal as well as the sick combat veteran is far more aggressive and hostile on his return to the country than when he was overseas in combat....

In combat, the mission of the fighter demands a stimulation of his aggressions. These he has been taught since early childhood to repress or displace, to modify for constructive purposes or to express only in sports and work. Many soldiers under the influence of a new standard of conduct, the military superego, are enabled to release their aggressions successfully in the process of killing, which is their purpose in the army. But, on returning from combat, they develop difficulties because renewal of inhibitions is not so easily effected. These men have no acceptable goal for their hostilities, no enemy to

kill. They often fight among themselves for the sake of fighting, to relieve tensions, without real hostility. Others displace their hostilities to officers, civilians or the army in all sorts of rebellious expressions and behavior....

Our Air Forces are fortunate in that combat is impersonal and a battle of machines. But strafing of troops and bombing of factories and cities evoke serious internal repercussions. Some men, who can endure little in the way of direct expression of hostility, succumb early and become psychiatric casualties; others have a higher threshold....

Aggressions in returnees are usually directed against superior officers.... He is like the little child whose reaction to the cruel fate of tripping and falling over a chair is to look up and blame the first human supporting figure who failed him with, "See what you made me do!" The whole weight of hostility directed in combat toward the enemy, deriving from repression of ambivalent feelings toward officers and comrades, is now released toward them directly. No longer is there a good father figure, the commanding officer, and a bad father figure, the enemy, but there is only one father figure, the superior officer, who must bear the brunt of the hostility of the regressed soldier.

The relationship to the brothers of the group was one of extreme altruism and everything was share and share alike. Hostile feelings toward individuals were so well repressed that antisemitism or antagonism to representatives of other minority groups was at a minimum overseas. The returned soldier is selfish. He thinks only of himself and has a revival of prejudices and other rationalized antagonisms.

CIVILIANS UNDER STRESS

Richard Titmuss (1907–1973), professor of social administration at the London School of Economics, was influential in shaping the British welfare state. The primarily self-educated son of a farmer who left school at the age of fourteen, Titmuss became interested, while working for a large insurance company, in the correlation between poverty and demography. During the war he advised the Ministry of Economic Warfare on German vital and medical statistics, and was well placed to observe the effect of the war on British society. One particular concern of "social experts" had been whether civilians would stand up to the pressure of aerial bombing, or if they would become demoralized and demand surrender (something analogous to the research on why combat units continued to fight despite casualties and stress). Civilian morale was the great unknown in an age of total war. Titmuss published many of his wartime observations in 1950 in *Problems of Social Policy*, and in this extract he reviews the surprising resilience of ordinary British citizens under the stress of "the Blitz."

The singular thing about the Second World War was that the subject of morale among the civilian population—and not merely the fighting part of it—was being considered long before anyone believed that the war was certain....

In simple terms, the experts foretold a mass outbreak of hysterical neurosis among the civilian population. It was expected that the conditions of life brought about by air raids would place an immediate and overwhelming strain upon the individual. Under this strain, people would regress to an earlier level of needs and desires. They would behave like frightened and unsatisfied children, and they would demand with the all-or-nothing vehemence of infants the security, food and warmth which the mother had given in the past. Many recommendations were accordingly made for the handling and treatment of these people in the event of war, one being that, to assist morale, instructional centres should be set up immediately a city had been raided so that householders might be taught how to make a habitable shelter out of a wrecked or partially wrecked house.

The civilian was compared unfavourably with the soldier. The latter was thought of as a member of a group purposely trained and taught to face tasks which involved the possibility of death. He was in uniform, and the strict discipline under which he lived would, it was believed, save him from too much consideration about his own safety....But the civilian, isolated, unattached and unorganised, would have no such powerful checks to his desire for self-preservation. He (and she) would be expected to risk death to fulfil some quite inglorious task, like keeping the firm's ledger up to date or tightening bolts in a factory. The flood-gates, it was said, might therefore be open to the full expression of the urge for self-preservation. 'There is real danger,' a psychiatrist wrote, 'that he (the civilian) will seek, not security, but infantile security.'

Richard M. Titmuss, *Problems of Social Policy* (London: His Majesty's Stationery Office, 1950), 337–350. Used by permission.

It is no exaggeration to say that in 1939 the leading mental health authorities in Britain feared a tremendous increase in disorders and emotional neurotic illnesses as soon as the Germans started to bomb....

It need hardly be said that what actually happened completely falsified not only the forecasts of the psychiatrists but the less pessimistic forebodings of officials....

The air raids of 1940–1 did not lead to a rise in the number of patients with such illnesses attending hospitals and clinics; in fact, there was a decrease. There was no indication of an increase in insanity, the number of suicides fell, the statistics of drunkenness went down by more than one-half, there was much less disorderly behaviour in the streets and public places, while only the juvenile delinquency figures registered a rise....

There may have been more anxiety, more general depression, but attendance at work ruled out an immediate collapse in standards or resort to what the psychiatrists called 'infantile security.'

The Research and Experiments Department of the Ministry of Home Security studied this question in detail....The main conclusion...was that absence from work for personal reasons was closely associated with the amount of house damage....

An outbreak of trekking, of nightly movements from target areas by thousands of people, which gave rise to much concern in the spring of 1941, was also investigated. It was found that, except for workers whose houses were seriously damaged, no more time...was lost by those who trekked as compared with those who continued to sleep at home. The fact that many people chose to trudge off into the country each evening did not, by itself, imply a deterioration in morale....Above all, they wanted to sleep; for sleep was forgetfulness and rest. And to sleep...was to behave normally; to lie awake was abnormal....

At no period during the war did more than about one person in seven in Metropolitan London spend the night in a tube station or public shelter. This peak was reached some time during September–October 1940 when Londoners were being 'battleconditioned.' In November, when the proportion had declined to one person in eight, the basements, railway arches, trenches and other public shelters were filled only to about forty per cent. of capacity. At this time, eight per cent. of the population were in public shelters, four per cent. in the tubes, one per cent. in the surface shelters—making thirteen per cent. in communal shelters—while twenty-seven per cent. were in...other domestic shelters. Thus, among every ten persons six were sleeping in their homes in November 1940.

It cannot be assumed because there was no panic, no rush to safety, that there was no anxiety. There was without doubt a great deal of fears and heartaches were inevitable in the circumstances, and many private terrors must have been stifled in the darkness....If they were not to behave as the psychiatrists had expected, most people had therefore to come to terms with bombing....

No objective or comprehensive explanation can be given of all the reasons, and combination of reasons, trivial and important, rational and irrational, which led so many families to decide during 1940–1 to stay where they were....

In the circumstances of 1940, the bases of sound morale among the civilian population rested on something more than the primary needs of life. Of course, the maintenance of food supplies, the provision and repair of homes, and security of employment were always of first importance. But other things vital in time of war mattered no less. Leadership was one, the sense of common effort and sacrifice was another. Self-control was easier when there was no awareness of injustice arising from the way in which the primary wants were met. The knowledge that large numbers of those who were privileged in the community were also carrying on with their work and facing the risks that ordinary people faced, the knowledge that such facilities as the evacuation and shelter schemes were available and were not limited to particular groups—here were important foundations of morale. The universal availability of services which often were not universally used had the function of 'shock-absorption.'

The rest centres, the feeding schemes, the casualty services, the compensation grants, and the whole apparatus of the post-raid services both official and voluntary occupied this role of absorbing shock. They took the edge off the calamities of damage and destruction; they could not prevent, but they helped to reduce, a great deal of distress....

The proximity of death, the spread of physical hardship, and the ubiquity of destructive forces which were more intelligible to the ordinary man than the working of economic laws, gave existence a different meaning, and old fears and responsibilities less significance....New aims for which to live, work that satisfied a larger number of needs, a more cohesive society, fewer lonely people; all these elements helped to offset the circumstances which often lead to neurotic illness....

The maintenance of physical contact between the members of a social unit also helped to meet another imperative need in time of war; the need to be related to the world outside, to ideas, values and social patterns that bestow a sense of 'belonging.'...

Many people discovered for themselves during the raids that the best prescription for stability was to keep the family together. Resistance to evacuation grew in strength after the first few weeks of London's bombing until, by November 1940, almost as many children were returning to London as were leaving....

All this is understandable if it is accepted that a stable society rests on the basis of stable family life. A threat to society implies a threat to the family, and when the physical hazards of air attack were present, families naturally tended to close their ranks. Staying at home, keeping the family together, and pursuing many of the ordinary activities of life made adjustment easier....

It was not altogether remarkable that people who were dug out of the ruins of their homes first asked, not for food or safety, but for their false teeth. Nor was it just an odd streak of personality that made mothers in rest centres and shelters more worried about awkward behaviour by their children than about death. The only possible way—as these mothers found—of dealing with death was to ignore it. Keeping ledgers up to date, worrying about false teeth, and correcting the manners of children affirmed the individual's confidence in life and, in the process, maintained morale.

RELIGION IN THE SKIES

After graduating from Harvard Law School in 1938, Philip P. Ardery (1914–) became an aviation cadet, graduating in April 1941. He then served in the 564th Bomb Squadron overseas, winning the Silver Star, Distinguished Flying Cross (twice), Air Medal (four times), and the French Cross of War (Croix de Guerre). Ardery became the commander of the Second Combat Bomb Wing for the D-day invasion. His array of medals hinted at how difficult it was for bomber crews to brave relentless German fighter planes, heavy antiaircraft fire, and unpredictable weather, all while flying in propeller-driven planes crammed with explosive contents of bombs and aviation fuel. What gave the crews the courage or determination to fly one mission after another in such circumstances, especially after they lost comrades with a terrifyingly predictable frequency? One obvious consolation was religion, confirming the old adage that there were no atheists in foxholes.

On every one of the first seven missions I made, the ship in which I was riding was shot up. Sometimes the damage was light and sometimes pretty serious, but at least I seemed to be something of a Jonah. McLaughlin, our plump and jovial Irishman from Syracuse, seemed to be my luckiest pilot. I took turns riding with all my pilots, and when I rode with Mac I told him I was glad to be assured of my luck on that mission. His ship was named *Ole Irish* and had a big green shamrock painted on it. It was officially called B for Baker. Mac was angry with me afterwards because his plane picked up its first holes on that mission.

Part of my reaction to my luck and general combat experience was to sense a resurgence of religion. Fellows who hadn't attended services in years found themselves going to Sunday services. My religion didn't take me to these services with regularity, but I went occasionally, not only for myself but to let the men in my squadron know I didn't consider attendance a sign of weakness. I felt if they saw me there it might help some of them to go who wanted to but were kept from going out of embarrassment.

In my case religion made me say short prayers before going to sleep at night, and sometimes during a fleeting instant at the height of combat. I think this undoubtedly made me a better combat officer. It comforted me so that I could sleep before missions, even though I had been briefed for the next mission and knew the assignment of the morning might be my last. It helped me say to myself with complete calm: "You can't live forever. You have had a great deal in your life-span already, much more than many people ever have. You would not shirk the duty of tomorrow if you could. Go into it calmly; don't try too hard to live. Don't ever give up hope; never let the fear of death strike panic in your mind and paralyze your reason. Death will find you sometime, if not tomorrow. Give yourself a chance." And then I would remember that very appropriate sentence of Shakespeare: "Cowards die many times before their deaths; the valiant never taste of death but once."

Philip Ardery, *Bomber Pilot: A Memoir of World War II* (Lexington: University of Kentucky Press, 1978), 92–93. Used by permission.

In Bengasi [Libya] we had no regular Protestant chaplain. One assigned to the Ninth Bomber Command used to come out for Sunday service. He was overworked by having about a dozen other services to perform each Sunday. Because I am a Protestant I tried to support this overworked man as best I could. Our Catholic boys were more fortunate because there was a Catholic chaplain assigned to our group. His name was Beck, and to my last day I shall never forget him. He had a shock of almost white-gray hair. He had twinkling blue eyes, and he was withal one of the most charming men I have ever met. He was unorthodox in his mode of religion. If there were no rabbi to perform the rites, Father Beck would preach a Jewish funeral service with as perfect form and dignity as any Catholic priest ever did. He would give all possible aid and comfort to the Protestant boys when no Protestant chaplain was available, and in giving he didn't push his religion upon them. But Father Beck played those Catholic boys like a great artist plays an organ. I know one of the upper-most thoughts in his mind was to make his men better, braver soldiers.

Father Beck flew on combat missions with us time after time until at length the group commander gave him a direct order to stop going. He slept in various tents with the enlisted men, and later when we had barracks he slept in their barracks. They would carry his cot and bedding from one sleeping place to the next, each group anxiously awaiting his time to visit them. The superstition was that a crew would not be shot down as long as he was sleeping in their quarters.

REVIVAL OF RUSSIAN ORTHODOXY

In the wake of the Russian Revolution in 1917, the victorious Bolsheviks set about dismantling the influence of the Orthodox Church, which they believed bore responsibility, along with the now deposed monarchy, for perpetuating an autocratic system that oppressed its people. A militant atheism was official policy in the 1920s and 1930s, and Stalin, as autocratic and oppressive a leader as could be found, remained deeply suspicious of any revival of religious influence as a potential threat to his own authority. Nonetheless, when German forces poured across the Soviet border on June 22, 1941, and a shaken Stalin was nowhere to be seen or heard, it was the head of Russian Orthodoxy, Metropolitan Sergei, who was first on the radio to call upon the faithful to defend the motherland. Under the stress of war, Stalin recognized that religious faith did have a role to play in persuading people to defend his regime, and the wartime years thus witnessed a more conciliatory attitude to the church on the part of his government.

Alexander Werth, *Russia at War, 1941–1945* (New York: Dutton, 1964), 429–430, 434–436. Used by permission.

The establishment of correct and even seemingly cordial relations between Church and
State had been one of the imperatives of Soviet
Government policy ever since the beginning of the
war. Even before the war, especially since the publication of the "Stalin" Constitution of 1936 which
guaranteed freedom of religious beliefs, the cruder
forms of anti-religious propaganda had been largely
abandoned....

The aim of the Soviet Government was to create
absolute national unity; and, with a very high proportion of soldiers in the Army coming from peasant
families, among whom religious traditions were still
strong, it was important to do nothing that would
offend their religious "prejudices." With government propaganda becoming more and more patriotic
and nationalist, complete with invocations of the
great national heroes of the past, including a saint
of the Orthodox Church—St. Alexander Nevsky—it
was impossible to treat the Church as a hostile element in what soon came to be known as "the Great
Patriotic War." It was, indeed, essential to secure the
utmost co-operation from the Church, and to induce
the clergy to do patriotic propaganda among the
faithful, and support the Soviet regime, rather than
look for salvation to the Germans who, despite all
the monstrosities of their occupation policy, still
gave some encouragement to the Orthodox Church
which they regarded (not unreasonably) as an element with serious grievances against the Soviet system. To the Soviet Government the Church was, in
effect, a potential Fifth Column [term for an internal
subversive movement], which it was imperative to
win over.

Some of the Orthodox clergy in the occupied
areas certainly collaborated with the Germans, or
pretended to—particularly during the earlier stages
of the war—while some members of the Ukrainian
church hierarchy were wholly subservient to Berlin to
the end. In 1941 and 1942 there were many instances
of the Germans posing as liberators of the Christian
faith in the occupied areas. General Guderian men-
tions, for example, the town of Glukhov, near
Briansk, where "the population asked our permission to use their church as a place of worship once
again. We willingly handed it over to them." In their
radio propaganda the Germans made much of this
"revival" of religion in the areas they had occupied,
and the fact that some priests were said to have joined
the partisans was insufficient to cancel out these
German claims entirely. Moscow was particularly
sensitive, in 1942, to hostile propaganda, especially
in the United States, on the ground that there was no
"freedom of religion" in Russia....

By 1943 there was already a great improvement.
The church attendance, especially on Easter night,
was extraordinarily high; whole streets adjoining the twenty-five or thirty churches in Moscow
were crowded with people who could find no room
inside. A Party member told me: "The Party and the
Komsomol have been much impressed by the number of people who went to church this Easter—much
more even than usual." One explanation was that
people knew that the Church was no longer frowned
upon by the authorities. Significantly, there were
many more soldiers in the churches in 1943 than
there had been in previous years.

The establishment of more "correct" relations with
the Church in 1942–3 was part of both a short-term
and a long-term policy. It was certainly part of that
drive for "complete national unity," which the grim
situation of 1942 demanded. The Church derived
considerable benefits from it and, in return, became
increasingly vocal in its loyalty to the regime, even
to the point of saying special prayers for Stalin, and
treating him as an "anointed of the Lord," though no
doubt in only a figurative way.

Internationally the "reconciliation" with the
Church served a great variety of purposes: it made
a good impression on the Allies, particularly the
United States; it made the Moscow Patriarchate play
the role of a sort of Greek-Orthodox Vatican, intoler-
ant of any suspect "sects."...

In September 1943 a sort of "concordat" was concluded between the Church and the State, after Stalin
had himself received all the three Metropolitans
[high-ranking Church officials from urban cen-
ters]...at the Kremlin. As a result of this meeting
the Church was allowed to elect its Patriarch and to
re-establish a proper ecclesiastical government, the
Holy Synod....The Church was also recognized as a
"juridical person" entitled to own property.

CHRISTIAN MORALITY IN WARTIME

An Anglican theologian and the Bishop of Chichester from 1929 until 1958, G. K. A. Bell (1883–1958) was an outspoken advocate of Christian morality throughout the war, even in cases where his uncompromising defense of principle left him isolated and unpopular. Bell is perhaps best known for his condemnation of both German and Allied bombing campaigns as immoral assaults upon innocent civilians. It has been speculated that Bell's willingness to court controversy cost him the premier position within the Anglican Church, the Archbishopric of Canterbury. Bell also did not hesitate to ally himself with Germany's Nonconfessing Church (*Bekennende Kirche*), which opposed Nazi efforts to make the churches compliant instruments of Nazi politics. He first met that church's driving force, Dietrich Bonhoeffer, in England in 1931, and when Bonhoeffer returned to England two years later, invited him to Chichester, where they discussed the fate of the German Evangelical Church under Hitler, the position of Germany's Jews, and the decision by the Nazis to force the Church to reject all converted Jews. Bell mobilized support in Britain against the Nazi exclusion of former Jews from the Church and convinced the Archbishop of Canterbury to protest the decision to the German ambassador.

The following extract, taken from essays and sermons Bell composed during the war, explores the moral tensions inherent in the adherence to a universalist faith in a period of national trial.

When war breaks out, there is always a great marshalling of the nation's forces. The Church, which stands within the nation, is expected to express its solidarity with the nation. Indeed, even if it were desired, it would be impossible to make a clean cut between Churchmen and citizens. There can be no contracting out of the national destiny. It is the Church of men, and there are no men save those belonging to nations. The Church has a share in all that affects the individual nation. It suffers in all the burdens which the nation must bear. What is the Church to do when there is a war?

We must insist on the distinction of functions. The Church has a specific task to perform at all times. It owes it to the nation, as well as to itself, to discharge that function to the best of its ability. If the Church has a function, war is not a time when it should be abandoned.

But we must interpret it further. There is first the question of right and wrong—the moral law. The Church, in the persons of its clergy, primarily represents the Gospel which brings forgiveness and salvation. But it witnesses also to eternal realities; and the moral law is both super-national and super-natural as the Gospel is. The Church then ought to declare both in peace-time and war-time, that there are certain basic principles which can and should be standards of both international and social order and conduct. Such principles are the equal dignity of all men, respect for human life, the acknowledgment of the solidarity for good and evil of all nations and races of the earth, fidelity to the plighted word, and

G. K. A. Bell, *The Church and Humanity (1939–1946)* (London: Longmans, Green & Co., 1946), 26–29. Used by permission.

the appreciation of the fact that power of any kind, political or economic, must be coextensive with responsibility. The Church therefore ought to declare what is just. It has a right to prophesy, to analyse the issues which lie behind a particular conflict, and to rebuke the aggressor. But two conditions are vital. The Church must be humble. It must acknowledge its own share in the guilt of the common injustice and lack of charity. Further, its witness must be disinterested and independent. It should speak only what the moral law compels it to speak, whether that is favourable or unfavourable to its country. Besides, the Church must guard and maintain those moral principles in the war itself. It must not hesitate, if occasion arises, to condemn the infliction of reprisals, or the bombing of civilian populations, by the military forces of its own nation. It should set itself against the propaganda of lies and hatred. It should be ready to encourage a resumption of friendly relations with the enemy nation. It should set its face against any war of extermination or enslavement, and any measures directly aimed at destroying the morale of a population.

But, although it must be free always to witness to basic moral principles, both in the social and in the international order, the characteristic function of the Church is of a different kind. And therefore the characteristic expression of its solidarity with the nation is also different. The Church stands for the Cross, the gospel of redemption. It cannot, therefore, speak of any earthly war as a 'crusade,' for the one thing which it is impossible to fight with earthly weapons is the Cross. Its supreme concern is not the victory of the national cause. It is a hard thing to say, but it is vital. Its supreme concern is the doing of the Will of God, whoever wins, and the declaring of the Mercy of God to all men and nations.... It is not only that the Church, if its clergy preach the gospel, offers a counterbalancing force of undoubted authority to the waves of national emotion, and so helps to preserve spiritual integrity. That is important. But what is still more important is the fact that the Church is the trustee of the gospel of redemption; and unless the gospel is preached, the Church is not the Church....

The Church may have a difficult task in wartime. But it has an extraordinary opportunity. Over against human selfishness and national divisions it sets the gospel of love of God and the community of Christians. And the Church is not a figment of man's mind, but a living spiritual reality, created by God.

"MUSCULAR CHRISTIANITY"

American-born theologian Reinhold Niebuhr (1892–1971), the son of a German Protestant émigré pastor, was an influential figure in the intellectual climate of American Protestantism from the 1920s until his death. A onetime member of the Socialist Party and a pacifist, Niebuhr became during the 1930s an ardent supporter of American intervention in World War II and an opponent of Nazism. Whatever the injunction to turn the other cheek or to avoid conflict wherever possible, Niebuhr worked to reconcile Christian principles with the moral imperative to take human life in defense of a higher good. Strongly believing that pacifism could not be a panacea for the evils of the world, including Hitler, in 1940 he wrote *Christianity and Power Politics* to advocate that America assist Britain in its struggle for survival.

Whenever the actual historical situation sharpens the issue, the debate whether the Christian Church is, or ought to be, pacifist is carried on with fresh vigor both inside and outside the Christian community. Those who are not pacifists seek to prove that pacifism is a heresy; while the pacifists contend, or at least imply, that the Church's failure to espouse pacifism unanimously can only be interpreted as apostasy, and must be attributed to its lack of courage or to its want of faith.

There may be an advantage in stating the thesis, with which we enter this debate, immediately. The thesis is, that the failure of the Church to espouse pacifism is not apostasy, but is derived from an understanding of the Christian Gospel which refuses simply to equate the Gospel with the "law of love." Christianity is not simply a new law, namely, the law of love. The finality of Christianity cannot be proved by analyses which seek to reveal that the law of love is stated more unambiguously and perfectly in the life and teachings of Christ than anywhere else. Christianity is a religion which measures the total dimension of human existence not only in terms of the final norm of human conduct, which is expressed in the law of love, but also in terms of the fact of sin....

All forms of religious faith are principles of interpretation which we use to organize our experience.... A religious faith which substitutes faith in man for faith in God cannot finally validate itself in experience. If we believe that the only reason men do not love each other perfectly is because the law of love has not been preached persuasively enough, we believe something to which experience does not conform. If we believe that if Britain had only been fortunate enough to have produced 30 per cent instead of 2 per cent of conscientious objectors to military service, Hitler's heart would have been softened and he would not have dared to attack Poland, we hold a faith which no historic reality justifies....

[A]n ethic of pure non-resistance can have no immediate relevance to any political situation; for in every political situation it is necessary to achieve justice by resisting pride and power. They [pacifists] therefore declare that the ethic of Jesus is not an ethic of non-resistance, but one of non-violent resistance; that it allows one to resist evil provided the resistance does not involve the destruction of life or property.

Reinhold Niebuhr, *Christianity and Power Politics* (New York: Charles Scribner's Sons, 1940), 1–2, 6, 9–11, 13–17, 28, 30. Used by permission.

There is not slightest support in Scripture for this doctrine of non-violence. Nothing could be plainer than that the ethic uncompromisingly enjoins non-resistance and not non-violent resistance. Furthermore, it is obvious that the distinction between violent and non-violent resistance is not an absolute distinction. If it is made absolute, we arrive at the morally absurd position of giving moral preference to the non-violent power which Doctor Goebbels wields over the type of power wielded by a general.... It is suggested that Christ ended his life on the Cross because he had not completely mastered the technique of non-violence, and for this reason be regarded as a guide who is inferior to Gandhi, but whose significance lies in initiating a movement which culminates in Gandhi....

No one is so blind as the idealist who tells us that war would be unnecessary "if only" nations obeyed the law of Christ, but who remains unconscious of the fact that even the most saintly life is involved in some measure of contradiction to this law....The pacifists do not know human nature well enough to be concerned about the contradictions between the law of love and the sin of man...[and] they do not see that because men are sinners that justice can be achieved only by a certain degree of coercion on the one hand, and by resistance to coercion and tyranny on the other hand. The political life of man must constantly steer between the Scylla of anarchy and the Charybdis of tyranny [allusion to the two sea monsters of Greek mythology who guarded a narrow channel, forcing sailors to choose between two equally dangerous and unpalatable alternatives].

If those who resist tyranny publish their scruples against violence too publicly the tyrannical power need only threaten the use of violence against non-violent pressure to persuade the resisters to quiescence. (The relation of pacifism to the abortive effort to apply non-violent sanctions against Italy in the Ethiopian dispute is instructive at this point.)

The refusal to recognize that sin introduces an element of conflict into the world invariably means that a morally perverse preference is given to tyranny over anarchy (war)....It is not unfair to assert that most pacifists who seek to present their religious absolutism as a political alternative to the claims and counter-claims, the pressures and counter-pressures of the political order, invariably betray themselves into this preference for tyranny. Tyranny is not war. It is peace, but it is a peace which has nothing to do with the peace of the Kingdom of God. It is a peace which results from one will establishing a complete dominion over other wills and reducing them to acquiescence.

One of the most terrible consequences of a confused religious absolutism is that it is forced to condone such tyranny as that of Germany in the nations which it has conquered and now cruelly oppresses. It usually does this by insisting that the tyranny is no worse than that which is practiced in the so-called democratic nations. Whatever may be the moral ambiguities of the so-called democratic nations, and however serious may be their failure to conform perfectly to their democratic ideals, it is sheer moral perversity to equate the inconsistencies of a democratic civilization with the brutalities which modern tyrannical States practise....

If we do not make discriminate judgments between social systems we weaken the resolution to defend and extend civilization. Pacifism either tempts us to make no judgments at all, or to give an undue preference to tyranny in comparison with the momentary anarchy which is necessary to overcome tyranny....

In its profoundest insights the Christian faith sees the whole of human history as involved in guilt, and finds no release from guilt except in the grace of God. The Christian is freed by that grace to act in history; to give his devotion to the highest values he knows; to defend those citadels of civilization of which necessity and historic destiny have made him the defender; and he is persuaded by that grace to remember the ambiguity of even his best actions. If the providence of God does not enter the affairs of men to bring good out of evil, the evil in our good may easily destroy our most ambitious efforts and frustrate our highest hopes.

GANDHI AND NONVIOLENCE

Must one fight fire with fire? Throughout his life, Mohandas K. Gandhi (1869–1948) wrestled with the dilemma of how people should respond to redress injustice, erase prejudice, and defeat tyranny. He repudiated violent means, even if the ends were peaceful, and advocated principled civil disobedience as the proper alternative. Such an approach, termed *Satyagraha* (literally "truth-force"), would embody an ultimately irresistible moral authority that went beyond mere passive resistance. Those who adopted a nonviolent stance (*ahimsa*) might be politically weak, but because they proceeded from a position of moral strength and unwavering conviction in the truth of their cause, they would compel those in power to concede. Gandhi developed this strategy in South Africa before 1914 to agitate for civil rights for the Indian community there, and by the eve of the Second World War, he was the preeminent spokesman for political change in British India. Many critics doubted that Gandhi could remain influential during a world war, or that his ideas on nonviolence could remain realistic as the fighting drew closer to India's borders. In the first extract, published in the weekly English-language newspaper *Harijan* on August 11, 1940, Gandhi responds to a skeptic by reaffirming the efficacy of nonviolence as a general principle. In the second, published in the same paper on April 12, 1942, Gandhi outlines the alternatives facing Indian citizens should (as then appeared likely) Japanese forces invade. His unwillingness to endorse resistance against a demonstrably brutal aggressor betrays the same moral certitude and consistency that baffled and exasperated the British rulers in India and led to Gandhi's frequent arrest and confinement. Nonetheless, one should not make the mistake of assuming that he hoped for a Japanese victory; on the contrary, Gandhi repudiated the expansionist aims and oppressive policies of the Axis regimes and desired an Allied triumph. To the British, however, that was scant consolation given Gandhi's insistence that they "Quit India," and they regarded his stance as not only naïve and misguided, but as a mortal threat to an empire in peril.

I

The correspondent doubts in substance the universal application of *ahimsa* [nonviolence], and asserts that society has made little progress towards it. Teachers like Buddha arose and made some effort with some little success perhaps in their lifetime, but society is just where it was in spite of them. *Ahimsa* may be good enough to be the duty of an individual; for society it is good for nothing, and India too will have to take to violence for her freedom.

The argument is, I think, fundamentally wrong. The last statement is incorrect inasmuch as the Congress has adhered to non-violence as the means for the attainment of *Swaraj* [self-rule]....It is only for protection against outside aggression that the Congress has maintained it would be necessary to have an army. And then even on this matter there was a considerable body of the members...who voted against the resolution. This dissent has got to be reckoned with when the question voted upon

M. K. Gandhi, "Is Non-Violence Impossible?" in Gandhi, *Non-Violence in Peace and War*, 2 vols. (Ahmedabad: Navajivan Publishing House, n.d.), 1:309–311. Used by permission.

is one of principle....Where there is no principle involved and there is a programme to be carried out, the minority has got to follow the majority. But where there is a principle involved, the dissent stands, and it is bound to express itself in practice when the occasion arises. That means that *ahimsa* for all occasions and all purposes has been recognized by a society, however small it may be, and that *ahimsa* as a remedy to be used by society has made fair strides....

If we turn our eyes to the time of which history has any record down to our own time, we shall find that man has been steadily progressing towards *ahimsa*. Our remote ancestors were cannibals. Then came a time when they were fed up with cannibalism and they began to live on chase. Next came a stage when man was ashamed of leading the life of a wandering hunter. He therefore took to agriculture and depended principally on mother earth for his food. Thus from being a nomad he settled down to civilized stable life, founded villages and towns, and from member of a family he became member of a community and a nation. All these are signs of progressive *ahimsa* and diminishing *himsa*. Had it been otherwise, the human species should have been extinct by now, even as many of the lower species have disappeared....

And yet violence seems to persist, even to the extent of thinking people like the correspondent regarding it as the final weapon. But, as I shown, history and experience are against him.

If we believe that mankind has steadily progressed towards *ahimsa*, it follows that it has to progress towards it still further. Nothing in this world is static, everything is kinetic. If there is no progression, then there is inevitable retrogression. No one can remain without the eternal cycle, unless it be God Himself.

The present war is the saturation point in violence. It spells to my mind also its doom. Daily I have testimony of the fact that *ahimsa* was never before appreciated by mankind as it is today.

M. K. Gandhi, "Non-Violent Resistance," in Gandhi, *Non-Violence in Peace and War*, 397–398.

II

Japan is knocking at our gates. What are we to do in a non-violent way? If we were a free country, things could be done non-violently to prevent the Japanese from entering the country. As it is, non-violent resistance could commence the moment they effected a landing. Thus non-violent resisters would refuse them any help, even water. For it is no part of their duty to help anyone steal their country....Suppose the Japanese compel resisters to give them water, the resisters must die in the act of resistance. It is conceivable that they will exterminate all resisters. The underlying belief in such non-violent resistance is that the aggressor will, in time, be mentally and even physically tired of killing non-violent resisters. He will begin to search what this new (for him) force is which refuses cooperation without seeking to hurt, and will probably desist from further slaughter. But the resisters may find that the Japanese are utterly heartless and that they do not care how many they kill. The non-violent resisters will have won the day inasmuch as they will have preferred extermination to submission.

But things will not happen quite so simply as I have put them. There are at least four parties in the country. First, the British and the army they have brought into being. The Japanese declare that they have no designs upon India. Their quarrel is only with the British. In this they are assisted by some Indians who are in Japan. It is difficult to guess how many, but there must be a fairly large number who believe in the declaration of the Japanese and think they will deliver the country from the British yoke and retire. Even if the worst happens, their fatigue of the British yoke is so great that they would even welcome the Japanese yoke for a change. This is the second party. The third are the neutrals, who though not non-violent will help neither the British nor Japanese.

The fourth and last are non-violent resisters. If they are only a few, their resistance will be ineffective except as an example for the future. Such resisters will calmly die wherever they are but will not bend the knee before the aggressor. They will not be deceived by promises. They do not seek deliverance from the British yoke through the help of a third party. They believe implicitly in their own way of fighting and no other....They believe that non-violence alone will lead men to do right under all circumstances. Therefore, if for want of enough companions non-violent resisters cannot reach the goal, they will not give up their way but pursue it to death.

The task before the votaries of non-violence is very difficult. But no difficulty can baffle men who have faith in their mission.

THE NEW IMPERATIVES OF EDUCATION

A good example of how the war affected American domestic attitudes in areas remote from any fighting (and, in all probability, equally remote from the prospect of an air raid mentioned in this pamphlet) is the renewed attention to the methods and purposes of education. The war would likely end before American schoolchildren were old enough to fight, but they might be viewed as vital future weapons in the nation's arsenal of democracy. At the same time, schools were urged to maintain their commitment to an American ideal of civic-mindedness, to foster a unity of purpose from the social melting point so decried by German teachers. That civic patriotism, however, had to be reinforced by the recognition that the country would be called upon to play a global role, and that the average student's horizons would have to broaden. Thus, the ideals of the war would have domestic consequences, while the war's realities would affect American ideals. The National Education Association, which traced its origins back before the Civil War, was a national umbrella for a network of affiliated state and local educational associations. It sought to promote better public schools and improved conditions for teachers. During the war, it took an active role, coordinating rationing of oil and sugar, promoting the sale of war bonds and defense savings stamps, and lobbying for the GI Bill (college opportunities for returning veterans). As an influential voice in educational policy, its outline of the proper goals of wartime education provides insight into schoolchildren's experience in the 1940s.

A child attending the elementary schools at this time will probably not see service in the armed forces. He will feel the war in a very personal way. His father will, perhaps, be overseas, and his mother may be working in some defense plant. When he comes to school, the opening exercises will start with the class saluting the flag, repeating together the Pledge of Allegiance, and singing patriotic songs. These school procedures are splendid and necessary but they do not mean that the elementary-school program should become a war program. Instead, the war activities should cause school procedures to take on new vigor and help in building morale. It is the task and privilege of teachers to organize the enthusiasm

National Education Association of the U.S., *Wartime Handbook for Education* (Washington, DC: National Education Association, 1943), 6–7, 18–19. Used by permission.

of the children in the school program, and in this way build not only for the present but for the postwar period....

The growth of children must continue to be skillfully guided. At the same time they must be protected as much as possible from the hazards and effects of war. Much can be done if the school and its community are in complete understanding. Some teachers are visiting the homes of every child in their classes, so as to establish a knowledge of the child's environment. Should an air raid take place such information will be particularly helpful.

Many of the suggestions listed below are being carried out in hundreds of schools:

1. *Obedience to expert authority*—In times of emergency, self-discipline and order are two of the major rules for survival. Children must learn that these two principles apply in their daily lives. The teacher, principal, or one of the older children (when given the authority) must be obeyed. During an air raid or similar emergency great danger and perhaps death can result if the principle of obedience to authority is not followed.

2. *Emphasize the fundamentals*—...Each child can learn something and learn it well. Therefore teach well each day. See that the child learns how to study.

In all the fundamental subjects teach for facts, skills, and accuracy. Cultural subjects should not be neglected, for these subjects aid the spiritual development of children.

3. *Teach how to read*—knowing how to read is more necessary now than it has ever been....

4. *Accuracy in arithmetic*—A thing is right or wrong. Our soldiers cannot aim their guns and be "almost correct" or "nearly right." Their aim must be true. Therefore, in our arithmetic let us teach the meaning of numbers, place greater emphasis on fractions and decimals, working continually for speed, smoothness, and ability. We shall have to drill if we are to accomplish perfection.

5. *This war is global*—Let us teach more thoroughly global geography. Continents, countries, cities, oceans, and seas are no longer vague names on a map. One child in the class may have a father in Australia, another, a brother in Iceland; thus, geography will take on a new and vital meaning.

6. *Stress history*—History, too, should receive a new impetus. Wars result from causes of long standing, and history helps to tell us why certain events happen and why they happen at a certain time or in a certain place.

7. *Health, physical fitness, and safety*—Teachers must develop good health habits among the children. Create a desire to have a well body; to eat proper foods; to practice safety procedures at school, at home, and on the playgrounds....

The present war and the coming peace confront the schools with new and especially critical responsibilities in education for democratic citizenship. Such education is needed by our young men and women in the armed services and by adults in civilian life, but it is also of special importance for children and youth in elementary and secondary schools in 1943—our young citizens whose lives are largely cast in this country's tomorrow and of whom many will soon be leaving their classrooms to serve in the Army, Navy, or in industry.

The chief, but not the exclusive, responsibility for citizenship education rests on the social studies. Accordingly, there is urgent need to alter curriculums in social studies in order to meet the new demands of wartime citizenship education....

1. *Americans must study the world at war*—Topics needing new or increased emphasis are democracy; American traditions and institutions; causes, issues, strategy, and aims of the war; total war and the individual; world geography; the United Nations; Asia and Latin America; our enemies and peace plans.

2. *The democratic way of life must be understood and appreciated by all citizens of democracy.* There should be in elementary and secondary schools study of dramatic, key episodes in the history of American democracy; biographies of men and women whose lives have advanced or personified the democratic tradition; great documents in American history; contrasts between democracy and dictatorship; civil liberties; and the responsibilities and self-disciplines as well as the privileges of citizenship.

3. *The worldwide setting of modern life must be emphasized.* The day of isolation has passed. Study of United States history should include study of

our nation's world relations; world history should include study of international organization and cooperation; elementary-school courses should include sympathetic study of other peoples, with increased attention especially for Canada, Latin America India, China, Russia, and the British Commonwealth of Nations; imperials and colonialism should be re-examined.

4. *Study of geography must be increased.* There is need for systematic instruction in use of maps, with emphasis on globes and polar projections. Continual reference to maps should be made in all social studies courses. Importance of natural resources in war and peace needs increased attention. Effects of aviation on concepts of political geography need to be pointed out. At least one full year of geography should be required of all secondary-school pupils.

5. *The economic tasks and impacts of war and reconstruction must be studied.* Topics of immediate importance are conservation; rationing; price control; public finance; war savings; inflation; relation of corporate organization, unionism, private enterprise, and governmental regulation to modern economy; and manpower.

6. *Racial and national prejudice and misunderstanding must be reduced.* Contributions of other races and nations should be studied; fallacies of Nazi racial theories should be exposed; the study of ethics and the moralities of great religions should be encouraged; restrictions on school study of the languages and cultures of the people with whom we are at war should be discouraged.

7. *Programs and principles for postwar reconstruction must be studied.* Historical study of past periods of postwar reconstruction is important; factors likely to influence the period to follow the present war should be analyzed; opportunities and responsibilities of youth in the postwar world should be forecast....

Art, like music, has a tremendously important contribution to make to the war effort, both in society and in the school. Enlightened educators realize that far from being a peacetime luxury, it is one of the most effective of the democratic weapons for fighting the war. Fascism, from the start, has always tried to destroy or to restrict the arts.

Today, art serves wartime needs—in government, in industry, and in military and civilian life. The output of factories has been speeded up by the use of "production drawings," which are large, freehand, visual interpretations of blueprints. "Production charts," like school bulletin-board displays, use cartoons, posters, and slogans to transmit morale-building ideas to workers. Military recruitment and government information agencies have always relied heavily on the poster as having more direct effect upon action than does the printed word alone. Our allies have found, as we are finding, that art does its part in relieving the tensions of a war-torn society, and we know that it will have its therapeutic effect in rehabilitation after the war.

RADIO ON THE HOME FRONT

From October 1 through 3, 1943, some 1,200 representatives from the worlds of movie production, script writing, the radio industry, and the scholarly study of the mass media met at Royce Hall on the campus of UCLA, under the auspices of the Hollywood Writers' Mobilization, to discuss what their respective industries had accomplished on behalf of the war effort over the past two years and how they could redirect their energies more effectively in the future. They envisioned a voluntary partnership with the government as the most effective way to promote the war, perhaps grudgingly accepting direction or advice from official bodies like the Office of War Information, but resisting any attempts at overt dictation or heavy-handed censorship. This strategy stands in sharp contrast to the perspective from which someone like Germany's Hans Fritzsche approached the issue of media and the war. Both the movie industry and radio found a receptive audience among the American public, and the combination of free enterprise and the business of "selling the war" proved a potent one that propelled both further into the spotlight in the postwar era.

There are some twenty-two governmental agencies and an equal number of semi-governmental agencies engaged in the prosecution of this war. It is only natural that every one of them, whether it be the War Production Board or the American Red Cross, should feel that its function and problems are the most important of all. At the beginning, all agencies quickly recognized the power of radio for the voicing of their problems to the public, and for the proper instruction of the public in wartime procedure. When forty or fifty agencies pursued radio at one time and made appeals for time for programs on the air, the result was chaos. Our bureau [Office of War Information] was formed by the President and charged with the duty of bringing order and coordination between the governmental agencies and the radio industry. Our purpose, then, was to make sure that every governmental problem was taken care of in turn, and to take meticulous care that we protect

the radio industry. Protect, by insisting that the value of the individual program must never be lessened by any decrease in entertainment value due to too much increase in war messages....

Since April, 1942,...[m]oney has been raised for War Bonds, Red Cross, and Community Chest. Conservation has been urged—tires, gasoline, "carry our own packages," etc. Salvage has been brought in—iron and steel, fats and grease, even binoculars and books. Food shortages have been explained. The problems of rationing have been outlined. Radio has been enormously helpful in the fight against black markets and hoarding. Men and women have been recruited for Army, Navy, Marines, Coast Guard, war plants and nurses' corps. V-mail has been explained and encouraged, as have victory gardens and the security of war information....

Now, how successfully have these things been done? Here are some figures.

Nat Wolff, "Radio on the Home Front" in *Writers' Congress: The Proceedings of the Conference held in October 1943 under the Sponsorship of the Hollywood Writers' Mobilization and the University of California* (Berkeley: University of California Press, 1944), 524, 526–527, 529–530.

1. Fat and grease salvage. In August, 1942, just over three million pounds per month were collected after several intensive campaigns. In March, 1943, over seven and a quarter million pounds per month. More than double.

2. V-mail. In January, 1943, a little over three million and a quarter letters. In April of this year, after an intensive network four-week campaign, just under nine million for the month.

3. Gasoline or mileage rationing, which was a very difficult problem, since it is very hard for people to understand the need for rationing gas and oil when they see it flowing in their backyards....In July, only 24 per cent of the Middle West admitted the necessity for rationing. The information program then started, and the results: in September, 42 per cent admitted the need, in November, 48 per cent, and in December, 67 per cent.

4. War bonds...[F]or the Second War Loan Drive, thirteen billion was the goal and eighteen billion was reached....

6. Nurse recruiting. A three-week drive increased enlistments over 100 per cent....

7. Victory gardens. The Department of Agriculture estimated there would be twelve million gardens—at the outside, fifteen million. The most recent Gallup poll estimates over twenty-one million victory gardens now....

The most effective selling is always done when people you know and believe are doing the selling. In other words, if you have spent months or years building up characters like Vic and Sade, Charlie McCarthy, Fibber McGee and Molly, Lum and Abner, or Amos and Andy, you can get the greatest possible result by having them take on the responsibility of the governmental problems at hand....On the other hand, if you use the announcers impersonally instead of your characters, the average audience reaction is "Turn it off, Bud—Here comes another doggone governmental talk."...

[T]he very nature of America itself can lull us all into a calm slumber when we should be on our toes and eager to get this thing over with. Bombs galvanize us into action, when it might well be too late. Let's make words do the galvanizing, and in time. You people who are thinking of life in terms of radio or other public media have in your hands the most powerful weapons in the world—the power not only of the instrument but of the American way of telling the truth....We know that guns and planes and tanks are going to win the war, but if your words can shorten it by one hour, you have served mankind well and have the right to call yourselves creators. This weapon is in your hands....

FILM AND PROPAGANDA

Film afforded viewers an escape from the strains of war and filmmakers an opportunity to shape popular attitudes to the conflict. The potential audience was enormous. In the United States alone, more than 100 million people (three-quarters of the population) viewed a movie each week during the war, and the industry, based in Hollywood, California, produced more than 400 titles during that period. In Britain, where urban centers were bombed and theaters damaged, cinemas still attracted a weekly average of 30 million viewers, or about half the population. One way that filmmakers sought to engage these audiences was by pairing newsreels on the war's events with cartoons about the underlying contrasts between friend and foe. *The Ducktators* (1942, in which Hitler, Mussolini, and Hirohito were portrayed as ducks taking over a barnyard), *Bugs Bunny Nips the Nips* (1944, a racist attempt at stereotyping the Japanese with short buck teeth and slanty eyes), and *Herr Meets Hare* (1945, in which Bugs Bunny took on Hermann Göring) were examples. Walt Disney studios also produced shorter films like *Der Führer's Face*, which won the 1942 Academy Award for its portrayal of ordinary Germans as militaristic stooges and Japanese as grinning buffoons. In fact, so beloved were Disney characters and films that "Mickey Mouse" served as the password for the Allied invasion on D-day, June 6, 1944. Regular feature-length films provided another avenue to interpret the culture of war in a perhaps less obvious fashion. *Since You Went Away* provided an idealized picture of American domestic life during the war, *Mission to Moscow* cast the country's formerly reviled Soviet allies in a more positive light, while *Mrs. Miniver* implied that Britain's previously entrenched hierarchies of class were being transcended by a new democratic wartime spirit of common purpose. In all of these films, the subliminal message was that eventual victory was both just and inevitable. Whether they portrayed what was actually happening was not the point. As the authors of one of the major studies of the subject conclude, "The genius of Hollywood was its ability to capture not American reality but American aspirations and make these seem real."

None of the other combatant nations matched the productivity of the American film industry, but they nonetheless bent their productions to the needs of the state. In the Soviet Union, for example, Sergei Eisenstein's classic *Alexander Nevsky*, which dealt with the thirteenth-century struggle between Teutonic knights and Novgorod's Russians, was effectively suppressed during the period of the German-Soviet nonaggression pact but resurfaced after June 1941 when its message of determined resistance to Germanic invasion was highly relevant. Even as the tide was turning in 1943, battlefield films were deemed potentially demoralizing, yet heroic partisan actions found their champion in Fridrikh Ermler's *She Defends the Motherland*. The film follows the transformation of a simple village wife, terrorized and widowed by the Nazis, who becomes a partisan leader and helps to liberate her country. In Germany, where Leni Riefenstahl's strikingly filmed *Triumph of the Will* virtually deified Hitler, sickeningly vicious anti-Semitic films like

Eric Knight, "Memorandum on Propaganda" (May 1942) in David Culbert, ed., *Film and Propaganda in America: A Documentary History*, 5 vols. (New York: Greenwood Press, 1990), 3:108–111, 114–117. Used by permission.

Jüd Süss and *Der Ewige Jude* sought to reinforce the sense of a life-or-death racial crusade for survival. Japanese films, on the other hand, illustrated some realities of war to inspire an "endearing empathy" among Japanese audiences, though the standard heroic fare of inspirational courage and self-sacrifice found expression in *The Story of Tank Commander Nishizumi*, produced by the Ministry of War.

There is general agreement, though, that state-sponsored or directed films were more heavy-handed and ultimately less effective than those left to private initiative, produced by cinematic professionals, and guided by an informal consensus among industry insiders, government censors, and military officials as to what constituted a beneficially patriotic approach. Most successful of all was Frank Capra, assigned to the Morale Branch of the OWI, who was commissioned in 1942 to make seven information films to explain to soldiers the principles behind American participation. The series, entitled simply *Why We Fight*, won the New York Film Critics Award for best documentary, and by 1945 had attracted nearly 54 million American viewers. The propaganda potential of film, so brilliantly realized by Capra, is delineated here by Eric Knight, a writer in the U.S. Army's Morale Branch, in a 1942 memorandum for his superiors. The second extract, by the iconoclastic artist and film critic Manny Farber (1917–2008), offers an extended review of the range of American wartime films.

I

Propaganda is the inculcation of a desired mental attitude in people. Hence any method of communication is a potential carrier of propaganda, and no medium of communication known to the human race can be ignored by the propagandist.

The eye and the ear can be reached by pamphlet and book, drama and screen story, radio and lecture, painting, statue, conversation. These media, and every last variation of mutation of them, are avenues of propaganda; from the weightiest and most abstract truth written by a philosopher down to the off-color story told by the night club comedian, or passed on in the smoking compartment of trains.

The enemy will assuredly use every one of these media in his attack against you. You will fail if you neglect to use every channel in your fight against him....

People in total war must have mental and moral sustenance no less than bodily sustenance. Without bodily sustenance, a nation must capitulate. But with sound moral and mental sustenance, a nation can and will continue with the will to win through even shortage of rations, housing and heating....

In all Democracies, initial war unity through patriotism is not enough. Democracy, being built on

individual free will, must have intellectual and moral unity. The populace must be convinced that its government made all possible efforts to solve the international problems by peaceful means; that is recourse to war was taken only when all such efforts were exhausted; that its fight is just and in keeping with national honor and attitudes of life; and that from victory in the war shall certainly come not only a period of sounder international stability, but also necessary advances in social, economic and cultural freedoms....

To achieve that victory the populace must be imbued with the will-to-fight and must also be taught how to conduct itself so that the war shall be won. And in total war this latter means education of every individual is almost every phase of his daily life....

In total war, there comes also totality of life-conduct and hence totality of propaganda influencing that life.

To achieve this totality places demands upon almost all the nations' creative workers in any of the propagandistic media. In Britain the constant conditioning of the public mind is carried on through a free press in which censorship is nearly always self-imposed, through paid Government advertisements in the daily press, through radio programs, through re-broadcasting of important speeches made in Parliament, through incessant posters, through organizational classes, and through films both long and short which the Government sponsors wholly or in part.

FILM IN PROPAGANDA

Film fails in wartime as propaganda in the enemy country. Although films have been dropped in this war by airplanes over enemy and occupied territory, film cannot compete with radio in reaching and influencing minds in the enemy populace.

But of all the media of expression film in many ways qualifies as the best means of spreading ideas and mental attitudes on the home front. The film is positive in approach and almost instantaneous in impact.

Film reaches the broadest of audiences. A man who cannot read or write can understand a film.

Silent film was the only true international language. John Bunny and Charlie Chaplin were as comprehensible to the Chinese and Hindus as to Americans and British. The birth of the talkie ruined the growing technique of the film as the one readily comprehensible international medium, and made it nationalistic in scope again. But it still remains as a medium capable of delivering impacts to all peoples. Foreign language sound tracks can easily be added.

Film carries more conviction than any other expressive medium because the onlooker believes—quite falsely—that the camera cannot lie.

The technician knows the camera can lie, fluently, by its angles, its own peculiar emphasis, and in cutting through its relation of the actual and the staged, and through its omissions....

FILM'S ROLE IN WARTIME AMERICA

In all internal propaganda, effectiveness lies through clear understanding of purpose. In propaganda films, virtuosity of technique, or "artistic" credit are not sufficient, if the primary objective is not attained (to implant in the subject mind the desired mental attitude).

This can be attained only by unmuddled understanding of the goals to be reached, of film methods which must carry the message, and use of mass mental attitudes and the processes of the human mind in which the message must be planted.

The purposes of such films in America will not differ greatly from those in Britain in broad aspects. American film can work for national moral unity by stating with conviction that:

1. The Government sought all possible means to solve international problems without recourse to war.
2. That war came because all such efforts were exhausted.
3. That the war is just and in keeping with national honor and systems of life.
4. That from victory shall come not only the needed era of sounder international stability; but also the desired advances in social, economic and cultural freedoms on the home front.

Of those four points, film can have much to say. The first—American peace efforts—can be readily dramatized. To state, however, that we sunk our warships, attended disarmament conferences, is not enough. It is the "defense" strategy—a mere justification of our attitude.

The positive attack comes through education films not merely showing our desire for peace, but rather stating clearly the full intention of the aggressor nations to solve world problems by brutal, undeclared attack and by ruthless force.

The second, that war came when all efforts for peace were exhausted, is easier of explanation here than in Britain. Britain declared war because another land was invaded. America came into the war because of a direct, bloody and savage attack upon American lives and forces. Pearl Harbor leaves the American mind needing little further statement of America's desire to stay at peace.

Pearl Harbor, however, can be destroyed as a symbol by meaningless repetition of the words. Overuse dulls words as well as razor-blades. Film can never over-emphasize the bloody deceit of Japan's attack, but it must seek continually new and powerful ways of saying it.

The third point, that the war is just and in keeping with national honor and our system of life, can again be best stated not by "defensive films" justifying our beliefs, but by savage and pitiless attack upon the aggressor nations' system of life....

The theory of "let's hate Hitler" will not sustain the necessary will-to-fight. Film must clarify the enemy not as a funny man with a moustache, but as thugs who beat and purged political and religious minorities, and as people who stood around in those lands watching, too craven to live like men or to risk death like men while eradicating the evil from their own national lives. The people who by acquiescence let loose Hitlerism and Fascism and Japanese imperialism upon the world, are even greater cowards and criminals than the men who trampled on their cowardice.

Film cannot state this too clearly in this present war. The cutting together of newsreel material of the earliest days of brutality in the aggressor nations, together with clear, truthful explanation of the progressive growth of world events, will reach to the desired effect.

The fourth aim—to state with conviction that victory will bring desired advances in life and freedom on the home front—is compatible with the democratic idea of a steadily advancing state of civilization. It is not enough to imply, even subconsciously, to the soldier and citizen that we are fighting to see that Germany behaves herself in this world (that is, that we die to restore for her the democratic freedoms she didn't have guts to retain for herself). The natural question in every mind is: "Yes, we want a better world, but we're part of this world and we want some share of the betterment, too." Either you say: "Be content with the share you've got," a static deadly answer; or we agree to even greater richness of life for the individual under democracy, and start to shape the still hazy forms which those improvements will take.

The broad aims, however, are clear: for one can turn to the Atlantic Charter of the President, as an official declaration of aims encompassing democratic progress. As these are officially extended and clarified and enlarged, one can define more exactly

Manny Farber, "Movies in Wartime," *The New Republic,* vol. 110, no. 1 (January 3, 1944), 16–20. Used by permission.

the "better world" which every fighting man desires as reward for his fighting.

II

The war movie comes in four shapes: the in-praise-of-a-branch-of-the-service film; half-fiction, half-historic accounts of actual battles; a kind that in the early parts of 1943 threatened to swamp the exhibitors, which shows the resistance of native populations in Europe to the conquerors; and home-front films. The first and second produced the best pictures, the fourth the worst and the third the most.

The ingredients of all servicemen films are identical psychologically. The central character, whether he is a bombardier in a Flying Fortress [American B-17 bomber] or the captain of a United Nations ship sailing supplies to Murmansk, has by the end of the picture become a hero of the war no matter how he started—as a sulker, the brother of the captain's hated rival, or an idiot. These heroes are treated in groups rather than as individuals, and though they are given a democratic texture of names like Winocki, O'Doul, Feingold and Ramirez, they are given only one personality. Winocki-O'Doul-Feingold-Ramirez is a man of average looks, on the handsome side, very friendly, short on ideas and emotions, philosophically on the Saroyan [American writer William Saroyan (1908–1981), whose stories emphasized optimistic responses to challenging or depressing situations] side of the street and capable of trading you a wisecrack. At an early point in the picture the hero finds he is fighting a righteous war, because he sees the Germans or the Japanese taking blood from children to use for their own soldiers, firing on survivors of ships they have torpedoed, behaving ruthlessly in Pearl Harbor or Czechoslovakia, ripping up a painting by Picasso or the house that Tolstoy lived in.

The only conflicts in the pictures arise out of someone's discontent with the way things are going, *e.g.,* that he should have been promoted instead of flunked out of pilot school, that he is too conceited, surly and know-it-all to be liked, or that he is asked to be officer of the day too many times in a row. And all this has a rotten effect on the group's morale. This conflict is resolved during the first battle, when the unruly one awakens to the fact that the Germans or

Japanese are bestial, that he would rather be fighting them than leave the service for a shore job, or when he finds that the captain is not the hard-boiled egg he supposed, because the captain asked him to play parchesi [*sic*]: (a popular board game from India)....Usually there is a father in the battle whose son is killed, or has to have his leg cut off, which is meant to imply that the war is as grim as could be imagined; and there is a mother, wife or sweetheart at home to read a letter from one of the soldiers, to show that the home front is behind the boys and to show the importance of the family tie. Death and destruction in war are diluted almost out of sight by various devices. Only one of the group would be killed, and so the death was hardly noticed, or the emphasis turned from individual dying to mass slaughter so that it became no longer a matter of men dying but endless streams of extras running wildly out into the open and falling down. Death would be further sterilized by switching immediately to more heroics, intense activity or scenes with a merry note.

This does not add up to saying that all the war movies are bad. It would be closer to say that they are all slight. Their scope in no way admitted all of the material that should be encountered in dealing with the problems they set up. Many of the best films took original material that was superficial and tawdry and made the best they could out of it...in them the living from moment to moment in war was splendidly realized; there were pieces of good dialogue and the beginnings of fine characterization. Yet it was all like a cheap watch that is kept running by expert attention but is doomed nevertheless to a short and not too happy life. There were films that started with sincere grasp of an actuality. But for one reason or another saw fit to erect an artificial, inadequate structure around it. Still, in films of this nature, like "Wake Island," the main procedure—the nature of one battle in the war—is still discernible and informative. The work of expert hands [producers, directors, writers, and actors] was always noticeable....Despite everything, Hollywood's mass of film will leave to posterity the greatest mirror of a kind that has ever been left of a war.

Though there was muttering in various quarters (including this one) about the quality of war films,

and though the public itself was heard to complain, it at the same time encouraged what it was getting....

People went to see anything. The figures for the 1942 year of the war shows that four and a quarter million more people went to the movies *weekly* than went in 1941, for five and a half cents more on average for a ticket. In 1941 the seven major film companies had made $36,000,000 more than they had in 1939 (when the foreign market was still there). For every twelfth American there was a movie seat—the others stood outside and waited for him to get up. The hardest time to get in was at 7:30 p.m. on Sunday.

The character of the movie audience has changed radically during the war years. It no longer seems to be the silent, rapt mass it once was: there is a noticeable quality of more or less cynical detachment, it has become a little more like the audience at a ball park where the crowd is broken up into pockets of people who do not give up their personality wholly to the spectacle but in one form or another express their own reactions—moviegoers nowadays are running conversations with one another, criticizing the film while watching it, taking the whole thing far less seriously than formerly. The reasons, and there are many, must have largely to do with the war: people have more money and are less fiercely intent on getting the most for it; they are living outside the settled equilibrium of home existence; they are going more frequently, less to see the movie than to get somewhere simply to sit down (this is particularly sadly applicable to servicemen and their girls); the crowds are younger and less frozen; longer hours of work for parents make the movie theatres improvised nurseries; and perhaps most of all, a curious atmosphere that wartime is to some extent vacation time, a transition period in which life is not quite the same as it has been before....

The most significant work in motion pictures during the war has been contributed by official government information services in England, Russia, Canada and this country which have communicated the actual life and temper of the war in factual films. Even this documentary arm which is the only one on the movie body that is alive and comparatively free, is forced to function within the social and political boundaries that prevailing opinion in each country sets for it. But within these boundaries the artist is given the freedom and means to express his subject matter with all the power and persuasion he possesses, and on the whole the limits have allowed material that is more adult and sensible than what is permitted in Hollywood. In the documentary film there is quality of straight, level communication with the audience on as high a level as the makers of the film know and it is this direct honesty that marks the principal difference of the documentary from the Hollywood film....

WAR BONDS AND MASS PERSUASION

Persuasive appeals to the masses were an integral part of the lead-up to the war (for instance, the apparently spellbinding oratory of Hitler and Mussolini) and, after its outbreak, to the effective mobilization of millions of armed men or cooperative civilians when mere compulsion alone could never have achieved such results. Why huge numbers of people willingly accepted certain statements or pursued certain actions was a question that fascinated social theorists. Robert K. Merton (1910–2003), a prominent Columbia University sociologist who had forsaken his teenage ambition to become a world-class magician, seized the opportunity to study the magic of mass persuasion by observing the response of American listeners to a one-day marathon appeal to buy war bonds on September 21, 1943. The appeal, carried on radio by the Columbia Broadcasting System (CBS), was spearheaded by the beloved singer Kate Smith (1907–1986), famous to generations of listeners for her stirring rendition of "God Bless America." The third in a series of such marathons, it was wildly successful, drawing in $39 million in pledges (compared to $1 million and $2 million for the first two efforts). The radio bond drive was particularly interesting because participants were not grouped together in a social setting and exposed to direct peer pressure (as would happen at a rally), but listened alone or with their families, yet they came forth in droves to proclaim their support for the war effort. Merton carefully analyzed the various aspects of the drive, producing a sociological classic and a thought-provoking study of how the American home front might define its role in the war.

As a consequence of its marathon structure, Smith's drive was an essay in persuasion, rather than propaganda. Though both seek to influence action, beliefs and attitude, persuasion differs from propaganda in two technical respects. It involves a higher degree of social interaction between the "persuader" and the "persuadee" and it permits the persuader to adapt his argumentation to the flow of reactions of the persons he is seeking to influence. The marathon enabled Smith to achieve a degree of *social interaction* and *flexibility of appeals* approximating that possible in face-to-face discussion, in a fashion ordinarily impossible for such an impersonal, mass medium of communication as the radio....

The usual run of separate and distinct appeals permits the radio audience only to *react* to the

Robert K. Merton, *Mass Persuasion: The Social Psychology of a War Bond Drive* (New York: Harper, 1946), 38–40, 45–47, 50–55. Used by permission.

speaker and his message. During the marathon, however, there was *reciprocal interplay,* for the audience was not only responding to Smith, but she was also responding to her audience and modifying her subsequent comments as a result. Many of her broadcasts during the day were based on information supplied by listeners who telephoned details about the circumstances of their bond-buying. Thus the usual radio monologue became something of a conversation. The essence of a two-way conversation is that what each says is modified by what the other has just said or by what one anticipates the other will say in return....

The interplay between Smith and her audience undoubtedly reinforced the sense of a personalized appeal and, reciprocally, the personal character of her messages helped further the sense of a conversational relationship....

Of the wide range of appeals that might have been utilized to persuade Americans to buy war bonds, the Smith drive selected a battery especially suited to her public personality and her audience. Analyzing her broadcasts, one is immediately struck by two omissions. In the first place, *nothing* was said about bonds as a *sound investment,* a nest egg of security, or a promise of good things to be bought after the war. In general, bond campaigns have tried to appeal to both patriotism and economic self-interest.... But this was evidently felt to be too materialistic and mercenary a view, and one out of accord with the dedicated spirit in which a Smith audience would buy bonds. By omitting this argument, the authors of her scripts were able to avoid the strain and incompatibility between the two mainlines of motivation: unselfish, sacrificing love of country and economic motives of sound investment....

[F]or many people the buying of war bonds is not like buying goods and services, or even like buying railroad bonds or preferred stocks. It is, rather, more nearly analogous to the monetary collections made in church which are thought of not as the wherewithal for the bread and butter of the minister, but rather as an "offering." To tinge such contributions with commercialism would profane the sentiments centered about war bonds, which have been termed "sacred" as compared with the more secular attitudes involved in the purchase of material goods for one's self. Patriotic feelings, like religious feelings, are usually, to those experiencing them, beyond the realm of the controversial, and any exhortation to contribute money in either of these fields would be tainted were it spoken of in terms of material advantages accruing to the contributor....

If Smith had nothing to say about bonds as sound investments or as a curb to inflation, what did she talk about? The answer to this question goes beyond casual impressions. The content of Smith's broadcasts was analyzed into recurring themes and the proportion of time devoted to each of these was taken as a crude measure of comparative emphases....

Keynoting her appeals was the theme of *sacrifice* to which Smith devoted fully half her broadcast time. Twenty-six per cent went to stories of the sacrifices of servicemen; almost as much, 20 per cent to the sacrifices of civilians and 5 per cent to the sacrifice of one civilian in particular, namely, Kate Smith herself.

Sixteen per cent of all Smith had to say dwelt upon the theme of *participation,* setting forth the view that the bond campaign was a common enterprise in which all of us could shuffle off our private egoisms and take part in a massive communal effort. Direct appeals to the families of servicemen accounted for 6 per cent of her broadcast time; a *familial* theme which defined war bonds as a means of getting the boys back home.

Whereas these themes dealt with bond-buying in general, the others were directly concerned with the Smith bond drive in particular. The twelve per cent of her time was devoted to the *competition* theme, which urged listeners to help Smith surpass her earlier bond sale records and to help their own community outdo others in purchasing bonds from her. The *facilitation* theme, accounting for 7 per cent, reminded her hearers of the ease with which they could telephone their bond pledges. And the *personal* theme, in which Smith conversationally referred to her private feelings and aspirations, was casually interwoven into 6 per cent of her broadcasts....

The attempt to fan into active flame the readiness of listeners to sacrifice for the war effort followed three lines. Foremost was *the sacrifice which the boys were making "over there."* The listener was urged to do as much for them as they were ready to do for us. . . .

[T]he act of buying a bond is redefined. It is imbued with pathos. It celebrates self-sacrifice. Removed from the plain and unadorned context of transactions in the marketplace, the bond purchase is sanctified as a sacrificial rite.

Never explicit, but insistently in the background, was the third theme of sacrifice. The Smith broadcasts repeatedly reminded listeners that *she herself was making no small sacrifice.* This was no mere indulgence in exalted expressions of sentiment: hers too was a sacrificial act. Throughout the presumed ordeal of an all-day broadcast, reminiscent perhaps of the dogged persistence of our men on the battlefield, Smith too was "carrying on."

The triangulation of sacrifice, this three-cornered pressure—the boys' sacrifice, other listeners' sacrifice, Smith's sacrifice manifested in the marathon—developed in many listeners a strong sense of unworthiness and guilt. They felt compelled to do something more to keep self-esteem. Only by matching the sacrifices of the other three—converting the triangle into a square, as it were—could tensions be relieved.

One of the compelling elements of this campaign was the sense of joining with others in a common effort. . . . The war, of course, and the bond drive as a whole invited participation, but these were so broad and impersonal that it was hard to derive much social response and satisfaction from what one did. The Smith war bond drive provided an occasion for joining in something specific, immediate and dramatic. It provided surcease from individuated, self-centered activity and from the sense that the war is too big for the individual's effort to count.

THE WELFARE STATE

During the nineteenth century, the prevailing view of poverty had been that it was largely the result of the moral failure of the poor themselves and that their relief was a matter for private charity rather than the responsibility of the state. A century later, especially during Britain's Liberal governments from 1906 onward, this attitude had softened, but there was still no universal right to social security assistance for illness, unemployment, or old age. After 1939, however, matters changed. The destruction wrought by German bombing, the upheaval of evacuation or migration, the documentation of health deficiencies by military authorities or factory managers intent on utilizing the maximum in manpower (or womanpower), all contributed to the growing recognition that government services which had evolved haphazardly in the past required a thorough overhaul. William Beveridge, a prominent economist and social reformer who had directed the London School of Economics, headed an official inquiry, and his 1942 report on *Social Insurance and Allied Services* was a sensation. It advocated government intervention to rid the land of five "giant evils": want, disease, ignorance, squalor, and idleness. Its proposals underlay the efforts of Clement Attlee's Labour government, elected in 1945, to fashion a true welfare state. Underlying this was a basic point, namely that a democratic government could not demand complete participation by its citizens in a warfare state without accepting responsibility for their welfare once the war was over.

[B]y the end of the Second World War the Government had, through the agency of newly established or existing services, assumed, and developed a measure of direct concern for the health and well-being of the population which, by contrast with the role of Government in the nineteen-thirties, was little short of remarkable. No longer did concern rest on the belief that, in respect to many social needs, it was proper to intervene only to assist the poor and those who were unable to pay for services of one kind and another. Instead, it was increasingly regarded as a proper function or even obligation of Government to ward off distress and strain among not only the poor but almost all classes of society. And, because the area of responsibility had so perceptibly widened, it was no longer thought sufficient to provide through various branches of social assistance a standard of service hitherto considered appropriate for those in receipt of poor relief—a standard inflexible in administration and attuned to a philosophy which regarded individual distress as a mark of social incapacity.

That all were engaged in war whereas only some were afflicted with poverty and disease had much to do with the less constraining, less discriminating scope and quality of the war-time social services. Damage to hoes and injuries to persons were not less likely among the rich than the poor and so, after the worst of the original defects in policy had been corrected—such as the belief that only the poor would need help when their homes were smashed—the assistance provided by the Government to counter the hazards of war carried little social discrimination,

Richard Titmuss, *Problems of Social Policy* (London: His Majesty's Stationery Office, 1950), 506–508. Used by permission.

and was offered to all groups in the community. The pooling of national resources and the sharing of risks were not always practicable nor always applied; but they were the guiding principles.

Acceptance of these principles moved forward the goals of welfare. New obligations were shouldered, higher standards were set....Better pensions were given to old people as a right and not as a concession. Certain groups—expectant and nursing mothers and young children—were singled out to receive extra allowances and special aids, not because they were rich or poor or politically vocal, but because common-sense, supported by science and pushed along by common humanity, said it was a good thing to do.

These and other developments in the scope and character of the welfare services did not happen in any planned or ordered sequence; nor were they a matter of deliberate intent. Some were pressed forward because of the needs of the war machine for more men and more work. Some took place almost by accident. Some were the result of a recognition of needs hitherto hidden by ignorance of social conditions. Some came about because war 'exposed weaknesses ruthlessly and brutally...which called for revolutionary changes in the economic and social life of the country.'...the evacuation of mothers and children and the bombing of homes during 1939–40 stimulated inquiry and proposals for reform long before victory was even thought possible. This was an important experience, for it meant that for five years of war the pressures for a higher standard of welfare and a deeper comprehension of social justice steadily gained in strength. And during this period, despite all the handicaps of limited resources in men and materials, a big expansion took place in the responsibilities accepted by the State for those in need.

The reality of military disaster and the threat of invasion in the summer of 1940 urged on these tendencies in social policy. The mood of the people changed and, in sympathetic response, values changed as well. If dangers were to be shared, then resources should also be shared. Dunkirk, and all that the name evokes, was an important event in the war-time history of the social services. It summoned forth a note of self-criticism, of national introspection, and it set in motion ideas and talk of principles and plans. *The Times*, in a remarkable leader [leading article] a few weeks after the evacuation of the British Expeditionary Force from the Continent, gave expression to these views. 'If we speak of democracy, we do not mean a democracy which maintains the right to vote but forgets the right to work and the right to live. If we speak of freedom, we do not mean a rugged individualism which excludes social organization and economic planning. If we speak of equality, we do not mean a political equality nullified by social and economic privilege. If we speak of economic reconstruction, we think less of maximum production (though this too will be required) than of equitable distribution.'

CHAPTER 10

THE INHUMANITY OF MAN

The Holocaust

THE FINAL SOLUTION A crematorium where the Nazis sought to dispose of the corpses of victims of the Holocaust.
Source: © Bettmann/CORBIS.

Death—through combat—is an inevitable part of war. Soldiers kill enemy soldiers as the most effective way to destroy their opponent's ability to wage war. Without death, there would be no victory, no peace, ironically, no life after any conflict. The Second World War, however, added a heinously chilling dimension to that reality, the Holocaust, in which the Nazis and their accomplices willingly and intentionally murdered millions of Jewish civilians. To that gruesome toll were added other innocent victims as well: ordinary Poles and Soviets, Jehovah's Witnesses, Freemasons, Gypsies (the Roma and Sinti), homosexuals, and the handicapped. These victims of religious, racial, sexual, and physical prejudice were vilified by the Nazis as weak, degenerate, and troublesome threats to

Germany's existence, and therefore unworthy of life and destined for elimination. Nazi attitudes were a lethal compound of social Darwinist, imperialist, militarist, and anti-Semitic impulses that had festered in the late nineteenth century and, in a troubled atmosphere of defeat and economic upheaval after 1918, metastasized to lend a ghastly urgency to growing fears of cultural and physical degeneration, of biological parasites and germs that would ravage the body politic and render Germany politically, culturally, and militarily impotent. If the Nazis did not invent these fears, they nevertheless ultimately played effectively upon them as an excuse to commit murder.

When Adolf Hitler and the NSDAP (Nazi Party) acceded to power on January 30, 1933, they set about laying the foundations for what the Führer envisioned as a "Thousand Year Reich." Slowly, carefully, and deviously the Nazis used both legitimate and illegal means to marginalize and dehumanize their "internal enemies." From early 1933 onward in the name of "racial purity," the Nazi state isolated, indeed demonized, those for whom there would be no place in the new Reich. Hitler reserved his greatest wrath for the Jews. His first response was to proceed by dubiously "legal" methods to legitimize discrimination. In 1935, the so-called Nuremberg Laws defined Jews not by religious practice but by "race," forbade Germans to shop at Jewish-owned stores, denied Jews the right to practice their professions, banned them from public places, outlawed marriage to or relations with "Aryan" Germans, and stripped them of their German citizenship. Emigration was at this point the preferred solution to the issue of unwanted Jews, and perhaps half of Germany's Jewish community left before the outbreak of the war.

Throughout the 1930s, Hitler and the Nazis employed violence to intimidate potential dissent into silence and break the social bonds that might sustain resistance. Concentration camps (*Konzentrationslager* or KZ) were erected, like Dachau, one of the first to be opened in March 1933, in which political opponents of the Nazi regime as well as "degenerates," that is, criminal elements and religious dissenters, were isolated from society and "reeducated" through hard labor, beatings, and torture. By 1935 concentration camps counted Jews among their prisoners as well. The prewar domestic reign of terror climaxed with the "Night of Broken Glass" or *Kristallnacht* (November 9–10, 1938) in which Germany's synagogues were desecrated and burned to the ground, and Jewish citizens beaten and robbed. By September 1939, when war finally came, the six-year record of the Nazi regime portended a bleak future for its opponents now that the last restraints of peace had faded.

Not only did the invasion of Poland on September 1 enable the Nazis to expand eastward to annex some of the *Lebensraum* (literally, "living space") they desired, it also afforded them the opportunity to put into practice their racialist ideology. Within a week, on September 7, Reinhard Heydrich, chief of the German Reich Security Main Office, instructed his SS (*Schutzstaffel*, Hitler's personal bodyguards) and special police units to "deal with" the members of the Polish intelligentsia and Catholic Church and to round up the Jews and confine them in ghettos in the larger cities. As a result, tens of thousands of Poles were murdered by the Nazis, while half a million Jews perished within the ghettos from forced labor, malnutrition, and disease. The ghettoization of eastern Europe's Jewry, however, was simply a stopgap measure, one that became all the more inadequate to the Nazis' purposes once the number of Jews under German control mushroomed with the rapid advance into Soviet territory from June 1941 onward under Operation Barbarossa. Despite further horrific initiatives, including the use of mobile gas units and widespread shootings of Jews in the forests, German anti-Semites had so far failed to find a sufficiently radical and total solution to their "Jewish question."

Moreover, in their developing war against the Jews, the Germans could count on the sympathy of some, and active assistance of others, as new territories came under their influence. Neither Poland nor the Ukraine, for example, had been immune to anti-Semitic attitudes or activities between the wars, and the latest conflict provided an opportunity for collaborators to come forward and act, even more brazenly and openly, on hatreds that had festered for generations. This pattern was repeated even in areas beyond the reach of the German military. In Palestine, the Grand Mufti of Jerusalem, Haj Amin al-Husseini, an ardent Pan-Arab nationalist, anti-Semite and Anglophobe, exploited Hitler's hatred of the Jews in the hope of expunging both British and Jewish influence from the Middle East. Al-Husseini helped to recruit Muslims (from Bosnia) for the Waffen-SS and influenced other Nazi sympathizers in the region. One of those men, Rashid Ali al-Kaylani (also known as Sayyad Rashid Ali al-Gillani), Iraq's prime minister during the 1930s, sanctioned a pogrom or *Farhud* on Baghdad's Jews in June 1941. On June 1, 1941, relatively peaceful relations between Muslims and Jews were interrupted by a *Kristallnacht*-style attack that left hundreds of Jews dead or injured, synagogues burned, and Jewish properties damaged. Al-Husseini's ultimate desire, to elicit from Germany a firm commitment to Arab independence, however, ultimately failed.

Within Europe, however, the success of the German military meant that the number of Jews under its control was escalating rapidly and exceeding its ability to deal with the situation through emigration, expulsion (wholesale transfer to Madagascar was briefly considered), confinement in ghettos, or ad hoc shootings and gassings. A more comprehensive and "efficient" approach was necessary. On December 12, 1941, the day after Germany declared war on the United States, Hitler privately commented in the Reich Chancellery that the moment had arrived to resolve the Jewish question without "sentimentality" or "pity." From the autumn of 1941 onward, the Nazis had initiated a program that in June 1942 would become known as Operation Reinhard. Named after SS General Reinhard Heydrich, chief of the Reich Security Main Office, who was assassinated by Czech partisans, and led by SS General Odilo Globcnik, the operation's objective was the deportation (euphemistically referred to as "resettlement") and murder of Polish Jews in newly constructed "killing centers"—Belzec, Sobibor, and Treblinka. These gas chambers and crematoria were established and operated by individuals who participated in the euthanasia program. On January 20, 1942, various officials met in the Berlin suburb of Wannsee to coordinate the deportation and eventual extermination of all of Europe's Jews. The "Final Solution" had begun.

Arriving daily in sealed train cars, some dead from asphyxiation, others barely clinging to life, Jews from across Europe entered the surreal world of Auschwitz-Birkenau, Chelmno, Majdanek, and other extermination camps located in Poland. There they were systematically gassed and their remains burned night and day in enormous furnaces that emitted a frightful stench. Jews and non-Jews alike also languished in forced labor camps where death was the only relief from unbearable labor conditions and malnutrition. In Germany, Buchenwald, Dachau, Dora/Mittelbau, Flossenbürg, Neuengamme, Ravensbrück, and Sachsenhausen served as labor camps; in Poland, Grossrosen and Plaszow; in Austria, Mauthausen; in France, Natzweiler/Struthof; and in Latvia, Kaiserwald. Transit and holding camps were located in Germany: Bergenbelsen, Oranienburg; in Czechoslovakia: Theresienstadt; and in the Netherlands: Westerbork.

While some 6 million Jews died in the Holocaust at the hands of the Nazis and their collaborators, some tens of thousands of righteous Gentiles risked their own lives to save as many Jews as possible. Some of these individuals' names are familiar to us, like the Swedish diplomat Raoul Wallenberg, who may have saved half of Budapest's Jews from the gas chambers; Oskar Schindler, the ethnic German industrialist whose business acumen and sheer humanity protected over 1,000 Jews in Poland by employing them in his factories; and Jan Karski (Jan Kosielewski), a courier for the Polish underground who brought firsthand information about the Holocaust to the West. Others are lesser known. Father Bruno (Henri Reynders), a Belgian Benedictine monk, established a clandestine network to hide Jewish children in Belgian abbeys to prevent them from being deported to the death camps. Abdol Hossein Sardari, a young Iranian politician in Paris, saved the lives of Iranian Jews resident in France, and some French Jews as well, to whom he issued Iranian passports. Sir Nicholas Winton, a British stockbroker, who, while on holiday in Prague, Czechoslovakia, rescued 669 Czech children before they were to have been taken to Nazi death camps. Of course, there were many others, ordinary civilians from various religious backgrounds and countries, whose courageous actions provided shelter, hope, and inspiration.

DEFINING GENOCIDE

The lawyer, human rights advocate, and linguist Raphael Lemkin, who had been born in Poland in 1900 to Jewish parents, became aware of the mistreatment of minorities as a young man. Following his studies at universities in both Poland and Germany, Lemkin accepted a position as a public prosecutor in Warsaw where he wrote books on law and helped to codify Polish penal codes. His contempt for ethnic cleansing, first aroused by the cruelties suffered by Armenians at the hands of the Turks in 1915, led him to urge the League of Nations in 1933 to prevent crimes perpetrated against any national, religious, and racial groups by banning mass slaughter. Lemkin's suggestion, however, was rejected, and his career was actually jeopardized by his bold stand. Upon Germany's invasion of Poland in 1939, Lemkin joined an underground movement in Poland's forests and in 1940 escaped to Sweden, where he lectured at the University of Stockholm and obtained for safekeeping copies of Nazi directives issued to occupied countries. Upon his arrival in the United States in 1941, Lemkin turned over the directives to the State and War Departments and, thanks to the assistance of an American colleague with whom he collaborated on a project in the early 1930s, began lecturing at Duke University. Between 1941 and 1943, Lemkin wrote *Axis Rule in Occupied Europe*, which was based upon his earlier attempts to warn the world about the dangers of allowing "genocide"—a word he coined from the Greek *genos*, meaning "race," and the Latin *cide*, meaning "killing"—to go unpunished. After the war he served as an advisor to Robert Jackson, the Nuremberg Trial judge, and worked arduously for the adoption by the United Nations of a treaty condemning genocide. Lemkin died in August 1959 after suffering a heart attack.

By "genocide" we mean the destruction of a nation or of an ethnic group. This word, coined by the author to denote an old practice in its modern development, is made from the ancient Greek word *genos* (race, tribe) and the Latin *cide* (killing)....Generally speaking, genocide does not necessarily mean the immediate destruction of a nation, except when accomplished by mass killings of all members of a nation. It is intended rather to signify a coordinated plan of different actions aiming at the destruction of essential foundations of the life of national groups, with the aim of annihilating the groups themselves. The objectives of such a plan would be disintegration of the political and social institutions, of culture, language, national feelings, religion, and the economic existence of national groups, and the destruction of the personal security, liberty, health, dignity, and even the lives of the individuals belonging to such groups. Genocide is directed against the national group as an entity, and the actions involved are directed against individuals, not in their individual capacity, but as members of the national group....

Genocide has two phases: one, destruction of the national pattern of the oppressed group; the other, the imposition of the national pattern of the oppressor. This imposition, in turn, may be made upon the

Reprinted by permission of the publisher from *Axis Rule in Occupied Europe*, Raphael Lemkin (Washington, DC: Carnegie Endowment for International Peace, 1944), 79–90. www.carnegieendowment.org.

oppressed population which is allowed to remain, or upon the territory alone, after removal of the population and the colonization of the area by the oppressor's own nationals. Denationalization was the word used in the past to describe the destruction of a national pattern. The author believes, however, that this word is inadequate because: (1) it does not connote the destruction of the biological structure; (2) in connoting the destruction of one national pattern, it does not connote the imposition of the national pattern of the oppressor; and (3) the denationalization is used by some authors to mean only deprivation of citizenship....

The techniques of genocide, which the German occupant has developed in the various occupied countries, represent a concentrated and coordinated attack upon all elements of nationhood. Accordingly, genocide is being carried out in the following fields:

POLITICAL

In...western Poland,...Luxemburg, and Alsace-Lorraine, local institutions of self-government were destroyed and a German pattern of administration imposed. Every reminder of former national character was obliterated. Even commercial signs and inscriptions on buildings, roads, and streets, as well as names of communities and of localities, were changed to a German form....

Special Commissioners for the Strengthening of Germanism are attached to the administration, and their task consists in coordinating all actions promoting Germanism in a given area. An especially active role in this respect is played by inhabitants of German origin who were living in the occupied countries before the occupation. After having accomplished their task as members of the so-called fifth column, they formed the nucleus of Germanism....

In order further to disrupt national unity, Nazi party organizations were established,...and their members from the local populations were given political privileges. Other political parties were dissolved....

In line with this policy of imposing the German national pattern, particularly in the incorporated

territories, the occupant has organized a system of colonization of these areas. In western Poland, especially, this has been done on a large scale. The Polish population has been removed from their homes in order to make place for German settlers who were brought in from the Baltic States, the central and eastern districts of Poland, Bessarabia, and from the Reich itself. The properties and homes of the Poles are being allocated to German settlers....

SOCIAL

The destruction of the national pattern in the social field has been accomplished in part by the abolition of local law and local courts and the imposition of German law and courts, and also by Germanization of the judicial language and of the bar. The social structure of a nation being vital to its national development, the occupant also endeavors to bring about such changes as may weaken the national spiritual resources. The focal point of this attack has been the intelligentsia, because this group largely provides national leadership and organizes resistance against Nazification. This is especially true in Poland and Slovenia [Slovene part of Yugoslavia], where the intelligentsia and the clergy were in great part removed from the rest of the population and deported for forced labor in Germany. The tendency of the occupant is to retain in Poland only the laboring and peasant class, while in the western occupied countries the industrialist class is also allowed to remain, since it can aid in integrating the local industries with the German war economy.

CULTURAL

In the incorporated areas the local population is forbidden to use its own language in schools and in printing....German teachers were introduced into the schools and they were compelled to teach according to the principles of National Socialism....

In order to prevent the expression of the national spirit through artistic media, a rigid control of all cultural activities has been introduced. All persons engaged in painting, drawing, sculpture, music, literature, and the theater are required to obtain a license for the continuation of their activities....Everyone of these activities is controlled through a special chamber and all these chambers are controlled by one chamber, which is called the Reich Chamber of Culture (*Reichskulturkammer*). The local chambers of culture are presided over by the propaganda chief of the National Socialist Party in the given area. Not only have national creative activities in the cultural and artistic field been rendered impossible by regimentation, but the population has also been deprived of inspiration from the existing cultural and artistic values....

ECONOMIC

The destruction of the foundations of the economic existence of a national group necessarily brings about a crippling of its development, even a retrogression. The lowering of the standard of living creates difficulties in fulfilling cultural-spiritual requirements. Furthermore, a daily fight literally for bread and for physical survival may handicap thinking in both general and national terms.

It was the purpose of the occupant to create such conditions as these among the peoples of the occupied countries, especially those peoples embraced in the first plans of genocide elaborated by him—the Poles, the Slovenes, and the Jews....

Participation in economic life is thus made dependent upon one's being German or being devoted to the cause of Germanism....

BIOLOGICAL

In the occupied countries "people of non-related blood," a policy of depopulation is pursued. Foremost among the methods employed for this purpose is the adoption of measures calculated to decrease the birthrate of the national groups of non-related blood, while at the same time steps are taken to encourage the birthrate of the *Volksdeutsche* living in these countries....

The birthrate of the undesired group is being further decreased as a result of the separation of males from females by deporting them for forced labor elsewhere. Moreover, the undernourishment of the parents, because of discrimination in rationing, brings about not only a lowering of the birthrate, but a lowering of the survival capacity of children born of underfed parents....

[T]he occupant is endeavoring to encourage the birthrate of the Germans. Different methods are adopted to that end. Special subsidies are provided in Poland for German families having at least three minor children. Because the Dutch and Norwegians are considered of related blood, the bearing, by Dutch and Norwegian women, of illegitimate children begotten by German military men is encouraged by subsidy....

PHYSICAL

The physical debilitation and even annihilation of national groups in occupied countries is carried out mainly in the following ways:

1. Racial Discrimination in Feeding

Rationing of food is organized according to racial principles throughout the occupied countries. "The German people come before all other peoples for food," declared Reich Minister Goering on October 4, 1942. In accordance with this program, the German population is getting 93 per cent of its pre-war diet, while those in the occupied territories receive much less: in Warsaw, for example, the Poles receive 66 per cent of the pre-war rations and the Jews only 20 per cent....

The result of racial feeding is a decline in health of the nations involved and an increase in the deathrate. In Warsaw, anemia rose 113 per cent among Poles and 435 among Jews. The deathrate per thousand in 1941 amounted in the Netherlands to 10 per cent; in Belgium to 14.5 per cent; in Bohemia and Moravia to 13.4....

2. Endangering of Health

The undesired national groups, particularly in Poland, are deprived of elemental necessities for preserving health and life. This latter method consists, for example, of requisitioning warm clothing and blankets in the winter and withholding firewood and medicine. During the winter of 1940–41, only a single room in a house could be heated in the Warsaw ghetto, and children had to take turns in warming themselves there. No fuel at all has been received since then by the Jews in the ghetto.

Moreover, the Jews in the ghetto are crowded together under conditions of housing inimical to health, and in being denied the use of public parks they are even deprived of the right to fresh air. Such measures, especially pernicious to the health of children, have caused the development of various diseases. The transfer, in unheated cattle trucks and freight cars, of hundreds of thousands of Poles from Incorporated Poland to the Government General, which took place in the midst of a severe winter, resulted in a decimation of the expelled Poles.

3. Mass Killings

The technique of mass killings is employed mainly against Poles, Russians, and Jews, as well as against leading personalities from the non-collaborationist groups in all the occupied countries. In Poland, Bohemia-Moravia, and Slovenia, the intellectuals are being "liquidated" because they have always been considered the main bearers of national ideals and at the time of occupation they were especially suspected of being the organizers of resistance. The Jews for the most part are liquidated within the ghettos, or in special trains in which they are transported to a so-called "unknown" destination....

RELIGIOUS

In Luxemburg, where the population is predominantly Catholic and religion plays an important role in national life, especially in the field of education, the occupant has tried to disrupt these national and religious influences. Children over fourteen years of age were permitted by legislation to renounce their religious affiliations for the occupant was eager to enroll such children exclusively in pro-Nazi youth organizations....Likewise in Poland, through the systematic pillage and destruction of church property and persecution of the clergy, the German occupying authorities have sought to destroy the religious leadership of the Polish nation.

MORAL

In order to weaken the spiritual resistance of the national group, the occupant attempts to create an atmosphere of moral debasement within this group. According to this plan, the mental energy of the group should be concentrated upon base instincts and should be diverted from moral and national thinking. It is important for the realization of such a plan that the desire for cheap individual pleasure be substituted for the desire for collective feelings and ideals based upon a higher morality....

EUTHANASIA

Senior colonel in the SS and the chief administrative officer in the Führer's Chancellery, Viktor Hermann Brack (1904–1948), along with Philip Bouhler, ran Hitler's secret euthanasia program, Operation T4, which was responsible for the deaths of thousands of innocent handicapped Germans by gassing. Beginning in the summer of 1939, Brack, along with Bouhler, set into motion a program ordered by Hitler to remove "physically impure" German children, an estimated 5,000 of which were taken to special pediatric clinics throughout Germany and Austria and murdered by starvation and by lethal injection of medication. In the autumn of 1939, orders were given to extend the program to adults. Before any official program was under way, SS units in occupied Poland in October 1939 shot some 4,000 mental patients in asylums and, between December 1939 and January 1940, gassed 1,558 patients in special mobile vans. These "successes" led to the implementation in April 1940 of the so-called Aktion T-4, named for the house at Tiergarten Strasse 4 in Berlin. Brack and his associates reviewed medical information on all asylum inmates and instances of birth deformities, generating forms marked with recommendations (+ to be killed; – to be granted a reprieve). Vans arrived at asylums ostensibly to transfer patients, but the unfortunate victims were gassed instead. From the end of 1939 until August 1940, at least 70,000 psychiatric patients within the German Reich were murdered. Brack was arrested after the war and tried by military tribunal at Nuremberg. The document that follows is a translation of Brack's deposition, given to Allied interrogators on October 14, 1946. Two years later, he was convicted and hanged.

1. I was born in Haaren, Germany, on November 9, 1904....In December 1929 I joined the NSDAP and at the same time the SS....In 1934...I was appointed...Chief of Staff (Stabsleiter) [chief of staff to Reichsleiter Bouhler] and later, in 1936, Chief of Department II of this office, located in Berlin. In accordance with my position, I held the title of *Reichsleiter* [Reich Leader, high-ranking Nazi office appointed by Hitler]. In this capacity, my duties were of administrative nature and personal representative to Bouhler as far as Department II was concerned.

2. By reason of this position and because of my personal contact with Bouhler, I obtained knowledge of the details of many of the activities in which Bouhler and various other high ranking personalities participated....Due to my position, I gained complete knowledge of the Euthanasia Program (Mercy Killing Program)....

THE EUTHANASIA PROGRAM

4. The Euthanasia Program was initiated in the Summer of 1939. Hitler issued a secret order to Prof. Dr. Karl Brandt, Reich Commissioner for Medical and Health Matters, and at that time personal physician to the Fuehrer, and to Phillip Bouhler, charging them with responsibility for the killing of human beings

---

Hermann Brack, "Testimony to Euthanasia and Forced Sterilization," in *The Nuremberg Trials* (*USA v. Karl Brandt et al.*), Document #426, Prosecution Document Book #6, Office of U.S. Chief Counsel. Used by permission.

who were not able to ? [illegible word], that is, the according of a mercy death to incurably insane persons.... On the basis of this order of Hitler, Bouhler and Brandt were to select doctors to carry out this program....

THE PROCEDURE

9. By order of Dr. Linden [from the Ministry of Interior], the directors of all insane asylums in the Reich had to fill out questionnaires for each patient within their institutions.... Then the questionnaires were forwarded to the Ministry of Interior to be distributed to the similar institutions.... The program was so arranged that photostats of each questionnaire were to be sent to four experts to determine the status of each patient.... Each of these experts [marked]... whether or not the patient could be transferred to an observation institution and eventually killed. Then the questionnaire was forwarded to a chief expert... [T]he chief expert also marked the questionnaire and then submitted it to Dr. Linden who ordered the insane asylum to transfer the patient to one of the observation institutions... Eglfing-Haar, Kempten, Jen, Buch Arnsberg.

10. At these institutions the patients were under observation of the doctor in charge for a period of from one to three months. The physician had the right to exempt the patient from the program if he decided that the patient was not incurable. If he agreed with the opinion of the chief expert, the patient was transferred to a so-called Euthanasia Institution. I can recall the names of the Euthanasia Institutions:

Grafeneck—under Dr. Schumann
Brandenburg—under Dr. Hannecke
Hartheim—under Dr. Rennaux
Sonnenstein—under Dr. Schmalenbach
Hadamar (I do not remember under whose leadership)
Berburg—under Dr. Behnke or Dr. Becker

In these institutions the patient was killed by means of gas by the doctor in charge. To the best of my knowledge, about fifty to sixty thousand persons were killed in this way in the period from Autumn 1939 to the Summer of 1941.

11. The order issued by the Fuehrer to Brandt and Bouhler was secret and never published. The Euthanasia Program itself was kept as secret as possible, and for this reason, relatives of persons killed in the course of the program were never told the real cause of death. The death certificates issued to the relatives carried fictitious causes of death such as heart failure. All persons subjected to the Euthanasia Program did not have an opportunity to decide whether they wanted a mercy death, nor their relatives contacted for approval or disapproval. The decision was purely within the discretion of the doctors....

12. Hitler's ultimate reason for the establishment of the Euthanasia Program in Germany was to eliminate those people confined to insane asylums and similar institutions who could no longer be of use to the Reich. They were considered useless eaters and Hitler felt that by exterminating these so-called useless eaters, it would be possible to relieve more doctors, male and female nurses, and other personnel, hospital beds and other facilities for the use of the Armed Forces.

REICH COMMITTEE FOR RESEARCH ON HEREDITARY DISEASES AND CONSTITUTIONAL SUSCEPTIBILITY TO SEVERE DISEASES

13. This committee, which was also a function of the Euthanasia Program, was an organization for the killing of children who were born mentally deficient or bodily deformed. All physicians assisting at births, midwives, and maternity hospitals were ordered by the Ministry of Interior to report such cases to the office of Dr. Linden in the Ministry of Interior. The experts in the medical section of Dr. Brandt's office were ordered to give their opinions in each case.... In many cases these children were to be operated upon in such a manner that the result was either complete recovery or death. Death resulted in a majority of these cases. The program was inaugurated in the summer of 1939. Bouhler told me that Dr. Linden had the order to ask for the consent of the parents of each child concerned. I do not know how long this program continued since I joined the Waffen-SS in 1942.

14. In 1941, I received an oral order to discontinue the Euthanasia Program. I received this order either from Bouhler or from Dr. Brandt. In order to preserve this personnel relieved of these duties and to have the opportunity of starting a new Euthanasia Program after the war, Bouhler requested, I think after a conference with Himmler, that I send this personnel to Lublin and put it at the disposal of SS Brigadefuehrer Globocnik [Odilo Globocnik, head of Aktion Reinhard and Himmler's immediate subordinate, was the administrator responsible for liquidation of Polish Jewry in the Warsaw and Bialystok ghettos as well as the deportation and extermination of European Jewry via concentration camps]. I then had the impression that these people were to be used in the extensive Jewish labor camps run by Globocnik. Later, however, at the end of 1942 or the beginning of 1943, I found out that they were used to assist in the mass extermination of the Jews, which was then already common knowledge in higher party circles.

15. Among the doctors who assisted in the Jewish extermination program, were Eberle and Schumann. Schumann performed medical experiments on prisoners in Auschwitz....The order to send these men to the East could have been given only by Himmler to Brandt, possibly through Bouhler.

THE STERILIZATION PROGRAM

16. In 1941, it was an "open secret" in high party circles that the powers that be intended to exterminate the entire Jewish population of Germany and the occupied countries. I and my collaborators, especially Dr. Hevelmann and Blankenburg, considered this intention of the party leaders not worthy of the German nation and mankind in general. Therefore, we decided to find another solution to the Jewish problem which would tend to be less radical than complete extermination of a race. We developed the idea to deport all Jews to a far-off place and I can recall that Dr. Hevelmann suggested the island of Madagascar for this purpose. In my office, we drafted such a plan and submitted it to Bouhler. Obviously, this plan was not acceptable, so we reached the conclusion that sterilization would be the answer to the Jewish problem. Since sterilization would be a complex program, we thought of sterilization by means of X-rays. In 1941, I proposed the sterilization of Jews by means of X-rays to Bouhler, but it was not accepted. Bouhler told me that such a program of sterilization by means of X-rays would not be feasible as Hitler was against it. I continued to work on this program and eventually submitted a new project to the Reichsfuehrer SS, Heinrich Himmler. Dr. Hevelmann submitted a report which indicated that the sterilization of human beings by means of X-rays was medically impossible....I do not know whether the sterilization of the Jews was actually carried out because, as I said before, I joined the Waffen-SS and had no further dealings with this matter.

ATROCITIES IN KAMENETS-PODOLSKY

Before the Wannsee Conference of January 20, 1942, paved the way for the annihilation of the Jews of Europe via concentration camps, the process of extermination was already under way by the spring of 1941 with the creation of Einsatzgruppen. The purpose of these units from the Security Services (*Sicherheitsdienst* or SD), likely established around the time plans were being made for Operation Barbarossa and answering directly to Himmler and Heydrich, was the murder of Jews, Gypsies, and Russian political commissars in the eastern territories. The Einsatzgruppen rounded up their victims, transported them to a central place, and then shot them. Mass shootings, often assisted by local anti-Semitic accomplices, occurred on a large scale throughout eastern Europe.

In July 1941, Hungary entered the war on the Axis side after Russia supposedly bombed the northern Hungarian town of Kassa. The attack on the town, however, may have been perpetrated by German forces eager to involve Hungary in the war so as to attain access to Romanian oil fields. The Arrow Cross, Hungary's most prominent fascist faction, welcomed its countrymen's entry on Germany's side and were eager to "deal" with the thousands of Jews who escaped to Hungary from German-occupied territories in Poland, Austria, Slovakia, and other Czech territories, as well as contend with the native Hungarian Jewish population. Jews were rounded up and transported over the border to the Kamenets-Podolsky (Ukraine), where they were eventually marched to the nearby forests and shot en masse by SS units. Over a three-day period in late August, more than 23,600 Jews were killed, making this the first large-scale massacre of Jews reaching a five-digit figure. So as to document their own experiences and that of fellow Jews in eastern Europe during World War II, Ilya Ehrenburg and Vasily Grossman, both war correspondents for the Red Army, compiled *The Black Book* in 1944 and 1945. It was originally published in Yiddish under the title *Murder of the People*. The following excerpt details some of the atrocities committed at Kamenets-Podolsky against the Jews in 1941 and 1942.

The preparation for the shooting of the Jewish population, without a doubt, was done ahead of time. And, as I later learned, it consisted of the following:

1. The concentration of the Jewish population.
2. The designation of the Jewish apartments (houses).
3. A compilation of precise lists.
4. The assembling of Jews from the different populated areas.
5. The selection of the day and place of the shooting....

Of the mass shootings of the Jewish population of citizens of the U.S.S.R. at Kamenets-Podolsky, which occurred in 1942, I am personally aware of two.

While serving with the gendarmery in Kamenets-Podolsky as company commander of the police squad, I participated with my subordinates for the first time in the mass shooting of the Jewish population of the

Captain Salog, "The Atrocities in Kamenets-Podolsky," in Ilya Ehrenburg and Vasily Grossman, *The Black Book*, trans. by John Glad and James S. Levine (New York: Holocaust Library, 1980), 529–537. Used by permission.

cities of Staraya Ushitsa and Studenitsa in August–September, 1942, and a second time in Kamenets-Podolsky. A mass shooting was carried out in the area of the Cossack barracks (the training Battalion) in November, 1942.

As the company commander, on the evening preceding the day of the shooting, I was ordered by the chief of the gendarmery, Lieutenant Reich, through the commander of the first company, Krubasik, to call out about fifty policemen from my company....

The order was given to take ten cartridges for each rifle plus a machine-gun cartridge belt in reserve. In addition, a portable machine gun and three automatic rifles were taken. About ten to twelve gendarmes and about fifty policemen...drove out. Members of the S.D. and of the criminal police drove out independently....

About one to one-and-one half kilometers before Staraya Ushitsa the vehicles were stopped, and the policemen were lined up. There Lieutenant Reich announced the purpose of the trip and its mission—to assemble the entire Jewish population of Staraya Ushitsa and Studenitsa and to deliver the Jews to a place of execution which was there, not far from the highway.

The entire Jewish population of Staraya Ushitsa was assembled in a square which was cordoned off by gendarmes and the police staff. All the males (adults and children, except for infants) were separated from the women, right there on the square. They were all ordered to sit down on the ground and not to speak to one another.

Attempts at conversation were stopped by a pre-emptory shout and a blow with a rifle butt or club.

The Chief of the S.D. and the chief of the gendarmery announced to the Jews that they were going to Kamenets-Podolsky....

The column's guard was organized this way: in front walked two gendarmes, five to seven steps from the first row of the column of Jews, on the sides there were about thirty to thirty-five policemen....

The false claim that the Jews were being taken to Kamenets-Podolsky was repeated several times throughout the journey....

The moment the column turned toward the pit there was a general outcry. No shouts, rifle-butting,

or kicks could stop these cries. The penetrating, shrill cries of the women were interwoven with the children's crying and the requests of the children for their mothers to take them in their arms....

The pit was approximately twelve by six meters and about one-and-a-half meters deep. On the side that was closer to Kamenets-Podolsky, the pit's entrance was about two meters wide, with a slope to the bottom, along which the condemned walked.

At this last part of their journey, the Jews, seeing that the order to send them to Kamenets-Podolsky was a deception, began to throw out cigarette cases, rings, and earrings. They ripped up documents, photographs, letters, papers with notes, and other things....

Fifteen to twenty meters from the pit...stood the closely packed mass of people who were condemned to death. Everyone, including the women and children, were stripped naked. Urged on by blows, five people at a time were directed to the pit.

Near the pit also stood several gendarmes who, in their turn, prodded the people with blows from their clubs or rifle butts into the pit toward the executioner. The executioner, whose first name was Paul (I don't know his surname), drank a fair amount of schnapps and ordered the victims to lie face down at the side of the pit opposite the entrance. The victims were killed with a point-blank shot in the back of the head. The following group of five lay down with their heads on the corpses of their fellow-Jews and were killed the same way....Standing over the top of the pit was a marker, a member of the criminal police; he marked off each group of five with a small cross.

The truth is that there were often instances when instead of five people, a family of six to eight people, in spite of orders to the contrary, and of being beaten half to death for a distance of fifteen to twenty meters, would nevertheless walk to the pit together; but the same small cross was written down just as if there had been only five people.

Not far from the pit stood the chief of the gendarmery, Lieutenant Reich, the chief of the S.D., whose surname I do not know, and commissar Reindl; during the course of the executions they would issue commands. In the interval between commands they encouraged their subordinates, sometimes laughing at successful blows which landed in great numbers on the heads and backs of the Jews who were already dazed; otherwise, they just stood stonefaced, silently watching the picture of the extermination. Sometimes they would turn away from the pit, put their hands in their pockets, and talk quietly about something among themselves....

Among the old men and women there were some who lost their senses. These people with wide-open, crazed eyes, paying no attention to the blows, walked on slowly, with their arms hanging at the side, stumbled, fell, got up again, and reaching the executioner, then stopped, stood stupefied, without saying a word or making a single movement. Only a forceful push from an automatic rifle or a kick from the executioner would get one of these victims to the bottom of the pit.

The small children, who were forcibly separated from their mothers, were thrown into the pit by the gendarmes up above....

Among the women there were no attempts to escape. While undressing, the condemned Jews ripped their good shoes and clothes to pieces and hid their valuables in the ground. The experienced members of the S.D., however, were on the alert for this and stopped the attempts to destroy valuables. The valuables covered up with soil or grass were handed over to a special collector—one of the S.D. persons.

Families, relatives, even acquaintances, when saying good-bye, shook each other's hands and kissed. Sometimes people, having embraced in a farewell kiss, stood several seconds under a shower of blows and pressed tightly one against the other, the whole family, carrying the children in their arms, walked to the pit....

Under the supervision of an S.D. man, the policemen began to shake and examine the clothes and shoes of those who had been shot. The clothes were examined with particular care. This was done because in the pleats of the clothes, in the linings, in the waist-bands of trousers they hoped to find valuables.

All valuables were put in a sack which was kept by an S.D. man....

New articles—dresses, kerchiefs, boots, shoes, coats as well as unfinished garments—were taken by the people who participated in the execution. Sometimes they tore things from each other's hands and argued violently.

Thus, on this day about four hundred citizens of the Soviet Union were shot—men and women of all ages, as well as children. The execution continued for approximately four hours (from 7:00 or 8:00 to 11:00 or 12:00).

THE YOUNGEST VICTIMS

Occasionally, conflict arose between the cold-blooded executioners (*Sonderkommando* and the SS) and the army regarding the treatment of the impending victims, especially when children were concerned. One notable incident occurred in mid-August 1941 following the murder of nearly 700 Jews at Bila (Bjelaja) Tserkva in the Ukraine near Kiev. About 90 young orphans (many of whom were infants) survived the massacre, only to be quarantined in a stifling hot building while awaiting their death sentence, guarded by young Ukrainian militiamen armed with clubs and rifles and close to some German soldiers. When some soldiers complained about the children's piercing shrieks, they called upon their military chaplains to investigate the conditions in which the children were being held. The protests of the chaplains (one Protestant, one Catholic) reached the General Staff Officer of the 295th Infantry Division, Lieutenant Colonel Helmuth Groscurth (1898–1943), who personally visited the children. Disturbed by what he saw, Groscurth wrote a report that reached the Commander of the Sixth Army, Field Marshal von Reichenau. Field Commander Riedl hosted a meeting with Paul Blobel (1894–1951), SS *Standartenführer*, commander of SK4a of Einsatzgruppen C [a mobile killing squad in the Ukraine subsequently responsible for carrying out the massacre at Babi Yar in Kiev], intelligence officer SS Obersturmführer August Haefner, Captain Luley, and Groscurth to discuss the "problems" in the operation that led to unnecessary sentimentality among the soldiers and clergymen. Groscurth's intervention, however, caused only a brief delay in the killing of the children, and the SS subsequently found more "orderly" ways in which to deal with eliminating young children.

On 20 August [1941] at 4:00 o'clock in the afternoon the two divisional clergymen reported to me about a house in the city in which approximately ninety Jewish children, who had been denied any food or water for about twenty-four hours, were located. They did so based upon the information of the clergyman of the military hospital who witnessed the conditions. They were intolerable; the attempt to have the local commander intervene, remained unsuccessful. The divisional clergyman reported that the conditions required an immediate remedy, that countless soldiers inspected the house and that the sanitary conditions were life-threatening, as a chief physician also confirmed.

As a result of this report I went with the Ordinance Officer, First Lieutenant Spoerhase, the divisional clergyman, Dr. Reuss, and the translator, specialist Tischuk, to the house that was set back about 50 meters [over 150 feet] from the street on a side street. The house was visible from the street; the whining of the children audible. About twenty non-commissioned officers and soldiers were in the courtyard. There were no guards in front of the house. A few armed Ukrainians stood around the courtyard. Children lay on the window-sills; the windows were not open. In the entrance hall of the first floor was a Ukrainian guard, who immediately opened the door to the room in which the children were housed. In the three adjoining rooms were

Helmut Krausnick and Harold C. Deutsch, eds., Helmuth Groscurth, *Tagebücher eines Abwehroffiziers, 1938–1940* (Stuttgart: Deutsche Verlags-Anstalt, 1970), 534–537. Used by permission.

*Translated by Marilyn Shevin-Coetzee.

additional Ukrainian guards with weapons. The room was filled with approximately ninety children and more women. In the lowest room, in which there were almost only infants, a woman was cleaning herself. An indescribable filth pervaded the remaining rooms; rags, diapers, rubbish lay all around. Countless flies covered the partially-naked children. Almost all the children were crying or whimpering. The stench was unbearable. A German-speaking woman maintained that she was completely innocent, never was interested in politics and wasn't Jewish. In the meanwhile a Oberscharführer [senior squad leader] of the SD came in, whom I asked what would become of the children. He admitted that the families of the children would be shot and that the children also should be done away with. I left without comment to see the local commander and demanded an explanation from him. He declared himself powerless; he had no influence upon the well-known decisions of the SD [and] proposed that I take the opportunity to speak with Field Commander, Lieutenant Colonel Riedl. I went to speak with the local commander and the ordinance officer. The Field Commander admitted that the leader of the Special Commandos had been by him, instructed him about his task and carried it out with the knowledge of the Field Commander. He had no influence on the decisions of the Obersturmführer. I asked the Field Commander whether he believed that the Obersturmführer received the order also from the highest rank to do away with the children....Thereupon I demanded that the area surrounding the house be cordoned off so that the troops would be unable to observe the process....I demanded further that the implementation of the transportation to the shooting must proceed inconspicuously. I declared myself ready to place troops of the division at the disposal should the guard strength of the Field Command Headquarters be insufficient. I declared further that I would instruct the army group about a decision whether the shooting of the children would be carried out. (Upon the instruction of the Field Commanders a number of children had already been done away with the day before and, no doubt, by the Ukrainian militia

upon the order of the SD.) The Field Commander consented....He wanted to stop the implementation of further measures until the army group made a decision [and] demanded a written order. I hesitated to interrupt the order because I assumed that the transport of the children would occur at night and until then a decision would be proposed by the army....The Field Commander explained, however, that the transport would happen shortly. Thereupon I ordered that the Field Commander should inform the head of the Special Commandos that he delay the transport until the army made a decision....

On 21 August at 11:00 a.m. Captain Luley appeared with Colonel [Standartenführer] of the SS Blobel....Before his arrival at the Division Captain Luley had viewed the village but without entering the house and the accommodations [where] the children were kept....

Captain Luley maintained that he was indeed an evangelical Christian but considered it better if the pastor concerned himself with the souls of the soldiers [and not the Jews]....Later in the course of the conversation the Field Commander took the opportunity to direct [it] to the ideological sphere and a discussion of the fundamental questions. He explained that he considered the extermination of the Jewish women and children an urgent necessity, regardless in what form it occurred. He emphasized repeatedly that...the removal of the children had been unnecessarily delayed twenty-four hours. The SS Colonel concurred with this opinion and added that it would be best if the troops, that snooped/spied, undertake the executions themselves and that the commander, who detained the measure [the execution], himself assume command of these troops. I rejected this demand in a calm manner, without commenting on it, so I could avoid any personal attacks....

Thereupon the specifics of the execution were established. They were supposed to follow on the 22nd at 8:00 p.m. I did not participate more in the specifics of this discussion. My request for the troops to stay away [from the execution] was carried out.

WANNSEE CONFERENCE

On January 20, 1942, senior officials of the Nazi regime met in the Berlin suburb of Wannsee to discuss a "final solution" of the Jewish question. Six months earlier, in July 1941, a euphoric Hitler had surveyed the string of German victories in Operation Barbarossa's opening stages and pledged to create a "German Garden of Eden" for German settlers in the conquered territories in the western reaches of the Soviet Union. But such "aspirations" were incompatible with the rapidly growing number of Jews (potentially an additional 4 million) coming under German control as Hitler's forces raced eastward. In accordance with Hitler's stated racial imperatives, they would have to be removed, "one way or another." On July 31, 1941, Hermann Göring directed Reinhard Heydrich (1904–1942), the chief of the Reich Security Main Office (RSHA), to make the necessary preparations for a radical solution entailing the complete removal of Jews from Germany and occupied countries and their deportation to camps in the East. Heydrich recognized that there were now too many Jews for German units simply to shoot them all (and, under such appalling circumstances, there had been difficulties with morale and the expenditure of ammunition). Once the German advance ground to a halt without capturing Moscow, the euphoria of the summer faded for good; neither territorial gains nor food supplies would be inexhaustible, and the momentum shifted from evacuation to extermination. Yet to assemble and transport millions of people, in the midst of war, with rail timetables and rolling stock already stretched thin by the logistical requirements of the army, was a formidable task. That is why Heydrich assembled representatives from various government agencies or departments (such as the Interior, Chancellery, Justice, Occupied eastern territories, and General Government in Poland) to brief them on what needed to be done. Within Germany itself, there would be potential problems in the roundup, so Heydrich devoted some time to explaining the legal definitions of who would be liable for deportation as a Jew (for most of the Jews of occupied Europe, such fine distinctions were irrelevant). Historians have suggested that not only did Heydrich organize the Wannsee Conference to help coordinate this massive undertaking, but he also sought to stake out his own authority (and that of his boss, Himmler) to oversee the extermination of the Jews. Adolf Eichmann (1906–1962) of the RSHA was ordered to take notes and produce a sanitized version (using euphemisms for killing), copies of which were then distributed to the participants. Fortunately, one of those copies survived and affords us a chilling look at the way genocide was to be instituted across a continent. Perhaps equally chilling is that not one word of dissent, skepticism, or regret was uttered; indeed, after the meeting, the participants continued a more frank discussion over cognac and brandy.

Adolf Eichmann, "Minutes from the Wannsee Conference, The Final Solution: January 20, 1942," in Jeremy Noakes and Geoffrey Pridham, eds., *Nazism, 1919–1945*, vol. 3 (Exeter: University of Exeter Press, 1988), 1127–1128, 1131–1134. Used by permission of University of Exeter Press.

The Chief of the Security Police and SD [Sicherheitsdienst, Security Service], SS Obergruppenführer Heydrich, began by announcing his appointment by the Reich Marshal as the person responsible for the preparation of the final solution of the European Jewish question and pointed out that this meeting was being held to achieve clarity in basic questions. The Reich Marshal's wish that he should be sent a draft on the organizational, technical, and material matters regarding the final solution of the European Jewish question made it necessary that all central authorities directly concerned with these questions should deal with them together in advance so as to ensure the coordination of the lines to be taken.

The supervision of the final solution was, regardless of geographical boundaries, centralized in the hands of the Reichsführer SS and Chief of the German Police (Chief of the Security Police and SD).

The Chief of the Security Police and SD then gave a brief review of the struggle which had been waged hitherto against these opponents. The basic elements were: (a) the exclusion of the Jews from the individual spheres of German life, (b) the exclusion of the Jews from the living space of the German people. In pursuit of these efforts, the acceleration of the emigration of Jews from the Reich territory was increased and systematically adopted as provisionally the only feasible solution....

In pursuance of the final solution, the Jews will be conscripted for labour in the east under appropriate supervision. Large labour gangs will be formed from those fit for work, with the sexes separated, which will be sent to these areas for road construction and undoubtedly a large number of them will drop out through natural wastage. The remainder who survive—and they will certainly be those who have the greatest powers of endurance—will have to be dealt with accordingly.... [From a eugenic point of view, this survival of the fittest Jews presented the greatest biological threat, and they had to be liquidated.]

In the process of carrying out the final solution, Europe will be combed through from west to east. The Reich territory, including the Protectorate of Bohemia and Moravia, will have to be dealt with first, if only because of the accommodation problem and other socio-political requirements.

The evacuated Jews will initially be brought in stages to so-called transit ghettos in order to be transported from there further east....

The timing for the start of the individual large-scale evacuation actions will be largely dependent on military developments....

The Nuremberg Laws would form, so to speak, the basis for carrying out the final solution project and the solving of the mixed marriages and *Mischling* questions is a precondition for the comprehensive resolution of this problem....

1. *Treatment of the Mischlinge 1. degree.*

Mischlinge 1. degree are to be treated as Jews for the purpose of the final solution. The following will be excluded from this treatment.

(a) *Mischlinge* 1. degree married to persons of German blood from whose marriage children (*Mischlinge* 2. degree) have been born. These *Mischlinge* 2. degree will essentially be treated as Germans.

(b) *Mischlinge* 1. degree who have been granted exemptions in certain spheres of life by the highest organs of the Party and State. Each individual case must be carefully examined and the possibility that the decision may this time go against the *Mischling* cannot be excluded....

The *Mischlinge* 1. degree who are exempted from evacuation will be sterilised in order to forestall any offspring and to resolve finally the *Mischlinge* problem. The sterilisation will be voluntary. It will, however, be a precondition for remaining in the Reich. The sterilised *Mischling* will then be freed from all restrictions to which he has hitherto been subjected.

2. *Treatment of Mischlinge 2. degree.*

The *Mischlinge* 2. degree will be treated as Germans as a matter of principle with the exception of the following cases in which the *Mischlinge* 2. degree will be placed on a par with the Jews.

(a) If the *Mischling* 2. degree is the offspring of a bastard marriage (both partners *Mischlinge*).

(b) A particularly unfavourable racial appearance of the *Mischling* 2. degree which gives him the outward appearance of a Jew.

(c) A particularly poor police and political assessment of the *Mischling* 2. degree which makes it clear that he feels and behaves like a Jew.

In these cases, however, exceptions should not be made even if the *Mischling* 2. degree is married to a person of German blood.

3. *Marriages between full Jews and persons of German blood.*

The decision on whether the Jewish partner should be evacuated or sent to an old people's ghetto must be decided from case to case depending on the effects of such a measure on the German relatives of this mixed marriage.

4. *Marriages between Mischlinge 1. degree and persons of German blood.*
(a) Without children.

If the marriage has not produced any children, the *Mischling* 1. degree will be evacuated or transferred to an old people's ghetto (Same treatment as with marriages between full Jews and persons of German blood. Point 3)

(b) With children.

If the marriage has produced children (*Mischlinge* 2. degree), in the event of their being treated as Jews they will be evacuated together with the *Mischling* 1. degree or transferred to a ghetto. In the event of these children being treated as persons of German blood (normal case), they are to be exempted from the evacuation as is the *Mischling* 1. degree as well.

5. *Marriages between Mischlinge 1. degree or Mischlinge 2. degree and Jews.*

In the case of these marriages, all parties, including the children, will be treated as Jews and therefore evacuated or transferred to a ghetto.

6. *Marriages between Mischlinge 1. degree and Mischlinge 2. degree.*

Both partners will be evacuated or transferred to an old people's ghetto irrespective of whether or not there are children, since such children generally display a stronger Jewish element than the Jewish *Mischlinge* 2. degree.

SS *Gruppenführer* Hofmann maintains that extensive use must be made of sterilization, particularly since if the *Mischling* is offered the choice of evacuation or sterilization he will prefer to undergo sterilization....

In order to simplify the *Mischling* problem one ought also to contemplate ways by which the legislator might say, for example: 'these marriages are dissolved.'...

State Secretary Dr. Buehler stated that the General Government would welcome it if the final solution of this question could begin in the General Government because the transport problem did not play a pre-eminent role here and labour factors would not hinder this operation. Jews should be removed from the territory of the General Government as quickly as possible because here in particular the Jew represented a significant threat as a carrier of epidemics and also, through systematic black market activities, was continually bringing the structure of the country into disorder. Moreover, the majority of the roughly two and a half million Jews in question were incapable of work.

State Secretary Buehler stated further...[h]e had one request—that the Jewish question in this area should be solved as soon as possible....

A POLISH WITNESS TO MASSACRE

Zygmunt Klukowski (1885–1959) was a Polish physician and director of Zamosc hospital in Szczebrzeszyn, a town located in the southeastern Polish province of Zamosc. An avid student of history as well as a Polish patriot, Klukowski kept a detailed diary of life during the Nazi occupation, recording the brutalities inflicted upon Poles and Jews of the region. In late 1942 and 1943 in the Zamosc area, the SS began to forcibly remove thousands of Poles, taking able-bodied teens and adults for forced labor inside Germany, moving the aged, disabled, and very young to other regions, while imprisoning still others in concentration camps. Some Polish children, too, were screened by the SS for their racial purity and possible adoption by German parents who participated in the Lebensborn program. Any resistance on the part of the Polish population was met with swift and severe retaliation by the Nazi authorities. Klukowski describes in the following passage the rounding up of Jews by the Gestapo in the spring of 1942.

May 8, 1942

Today we survived a terrible day. I still have not come to myself after this ordeal....

Around 3 p.m. a real hell started in town. From Zamosc there arrived a group of gestapo. They ordered the *Judenrat* [local Jewish councils created by Nazis to enforce compliance with Nazi policies] to provide 100 Jews for forced labor, giving only one hour for this to happen. After one hour passed, the gestapo, with help from the gendarmes, started catching the Jews, but they really began a mass shooting. The shooting could be heard throughout the city. They shot people like ducks, killing them not only on the streets but also in their own houses—men, women, and children, indiscriminately....I will say that the number killed was over 100....

After a short while I began to think: I have had instructions from the German county administrator not to give any medical aid to Jews. So I called the police station and I was told that Jews are not my

business. Then I called the county doctor in Bilgoraj. He told me the hospital has no right to give any help to the Jews since a Jewish doctor is in the city, and even more so during a mass action by the Germans. I posted a few people at the hospital entrance to explain that we are not allowed to admit any Jews.

I was lucky that I did so. There is no way I would have been able to save Jews, and certainly I would have been arrested and executed. Around 4 p.m. two gestapo men...entered the hospital lobby,...armed with machine guns, and asked if I had admitted or given help to any Jews. I told them no....

Around 5 p.m. the gestapo left Szczebrzeszyn. The Jews are terrified. Women are crying and tearing their clothes....Dr. Bolotny, the only Jewish physician in town, came to me begging for help. He could not do the work alone with so many wounded, some critically. I am saddened that I had to refuse to give any help at all. I did this only because of strict orders by the Germans. This was against my own feeling and against a physician's duties. With my eyes I can still see the wagons filled with the dead, one Jewish woman walking along with her dead child in her arms, and many wounded lying on the sidewalks across from my hospital, where I was forbidden to give them any help.

May 9, 1942

Today the only topic of discussion is yesterday's massacre....

This morning a number of Jews attempted to escape from the city, but they were stopped by other Jews who were afraid that a mass escape would give the Germans an excuse for more killing. At 8 a.m. sixty Jews were taken for labor in Kulikowo. We all feel that this is not yet the end....

The way some Poles behave is completely out of line. During the massacre some even laughed. Some went sneaking into Jewish houses from the back, searching for what could be stolen.

Here is something different: the gestapo ordered the *Judenrat* to pay 2,000 zloty and 3 lbs. of coffee for the ammunition used to kill Jews....

August 8, 1942

11 a.m. In town the atmosphere is very tense. Last night it was clear that Jewish lives are in jeopardy....

German patrols increased throughout the night. Around 1 a.m. I was awakened by unusually loud noises on the street. I heard shouting in German, Polish, and Yiddish....

In the morning I left the hospital to try and find out what had happened. All Jews must report at 8 a.m. across from the *Judenrat*. They are allowed to take 15 lbs. of baggage, food for five days, and 1,500 zloty per person. The mayor informed me that 2,000 Jews will be deported east to the Ukraine. Railroad workers said that a large train with fifty-five cars is ready at the station. So far there are no volunteers, so the Germans began mass arrests. I asked a gendarme what would happen if the Jews did not show up. His answer was, 'We will kill them here.'

It is 7 p.m. Without interruption, throughout the entire day, patrols of gestapo, gendarmes, *Sonderdienst* [special auxiliary force of ethnically-German Poles

to assist Nazis with local administration and policing of the General Government in Poland], blue police, along with members of the *Judenrat* and the so-called Jewish Militia, patrolled the city. They searched houses, including basements and attics. Most Jewish houses are empty now, so city personnel began removing the belongings, loaded everything onto horse-drawn wagons, and took them for storage in warehouses around city hall. Most of the Jews are still hiding. Some Poles are helping the Germans search for Jews. In town the tension is growing.

August 8, 9 p.m.

Around 8 p.m. the Germans began moving the Jews from the marketplace. Some Jews attempted to escape, but the German police stopped them. The shooting started a panic among the people standing near the streets, so everyone began running.

Several hundred Jews were taken to the railroad station. Some older men and women who were unable to walk quickly were beaten by the gendarmes....

From Bilgoraj and a few surrounding villages around 1,000 Jews were taken to the railroad station. So far in Szczebrzeszyn thirteen Jews were killed. No one believes that the Jews will be moved to the Ukraine. They will all be killed....

August 10

Yesterday no Jews were seen on the city streets. Late in the evening three more Jews were shot. I learned that the train carrying the Jews went to Belzec [concentration camp about 100 miles southeast of Warsaw that began construction in November 1941 and operation in March 1942 and was closed in 1943 and then was razed to the ground; an estimated 600,000 Jews were killed there]. They have probably been killed by now.

October 21

Today I planned to try to go to Zamosc again. I woke up very early to be ready, but around 6 a.m. I heard noise and through the window saw unusual movement. This was the beginning of the so-called displacement of Jews, in reality a liquidation of the entire Jewish population in Szczebrzeszyn.

From early morning until late at night we witnessed indescribable events. Armed SS soldiers, gendarmes, and blue police ran through the city looking for Jews. Jews were assembled in the marketplace. The Jews were taken from their houses, barns, cellars, attics, and other hiding places. Pistols and gunshots were heard throughout the entire day. Sometimes hand grenades were thrown into the cellars. Jews were beaten and kicked; it made no difference whether they were men, women, or small children.

By 3 p.m. more than 900 Jews had been assembled. The Germans began moving them to the outskirts of the city....The action didn't stop even after they were taken out of town. The Germans still carried on the search for Jews. It was posted that the penalty for hiding Jews is death, but for showing their hiding places special rewards will be given.

All Jews will be shot. Between 400 and 500 have been killed. Poles were forced to begin digging graves in the Jewish cemetery. From information I received approximately 2,000 people are in hiding. The arrested Jews were loaded onto a train at the railroad station to be moved to an unknown location.

It was a terrifying day....You cannot even imagine the barbarism of the Germans. I am completely broken and cannot seem to find myself....

October 22

The action against the Jews continues. The only difference is that the SS has moved out and the job is now in the hands of our own local gendarmes and the blue police. They received orders to kill all the Jews, and they are obeying them. At the Jewish cemetery huge trenches are being dug and Jews are being shot while lying in them....

LIDICE

In June 1942, the tiny, quiet village of Lidice (Liditz) in the Czech Republic (former Czechoslovakia), hostile toward Nazi occupation and receptive to partisans, became a scapegoat in Hitler's war against resistance. While being driven on May 27, 1942, from his villa to his office in Prague, Reinhard Heydrich, the *Reichsprotektor* of the Protectorate of Bohemia and Moravia (which German forces had occupied in 1939), was shot by two Czech resistance fighters, who had served with the Polish forces in Britain. Heydrich died of his wounds a week later on June 4. Enraged by the assassination of one of his high-ranking officials, Hitler ordered a massive campaign of retaliation against the Czechs, starting with Lidice (chosen for its reluctance to embrace Nazi rule). On June 10, German security police surrounded the village to prevent Lidice's inhabitants from leaving, rounded them up, and shot fifty men all over the age of fifteen. Seven women and nineteen men who were working in a mine during the roundup were sent to Prague where they were shot as well. The village's remaining women were sent to Ravensbrück concentration camp, the children to Poland where they were evaluated for their "racial" worthiness. About 340 villagers in all were murdered, and the village was burned to the ground. Another village, Lezaky, suffered a similar fate as Lidice. After learning of the details of the massacre, Winston Churchill suggested that the Royal Air Force destroy three German villages in revenge for Lidice, but his plan was rejected by members of his cabinet and never undertaken.

On June 9th, 1942 the village of Lidice was, on orders of the Gestapo, surrounded by soldiers having arrived…in ten large lorries [trucks]. They allowed everyone into the village but no one out of it. A twelve-year old boy tried to run away. A soldier shot him. One woman tried to escape; a bullet in the back frustrated her flight and her corpse was found in the fields after the harvest. The Gestapo dragged the women and children to the school.

The morning of June 10th, brought the last day to Lidice and its inhabitants. The men were already shut up in the cellar, barn and stable of the Horak farm. They foresaw their fate and awaited it calmly. The 73 year-old priest STERNBECK strengthened them with the world of God.

A firing squad of 30 gendarmes (a branch of the so-called Ordnungspolizei) had arrived from Prague at 3:30 in the morning. They began their cruel work before 7 o'clock in the morning when K.H. Frank [Karl Hermann Frank was Higher SS and Police Leader, Bohemia/Moravia] had also arrived. When FRANK got out of his car the commander of the Squad reported to him. FRANK turned to the gendarmes and said: "Carry on with your work." Later he intimated that none of the gendarmes must disclose what had happened at Lidice or else he would be shot. The first house on the highroad was occupied by the Gestapo. In front of it SS Hauptsturmführer [SS Captain] WEISMANN informed the firing squad that it was the will of the Fuehrer they were about to carry out.

Trial of the Major War Criminals before the International Military Tribunal (Nuremberg, 1947), 514–516. Used by permission.

From the Horak farm the men were led out into the garden behind the barn in tens and shot. The massacres lasted from morning until 4 o'clock in the afternoon. Afterwards the executioners had themselves photographed with the corpses on the execution ground. The pictures show both boys and older men. They show that they had put straw on the wall so that the bullets should not rebound.

At the same time, 7 o'clock in the morning, the first building...was set on fire and after that one house after another was burned to the ground by the Gestapo. They brought two barrels of petrol and in front of each house poured out a pailful to light the fires.

On June 11th, 20 Jews came from Terezin [also known by its German name of Terezienstadt, it was a city thirty-five miles northwest of Prague, Czechoslovakia, which served as a transit camp for Czech Jews, the majority of whom were then deported to death camps] who had to dig graves near the place of execution and throw in the corpses head to toe and side by side. Afterwards quicklime was poured over the corpses which were then covered by boards. Then the corpses taken from the cemetery were placed in the same graves and the cemetery wiped out.

On June 12th, German pioneers fitted into the walls of the centuries old church of St. Martin, explosive charges....A few month later fields covered the ground where Lidice had stood.

The fate of the men of Lidice has been described. 172 men and youths from 16 years upwards were shot on June 10th, 1942. Another 19 who worked in coalmines of Kladno on June 9th and 10th, were taken to Prague and shot.

7 women from Lidice were shot in Prague as well. The others, the remaining 195 were deported to the Ravensbrueck concentration camp [situated about fifty miles north of Berlin and was used primarily for women] ca. 42 died from ill-treatment, 7 were gassed and 3 are missing.

4 of these women were taken from Lidice to a maternity home in Prague, their newly born children murdered and the mothers then sent to Ravensbrück.

The children of Lidice were taken from their mothers a few days after the destruction of the village. 90 were sent to Lodz in Poland and from there to Gneisenau concentration camp (in the so-called Wartheland). So far no trace of these children has been discovered. 7 of the youngest (less than a year old) were taken to a German children's hospital in Prague and after examination by "racial experts" sent to Germany. They were to be brought up as Germans and were given German names. Every trace of them has been lost.

Two of three children were born in Ravensbrück concentration camp. They were killed immediately after their birth.

The belongings of the population of Lidice were "confiscated." Already on June 9th the Gestapo seized money, saving books and other valuables. In the early morning of June 10th the cattle was driven off and furniture, tools etc., removed to the Bustehrad Court. The land fell to the Reich.

In an official report of 10.6.42 published in the newspaper *Der Neue Tage* on June 11th, 1942, No. 159 (Annex 18) it was maintained "that the population of the village of Lidice aided and abetted the perpetrators" (i.e., the persons who participated in the attempt on HEYDRICH), further that "illegal publications, dumps of arms and ammunition" [and]... "an illegal transmitter" were discovered in Lidice and eventually that "the inhabitants of the locality were in the active service of the enemy abroad."

From a proclamation of 13.6.42 published in the newspaper *Der Neue Tag* on June 14th, 1942, No. 162 (Annex 19) we learn that neither the interrogation of the inhabitants of Lidice, nor their massacre and the destruction of the village, led the German authorities to any trace of the perpetrators. Again they promised rewards to anyone supplying them with appropriate information and threatened all those violating the obligation to inform the police, to be shot with their family.

THE WARSAW GHETTO

Germany's invasion of Poland in September 1939 left the lives of more than 2 million Polish Jews in jeopardy. Just prior to the war's outbreak, Nazi officials had discussed the idea of rounding up Poland's Jews and placing them in ghettos, cordoned-off areas within cities like Lodz, Warsaw, Krakow, and Lublin, where Jews were physically isolated from Gentile society. The ghettos were intended as temporary solutions for the "Jewish question." Among the first Polish ghettos (beginning February 8, 1940) was the industrial city of Lodz (renamed by the Nazis as Litzmannstadt in honor of General Karl Litzmann, who captured the city in World War I), home to Poland's second largest Jewish community. On October 12, 1940, the Nazis decreed the ghettoization of Poland's largest Jewish population, Warsaw, and sealed it in November 1940. Lacking running water, working sewer systems, food, and basic medical supplies, these and other ghettos throughout eastern Europe became death traps for the individuals confined within their wretched walls. Resistance to the Nazis from within the ghetto walls was extremely difficult to organize in light of Nazi regulations and policing, yet underground resistance movements did exist, as was the case in the Warsaw ghetto.

In 1942, as the Nazi deportations to death camps at Chelmno and Treblinka began, a group of young Jews in the Warsaw ghetto, determined to take a stand against their tormentors, created the ZOB (Zydowska Organizacja Bojowa, or Jewish Fighting Organization), led by Mordecai Anielewicz. On April 19, 1943, the day in which Himmler's forces planned to liquidate the remaining Jews in the Warsaw ghetto as a birthday present for the Führer, and on the eve of the Jewish holiday of Passover, the ZOB launched its own surprise attack. Armed with only a few guns, hand grenades, and improvised Molotov cocktails, the woefully outnumbered and undersupplied members of the resistance managed some modicum of revenge against the SS forces (under the command of SS and Police General Jürgen Stroop). Of the nearly 60,000 Jews who remained in the ghetto before the uprising started, only 100 survived; the rest either were deported to concentration camps or were killed in the fighting.

The two selections that follow chronicle the indescribable horrors Jews faced within the confines of the Warsaw ghetto. The first piece was written by Emmanuel Ringelblum (1900–1944), a Polish-Jewish historian who chronicled Jewish life in the Warsaw ghetto. While forced to live with his family in the ghetto, Ringelblum along with a number of other Jews (collectively known as Operation Oneg Shabbat, meaning "the joy of Sabbath") secretly collected items such as diaries, documents, and papers about Jewish life in it to preserve for future generations. Ringelblum also was active in a number of other groups in the ghetto, including one devoted to obtaining food for starving residents. In spring 1943, this collection was placed in three milk cans and metal boxes and hidden in various cellars in buildings. Ringelblum and his family managed to escape the ghetto and were hidden on the so-called Aryan side. Unfortunately, their hiding place was discovered, and the Ringelblums, along with the Polish family that hid them, were executed by the Nazis in March 1944.

The second eyewitness to the Warsaw ghetto was Marysia Warman (her actual name was Bronislawa Feinmesser). Born in Warsaw in 1919, Warman grew up in an assimilated Jewish family that spoke Polish rather than Yiddish as a primary language and chose to live in a non-Jewish neighborhood of the city. In 1942, while working as an assistant to Polish physicians in a Warsaw ghetto hospital, she joined the clandestine ZOB. In the second selection, Warman describes conditions within the ghetto, the assistance rendered by some righteous Poles to Jews within the ghetto's confines, and her activities as a courier for the underground organization. Warman's observations are acute, though her experience was not typical. She enjoyed a degree of mobility available to very few Jews, and was one of the fortunate few Polish Jews to have survived the war.

I

November 8, 1940

My dear,
There's been the growth of a strong sense of historical consciousness recently. We tie in fact after fact from our daily experience with the events of history. We are returning to the Middle Ages....The Jews created another world for themselves in the past, living in it forgot the troubles around them, allowed no one from the outside to come in. As for parallels: The present expulsion is one of the worst in Jewish history, because in the past there were always critics of refuge. Someone said to me: "It's bad to read Jewish history, because you see that the good years were few and far between. There were always troubles and pogroms."...

November 19, 1940

The Saturday the Ghetto was introduced (16th of November) was terrible. People in the street didn't know it was to be a closed Ghetto, so it came like a thunderbolt. Details of German, Polish and Jewish guards stood at every street corner searching passersby to decide whether or not they had the right to pass. Jewish women found the markets outside the ghetto closed to them. There was an immediate shortage of bread and other produce. There's been a real orgy of high prices ever since. There are long queues in front of every food store, and everything is bought up.... Neither Saturday nor Sunday did the Jewish doctors get passes. The Jewish Council levies a tax of five zlotys per pass.— Saturday Jewish workers were not allowed to leave the city on their outside work details. On the first day after the Ghetto was closed, many Christians brought bread for their Jewish acquaintances and friends. This was a mass phenomenon. Meanwhile, Christian friends are helping Jews bring produce into the Ghetto....

[T]hose who are slow to take their hats off to Germans are forced to do calisthenics using paving stones or tiles as weights. Elderly Jews, too, are ordered to do push-ups. They tear paper up small, scatter the pieces in the mud, and order people to pick them up, beating them as they stoop over. In the Polish quarter Jews are ordered to lie on the ground and they walk over them....A wave of evil rolled over the whole city, as if in response to a nod from above....

Many Jews make their living outside the Ghetto, and now they're cut off from it....

A Christian was killed today, the 19th of November, for throwing a sack of bread over the Wall....The Ghetto game is continuing. It is said that the electricity has been turned off in the Lodz Ghetto. Jews have to sit in the dark there....

August 26, 1941

There is a marked, remarkable indifference to death, which no longer impresses. One walks past corpses with indifference. It is rare for anyone to visit the

---

Emmanuel Ringelblum, *Notes from the Warsaw Ghetto,* as reprinted in Robert Chazen and Marc Lee Raphael eds., *Modern Jewish History: A Source Reader* (New York: Schocken, 1974), 284–285, 287–289, 292–293, 295–296.

hospital to inquire after a relative. Nor is there much interest in the dead at the graveyard.

Next to hunger, typhus is the question that is most generally absorbing for the Jewish populace. It has become the burning question of the hour. The graph line of typhus cases keeps climbing. For example, now, the middle of August, there are some six or seven thousand patients in [private] apartments, and about nine hundred in hospitals....

The patients die from hunger in the hospital, because they get nothing to eat but a little soup and some other minor nourishment. The patients don't die from typhus, really, but because of their weakened condition....[T]he lice are omnipresent. They literally fly through the air, and it is almost impossible to avoid them....The problem of [disposing of] corpses is a pressing one in the houses of the poor. Not having the money to bury their dead, the poor often throw the corpses in the street. Some houses shut their gates and refuse to permit tenants [with a corpse at home] to leave until they have had the body buried. On the other hand, the police chiefs, not wanting to bother with the formalities connected with [disposing of] corpses, simply throw the bodies from one streetcar to the next. The bodies are buried in mass graves at the graveyard, where there are tremendously high sand mounds in the old section. On hot summer days, the stench from these mass graves is so strong you have to hold your nose when you pass....

May 8, 1942

The period ending that fateful Friday, April 18, may be termed "the period of legal conspiracy." All the political parties in the Ghetto conducted activities that were practically semilegal. Political publications sprouted like mushrooms after rain....The political leaflets and communiqués used to be read in offices, factories, and similar public places.

Marysia Warman, "Warsaw Ghetto," in Brana Gurevitsch, ed., *Mothers, Sisters, Resisters: Oral Histories of Women Who Survived the Holocaust* (Tuscaloosa: University of Alabama Press, 1998), 277–280, 282, 287–288. Used by permission.

The various parties used to hold their meetings practically in the open halls. They even had big public celebrations. At one such meeting, a speaker addressing an audience of 150 preached active resistance....

We had even begun to debate and insult one another, as in the good old prewar days....Everyone imagined that the Germans were indifferent to what the Jews were thinking and doing in their Ghetto. We thought that all that the Germans were concerned about was ferreting out Jewish merchandise, money, currency—that they were uninterested in intellectual matters. We turned out to be sadly mistaken. That bloody Friday, when the publishers and distributors of illegal publications were executed, proved that our political constellation is not a subject of indifference to Them, particularly when it has some connection with what is happening in the Polish, non-Jewish part of Warsaw....

Bloody Friday has had strong repercussions. The illegal press has stopped publishing. There has been a significant weakening of political activity. The interest in social undertakings has slackened. It was a hard blow to people's spirits; half the city spends the night away from home these days. Anyone who had anything at all to do with any kind of community work is terrified.

II

When the ghetto was established, Dr. Braude-Hellerowa, director of the Berson and Bauman children's hospital, whom I knew very well, hired me as a telephonist. I lived in the hospital. I slept in the operating room on the operating table. I became very, very friendly with almost all the personnel. In the evening, after my work in the office, I stayed in the hospital, and I worked as a nurse, although I was not qualified or registered, but I worked with the children, giving them food, changing their hospital clothes, even giving injections, massages, various things....

As the Germans reduced the area of the ghetto the hospital had to move several times. Finally, it moved to the *Umschlagplatz* [transfer point or point of departure in Warsaw from which hundreds of thousands of Jews were herded into freight trains like cattle for a final journey to concentration camps], where all the

Jewish people went to the train, and all the children were taken to the camp, to Treblinka. It didn't look like a hospital; it was in a school building; conditions were terrible.

At the beginning, in 1941 and part of 42, there was a nursing school and medical school in the ghetto. I attended this medical school for two years....

I wasn't in touch with many people. I was busy working all day long. My mother and my sister lived far away from the hospital in the ghetto. Once or twice a week I went to see my mother and sister. On the way, through the ghetto streets, I saw plenty of people, mostly children, lying in the street, swollen with hunger, begging for food, or dead, covered with newspaper. There were some stores; I bought food with my salary from the hospital and brought some to my mother and sister.

The director of this children's hospital, Dr. Anna Braude-Hellerowa, was absolutely committed to helping the children of the ghetto swollen from hunger, dying on the street, transported at the last moment to the hospital. Some of them recovered; most of them died in the hospital. The children, especially from Orthodox families, hardly spoke Polish, and communication with such sick children was very, very difficult. Besides typhus, the majority of the children were dying of hunger. It was terrible.

Dr. Braude-Hellerowa established this hospital many years before the war....Dr. Braude-Hellerowa was an absolutely fantastic person. She was completely devoted to the children, even the children who were too sick without any hope of recovery. The children were the most important thing for her. She didn't leave them until the end....

We had a commissar of the hospital, Dr. Waclaw Skonieczny, who was appointed by the Germans. He was a very nice, very honest man. He was probably a *Volksdeutscher*. Thanks to his help with medicine for the hospital, with food, with different things, the hospital could exist....I got a pass from him to leave the ghetto to go to the Aryan side. I don't remember whose idea it was. Maybe I spoke to him; maybe the head nurse spoke to him. With that pass I went from the ghetto to the Aryan side and back. The

pass allowed me to do things for the hospital on the Aryan side....

On July 22, 1942, they gathered the population of the Warsaw ghetto in the front of the *Judenrat*. Dr. Braude-Hellerowa got a few life passes for all the employers of the hospital, which meant that they wouldn't be sent to the *Umschlagplatz* [reloading point] and that they had a right to live in the ghetto. It is very difficult to say exactly, but for approximately two hundred employees of the hospital, doctors, nurses, supporting personnel, and so on, she got around twenty-five to thirty of these passes. How can one person decide who has a right to live and who will die? It was an enormously difficult decision, but she had to distribute those tickets of life. The *Umschlagplatz*, where all the ghetto people were gathered, had an entrance with guards, and only the people with those passes had the right to go outside this place. All other people were taken to the trains. Dr. Braude-Hellerowa didn't give those life passes to her closest colleagues, to her friends, to the doctors, to many people who used to work for the hospital. Her decision, which was very characteristic of her, was to give those passes to the youngest ones. Among others, I got this pass, although I didn't have an important position in this hospital....She didn't even give her family members any passes!...She didn't keep one for herself either....

I was not aware of preparations for an uprising. It was a surprise for me. I knew that arms, revolvers, were being smuggled into the ghetto. But that was really secret. Nobody knew about that except for the people who took part in organizing and preparing for the ghetto uprising....

I started to work for the Bund organization. My duties were: finding hiding places, organizing false documents, distributing money, paying rent to the landlords; these were my main tasks....Our room was the location for the Bund organization gatherings. When these gatherings took place we girls (Inka [Dr. Adina Szwajger] and I) didn't take part; we left the apartment. They told us when we should come back. The meetings were secret. In this room we stored files, documents, underground literature and plenty of money we distributed. It was decided that in this room we would not hide people. We would follow all the conspiracy rules. But it wasn't always possible because sometimes if someone was without a roof for the night we couldn't send them out on the street after curfew; we had to hide them. We tried not to, but if it was absolutely necessary we had to.

We were out in the city from very early morning until the curfew. We were always exhausted, completely, because everyday we were in danger of being recognized. Remember that I was born in Warsaw, and I used to live in the center of the city, and plenty of people knew me. This was not a question of Jewish looks or language. Thanks to my language and looks I could pass easily; until I met somebody who could denounce me, I could walk around freely....

I have to tell you about the people who were helping us. There were many, many different kinds of people. There were Christian people who were very religious, and they thought that they were doing what God told them to do. There were people who wanted money because they didn't have any source of income to live on except their apartment....

One woman, the wife of a Polish officer who was in a camp in Germany, took a lot of money from us for each person. She fed them, she hid them. She fed them very poorly, but somehow she was reliable....

During the ghetto uprising I was already on the Aryan side. The only thing I could do was take care of the people who escaped from the ghetto, to find some place to hide them to make documents for them, and to give them money....

When the Polish uprising broke out Antek [Yitzhak Zuckerman, one of the leaders of the ZOB, which led the uprisings] and Marek [Edelman] [another ZOB leader of the uprising] went to higher officers in the Polish army and asked them to take us as a group, as the Jewish Fighting Organization. They refused. Individually, please come, but not as a group; we won't give you any commander.... First we fought in the Old Town, hiding at night in the cellar together. There was heavy fighting. We had ammunition, guns. I didn't fight; the men fought. The women didn't fight. There were maybe six or eight women. There was heavy, heavy bombarding, and the old city was leveled to the ground.

Then we decided that there was no sense in remaining there, and somehow they found a guide to lead us to the Zoliborz quarter of Warsaw through the sewers. The water was going with such speed and rising higher and higher. It was very difficult even for a strong person to stand or walk. I had a bundle with my personal things, some photographs, some documents.... When we came to Zoliborz, it was so beautiful and peaceful. We thought the quiet would last forever.

At the beginning, we were located in some houses.... We were there almost a month, and at the beginning of October we learned that the uprising was finished. The *Armia Krajowa* [the Home Army, Polish resistance movement] surrendered, and its troops were treated as prisoners of war.

HIMMLER AND THE FINAL SOLUTION

Born in Munich, the son of a Catholic schoolmaster who had been a tutor to the Bavarian crown prince, Heinrich Himmler (1900–1945) led the Gestapo and Waffen-SS and served as Hitler's Minister of the Interior from 1943 until 1945. Himmler was in his early twenties when he became involved in far right-wing politics, participating in the failed November 1923 Beer Hall Putsch in Munich and joining the NSDAP. By 1929 he was appointed head of the SS, helped to organize (along with Reinhard Heydrich) the Security Service (SD), established the first concentration camp—Dachau—in 1933, masterminded the purge of rival organization SA in June 1934, and became the chief of the Gestapo in addition to his position as leader of the SS in 1936. Perhaps as a way of compensating for his slight physique and pedestrian looks, Himmler promoted the idea of Aryan supremacy through his Lebensborn breeding centers where SS men with meticulous Aryan bloodlines were matched with Aryan women of supposedly equally pure heritage to produce a super-race of Germans. With Germany's annexation of Polish territory in the autumn of 1939 Himmler oversaw all racial matters and ultimately, in 1943, the Final Solution. Captured on May 23, 1945, by the Allies after trying unsuccessfully to escape in disguise, Himmler committed suicide by poison to avoid trial. The following selection is an excerpt taken from a three-hour-long speech delivered by Himmler in the city of Posen to a group of SS officers in which he spoke openly about the killing of the Jews.

I also want to talk to you quite frankly about a very grave matter. We can talk about it quite frankly among ourselves and yet we will never speak of it publicly. Just as we did not hesitate on 30 June 1934 [reference to the purge known as the Night of the Long Knives in Bad Wiessee of the SA or Sturmabteilung, a Nazi paramilitary association, that was viewed by Hitler and other close associates as a potential threat to their power] to do our duty as we were bidden, and to stand comrades who had lapsed up against the wall and shoot them, so we have never spoken about it and will never speak of it. It was that tact which is a matter of course, and which I am glad to say is inherent in us, that made us never discuss it among ourselves, never speak of it. It appalled everyone, and yet everyone was certain that he would do it the next time if such orders should be issued and it should be necessary.

I am referring to the Jewish evacuation programme, the evacuation of the Jewish people. It is one of those things which are easy to talk about. The Jewish people will be exterminated, says every party comrade, it's clear, it's in our programme. Elimination of the Jews, extermination and we'll do it. And then they come along, the worthy eighty million Germans, and each one of them produces his decent Jew. It's clear the others are swine, but this one is a fine Jew. Not one of those who talk like that has watched it happening, not one of them has been through it. Most of you will know what it means

Heinrich Himmler, "On Extermination; Speech to SS Leaders on 4 October 1943 in Posen," in Jeremy Noakes and Geoffrey Pridham, eds., *Nazism, 1919–1945*, vol. 3 (Exeter: University of Exeter Press, 1988), 1199–1200. Used by permission.

when a hundred corpses are lying side by side, or five hundred or a thousand are lying there. To have stuck it out and—apart from a few exceptions due to human weakness to have remained decent, that is what has made us tough. This is a glorious page in our history and one that has never been written and can never be written. For we know how difficult we would have made it for ourselves, if on top of the bombing raids, the burdens and the deprivations of war, we still had Jews today in every town as secret saboteurs, agitators and troublemakers. We would now probably have reached the 1916–17 stage when the Jews were still part of the body of the German nation.

We have taken from them what wealth they had. I have issued a strict order, which SS Obergruppenfuehrer Pohl [chief of the administrative office of the SS] has carried out, that this wealth should, as a matter of course, be handed over to the Reich without reserve. We have taken some of it for ourselves. Individual men who have lapsed will be punished in accordance with an order I issued at the beginning which gave this warning: Whoever takes so much as a mark of it is a dead man. A number of SS men—there are not very many of them—have fallen short, and they will die, without mercy. We had the moral right, we had the duty to our people, to destroy this people which wanted to destroy us. Be we have not the right to enrich ourselves with so much as a fur, a watch, a mark, a cigarette or anything else. We have exterminated a bacterium because we do not want in the end to be infected by the bacterium and die of it. I will not see so much as a small area of sepsis appear here or gain a hold. Wherever it may form we will cauterize it. All in all, we can say that we have fulfilled this most difficult duty for the love of our people. And our spirit, our soul, our character has not suffered injury from it....

THE HOLOCAUST IN GREECE

By 1943, organized Jewish communities had existed in Greece for more than 2,000 years. Within a single year, they would be all but wiped out. Between 60,000 and 70,000 Greek Jews perished under German persecution, or about 80 percent of the country's Jewish population. German efforts were facilitated by the long-standing concentration of Greek Jews in the city of Thessaloniki, the largest urban Sephardic community in the world, which made it easier to round up and deport the victims. Nonetheless, some Jews were saved because of the sympathetic response of ordinary civilians, the outspoken opposition to the deportations by members of the Greek Orthodox Church (especially Archbishop Damaskenos) and their willingness to issue false baptismal certificates, as well as the refusal of Italian authorities to hand over Jews from the areas of Greece they had occupied. This report from a Greek eyewitness gives a clear account of the sequential stages by which the Germans isolated and destroyed the Jewish community.

"Report of P. Kontopoulos, Student of Chemistry, about the Persecution of Jewish Greek Citizens," in Photini Costantopoulou and Thanos Veremis, eds., *Documents on the History of the Greek Jews: Records from the Historical Archives of the Ministry of Foreign Affairs*, 2nd ed., 1999 Kastaniotis Editions, Athens, 257–260. Used by permission.

15 September 1943

The persecution of the Jews began in Thessaloniki, the centre of the Jewish population of northern Greece, in mid-February 1943 by means of specially-dispatched German Police forces belonging to the SS Battalions which had already swept away the Jews of all the other European countries conquered by the Germans.

The measures taken against the Jews were comparatively mild at first, reaching their climax in June 1943, when the Jews were openly tortured before the eyes of all the Greek population.

Measure 1: The Jewish Community...handed over to the Rosenberg Gestapo Battalions all the registers of the Jewish Community of Thessaloniki. This was the greatest mistake made by the Jews, since it was the beginning of the disaster that came upon them later....

Measure 2: Two weeks later, all the Jews of Greek citizenship were instructed to present themselves at the offices of the Jewish Community, where they were issued with Stars of David, yellow in colour, measuring approximately 10 × 10 cm., and bearing their register number in the centre. All Jews, regardless of sex and age (over the age of 3 years), were obliged to wear the Star. All the Gestapo's orders were issued to the Jews solely and exclusively via the Jewish Community, and not via the Greek newspapers.

For the time being, the Rallis (Greek) Government appeared to be completely ignorant of the situation.

Measure 3: Five days later, all the Jews were instructed to assemble within five districts selected by the Jewish Community. This assembly had to take place within 4 days and at least 5 persons had to live in each room. Of the districts selected, three were exclusively Jewish...while the other two, in the centre of the city, were also inhabited by very many Greek families.

This move was the first hardship to which the Jews were subjected, because in early March, a time of continual rain and amid the cold, they were compelled to leave their houses and assemble as best they might, usually in the basements of houses—and in conditions of severe crowding, given that there was a complete shortage of housing in view of the German requisitioning. The Jewish houses and shops were sealed by the Germans, who held these buildings in their own exclusive possession.

At this time, the Germans issued an order forbidding the Greeks to undertake the protection of Jewish property and to engage in commercial transactions of any kind with them.

Measure 4: Once the Jews had been enclosed within the above areas, and after three days had elapsed, an order was issued forbidding all Jews from leaving these areas. The streets leading to the outside world were guarded by Greek gendarmes and Jewish civil guards. Entry into the areas was permitted to all the Greeks, who began to pass supplies to their Jewish friends and to help them in all possible ways.

Measure 5: Special detachments of the Jewish militia, escorted by Germans, were sent to all the cities of northern Greece, Thrace and the Greek islands to bring all the Jews living there into the Jewish camps in Thessaloniki.

Measure 6: Under the escort of Jewish civil guards and with special permission from the Germans, all the Jews owning shops were taken into the city one by one, every day, to hand over their keys to the German authorities. The Germans immediately began to empty and strip the most important Jewish shops. The Jewish goods were loaded on whole convoys of German trucks and taken to the German warehouses.

Measure 7: Deportation to Poland. The first group was from the Baron Hirsch camp, which was closest to the railway station and was the only camp to have been surrounded with barbed wire and guarded only by German soldiers. The first train was loaded with approximately 3,000 persons of all social classes, regardless of sex, age or condition of health. The Jews were loaded into the train like animals. 70 persons being crammed into each ordinary goods wagons of the Greek railways....

In these circumstances, the Greek people did as much as they could to help their brothers the Greek Jews, and more than just a few Greeks are still rotting in prison, awaiting trial, in the German concentration camps. In addition, many Greeks adopted Jewish children, and equally as many are still hiding Jewish families, at the risk of their own lives. Special mention should be made of the action taken by the Metropolitan Bishop of Thessaloniki, who called on the German military commander and begged him, on behalf of all mankind, to make the measures taken against the Jews and their deportation more humane. The military commander's answer was that his orders came from a higher authority and he was completely powerless to intervene. The general attitude of the Greek population, and of the Greek guerrillas (EAM), who took into their ranks their comrades-in-arms from Albania, was outstanding.

VON MOLTKE'S THOUGHTS ON RESISTANCE

An important figure in the German resistance against Hitler, Helmut James von Moltke (1907–1945) descended from a well-known Prussian noble family on his father's side and a highly respected South African family of British descent on his mother's. In 1929, von Moltke interrupted his law studies to run his family's estate in Kreisau (located today in Poland), returning to Berlin to complete his studies in 1931 and marrying Freya Deichmann, a fellow law student and daughter of a banker from Cologne, whom he had met earlier. Von Moltke's opposition to the Nazi regime was already apparent in 1935 when he chose to open his own law practice rather than accept a judgeship that would have required him to join the NSDAP. As an expert in international law, von Moltke assisted victims of Nazi persecution to emigrate and befriended individuals who later would be crucial to his anti-Nazi resistance group, the Kreisau Circle (Kreisauer Kreis), which he founded. Upon the outbreak of the Second World War, von Moltke joined the Military Intelligence Service (Abwehr) where he served as a legal advisor to the High Command (OKW) and traveled throughout occupied Europe with access to secret information that he used to recruit others opposed to Hitler's regime. Von Moltke's strong religious beliefs, however, precluded him from supporting the assassination of Hitler and reinforced his commitment to the creation of a new Germany based on the rule of law and protective of religious freedom and human rights. In January 1944 he was arrested by the SS, thrown into a number of prisons and concentration camps where he was interrogated and tortured, and was finally executed one year later in January 1945. Throughout the war, von Moltke corresponded with his wife, Freya, about Nazi persecution of the Jews and the war's conduct.

From *Letters to Freya, 1939–1949* by Helmuth James Von Moltke, pp. 282–288, translation copyright © 1990 by Alfred A. Knopf, a division of Random House, Inc. Used by permission of Alfred A. Knopf, a division of Random House, Inc.

25 March 1943

[F]rom the point of view of politics the same rule applies in dictatorships or tyrannies as in democracies: you can only get rid of one government if you can offer another government, and that means, that the mere process of destroying the third realm [Third Reich] can only get under way if you at least are able to propound an alternative. This view is not in sight of the man with the secret service point of view, and this lack can have very grave consequences not only for the post-war period but also for the chances of destroying the third realm with assistance from inside.

By the way, this argument has been propounded to me by more than one man from the underground organizations in the various occupied countries.

People outside Germany do not realize the following handicaps under which we labour and which distinguish the position in Germany from that of any other of the occupied countries: lack of unity, lack of men, lack of communication.

Lack of unity: In all countries under Hitler but Germany and France the people are practically united. If it be in Norway or Poland, in Greece, Jugoslavia or Holland the vast majority of the people are one in mind. There are a great many people who have profited from the third realm and who know that their time will be up with the third realm's end. This category does not only comprise some few hundred people, no it runs into hundreds of thousands and in order to swell their number and to create new posts of profit everything is corrupted.—Further there are those who supported the Nazis as a counterbalance against foreign pressure and who cannot now easily find their way out of the tangle; even where they believe the Nazis to be in the wrong they say that this wrong is counterbalanced by a wrong done to us before.—Thirdly there are those who—supported by Göbbel's propaganda and by British propaganda—say: if we lose this war we will be eaten up alive by our enemies and therefore have to stand this through with Hitler and have to put him right, i.e., get rid of him thereafter: it is impossible to change horses in mid-stream....Therefore while, practically speaking, you can trust every Dutchman, Norwegian, etc., as to his intentions, you have to probe deep into every

German before you find out whether or not you can make use of him, the fact that he is an anti-nazi is not enough.

Lack of men: In our country, we have, practically speaking, no young men left, men of the age groups which make revolutions, or are at least its spearhead. You have got young or at least fairly young workers in your home [Britain] factories, you have your young men training in your own country. All this is different with us; all our young men, even those in training, are far beyond our frontiers. Instead we have got more than 8 million foreign and potentially hostile workers in the country, and their numbers are going to be swelled to 10 millions and not a man younger than the age group of 1899 in the country. The exceptions to this rule are, but for the secret police and the SS, negligible. And those who still are there and are active are terribly overworked and have no strength. The women, if they are not engaged in war work of one kind or another, are fully occupied—physically but especially mentally—in keeping their houses in order. The worse the economic strain gets the less likely a revolution becomes, because people are so occupied in simply living....

Lack of communication: This is the worst. Can you imagine what it is like if you

a. cannot use the telephone,
b. cannot use the post,
c. cannot send a messenger, because you probably have no one to send, and if you have you cannot give him a written message as the police sometimes searches people in trains, trams, etc., for documents.
d. cannot even speak with those with whom you are completely *d'accord* [in agreement with], because the secret police have methods of questioning where they first break the will but leave the intelligence awake, thereby inducing the victim to speak out all he knows; therefore you must limit information to those who absolutely need it;
e. cannot even rely on rumour or a whispering-campaign to spread information as there is so effective a ban on communications of all kind that a whispering campaign started in Munich may never reach Augsburg.

There is only one reliable way of communicating news, and that is the London wireless, as that is listened in to by many people who belong to the opposition proper and by many disaffected party members.

Some of this devilish machinery has been invented by the Nazis, but some of it has been produced by war itself. But this machinery is used to great effect by the ruling class. Their first aim is to keep the army out of touch with the political trends in the country. They succeed in this to a great extent. None but men on leave and those manning anti-aircraft guns are in the country. When on leave they do not want to be bothered and their relatives do not want to bother them. When out of the country, the information they get by post is very scanty as their womenfolk dare not write to them for fear of repressive measures which are and have been taken....Their mind is occupied with the enemy as fully as the housewife's is occupied with her requirements....

But even in Germany people do not know what is happening. I believe that at least 9tenths of the population do not know that we have killed hundreds of thousands of Jews. They go on believing they just have been segregated and lead an existence pretty much like the one they led, only farther to the east, where they came from. Perhaps with a little more squalor but without air raids. If you told these people what has really happened they would answer: you are just a victim of British propaganda; remember what ridiculous things they said about our behaviour in Belgium in 1914/18 [reference to alleged atrocities committed by German troops against Belgian civilians during World War I].....

We have now 19 guillotines working at considerable speed without most people even knowing this fact, and practically nobody knows how many are beheaded per day. In my estimation there are about 50 daily, not counting those who die in concentration camps.—Nobody knows the exact number of concentration camps or of their inhabitants. We have got a concentration camp only a few miles from our farm, and my district-commissioner told me that he only learnt of the fact that there was a concentration camp in his district when he was asked for orders to stop an epidemic of typhoid from spreading to a neighbouring village; but that time the camp had existed for months. Calculations on the number of KZ-inhabitants [abbreviation for *Konzentrationslager*, or concentration camps] vary between 150,000 and 350,000. Nobody knows how many die per day. By chance I have ascertained that in one single month 160 persons died in the concentration camp of Dachau. We further know fairly reliably that there are 16 concentration camps with their own cremation apparatus. We have been informed that in Upper Silesia a big KZ is being built which is expected to be able to accommodate 40 to 50,000 men, of whom 3 to 4000 are to be killed per month. But all this information comes to me, even to me, who is looking out for facts of this nature, in a rather vague and indistinct and inexact form. We only know for certain, that scores, probably many hundreds of Germans are killed daily by various methods, and that these people die not a glorious death, as those in the occupied countries do, knowing that their people consider them heroes, but an ignominious death knowing that they are classed among robbers and murderers.

What is happening to the opposition, the men "of whom one hears so much and notices so little" as a headline in a paper lately said.

Well, first of all, it loses men, at a considerable rate. The quickly-working guillotines can devour a considerable number of men. This is a serous matter, not alone because of the loss of life....The worst is that this death is ignominious. Nobody really takes much notice of the fact, the relatives hush it up, not because there is anything to hide, but because they would suffer the same fate at the hands of the Gestapo if they dared telling people what has happened. In other countries suppressed by Hitler's tyranny even the ordinary criminal has a chance of being classified as a martyr. With us it is different: even the martyr is certain to be classed as an ordinary criminal. That makes death useless and therefore is a very effective deterrent....

Thirdly the opposition is saving individual lives. We cannot prevent the ferocious orders from being given, but we can save individuals. And this is done in all walks of life. People who have been officially executed still live, others have been given sufficient warning to escape in time. This is especially so in occupied countries: there is no denying the mass-murders, but once the balance is drawn, people will perhaps realize that many thousands of lives have been saved by the intervention of some German, sometimes a private and sometimes a general, sometimes a workman and sometimes a high-ranking official.

Fourthly the opposition has made many mistakes. The main error of judgement (*sic*) has been the reliance placed on an act by the generals. This hope was forlorn from the outset, but most people could never be brought to realize this fact in time. The same reasons which made it impossible for the French Generals to get rid of Napoleon prevent this happening in Germany....The main sociological reason is that we need a revolution, not a coup d'état, and no revolution of the kind we need will give generals the same scope and position as the Nazis have given them, and give them today.

Fifthly the opposition has done two things which, I believe, will count in the long run: the mobilization of the churches and the clearing of the road to a completely decentralized Germany. The churches have done great work these times. Some of the sermons of the more prominent Bishops, Catholic as well as Protestant, have become known abroad, especially two sermons of the Bishop of Berlin, Count Preysing of May 16th (?) 1942 and December 20th, 1942. But the most important part of the churches' work has been the continuous process by which the whole clergy, practically without exception, have upheld the great principles in spite of all the intense propaganda and the pressure exerted against them. I do not know of a single parson who in a church demolished by British bombs held a sermon with an anti-British strain. And the churches are full Sunday after Sunday. The state dare not touch the churches at present, and in order to get over this difficulty the churches have been requisitioned in many places for storing furniture saved from bombed houses; thereby the state hopes to make church-work slowly impossible.

The breaking down of the idea of a highly centralized German state has made considerable progress. While two years ago the idea of a completely decentralised Germany was considered a utopia it is today nearly a commonplace. This will ease the transitory period between war and peace, and may, perhaps, make a meeting of the minds possible.

TREBLINKA

Treblinka, some sixty miles from Warsaw, was one of four Aktion Reinhard death camps established in the summer of 1942 for the purpose of exterminating European Jewry. About 800,000 Jews, many of them from the Warsaw ghetto, were killed at Treblinka, but the camp was also notable for the revolt by prisoner work details in August 1943. Although the uprising was brutally suppressed, the resisters killed a number of guards and seriously damaged camp buildings. By October–November 1943, the camp ceased to operate and the SS tried to obliterate any evidence that it had existed. In July 1944, when Soviet forces overran the location, it had reverted to a farm. Fortunately, Vasily Grossman, who was accompanying the Soviet troops, managed to locate some forty survivors, as well as local Polish peasants, and on the basis of his interviews with them was able to reconstruct the horrors that had occurred there. So painstaking and incriminating was Grossman's account that it was entered into evidence at the Nuremberg Trials. Grossman himself was so sickened by the ordeal that the normally resolute and indefatigable journalist, a veteran of numerous grueling campaigns, collapsed from nervous exhaustion.

They stepped into a straight alley, with flowers and fir trees planted along it. It was 120 metres long and two metres wide and led to the place of execution. There was wire on both sides of this alley, and guards in black uniforms and SS men in grey ones were standing and those who were walking in front with their hands up could see the fresh prints of bare feet in this loose sand: small women's feet, very small children's ones, those left by old people's feet. These ephemeral footprints in the sand were all that was left of thousands of people who had walked here recently, just like the four thousand that were walking now, like the other thousands who would walk here two hours later, who were now waiting for their turn at the railway branch in the forest. People who'd left their footprints had walked here just like those who walked here yesterday, and ten days ago, and a hundred days ago, like they would walk tomorrow, and fifty days later, like the people did throughout the thirteen hellish months of Treblinka's existence.

The Germans called this alley 'The Road of No Return.'...People, their hands still raised, walked in silence between the two lines of guards, under the blows of sticks, sub-machine-gun butts, rubber truncheons. Children had to run to keep up with the adults....[A]n SS man called Zepf...specialized in killing children. This beast, who possessed a massive physical strength, would suddenly seize a child out of the crowd, and either hit the child's head against the ground waving the child like a cudgel, or tear the child in two halves....

At this moment, the SS men would unleash the trained dogs, who threw themselves on the crowd and tore the naked bodies with their teeth. SS men were beating people with sub-machine-gun butts, urging on petrified women, and shouting wildly: 'Schneller! Schneller! [faster! faster!] Schmidt's assistants at the entrance to the building drove people through the open doors into the gas chambers....

In the terribly crowded state, which was bone-crushing, their chests were unable to breathe, they were standing squashed against one another, with the last sticky death-sweat pouring down, they were standing there as one body....

Schmidt's assistants looked into the peepholes twenty to twenty-five minutes later. The time came to open the door of chambers leading to the platforms. Prisoners in overalls would start the unloading. As the floor sloped towards the platforms, the bodies fell out by themselves....

The corpses were examined by SS men. If someone was discovered to be still alive, was moaning or moved, this person was shot with a pistol. Then the crews armed with dentist's tongs would set to work wrenching platinum and gold teeth out of dead people's mouths. The teeth were then sorted according to their value, packed into boxes and sent to Germany....

The corpses were loaded on to the cars and taken to the enormous moat-graves. There, they were laid down in rows, closely, side by side. The moat would be left unfilled with earth, waiting.

CHAPTER 11

OUT OF THE "DARK AND DEADLY VALLEY"*

FLEETING FELLOWSHIP The high hopes and cooperative spirit evoked by this meeting of advancing Soviet and American troops in April 1945 were soon dashed by the realities of great power rivalry in the Cold War.
Source: © Bettmann/CORBIS.

The war ended in both the European and Pacific theaters on the heels of dramatic events. On April 30, 1945, an unrepentant Adolf Hitler, confined to his underground bunker in central Berlin as Soviet troops inexorably closed in, committed suicide. German news organizations, spreading lies to the very end, falsely reported that he had been killed in action, supposedly in defense of a once proud capital that his war had reduced to rubble. In Japan, the landscape was similar, with most urban centers burned to the ground, and, in early August 1945, two cities, Hiroshima and Nagasaki, laid waste by atomic bombs. Neither country could continue to wage war. Hitler's chosen successor, the U-boat admiral Karl Dönitz, sued for peace and the surrender on May 8 forever enshrined that date to be designated "Victory in Europe" or "V-E day." In Tokyo, the emperor's intervention was crucial in reconciling a divided cabinet to surrender, a decision which led to August 15 becoming "Victory over Japan" or "V-J day." The famous formal surrender ceremony on the deck of the battleship *Missouri* took place on September 2, 1945.

But if the formal conclusion of the war signaled an end to hostilities, it marked only the beginning of several new and extremely perplexing challenges. As had been the case some three decades earlier, none of the victorious Allies wanted to be threatened again, and they vowed to do a better job this time of preventing a recurrence of aggression. To America and Britain, this meant that both defeated countries would have to be "purified" of their aggressive militarism: the surviving leaders stripped of their powers and punished for their transgressions, their military services deprived of whatever war-making capabilities they retained, and the societies themselves democratized in ways that, after a period of probation, would enable their eventual return within the accepted civilized family of nations. The Soviets fully concurred about the desirability of removing those who had exercised power in Germany or Japan, of trying the worst offenders (the barbarity of this war was indisputable), and disarming the countries. The democratization of the successor regimes never figured as one of Stalin's goals, however, for he considered that the best guarantee of the security of the Soviet Union lay in the creation of sympathetic puppet states in eastern Europe whose compliance with Moscow's interests was enforced by the might of the Red Army.

A second important challenge was to rebuild the devastated economies and infrastructure, as well as the shattered lives, in the various battle-torn countries. This agenda was every bit as imperative for the victorious Soviet Union as for the defeated Axis powers, and much of the European continent and Asia had witnessed widespread destruction as well. The human toll had been staggering, with perhaps 60 million people killed and an equal number uprooted from their prewar states. Only the United States was in a position to offer the necessary economic assistance, the key component of which would be the Marshall Plan inaugurated in 1947. For America to play that role, though, and to immerse itself in the task of restoring the victors and rehabilitating the vanquished meant following a very different path from the isolationist stance it had adopted after World War I. That greater involvement after World War II, coupled with the fact that American aid and expertise was

---

*Winston Churchill in the House of Commons, January 22, 1941

geared to the redevelopment of capitalist economies in the face of communist suspicion, helps to explain the different configuration of international relations after 1945. Instead of a resurrected balance of power, the postwar world was a bipolar one, caught in the evolving confrontation between two superpowers. American leaders were determined not to have exchanged one expansionist dictatorship (Hitler's) for another (Stalin's) and sought to contain Soviet influence at key points around the globe. Two armed camps, bound by alliances (North Atlantic Treaty Organization [NATO] and the Warsaw Pact) and divided by an "iron curtain" of the Soviets' devising that bisected Germany in two, faced each other in a "cold war" that periodically showed dangerous signs of flaring up into something much hotter that could, with recourse to nuclear weapons, spell global oblivion. The overwhelming power of the U.S. military, the more interventionist role articulated by the Truman administration, and the allure of the nation's commitment to individual liberty, political democracy, and free enterprise as a model for imitation, all persuaded a number of observers that the succeeding decades would make the twentieth a decidedly "American century."

Yet if America's more engaged role in world affairs as a superpower was one significant legacy of the war, its influence, and that of its allies, would not go unchallenged. The Japanese onslaught in the Pacific had shaken European colonial dominion to its very roots, and the European powers themselves were in no position to exercise imperial power in the ways to which they had been accustomed before 1939. Military service provided thousands of African and Asian recruits with a fresh perspective on their situation, as well as the education, discipline, and determination to reshape it. Moreover, the central role of the avowedly Marxist-Leninist Soviet Union in defeating the hitherto unstoppable German armies seemingly vindicated the power of communism to inspire and organize peoples, and around the globe liberation movements emerged to put those theories to the test. In Algeria and Indochina (Vietnam), in Cuba and across Africa, the unsettling and transformative influence of the war would be felt, and the clock could not be turned back.

NAZIS TO THE BITTER END?

As Allied armies closed in on Hitler's tottering state, their soldiers wondered just what they would find. Were most German civilians ardent Nazis who would resist to the bitter end? Or had most been coerced into compliance with the brutal dictatorship? Or would the Americans find political chameleons, a people who claimed innocence now, but who had once accepted or applauded the Nazi emphasis on conquest and social purity? Could one even make such broad generalizations about actions in the past, attitudes in the present, or, ominously, the prospects for building a stable democracy in the future upon the ashes of hatred? The U.S. Army was eager to learn what it could about popular attitudes in the Nazi regime (and to identify those who merited criminal prosecution), and it relied upon a cadre of officers (often, though not exclusively, émigrés) whose fluency in German could elicit some initial answers. Saul Padover (1905–1981) had been born in Vienna and, after emigrating to America, earned a Ph.D. from the University of Chicago. He put his services at the disposal of the army to interrogate Germans in a variety of walks of life, and here he describes the popular mood in Germany as the war wound down. Padover himself went on to a distinguished career teaching political science at the New School for Social Research in New York.

Defeatism is rife in the Reich. There is no evidence of any last-ditch sentiment; the majority of the people hope for a quick end of the war. They are prepared to accept an Allied occupation, and even to pay the price of defeat. There seems to be a latent and possibly deep-rooted sense of guilt owing to the brutalities committed by the German armies in Europe, particularly against the Slavs and the Jews. Many Germans have resigned themselves to the idea of *"Vergeltung"* [retribution] and their only hope is that the Americans would moderate the fury of those who have reasons to punish them. Many believe that they will have to do heavy labor abroad, others think that German youth will be sent to Siberia. As for sniping and other forms of opposition against an Allied occupation, reliable informants dismiss such a notion with a certain amount of contempt. German civilians will offer no resistance to us....

At the end of November 1944, we wrote a summary of our work among the Germans. So far as I know, this was the first comprehensive study of the German mind in wartime based on first-hand investigation....

Catholics

Rhinelanders always make the claim...that the Rhineland is "anti-Nazi" because it is Catholic.

As a rule, religion did not determine a person's acceptance or rejection of Nazism. A number of high Catholic dignitaries were not in favor of Hitlerism, but the Nazi Party contains a great number of

Saul K. Padover, *Experiment in Germany: The Story of an American Intelligence Officer* (New York: Duell, Sloan & Pearce, 1946), 18, 110–112, 115–118. Used by permission.

Catholics. The leading Nazis, Hitler and Goebbels, came from Catholic homes and environments.

In the overwhelmingly Catholic town of Roetgen (pop. 2600), we found about one third of the population to have been Nazi. Many of them still are Nazis, despite the American occupation....There is perhaps a greater pro-Allied feeling in the Rhineland than in the rest of Germany, mainly because the area is heavily industrialized and sees no economic future in a defeated Reich....

Jews

Despite Nazi anti-Semitic agitation without parallel in history, we found an astonishing absence of anti-Semitism even among those who accepted the Nazi *Weltanschauung* [view of the world] in part or wholly. There seems to prevail a strange sense of guilt about the Jews, an uneasy feeling, and frequently an open admission, that a great wrong has been committed. There is also a fear of revenge and a dread of hearing the worst about the horrors that have been inflicted on the Jews in Poland....

Attacking the Jews was Hitler's "greatest error." All the blame is being put on the Führer in an attempt to escape moral responsibility....

Russians

Everybody, except old-time Marxists, suffers from a phobia about the Russians. This is true of workers as well as of bourgeois, of the young and of their elders. This Russophobia is more than Nazi propaganda, more than the ancient hostility of Teuton towards Slav, more even than the ordinary fear of an enemy at the frontiers. The dread of the Russians seems to be a dread of retribution....Germans seem to know much more about what happened in Russia than they care to admit, and they take out their fear and their guilt in name calling. The Russians are "uncultivated," "barbarous," "greasy."...

Hate Germans, flatter Americans—such seems to be the Germans' present technique. Their sole hope lies with the Americans. By dividing the allies, they expect to escape severe retribution....

No Resistance

Of all the people interrogated, only two expressed a desire to fight the Nazis physically and overtly....All the others who uttered strong or violent sentiments were otherwise passive and emotionally incapable even of contemplating the possibility of active resistance. Those who complained bitterly against the Nazis said of resistance,—"But it is impossible! The terror is too great. For the slightest activity or criticism you get sent to a concentration camp or shot." When it was pointed out that the terror was equally great in France, and that hundreds of thousands of Frenchmen took up arms against the Gestapo and fought the German for years, there was invariably the reply—"Ah yes, the Frenchmen! We Germans are different. We are not revolutionary people."

Nearly all those who are hostile to the Nazi regime complain of their personal sufferings. They overflow with self-pity. Investigation revealed that these complaints and expressions of self-pity are a more or less conscious technique of justifying an acceptance and toleration of Nazism....

This self-pity and self-centeredness is tied up with their refusal (or psychological inability) to fight the Nazi regime or even to carry on sabotage. Whatever the reason...adult Germans give the impression of being a cowed people, incapable of independent action or of courageous resistance....

War Guilt

Even the Nazi Party members and Nazi sympathizers agree that Hitler started the war....

Non-Nazis put all the blame on Hitler and the Nazi Party, rather than on the German nation. Again and again people said: "The war began because Hitler always wanted more." If only Hitler had been satisfied with the Rhineland, the Saar, the Sudetenland, and Austria! But his appetite grew with the eating....No one blamed the German people's historic inclination to organized violence and profound respect for martial values for the Reich's present plight. Hitler and the Nazis are now the sole scapegoats for a losing war that every German fears will end in disaster, for a war that most German supported passively or actively, and still do....

Psychologically the German people is now prepared to escape punishment and moral responsibility by offering to the world as a scapegoat who only a short while ago was a demi-god. Most Germans admitted that they accepted the war of 1939 with no opposition and the victories of 1940 with great enthusiasm. The war brought prosperity, and the victories booty. Hitler was then a revered hero. The profound change in attitude—a change amounting almost to a traumatic shock—came with Stalingrad. When the Red Army buried the Wehrmacht's hope for victory in Russia, people began to turn against Hitler, passively of course, and to doubt the wisdom of his leadership. The Red Army not only destroyed Hitler's legions but also his prestige. The more the Germans began to doubt the Führer's military qualities, the more they tended to trust the generals.

In this tendency to shift responsibility and to refuse to share reverses with the chosen Leader, one detects no gleam of self-guilt, no awareness that war as such is evil, no realization that there may be something quite wrong with the Germans. No one criticized aggression as such. The only criticism was of aggression that failed. Hitler is blamed for losing the war, not for starting it.

LIBERATING THE DEATH CAMPS

Only when advancing Allied forces began to liberate the concentration camps did the full horror of what the Nazi regime had been doing begin to impress itself upon the world's conscience. Not far from the idyllic city of Weimar (home of Goethe and Germany's "other," more tolerant tradition) was the camp of Buchenwald (the "beech forest"). Troops from the American Sixth Armored Division reached Buchenwald on April 11, 1945, just after camp prisoners had overthrown those guards who had remained. A day later, newsman Edward R. Murrow, already revered for his calm reports from bomb-ravaged London, visited Buchenwald, and on April 15 he gave this famous broadcast. Fred Friendly, president of CBS News, recalled it as "the best piece of television journalism ever done." So powerful and evocative were Murrow's images that listeners could picture for themselves (without television) the dreadful conditions he was describing. It is worth noting that conditions at Buchenwald were "better" than elsewhere because it was not an extermination camp; for the most part, it held dissidents, political prisoners, and other alleged enemies of the Nazi state, and its inmates were not marked for immediate death. Perhaps 56,000 died over the eight-year span of the camp's operation (roughly a quarter of those who at anytime were confined there). Some 20,000 emaciated survivors remained there to greet the American forces.

Edward R. Murrow, "Radio Address: Liberating the Nazi Death Camps," in Brewster Chamberlin and Marcia Feldman, eds., *The Liberation of the Nazi Concentration Camps 1945: Eyewitness Accounts of the Liberation* (Washington, DC: U.S. Holocaust Memorial Council, 1987), 42–44. Used by permission.

Permit me to tell you what you would have seen and heard had you been with me on Thursday. It will not be pleasant listening. If you are at lunch or if you have no appetite to hear what Germans have done, now is a good time to switch off the radio, for I propose to tell you of Buchenwald.

It is on a small hill about four miles outside Weimar, and it was one of the largest concentration camps in Germany. And it was built to last....

And now, let me tell this in the first person, for I was the least important person there, as you shall hear. There surged around me an evil-smelling horde; men and boys reached out to touch me. They were in rags and the remnants of uniforms. Death had already marked many of them, but they were smiling with their eyes....

When I entered [the barracks], men crowded around, tried to lift me to their shoulders. They were too weak....Many of them could not get out of bed. I was told that this building had once stabled 80 horses; there were 1,200 men in it, five to a bunk. The stink was beyond all description.

When I reached the center of the barracks, a man came up and said, 'You remember me; I'm Peter Zenkl, one-time mayor of Prague.' I remembered him but did not recognize him....

I asked how many men had died in that building during the last month. They called the doctor. We inspected the records. There were only names in the little black book, nothing more. Nothing of who these men were, what they had done or hoped. Behind the names of those who had died there was a cross. I counted them. They totaled 242—242 out of 1,200 in one month.

As I walked down to the end of the barracks, there was applause from the men too weak to get out of bed. It sounded like the hand-clapping of babies, they were so weak....

In another part of the camp they showed me the children, hundreds of them. Some were only six. One rolled up his sleeve, showed me his number. It was tattooed on his arm—D6030 it was. The others showed me their numbers. They will carry them till they die....

We crossed to the courtyard. Men kept coming up to speak to me and to touch me—professors from Poland, doctors from Vienna, men from all Europe, men from the countries that made America.

We went to the hospital; it was full. The doctor told me that 200 had died the day before. I asked the cause of death; he shrugged and said, 'Tuberculosis, starvation, fatigue, and there are many who have no desire to live. It is very difficult.'...

I asked to see the kitchen; it was clean. The German in charge had been a Communist, had been at Buchenwald for nine years, had a picture of his daughter in Hamburg—hadn't seen her for almost 12 years, and if I got to Hamburg would I look her up? He showed me the daily ration—one piece of brown bread about as thick as your thumb; on top of it a piece of margarine as big as three sticks of chewing gum. That and a little stew was what they received every 24 hours.

He had a chart on the wall, very complicated it was. There were little red tabs scattered through it. He said that was to indicate each 10 men who died. He had to account for the rations. And he added, 'We are very efficient here.'

We went again into the courtyard, and as we walked, we talked. The two doctors, the Frenchman and the Czech, agreed that about 6,000 had died during March. Kerscheimer, the German, added that back in the winter of '39, when the Poles began to arrive without winter clothing, they died at the rate of approximately 900 a day....

Dr. Heller, the Czech, asked if I would care to see the crematorium. He said it wouldn't be very interesting because the Germans had run out of coke some days ago and had taken to dumping the bodies into a great hole nearby....

We entered. It was floored with concrete. There were two rows of bodies stacked up like cordwood; they were thin and very white. Some of the bodies were terribly bruised, though there seemed to be little flesh to bruise. Some had been shot through the head, but they bled but little. All except two were naked. I tried to count them as best I could, and arrived at the conclusion that all that was mortal of more than 500 men and boys lay there in two neat piles.

There was a German trailer which must have contained another 50, but it wasn't possible to count them. The clothing was piled in a heap against the wall. It appeared that most of the men and boys had died of starvation; they had not been executed. But the manner of death seemed unimportant—murder had been done at Buchenwald. God alone knows how many men and boys have died there during the last 12 years. Thursday I was told that there were more than 20,000 in the camp; there had been as many as 60,000. Where are they now?...

I pray you to believe what I have said about Buchenwald. I have reported what I saw and heard, but only part of it; for most of it I have no words.

A MOTHER PONDERS THE WAR'S END

Nella Last, a Barrow-in Furness housewife married to a joiner/shop-fitter, was a volunteer for Mass Observation who began keeping a diary in September 1939. She meticulously recorded the details of daily life among the ordinary inhabitants of that shipbuilding town in northern England, right down to the distinctive accents of her friends. She had a sharp eye for the war's subversive impact on gender roles, even as she witnessed the resilience of traditional attitudes. Although Last lived thousands of miles from the events of the Pacific campaign, she also readily grasped the awesome implications of the new atomic bomb.

Wednesday, 25 July 1945

I felt tired, but ironed my washing, as I'm going out to the Centre in the morning. My husband is very sulky about it. He said, 'When the war got over, I thought you would always be in at lunch-time.' I said, 'Well, you always have a good lunch left—much better than many men whose wives are always at home.' He said, 'Well, I like you there always.' No thought as to either my feelings or to any service I could be doing. I thought of the false sentiment my generation had been reared with, the possessiveness which stood at the hallmark of love, with no regard to differences in temperament, inclination or ideals—when the 'head of the house' *was* a head, a little dictator in his own right; when a person of limited vision, or just plain fear of life, could crib and confine more restless spirits. I looked at my husband's petulant face, and thought that, if I'd never done anything else for my lads, at least I'd left them alone and had never given advice at pistol-point, shrinking from imposing my will in any way. A little chill fell on me—not from the dusk which was creeping on the garden, either. Rather did it blow from the past, when to go anywhere without my husband was a heinous crime—and he went practically nowhere! I had a pang as I wondered what I would do when all my little war activities stopped, when he *could* say plaintively, '*Must* you go?' or 'I don't feel like...'—and I wondered if my weak streak would crop up as strong as ever, and I'd

Nella Last's War: A Mother's Diary, 1939–45, Richard Broad and Suzy Fleming, eds., (London: Sphere Books LTD, 1983; reprinted Profile Books, 2006), 209–301. Used by permission.

give in for peace and to that unspoken, but *very* plain, Victorian-Edwardian accusation, 'I feed and clothe you, don't I? I've a right to say what you do.' It's not 'love,' as the sloppy Vic-Eds. [Victorians/Edwardians] sang, it's sheer poverty of mind and fear of life. If you love a person in the real sense, you want them to be happy, not take them like butter and spread them thinly over your own bread, to make it more palatable for yourself.

Sunday, 5 August 1945

When I wrote that date, my mind swung back: two world wars in my comparatively short life—and this one not yet over. Sometimes I think it never will be-that, in spite of all our talk of 'helping the Germans to be a nation among nations again,' their hatred of what we had to do to their towns and cities, industry and life in general, will smoulder and burn till the winds of chance blow it into a fierce flame. My husband says, 'I cannot see it. We stood by foolishly last time while huge armies were formed and drilled—we will never be such fools again.' Me, I think of a devoted band of fanatical clever ones, working in secret in the heart of some underground lab, splitting atoms and such. This war has taught us that man is finished as the deciding factor in future wars. The V-bombs showed, in a dawn of horror, weapons that no country could leave out of future developments. Just a *very* few people could smash civilization in the future; it would not need marching armies....

Tuesday, 7 August 1945

I'd a very broken night—dreaming of changes . . . and woke feeling tired. . . . My husband had looked in and seen I was sleeping, and I wakened with a start as old Joe called upstairs—he had come through the door between the two cottages. He shouted, 'Arta waken, lass?' I slipped on my dressing-gown and went downstairs, wondering whatever could be the matter. His white thick hair . . . seemed to be on end as he rubbed it with one hand and brandished the 'Daily Mail' in the other. He said, 'By Goy, lass, but it looks as if some of your daft fancies and fears are reet. Look at this'—and it was the article about the atomic bombs. I've rarely seen him so excited—or upset. He said, 'Read it—why, this will change allt' world. Ee I wish I wor thutty years younger and could see it aw.' I felt sick—I wished I was thirty years older, and out of it all. My husband began to wonder if it would influence all power—cars chiefly—in some way taking the place of petrol. . . .

Wednesday, 8 August 1945

We talked about the atomic bomb. It seems to have frightened Mrs. Howson very much. Our talk had a very Wellsian turn [reference to British science fiction writer H. G. Wells whose 1898 novel, *The War of the Worlds*, featured Martians equipped with destructive death rays]. We wondered if it was at all possible for German scientists to be hiding anywhere, and if they could send a revenge plane to wreck England—or American cities! We followed our fantastic themes of super 'werewolves' till we felt dizzy and were rather scared. This atomic bomb business is so dreadful. Was it something like this that happened when Atlantis disappeared under the sea, and the Age of Mythology began?

THE GERMAN PROBLEM

Henry Morgenthau Jr. (1891–1967) was the brilliant Secretary of the Treasury for eleven years in Roosevelt's cabinet. He was an exceptionally successful fund-raiser whose effective bond drives both provided money for the American war effort and moderated wartime inflation. His view of how to treat postwar Germany was deeply influenced by the failure of the Versailles Treaty and its disarmament clauses (which limited Germany's military to 100,000 men and prohibited certain classes of weapons) to restrain Germany from launching a second aggressive war within a quarter century. Having been deeply involved in agriculture, as a dairy farm owner and chairman of the Federal Farm Board, Morgenthau believed that a pastoral Germany dotted with farms and deprived of heavy industry would be stable, prosperous, and content, a better partner to its European neighbors in a search for lasting peace. Morgenthau also advocated that Germany be divided into two states, northern and southern, to minimize its potential power. He failed, however, to anticipate the division of Germany on an east-west axis, or the tensions that would escalate with the Soviet Union.

In September, 1944, President Franklin D. Roosevelt asked me to outline for him a program for the treatment of Germany after her defeat. He wished to take such a document to the Quebec Conference [September 12–16, 1944, second of two Allied conferences held in Quebec, in which plans for Germany's future were discussed] which was to be held in a few days, and he knew that I had devoted a good deal of thought and study to the subject....

Only a few weeks before the President made his request, I had been in London, and the sight of that bombed city with its courageous people had deepened my convictions, as I think it must have deepened the convictions of anyone who saw London in wartime. It prompted the theme of a broadcast I made on the eve of my departure and in which I said:

> There can be no peace on earth—no security for any man, woman or child—if aggressor nations like Germany and Japan retain any power to strike at their neighbors. It is not enough for us to say, 'we will disarm Germany and Japan and *hope* that they will learn to behave themselves as decent people.' Hoping is not enough.

That was the spirit in which I drew up the plan which Mr. Roosevelt had requested. I know that was the spirit in which he received it....This book is an elaboration of the program which I then submitted to the President for his use....

In writing this book, I have been motivated entirely by the conviction that the purpose of our program for dealing with Germany should be peace. And that should be its only purpose. The peoples of the earth have a right to demand of their peace makers that another generation of youth shall not have to be maimed and die in the defense of human freedom....

My own program for ending the menace of German aggression consists, in its simplest terms, of depriving Germany of all heavy industries. The reason for selecting heavy industries is that with them Germany can quickly and terribly convert once more to war. Without them, no matter how savage her aggressive aims can be, she cannot make war.

For longer than living men can remember, the greatest threat to peace anywhere in the world has been Germany's lust for armed conquest. Even more than the German Army, that lust has found its release through German heavy industry. It was done in two ways, both of which will be not only possible but probable again if we permit Germany to retain the basic means of aggression.

First, of course, was the actual manufacture of the weapons of modern war. The guns, planes, tanks, submarines which a Germany with heavy industry could produce fifteen or twenty years from now would be as far beyond present weapons as ours today are beyond those of 1917. We had just a taste of that future in the jet planes and buzz bombs of last year. If Germany keeps the means to perfect such weapons, she will use them.

The second role of heavy industry in the German plan of aggression was and will be economic Blitzkrieg. This can be and has been as demoralizing as the military article. The heavy hand of German power was laid upon the economy of her neighbors— and throughout Europe industries withered, scarcity grew, fear multiplied.

Any country's war potential these days can be measured by its heavy industries much more accurately than by the size of its army, navy and air force at any given moment. In four years the peacetime industrial machine of the United States was converted into a weapon that dwarfed Germany's once famous Luftwaffe, Wehrmacht and the rest....That

being so, it would seem rather obvious that to disarm Germany in any real sense of the word is to remove the industries that would make rearmament possible. It is all very well to confiscate guns, planes, tanks, submarines, military installations and so on. It is even more important to remove or destroy the German plants where new and more horrifying weapons of war could be forged. It is most important of all to keep those plants from being rebuilt.

Germany's real armament is a triple threat of metallurgical, chemical and electrical industries. The prewar Reich dominated Europe in those fields. Therefore, she dominated Europe militarily as well until she challenged even greater industrial powers. Without these factories, the Germans could not have indulged their lust for conquest in 1914 or 1939. Without these factories, they could not do it again....

In de-industrializing Germany, the factories taken from her would be rebuilt in other parts of Europe. They would constitute some reparation for damage done, but they would also help balance Europe better industrially so that the Continent need never again be overshadowed by the machine power of a single nation. Devastated countries should have priority in claiming Germany's industrial equipment....

Machinery can be moved or broken up for scrap; buildings can be demolished; workers can be sent to other jobs. But coal in the ground is not so easily disposed of. The Ruhr Valley had 70 per cent to 80 per cent of Germany's coal production...[and] the existence of this coal was the reason why the Ruhr became the greatest single industrial center in Europe....

The coal cannot be taken away from the Ruhr (except by the trainload as it is mined), so the Ruhr should be taken away from Germany. Annexed to any other country, it would be a perpetual storm center, but it could safely be placed under the control of a governing body established by the League of Nations....

Germany's road to peace leads to the farm. The men and women in the German labor force can best serve themselves and the world by cultivating German soil. Such a program offers security to us as well as food for Germany and her neighbors.

A great deal of the discussion as to whether or not the German people could exist without heavy industry...can be settled only through studying the facts about Germany's labor force, the farmland available and the potential production under principles of modern scientific land use.

Such a study leads inescapably to the conclusion that Germany without heavy industry has the manpower and the acreage to feed her people. It will involve hardship and hard work for several years....The main consideration, however, is not discomfort and toil for Germany but peace for the world. If it were true, as some people have asserted, that thirty million Germans would starve through the elimination of their heavy industry, their misery would become a menace to peace. But a study of the facts shows that their best chance of getting an adequate diet within a reasonable time is by growing their own food and not by returning to steel mills and synthetic plants....

The elementary lesson for the German people is that there is no use planning and working for war because they will not have the means to wage it....When the majority of the German people are small farmers, they will be a bit less susceptible to the lure of militarism. The owners of land, especially the owners who actually work it themselves, are likely to have little time for other occupations and to be impatient of military service which calls their sons from home at harvest time.

AMERICA'S PLANS FOR POSTWAR GERMANY

In 1946 it was hard to find evidence that Germany was making particular progress toward economic recovery or political stability. It remained weak, beset by hunger, and American officers on the scene, like General Lucius Clay, worried that poor conditions not only favored the growth of communist agitation and further destabilization, but might also persuade reluctant American taxpayers that it was simply not worth maintaining an American military presence there. This speech in September 1946 by Truman's Secretary of State, James F. Byrnes (1879–1972), laid the foundation for a postwar partnership by reiterating America's commitment to work toward a free, prosperous, and democratic Germany. Often referred to as "the speech of hope," Byrnes' address was welcomed by European opinion as a repudiation of Morgenthau's policy of economic retribution and an indication that, unlike after the previous world war, this time America would not shirk its world role. In retrospect, Byrnes' speech can be seen as laying the groundwork for the Marshall Plan of economic assistance to spur European recovery.

"Restatement of Policy on Germany," Speech by Secretary of State Byrnes at Stuttgart, September 6, 1946, http://usa.usembassy.de/etexts/ga4–460906.htm. Used by permission.

have come to Germany to learn at first hand the problems involved in the reconstruction of Germany and to discuss with our representatives the views of the United States Government as to some of the problems confronting us. We in the United States have given considerable time and attention to these problems because upon their proper solution will depend not only the future well-being of Germany, but the future well-being of Europe. We have learned, whether we like it or not, that we live in one world, from which world we cannot isolate ourselves. We have learned that peace and well-being are indivisible and that our peace and well-being cannot be purchased at the price of peace or the well-being of any other country....

The American people want peace. They have long since ceased talk of a hard or a soft peace for Germany. This has never been the real issue. What we want is a lasting peace. We will oppose soft measures which invite the breaking of the peace. In agreeing at Potsdam that Germany should be disarmed and demilitarized and in proposing that the four major powers should by treaty jointly undertake to see that Germany is kept disarmed and demilitarized for a generation, the United States is not unmindful of the responsibility resting upon it and its major Allies to maintain and enforce peace under the law....

The United States, therefore, is prepared to carry out fully the principles outlined in the Potsdam Agreement on demilitarization and reparations. However, there should be changes in the level of industry agreed upon by the Allied Control Commission if Germany is not to be administered as an economic unit as the Potsdam Agreement contemplates and requires.

The basis of the Potsdam Agreement was that, as part of a combined program of demilitarization and reparations, Germany's war potential should be reduced by elimination and removal of her war industries and the reduction and removal of heavy industrial plants. It was contemplated this should be done to the point that Germany would be left with levels of industry capable of maintaining in Germany average European living standards without assistance from other countries....

The carrying out of the Potsdam Agreement has, however, been obstructed by the failure of the Allied

Control Council to take the necessary steps to enable the German economy to function as an economic unit....The equitable distribution of essential commodities between the several zones so as to provide a balanced economy throughout Germany and reduce the needs for imports has not been arranged....The United States is firmly of the belief that Germany should be administered as an economic unit and that zonal barriers should be completely obliterated so far as the economic life and activity in Germany are concerned.

The conditions which now exist in Germany make it impossible for industrial production to reach the levels which the occupied powers agreed were essential for a minimum German peacetime economy. Obviously, if the agreed levels of industry are to be reached, we cannot continue to restrict the free exchange of commodities, persons, and ideas throughout Germany....

While Germany must be prepared to share her coal and steel with the liberated countries of Europe dependent upon these supplies, Germany must be enabled to use her skills and her energies to increase her industrial production and to organize the most effective use of her raw materials. Germany must be given a chance to export goods in order to import enough to make her economy self-sustaining. Germany is a part of Europe and recovery in Europe and particularly in the states adjoining Germany, will be slow indeed if Germany with her great resources of iron and coal is turned into a poor house.

When the ruthless Nazi dictatorship was forced to surrender unconditionally, there was no German government with which the Allies could deal. The Allies had temporarily to take over the responsibilities of the shattered German state, which the Nazi dictatorship had cut off from any genuine accountability to the German people. The Allies could not leave the leaders or minions of Nazism in key positions, ready to reassert their evil influence at first opportunity. They had to go.

But it was never the intention of the American Government to deny to the German people the right to manage their own internal affairs as soon as they were able to do so in a democratic way, with genuine respect for human rights and fundamental freedoms. The Potsdam Agreement...

bound the occupying powers to restore local self-government and to introduce elective and representative principles into the regional, provincial, and state administration as rapidly as was consistent with military security and the purposes of the military occupation. The principal purposes of the military occupation were and are to demilitarize and de-Nazify Germany but not raise artificial barriers to the efforts of the German people to resume their peacetime economic life.

THE NUREMBERG TRIALS

Between 1945 and 1946, Nuremberg, Germany, a Franconian city infamous for its Nazi rallies, became the site for Nazi war trials. In the Palace of Justice, where only a decade earlier the Nazi regime had enacted its racial laws, judges from the United States, Great Britain, France, and the Soviet Union presided over the proceedings. Led by United States Supreme Court Justice Robert H. Jackson (1892–1954) as Chief Counsel for the United States, the Allied judges indicted twenty-four men (excluding Hitler, Himmler, and Goebbels, who had all committed suicide), twenty-one of whom appeared before the court to be tried for their crimes. Eleven defendants, including Hermann Göring, Hans Frank, Wilhelm Frick, Alfred Rosenberg, and Joachim von Ribbentrop, received death sentences, seven others were given prison terms, while three more were acquitted for their crimes. What follows is an excerpt from Jackson's opening address at the Nuremberg Trials. In confronting face-to-face the men charged with horrific "crimes against humanity" and thereby giving voice to their victims, Jackson bore an awesome responsibility. His task was further complicated by the fact that moral outrage was by itself an insufficient standard, given that this was to be a legal tribunal whose proceedings would condemn to posterity the staggering depths of Nazi depravity. By all accounts, Jackson shouldered his unenviable burden with enviable eloquence and insight, a performance subsequently hailed as a landmark in international law.

The privilege of opening the first trial in history for crimes against the peace of the world imposes a grave responsibility. The wrongs which we seek to condemn and punish have been so calculated, so malignant, and so devastating, that civilization cannot tolerate their being ignored, because it cannot survive their being repeated. That four great nations, flushed with victory and stung with injury stay the hand of vengeance and voluntarily submit their captive enemies to the judgment of the law is one of the most significant tributes that Power has ever paid to Reason.

This Tribunal, while it is novel and experimental, is not the product of abstract speculations nor is it

Robert H. Jackson, "Opening Address before the Nuremberg Trials," November 21, 1945, *Trial of the Major War Criminals before the International Military Tribunal* (Nuremberg: International Military Tribunal, 1947) 2:98–103, 104–105, 153–154. Used by permission.

created to vindicate legalistic theories. This inquest represents the practical effort of four of the most mighty of nations, with the support of 17 more, to utilize international law to meet the greatest menace of our times—aggressive war. The common sense of mankind demands that law shall not stop with the punishment of petty crimes by little people. It must also reach men who possess themselves of great power and make deliberate and concerted use of it to set in motion evils which leave no home in the world untouched. It is a cause of that magnitude that the United Nations will lay before Your Honors....

What makes this inquest significant is that these prisoners represent sinister influences that will lurk in the world long after their bodies have returned to dust. We will show them to be living symbols of racial hatreds, of terrorism and violence, and of the arrogance and cruelty of power. They are symbols of fierce nationalisms and of militarism, of intrigue and war-making which have embroiled Europe generation after generation, crushing its manhood, destroying its homes, and impoverishing its life. They have so identified themselves with the philosophies they conceived and with the forces they directed that any tenderness to them is a victory and an encouragement to all the evils which are attached to their names. Civilization can afford no compromise with the social forces which would gain renewed strength if we deal ambiguously or indecisively with the men in whom those forces now precariously survive....

Never before in legal history has an effort been made to bring within the scope of a single litigation the developments of a decade, covering a whole continent, and involving a score of nations, countless individuals, and innumerable events. Despite the magnitude of the task, the world has demanded immediate action.... [L]ess than 8 months ago today the courtroom in which you sit was an enemy fortress in the hands of German SS troops. Less than 8 months ago nearly all of our witnesses and documents were in enemy hands....

Unfortunately, the nature of these crimes is such that both prosecution and judgment must be by victor nations over vanquished foes. The world-wide scope of the aggressions carried out by these men has left but few real neutrals....The former high station of these defendants, the notoriety of their acts, and the adaptability of their conduct to provoke retaliation make it hard to distinguish between the demand for a just and measured retribution, and the unthinking cry for vengeance which arises from the anguish of war. It is our task, so far as humanly possible, to draw the line between the two. We must never forget that the record on which we judge these defendants today is the record on which history will judge us tomorrow. To pass these defendants a poisoned chalice is to put it to our own lips as well. We must summon such detachment and intellectual integrity to our task that the Trial will commend itself to posterity as fulfilling humanity's aspirations to do justice....

If these men are the first war leaders of a defeated nation to be prosecuted in the name of the law, they are also the first to be given a chance to plead for their lives in the name of the law. Realistically, the Charter of this Tribunal, which gives them a hearing, is also the source of their only hope. It may be that these men of troubled conscience, whose only wish is that the world forget them do not regard a trial as a favor. But they do have a fair opportunity to defend themselves—a favor which these men, when in power, rarely extended to their fellow countrymen. Despite the fact that public opinion already condemns their acts, we agree that here they must be given a presumption of innocence, and we accept the burden of proving criminal acts and the responsibility of these defendants for their commission.

When I say that we do not ask for convictions unless we prove crime, I do not mean mere technical or incidental transgression of international conventions. We charge guilt on planned and intended conduct that involves moral as well as legal wrong. And we do not mean conduct that is a natural and human, even if illegal, cutting of corners, such as many of us might well have committed had we been in the defendants' positions. It is not because they yielded to the normal frailties of human beings that we accuse them. It is their abnormal and inhuman conduct which brings them to this bar.

We will not ask you to convict these men on the testimony of their foes. There is no count in the Indictment that cannot be proved by books and records. The Germans were always meticulous record keepers, and these defendants had their share of the Teutonic passion for thoroughness in putting things on paper. Nor were they without vanity. They arranged frequently to be photographed in action. We will show you their own films. You will see their own conduct and hear their own voices as these defendants re-enact for you, from the screen, some of the events in the course of the conspiracy.

We would also make clear that we have no purpose to incriminate the whole German people. We know that the Nazi Party was not put in power by a majority of the German vote. We know it came to power by an evil alliance between the most extreme of the Nazi revolutionists, the most unrestrained of the German reactionaries, and the most aggressive of the German militarists. If the German populace had willingly accepted the Nazi program, no Stormtroopers would have been needed in the early days of the Party and there would have been no need for concentration camps or the Gestapo, both of which institutions were inaugurated as soon as the Nazis gained control of the German State. Only after these lawless innovations proved successful at home were they taken abroad.

The German people should know by now that the people of the United States hold them in no fear, and in no hate. It is true that the Germans have taught us the horrors of modern warfare, but the ruin that lies from the Rhine to the Danube shows that we, like our Allies, have not been dull pupils. If we are not awed by German fortitude and proficiency in war, and if we are not persuaded of their political maturity, we do respect their skill in the arts of peace, their technical competence, and the sober, industrious, and self-disciplined character of the masses of the German people....

In general, our case will disclose these defendants all uniting at some time with the Nazi Party in a plan which they well knew could be accomplished only by an outbreak of war in Europe. Their seizure of the German State, their subjugation of the German people, their terrorism and extermination of dissident elements, their planning and waging of war, their calculated and planned ruthlessness in the conduct of warfare, their deliberate and planned criminality toward conquered peoples—all these are ends for which they acted in concert; and all these are phases of the conspiracy, a conspiracy which reached one goal only to set out for another and more ambitious one. We shall also trace for you the intricate web of organizations which these men formed and utilized to accomplish these ends. We will show how the entire structure of offices and officials was dedicated to the criminal purposes and committed to the use of the criminal methods planned by these defendants and their co-conspirators, many of whom war and suicide have put beyond reach.

It is my purpose to open the case, particularly under Count One of the Indictment, and to deal with the Common Plan or Conspiracy to achieve ends possible only by resort to Crimes against Peace, War Crimes, and Crimes against Humanity. My emphasis will not be on individual barbarities and perversions which may have occurred independently of any central plan....

The case as presented by the United States will be concerned with the brains and authority back of all the crimes. These defendants were men of station and rank which does not soil its own hands with blood. They were men who knew how to use lesser folk as tools. We want to reach the planners and designers, the inciters and leaders without whose evil architecture the world would not have been for so long scourged with the violence and lawlessness, and wracked with the agonies and convulsions, of this terrible war....

DISPLACED JEWS IN OCCUPIED GERMANY

At the war's conclusion, many of its survivors were scattered far from their original homes or countries of origin. Some were refugees who had fled the fighting in one campaign or another, and now struggled to make do with what little they had been able to carry with them in the haste of evacuation. Others had been forcibly moved: inmates from concentration camps, prisoners of war, workers who had been conscripted for forced labor, and, most poignant of all, those who miraculously had survived the death camps. Most were in a very vulnerable position, the result of malnutrition and maltreatment, and all faced a precarious and uncertain future in a continent devastated by the destruction of cities and urban infrastructure, not to mention the main transportation networks. It was assumed that refugees or prisoners would be repatriated, but many of these "displaced persons" (or DPs) as they were called, had no desire to return to a former home in which they had been, or now likely would be, discriminated against or repressed (as in communist regimes). Indeed, some 12 million ethnic Germans were forcibly expelled from their communities in Polish, Czech, or Soviet territory, partly because of the obvious tensions with their neighbors, partly to prevent any recurrence of a German government justifying territorial expansion as a legitimate inclusion of such groupings of its ethnic compatriots. Anywhere from 10 to 30 million or more Europeans were displaced by the war (estimates vary widely because of the sheer difficulty in tracking shattered, dispersed families amid fragmentary documentary evidence), and many of them were grouped in temporary camps to await the resolution of their situations. In the most difficult circumstances of all were Holocaust survivors, whose lives had been torn apart. Earl G. Harrison (1899–1955), an American attorney and a former Commissioner of Immigration and Naturalization, was appalled that these Jewish victims of the war were now being made to suffer again as administrative obstacles delayed their ability to depart the DP camps and emigrate to Palestine or the United States. His report would prompt some action, including legislation in 1948 permitting the admission of 200,000 Jewish refugees.

I. GERMANY AND AUSTRIA

CONDITIONS

(1) Generally speaking, three months after V-E Day [Victory in Europe day; on May 7 in Rheims, France, and May 8, 1945, in Berlin, Germany signed the unconditional surrender] and even longer after the liberation of individual groups, many Jewish displaced persons and other possibly non-repatriables are living under guard behind barbed-wire fences, in camps of several descriptions (built by the Germans for slave-laborers and Jews), including some of the most notorious of the concentration camps, amidst crowded, frequently unsanitary and generally grim conditions, in complete idleness, with no opportunity, except surreptitiously, to communicate with the outside world, waiting, hoping for some word of encouragement and action in their behalf.

"The Treatment of Displaced Jews in the United States Zone of Occupation in Germany, 1945: Report of Earl G. Harrison to President Truman," http://www.sunsite.unc.edu/pha/policy/1945/540929a.html. Used by permission.

(2) While there has been marked improvement in the health of survivors of the Nazi starvation and persecution program, there are many pathetic malnutrition cases both among the hospitalized and in the general population of the camps. The death rate has been high since liberation, as was to be expected. One Army Chaplain, a Rabbi, personally attended, since liberation 23,000 burials (90 per cent Jews) at Bergen Belsen [former prisoner of war and concentration camp located about thirty-five miles northeast of Hannover, Germany] alone, one of the largest and most vicious of the concentration camps, where, incidentally, despite persistent reports to the contrary, fourteen thousand displaced persons are still living, including over seven thousand Jews. At many of the camps and centers including those where serious starvation cases are, there is a marked and serious lack of needed medical supplies.

(3) Although some Camp Commandants have managed, in spite of the many obvious difficulties, to find clothing of one kind or another for their charges, many of the Jewish displaced persons, late in July, had no clothing other than their concentration camp garb—a rather hideous striped pajama effect—while others, to their chagrin, were obliged to wear German S.S. uniforms. It is questionable which clothing they hate the more.

(4) With a few notable exceptions, nothing in the way of a program of activity or organized effort toward rehabilitation has been inaugurated and the internees, for they are literally such, have little to do except to dwell upon their plight, the uncertainty of their future and, what is more unfortunate, to draw comparisons between their treatment "under the Germans" and "in liberation." Beyond knowing that they are no longer in danger of the gas chambers, torture, and other forms of violent death, they see—and there is—little change. The morale of those who are either stateless or who do not wish to return to their countries of nationality is very low. They have witnessed great activity and efficiency in returning people to their homes but they hear or see nothing in the way of plans for them and consequently they wonder and frequently ask what "liberation" means. This situation is considerably accentuated where, as in so many cases, they are able to look from their crowded and bare quarters and see the German civilian population, particularly in the rural areas, to all appearances living normal lives in their own homes.

(5) The most absorbing worry of these Nazi and war victims concerns relatives—wives, husbands, parents, children. Most of them have been separated for three, four or five years and they cannot understand why the liberators should not have undertaken immediately the organized effort to reunite family groups. Most of the very little which has been done in this direction has been informal action by the displaced persons themselves with the aid of devoted Army Chaplains, frequently Rabbis, and the American Joint Distribution Committee [Jewish relief agency, originally founded in 1914 by Henry Morgenthau, that assisted European Jews during and after the war]....

(6) It is difficult to evaluate the food situation fairly because one must be mindful of the fact that quite generally food is scarce and is likely to be more so during the winter ahead. On the other hand, in presenting the factual situation, one must raise the question as to how much longer many of these people, particularly those who have over such a long period felt persecution and near starvation, can survive on a diet composed principally of bread and coffee, irrespective of the caloric content. In many camps, the 2,000 calories included 1,250 calories of a black, wet and extremely unappetizing bread. I received the distinct impression and considerable substantiating information that large numbers of the German population—again principally in the rural areas—have a more varied and palatable diet than is the case with the displaced persons....

(7) Many of the buildings in which displaced persons are housed are clearly unfit for winter use and everywhere there is great concern about the prospect of a complete lack of fuel. There is every likelihood that close to a million displaced persons will be in Germany and Austria when winter sets in. The outlook in many areas so far as shelter, food and fuel are concerned is anything but bright....

IV. CONCLUSIONS AND RECOMMENDATIONS

As matters now stand, we appear to be treating the Jews as the Nazis treated them except that we do not exterminate them. They are in concentration camps in large numbers under our military guard instead of S.S. troops. One is led to wonder whether the German people, seeing this, are not supposing that we are following or at least condoning Nazi policy....

I wish to repeat that the main solution, in many ways the only real solution, of the problem lies in the quick evacuation of all non-repatriable Jews in Germany and Austria, who wish it, to Palestine. In order to be effective, this plan must not be long delayed. The urgency of the situation should be recognized. It is inhuman to ask people to continue to live for any length of time under their present conditions....

JAPANESE BIOLOGICAL WARFARE

In 1925 the Geneva Convention banned both chemical and biological warfare. In defiance, Japan, under the guidance of Dr. Shiro Ishii (1892–1959), a member of the Army Medical Corps, initiated its own program to develop and test chemical and biological weapons during the 1930s and 1940s. In contrast to the United States and Great Britain, which tested biological weapons on animals during World War II, Ishii promoted a program in which humans, more specifically enemies of the Japanese state (Chinese, Russians), became the guinea pigs in the name of scientific research. Following Japan's invasion of Manchuria, Ishii began his experiments on germ warfare, using Chinese as his victims. Disguised as a water purification unit, Japan's infamous Unit 731 built a large complex outside the city of Harbin in Manchuria in which at least 9,000 people were subjected to, and died from, inhumane tests conducted on them. In 1942 new tests were conducted in which the Japanese air-dropped rats and fleas carrying bubonic plague as well as anthrax spores upon Chinese soldiers and civilians in the villages. Cholera and typhoid cultures were also dropped by airplane into water supplies. It has been estimated that roughly 200,000 deaths were caused by these various kinds of experimentation. The United States was an intended victim of Japanese biological warfare. In 1945 plans were also drawn up to float balloon bombs to carry various diseases across the ocean to the West Coast as well as use kamikaze pilots to dump plague-infected fleas on San Diego. American officials were eager to gain access to the Japanese research (and to deny it to the Soviets) and sought to keep much of Unit 731's work secret, even if this meant not punishing the principal perpetrators. Ishii, for example, went free in return for his assistance. The Soviets, who were no less fascinated by the implications of the Japanese research on biological warfare, placed twelve captured Japanese army personnel from the unit on trial in Khabarovsk, Siberia, in December 1949. It is the transcripts from that trial, excerpted next, that afford a glimpse into the shadowy work of Unit 731.

Materials on the Trial of Former Servicemen of the Japanese Army Charged with Manufacturing and Employing Bacteriological Weapons (Moscow: Foreign Languages Publishing House, 1950), 285–286, 321–324, 352–358. Used by permission.

EVENING SITTING, DECEMBER 26, 1949, EXAMINATION OF ACCUSED NISHI

STATE PROSECUTOR: Accused Nishi, what positions did you hold in Detachment 731, and at what times?

ACCUSED NISHI: From January 1943 to July 1944, I was Chief of Detachment 731's branch in the town of Sunyu. From July 1944 to July 1945, I was Chief of Training Division of Detachment 731.

QUESTION: What did Detachment 731 do? What were its functions?

ANSWER: Most of the work of Detachment 731 was concerned with preparation for waging bacteriological warfare....

QUESTION: What bacteriological means did Detachment 731 employ?

ANSWER: Its accepted weapons were the germs of plague, anthrax and gas gangrene.

QUESTION: Which of these disease carriers were considered the most effective?

ANSWER: Plague bacteria.

QUESTION: What methods of employing these bacteriological means were adopted by the detachment?

ANSWER: First, spraying bacteria from aircraft, second, dropping of porcelain bacteria bombs.

QUESTION: Were plague fleas employed to infect human beings?

ANSWER: Yes, they were employed in China....

QUESTION: Will you tell the Court about the sweets which were prepared...?

ANSWER: They were not sweets, but ordinary chocolates, which were to be stuffed with bacteria and then wrapped in papers. The chocolates were to be of round shape....

QUESTION: What bacteria were these chocolates infected with?

ANSWER: ...the chocolates contained the bacteria of anthrax. The chocolates were intended for sabotage actions.

QUESTION: Will you tell us what you know about the practical employment of bacteriological means of warfare by Detachment 731?

ANSWER: I heard that the bacteriological weapon was employed against China in 1940. In August and September 1940, when I was at the headquarters of the Water Supply and Prophylaxis Administration in Peking, I heard there that bacteria were used in the Nimpo area, in Central China....

EVENING SITTING, DECEMBER 27, 1949, EXAMINATION OF ACCUSED MITOMO

STATE PROSECUTOR: Accused Mitomo, when did you first join Detachment 100?

ANSWER: I joined Detachment 100 in April 1941....

QUESTION: Tell us what activities were conducted by the 6th Section of the 2nd Division of Detachment 100.

ANSWER: The main function...was to devise methods of bacteriological warfare and sabotage and the production of bacteria on a mass scale. This research was made in preparation for bacteriological warfare against the Soviet Union.

QUESTIONS: What germs primarily were studied?

ANSWER: Glanders, anthrax, cattle and sheep plague....

QUESTION: What were your functions in the 6th Section?

ANSWER: I was engaged, in the main, in cultivating the glanders germ. I also took part in experiments on human beings....

QUESTION: Tell us all you know about the experiments on human beings performed in Detachment 100.

ANSWER: Experiments on human beings were performed in August–September 1944. These experiments took the form of giving the experimentees, without their knowledge, soporific drugs and poisons. The experimentees included 7–8 Russians and Chinese. Korean bindweed, heroic and castor-oil seed were among the poisons used in the experiments. These poisons were put in the food.

The poisoned food was given to the experimentees five or six times over a period of two weeks. Korean bindweed was used mostly in soups, I think heroin in porridge, while tobacco was mixed with heroin and bactal. After eating the soup mixed with Korean bindweed the experimentees dropped off into a deep five-hour sleep 30 minutes or an hour later. After two weeks the experimentees were so weak that they could no longer be used.

QUESTION: What happened to them then?

ANSWER: For purposes of secrecy all the experimentees were put to death.

QUESTION: How?

ANSWER: There was the case of a Russian experimentee who...was put to death with an injection of one-tenth of a gram of potassium cyanide....

EVENING SITTING: DECEMBER 28, EXAMINATION OF WITNESS FURUICHI

PRESIDENT OF THE COURT: Witness Furuichi, I warn you of your liability to criminal prosecution for giving false testimony. In court you must speak nothing but the truth.

WITNESS FURUICHI: I understand that....

STATE PROSECUTOR: Witness Furuichi, tell us, under what circumstances, and when, you began to serve in Detachment 731?

WITNESS FURUICHI: I joined Detachment 731 in July 1941....

QUESTION: What have you to say about the work Detachment 731 as a whole was engaged in?

ANSWER: Although outwardly Detachment 731 was the Prophylaxis and Water Supply Administration, actually, it prepared for the conduct of bacteriological sabotage....

QUESTION: Did you take part in any expedition carried out by Detachment 731?

ANSWER: Yes, in 1942, I took part in an expedition into Central China.

QUESTION: Tell us, what were the objects of this expedition and what did you yourself do during this expedition?

ANSWER: The chief object of the expedition into Central China was to carry on sabotage against the Chinese troops and the civilian population in the region of the town of Yushan.

   In July 1942, a group from Detachment 731...arrived in Central China, in the city of Nanking....The final number of men in our expedition was 150–160....

QUESTION: What did the expedition do in Central China?

ANSWER: The work of the expedition in which I took part consisted in the following: this was a bacteriological attack by contaminating water sources, wells and buildings with the germs of typhoid and paratyphoid....The bacteria were put into peptone bottles and these bottles were placed in boxes marked "Water Supply." These boxes were sent to Nanking by aeroplane....

QUESTION: What did you yourself do during these acts of sabotage?

ANSWER: I helped to throw the flasks containing bacteria into wells, marshes and the homes of civilians.

   At that time there were...two camps for Chinese war prisoners, numbering about three thousand. Three thousand rolls were especially made; members of the expedition took part in making these rolls. A little later, these rolls were contaminated with bacteria with the aid of a syringe....

QUESTION: What was done with the Chinese war prisoners after they had eaten these germ-contaminated rolls?

ANSWER: They were released from the camp in order to cause an epidemic of typhoid and paratyphoid....

QUESTION: Tell us, do you know anything about the experiments performed on the detachment's proving ground near Anta Station?

ANSWER: Yes.

QUESTION: Tell the Court what you know.

ANSWER: Experiments on the proving ground at Anta Station were performed in 1944, in the autumn and winter. In these experiments the germs of typhoid and plague, and also of anthrax were used....

QUESTION: Tell us, were freezing experiments performed in Detachment 731?

ANSWER: Yes. I saw such experiments performed....

QUESTION: Tell us about the experiments in freezing human beings.

ANSWER: Experiments in freezing human beings were performed every year in the detachment, in the coldest months of the year: November, December, January and February. The technique of these experiments was as follows: the experimentees were taken out into the frost at night, at about 11 o'clock, and compelled to dip their hands into a barrel of cold water. Then they were compelled to take their hands out and stand with wet hands in the frost for a long time. Or else the following was done: the people were taken out dressed but with bare feet and compelled to stand at night in the frost in the coldest period of the year.

When these people had gotten frostbite, they were taken to a room and forced to put their feet in water of 5 C. temperature, and then the temperature was gradually increased....

QUESTION: What other experiments and tests were made on human beings?

ANSWER: I know that [a] researcher...performed experiments in applying ulcerating gas to people....

QUESTION: In what condition were these people? What symptoms of illness did they show?

ANSWER: I saw people with big ulcers on their hands and feet....

THE TOKYO WAR TRIALS

Postwar trials of war criminals were a nonnegotiable part of the broader demand for unconditional surrender embodied in the Potsdam Declaration conveyed to Japan in July 1945. Modeled on the trials conducted in Germany, the International Military Tribunal for the Far East met from May 1946 until November 1948. It was beset with a number of problems, however. The Soviet judge understood neither English nor Japanese and found it hard to follow the proceedings. The emperor, Hirohito, in whose name the war had been conducted, was not prosecuted. Efforts to try the principal defendants (Japan's military and political leaders) on charges of committing crimes against peace and waging aggressive war were complicated by the fact that no accepted definition of these issues as a violation of international law had existed at the time, raising the question of whether the Allies were not ex post facto changing the law to suit their purposes. Eight of the eleven tribunal justices supported the final judgment, including the execution of seven defendants (most notably, former general and prime minister Hideki Tojo). The Indian justice at the tribunal, Judge Radhabinod Pal (1886–1967), was one of the dissenters. He surprised and perplexed his colleagues by voting for acquittal in every instance. Pal did not dispute that the Japanese had done terrible things during the war, but he regarded the tribunal as a punitive exercise in which the victors imposed their own warped justice, while avoiding censure for the crimes that they had inflicted upon the vanquished, such as the use of atomic bombs. As a result of his dissent, Pal was revered by Japanese ultranationalists and honored with a memorial in Tokyo's Yasukuni Shrine to the nation's war dead. Despite the controversy surrounding the validity of the tribunal's actions, many Western observers felt that it had been an essential element in documenting the atrocious conduct of the Japanese military toward soldiers, prisoners, and civilians.

Judge R. Pal, "Judgment, " in B. V. A. Roeling and C. F. Rueter, eds., *The Tokyo Judgment: The International Military Tribunal for the Far East* (Amsterdam: Apa-University Press Amsterdam, 1977), 2 vols., 2:574–575, 577, 1035. Used by permission.

As to the "widening sense of humanity" prevailing in international life, all I can say is that at least before the Second World War the powerful nations did not show any such sign....If we take the fact that there still continued domination of one nation by another, that servitude of nations still prevailed unreviled and that domination of one nation by another continued to be regarded by the so-called international community only as a domestic question for the master nation, I cannot see how such a community can even pretend that its basis is humanity. In this connection I cannot refrain from referring to what Mr. Justice Jackson asserted in his summing up of the case at Nuremberg. According to him, a preparation by a nation to dominate another nation is the worst of crimes. This may be so now. But I do not see how it could be said that such an attempt or preparation was a crime before the Second World War when there was hardly a big power which was free from that taint. Instead of saying that all the powerful nations were living a criminal life I would prefer to hold that international society did not develop before the Second World War so as to make this taint a crime.

The atom bomb during the Second World War, it is said, has destroyed selfish nationalism and the last defense of isolationism more completely than it razed an enemy city. It is believed that it has ended one age and begun another—the new and unpredictable age of soul. "Such blasts as leveled Hiroshima and Nagasaki on August 6 and 9, 1945, never occurred on earth before—nor in the sun or stars, which burn from sources that release their energy much more slowly than does uranium." So said John J. O'Neill, the science editor, *New York Herald Tribune*. "In a fraction of a second the atomic bomb that dropped on Hiroshima altered our traditional economic, political, and military values. It caused a revolution in the technique of war that forces immediate reconsideration of our entire national defense problem." Perhaps these blasts have brought home to mankind "that every human being has a stake in the conduct not only of national affairs but also of world affairs." Perhaps these explosives have awakened within us the sense of unity of mankind, the feeling that: "we are a unity of humanity, linked to all our fellow human beings, irrespective of race, creed or color, by bonds which have been fused unbreakably in the diabolical heat of those explosions."

All this might have been the result of these blasts. But certainly these feelings were non-existent at the time when the bombs were dropped. I, for myself, do not perceive any such feeling of broad humanity in the justifying words of those who were responsible for their use. As a matter of fact, I do not perceive much difference between what the German Emperor is alleged to have announced during the First World War in justification of the atrocious methods directed by him in the conduct of that war and what is being proclaimed after the Second World War in justification of these inhuman blasts....

I know that as a judge, it is not for me to preach the need for a wider social consciousness or to propound practical solutions for the problems involved in the material interdependence of the modern world. Yet the international relation has reached a stage where even a judge cannot remain silent though the task that is given him is only one of formulation, classification and interpretation....[I]t is high time that international law should recognize the individual as its ultimate subject and maintenance of his rights as its ultimate end....A law of nations effectively realizing that purpose would acquire a substance and a dignity which would go far toward assuring its ascendancy as an instrument of peace and progress. This certainly is to be done by a method very different from that of trial of war criminals from amongst the vanquished nations....

For the reasons given in the forgoing pages, I would hold that each and everyone of the accused must be found not guilty of each and everyone of the charges in the indictment and should be acquitted of all those charges. I have not considered whether or not any of the wars against any of the nations covered by the indictments was aggressive. The view of law that I take as to the criminality or otherwise of any war makes it unnecessary for me to enter into this question.

Further, I have indicated the difficulty that I feel in defining "aggressive war," keeping in view the generally prevalent behavior of the powers in international life.... I believe this [the argument that under Article 43 of the 1907 Hague Convention, victorious powers had the right to isolate or arrest defeated leaders in the interest of postwar stability] is really an appeal to the political power of the victor nations with a pretense of legal justice.

AMERICAN POLICY FOR POSTWAR JAPAN

Although Japanese hard-liners had bitterly opposed the prospect of an Allied occupation of the home islands, Emperor Hirohito's broadcast of surrender on August 15, 1945, erased any doubts that after the end of the war the Japanese might escape the presence of American soldiers on their soil. As Supreme Commander of the Allied Powers (or SCAP), General Douglas MacArthur (1880–1964) headed the occupation, which sought to restore the stability and prosperity of the shattered nation while at the same time disarming, demilitarizing, and democratizing it. The imperious American general found a useful partner in Emperor Hirohito, who willingly shed his traditional aura as a divine figure and embraced the new role of a largely ceremonial constitutional monarch. Yet even with the retention of the imperial throne, MacArthur's task of reforming and reconstructing an entire society was a daunting one, as his orders from the Joint Chiefs of Staff make clear.

The ultimate objective of the United Nations with respect to Japan is to foster conditions which will give the greatest possible assurance that Japan will not again become a menace to the peace and security of the world and will permit her eventual admission as a responsible and peaceful member of the family of nations. Certain measures considered to be essential for the achievement of this objective have been set forth in the Potsdam Declaration. These measures include, among others, the carrying out of the Cairo Declaration and the limiting of Japanese sovereignty to the four main islands [Hokkaido, Honshu, Kyushu, and Shikoku] and such minor islands as the Allied powers determine; the abolition of militarism and ultra-nationalism in all their forms; the disarmament and demilitarization of Japan, with continuing control over Japan's capacity to make war; the strengthening of democratic tendencies and processes in governmental, economic and social institutions; and the encouragement and support of liberal political tendencies in Japan. The United States desires that the Japanese Government conform as closely as may be to principles of democratic self-government, but it is not the responsibility of the occupational forces to impose on Japan any form of government not supported by the freely expressed will of the people....

"Basic Initial Post-Surrender Directive to Supreme Commander for the Allied Powers for the Occupation and Control of Japan," November 8, 1945, as reprinted from www.ndl.go.jp/constitution/e/shiryo/01/036/036tx.html, 123, 125–127, 132, 139–142. Used by permission.

Where action is necessary in order to carry out the surrender, you have the right to act directly from the outset. Otherwise, subject always to your right as the Supreme Commander to take direct action in the event of the unwillingness or failure of the Emperor or other Japanese authority to act effectively, you will exercise your supreme authority through the Emperor and Japanese government machinery, national and local. The policy is to use the existing form of government in Japan, not to support it. Changes in the direction of modifying the feudal and authoritarian tendencies of the government are to be permitted and favored....

By appropriate means you will make clear to all levels of the Japanese population the fact of their defeat. They must be made to realize that their suffering and defeat have been brought upon them by the lawless and irresponsible aggression of Japan, and that only when militarism has been eliminated from Japanese life and institutions will Japan be admitted to the family of nations. They must be told that they will be expected to develop a non-militaristic and democratic Japan which will respect the rights of other nations and Japan's international obligations. You will make it clear that military occupation of Japan is effected in the interests of the United Nations and is necessary for the destruction of Japan's power of aggression and her war potential and for the elimination of militarism and militaristic institutions which have brought disaster on the Japanese....

Local, regional and national agencies of governmental administration, excluding those functions and responsibility inconsistent with the purposes of the occupation, will be permitted to continue to function after the removal of officials who are unacceptable.... [I]n no circumstances will persons be allowed to hold public office or any other positions of responsibility or influence in public or important private enterprise who have been active exponents of militant nationalism and aggression, who have been influential members of any Japanese ultra-nationalistic terroristic or secret patriotic society,...or who manifest hostility to the objectives of the military occupation....

You will establish such minimum control and censorship of civilian communications including the mails, wireless, radio, telephone, telegraph and cables, film and press as may be necessary in the interests of military security and the accomplishment of the purposes set forth in this directive. Freedom of thought will be fostered by the dissemination of democratic ideals and principles through all available media of public information.

You will immediately place under control all existing political parties, organizations and societies. Those whose activities are consistent with the requirements of the military occupation and its objectives should be encouraged. Those whose activities are inconsistent with such requirements and objectives should be abolished. Subject to the necessity of maintaining the security of the occupying forces, the formation and activities of democratic political parties with rights of assembly and public discussion will be encouraged. Free elections of representative local governments should be held at the earliest practicable date, and at the regional and national levels as directed, after consideration of your recommendation, through the Joint Chiefs of Staff. Your action in connection with the program referred to in this subparagraph should be taken in the light of one of the ultimate objectives of the occupation, the establishment, in accordance with the freely expressed will of the Japanese people, of a peacefully inclined and responsible government....

As soon as practicable educational institutions will be reopened. As rapidly as possible, all teachers who have been active exponents of militant nationalism and aggression and those who continue actively to oppose the purposes of the military occupation will be replaced by acceptable and qualified successors....

You will not assume any responsibility for the economic rehabilitation of Japan or the strengthening of the Japanese economy. You will make it clear to the Japanese people that: a. you assume no obligations to maintain, or have maintained, any particular standard of living in Japan, and b. that the standard of living will depend upon the thoroughness with which Japan rids itself of all militaristic ambitions, redirects the use of its human and natural resources wholly and solely for purposes of peaceful living, administers adequate economic and financial controls, and cooperates with the occupying forces and the governments they represent....

It is the intent of the United States Government to encourage and show favor to: a. policies which permit a wide distribution of income and of ownership of the means of production and trade. b. The development organizations in labor, industry, and agriculture organized on a democratic basis....

Accordingly, you will: 1. Require the Japanese to establish a public agency responsible for reorganizing Japanese business in accordance with the military and economic objectives of your government. You will require this agency to submit, for approval by you, plans for dissolving large Japanese industrial and banking combines or other large concentrations of private business control.... 4. Abrogate all legislative or administrative measures which limit free entry of firms into industries to be reorganized where the purpose or effect of such measures is to foster and strengthen private monopoly....

You will assure that all practicable economic and police measures are taken to achieve the maximum utilization of essential Japanese resources in order that imports into Japan may be strictly limited. Such measures will include production and price controls, rationing, control of black markets, fiscal and financial control and other measures directed toward full employment of resources, facilities and means available in Japan.

JAPAN ADJUSTS TO OCCUPATION

Japan's occupation did not end until the Treaty of San Francisco, signed in September 1951, went into effect in 1952, after which Japan regained its status as an independent nation. Even after just six years, it was clear that the occupation had succeeded in several of its tasks: it broke the power of the militarist cabal, it preserved Japan from communist influence or subversion, and it nourished a stable and outwardly democratic polity. It was less effective in restructuring the economy, curtailing the influence of the *Zaibatsu* (the business conglomerates), or neutralizing the old elites, many of whose members resumed a more public role in the 1950s. Russell Brines (1911–1982) was an experienced journalist who covered the war in Asia for the Associated Press and continued to report on the region throughout the Korean War. Here he tries to convey how the average Japanese citizen viewed the American presence during the first half of the occupation.

The Japanese blew hot and cold through the five main occupation seasons.

First was the period of confusion and apprehension. It began with the ill-understood imperial surrender rescript and lasted through the early months of the bloodless invasion. This was the time when the streets were deserted at night and women scuttled to safety from husky foreign visitors. It was an era of whispered stories about rape and robbery. The Japanese were constantly apprehensive over the next new innovation to be ordered by headquarters, which might alter familiar institutions or destroy the prized pattern of antiquity.

Russell Brines, *MacArthur's Japan* (Philadelphia: J. B. Lippincott Co., 1948), 270–277. Used by permission.

This was succeeded by the era of gratitude. The Japanese realized with a rush that they had become the most fortunate losers in military history and that a totally unexpected, benevolent occupation was underway. Jiro Tanaka, the Average Man, turned his adulation of authority from the emperor to General MacArthur and his respect for power from his own leaders to the conquerors. Whatever came from headquarters was welcomed or, at least, not openly opposed....

Then came hope and confidence, a beckoning future. The movement for a peace treaty, started by General MacArthur, quickly won support, except from Russia, as usual....The treaty could be signed quickly, and at once the weight of uncertainty would be removed. Mr. Tanaka did not visualize a small, poor country with conditions unchanged from the present, or worse. He thought that, with a treaty, food would flow immediately to the markets, and a man would no longer be forced to live on useless currency or haggle for a livelihood....

The Japanese had their own ideas about democracy and its progress. "See, we have reformed," they often said. "We have democracy now, and we are very grateful. But the occupation, it is costing much money." After all, it was an easy task for an old country like Japan to adopt democracy. In fact, it was difficult sometimes to understand why other nations had taken centuries to become democracies. Every day some Japanese proved the point. A lot of them could write names on a ballot. The labor unions had put the bosses in their places. The emperor had become a transcontinental commuter, and he waved to everyone. What else was necessary? After all, it was appearance that mattered....

He regarded the basic idea of occupation pretty much in personal terms. The GI's had done nothing to him personally, so he was inclined to consider them as pretty nice boys....Mr. Tanaka had been known to say many times that he was glad to have husky young men with a lot of guns around him in case the communists or the "bad" labor unions got ambitious.

But then his government announced for the first time how much the occupation was costing. The government also said the occupation took many of the materials Japan needed for foreign trade. Mr. Tanaka had heard this factor was responsible for the fact that his money wouldn't buy anything. It was also reported to be the cause of his high taxes, which took about one fourth of every month's pay. Hmm!...

When it came to big issues, Mr. Tanaka's mind was quite clear. The United States needed Japan and was making every effort to win her friendship. Japan had surprised everyone by the way she performed under the occupation, and the whole world was looking to her for leadership in the crisis. Why, it was well known that Japan was one of the last bulwarks against communism! And she was a pioneer, by her constitution, in the quest for peace. Therefore, with some shrewd bargaining, the Japanese would be strong again very soon. Everybody abroad had forgotten the war and was intent upon new problems. So the Japanese had nothing for which to apologize....

He had thought a lot about the first days of peace. He remembered how, when the Americans were about to come in, Mrs. Tanaka had put on her baggiest pair of pants to keep from being accosted. Now she wore makeup and fixed her hair all the time and looked as if she wanted to be accosted.

Mr. Tanaka also was a bit worried about his eldest daughter. Since she had been going around with that young American soldier, she kept insisting that she was going to choose her own husband. Imagine an eighteen-year-old girl knowing more about marriage and husbands than her own father! The younger children also had shown a lamentable inclination to argue with him about life. It was something they had picked up at school. Mr. Tanaka was not worried, however. If this fad did not wear off, he could stop it easily enough by exercising his authority as head of the house. But all these things made him think that, whatever democracy was, it caused a lot of arguments....

But democracy also laughed a lot. Mr. Tanaka could not remember when he had seen so many smiles or so much giggling as when the GI's walked, rather shamelessly, down the street with Japanese girls. He could not see much for amusement in these times, but it was good to get away from the heaviness of the war when everybody had had a long face and tight lips. Maybe it was baseball that made the soldiers happy. It was a good game, except that Mr. Tanaka wished his own team, the Tokyo Giants, would lose less frequently and save him face now and then. The movies might also be responsible; Mr. Tanaka preferred the more solid dramas which made his wife cry and kept his young son quiet.

In all honesty, he was shocked and somewhat angry at all the lipstick and powder and short skirts and wrinkled stockings. He didn't like to see women smoke on the streets, and the great gangs of street-walkers sickened him, not so much on moral grounds, for he was no philosopher and had been familiar with the large, sprawling licensed quarters of the Yoshiwara which the bombers destroyed. But there was no charm in sidewalk barter. He was offended also by the flood of uncouth pornographic literature and the pimply college students who rushed to buy it. This was linked in his mind with the harsh jazz music he heard over the radio, that sounded like a freight car with a flat wheel. Mr. Tanaka was rather disgusted by the explanation that all this was democratic and that youth was going the way it was out of a new freedom that made them curious. Democracy, it seemed, could be uncouth....

Mr. Tanaka knew he was only an average man and expected to be no more. But it warmed him to know there were some in Japan who perpetuated the old culture, with an occasional pause to view the things they told him were beautiful or to write about them. He had heard it said that the new times and the rush

of new ideas would destroy Old Japan, all of which he could not understand but valued. Democracy, quite evidently, could be Japanese.

No, it was very plain that democracy had borrowed a lot from Japan. Therefore one did not have to change very much to be a democrat. Once it had been feared the Americans would completely remake the whole country, and the press mentioned the "rights of the people" as if they were machine guns to mow down the old officials and wipe out their mean little tricks. Mr. Tanaka still had the same corner policeman, the same district tax collector and he had voted for the same Neighborhood Association leader....

Mr. Tanaka thought more about democracy when he saw shiny new busses and sedans from the window of his crowded, dirty train than when he read vague generalities about it in his newspaper. He wondered if Japan, too, could reach wealth through it.

On the whole, Mr. Tanaka thought things had gone off quite well. He heard many Americans still hated the Japanese, but you wouldn't get that idea from seeing the soldiers in Japan. Still, it was unpleasant for a proud Japanese to be under an occupation force. That was one reason Mr. Tanaka hoped the peace treaty would come soon, and his country again would become a major power.

REVOLUTION AND LIBERATION IN INDOCHINA

By 1945, Indochina had been under French colonial rule for a century. The situation was a complex one, however, for while the Japanese military's aggressive campaigns and search for raw materials in Southeast Asia made Vietnam an obvious target, the ruling French Vichy government was a puppet of Nazi Germany, which in turn was allied with Japan. In 1941 the Japanese occupied the country and exploited its people and resources, but left the French administration largely intact in principle, if weak in practice. The war witnessed the emergence and growth of a communist guerilla movement, the Viet Minh, dedicated to national liberation, which meant expelling both the French and the Japanese. The most prominent leader of the Viet Minh was the French-educated Ho Chi Minh (1890–1969), and he was successful in attracting American support (through the OSS) for resisting the Japanese occupation. The Viet Minh were especially successful in the northernmost of the three principal Vietnamese regions (Tongking). This resolution, adopted there in April 1945 after the Japanese had abolished the French administration the month before, illustrates how the idea of fighting oppression in the form of fascism galvanized subject populations across the region. Once the genie of democratic government was out of the bottle, so to speak, it could not be easily stuffed back in; it could, in fact, be turned against any country, not just Germany or Japan.

The Revolutionary Military Conference of Tongking has opened at a time when, in the international arena, the war between the aggressive camp and the non-aggressive camp has entered a decisive stage, and immediately after the staging of a Japanese coup in our country. Following that coup there developed in our country a wide anti-Japanese Movement for National Salvation, which has drawn into the struggle the broadest strata of the population.

At the same time shots fired by the guerrillas of our National Liberation Army have heralded the beginning of the armed struggle of the Vietnamese people against the Japanese oppressors....

Simultaneously with the war against Fascism there is growing a revolutionary liberation movement throughout the world. Almost all the countries of Europe, which were enslaved by Germany, have been liberated. "National independence!" is the main slogan of the present revolutionary movement.

This movement is also a movement for the <u>new democracy</u>. Masses of workers and peasants have risen in order to break the fetters of bourgeois democracy. From Finland to Belgium, from Rumania to Italy—everywhere Communists are participating in the Government. In France, in particular, two parties, the Communist and the Socialist, have concluded an alliance and have forced the Government of de Gaulle to accept a wide economic programme and to establish a truly democratic system.

In East Asia the Chinese are continuing their resistance. Under the influence of the popular

"The Resolution of the Revolutionary Military Conference of Tong King," in Rima Rathausky, ed., *Documents of the August 1945 Revolution in Vietnam* (Canberra: Australian National University, 1963), 14–17, 20. Used by permission.

movements and progressive tendencies throughout the world China is becoming more and more democratic. The Government in Chungking [China's wartime capital also known as Chongqing, located in southeast Sichuan Province] has been partially reconstructed. The talks between the Kuomintang and the Communist Party of China have brought some results.

Following the example of the Chinese people, the Korean people have intensified their struggle for independence. Notwithstanding the disappointing differences between the Hindus and the Moslems within the National Congress, India has finally taken part in the war against the Japanese Fascists.

The entire East has arisen in order to participate in the destruction of Japanese Fascism. It is full of determination to make use of the existing situation to gain the right to national independence and to establish a system of new democracy.

In a word, at present there is taking place throughout Europe and Asia a struggle to the death between the aggressive camp and the non-aggressive camp. Though the defeat of Japanese Fascism is not so close as the defeat of Hitlerism, nevertheless it is also not far off. Thanks to the sacrifices made by the whole of mankind in the fight against Fascism, a new world is being built, the world of new democracy. This extremely favourable objective situation serves as a strong impetus to the Vietnamese revolutionary movement and constitutes one of the conditions ensuring the success of our revolutionary struggle for national liberation....

The Anti-Japanese Movement is growing, and this is resulting in a considerable broadening of Viet Minh [nationalist organization known as the League for the Independence of Vietnam, founded by Ho Chi Minh for the purpose of creating an independent Vietnam] organizations. In certain regions the number of Viet Minh adherents after the "coup" increased sixfold. In various districts there were formed Liberation Committees and Revolutionary People's Committees with the task of taking into their hands local authority and calling upon the population to fight against the Japanese.

HO CHI MINH APPEALS TO TRUMAN

After the Japanese surrender in August 1945, the way was clear for Ho Chi Minh and the communist Viet Minh to concentrate upon dismantling French colonial rule in Indochina. Riots and demonstrations in the ensuing power vacuum culminated in the so-called August Revolution and Ho's proclamation of the Democratic Republic of Vietnam on September 2, 1945. By February 1946, the situation was deteriorating for Ho's fledgling government as the French sought to restore their authority in the country. In response, Ho Chi Minh appealed to the United States to exercise pressure upon France to withdraw, and he couched his appeal in terms of the solidarity of freedom-loving people fighting oppression, a rhetorical aim the Allies had embraced during the war.

Dear Mr. President:

I avail myself of this opportunity to thank you and the people of the United States for the interest shown by your representatives at the United Nations Organization in favour of the dependent peoples.

Our VIETNAM people, as early as 1941, stood by the Allies' side and fought against the Japanese and their associates, the French colonialists.

From 1941 to 1945 we fought bitterly, sustained by the patriotism of our fellow-countrymen and by the promises made by the Allies at YALTA, SAN FRANCISCO and POTSDAM.

When the Japanese were defeated in August 1945, the whole Vietnam territory was united under a Provisional Republican Government which immediately set out to work. In five months, peace and order were restored, a democratic republic was established on legal bases, and adequate help was given to the Allies in the carrying out of their disarmament mission.

But the French colonialists, who betrayed in war-time both the Allies and the Vietnamese, have come back and are waging on us a murderous and pitiless war in order to reestablish their domination. Their invasion has extended to South Vietnam and is menacing us in North Vietnam. It would take volumes to give even an abbreviated report of the crises and assassinations they are committing everyday in the fighting area.

This aggression is contrary to all principles of international law and the pledges made by the Allies during the World War. It is a challenge to the noble attitude shown before, during and after the war by the United States Government and the People. It violently contrasts with the firm stand you have taken in your twelve point declaration, and with the idealistic loftiness and generosity expressed by your delegates to the United Nations Assembly, MM [Misters] BYRNES, STETTINIUS, and J.F. DULLES.

The French aggression on a peace-loving people is a direct menace to world security. It implies the complicity, or at least the connivance of the Great Democracies. The United Nations ought to keep their words. They ought to interfere to stop this unjust war, and to show that they mean to carry out in peace-time the principles for which they fought in war-time.

Our Vietnamese people, after so many years of spoliation and devastation, is just beginning its building-up work. It needs security and freedom,

"Letter of Ho Chi Minh to President Truman, February 16, 1946," in *The United States and Vietnam: 1944–1947* (Washington, DC: U.S. Government Printing Office, 1972), 10–11. Used by permission.

first to achieve internal prosperity and welfare, and later to bring its small contribution to world-reconstructions.

This security and freedom can only be guaranteed by our independence from any colonial power, and our free cooperation with all other powers. It is with this firm conviction that we request of the United States as guardians and champions of World Justice to take a decisive step in support of our independence.

What we ask has been graciously granted to the Philippines. Like the Philippines our goal is full independence and full cooperation with the UNITED STATES. We will do our best to make this independence and cooperation profitable to the whole world.

AFRICA SPEAKS

Unlike in the First World War, sub-Saharan Africa was not the scene of fighting between British and German forces. From 1939 onward, however, British East Africa was the scene of a campaign that would eventually drive Italian occupying troops out of Abyssinia. Robert H. Kakembo, a Ugandan, served in the King's African Rifles, and though his region may have experienced less in the way of prolonged combat, it was nonetheless profoundly affected by the military's mobilization. Indeed, throughout colonial Africa and Southeast Asia, the prestige of the imperial powers was diminished by wartime defeats or episodes of obvious incompetence. In the case of Britain in particular, it was clear the extent to which its very survival depended on the loyalty of its colonial subjects. As those very subjects donned uniforms in a struggle, they were told, to defend freedom against tyranny, and as they met and mingled with other subordinate groups, it grew more difficult for the European empires to anticipate returning to business as usual once the war was over. In Africa, within twenty years of 1945, nearly all of the continent would be independent, freed from colonial domination. Kakembo's memoirs, though measured in tone, give a clear indication of the war's incendiary and liberating effects on the consciousness of ordinary Africans.

My five years of service in the army, that is, since September 1939, has shown me without doubt that the Army, the war, in spite of its many drawbacks, is the best practical school one can ever go to. No university rivals the war as a teacher of sociology and geography. The war is a great molder of character. It makes men realize their manliness for the first time in their lives. It makes men men. It is a great leveler of men, but I would not care to make it my career.

It was this war that brought most of the East and Central African tribes together for the first time in history of Africa.... Now, during this war, not only do we meet men from other parts of Africa, but we have been up and down those countries. It will be recorded by historians that it was during the war that the African started to think more in terms of a race than as a tribe. The words 'the African,' 'the native,' are showing us that we are all one and the same race....

R. H. Kakembo, *An African Soldier Speaks* (London: Edinburgh House Press, 1946), 19, 22–24, 46. Used by permission.

Now the African soldier has learned to read and write; he is used to reading newspapers, to listening to wireless broadcasts, to seeing films, to playing games, both outdoor and indoor ones. The question is, will this man, the widely travelled and educated soldier go back and be satisfied to go back home to his village and live in the same old dull conditions that he lived in before the war? You know as well as I do that we have men demobilized from the forces who have been highly trained in all branches of warfare of a mechanized army, which is producing an outlook and an intensification of mentality that will never submit to the neglect that the uneducated masses, back home in the villages, undergo.

I would like to urge our trustees to direct their mind not to plan for getting rid of the demobilized soldier as quickly as possible, but to the laying of a new foundation for society—now. I speak with experience when I say that things will never be as they used to be before the war....

The civilians too are not unchanged by the effects of this total war. The war has brought about a great industrial revolution and agricultural improvement. The favourable prices, the assured market, the Allies' continuous demand for greater output—all these have brought about a great revolution in the ordinary life of the African, and he is not going back to where he started in 1939....

Having fought for liberty, equality and for all the four freedoms expressed in the Atlantic Charter, we are determined not to remain behind in the world race. We have every right to claim a share in the future advantages and opportunities of development. We have a very long way to go to catch up with the senior races, but the war has shown the world that we are men, and given the opportunity, we are a match of anybody else in the world. I speak with the Rt. Hon. Winston Churchill: Give us the tools and we will finish the job.

"THE LONG TELEGRAM" AND CONTAINMENT

By early 1946, it was becoming increasingly clear that the wartime alliance of the United States and the Soviet Union marked only the temporary convergence of states with fundamentally differing interests. Now that Germany was defeated and the war was over, there was nothing to restrain the former allies from emerging as open and bitter rivals. A highly influential analysis of how the United States should respond to postwar realities was embodied in this 5,300-word "long telegram" from George Kennan (1904–2005), an American diplomat in Moscow to James Byrnes, the Secretary of State. Kennan sought to explain what he had observed of the Soviet government's worldview and how that perspective would shape Soviet policy. He regarded Stalin's government as insecure and suspicious, driven by communist ideology, and therefore inherently expansionist. The correct American response was a policy of "containment," to stymie Soviet pressure on areas of strategic importance to the United States. Kennan's views, later expanded into a famous journal article on "The Sources of Soviet Conduct" in the July 1947 issue of *Foreign Affairs*, helped to justify the idea of continual American vigilance during the cold war and President Truman's commitment "to support free peoples who are resisting attempted subjugation by armed minorities or by outside pressures" (the so-called Truman Doctrine).

Courtesy of the Harry S. Truman Library

SECRET

Moscow, February 22, 1946 @ 9 p.m. [received February 22 @ 3:52 p.m.]

PART 1: BASIC FEATURES OF POST WAR SOVIET OUTLOOK, AS PUT FORWARD BY OFFICIAL PROPAGANDA MACHINE ARE AS FOLLOWS:

(a) USSR [Union of Soviet Socialist Republics] still lives in antagonistic "capitalist encirclement" with which in the long run there can be no permanent coexistence....

(b) Capitalist world is beset with internal conflicts, inherent in nature of capitalist society. These conflicts are insoluble by means of peaceful compromise. Greatest of them is that between England and US.

(c) Internal conflicts of capitalism inevitably generate wars. Wars thus generated may be of two kinds: intra-capitalist wars between two capitalist states, and wars of intervention against socialist world. Smart capitalists, vainly seeking escape from inner conflicts of capitalism, incline toward latter.

(d) Intervention against USSR, while it would be disastrous to those who undertook it, would cause renewed delay in progress of Soviet socialism and must therefore be forestalled at all costs.

(e) Conflicts between capitalist states, though likewise fraught with danger for USSR, nevertheless hold out great possibilities for advancement of socialist cause, particularly if USSR remains militarily powerful, ideologically monolithic and faithful to its present brilliant leadership.

(f) It must be borne in mind that capitalist world is not all bad. In addition to hopelessly reactionary and bourgeois elements, it includes (1) certain wholly enlightened and positive elements united in acceptable communistic parties and (2) certain other elements...whose reactions, aspirations and activities happen to be "objectively" favorable to interests of USSR. These last must be encouraged and utilized for Soviet purposes....

So much for premises. To what deductions do they lead from standpoint of Soviet policy? To following:

(a) Everything must be done to advance relative strength of USSR as factor in international society. Conversely, no opportunity must be missed to reduce strength and influence, collectively as well as individually, of capitalist powers.

(b) Soviet efforts, and those of Russia's friends abroad, must be directed toward deepening and exploiting of differences and conflicts between capitalist powers. If these eventually deepen into an "imperialist" war, this war must be turned into revolutionary upheavals within the various capitalist countries....

PART 2: BACKGROUND OF OUTLOOK

Before examining ramifications of this party line in practice there are certain aspects of it to which I wish to draw attention....

[I]t does not represent natural outlook of Russian people. Latter are, by and large, friendly to outside world, eager for experience of it, eager to measure against it talents they are conscious of possessing, eager above all to live in peace and enjoy fruits of their own labor. Party line only represents thesis which official propaganda machine puts forward with great skill and persistence to a public often remarkably resistant in the stronghold of its innermost thoughts. But party line is binding for outlook and conduct of people who make up apparatus of power—party, secret police and Government—and it is exclusively with these that we have to deal....

It indicates that Soviet party line is not based on any objective analysis of situation beyond Russia's borders; that it has, indeed, little to do with conditions outside of Russia; that it arises mainly from basic inner-Russian necessities which existed before recent war and exist today.

At bottom of Kremlin's neurotic view of world affairs is traditional and instinctive Russian sense of insecurity. Originally, this was insecurity of a peaceful agricultural people trying to live on vast exposed plain in neighborhood of fierce nomadic peoples. To this was added, as Russia came into contact with economically advanced West, fear of more competent, more powerful, more highly organized societies in that area.... For this reason they have always feared foreign penetration, feared direct contact between Western world and their own, feared what would happen if Russians learned truth about world without or if foreigners learned truth about world within....

PART 3: PROJECTION OF SOVIET OUTLOOK IN PRACTICAL POLICY ON OFFICIAL LEVEL . . .

On official plane we must look for following:

(a) Internal policy devoted to increasing in every way strength and prestige of Soviet state: intensive military-industrialization; maximum development of armed forces; great displays to impress outsiders; continued secretiveness about internal matters, designed to conceal weaknesses and to keep opponents in dark.

(b) Wherever it is considered timely and promising, efforts will be made to advance official limits of Soviet power. For the moment, these efforts are restricted to certain neighboring points conceived of here as being of immediate strategic necessity, such as Northern Iran, Turkey....

(c) Russians will participate officially in international organization where they see opportunity of extending Soviet power or of inhibiting or diluting power of others. Moscow sees in UNO [United Nations Organization] not the mechanism for a permanent and stable world society founded on mutual interest and aims of all nations, but an arena in which aims just mentioned can be favorably pursued. As long as UNO is considered here to serve this purpose, Soviets will remain with it.... I reiterate, Moscow has no abstract devotion to UNO ideals. Its attitude to that organization will remain essentially pragmatic and tactical.

(d) Toward colonial areas and backward or dependent peoples, Soviet policy, even on official plane, will be directed toward weakening of power and influence and contacts of advanced Western nations, on theory that in so far as this policy is successful, there will be created a vacuum which will favor Communist-Soviet penetration....

(e) Russians will strive energetically to develop Soviet representation in, and official ties with, countries in which they sense strong possibilities of opposition to Western centers of power. This applies to such widely separated points as Germany, Argentina, Middle Eastern countries, etc.

(f) In international economic matters, Soviet policy will really be dominated by pursuit of autarchy for Soviet Union and Soviet-dominated adjacent areas taken together....

PART 5: PRACTICAL DEDUCTIONS FROM STANDPOINT OF US POLICY

In summary, we have here a political force committed fanatically to the belief that with US there can be no permanent *modus vivendi* that is desirable and necessary, that the internal harmony of our society be disrupted, our traditional way of life be destroyed, the international authority of our state be broken, if Soviet power is to be secure. This political force has complete power of disposition over energies of one of world's greatest peoples and resources of world's richest national territory, and is borne along by deep and powerful currents of Russian nationalism. In addition, it has an elaborate and far flung apparatus for exertion of its influence in other countries, an apparatus of amazing flexibility and versatility, managed by people whose experience and skill in underground methods are presumably without parallel in history.... Problem of how to cope with this force is undoubtedly greatest task our diplomacy has ever faced and probably greatest it will ever have to face....

THE IRON CURTAIN

When Winston Churchill went to Fulton, Missouri, in President Harry Truman's home state, to receive an honorary degree from Westminster College, he was no longer prime minister. In fact, when he addressed the crowd there on March 5, 1946, he did not do so in any official capacity for the British government (he was now leader of the opposition to Attlee's Labour government), but could still draw upon the immense affection and respect with which he was regarded in the United States. Truman agreed to accompany and introduce him, so Churchill knew he would have an attentive and influential audience. Part of his intention that day was to warn, as he had warned in the 1930s, of the threat of tyranny, in this case from Stalin's Soviet regime. Churchill also wanted to ensure that Britain and America would retain what he called their "special relationship" and not drift apart or see the United States retreat again into isolation. Although he regarded his message as one elaborating the "sinews of peace" that could ensure a stable world order, Churchill was heavily criticized for having escalated tensions with the Soviets and accentuated the slide into the cold war.

The United States stands at this time at the pinnacle of world power. It is a solemn moment for the American Democracy. For with primacy in power is also joined an awe-inspiring accountability to the future....

What then is the overall strategic concept which we should inscribe today? It is nothing less than the safety and welfare, the freedom and progress, of all the homes and families of all the men and women in all the lands. And here I speak particularly of the myriad cottage or apartment homes where the wage-earner strives amid the accidents and difficulties of life to guard his wife and children from privation and bring the family up in the fear of the Lord, or upon ethical conceptions which often play their potent part.

To give security to these countless homes, they must be shielded from the two giant marauders, war and tyranny.... The awful ruin of Europe, with all its vanished glories, and of large parts of Asia glares us in the eyes. When the designs of wicked men or the aggressive urge of mighty States dissolve over large areas the frame of civilized society, humble folk are confronted with difficulties with which they cannot cope....

A world organization has already been erected for the prime purpose of preventing war. UNO, the successor of the League of Nations, with the decisive addition of the United States...is already at work. We must make sure that its work is fruitful, that it is a reality and not a sham, that it is a force for action, and not merely a frothing of words, that it is a true temple of peace in which the shields of many nations can some day be hung up, and not merely a cockpit in a Tower of Babel....

The United Nations Organization must immediately begin to be equipped with an international

Sir Winston Churchill, "The Iron Curtain Speech," March 5, 1946, in David Cannadine, ed., *Blood, Toil, Tears and Sweat: The Speeches of Winston Churchill* (Boston: Houghton Mifflin, 1989), 296–308. Used by permission.

armed force.... I propose that each of the Powers and States should be invited to delegate a certain number of air squadrons to the service of the world organization. These squadrons would be trained and prepared in their own countries, but would move around in rotation from one country to another. They would wear the uniform of their own countries but with different badges. They would not be required to act against their own nation, but in other respects they would be directed by the world organization. This might be started on a modest scale and would grow as confidence grew....

Now I come to the second danger of these two marauders which threatens the cottage, the home, and the ordinary people—namely, tyranny. We cannot be blind to the fact that the liberties enjoyed by individual citizens throughout the British Empire are not valid in a considerable number of countries, some of which are very powerful. In these States control is enforced upon the common people by various kinds of all-embracing police governments. The power of the State is exercised without restraint, either by dictators or by compact oligarchies operating through a privileged party and a political police. It is not our duty at this time when difficulties are so numerous to interfere forcibly in the internal affairs of countries which we have not conquered in war. But we must never cease to proclaim in fearless tones the great principles of freedom and the rights of man which are the joint inheritance of the English-speaking world and which through Magna Carta, the Bill of Rights, the Habeas Corpus, trial by jury, and the English common law find their most famous expression in the American Declaration of Independence.

All this means that the people of any country have the right, and should have the power by constitutional action, by free unfettered elections, with secret ballot, to choose or change the character or form of government under which they dwell; that freedom of speech and thought should reign; that courts of justice, independent of the executive, unbiased by any party, should administer laws which have received the broad assent of large majorities or are consecrated by time and custom. Here are the title deeds of freedom which should lie in every cottage home. Here is the message of the British and American peoples to mankind. Let us preach what we practise—let us practise what we preach.

I have now stated the two great dangers which menace the homes of the people: War and Tyranny. I have not yet spoken of poverty and privation which are in many cases the prevailing anxiety. But if the dangers of war and tyranny are removed, there is no doubt that science and co-operation can bring in the next few years to the world...an expansion of material well-being beyond anything that has yet occurred in human experience....

Neither the sure prevention of war, nor the continuous rise of world organization will be gained without what I have called the fraternal association of the English-speaking peoples. This means a special relationship between the British Commonwealth and Empire and the United States....It should carry with it the continuance of the present facilities for mutual security by the joint use of all Naval and Air Force bases in the possession of either country all over the world....

Would a special relationship between the United States and the British Commonwealth be inconsistent with our overriding loyalties to the World Organization? I reply that, on the contrary, it is probably the only means by which that organization will achieve its full stature and strength....Special associations between members of the United Nations which have no aggressive point against any other country, which harbour no design incompatible with the Charter of the United Nations...are beneficial and...indispensable....

A shadow has fallen upon the scenes so lately lighted by the Allied victory. Nobody knows what Soviet Russia and its Communist international organization intends to do in the immediate future, or what are the limits, if any, to their expansive and proselytizing tendencies....We understand the Russian need to be secure on her western frontiers by the removal of all possibility of German aggression. We welcome Russia to her rightful place among the leading nations of the world....It is my duty, however...to place before you certain facts about the present position in Europe.

From Stettin in the Baltic to Trieste in the Adriatic, an iron curtain has descended across the Continent. Behind that line lie all the capitals of the ancient states of Central and Eastern Europe. Warsaw, Berlin, Prague, Vienna, Budapest, Belgrade, Bucharest and Sofia, all these famous cities and the populations around them lie in what I must call the Soviet sphere, and all are subject in one form or another, not only to Soviet influence but to a very high and, in many cases, increasing measure of control from Moscow....The Russian-dominated Polish Government has been encouraged to make enormous and wrongful inroads upon Germany, and mass expulsions of millions of Germans on a scale grievous and undreamed-of are now taking place. The Communist parties, which were very small in all these Eastern States of Europe, have been raised to pre-eminence and power far beyond their numbers and are seeking everywhere to obtain totalitarian control. Police governments are prevailing in nearly every case, and so far, except in Czechoslovakia, there is no true democracy....

If now the Soviet Government tries, by separate action, to build up a pro-Communist Germany in their areas, this will cause new serious difficulties in the British and American zones, and will give the defeated Germans the power of putting themselves up to auction between the Soviets and the Western Democracies. Whatever conclusions may be drawn from these facts...this is certainly not the Liberated Europe we fought to build up. Nor is it one which contains the essentials of permanent peace.

The safety of the world requires a new unity in Europe, from which no nation should be permanently outcast....Surely we should work with conscious purpose for a grand pacification of Europe, within its Charter....

In front of the iron curtain which lies across Europe are other causes for anxiety. In Italy the Communist Party is seriously hampered by having to support the Communist-trained Marshal Tito's claims to former Italian territory at the head of the Adriatic. Nevertheless, the future of Italy hangs in the balance. Again one cannot imagine a regenerated Europe without a strong France. All my public life I have worked for a strong France and I never lost faith in her destiny, even in the darkest hours. I will not lose faith now. However, in a great number of countries, far from the Russian frontiers and throughout the world, Communist fifth columns are established and work in complete unity and absolute obedience to the directions they receive from the Communist centre. Except in the British Commonwealth and in the United States where Communism is in its infancy, the Communist parties or fifth columns constitute a growing challenge and peril to Christian civilization....

The outlook is also anxious in the Far East and especially in Manchuria. The Agreement which was made at Yalta, to which I was a party, was extremely favourable to Soviet Russia, but it was made at a time when no one could say that the German war might not extend all through the summer and autumn of 1945 and when the Japanese war was expected to last for a further eighteen months from the end of the German war....

On the other hand I repulse the idea that a new war is inevitable; still more that it is imminent. It is because I am sure that our fortunes are still in our own hands and that we hold the power to save the future, that I feel the duty to speak out now that I have the occasion and the opportunity to do so. I do not believe that Soviet Russia desires war. What they desire is the fruits of war and the indefinite expansion of their power and doctrines....What is needed is a settlement, and the longer this is delayed, the more difficult it will be and the greater our dangers will become.

From what I have seen of our Russian friends and Allies during the war, I am convinced that there is nothing they admire so much as strength, and there is nothing for which they have less respect than for weakness, especially military weakness. For that reason the old doctrine of a balance of power is unsound....If the Western Democracies stand together in strict adherence to the principles of the United Nations Charter, their influence for furthering those principles will be immense and no one is likely to molest them. If, however, they become divided or falter in their duty and if these all-important years are allowed to slip away then indeed catastrophe may overwhelm us all....

Let no man underrate the abiding power of the British Empire and Commonwealth....If the population of the English-speaking Commonwealths be added to that of the United States with all that such co-operation implies in the air, on the sea, all over the globe and in science and in industry, and in moral force there will be no quivering, precarious balance of power to offer its temptation to ambition or adventure. On the contrary, there will be an overwhelming assurance of security. If we adhere faithfully to the Charter of the United Nations and walk forward in sedate and sober strength seeking no one's land or treasure, seeking to lay no arbitrary control upon the thoughts of men; if all British moral and material forces and convictions are joined with your own in fraternal association, the highroads of the future will be clear, not only for us but for all, not only for our time, but for a century to come.

THE AMERICAN CENTURY

With the mobilization of its vast economic and military resources, which would prove sufficient to help secure the defeat on formidable foes across two oceans, the United States would emerge from the war as the dominant power. Would it play a role in foreign affairs commensurate with that strength? Even before Pearl Harbor, as conflict raged in Europe and China, some Americans were convinced that their nation had been called upon to exercise its beneficial influence around the world, to ensure that the twentieth century would become the "American Century." One impassioned advocate of this view was Henry Luce (1898–1967), the prominent founder and publisher of *Time* and *Life* magazines. Born in China to American Presbyterian missionaries, Luce with a missionary zeal of his own insisted that the United States could become the world's Good Samaritan, leading by example and intervening to foster improved conditions on other continents.

Once we cease to distract ourselves with lifeless arguments about isolationism, we shall be amazed to discover that there is already an immense American internationalism. American jazz, Hollywood movies, American slang, American machines and patented products, are in fact the only things that every community in the world, from Zanzibar to Hamburg, recognizes in common. Blindly, unintentionally, accidentally and really in spite of ourselves, we are already a world power in all the trivial ways—in very human ways. But there is a great deal more than that. America is already the intellectual, scientific and artistic capital of the world....America's worldwide experience in commerce is also far greater than most of us realize.

Most important of all, we have that indefinable, unmistakable sign of leadership; prestige. And unlike the prestige of Rome or Genghis Khan or 19th Century England, American prestige throughout the world is faith in the good intentions as well as in the

Henry Luce, "The American Century," *Life* (February 17, 1941), 61–65. Copyright 1941 Life Inc. Reprinted with permission. All rights reserved.

ultimate intelligence and ultimate strength of the whole American people....

As America enters dynamically upon the world scene, we need most of all to seek and to bring forth a vision of America as a world power which is authentically American and which can inspire us to live and work and fight with vigor and enthusiasm. And as we come now to the great test, it may yet turn out that in all our trials and tribulations of spirit during the first part of this century we as a people have been painfully apprehending the meaning of our time and now in this moment of testing there may come clear at last the vision which will guide us to the authentic creation of the 20th Century—our Century....

First, the economic. It is for America and for America alone to determine whether a system of free economic enterprise—an economic order compatible with freedom and progress—shall or shall not prevail in this century. We know perfectly well that there is not the slightest chance of anything faintly resembling a free economic system prevailing in this country if it prevails nowhere else.... [W]e have to decide whether or not we shall have for ourselves and our friends freedom of the seas—the right to go with our ships and our ocean-going airplanes where we wish, when we wish and as we wish. The vision of America as the principal guarantor of the freedom of the seas, the vision of America as the dynamic leader of world trade, has within it the possibilities of such enormous human progress as to stagger the imagination.... Our thinking of world trade today is on ridiculously small terms. For example, we think of Asia as being worth only a few hundred millions a year to us. Actually, in the decades to come Asia will be worth to us exactly zero—or else it will be worth to us four, five, ten billions of dollars a year. And the latter are the terms we must think in, or else confess a pitiful impotence.

Closely akin to the purely economic area and yet quite different from it, there is the picture of an America which will send out through the world its technical and artistic skills. Engineers, scientists, doctors, movie men, makers of entertainment, developers of airlines, builders of roads, teachers, educators. Throughout the world, these skills, this training, this leadership is needed and will be eagerly welcomed, if only we have the imagination to see it and the sincerity and good will to create the world of the 20th Century.

But now there is a third thing which our vision must immediately be concerned with. We must undertake now to be the Good Samaritan of the entire world. It is the manifest duty of this country to undertake to feed all the people of the world who as a result of this worldwide collapse of civilization are hungry and destitute—all of them, that is, whom we can from time to time reach consistently with a very tough attitude toward all hostile governments. For every dollar we spend on armaments, we should spend at least a dime in a gigantic effort to feed the world—and all the world should know that we have dedicated ourselves to this task. Every farmer in America should be encouraged to produce all the crops he can, and all that we cannot eat—and perhaps some of us could eat less—should forthwith be dispatched to the four quarters of the globe as a free gift, administered by a humanitarian army of Americans, to every man, woman and child on this earth who is really hungry.

But all this is not enough: All this will fail and none of it will happen unless our vision of America as a world power includes a passionate devotion to great American ideals. We have some things in this country which are infinitely precious and especially American—a love of freedom, a feeling for the equality of opportunity, a tradition of self-reliance and independence and also of co-operation. In addition to ideals and notions which are especially American, we are the inheritors of all the great principles of Western civilization—above all Justice, the love of Truth, the ideal of Charity....

America as the dynamic center of ever-widening spheres of enterprise, America as the training center of the skillful servants of mankind, America as the Good Samaritan, really believing again that it is more blessed to give than to receive, and America as the powerhouse of the ideals of Freedom and Justice—out of these elements surely can be fashioned a vision of the 20th Century to which we can and will devote ourselves in joy and gladness and vigor and enthusiasm.

CHAPTER 12

COMMEMORATING WORLD WAR II

Confronting the Past, Writing the Future

REMEMBERING THOSE WHO SERVED America's national World War II memorial, not authorized until 1993, finally opened to the public in April 2004. Advocates had fought hard to secure a spot on the National Mall in Washington DC, and the requisite funding.
Source: Photograph by Richard Becker.

"Who controls the past controls the future. Who controls the present controls the past." George Orwell's omniscient comment in his gripping novel *1984*, written in 1949, serves as a reminder about both the importance of and dangers associated with historical commemoration. Because by nature, memory is fragile, fleeting, unstable and subjective, open, fluid and contestable, nations seek to create collective memories that provide common identities through past events as well as shared visions for the future. Before consensus is reached on how events are to be collectively remembered, however, contention and conflict can arise, especially when the construction of memorials or museums is involved.

Which aspect(s) of a certain event should be remembered, how much content should be included, for whom is it meant, what present and future generations will learn from it- these are questions confronting officials entrusted with the task of collecting historical memories and institutionalizing them for posterity. As World War II's veterans and survivors fall victim to the natural process of aging, both the victors and the vanquished have rushed to ensure that their legacies be preserved.

The experiences of World War II are disseminated through a variety of media. Throughout the world, museums and memorials serve as permanent physical reminders, traveling exhibits bring the war to schoolchildren, films and documentaries expose the public to the horrors of war, and works of literature allow for a more private and intimate approach. By the late twentieth century, prominent Holocaust museums, World War II memorials/museums, and/or postwar peace museums (or the blueprints for them) had emerged in Australia, Austria, Canada, Denmark, France, Germany, India, Israel, Korea, the Netherlands, Japan, Soviet Union, Spain, and the United Kingdom. China opened its "Chinese People's Resistance Against Japanese Aggression" national war memorial on June 6, 1987, one day prior to the fiftieth anniversary of the Marco Polo Bridge incident. Dedicated to the history of that nation's resistance against Japan, the memorial instructs the public on the atrocities and by so doing reinforces nationalistic sentiments. Poland, too, has hinted that it hopes to build a World War II museum in Gdansk to educate its public.

If museums have come to be viewed as potential agents of positive social change, as a means by which xenophobia might be combated and cultural and religious understanding promoted, their messages, nevertheless, can still stimulate controversy over *how* a nation remembers the conflict. Delayed by nearly two decades and covering an entire city block between the Brandenburg Gate and the site of Hitler's bunker, the Berlin Holocaust Memorial that finally opened in May 2005 met with immediate criticism. Critics disliked the design—a field of 2,711 concrete pillars (roughly the size of at least two football fields), planted in undulating waves and representing the 6 million murdered Jews—and questioned the absence of direct representations of victims (both Jewish and Gentile) of the Holocaust while lambasting the selection of the Degussa company (whose product Zyklon B gas had been used to asphyxiate Jews and Gentiles in the death camps) to graffiti-proof the monument. In Korea, the raison d'être behind Korea's History Museum of Japanese Military Comfort Women (1998), the first museum to highlight the evils of sex slavery during World War II, continues to be denied by the Japanese government. In 2005, the pilgrimage of some of Japan's most prominent lawmakers to the Yasukuni Shrine (built originally in 1869 to worship the "fallen" spirits of the Shinto religion), where more than 1,000 Japanese World War II criminals' names were enshrined, provoked outrage throughout Asia where bitter memories of Japanese occupation remained.

Visual culture, too, in film and television, was enlisted to represent the war to contemporary audiences, and it afforded an opportunity, tentatively, to explore more difficult issues. One seminal event was in April 1978 when NBC aired a 9½-hour-long American miniseries, *The Holocaust*, shot on location in Europe. The network, which had worried that the gravity of subject might repel viewers, was pleasantly surprised to attract an audience over 100 million, although it endured criticism from some Holocaust survivors, notably Elie Wiesel, who complained that it trivialized, simplified, distorted, and commercialized the tragedy. The series producers, on the other hand, maintained that, whatever the form, the substance of the series raised awareness of the Holocaust throughout Europe and the United States. They pointed to the fact that the series' broadcast in Germany in January 1979, which attracted roughly half of the West German adult population, resulted in the extension of the statute of limitations for Nazi war crimes that was scheduled to expire at the end of 1979. With the ground thus prepared, six years later television could broadcast Claude Lanzmann's harrowing documentary *Shoah* (the Hebrew word for Holocaust). Lanzmann personally interviewed actual survivors, witnesses, and persecutors, and filmed them against the actual backdrop of the concentration camps to convey a sense of intimacy, realism, and historical accuracy.

By the last decade of the twentieth century, World War II was big business on American screens, as films like *Saving Private Ryan* (1998) portrayed the nation's "good war" in which unpretentious American boys reluctantly fought in a fundamentally decent way to end the war and return as quickly as possible to their homes and farms. Awkward aspects, such as the persistence of racism or the cost to enemy civilians, were either ignored or glossed over. In 2007 the nation was treated to another long documentary, Ken Burns' fifteen-hour documentary, *The War*, which personalized the conflict to provide a more intimate portrait of a war that was indisputably "just" but nonetheless complex, even on a moral level. Burns effectively interspersed actual footage with newsreels, home movies, and personal photos, but his initial portrait of veterans and civilians from four communities (Danbury, Mobile, Sacramento, and St. Paul) violated the newer image of the war as one of national multi-cultural consensus by omitting any serious discussion of Hispanic-American participation and exaggerated the American contribution to victory in Europe. It reflected the more individual scale and private orientation that increasingly colored public memories of the war.

REMEMBERING D-DAY AND THE BOYS OF POINTE DU HOC

After the debacle of Vietnam, military commemorations did not always engage the fullest support or attention of the American people. Even the Second World War, which had been a staple of popular culture in the 1960s, had begun to fade. That consignment to the margins changed dramatically from the mid-1980s onward. In part, the commemorations of the fortieth anniversary of crucial events (and Allied victories) late in the war, as well as of the conclusion of the conflict, refocused attention on the war. One of the key episodes occurred when President Ronald Reagan (1911–2004), always an eloquent orator, delivered this speech in Normandy, France, to commemorate the capture on D-day, by the American Second Ranger Battalion, of the heights of Pointe du Hoc. Atop 100-foot-high sheer cliffs lay German emplacements for six 155 mm heavy guns which, if not destroyed, could devastate the landing zone at Omaha Beach four miles to the east. In a legendary display of skill and courage, the Rangers used ropes, ladders, and grapples to scale the cliffs and seize their objective. Although the guns had been moved a mile inland, the Rangers managed to both secure the original position (which was still useful for observation and fire from lighter weapons) and destroy the heavy guns in their new location. Reagan, in an evocative speech crafted by Peggy Noonan and set against the backdrop of the Normandy cliffs, paid due tribute to the bravery of the Rangers but also reemphasized America's determination to stand with its European allies in the defense of freedom. Timed to head the evening newscasts for an American audience, the speech was highly successful and touched on themes that Reagan would reiterate during his campaign for reelection that would culminate in a landslide victory in November 1984. From this point onward, momentum would accumulate to pay homage to World War II veterans as "the greatest generation" and to highlight the American contribution to victory, even in the European theater.

We're here to mark that day in history when the Allied armies joined in battle to reclaim this continent to liberty. For four long years, much of Europe had been under a terrible shadow. Free nations had fallen, Jews cried out in the camps, millions cried out for liberation. Europe was enslaved, and the world prayed for its rescue. Here in Normandy the rescue began. Here the Allies stood and fought against tyranny in a giant undertaking unparalleled in human history.

We stand on a lonely, windswept point on the northern shore of France. The air is soft, but forty years ago at this moment, the air was dense with smoke and the cries of men, and the air was filled with the crack of rifle fire and the roar of cannon. At dawn, on the morning of the sixth of June, 1944, 225

"Ronald Reagan's Speech at Pointe du Hoc Commemorating the Fortieth Anniversary of the Normandy Invasion, June 6, 1984," as reprinted from *The Public Papers of Ronald Reagan*, online version. Used by permission.

Rangers jumped off the British landing craft and ran to the bottom of these cliffs. Their mission was one of the most difficult and daring of the invasion: to climb these sheer and desolate cliffs and take out the enemy guns. The Allies had been told that some of the mightiest of these guns were here and they would be trained on the beaches to stop the Allied advance.

The Rangers looked up and saw the enemy soldiers at the edge of the cliffs shooting down at them with machine guns and throwing grenades. And the American Rangers began to climb. They shot rope ladders over the face of these cliffs and began to pull themselves up. When one Ranger fell, another would take his place. When one rope was cut, a Ranger would grab another and begin his climb again. They climbed, shot back, and held their footing. Soon, one by one, the Rangers pulled themselves over the top, and in seizing the firm land at the top of these cliffs, they began to seize back the continent of Europe. Two hundred and twenty-five came here. After two days of fighting, only ninety could still bear arms.

Behind me is a memorial that symbolizes the Ranger daggers that were thrust into the top of these cliffs. And before me are the men who put them there.

These are the boys of Pointe du Hoc. These are the men who took the cliffs. These are the champions who helped free a continent. These are the heroes who helped end a war.

Gentlemen, I look at you and I think of the words of Stephen Spender's poem, You are men who in your "lives fought for life…and left the vivid air signed with" your honor.

I think I know what you may be thinking right now—thinking "we were just part of a bigger effort; everyone was brave that day." Well, everyone was. Do you remember the story of Bill Millin of the 51st Highlanders? Forty years ago today, British troops were pinned down near a bridge, waiting desperately for help. Suddenly, they heard the sound of bagpipes, and some thought they were dreaming. Well, they weren't. They looked up and saw Bill Millin with his bagpipes, leading the reinforcements and ignoring the smack of the bullets into the ground around him.

Lord Lovat was with him—Lord Lovat of Scotland, who calmly announced when he got to the bridge, "Sorry I'm a few minutes late," as if he'd been delayed by a traffic jam, when in truth he'd just come from the bloody fighting on Sword Beach [code name for one of five primary landing beaches in the initial phase of the Allied invasion of Normandy], which he and his men had just taken.

There was the impossible valor of the Poles who threw themselves between the enemy and the rest of Europe as the invasion took hold, and the unsurpassed courage of the Canadians who had already seen the horrors of war on this coast. They knew what awaited them there, but they would not be deterred. And once they hit Juno Beach [also known as the Canadian beach, landing site for the Third Canadian Infantry Division on the Normandy coast during D-day] they never looked back.

All of these men were part of a roll call of honor with names that spoke of a pride as bright as the colors they bore: the Royal Winnipeg Rifles, Poland's 24th Lancers, the Royal Scots Fusiliers, the Screaming Eagles, the Yeomen of England's armored divisions, the forces of Free France, the Coast Guard's "Matchbox Fleet" and you, the American Rangers.

Forty summers have passed since the battle that you fought here. You were young the day you took these cliffs; some of you were hardly more than boys, with the deepest joys of life before you. Yet, you risked everything here. Why? Why did you do it? What impelled you to put aside the instinct for self-preservation and risk your lives to take these cliffs? What inspired all the men of the armies that met here? We look at you, and somehow we know the answer. It was faith and belief; it was loyalty and love.

The men of Normandy had faith that what they were doing was right, faith that they fought for all humanity, faith that a just God would grant them mercy on this beachhead or on the next. It was the deep knowledge—and pray God we have not lost it—that there is a profound, moral difference between the use of force for liberation and the use of force for conquest. You were here to liberate, not to conquer, and so you and those others did not doubt your cause. And you were right not to doubt.

You all knew that some things are worth dying for. One's country is worth dying for, and democracy is worth dying for, because it's the most deeply honorable form of government ever devised by man. All of you loved liberty. All of you were willing to fight tyranny, and you knew the people of your countries were behind you.

The Americans who fought here that morning knew word of the invasion was spreading through the darkness back home. They fought—or felt in their hearts, though they couldn't know in fact, that in Georgia they were filling the churches at 4 a.m., in Kansas they were kneeling on their porches and praying, and in Philadelphia they were ringing the Liberty Bell.

Something else helped the men of D-Day: their rockhard belief that Providence would have a great hand in the events that would unfold here; that God was an ally in this great cause. And so, the night before the invasion, when Colonel Wolverton asked his parachute troops to kneel with him in prayer he told them: Do not bow your heads, but look up so you can see God and ask His blessing in what we're about to do. Also that night, General Matthew Ridgway on his cot, listening in the darkness for the promise God made to Joshua: "I will not fail thee nor forsake thee."

These are the things that impelled them; these are the things that shaped the unity of the Allies.

When the war was over, there were lives to be rebuilt and governments to be returned to the people. There were nations to be reborn. Above all, there was a new peace to be assured. These were huge and daunting tasks. But the Allies summoned strength from the faith, belief, loyalty, and love of those who fell here. They rebuilt a new Europe together.

There was first a great reconciliation among those who had been enemies, all of whom had suffered so greatly. The United States did its part, creating the Marshall Plan to help rebuild our allies and our former enemies. The Marshall Plan led to the Atlantic Alliance—a great alliance that serves to this day as our shield for freedom, for prosperity, and for peace.

In spite of our great efforts and successes, not all that followed the end of the war was happy or planned. Some liberated countries were lost. The great sadness of this loss echoes down to our own time in the streets of Warsaw, Prague, and East Berlin. Soviet troops that came to the center of this continent did not leave when peace came. They're still there, uninvited, unwanted, unyielding, almost forty years after the war. Because of this, Allied forces still stand on this continent. Today, as forty years ago, our armies are here for only one purpose—to protect and defend democracy. The only territories we hold are memorials like this one and graveyards where our heroes rest.

We in America have learned bitter lessons from two world wars: It is better to be here ready to protect the peace, than to take blind shelter across the sea, rushing to respond only after freedom is lost. We've learned that isolationism never was and never will be an acceptable response to tyrannical governments with an expansionist intent.

But we try always to be prepared for peace; prepared to deter aggression; prepared to negotiate the reduction of arms; and, yes, prepared to reach out again in the spirit of reconciliation. In truth, there is no reconciliation we would welcome more than a reconciliation with the Soviet Union, so, together, we can lessen the risks of war, now and forever.

It's fitting to remember here the great losses also suffered by the Russian people during World War II: Twenty million perished, a terrible price that testifies to all the world the necessity of ending war. I tell you from my heart that we in the United States do not want war. We want to wipe from the face of the Earth the terrible weapons that man now has in his hands. And I tell you, we are ready to seize the beachhead. We look for some sign from the Soviet Union that they are willing to move forward, that they share our desire and love for peace, and that they will give up the ways of conquest. There must be a changing there that will allow us to turn our hope into action.

We will pray forever that some day that changing will come. But for now, particularly today, it is good and fitting to renew our commitment to each other, to our freedom, and to the alliance that protects it.

We are bound today by what bound us forty years ago, the same loyalties, traditions, and beliefs. We're bound by reality. The strength of America's allies is vital to the United States, and the American security guarantee is essential to the continued freedom of

Europe's democracies. We were with you then; we are with you now. Your hopes are our hopes, and your destiny is our destiny.

Here, in this place, where the West held together, let us make a vow to our dead. Let us show them by our actions that we understand what they died for. Let our actions say to them the words for which Matthew Ridgway listened: "I will not fail thee nor forsake thee."

Strengthened by their courage, heartened by their value [valor], and borne by their memory, let us continue to stand for the ideals for which they lived and died.

Thank you very much, and God bless you all.

GERMANY COMMEMORATES THE FORTIETH ANNIVERSARY OF DEFEAT

The events during May 1985 in the Federal Republic of Germany (West Germany) marking the fortieth anniversary of the end of the war were controversial. Some conservative German intellectuals deplored the fact that their country was still burdened with guilt for unleashing an aggressive war and undertaking the Holocaust, and they sought to define a more positive historical record that could make German citizens proud of their country and its achievements. In short, they hoped to normalize the nation's problematic relation with its history and memory, and bring civic pride into line with that of other European nations. German chancellor Helmut Kohl hoped to dramatize the reconciliation between former antagonists with a ceremony at a German military cemetery, and applied pressure on American president Ronald Reagan to agree to a joint visit to one at the town of Bitburg, near an American air base and the border with Luxemburg. Unfortunately for Reagan, who insisted that young German soldiers were as much victims of the war as those in concentration camps, the Bitburg cemetery contained the graves of forty-nine members of the Waffen-SS. To pay tribute to such men as victims outraged American public opinion, and many in the United States called upon Reagan to cancel his trip to Bitburg. Yet Reagan refused to abandon Kohl, who had accepted the controversial American deployment of Pershing missiles on German soil, and he went ahead with the cemetery visit, now cut short to a mere eight minutes on May 5, 1985, and coupled with a concentration camp stop as well. It was in this atmosphere that the Federal Republic's president, Richard von Weizsaecker (1920–), faced the delicate task of addressing the German legislature on V-E day (May 8, "Victory in Europe" day) and divining its meaning forty years after the fact. Although his role as president was a ceremonial one, Weizsaecker knew that his remarks would be considered as reflective of the country's official posture toward its past, and he was determined to be, as a *New York Times* correspondent dubbed him, "the custodian of

"Speech by Richard von Weizsaecker, President of the Federal Republic of Germany, in the *Bundestag* during the Ceremony Commemorating the 40th Anniversary of the End of the War in Europe and of National Socialist Tyranny, May 8, 1985," as reprinted in Geoffrey Hartman, ed., *Bitburg in Moral and Political Perspective* (Bloomington: Indiana University Press, 1986), 262–268. Used by permission.

the nation's moral conscience." Weizsaecker's father had been a Nazi diplomat, and he himself had served in the German army during the war, but he refused to treat Germany's surrender as a defeat to be met with an embarrassed silence. Rather, it was, as he reminded the parliamentarians of the Federal Republic's thriving democracy, a "liberation" for Germans as much as for the populations of occupied Europe. And because he did not ignore the ghastly consequences of Hitler's regime, his more balanced appraisal was widely hailed as a milestone on West Germany's route to coming to terms with its past. Interestingly, in East Germany (the German Democratic Republic, or DDR), the state was defined as one of the victors in the triumph of socialism over fascism and so, publicly at least, it was not obligated to confront responsibility for past crimes.

I

Many nations are today commemorating the date on which World War II ended in Europe. Every nation is doing so with different feelings, depending on its fate. Be it victory or defeat, liberation from injustice and alien rule or transition to new dependence, division, new alliances, vast shifts of power—May 8, 1945, is a date of decisive historical importance for Europe.

We Germans are commemorating that date amongst ourselves, as is indeed necessary. We must find our own standards. We are not assisted in this task if we or others spare our feelings. We need and we have the strength to look truth straight in the eye—without embellishment and without distortion.

For us, the 8th of May is above all a date to remember what people had to suffer. It is also a date to reflect on the course taken by our history. The greater honesty we show in commemorating this day, the freer we are to face the consequences with due responsibility. For us Germans, May 8 is not a day of celebration. Those who actually witnessed that day in 1945 think back on highly personal and hence highly different experiences. Some returned home, others lost their homes. Some were liberated, while for others it was the start of captivity. Many were simply grateful that the bombing at night and fear had passed and that they had survived. Others felt first and foremost grief at the complete defeat suffered by their country. Some Germans felt bitterness about their shattered illusions, while others were grateful for the gift of a new start....

The 8th of May was a day of liberation. It liberated all of us from the inhumanity and tyranny of the National Socialist regime.

Nobody will, because of that liberation, forget the grave suffering that only started for many people on May 8. But we must not regard the end of the war as the cause of flight, expulsion and deprivation of freedom. The cause goes back to the start of the tyranny that brought about war. We must not separate May 8, 1945, from January 30, 1933.

II

May 8 is a day of remembrance. Remembering means recalling an occurrence honestly and undistortedly so that it becomes part of our very beings. This places high demands on our truthfulness.

Today we mourn all the dead of the war and the tyranny. In particular we commemorate the six million Jews who were murdered in German concentration camps. We commemorate all nations who suffered in the war, especially the countless citizens of the Soviet Union and Poland who lost their lives. As Germans, we mourn our own compatriots who perished as soldiers, during air raids at home, in captivity or during expulsion. We commemorate the Sinti and Romany Gypsies, the homosexuals and the mentally ill who were killed, as well as the people who had to die for their religious or political beliefs. We commemorate the hostages who were executed. We recall the victims of the resistance movements in all the countries occupied by us. As Germans, we pay homage to the victims of the German resistance—among the public, the military, the churches, the workers and trade unions, and the Communists. We commemorate those who did not actively resist, but preferred to die instead of violating their consciences....

III

There is no such thing as the guilt or innocence of an entire nation. Guilt is, like innocence, not collective, but personal. There is discovered or concealed individual guilt. There is guilt which people acknowledge or deny. Everyone who directly experienced that era should today quietly ask himself about his involvement then.

The vast majority of today's population were either children then or had not been born. They cannot profess a guilt of their own for crimes that they did not commit. No discerning person can expect them to wear a penitential robe simply because they are Germans. But their forefathers have left them a grave legacy. All of us, whether guilty or not, whether old or young, must accept the past. We are all affected by its consequences and liable for it. The young and old generations must and can help each other to understand why it is vital to keep alive the memories. It is not a case of coming to terms with the past. That is not possible. It cannot be subsequently modified or made not to have happened. However, anyone who closes his eyes to the past is blind to the present. Whoever refuses to remember the inhumanity is prone to new risks of infection.

The Jewish nation remembers and will always remember. We seek reconciliation. Precisely for this reason we must understand that there can be no reconciliation without remembrance. The experience of millionfold death is part of the very being of every Jew in the world, not only because people cannot forget such atrocities, but also because remembrance is part of the Jewish faith. . . .

IV

The 8th of May marks a deep cut not only in German history but in the history of Europe as a whole. The European civil war had come to an end, the old world of Europe lay in ruins. . . . The meeting of American and Soviet Russian soldiers on the Elbe became a symbol for the temporary end of a European era. . . .

In the course of that war the Nazi regime tormented and defiled many nations. At the end of it all only one nation remained to be tormented, enslaved and defiled; the German nation. Time and again Hitler had declared that if the German nation was not capable of winning the war it should be left to perish. The other nations first became victims of a war started by Germany before we became the victims of our own war.

The division of Germany into zones began on May 8. In the meantime the Soviet Union had taken control in all countries of Eastern and South Eastern Europe that had been occupied by Germany during the war. . . . The division of Europe into two different political systems took its course. . . . In a sermon in East Berlin commemorating the 8th of May, Cardinal Meissner said: "the pathetic result of sin is always division." . . .

V

We cannot commemorate the 8th of May without being conscious of the great effort required on the part of our former enemies to set out on the road of reconciliation with us. Can we really place ourselves in the position of relatives of the victims of the Warsaw Ghetto or of the Lidice massacre? And how hard must it have been for the citizens of Rotterdam or London to support the rebuilding of our country from where the bombs came which not long before had been dropped on their cities? To be able to do so they had gradually to gain the assurance that the Germans would not again try to make good their defeat by use of force.

THE SOVIET UNION AND THE USES OF VICTORY

"The Great Patriotic War" was how the Soviets officially described the conflict they had waged against Hitler's Germany, and they had little use for the terms (like "World War II" or "Second World War") conventionally used in the West to label the war. By so doing, the Soviets simultaneously linked their struggle with the ultimately successful "Patriotic War" to repel Napoleon's invasion in 1812 and conceptually marginalized the operations by other combatants in Europe, North Africa, and the Pacific. No other nation had endured such frightful absolute numbers of casualties (though other states, such as Poland, had lost a proportionately higher number of their citizens), but the emphasis on remembering the war in a certain way was carefully calibrated by the Soviet government. Victory over the Germans between 1941 and 1945 lent a badly needed veneer of legitimacy to a Soviet system which appeared to have lost the postwar peace. Its living standards lagged behind the prosperity of the West, its Communist Party–based autocracy belied its claims of socialist harmony and equality, and its domination of eastern Europe (periodically enforced at gunpoint by the Soviet army) affronted the supposed independent sovereignty of states like Hungary, Poland, Czechoslovakia, and the German Democratic Republic (East Germany). Even after Stalin's system has crumbled and the old generation has faded from the scene, memory of the war plays an important role, as Lev Gudkov, a contemporary Russian sociologist, reminds us.

In this article, I shall examine the character of the collective "memory of the war" or the role of representations of the war in the system of the contemporary Russian national identity.

What needs to be noted at the outset is that the mass, i.e., non-specialized, "general" or "lower-class" consciousness is deprived of "memory." Public opinion doesn't retain the experience of separate individuals; their experience is neither preserved nor transmitted. All that individuals go through, and above all their unreflected suffering, vanishes unless it is taken up by specialized institutions, unless it is channeled into other means of cultural reproduction and, accordingly, unless private opinions are sanctioned by some authority that ranks as supraindividual. This is why today we should speak not so much of memory but rather of the reproduction of "memory": at present, people who lived through the war make up no more than 6–7 per cent of the population, they are mainly elderly and little educated women, most of whom have neither the means, opportunities, nor, most importantly, any motivation for transmitting such experience.

Mass attitudes towards the war virtually liken it to traditional, almost Biblical acts of God—famine, pestilence, floods, or earthquakes, with unclear causes and terrible consequences. The un-worked-through and uninterpreted mass experience of the war is preserved in such amorphous and extremely indefinite categories that retain only a highly general assessment of the events of those now-distant years. People consider the "patriotic war"…above all

Lev Gudkov, "The Fetters of Victory: How the War Provides Russia with Its Identity," www.eurozine.com/articles/2005-05-03-gudkov-en.html. Used by permission.

"great," then "bloody," "tragic," "terrible," much less frequently "heroic," "long," and even less frequently "mean."

Collective memory (mass consciousness) has virtually repressed an entire level of experience: the cheerless everyday life during the war and the post-war years, the coercive labour, the chronic hunger and poverty, the overcrowded conditions of life. All of this has dissipated, as has the memory of the maimed invalids (or, as they were called in the post-war years, the "samovars"—human stumps on little wheels that were a fixture of the street bustle as late as the first half of the 1950s). All of this is now seen as burdensome and unnecessary, as were the invalids in the post-war period (they were left to the mercy of fate, people were ashamed of them, turned away from them, hid them with an unpleasant feeling of guilt and a sense of "the ugliness of life"—everything was done to keep them out of the official gala picture of peace-time life). All of this has left only an unconscious fear in public memory, a fear that often expresses itself as a fear of a new (world- or civil-) war, and forms the background to mass assessments of the quality of life, to the sluggish resistance against attempts to heroize anything that goes beyond the war theme, to people's passive endurance—in brief, to everything that used to be expressed in the familiar Soviet sigh: "If only there was no war!" These components of mass consciousness have become a "collective unconscious" and are not disappearing, although their significance is gradually diminishing.

In total contrast to this diffuse state of memory, an extremely structured social attitude towards the war is incarnated and consolidated in the main symbol that integrates the nation: victory in the war, victory in the Great Patriotic War [GPW]. In the opinion of Russia's inhabitants, this is the most important event in their history; it is the basic image of national consciousness. No other event compares with it. In the list of the most important events that determined Russia's fate in the twentieth century, victory in the GPW is named by 78 per cent of those surveyed. In recent years, especially after Putin came to power, the significance of victory has only increased. In 1996, 44 per cent of those surveyed

(a relative majority) mentioned it in response to the question, "What makes you personally most proud of our history?"; in 2003 the figure was 87 per cent. There is nothing else left to take pride in: the disintegration of the USSR and the failure of the post-Soviet reforms, the noticeable weakening of mass hopes, and the disappearance of the illusions of Perestroika [restructuring under Mikhail Gorbachev] have furnished the content of a traumatic experience of national failure.

An interconnected process is at work here: as pride in Soviet achievements (the Revolution, the construction of a new society, the creation of a New Man, the demonstrative results of Soviet industrialization, the military might of the superpower, and the related strength of science and technology) is eroding, the symbolic weight of Victory is increasing. Both the imperial cultural heritage (including "sacred" Russian literature) and the ideological symbols of socialism (which today are only preserved by older generations in the form of nostalgia for an idealized past) are increasingly losing out to Victory. All components of the positive collective unity of the idea of "us" are eroding. After their devaluation has brought to the fore a range of complexes of hurt self-esteem and inferiority, Victory now stands out as a stone pillar in the desert, the vestige of a weathered rock. All the most important interpretations of the present are concentrated around Victory; it provides them with their standards of evaluation and their rhetorical means of expression.

Therefore, every time people mention "Victory," what they mean is a symbol that appears to the vast majority of those surveyed, and thus to society as a whole, as a central element of collective identity, a point of reference, a gauge that sets a certain perspective for evaluating the past and, partly, for understanding the present and the future. The victory of 1945 is not simply the central junction of meaning of Soviet history, which started with the October Revolution and ended with the collapse of the USSR; it is in fact the only positive anchor point for post-Soviet society's national consciousness....Victory in the war retrospectively legitimizes the Soviet totalitarian regime as a whole and uncontrolled rule as such; justifies the "costs" of Soviet history and the accelerated military-industrial modernization—the repressions, famines, poverty, and enormous numbers of deaths after collectivization—and creates a version of the past that has no alternative and provides the only possible and significant framework for interpreting history.

In the eyes of Russian society, the war and its victims sacralized not only the army as one of the central, fundamental social institutions, the carcass of the entire Soviet and post-Soviet regime, but also the very principle of a "vertical" construction of society, a mobilizational, command-hierarchical model of social order that does not bestow any autonomy or value upon a private existence or group interests that are independent of the "whole." . . . Memories of the war are required above all to legitimate a centralized and repressive social order; they are built into a general post-totalitarian traditionalization of culture in a society that has not been able to cope with budding social change. That is why the Russian authorities constantly have to return to those traumatic circumstances of its past that reproduce key moments of national mobilization.

THE HOLOCAUST MUSEUM

During the first two postwar decades, the Holocaust did not figure that prominently in the ways in which the war was remembered or commemorated. Many of the survivors preferred to focus on getting on with their lives, rather than recalling a horrific and perilous experience when even survival seemed a matter of sheer chance. They hoped to spare their own children the nightmares they had endured. And they preferred not to focus on an episode of Jewish vulnerability, especially when the tiny state of Israel was dwarfed by neighbors bent on its destruction. With the passage of time, however, the dwindling number of survivors who could testify to Nazi genocide, and (after its victory in the 1967 war) the apparent survival of Israel, the Holocaust regained prominence as a topic of public discussion and scholarly research. In the United States, escalating pressure for a permanent memorial to the victims led in 1978 to the appointment by President Jimmy Carter of a commission chaired by Elie Wiesel (1928–), a future Nobel laureate, prominent author and activist, and survivor of Auschwitz and Buchenwald. As the most public exponent of Holocaust remembrance, Wiesel faced a difficult challenge: some skeptics complained that any memorial should be built closer to the scene of events in Europe rather than America, while other critics objected to singling out Jewish victims of Hitler's regime and neglecting Gypsies, the mentally deficient, homosexuals, or political dissidents (not to mention "ordinary" civilians in occupied countries) who suffered at the hands of the Nazis. The report from the President's Commission on the Holocaust, presented in September 1979, laid out the premises for what would become the United States Holocaust Memorial Museum. Approved by Congress in 1980, the museum would be built in central Washington DC on a site on the National Mall according to a widely praised design by architect James Ingo Freed. It would open to the public in 1993. The following excerpt, from the report the presidential commission prepared under Wiesel's guidance, describes the two guiding principles the museum was intended to address.

The Commission's efforts have been undertaken in the service of memory, with the conviction that in remembrance lie the seeds of transformation and renewal. Throughout the Commission's work, two guiding principles have provided the philosophical rationale. They are: (1) the uniqueness of the Holocaust; and (2) the moral obligation to remember.

THE UNIQUENESS OF THE HOLOCAUST

The Holocaust was the systematic, bureaucratic extermination of six million Jews by the Nazis and their collaborators as a central act of state during the Second World War; as night descended, millions of other peoples were swept into this net of death. It was a crime unique in the annals of human history, different not only in the quantity of violence—the

"Report of the President's Commission on the Holocaust (September 27, 1979)," from www.ushmm.org. Used by permission.

sheer numbers killed—but in its manner and purpose as a mass criminal enterprise organized by the state against defenseless civilian populations. The decision was to kill every Jew everywhere in Europe: the definition of Jew as target for death transcended all boundaries. There is evidence indicating that the Nazis intended ultimately to wipe out the Slavs and other peoples; had the war continued or had the Nazis triumphed, Jews might not have remained the final victims of Nazi genocide, but they were certainly its first.

The concept of annihilation of an entire people...was unprecedented; never before in human history had genocide been an all-pervasive government policy unaffected by territorial or economic advantage and unchecked by moral or religious constraints....Jews were particular targets despite the fact that they possessed no army and were not an integral part of the military struggle. Indeed, the destruction frequently conflicted with and took priority over the war effort. Trains that could have been used to carry munitions to the front or to retrieve injured soldiers were diverted for the transport of victims to the death camps....Clearly, genocide was an end in itself independent of the requisites of war....

The Holocaust was not a throwback to medieval torture or archaic barbarism but a thoroughly modern expression of bureaucratic organization, industrial management, scientific achievement, and technological sophistication. The entire apparatus of the German bureaucracy was marshaled in the service of the extermination process....

The Holocaust could not have occurred without the collapse of certain religious norms; increasing secularity fueled a devaluation of the image of the human being created in the likeness of God. Ironically, although religious perspectives contributed to the growth of anti-Semitism and the choice of Jews as victims, only in a modern secular age did anti-Semitism lead to annihilation....

Whether the product of technology or a reaction against it, the horror of the Holocaust is inextricably linked to the conditions of our time. By studying the Holocaust, we hope to help immunize modern man against the disease particular to the twentieth century which led to this monstrous aberration.

THE MORAL OBLIGATION TO REMEMBER

The American philosopher George Santayana has warned that those who forget history are condemned to repeat it. The Holocaust reveals a potential pathology at the heart of Western civilization together with the frightening consequences of the total exercise of power. Remembering can instill caution, fortify restraint, and protect against future evil or indifference. The sense of outrage in the face of the Holocaust expressed in the declaration "Never Again"—neither to the Jewish people nor to any other people—must be informed by an understanding of what happened and how....

PROPOSALS AND PROJECTS:

Because of the magnitude of the Holocaust, its scope and the critical issues it raises, the Commission recommends establishment of a living memorial that will speak not only of the victims' deaths but of their lives, a memorial that can transform the living by transmitting the legacy of the Holocaust.

The Commission recommends that the three components of such a living memorial be:

* A memorial/museum
* An educational foundation
* A Committee on Conscience

While a monument alone may commemorate the victims, no structure can fully reveal the process that culminated in extermination; nor can it document the awesome dimensions of the crime or analyze its causes and implications. While no monument in and of itself can speak to the present or inform the future, the Commission does recommend the erection of a physical structure as a setting for a living memorial.

NATIONAL HOLOCAUST MEMORIAL/MUSEUM

The Commission recommends that a National Holocaust Memorial/Museum be erected in Washington, D.C. The museum must be of symbolic and artistic beauty, visually and emotionally moving in accordance with the solemn nature of the Holocaust.

The Commission proposes that the museum become a Federal institution, perhaps an autonomous bureau of the Smithsonian Institution offering extension services to the public, to scholars, and to other institutions.

The museum would present the Holocaust through pictorial accounts, films, and other visual exhibits within a framework that is not merely reportorial but analytic, encouraging reflection and questioning. Furthermore, the museum would provide a fluid medium in which to apply historical events to contemporary complexities; its presentations would not be static but designed to elicit an evolving understanding. Recent technological innovations in computers and information banks now make it possible for museum visitors to become active learners and inquirers.

Museum exhibits would focus on the six million Jews exterminated in the Holocaust and millions of other victims. Changing displays would allow for emphasis on areas of current concern.

Special emphasis would also be placed on the American aspect of the Holocaust—the absence of American response (exclusion of refugees, denials of the Holocaust, etc.), the American liberation of the camps, the reception of survivors after 1945, the lives rebuilt in this country and their contribution to American society and civilization, the development of a new sensitivity to the Holocaust, and the growing respect for the multi-ethnic, multi-dimensional aspects of American culture. Also incorporated would be the life and culture of the victims and not just the destruction process. Similarly, the museum would depict the extraordinary efforts to preserve human dignity and life during the Holocaust, the heroic resistance efforts, and the response of renewed life after the Event.

The museum would house a library, an archive of Holocaust materials, computer linkage to existing centers of Holocaust documentation, and a reference staff. Such facilities would enable both the general public and specialized scholars to study the record of the Holocaust....

JAPAN AND THE WAR'S CONTESTED MEMORY

Over the more than sixty years since its defeat, Japan has had more difficulty in coming to terms with its role in the war than its Axis partner and fellow vanquished power, Germany. Repeatedly, prominent Japanese politicians and intellectuals have downplayed the degree to which Japanese aggression in China and the Pacific initiated hostilities in Asia, or to which Japanese conduct toward civilians and prisoners violated accepted "laws of warfare" and constituted crimes against humanity (or against "peace" as it was sometimes framed). As recently as 2006–2007, the Japanese prime minister, Shinzo Abe (1954–), reiterated his doubts that the "comfort women" had been coerced into service by Japan's government or that Japan's wartime military elite had committed crimes under Japanese law. In part, the widespread reluctance to admit to wartime transgressions stems from the strong conviction by many Japanese that they too were victims, of blockade, fire-bombing, and atomic attack, and that American intransigence and economic embargoes in the 1930s had left Japan no alternative but to fight for its very survival. The retention by the occupying Americans of Emperor Hirohito, in whose name the war was fought and administered, without trial for war crimes, also encouraged the belief that Japan bore no special responsibility for violations of accepted wartime conduct, but merely acted, out of necessity, as had other nations during the conflict. Nowhere is this sense more pronounced than in the history textbooks in which younger generations of Japanese students are first exposed to the issues surrounding their nation's participation in the war. Some left-wing historians have challenged the prevailing consensus and tried to ensure that the textbooks are more accurate and do not gloss over the horrors like the "rape of Nanking" or Unit 731. In the following article, Gavan McCormack, a historian of Japan at the Australian National University, charts the conflict over the nation's historical memory of the war.

In practice nothing is negated by the "liberals" with more vehemence than the comfort women—their existence, their servile status under the imperial Japanese army, their suffering, and their entitlement to any apology or compensation from the Japanese state. Because the story they tell does not function to increase the sense of "pride in the history of our nation," it should not be told, and those who tell it are bad (*akudama*) for doing so. Furthermore, the basis of the negation appears to be essentially a priori rather than empiricist, in the sense that it rests on the passionate belief that the Japanese state *could not possibly have been* involved in the crime of abduction and slavery on a large scale; therefore the claim is utterly false and abhorrent, and the recounting of the material in school textbooks amounts to "anti-Japanese" and "masochistic" behavior, which can only serve to "corrode, pulverize, melt and disintegrate"

Gavan McCormack, "The Japanese Movement to 'Correct' History," in Laura Hein, ed., *Censoring History: Citizenship and Memory in Japan, Germany and the United States* (Armonk, NY: M. E. Sharpe, 2000), 59–63. Used by permission.

Japan. Schools that teach "false history" of comfort women become like a giant "Kamikuishikimura [the headquarters of the Aum sect], a mind control center staining the entire nation with anti-Japanese ideology." For Fujioka, the comfort women issue is "an unfounded scandal created in the 1990s for the political purpose of bashing Japan." It is even "a grand conspiracy for the destruction of Japan, in collaboration with foreign elements." If such a falsehood were to be included in school texts Japan would come to be seen as "a lewd, foolish and rabid race without peer in the world."

However emotional the deep commitment indicated by such formulations of its position, the Liberal View of History Group does also try to cast its appeal in scientific and empiricist terms, and for this it relies heavily on the services of a professional historian well known and respected for his work on war history, Hata Ikuhiko. In addressing the complex issues of the wartime comfort women, the case as constructed by Hata and Fujioka is that the comfort women were professional prostitutes, earning more than a general in the imperial Japanese army, or as much as 100 times the pay of their soldier customers. Hata describes the work as "high risk, high return." In launching their suits for compensation now, the women are described as motivated by greed and desire for money, seeing their suits as a chance to "win the lottery." Hata and Fujioka insist there is no documentary evidence of compulsion or official responsibility, and they reject the evidence of the women themselves as not on oath or subject to constraints of perjury laws. They propose an analogy to illustrate the relationship between the privately run comfort stations and the (iango) imperial Japanese army, seeing the comfort stations as akin to the restaurants within the Ministry of Education building, physically within the premises and subject to certain constraints of payment of rent, health controls, and the like but fundamentally independent in terms of management and treatment of their staff. As the Ministry of Education is not responsible for the services or the labor relations in restaurants housed within its building, so, they argue, the Japanese army cannot be held responsible for the conduct of the sex business in the old Japanese empire at a time when prostitution was legal anyway and standards and values were very different from what they are today.

Hata also advances an argument on financial grounds: that if responsibility to compensate the women were officially recognized, meeting the claims might cripple the Japanese state. At a figure of, say, 3 million yen for each act of rape to which they were subjected, and taking account of the number of such acts of rape over the years, he estimates that each woman could be entitled to payments of up to 70 billion yen, in which case the overall claim would soon rival the Japanese national debt. It is bizarre that the argument should here shift ground from principle and truth to financial considerations and convenience, but such swings are characteristic of a discourse only thinly grounded in logic or moral principle.

Underlying these protestations about the women is the question of how to characterize the Japanese state. Fujioka and his colleague Nishio Kanji in particular argue that, although Japan may be compared with other modern states, all of which have committed various crimes or excesses, it is fundamentally different from Nazi Germany. Nishio goes to great lengths to protest that, even if what he describes as "Japan's theocratic state under the emperor as high priest" may have fought "a slightly high-handed patriotic war"..., it certainly did not commit "crimes against humanity" such as would warrant its inclusion with Nazi Germany in the category of "historically unprecedented terror state." Fujioka adds that it was neither a terror state nor a "grotesque sex-crime state."

The difficulty with this claim is that although genocidal intent as such was unique to the Nazis, the casualties and destruction in the Asian war overall matched and even exceeded those on the European front. The crimes were also as abhorrent, particularly in regard to the comfort women but also to the crimes of the Japanese medical and scientific elites (most shockingly known from the record of Unit 731), and there were similarities in racial ideology and the "science" of eugenics, and more generally in relation to wartime "forced labor."...In many respects Nazi and Japanese ideology and practice were similar, and indeed in some respects Japan was guilty of crimes that even the Nazis did not commit—bacteriological and gas warfare, trading in opium to finance the activities of its puppet governments, and (also in China) the forced evacuation of vast areas of all population....

Unlike the former Nazi and present German governments, which are divided by a historical chasm, however, the present Japanese state enjoys a high measure of continuity with its wartime predecessor....If the analogy is pursued, it becomes clear that the sort of views upheld by Fujioka and his colleagues—denying the comfort women, denying Nanjing, and denying other atrocities associated with Unit 731—are generically one with those that in the German (and French) case would be proscribed under the legislation forbidding Holocaust denial.

JAPAN'S COMFORT WOMEN

The abduction and forced recruitment of young females of various ethnic and national backgrounds (Korean, Chinese, Taiwanese, Filipino, Japanese, and Dutch, among others) by the Japanese military as concubines for Japanese troops abroad remains unacknowledged by the Japanese six decades after the war. Known as "comfort women," these unfortunate females (including some preteens) were forced to administer to the sexual needs of Japanese officers and enlisted men alike and threatened with punishment and even death should they attempt to escape their horrible fate. The number of "comfort women" is estimated upwards of 200,000, with the majority of them Koreans. Although evidence documenting the abuses of these "comfort women" was gathered in the wake of the war, none was introduced or used in the Tokyo war crimes trials to punish those responsible. Only on the fiftieth anniversary of the attack on Pearl Harbor in December 1991 did a group of surviving comfort women confront the Japanese government by filing a class-action lawsuit against it. While the Japanese government issued an apology in 1993 for overseeing the brothels, its recent prime minister, Shinzo Abe, in March 2007 continued to deny that women had been forced into sexual slavery by the Japanese. What follows is an excerpt from the reminiscences of one such unfortunate woman, Yi Okpun, a twelve-year-old Korean.

The soldiers occupied an elementary school [in Taiwan] not far from the escarpment. It was a single-storey building with 17 classrooms. Each classroom was divided into three by wooden boards. There were about 40 women there. In front of the school was a sign saying, 'Commando Unit Comfort Station.' The distance from the barracks to the station seemed to me to be about 2 km.

On Saturdays, the Japanese soldiers formed long queues outside the school building. The ends of the queues were sometimes invisible. They each had a piece of paper with a red chop mark on it. They came

Yi Okpun, "Taken Away at Twelve," in Keith Howard, ed., *True Stories of the Korean Comfort Women* (London: Cassell, 1995), 98–101. Used by permission.

from 9:00 a.m. until midnight on both Saturday and Sunday. Sometimes, after the soldiers had returned to barracks, officers came and stayed the night, leaving at about 5:00 a.m. On such nights we got no sleep. Each woman had to serve 20 to 30 soldiers a day. We were already very weak, but going without good food and being forced to serve so many men left some of us half dead. If anyone was too weak to work, the receptionist dragged them out and put a more healthy woman in their cubicle. Three to five weak women were typically kept in a back room without any food. If they thought such a woman could not recover her health with herbal tonics and medicines, she would be loaded on to a truck and taken to a mountain. She never came back. Anyone who died was also carted away to the mountain, the bodies left there, barely covered with grass.

If you wanted to survive, you had to be tactful. If we made faces at the men we were taken to a confinement room by the receptionist, so we smiled regardless of whether we felt like doing so. Each man was given 30 minutes in the cubicle, and I would try to prolong the time in an effort to lessen the number I had to serve, even to lessen the number by one. At first, I got away with this, but later on I was too exhausted to do anything but lie still like the dead with my face turned to the wall, avoiding his stare.... For my first eight months I only served Yamamoto, the captain of the unit. But once he was transferred to Tayoko, I had to join the other women and serve 20 or 30 men a day. It was better to serve officers, as they would order the proprietor and receptionist not to send anyone else to me until they were spent and satisfied.

During my time there I was called both Haruko and Kohana, whichever name the men chose. We took turns to cook our meals, typically rising at 5:00 a.m. We ate rice with some vegetables or pickled radish as side dishes. Since we were given food only twice a day, we were always hungry. We had breakfast in the kitchen at 9:00 a.m. and supper at 6:00 p.m. We often looked at each other's rice bowl, wishing we could have some of our neighbour's food as well. If one of us was ill or looked extremely hungry, we would each give them a spoonful from our own bowls behind the backs of the Japanese. But if we were caught sharing food, both sharers and recipient got a severe beating.

The Japanese had their own rations and didn't have to eat such meager food as we received....

The cubicles were just large enough for two people to lie down in, and we each had two blankets for bedding. There was a small box for clothes and possessions and a dustbin in each room. Toilet paper was provided.

The soldiers all used condoms. We had a medical examination twice a month for venereal disease in a big room resembling a warehouse more than a hospital.... If the surgeon found any of us had caught a disease, he gave us an injection. The shot was so strong that we couldn't eat properly afterwards. It was said that the drug was strong enough to separate the womb from the body. We didn't have any cosmetics, and we were given two pairs of baggy trousers for our clothes in winter, spring and summer. There was a war raging, so we were not allowed to go out. Nevertheless, Yamamoto did take me out occasionally, and we went twice to a Chinese restaurant. Because of the war we had to cut hay during the weekdays, wearing a military uniform topped by a cap. Each of us was told to cut a certain amount of hay....

On weekday evenings we were made to sing, dance and play the violin in the bomb shelter. Even there we weren't allowed to sleep properly.... The shelter was huge, 4 km long, big enough to accommodate all the soldiers. We were taught how to play the violin by the soldiers so that we could entertain them. They had eight instruments. If we couldn't play well, we were beaten. The men drank heavily and would quickly become very violent....

I still have a photograph taken when I was 19. In it I am working, dressed in military uniform. The woman in a dress standing behind me came from Sariwon, Korea. In the original photograph there were many Japanese soldiers surrounding us, but since I hated them I have since cut them out.

The war was coming to an end, and Japan was thrown on the defensive. The soldiers moved about in a frantic muddle. They fought during the day, and at night they hid in caves. As the American bombing raids became more frequent soldiers could no longer come to the school. Instead, they would abuse us in the caves at night....

When I recall my life, I feel an unspeakable anger rising in my throat. Whenever any of us were beaten by the soldiers for having shared our rice, I used to grind my teeth together, saying to myself: 'One day I am going to kill you all. I will wipe out your descendents.' At the same time I used to ask myself 'Why is life so tough? Why can't I have my life, instead of living so wretchedly?' I lived each day hating myself that I continued to live. One morning I left the shelter at 3:00 a.m. while the others were fast asleep. I went to the seashore, intending to throw myself into the water, but I didn't have the courage. I tiptoed back and never told anyone.

HIROSHIMA, CULTURE WARS, AND THE *ENOLA GAY*

In the early 1990s, the National Air and Space Museum, the most popular of the Smithsonian Institution complex of museums in Washington DC, determined to mark the upcoming anniversary of the end of World War II with a special exhibition. At the center of the proposed exhibit would be the forward section of the restored *Enola Gay*, the B-29 bomber that had dropped the first atomic bomb on Hiroshima. Martin Harwit, a Cornell University astrophysicist who had been appointed the museum's director in 1987, as well as the staff of curators, intended to use the didactic opportunity afforded by the anniversary and the availability of the famous airplane to engage visitors with a thought-provoking look at the war's final stages and prompt them to reconsider their attitudes toward the use of atomic weapons on Japan. The first document in the readings that follow is an internal museum memorandum from July 1993 reflecting the curatorial staff's initial conception of the exhibition. By January 1994, museum historians had completed a first draft of the "script," the captions that would accompany the artifacts and visual images in the proposed exhibit. It was common, given the museum's highly visible role and dependence upon public funding, for it to circulate proposals or scripts to interested parties for their reaction. In this case, the proposed script ignited a firestorm of critical reaction, especially from veterans' groups, which had often felt that the museum favored achievements in civilian aviation over the exploits of military pilots. In the forefront of opposition to the museum's plan was the Air Force Association, a private organization separate from the U.S. Air Force, but an influential one comprising many veterans and acting as a powerful advocate for the past heritage and future influence of airpower. The second document, originally published in that association's magazine by its editor-in-chief, was a scathing condemnation of the proposed exhibition as a slap in the face at the integrity, professionalism, and patriotism of the bomber crews in particular, and the whole American war effort against Japan in general. By this point, however, opposition was widening. It was not just veterans who felt the Smithsonian was committed to a specifically liberal view of history that denigrated the military. In November 1994, a new Republican majority took control of Congress (which appropriated funds for the museum), its ascent fueled by the so-called culture wars over political correctness, multiculturalism, gender and sexual orientation, and so forth.

Republican House Speaker Newt Gingrich insisted that most Americans were "sick and tired of being told by some cultural elite that they ought to be ashamed of their country," while the *Wall Street Journal* complained that museums now had fallen under the sway of "academics unable to view American history as anything other than a woeful catalog of crimes and aggressions against the helpless peoples of the earth." Harwit and the museum staff sought to make concessions, revising the script where it seemed unduly critical of the U.S. efforts and overly sympathetic to the Japanese, but these foundered over the fact that it was not merely the accompanying captions, but the underlying conception of the exhibition and its powerful images that offended so many. In January 1995, more than eighty members of Congress called for Harwit's dismissal, and 20,000 subscribers to *Smithsonian Magazine* voiced their displeasure with the museum's plans. Harwit himself recognized that there was no way to reconcile commemoration of military veterans' dedicated and honorable service (that veterans expected the museum to undertake) with the searching reevaluation of the causes and consequences of the decision to drop the atomic bomb that the museum had intended to provoke. Harwit's growing recognition of that dilemma, expressed in a letter to the *Washington Post*, is the third selection.

I

Beginning in May 1995, the National Air and Space Museum will mount an exhibit about the end of the Second World War, the development of the atomic bomb, and the onset of the Cold War. Museum staff members recognize that this subject is marked by strong feelings and a broad range of opinion. The primary goal of this exhibition will be to encourage visitors to undertake a thoughtful and balanced re-examination of these events in the light of the political and military factors leading to the decision to drop the bomb, the human suffering experienced by the people of Hiroshima and Nagasaki and the long-term implications of the events of August 6 and 9, 1945....

The main theme of...[the first] unit will be the increasing bitterness and brutality of a war that was also, for Americans, a war of vengeance for Pearl Harbor.... "A Fight to the Finish" will...[include] a view of the Japanese Okha suicide bomb hanging overhead and diving toward the visitor. The kamikaze attacks expressed and symbolized the bitter resistance of the Japanese forces, which contributed to American racial and cultural perceptions and the assumption that war would end with a fight to

the finish on the beaches and in the home islands of Japan....This section will point out that air raids killed at least half a million Japanese civilians in the last six months of the war—about as many as in five years of bombing Germany. These raids were an important context for the decision to use the atomic bomb without warning on Japanese cities.

...[The second] section, which forms the intellectual heart of the exhibit...show[s] that there may have been no decision to drop the bomb in the usual sense, but rather there was a process of moving toward use that was difficult to deflect. Neither the atomic bomb nor an invasion was probably needed to end the Pacific war, but this is much more obvious in hindsight than it was at the time....

The second unit stops at the point where the dropping of the bomb is inevitable; the exhibit now turns to how the weapon was to be delivered. When visitors walk into this unit, they will immediately see the nose of the "Enola Gay," plus some view of the rest of the gigantic forward fuselage, which is about 18 meters (56 ft) long and 3 meters (10 ft) in diameter....The theme of Unit 3 is thus the creation of the instruments for delivering the bomb....

The Crossroads: The End of World War II, the Atomic Bomb, and the Onset of the Cold War (National Air and Space Museum, Smithsonian Institution, Exhibition Planning Document, July 1993) at www.afa.org/media/enolagay/07-93.html. Reprinted by permission from *AIR FORCE Magazine*, published by the Air Force Association.

When visitors go from Unit 3 to Unit 4, they will be immediately hit by drastic change of mood and perspective: from well-lit and airy to gloomy and oppressive. The aim will be to put visitors on the ground during the atomic bombings of the two cities. The opening of "Hiroshima/Nagasaki" must convey that stunning, searing moment of the initial flash, heat and burns through pictures, through the words of survivors themselves and through bomb-damaged artifacts....

If Unit 2 is the intellectual heart of the exhibit, Unit 4 is its emotional center. Photos of victims, enlarged to life-size, stare out at the visitor. Photographs of dead bodies will, however, be presented in such a way that parents can choose whether or not to allow their children to see them. The emphasis will be on the personal tragedy of this experience. The people of Hiroshima and Nagasaki will tell their own stories....Among the artifacts that could be used, if permission were granted, are a school girl's lunchbox with completely burned contents, burned and shredded clothing, and melted and broken religious objects.

II

The *Enola Gay*'s task was a grim one, hardly suitable for glamorization. Nevertheless, many visitors may be taken aback by what they see. That is particularly true for World War II veterans who had petitioned the museum to display the historic bomber in a more objective setting.

The restored aircraft will be there all right, the front fifty-six feet of it, anyway. The rest of the gallery space is allotted to a program about the atomic bomb. The presentation is designed for shock effect. The museum's exhibition plan notes that parents might find some parts unsuitable for viewing by their children, and the script warns that "parental discretion is advised."

For what the plan calls the "emotional center" of the exhibit, the curators are collecting burnt watches, broken wall clocks, and photos of victims—which

will be enlarged to life size—as well as melted and broken religious objects. One display will be a schoolgirl's lunch box with remains of peas and rice reduced to carbon. To ensure that nobody misses the point, "where possible, photos of the persons who owned or wore these artifacts would be used to show that real people stood behind the artifacts." Survivors of Hiroshima and Nagasaki will recall the horror in their own words.

The Air and Space Museum says it takes no position on the "difficult moral and political questions" involved. For the past two years, however, museum officials have been under fire from veterans groups who charge that the exhibition plan is politically biased.

The exhibition plan the museum was following as recently as November picked up the story of the war in 1945 as the end approached. It depicted the Japanese in a desperate defense of their home islands, saying little about what had made such a defense necessary. US conduct of the war was depicted as brutal, vindictive, and racially motivated.

The latest script, written in January, shows major concessions to balance. It acknowledges Japan's "naked aggression and extreme brutality" that began in the 1930s. It gives greater recognition to US casualties. Despite some hedging, it says the atomic bomb "played a crucial role in ending the Pacific war quickly." Further revisions to the script are expected.

The ultimate effect of the exhibition will depend, of course, on how the words are blended with the artifacts and audiovisual elements. And despite the balancing material added, the curators still make some curious calls.

"For most Americans," the script says, "it was a war of vengeance. For most Japanese, it was a war to defend their unique culture against Western imperialism." Women, children, and mutilated religious objects are strongly emphasized in the "ground zero" scenes from Hiroshima and Nagasaki. The museum says this is "happenstance," not a deliberate ideological twist....

In a letter to Dr. Harwit last fall, Gen. Monroe W. Hatch, Jr. (USAF Ret.), Air Force Association executive director, said the museum's plan "treats Japan and the United States as if their participation in the

---

John T. Correll, "Air Force Association Special Report: The Smithsonian and the Enola Gay," March 15, 1994, at www.afa.org/media/enolagay/02–001.html. Used by permission.

war were morally equivalent. If anything, incredibly, it gives the benefit of opinion to Japan, which was the aggressor." What visitors would get from such an exhibition, General Hatch said, was "not history or fact, but a partisan interpretation."

III

Forty-nine years ago this weekend, the United States dropped an atomic bomb on Hiroshima and then another on Nagasaki. A year from now, on the 50th anniversary, Americans will commemorate these pivotal events. But we lack a national consensus on what to say.

Two divergent but widely held views define the dilemma. One view sprang up as soon as the bombs exploded and the war ended. Its proponents are united on the main details that need to be included in their story. Properly told, it appeals to our national self-image. The other point of view, slower in coming to the fore, is more analytical, critical in its acceptance of facts and concerned with historical context. It is complex and, in the eyes of some, discomforting.

The first view recalls the morning of Aug. 6, 1945, when three B-29 Superfortresses arrived over Japan's Inland Sea. One of the aircraft, the Enola Gay, named for the pilot's mother, approached its Hiroshima target, released its heavy payload, then veered to distance itself from the bomb. Seconds later, at 8:15 a.m. the atomic bomb exploded over Hiroshima. The crew was stunned by the sight. The blast rocked the aircraft. The 29-year old pilot, Col. Paul W. Tibbets, commander of the 509th composite Group, which was trained and tasked to deliver the bomb, was awed by the sight of the burning, devastated city below. To his copilot he remarked, "I think this is the end of the war." Five days and another atomic bomb later, Japan surrendered.

Our troops were ecstatic. They would not have to die by the many tens of thousands in a bloody invasion of Japan. They'd go home instead, settle down with their sweethearts, have children and lead normal lives. They had been asked to save the world for

democracy, had accepted the challenge at great personal risk, and had come through victorious.

Approaching the 50th anniversary of Hiroshima next year, these same men, now in their seventies, have asked the National Air and Space Museum, into whose care the Enola Gay was entrusted after the war, to put their aircraft on exhibition. They want the museum to tell their story the way they have always told and retold it—a story of fighting a ruthless enemy, perpetrator of barbaric massacres in China, the infamous attack at Pearl Harbor, the death march at Bataan, torture and executions in prison camps, kamikaze raids on our warships and deaths by the thousands for every Pacific island wrested away; a story of the world's top physicists working in secrecy to perfect a mighty weapon; a story of a powerful new aircraft, designed, built and first flown in just 24 months; a story of ordinary citizens, men and women, working together to defeat a ferocious enemy.

These are the themes emphasized by those who fought so hard to secure freedom for their children and grandchildren.

Those children and grandchildren by now are mature citizens. For them the atomic bomb has added associations: ICBMs, megaton warheads, the DEW line, 45-minute warnings, first strike, Mutually Assured Destruction, nuclear winter....Theirs was not a world of two small atomic bombs but of 50,000, many of which are 1,000 times more powerful than those that destroyed Hiroshima and Nagasaki. Next year these younger people will not only commemorate a bomb that ended the most terrible war, but also they will have reason to celebrate the restraint that has prevailed for half a century in which no man, woman or child has been killed by an atomic bomb. They want to extend that record to all time.

The Enola Gay symbolizes the end of one era and the beginning of another. For an older generation, the aircraft meant the end of World War II; for younger people it ushered in the nuclear age. The postwar generations respect their fathers for the sacrifices they made, but they also realize that the nuclear bombs that saved their fathers' lives continue to threaten their own and their children's.

Martin Harwit, "The Enola Gay: A Nation's, and a Museum's, Dilemma," *Washington Post* (August 7, 1994), C9. Used by permission.

These conflicting views pose the dilemma the National Air and Space Museum faces as we prepare an exhibition of the Enola Gay for 1995. We want to honor the veterans who risked their lives and those who made the ultimate sacrifice. They served their country with distinction. But we must also address the broader questions that concern subsequent generations—not with a view to criticizing or apologizing or displaying undue compassion for those on the ground that day, as some may fear, but to deliver an accurate portrayal that conveys the reality of atomic war and its consequences.

To that end, the museum proposes to tell the full story surrounding the atomic bomb and the end of World War II; to recall the options facing a newly installed President Truman, who had never heard of the bomb until the day he was sworn in; to examine the estimates of the casualties Truman anticipated if U.S. troops had to invade Japan; to consider the extent to which his wish to impress a threatening Soviet Union influenced his decision to drop the bomb; to exhibit the destruction and suffering on the ground at Hiroshima and Nagasaki; and to recall the escalating numbers of weapons in the superpowers' nuclear arsenals during the Cold War, and their current decline.

Faced with a number of alternatives, the museum has chosen to provide not an opinion piece but rather the basic information that visitors will need to draw their own conclusions. This is our responsibility, as a national museum in a democracy predicated on an informed citizenry.

We have found no way to exhibit the Enola Gay and satisfy everyone. But a comprehensive and thoughtful discussion can help us learn from history. And that is what we aim to offer our visitors.

WORLD WAR II TIMELINE

1931

JANUARY 12   Oversight by the Allied Military Control Committee of German military demobilization ends

SEPTEMBER 16   Japanese troops begin invasion and occupation of Manchuria

DECEMBER 10   Spain adopts a new constitution, establishes a republic under a president, and separates Church and State

1932

JANUARY 2   Japan proclaims the establishment of the Republic of Manchukuo in China

FEBRUARY 5   Japan extends its occupation to central Manchuria

JULY 25   The USSR signs a series of nonaggression pacts with Estonia, Finland, and Poland

NOVEMBER 8   Franklin D. Roosevelt is elected president of the United States after defeating incumbent president Herbert Hoover in a landslide election victory

1933

JANUARY 30   Adolf Hitler becomes chancellor of Germany

MARCH 22   Dachau concentration camp opens for incarceration of "political prisoners"

MARCH 27   The Enabling Act in Germany gives Hitler's government dictatorial powers

APRIL 1   Germany imposes national boycott of Jewish businesses and professionals

JULY 14   The National Socialist Party (NSDAP) becomes the only legal political party in Germany, following the dissolution of all other political parties

OCTOBER 23   Germany withdraws from the League of Nations and the Disarmament Conference

1934

JANUARY 26   Germany and Poland sign a nonaggression pact for ten years

AUGUST 2   Hitler proclaims himself both Führer and Reichskanzler

DECEMBER 19   Japan refuses to limit the size of its fleet in violation of naval treaties of 1922 and 1930

1935

MARCH 1   The League of Nations return the Saar to Germany, marking the beginning of German territorial expansion under Hitler

MARCH 16   In defiance of the Versailles Treaty, Germany refuses to adhere to its disarmament clauses and initiates conscription

SEPTEMBER 15   Germany enacts the Nuremberg Racial Laws, barring Jews from citizenship

OCTOBER 3   Italy invades Ethiopia

1936

MARCH 7   Germany violates the terms of the Versailles Treaty and Locarno Pacts of 1925 by remilitarizing the Rhineland

MAY 5   Italian forces enter Ethiopia's capital, Addis Ababa, forcing Emperor Haile Selassie to flee and ending the Ethiopian war

JULY   Sachsenhausen concentration camp opens

JULY 17–18   The Spanish Civil War begins when the Spanish military launches a coup against the Republican government with the support of the German and Italian governments

OCTOBER 25   Hitler and Mussolini announce a Rome-Berlin alliance (Axis)

1937

JANUARY 19   Japan refuses to adhere to the naval limitations of the Washington Conference Treaty of 1921

JANUARY 27   Nationalists and Communists in China agree to combine forces against the Japanese

MAY 1   President Roosevelt signs the Neutrality Act banning the American government and businesses from providing weapons or financial assistance to belligerent nations

JULY 7   Clash occurs between Japan and Chinese troops at the Marco Polo Bridge near Peking (now Beijing); Japan seizes control of the city on July 28

JULY 15   Germany opens Buchenwald concentration camp

NOVEMBER 5   Hossbach Memorandum: Colonel Friedrich Hossbach takes minutes at a secret conference in the Reich Chancellery in Berlin during which Hitler reportedly discusses his expansionist plans

DECEMBER 11   Italy withdraws from the League of Nations

DECEMBER 13   Japanese troops enter Chinese city of Nanjing (Nanking) and begin campaign of murder, rape, and looting

1938

MARCH 11–13   The *Anschluss*—Germany incorporates Austria

MARCH 26   The Japanese government passes the National Mobilization Bill, giving the state dictatorial powers in Japan's economy

MARCH 28   The Japanese establish a puppet regime in Nanking

APRIL 30   The Swiss government appeals to the Council of the League of Nations to recognize Switzerland's neutrality

AUGUST 8   Germany begins construction of Mauthausen concentration camp in Austria

SEPTEMBER 12	Adolf Hitler demands that the Czechoslovak government give Sudeten Germans the right of self-determination
SEPTEMBER 15	British prime minister Neville Chamberlain flies to Germany to meet with Hitler to discuss Czechoslovakia; Hitler demands the annexation of the German regions of Czechoslovakia, threatening war if his conditions are not met
SEPTEMBER 29	Germany, Italy, Great Britain, and France sign the Munich agreement, according Hitler his demands for Czechoslovakia and making Germany the strongest power in Europe
NOVEMBER 9–10	*Kristallnacht* ("Night of the Broken Glass") in which Germany's synagogues are pillaged and burned
DECEMBER 31	The U.S. Department of State refuses to recognize Japan's "New Order" in the Far East

1939

JANUARY 30	Hitler addresses the Reichstag, warning ominously of the "annihilation of the Jews" should war break out in Europe
MARCH 14–15	The Slovaks declare independence and form a republic; Germans create the protectorate of Bohemia and Moravia
MARCH 28	The Spanish Civil War ends when Franco's Nationalist troops enter Madrid, defeating the Republican forces
MARCH 31	France and Great Britain guarantee the integrity of the borders of the Polish state
APRIL 7	Italy begins its invasion of Albania and then annexes it
MAY 8	Spain withdraws from the League of Nations
MAY 22	Germany and Italy form the "Pact of Steel"
AUGUST 23	German-Soviet nonaggression treaty (Nazi-Soviet Pact) divides Poland into spheres of influence
SEPTEMBER 1	Germany invades Poland
SEPTEMBER 3	France, Britain, Australia, and New Zealand declare war on Germany
SEPTEMBER 10	Canada declares war on Germany
SEPTEMBER 17	Soviet Union invades Poland
SEPTEMBER 21	Reinhard Heydrich orders establishment of ghettos in German-occupied Poland
SEPTEMBER 27	Warsaw surrenders to German forces
OCTOBER 28	First Polish ghetto (Piotrkow) is established
NOVEMBER 23	Jews in occupied Poland are forced to wear an armband or yellow star for identification as Jews
NOVEMBER 30	Soviet Union attacks Finland in the "Winter War"

1940

JANUARY 26	The United States abrogates its commercial treaty with Japan that had been in effect since 1911
MARCH 12	Finland surrenders and signs treaty with Soviet Union
APRIL 9	Germany invades Denmark and Norway
MAY 7	Germany seals Lodz ghetto

MAY 10	Germany invades France, the Netherlands, Belgium, and Luxemburg
MAY 14	The city of Rotterdam is bombed by the Germans
MAY 15	The Netherlands surrender to the Germans
MAY 20	Germany establishes concentration camp at Auschwitz
MAY 28	Belgium surrenders to Germany
JUNE 10	Italy joins Germany in the war and declares war on France and Britain; German occupation of Norway is complete
JUNE 14	German troops march into Paris
JUNE 14–18	The Soviet Union occupies the Baltic States
JUNE 15	President Roosevelt establishes the National Defense Research Committee (headed by Dr. Vannevar Bush) with the purpose of planning and organizing American defense preparations
JUNE 17	Marshal Philippe Pétain sues for peace with Germany
JUNE 22	France signs armistice with Germany; Germany occupies the northern half of France
JUNE 23	Charles de Gaulle, who has escaped from France to London, declares himself leader of the Free French movement
JULY 2	Collaborator Marshal Pétain establishes Vichy France
JULY 10	Marshal Pétain and Pierre Laval are granted authoritarian powers under the Vichy government
JULY 20	President Roosevelt signs bill establishing a "two-ocean navy" to combat threats to the United States around the world
JULY–OCTOBER	Battle of Britain
AUGUST 3–6	The Soviet Union annexes the Baltic States
AUGUST 3	Vichy France passes anti-Jewish racial laws
AUGUST 17	Germany establishes a total naval blockade around the British Isles
SEPTEMBER 27	Rome-Berlin-Tokyo Axis forms
OCTOBER 3	The Warsaw ghetto is opened
OCTOBER 23	Hitler fails to persuade General Francisco Franco to bring Spain into the war
OCTOBER 28	Italy invades Greece
OCTOBER 29	U.S. government conducts the first peacetime draft lottery in American history
NOVEMBER 16	Germans seal the Warsaw ghetto
NOVEMBER 20	Hungary joins the Axis
DECEMBER 18	Hitler finalizes plan for "Operation Barbarossa," the plan for the invasion of the Soviet Union

1941

JANUARY 6	President Roosevelt delivers his "Four Freedoms" speech
JANUARY 20	Mussolini allows German troops into Italy to help bolster Italian military efforts
JANUARY 21–26	Anti-Jewish riots erupt in Romania
MARCH 1	Bulgaria joins the Axis powers and German troops enter Sofia, its capital

MARCH 11	Congress passes the Lend-Lease Act, allowing the president to provide economic and military support to nations whose defense is vital to the United States
MARCH 24	General Erwin Rommel and the Afrika Korps are dispatched to Libya by Germany to shore up the Italian forces in Libya
APRIL 6	Germany invades Yugoslavia and Greece to secure the Axis position in the Balkans; British troops liberate Addis Ababa from the Axis
APRIL 13	The Soviet Union and Japan sign a Treaty of Neutrality, pledging both to remain neutral in the event of a war with a third party
APRIL 17	Yugoslavia capitulates to the Germans
APRIL 21	In a meeting in Singapore, American, British, and Dutch military officials develop a strategic plan for combined operations against Japan in the event the Japanese attack the United States
APRIL 23	Greece surrenders to Germany
MAY 2	Rashid Ali of Iraq invites German aid in his country; Britain responds by sending forces into Iraq to overthrow the pro-Axis regime
MAY 27	Following a German U-boat sinking of an American merchant ship off the coast of Brazil, President Roosevelt declares an unlimited state of national emergency in the United States
JUNE 18	Germany and Turkey sign a nonaggression pact
JUNE 22	Operation Barbarossa begins against the Soviet Union (through December)
JULY 2	The Nationalist Chinese government severs diplomatic relations with the Axis powers
JULY 13	Britain agrees to provide military assistance to aid the Russians against the Germans
JULY 24	The Vichy government gives Japan permission to establish military control over French Indochina
JULY 26	President Roosevelt freezes all Japanese credits in the United States and cuts off trade with it in response to the Japanese occupation of French Indochina
AUGUST 9–12	British prime minister Winston Churchill and President Roosevelt meet off the coast of Canada in Newfoundland to discuss wartime objectives and postwar peace plans; the result is the Atlantic Charter, which they announce on August 14
AUGUST 17	President Roosevelt warns the Japanese ambassador to the United States that it will take action to safeguard American rights and interests in the Far East if the Japanese take new military actions in the region
AUGUST 25	British and Soviet forces invade Iran in the hope of overthrowing the pro-Axis government of Riza Shah; Lebanon, Syria, and Iraq are already under British control (since June–July 1941)
SEPTEMBER 28–29	Massacre of Jews in a ravine at Babi Yar, located just outside of Kiev; at least 34,000 are murdered
OCTOBER 11	President Roosevelt privately proposes to Winston Churchill that the United States and Britain work together to develop an atomic bomb
OCTOBER 17	The American destroyer USS *Kearny* is torpedoed by a German U-boat off the coast of Iceland, killing eleven American sailors

OCTOBER 27	Pro-Axis general Hideki Tojo becomes Japan's new prime minister and minister of war
NOVEMBER 18	The Japanese Diet approves a resolution of hostility against the United States
NOVEMBER 26	Lebanon declares its independence from France
NOVEMBER 27	The United States warns the British of imminent war with Japan
NOVEMBER 28	The Mufti of Jerusalem, Haj Amin al-Husseini, meets with Hitler in Berlin to try to obtain his support for the Arabs in their conflict with the Jews in Palestine
DECEMBER 6	President Roosevelt appeals to Emperor Hirohito of Japan to prevent a war between his country and the United States
DECEMBER 7	Japanese planes attack the U.S. naval base at Pearl Harbor, Hawaii
DECEMBER 8	The United States declares war against Japan; Japanese troops land on the Malay Peninsula and Thailand; Chelmno death camp becomes operational
DECEMBER 10	Japanese troops land in the Philippines
DECEMBER 11	Germany and Italy declare war on the United States; the British launch their second offensive against the Axis in Libya
DECEMBER 20	Britain declares war on Japan after the Japanese attack Malaya and Hong Kong
DECEMBER 21	Japan and Thailand sign a ten-year Treaty of Alliance
DECEMBER 22–28	Winston Churchill visits Washington DC to confer with President Roosevelt on Anglo-American strategy in the war effort; they agree to concentrate resources against the Axis in Europe while simultaneously pursuing a policy of containment in the Far East
DECEMBER 25	Japanese forces seize control of Hong Kong from the British
1942	
JANUARY 1	Twenty-six nations sign the United Nations Declaration in Washington DC, affirming the principles of the Atlantic Charter
JANUARY 2	The Supreme Command for American, British, Dutch, and Australian Forces in the Far East (ABDACOM) is created with British general Sir Archibald P. Wavell as its appointed commander
JANUARY 2–MAY 6	Japanese forces capture Manila in the Philippines, forcing American and Filipino forces to retreat to the Bataan Peninsula
JANUARY 11	Japanese forces begin the occupation of the Dutch East Indies
JANUARY 12	The United States and Mexico establish a joint defense commission to coordinate defense planning
JANUARY 15–28	In Rio de Janeiro, Brazil, the United States meets with Latin American countries to ensure that they declare war on the Axis powers and sever all relations with them; only Chile and Argentina object
JANUARY 20	The Wannsee Conference takes place in a villa in Berlin, where plans are drawn up for the "Final Solution" of the Jews
JANUARY 25	Thailand declares war on the United States and Great Britain
FEBRUARY 8	Japan begins its invasion of Burma
FEBRUARY 15	Singapore falls to the Japanese

FEBRUARY 19	President Roosevelt signs Executive Order 9066, authorizing the internment of tens of thousands of American citizens of Japanese ancestry and resident aliens from Japan
MARCH	Operation Reinhard begins with the purpose of killing the General Government of Poland's 3 million Jews by means of carbon monoxide gas; Belzec death camp is opened
APRIL 9	American and Filipino troops are forced to surrender to the Japanese on the Bataan Peninsula
APRIL 11	The British offer autonomy to India after the war as long as it supports the Allied war effort
MAY 27	Reinhard Heydrich, Protector of Bohemia and Moravia, head of the Reich Security Main Office (RSHA), and coordinator of the "Final Solution," is assassinated by Czech resistance fighters
JUNE 4–7	Battle of Midway leads to restoration of the balance of power in the Pacific and allows U.S. forces to go on the offensive
JULY 6	Argentina declares its neutrality in the war
JULY 22	Treblinka concentration camp is established
AUGUST 12–16	Winston Churchill and U.S. ambassador W. Averell Harriman inform Soviet premier Josef Stalin that the premier's desire for the opening of a second front is impossible at the moment
AUGUST 13	Brigadier General Leslie Groves is appointed to head the Manhattan Project for the development of an atomic bomb
AUGUST 30	Germany annexes the Grand Duchy of Luxemburg
OCTOBER 23	The British under General Bernard L. Montgomery launch a major offensive against Rommel's Afrika Korps in western Egypt
NOVEMBER 8	Commanded by General Dwight D. Eisenhower, U.S. British and Allied forces land at several cities in Morocco and Algeria to gain control of North Africa from Vichy France
NOVEMBER 11	Admiral Jean-François Darlan, representative of Vichy France, signs an armistice with the Allies, ending the fighting in Morocco and Algeria
NOVEMBER 27	Marshal Pétain appoints Pierre Laval his successor in the Vichy government
DECEMBER 1	Supported by the Americans and British, Admiral Jean-François Darlan becomes Chief of State in French North Africa; Darlan is assassinated only weeks later on December 24
DECEMBER 2	Scientists working on the Argonne Project at the University of Chicago achieve the first self-sustaining nuclear reaction

1943

JANUARY 14–24	Following the Allied invasion of North Africa, Roosevelt, Churchill, de Gaulle, and Giraud meet in Casablanca to plan an offensive against the Axis that would result in its unconditional surrender; the opening of a second front is agreed to in principle
JANUARY 16	The new Iraqi government declares war on the Axis powers
JANUARY 20	Chile ends diplomatic relations with Germany and Japan

JANUARY 24	British troops capture Tripoli and force the Axis to retreat westward into Tunisia
JANUARY 30	Ernst Kaltenbrunner succeeds the deceased Heydrich as head of the Reich Security Main Office and the "Final Solution"
FEBRUARY 2	The Red Army wins a critical victory in Stalingrad, forcing the remaining 80,000 Axis troops to surrender and ending a battle that began summer 1942
APRIL 19	Warsaw ghetto uprising begins as Germans try to liquidate its 70,000 inhabitants
MAY 12–25	At the Anglo-American Trident Conference in Washington DC, Churchill and Roosevelt agree to open a second front in Europe and to prepare for a landing on the coast of Normandy on May 1, 1944
JUNE	Himmler orders the liquidation of all ghettos in Poland and the Soviet Union
JULY 10–AUGUST 17	Under the command of General Dwight Eisenhower, American, British, and Canadian forces from North Africa mount the invasion of Sicily
JULY 25	Mussolini is forced to resign and placed under house arrest; Marshal Pietro Badoglio becomes the new Italian premier
JULY 28	Marshal Badoglio begins secret armistice negotiations with the Allies
AUGUST 11–25	Churchill and Roosevelt meet at First Quebec Quadrant Conference to plan the second front in Europe and reaffirm the date for the Normandy landing
SEPTEMBER 3	Italy signs secret armistice with the Allies in Algiers; amphibious invasion of southern Italy by British Eighth Army begins
SEPTEMBER 11	The new Iranian government declares war against Germany; Germany learns of Italy's surrender to the Allies and seizes control of major cities in central and northern Italy
SEPTEMBER 12	German paratroopers rescue Mussolini from Italian imprisonment and bring him to Berlin; the intent of the raid is to restore him to power in German-occupied northern Italy
SEPTEMBER 13	General Chiang Kai-shek is elected president of the Republic of China by the Central Executive Committee and permitted to retain his post as commander-in-chief of the army
SEPTEMBER 15	Mussolini announces the establishment of the Socialist Republic of Italy in the German-controlled northern sector of the country
OCTOBER 13	Italy declares war against Germany
OCTOBER 19–30	High-ranking representatives of the U.S., British, and Soviet governments (Cordell Hull, Anthony Eden, and V. M. Molotov) and military officials meet to discuss strategy; Soviets dissatisfied over the Polish government-in-exile; the Soviets are promised the opening of a second European front, and in return Stalin promises to enter the war against Japan once Germany is defeated
OCTOBER 21	Subhas Chandra Bose, former leader of the Indian National Congress, insists that Gandhi's nonviolence policy will not lead to Indian independence from Britain, allies with the Axis powers in the hope of removing the British from Indian soil

NOVEMBER 8	Lebanon proclaims its independence from France only to have its government leaders arrested by French authorities; on November 22, however, in the face of growing international pressure, France grants Lebanon its independence
NOVEMBER 28– DECEMBER 2	Roosevelt, Churchill, and Stalin meet face-to-face in Teheran to discuss strategy and postwar planning
DECEMBER 1	Roosevelt, Churchill, and Chiang Kai-shek declare in the Cairo Declaration that the Japanese will be forced to surrender unconditionally and return all its Pacific Island possessions taken since 1914 as well as all Chinese territory it had seized; Korea would also be granted its independence at a later date
DECEMBER 4–6	Roosevelt, Churchill, and Ismet Inonu meet in Cairo to discuss eastern Mediterranean issues; Turkey refuses, however, to be brought into the war against the Axis

1944

JANUARY 20– FEBRUARY 8	African leaders from French West and Equatorial Africa meet in Brazzaville (capital of the French Congo) to lobby for reforms in French colonial rule with the hope of ultimately obtaining independence from France
JANUARY 31– FEBRUARY 20	American troops launch amphibious assaults, giving them control of the Marshall Islands
MARCH 19	After Hungary tries to negotiate a separate armistice with the Allies, Germany sends troops into Hungary and establishes a pro-German puppet government, which cooperates with the Germans in the deportation of Hungarian Jews
JUNE 4	The U.S. Fifth Army enters Rome, which becomes the first European capital to be liberated from the Axis
JUNE 6	Under the command of General Dwight Eisenhower, Operation Overlord begins with U.S., British, and Canadian forces landing on the beaches of Normandy, France
JUNE 13	Germany launches the V-1 pilotless aircraft against Britain
JULY 1–22	In Bretton Woods, New Hampshire, representatives from the Allied nations meet to plan for the postwar international financial system and propose the creation of an International Monetary Fund and an International Bank for Reconstruction and Development (renamed the World Bank) to assist with the postwar's economic and political stability
JULY 13–AUGUST	American, British, and Canadian forces advance into northern France, liberating Paris on August 23
JULY 18	General Hideki Tojo and his cabinet resign in Japan, following major Allied advances against the Japanese in the Pacific
JULY 20	An assassination attempt against Hitler by Claus von Stauffenberg and members of the German military fails
JULY 24	Russians liberate Majdanek
AUGUST 21– OCTOBER 9	Delegates from the United States, Great Britain, the Soviet Union, and China meet at Dumbarton Oaks in Washington DC to discuss the creation of the United Nations as the replacement for the League of Nations
AUGUST 23	Romania surrenders and is occupied by the Red Army
AUGUST 25	Romania declares war on Germany

SEPTEMBER 4	Brussels and Antwerp are liberated from German occupation
SEPTEMBER 7	The Germans launch their new V-2 rockets on London
SEPTEMBER 12–16	Roosevelt and Churchill meet at Second Quebec Conference to discuss the zones of occupation after Germany's defeat as well as the plan of Secretary of the Treasury, Henry Morgenthau, for Germany's postwar economy
SEPTEMBER 24– OCTOBER 13	British land in Greece, liberating Athens on October 13
OCTOBER 9–19	In Moscow, Churchill and Stalin agree to a plan for the division of the Balkans into spheres of influence; the Soviets will control Bulgaria, Hungary, and Romania, the British will control Greece
OCTOBER 23	General Charles de Gaulle is recognized officially by the Allies as the leader of the French provisional government
DECEMBER 16– JANUARY 25, 1945	Hitler decides to launch a surprise counteroffensive through the Ardennes to strike a final blow against the Allies in what becomes the Battle of the Bulge; by the end of January the Allies recoup all ground that had been lost

1945

JANUARY 6	Turkey breaks off diplomatic relations with Japan
JANUARY 9	U.S. forces attempt to reclaim most of the Philippine Islands, which they do by July 5
JANUARY 17	Soviet army launches offensive and captures Warsaw
JANUARY 20	Hungary concludes an armistice with Allies and supports the war against Germany
JANUARY 27	Soviet troops liberate Auschwitz and its 7,000 prisoners
JANUARY 30– FEBRUARY 3	Roosevelt and Churchill meet on the island of Malta (Malta Conference) to plan the final campaign against the Germans and discuss how to deal with the Soviets
FEBRUARY 7–12	Roosevelt, Churchill, and Stalin meet in Yalta (Yalta Conference) on the Crimean Peninsula to discuss postwar planning, including the division of Germany, the fate of eastern Europe, and the creation of the United Nations
FEBRUARY 12	The Polish government-in-exile protests against Soviet actions against the Polish population, including deportation and transfers across the border
FEBRUARY 19	U.S. Marines storm ashore on Iwo Jima (located halfway between the Mariana Islands and Japan)
FEBRUARY 23	Turkey declares war against Germany and Japan
FEBRUARY 24	Egyptian prime minister Ahmed Pasha announces his country's declaration of war against Germany and Japan and is assassinated later that same day
MARCH 3	Finland signs an armistice with the Soviet Union and declares war on Germany
MARCH 27	Argentina declares war on Germany and Japan
APRIL 1–JUNE 22	In Operation Iceberg, U.S. troops land on Okinawa (large island just 340 miles from mainland Japan), initiating the Battle of Okinawa, the fight for a strategic foothold on the island
APRIL 12	President Roosevelt dies suddenly at his retreat in Warm Springs, Georgia

APRIL 13	Soviet army launches final offensive against Germany in Berlin, entering the city on April 20
APRIL 25–JUNE 26	Representatives from fifty countries meet in San Francisco at the United Nations Conference on International Organization to draw up the United Nations Charter, which is signed on June 26
APRIL 28	Mussolini is captured by Italian anti-Fascist forces and executed after trying to escape to Switzerland
APRIL 30	Adolf Hitler and his wife of one day, Eva Braun, commit suicide in Hitler's bunker in Berlin beneath the Reich Chancellery
MAY 1	Admiral Karl Dönitz emerges as Germany's new leader and begins surrender negotiations with the Allies
MAY 7	Admiral Dönitz accepts the Allied surrender terms unconditionally
MAY 8	Roosevelt's successor, former vice president and now President Harry Truman, and Churchill proclaim the end of war in Europe with V-E day; Algerian Nationalists, demanding an autonomous Algeria, clash with French forces
MAY 9–23	The Allies disarm the German army and, two weeks later, the provisional German government
MAY 10	President Edvard Benes returns from exile to establish a new government in Czechoslovakia and executes Nazi collaborators
JUNE 5	The European Advisory Commission assumes power over Germany and divides it into four zones of occupation: American, British, French, and Soviet
JUNE 9	Japan announces it will fight to the very end rather than accept unconditional surrender
JUNE 28	The Poles form a National Unity Government, consisting of members of the Polish government-in-exile and socialists backed by the Soviet Union
JULY 3	Berlin is to be divided into three zones: American, British, and Soviet
JULY 5	Liberation of the Philippines by American forces
JULY 17–AUGUST 2	Truman, Churchill, Clement Attlee (who replaced Churchill), and Stalin meet in Berlin to plan the postwar world and demand that Japan surrender or face horrible consequences
AUGUST 6	The *Enola Gay* drops an atomic bomb (nicknamed "Little Boy") on Hiroshima, Japan, at approximately 8:15 A.M.
AUGUST 8	Soviet government declares war on Japan
AUGUST 9	A second atomic bomb (nicknamed "Fat Man") is dropped on Nagasaki, Japan, at 11:02 A.M.
AUGUST 10	Emperor Hirohito overrules his military leaders, forcing them to accept surrender as long as he is allowed to retain the position of head of state
AUGUST 12	Allies agree to accept Japanese surrender and allow the emperor to remain in a purely ceremonial role, relinquishing his "divine" status
AUGUST 15	Emperor Hirohito broadcasts via radio Japan's surrender to the Allies; this was the first time the Japanese had heard his voice; President Truman announces victory over Japan (V-J day) and the end of the Pacific War
SEPTEMBER 2	Vietnam, led by Ho Chi Minh, declares its independence from French rule
SEPTEMBER 19	Britain proposes to begin negotiations on Indian autonomy
OCTOBER 24	The United Nations officially comes into existence

WORLD WAR II BIBLIOGRAPHY

GENERAL WORKS

Michael Bess, *Choices under Fire: Moral Dimensions of World War II* (New York: Knopf, 2006)

Joanna Bourke, *The Second World War: A People's History* (Oxford: Oxford University Press, 2002)

Peter Calvocoressi, Guy Wint, and John Pritchard, *The Penguin History of the Second World War* (London: Penguin, 1999; 3rd rev. ed., 2001)

Roger Chickering, Stig Förster, and Bernd Greiner, eds., *A World at Total War: Global Conflict and the Politics of Destruction* (New York: Cambridge University Press, 2005)

Norman Davies, *No Simple Victory: World War II in Europe, 1939–1945* (New York: Viking, 2007)

I. C. B. Dear and M. R. D. Foot, *Oxford Companion to World War II* (Oxford: Oxford University Press, 2005)

John Ellis, *World War II: A Statistical Survey* (New York: Facts on File, 1993, 1995)

Niall Ferguson, *The War of the World* (London: Penguin, 2006)

John Keegan, *The Second World War* (New York: Viking, 1989)

Ian Kershaw, *Fateful Choices: Ten Decisions that Changed the World, 1940–1941* (London: Penguin, 2007)

John Lukacs, *The Second World War: Its Legacy* (New Haven, CT: Yale University Press, 2009)

Evan Mawdsley, *World War II: A New History, 1937–1945* (Cambridge: Cambridge University Press, 2009)

Mark Mazower, *Hitler's Empire: How the Nazis Ruled Europe* (London: Penguin, 2008)

Williamson Murray and Allan R. Millett, *A War to be Won: Fighting the Second World War* (Cambridge, MA: Belknap Press, 2000)

R. J. Overy, *The Dictators: Hitler's Germany and Stalin's Russia* (New York: W. W. Norton, 2004)

———., *Why the Allies Won* (New York: W. W. Norton, 1995)

Mark P. Parillo, ed., *We Were in the Big One: Experiences of the World War II Generation* (Wilmington, DE: Scholarly Resources, 2002)

R. A. C. Parker, *The Second World War: A Short History* (Oxford: Oxford University Press, 1985; rev. ed. 2002)

Robert O. Paxton, *The Anatomy of Fascism* (New York: Knopf, 2004)

Margaret E. Wagner et al., *The Library of Congress World War II Companion* (New York: Simon & Schuster, 2007)

Gerhard L. Weinberg, *A World at Arms: A Global History of World War II* (Cambridge: Cambridge University Press, 1994; 2nd ed. 2005)

ORIGINS

Michael A. Barnhart, *Japan Prepares for Total War: The Search for Economic Security, 1919–1941* (Ithaca, NY: Cornell University Press, 1988)

P. M. H. Bell, *The Origins of the Second World War in Europe* (London: Longman, 1986)

Akira Iriye, *The Origins of the Second World War in Asia and the Pacific* (London: Longman, 1987)

Gordon Martel, ed., *The Origins of the Second World War Reconsidered* (London: Allen & Unwin, 1986)

A. J. P. Taylor, *The Origins of the Second World War* (London: Hamilton, 1961)

D. C. Watt, *How War Came: The Immediate Origins of the Second World War, 1938–1939* (New York: Pantheon, 1989)

Jonathan Wright, *Germany and the Origins of the Second World War* (Houndmills: Palgrave Macmillan, 2007)

CAMPAIGNS AND BATTLES

Antony Beevor, *Stalingrad* (New York: Viking, 1998)

———., *The Fall of Berlin 1945* (New York: Viking, 2002)

———., *D-Day: The Battle for Normandy* (New York: Viking, 2009)

Thomas J. Cutler, *The Battle of Leyte Gulf* (New York: HarperCollins, 1994)

John Erickson, *The Road to Stalingrad* (New York: Harper & Row, 1975)

———., *The Road to Berlin: Continuing the History of Stalin's War with Germany* (Boulder, CO: Westview Press, 1983)

Richard B. Frank, *Guadalcanal* (New York: Random House, 1990)

David Glantz and Jonathan House, *The Battle of Kursk* (Lawrence: University of Kansas Press, 1995)

Evan Mawdsley, *Thunder in the East: The Nazi-Soviet War, 1941–1945* (Oxford: Oxford University Press, 2006)

Rolf-Dieter Müller and Gerd R. Überschär, *Hitler's War in the East, 1941–1945* (Providence, RI: Berghahn Books, 1997; rev. 3rd ed., New York: Berghahn Books, 2008)

Hugh Sebag-Montefiore, *Dunkirk: Fight to the Last Man* (Cambridge, MA: Harvard University Press, 2006)

David Stahel, *Operation Barbarossa and Germany's Defeat in the East* (Cambridge: Cambridge University Press, 2009)

Mark Stoller, *Allies in War: Britain and America Against the Axis Powers, 1940–1945* (London: Hodder Arnold, 2005)

Wolfgang Wette, *Wehrmacht: History, Myth, Reality* (Cambridge, MA: Harvard University Press, 2006)

Olivier Wieviorka, *Normandy: The Landings to the Liberation of Paris* (Cambridge, MA: Harvard University Press, 2008)

AERIAL WAR

Conrad C. Crane, *Bombs, Cities and Civilians: American Air Power Strategy in World War II* (Lawrence: University of Kansas Press, 1993)

Tami Biddle Davis, *Rhetoric and Reality in Air Warfare: The Evolution of British and American Ideas about Strategic Bombing, 1914–1945* (Princeton, NJ: Princeton University Press, 2002)

Williamson Murray, *Luftwaffe* (London: Allen & Unwin, 1985)

Richard J. Overy, *The Air War, 1939–1945* (New York: Stein & Day, 1980)

———., *The Battle of Britain: the Myth and the Reality* (New York: W. W. Norton, 2001)

Ronald Schaffer, *Wings of Judgment: American Bombing in World War II* (New York: Oxford University Press, 1985)

Michael Sherry, *The Rise of American Air Power: The Creation of Armageddon* (New Haven, CT: Yale University Press, 1987)

Marilyn B. Young and Yuki Tanaka, eds., *Bombing Civilians: A Twentieth-Century History* (New York: New Press, 2009)

NAVAL WAR

Corelli Barnett, *Engage the Enemy More Closely: The Royal Navy in the Second World War* (New York: W. W. Norton, 1991)

Clay Blair, *Silent Victory: The U.S. Submarine War Against Japan* (Philadelphia: Lippincott, 1975)

———., *Hitler's U-Boat War: The Hunters, 1939–1942* (New York: Random House, 1996)

———., *Hitler's U-Boat War: The Hunted, 1942–1945* (New York: Random House, 1998)

Paul S. Dull, *Battle History of the Imperial Japanese Navy, 1941–1945* (Annapolis, MD: U.S. Naval Institute Press, 1978)

Nathan Miller, *War at Sea: Naval History of World War II* (New York: Oxford University Press, 1995)

Mark P. Parillo, *The Japanese Merchant Marine in World War II* (Annapolis, MD: U.S. Naval Institute Press, 1993)

Dan Van der Vat, *The Atlantic Campaign: World War II's Great Struggle at Sea* (New York: Harper & Row, 1988)
———., *The Pacific Campaign: World War II, the U.S.-Japanese Naval War, 1941–1945* (New York: Simon & Schuster, 1991)

COUNTRIES AND REGIONS

Africa

John Bierman and Colin Smith, *War Without Hate: The Desert Campaign of 1940–1943* (New York: Penguin, 2002)
Ashley Jackson, *Botswana, 1939–1945: An African Country at War* (Oxford: Clarendon Press, 1999)
David Killingray and Richard Rathbone, eds., *Africa and the Second World War* (Basingstoke: Macmillan, 1986)
Martin Kitchen, *Rommel's Desert War: Waging World War II in North Africa, 1941–1943* (Cambridge: Cambridge University Press, 2009)

Asia

Christopher Bayly and Tim Harper, *Forgotten Armies: The Fall of British Asia, 1941–1945* (Cambridge, MA: Harvard University Press, 2005)
———., *Forgotten Wars: Freedom and Revolution in Southeast Asia* (Cambridge, MA: Harvard University Press, 2007)
Timothy Brook, *Collaboration: Japanese Agents and Local Elites in Wartime China* (Cambridge, MA: Harvard University Press, 2005)
Robert Butow, *Japan's Decision to Surrender* (Stanford, CA: Stanford University Press, 1954)
Richard Calichman, *Overcoming Modernity: Cultural Identity in Wartime Japan* (New York: Columbia University Press, 2008)
Haruko T. Cook and Theodore F. Cook, eds., *Japan at War: An Oral History* (New York: New Press, 1992)
Gavan Davis, *Prisoners of the Japanese* (New York: Morrow, 1994)
John Dower, *War without Mercy: Race and Power in the Pacific War* (New York: Pantheon, 1986)
Edward Dreyer, *China at War, 1901–1949* (London: Longman, 1995)
Richard B. Frank, *Downfall: the End of the Imperial Japanese Empire* (New York: Random House, 1999)
Tsuyoshi Hasegawa, *Racing the Enemy: Stalin, Truman, and the Surrender of Japan* (Cambridge, MA: Belknap Press, 2005)

Eri Hotta, *Pan-Asianism and Japan's War, 1931–1945* (London: Palgrave Macmillan, 2007)
Akira Iriye, *Power and Culture: The Japanese-American War, 1941–1945* (Cambridge, MA: Harvard University Press, 1981)
Stephen R. MacKinnon, *Wuhan, 1938: War, Refugees, and the Making of Modern China* (Berkeley: University of California Press, 2008)
Stephen R. Mackinnon, Diana Lary, and Ezra F. Vogel eds., *China at War: Regions of China, 1937–45* (Stanford, CA: Stanford University Press, 2007)
E. Bruce Reynolds, *Thailand's Secret War: The Free Thai, OSS, and SOE during World War II* (Cambridge: Cambridge University Press, 2005)
Andrew J. Rotter, *Hiroshima: The World's Bomb* (New York: Oxford University Press, 2008)
Michael Schaller, *The U.S. Crusade in China, 1939–1945* (New York: Columbia University Press, 1979)
Peter Schrijvers, *The GI War against Japan: American Soldiers in Asia and the Pacific during World War II* (New York: New York University Press, 2002)
Jagdish N. Sinha, *Science, War, and Imperialism: India in the Second World War* (Boston: Brill, 2008)
Ronald Spector, *The Eagle against the Sun: The American War with Japan* (New York: Macmillan, 1985)
Christopher Thorne, *Allies of a Kind: The United States and the War Against Japan, 1941–1945* (New York: Oxford University Press, 1985)

Austria

Robert H. Keyserlingk, *Austria in World War II: An Anglo-American Dilemma* (Kingston: McGill-Queen's University Press, 1988)
Tim Kirk, *Nazism and the Working Class in Austria: Industrial Unrest and Political Dissent in the National Community* (Cambridge: Cambridge University Press, 1996)

Britain

Paul Addison, *The Road to 1945* (London: Jonathan Cape, 1975)
Steven Brooke, *Labour's War: The Labour Party during the Second World War* (Oxford: Clarendon Press, 1992)
Angus Calder, *The People's War: Britain, 1939–1945* (New York: Pantheon, 1969)
Tom Harrisson, *Living through the Blitz* (New York: Schocken, 1976)
David Reynolds, *Rich Relations: The American Occupation of Britain, 1942–1945* (New York: Random House, 1995)

Sonya O. Rose, *Which People's War? National Identity and Citizenship in Wartime Britain* (Oxford: Oxford University Press, 2003)

Andrew Thorpe, *Parties at War: Political Organization in Second World War Britain* (New York: Oxford University Press, 2009)

Clair Wills, *That Neutral Island: A Cultural History of Ireland During the Second World War* (Cambridge, MA: Belknap Press, 2007)

Colonial Empires

Ruth Ginio, *French Colonialism Unmasked: The Vichy Years in French West Africa* (Lincoln: University of Nebraska Press, 2006)

Ashley Jackson, *The British Empire and the Second World War* (London: Hambledon Continuum, 2006; new ed. 2007)

Martin Thomas, *The French Empire at War, 1940–1945* (Manchester and New York: Manchester University Press and St. Martin's, 1998)

Eastern Europe

Karel Berkhoff, *Harvest of Despair: Life and Death in Ukraine under Nazi Rule* (Cambridge, MA: Harvard University Press, 2004)

Chad Bryant, *Nazi Rule and Czech Nationalism* (Cambridge, MA: Harvard University Press, 2007)

Mark Cornwall, *Czechoslovakia in a Nationalist and Fascist Europe, 1918–1948* (Oxford: Oxford University Press, 2007)

Cecil D. Eby, *Hungary at War: Civilians and Soldiers in World War II* (University Park: Penn State Press, 1998, 2007)

Marko Attila Hoare, *Genocide and Resistance in Hitler's Bosnia: The Partisans and the Chetniks, 1941–1943* (Oxford: Oxford University Press, 2006)

Steven Pavlowitch, *Hitler's New Disorder: The Second World War in Yugoslavia* (New York: Columbia University Press, 2008)

P. T. Rutherford, *Prelude to the Final Solution: The Nazi Program for Deporting Ethnic Poles, 1939–1941* (Lawrence: University Press of Kansas, 2007)

Ben Shephard, *War in the Wild East: The German Army and Soviet Partisans* (Cambridge, MA: Harvard University Press, 2004)

France

Hanna Diamond, *Fleeing Hitler: France 1940* (Oxford: Oxford University Press, 2007)

Hanna Diamond and Simon Kitson, eds., *Vichy, Resistance, Liberation: New Perspectives on Wartime France* (Oxford: Berg, 2005)

Shannon L. Fogg, *The Politics of Everyday Life in Vichy France: Foreigners, Undesirables, and Strangers* (Cambridge: Cambridge University Press, 2008)

Robert Gildea, *Marianne in Chains: Daily Life in the Heart of France during the German Occupation* (New York: Metropolitan Books, 2003)

Gerhard Hirschfeld and Patrick Marsh, *Collaboration in France: Politics and Culture during the Nazi Occupation, 1940–1944* (Oxford: Berg, 1989)

Julian Jackson, *France: The Dark Years, 1940–1944* (Oxford: Oxford University Press, 2001; new ed., 2003)

———., *The Fall of France: The Nazi Invasion of 1940* (Oxford: Oxford University Press, 2003)

H. R. Kedward, *Occupied France: Collaboration and Resistance, 1940–1944* (Oxford: Blackwell, 1985)

Simon Kitson, *The Hunt for Nazi Spies: Fighting Espionage in Vichy France* (Chicago: University of Chicago Press, 2008)

Michael R. Marrus and Robert O. Paxton, *Vichy France and the Jews* (New York: Basic Books, 1981; Stanford University Press, 1995)

Ernest R. May, *Strange Victory: Hitler's Conquest of France* (New York: Hill & Wang, 2000)

Robert O. Paxton, *Vichy France* (New York: Knopf, 1972; rev. ed. Columbia University Press, 2001)

Richard Vinen, *The Unfree French: Life under the Occupation* (New Haven, CT: Yale University Press, 2006)

Germany

Omer Bartov, *The Eastern Front, 1941–1945: German Troops and the Barbarisation of Warfare* (New York: St. Martin's, 1986)

———., *Hitler's Army: Soldiers, Nazis, and War in the Third Reich* (New York: Oxford University Press, 1991)

Michael Burleigh, *The Third Reich: A New History* (London: Macmillan, 2000)

Michael Burleigh and Wolfgang Wippermann, *The Racial State: Germany, 1933–1945* (Cambridge: Cambridge University Press, 1993)

Jane Caplan, ed., *Nazi Germany* (Oxford: Oxford University Press, 2008)

David F. Crew, *Hitler and the Nazis: A History in Documents* (New York: Oxford University Press, 2005)

Richard J. Evans, *The Coming of the Third Reich* (London: Penguin, 2003)

———., *The Third Reich in Power* (London: Penguin, 2005)

———., *The Third Reich at War, 1939–1945* (London: Penguin, 2008)

Jörg Friedrich, *The Fire: The Bombing of Germany, 1940–1945* (New York: Columbia University Press, 2006)

Stephen G. Fritz, *Endkampf: Soldiers, Civilians, and the Death of the Third Reich* (Lexington: University of Kentucky Press, 2004)

———., *Frontsoldaten: The German Soldier in World War II* (Lexington: University of Kentucky Press, 1995)

Peter Fritzsche, *Life and Death in the Third Reich* (Cambridge, MA: Belknap Press, 2008)

———., *Germans into Nazis* (Cambridge, MA: Harvard University Press, 1998)

Detlef Garbe, *Between Resistance and Martyrdom: Jehovah's Witnesses in the Third Reich* (Madison: University of Wisconsin Press, 2007)

Robert Gellately, *The Gestapo and German Society: Enforcing Racial Policy, 1933–1945* (Oxford: Oxford University Press, 1990)

———., *Backing Hitler: Consent and Coercion in Nazi Germany* (Oxford: Oxford University Press, 2001)

Robert Gellately and Nathan Stoltzfus, eds., *Social Outsiders in Nazi Germany* (Princeton, NJ: Princeton University Press, 2001)

Neil Gregor, *Daimler-Benz in the Third Reich* (New Haven, CT: Yale University Press, 1998)

Peter Hayes, *Industry and Ideology: IG Farben in the Nazi Era* (Cambridge: Cambridge University Press, 1987)

Marion A. Kaplan, *Between Dignity and Despair: Jewish Life in Nazi Germany* (New York: Oxford University Press, 1998)

Michael Kater, *Hitler Youth* (Cambridge, MA: Harvard University Press, 2004)

Ian Kershaw, *Popular Opinion and Political Dissent in the Third Reich: Bavaria, 1933–1945* (Oxford: Oxford University Press, 1983)

Tim Kirk, *Nazi Germany* (Houndmills: Palgrave Macmillan, 2006)

Claudia Koonz, *The Nazi Conscience* (Cambridge, MA: Belknap Press, 2003)

Victor Klemperer, *I Will Bear Witness: A Diary of the Nazi Years*, 2 vols. (New York: Modern Library, 1999-2001)

Robert J. Lifton, *The Nazi Doctors: Medical Killing and the Psychology of Genocide* (New York: Basic Books, 1986, 2000)

Alan Milward, *The German Economy at War* (London: Athlone Press, 1965)

Jonathan Petropoulos, *Royals and the Reich: The Princes von Hessen in Nazi Germany* (New York: Oxford University Press, 2006)

Lisa Pine, *Hitler's National Community: Society and Culture in Nazi Germany* (Oxford: Oxford University Press, 2007)

Raffael Scheck, *Hitler's African Victims: The German Army Massacres of Black French Soldiers in 1940* (Cambridge: Cambridge University Press, 2006)

Kevin Spicer, *Hitler's Priests: Catholic Clergy and National Socialism* (DeKalb: Northern Illinois University Press, 2008)

Adam Tooze, *The Wages of Destruction: The Making and Breaking of the Nazi Economy* (London: Allen Lane, 2006)

Nikolaus Wachsmann, *Hitler's Prisons: Legal Terror in Nazi Germany* (New Haven, CT: Yale University Press, 2004)

Greece

Mark Mazower, *Inside Hitler's Greece: The Experience of Occupation, 1941–44* (New Haven, CT: Yale University Press, 1993)

Italy

R. J. Bosworth, *Mussolini's Italy: Life Under the Dictatorship, 1915–1945* (New York: Penguin, 2006)

John Gooch, *Mussolini and his Generals: The Armed Forces and Fascist Foreign Policy, 1922–1940* (Cambridge: Cambridge University Press, 2008)

Macgregor Knox, *Hitler's Italian Allies: Royal Armed Forces, Fascist Regime, and the War of 1940–43* (Cambridge: Cambridge University Press, 2000)

———., *Mussolini Unleashed, 1939–1941: Politics and Strategy in Fascist Italy's Last War* (Cambridge: Cambridge University Press, 1982)

Philip Morgan, *The Fall of Mussolini: Italians and the War, 1940–1945* (Oxford: Oxford University Press, 2007)

Davide Rodogno, *Facism's European Empire: Italian Occupation during the Second World War* (Cambridge: Cambridge University Press, 2006)

Joshua D. Zimmerman, *The Jews of Italy under Fascist and Nazi Rule, 1922–1945* (Cambridge: Cambridge University Press, 2005)

Latin America

Max Paul Friedman, *Nazis and Good Neighbors: The United States Campaign against the Germans of Latin America in World War II* (Cambridge: Cambridge University Press, 2003)

R. A. Humphreys, *Latin America and the Second World War*, 2 vols. (Atlantic Highlands, NJ: Humanities Press, 1981–1982)

Thomas M. Leonard and John F. Bratzel, eds., *Latin America during World War II* (Lanham, MD: Rowman & Littlefield, 2007)

Netherlands

Bob Moore, *Victims and Survivors: The Nazi Persecution of the Jews in the Netherlands, 1940–1945* (London: Arnold, 1997)

Werner Warmbrunn, *The Dutch under German Occupation* (Stanford, CA: Stanford University Press, 1983)

Soviet Union

John Barber and Mark Harrison, *The Soviet Home Front: A Social and Economic History of the USSR in World War II* (London: Longman, 1991)

Chris Bellamy, *Absolute War: Soviet Russia in the Second World War* (New York: Knopf, 2007)

Boris Gorbachevsky, *Through the Maelstrom: A Red Army Soldier's War on the Eastern Front, 1942–1945* (Lawrence: University Press of Kansas, 2008)

Catherine Merridale, *Ivan's War: Life and Death in the Red Army, 1939–1945* (New York: Metropolitan Books, 2006)

Robert W. Thurston and Bernd Bonwetsch, *The People's War: Responses to World War II in the Soviet Union* (Urbana: University of Illinois Press, 2000)

Amir Weiner, *Making Sense of War: The Second World War and the Fate of the Bolshevik Revolution* (Princeton, NJ: Princeton University Press, 2001)

United States

Luis Alvarez, *The Power of the Zoot: Youth Culture and Resistance during World War II* (Berkeley: University of California Press, 2008)

Rick Atkinson, *An Army at Dawn: The War in North Africa, 1942–1943* (New York: Henry Holt, 2002)

———., *The Day of Battle: The War in Sicily and Italy, 1943–1944* (New York: Henry Holt, 2007)

Robert Dallek, *Franklin D. Roosevelt and American Foreign Policy, 1932–1945* (New York: Oxford University Press, 1979)

Roger Daniels, *Prisoners on Trial: Japanese Americans in World War II* (New York: Hill & Wang, 1993)

Lewis A. Erenberg and Susan Hirsch, eds., *The War in American Culture: Society and Consciousness during World War II* (Chicago: University of Chicago Press, 1996)

Richard Griswold del Castillo, *World War II and Mexican American Civil Rights* (Austin: University of Texas Press, 2008)

David Kennedy, *Freedom from Fear: The American People in Depression and War, 1929–1945* (New York: Oxford University Press, 1999)

Lee Kennett, *GI: The American Soldier in World War II* (New York: Scribner's, 1987)

Nelson Lichtenstein, *Labor's War at Home: The CIO in World War II* (New York: Cambridge University Press, 1982)

Gerald Linderman, *The World Within War: America's Combat Experience in World War II* (New York: Free Press, 1997)

Judy Barrett Litoff and David Smith, eds., *Dear Boys: World War II Letters from a Woman Back Home* (Jackson, MS.: University Press of Mississippi, 1991)

Sean L. Malloy, *Atomic Tragedy: Henry L. Stimson and the Decision to Use the Bomb Against Japan* (Ithaca, NY: Cornell University Press, 2008)

Eric L. Muller, *American Inquisition: The Hunt for Japanese American Disloyalty in World War II* (Chapel Hill: University of North Carolina Press, 2007)

William L. O'Neill, *Democracy at War: America's Fight at Home and Abroad in World War II* (New York: Free Press, 1993)

Kenneth D. Rose, *Myth and the Greatest Generation: A Social History of Americans in World War II* (New York: Routledge, 2008)

Andrew Jon Rotter, *Hiroshima: The World's Bomb* (Oxford: Oxford University Press, 2008)

Ben Shephard, *A War of Nerves: Soldiers and Psychiatrists in the Twentieth Century* (Cambridge, MA: Harvard University Press, 2001)

Martin J. Sherwin, *A World Destroyed: The Atomic Bomb and the Grand Alliance* (New York: Knopf, 1975)

Ronald Smelser and Edward J. Davies II, *The Myth of the Eastern Front: The Nazi-Soviet War in American Popular Culture* (Cambridge: Cambridge University Press, 2008)

K. Scott Wong, *Americans First: Chinese Americans and the Second World War* (Philadelphia: Temple University Press, 2008)

Emilio Zamora, *Claiming Rights and Righting Wrongs in Texas: Mexican Workers and Job Politics during World War II* (College Station: Texas A&M University Press, 2009)

BIOGRAPHY

Paul Addison, *Churchill: The Unexpected Hero* (Oxford: Oxford University Press, 2005)

Steven E. Ambrose, *Eisenhower*, 2 vols. (New York: Simon & Schuster, 1983–1984)

Geoffrey Best, *Churchill: A Study in Greatness* (London: Hambledon, 2001)

Herbert P. Bix, *Hirohito and the Making of Modern Japan* (New York: HarperCollins, 2000)

R. J. B. Bosworth, *Mussolini* (London: Arnold; New York: Oxford University Press, 2002)

James MacGregor Burns, *Roosevelt: The Soldier of Freedom* (New York: Harcourt Brace, 1970)

Alvin D. Coox, *Tojo* (New York: Ballantine Books, 1975)

Richard B. Frank, *MacArthur* (New York: Palgrave Macmillan, 2007)

Robert Gellately, *Lenin, Stalin, and Hitler: The Age of Social Catastrophe* (New York: Knopf, 2007)

Nigel Hamilton, *Monty: The Making of a General, 1887–1942* (New York: McGraw-Hill, 1981)

———., *Master of the Battlefield: Monty's War Years, 1942–1944* (New York: McGraw-Hill, 1983)

———., *Monty: Final Years of the Field Marshal, 1944–1976* (New York: McGraw-Hill, 1986)

Ian Kershaw, *Hitler, 1889–1936: Hubris* (London: Penguin, 1998)

———., *Hitler, 1936–1945: Nemesis* (London: Penguin, 2000)

Forrest Pogue, *George C. Marshall: Ordeal and Hope, 1939–42* (New York: Viking, 1963)

———., *George C. Marshall: Organizer of Victory, 1943–1945* (New York: Viking, 1973)

Simon Sebag-Montefiore, *Stalin: The Court of the Red Tsar* (New York: Knopf, 2004)

ECONOMIC MOBILIZATION

Wolf Gruner, *Jewish Forced Labor under the Nazis: Economic Needs and Racial Aims, 1938–1944* (New York: Cambridge University Press, 2006)

W. K. Hancock and M. Gowing, *The British War Economy* (London: H.M.S.O., 1949)

Mark Harrison, ed., *The Economics of World War II: Six Great Powers in International Comparison* (Cambridge: Cambridge University Press, 1998)

Ulrich Herbert, *Hitler's Foreign Workers: Enforced Foreign Labor in Germany under the Third Reich* (Cambridge: Cambridge University Press, 1997)

Alan Milward, *The German Economy at War* (London: Athlone Press, 1965)

———., *War, Economy, and Society, 1939–1945* (Berkeley: University of California Press, 1977)

J. Adam Tooze, *The Wages of Destruction: The Making and Breaking of the Nazi Economy* (New York: Viking, 2007)

Ina Zweininger-Bargielowska, *Austerity in Britain: Rationing, Controls, and Consumption, 1939–1955* (Oxford: Oxford University Press, 2000)

WOMEN AND GENDER

Allan Berubé, *Coming Out Under Fire: The History of Gay Men and Women in World War Two* (New York: Free Press, 1990)

D'Ann Campbell, *Women at War with America: Private Lives in a Patriotic Era* (Cambridge, MA: Harvard University Press, 1984)

Robert Gellately and Nathan Stoltzfus, eds., *Social Outsiders in Nazi Germany* (Princeton, NJ: Princeton University Press, 2001)

Victoria de Grazia, *How Fascism Ruled Women: Italy, 1922–1945* (Berkeley: University of California Press, 1991)

Susan Hartmann, *The Homefront and Beyond: American Women in the 1940's* (Boston: Twayne, 1982)

Elizabeth Harvey, *Women and the Nazi East: Agents and Witnesses of Germanization* (New Haven, CT: Yale University Press, 2003)

Marion Kaplan, *Between Dignity and Despair: Jewish Life in Nazi Germany* (New York: Oxford University Press, 1998)

Claudia Koonz, *Mothers in the Fatherland: Women, the Family, and Nazi Politics* (New York: St. Martin's Press, 1987)

Dalia Ofer and Lenore J. Weitzman, *Women in the Holocaust* (New Haven, CT: Yale University Press, 1998)

Alison Owings, ed., *German Women Recall the Third Reich* (New Brunswick, NJ: Rutgers University Press, 1993)

Richard Plant, *The Pink Triangle: The Nazi War against Homosexuals* (New York: Henry Holt, 1986)

Catherine S. Ramírez, *The Woman in the Zoot Suit: Gender, Nationalism, and the Cultural Politics of Memory* (Durham, NC: Duke University Press, 2009)

Dagmar Reese, *Growing Up Female in Nazi Germany*, trans. William Templer (Ann Arbor: University of Michigan Press, 2006)

Jill Stephenson, *Women in Nazi Germany* (London: Longman, 2001)

Matthew Stibbe, *Women in the Third Reich* (London: Arnold, 2003)

Toshiyuki Tanaka, *Japan's Comfort Women: Sexual Slavery and Prostitution during World War II and the US Occupation* (London: Routledge, 2002)

FILM/THE ARTS

Jeanine Basinger, *The World War II Combat Film: Anatomy of a Genre* (New York: Columbia University Press, 1986)

Jo Berg, *Film Propaganda in Britain and Nazi Germany: World War II Cinema* (Oxford: Berg, 2007)

John W. Chambers II and David Culbert, eds., *World War II: Film and History* (New York: Oxford University Press, 1996)

Heidi Fehrenbach, *Cinema in Democratizing Germany: Reconstructing National Identity after Hitler* (Chapel Hill: University of North Carolina Press, 1995)

Gerd Horten, *Radio Goes to War: The Culture Politics of Propaganda During World War II* (Berkeley: University of California Press, 2002)

Jonathan Huener and Francis R. Nicosia, eds., *The Arts in Nazi Germany: Continuity, Conformity, Change* (Oxford: Berghahn Books, 2006)

Annette Insdorf, *Indelible Shadows: Film and the Holocaust* (Cambridge: Cambridge University Press, 2002)

Michael Kater, *The Twisted Muse: Musicians and their Music in the Third Reich* (New York: Oxford University Press, 1997)

Clayton Koppes and Gregory D. Black, *Hollywood Goes to War: How Politics, Profits, and Propaganda Shaped World War II Movies* (New York: Free Press, 1987)

Michael Paris, ed., *Repicturing the Second World War: Representations in Film and Television* (Houndmills: Palgrave Macmillan, 2007)

David Welky, *The Moguls and the Dictators: Hollywood and the Coming of World War II* (Baltimore, MD: Johns Hopkins University Press, 2008)

Allan M. Winkler, *The Politics of Propaganda: The Office of War Information* (New Haven, CT: Yale University Press, 1978)

HOLOCAUST

Shlomo Aronson, *Hitler, the Allies, and the Jews* (Cambridge: Cambridge University Press, 2004)

Abraham Ascher, *A Community under Siege: The Jews of Breslau under Nazism* (Stanford, CA: Stanford University Press, 2007)

David Bankier, *The Germans and the Final Solution: Public Opinion under Nazism* (Oxford: Oxford University Press, 1992)

David Bankier and Israel Gutman, eds., *Nazi Europe and the Final Solution* (Jerusalem: Yad Vashem, 2003)

Omer Bartov, *Murder in Our Midst: The Holocaust, Industrial Killing, and Representation* (New York: Oxford University Press, 1996)

———., *Mirrors of Destruction: War, Genocide and Modern Identity* (Oxford: Oxford University Press, 2000)

———., *Germany's War and the Holocaust: Disputed Histories* (Ithaca, NY: Cornell University Press, 2003)

Yehuda Bauer, *Rethinking the Holocaust* (New Haven, CT: Yale University Press, 2001)

Doris L. Bergen, *War and Genocide: A Concise History of the Holocaust* (Lanham, MD: Rowman & Littlefield, 2003)

Steven B. Bowman, *The Agony of Greek Jews, 1940–1945* (Stanford, CA: Stanford University Press, 2008)

Ray Brandon and Wendy Lower, eds., *The Shoah in Ukraine: History, Testimony, Memorialization* (Bloomington: Indiana University Press, 2008)

Richard Breitman, Norman Gode, Timothy Naftali, Robert Wolfe, eds., *U.S. Intelligence and the Nazis* (Cambridge: Cambridge University Press, 2005)

Richard Breitman, *Architect of Genocide: Himmler and the Final Solution* (New York: Knopf, 1991)

———., *Official Secrets: What the Nazis Planned, What the British and Americans Knew* (New York: Hill & Wang, 1998)

Christopher Browning, *Ordinary Men: Reserve Police Battalion 101 and the Final Solution in Poland* (New York: HarperCollins, 1992)

Christopher R. Browning, Richard S. Hollander, and Nechama Tec, eds., *Every Day Lasts a Year: A Jewish Family's Correspondence from Poland* (New York: Cambridge University Press, 2007)

Christopher R. Browning and Jürgen Matthäus, *The Origins of the Final Solution: The Evolution of Nazi Jewish Policy, September 1939–March 1942* (Lincoln: University of Nebraska Press, 2004)

Martin Dean, *Robbing the Jews: The Confiscation of Jewish Property in the Holocaust, 1933–1945* (Cambridge: Cambridge University Press, 2008)

Debórah Dwork, *Children with a Star: Jewish Youth in Nazi Europe* (New Haven, CT: Yale University Press, 1991)

Debórah Dwork and R. J. van Pelt, *Holocaust: A History* (New York: W. W. Norton, 2002)

Eric Ehrenreich, *The Nazi Ancestral Proof: Genealogy, Racial Science, and the Final Solution* (Bloomington: Indiana University Press, 2007)

Barbara Epstein, *The Minsk Ghetto, 1941–1943: Jewish Resistance and Soviet Internationalism* (Berkeley: University of California Press, 2008)

Frieda Forman, *Jewish Refugees in Switzerland during the Holocaust: A Memoir of Childhood and History* (London: Vallentine Mitchell, 2009)

Henry Friedländer, *The Years of Extermination: Nazi Germany and the Jews, 1939–1945* (New York: HarperCollins, 2007)

———., *The Origins of Nazi Genocide: From Euthanasia to the Final Solution* (Chapel Hill: University of North Carolina Press, 1995)

Daniel J. Goldhagen, *Hitler's Willing Executioners: Ordinary Germans and the Holocaust* (New York: Knopf, 1996)

Israel Gutman, *Resistance: The Warsaw Ghetto Uprising* (Boston: Houghton Mifflin, 1994)

Israel Gutman, ed., *Encyclopedia of the Holocaust*, 4 vols. (New York: Macmillan, 1990)

Patrick Henry, *We Know Only Men: The Rescue of Jews in France during the Holocaust* (Washington, DC: Catholic University Press, 2007)

Jeffrey Herf, *The Jewish Enemy: Nazi Propaganda during World War II and the Holocaust* (Cambridge, MA: Belknap Press, 2006)

Raul Hilberg, *The Destruction of the European Jews* (Chicago: Quadrangle Books, 1961; 3rd ed. Yale University Press, 2003)

———., *Perpetrators, Victims, Bystanders: The Jewish Catastrophe, 1933–1945* (London: Secker & Warburg, 1992)

Gordon J. Horwitz, *Ghettostadt: Lodz and the Making of a Nazi City* (Cambridge, MA: Harvard University Press, 2008)

Radu Ioanid, *The Holocaust in Romania: The Destruction of Jews and Gypsies under the Antonescu Regime, 1940–1944* (Chicago: Ivan R. Dee, 2000)

Thomas Pegelow, *The Language of Nazi Genocide. Linguistic Violence and the Struggle of Germans of Jewish Ancestry* (Cambridge: Cambridge University Press, 2009)

Ian Kershaw, *Hitler, the Germans, and the Final Solution* (New Haven, CT: Yale University Press, 2008)

Victor Klemperer, *I Will Bear Witness: A Diary of the Nazi Years*, 2 (vols.) (New York: Modern Library, 1999–2001)

Robert J. Lifton, *The Nazi Doctors: Medical Killing and the Psychology of Genocide* (New York: Basic Books, 1986, 2000)

Peter Longerich, *The Nazi Persecution and Murder of the Jews* (Oxford: Oxford University Press, 2010)

Wendy Lower, *Nazi Empire Building and the Holocaust in Ukraine* (Chapel Hill: University of North Carolina Press, 2005)

Kristen Renwick Moore, *The Hand of Compassion: Portraits of Moral Choice during the Holocaust* (Princeton, NJ: Princeton University Press, 2004)

Michael Phayer, *Pius XII, the Holocaust, and the Cold War* (Bloomington: Indiana University Press, 2007)

———., *The Catholic Church and the Holocaust, 1930–1965* (Bloomington: Indiana University Press, 2000)

Hans Safrian, *Eichmann's Men* (Cambridge: Cambridge University Press, 2009)

Flora M. Singer, *Flora: I was but a Child* (New York: Yad Vashem, 2007)

Jonathan Steinberg, *All or Nothing: The Axis and the Holocaust, 1941–1943* (London: Routledge, 1990)

Alan E. Steinweis, *Studying the Jew: Scholarly Antisemitism in Nazi Germany* (Cambridge, MA: Harvard University Press, 2008)

Susan Zuccotti, *The Italians and the Holocaust: Persecution, Rescue, and Survival* (New York: Basic Books, 1987)

———., *The Holocaust, the French, and the Jews* (New York: Basic Books, 1993)

RESISTANCE

Peter Hoffman, *The History of German Resistance 1933–1945* (Cambridge, MA: MIT Press, 1970)

Tim Kirk and Anthony McElligott, eds., *Opposing Fascism: Community, Authority and Resistance in Europe* (Cambridge: Cambridge University Press, 1999)

Klemens von Klemperer, *German Resistance against Hitler: The Search for Allies Abroad, 1938–1945* (Oxford: Oxford University Press, 1993)

David Clay Large, *Contending with Hitler: Varieties of German Resistance in the Third Reich* (Cambridge: Cambridge University Press, 1991)

Hans Mommsen, *Alternatives to Hitler: German Resistance Under the Third Reich* (Princeton, NJ: Princeton University Press, 2003)

———., *Germans against Hitler: The Stauffenberg Plot and Resistance under the Third Reich* (London: I.B.Tauris, 2009)

Bob Moore, *Resistance in Western Europe* (Oxford: Berg, 2000) *Germans against Hitler: The Stauffenberg Plot and Resistance under the Third Reich* (London: I.B. Tauris, 2009)

Nathan Stoltzfus, *Resistance of the Heart: Intermarriage and the Rosenstrasse Protest in Nazi Germany* (New York: W. W. Norton, 1996)

Nechama Tec, *Defiance: The Bielski Partisans* (New York: Oxford University Press, 2008; originally published 1993)

POSTWAR

Thomas Childers, *Soldier from the War Returning: The Greatest Generation's Troubled Homecoming from World War II* (Boston: Houghton Mifflin, 2009)

István Deák, Jan T. Gross, and Tony Judt, eds., *The Politics of Retribution in Europe: World War II and Its Aftermath* (Princeton, NJ: Princeton University Press, 2000)

John Dower, *Embracing Defeat: Japan in the Wake of World War II* (London: Allen Lane, 1999)

John Lewis Gaddis, *The Cold War: A New History* (New York: Penguin, 2005)

William I. Hitchcock, *Liberation 1945: The Allies, the People of Europe, and the Troubled Road to Freedom* (New York: Free Press, 2008)

TRIALS

Donald Bloxham, *Genocide on Trial: War Crimes Trials and the Formation of Holocaust History and Memory* (Oxford: Oxford University Press, 2001)

Robert Cryer and Neil Boister, *The Tokyo International Military Tribunal* (New York: Oxford University Press, 2008)

Patricia Heberer and Jürgen Matthäus, eds., *Atrocities on Trial: Historical Perspectives on the Politics of Prosecuting War Crimes* (Lincoln: University of Nebraska Press, 2008)

Yuma Totani, *The Tokyo War Crimes: The Pursuit of Justice in the Wake of World War II* (Cambridge, MA: Harvard University Press, 2008)

MEMORY

Günter Bischof and Anton Pelinka, eds., *Austrian Historical Memory and National Identity.* Contemporary Austrian Studies, vol. 5 (New Brunswick, NJ: Transaction Publishers, 1997)

R. J. B. Bosworth, *Explaining Auschwitz and Hiroshima: History Writing and the Second World War, 1945–1900* (London: Routledge, 1993)

John Breen, ed., *Yasukuni, the War Dead and the Struggle for Japan's Past* (New York: Columbia University Press, 2008)

Ian Buruma, *The Wages of Guilt: Memories of War in Germany and Japan* (New York: Farrar, Straus & Giroux, 1994)

Richard J. Evans, *Lying about Hitler: History, Holocaust, and the David Irving Trial* (New York: Basic Books, 2001)

Philipp Gassert and Alan E. Steinweis, eds., *Coping with the Nazi Past: West German Debates on Nazism and Generational Conflict, 1955–1975* (New York: Berghahn Books, 2006)

Frank Gibney, ed., *Sensô: Japanese Remember the War* (New York: St. Martin's, 1995)

Pieter Lagrou, *The Legacy of Nazi Occupation: Patriotic Memory and National Recovery in Western Europe, 1945–1965* (Cambridge: Cambridge University Press, 2000)

Edward T. Linenthal, *Preserving Memory: The Struggle to Create America's Holocaust Museum* (New York: Viking, 1995)

Edward T. Linenthal and Tom Engelhardt, eds., *History Wars: The Enola Gay and other Battles for the American Past* (New York: Metropolitan Books, 1996)

Deborah Lipstadt, *History on Trial: My Day in Court with David Irving* (New York: Ecco, 2005)

———., *Denying the Holocaust: The Growing Assault on Truth and Memory* (New York: Free Press, 1993)

Charles S. Maier, *The Unmasterable Past: History, Holocaust, and German National Identity* (Cambridge, MA: Harvard University Press, 1988)

Harold Marcuse, *Legacies of Dachau. The Uses and Abuses of a Concentration Camp, 1933-2001* (Cambridge: Cambridge University Press, 2001)

Chloe Paver, *Refractions of the Third Reich in German and Austrian Fiction and Film* (New York: Oxford University Press, 2007)

David Reynolds, *In Command of History: Churchill Fighting and Writing the Second World War* (New York: Random House, 2005)

Gavriel D. Rosenfeld, *The World Hitler Never Made: Alternate History and the Memory of Nazism* (Cambridge: Cambridge University Press, 2005)

Henry Rousso, *The Vichy Syndrome: History and Memory in France since 1944* (Cambridge, MA: Harvard University Press, 1991)

Philip Seaton, *Japan's Contested War Memories: The "Memory Rifts" in Historical Consciousness of World War II* (London: Routledge, 2007)

Ronald Smelser and Edward J. Davies II, *The Myth of the Eastern Front: The Nazi-Soviet War in American Popular Culture* (Cambridge: Cambridge University Press, 2008)

Susan Rubin Suleiman, *Crises of Memory and the Second World War* (Cambridge, MA: Harvard University Press, 2006)

Studs Terkel, *The "Good War": An Oral History of World War Two* (New York: Pantheon, 1984)

Peter Utgaard, *Remembering and Forgetting Nazism: Education, National Identity, and the Victim Myth in Postwar Austria* (Oxford & New York: Berghahn Books, 2003)

Zoe Vania Waxman, *Writing the Holocaust: Identity, Testimony, Representation* (New York: Oxford University Press, 2007)

James E. Young, *The Texture of Memory: Holocaust Memorials and Meaning* (New Haven, CT: Yale University Press, 1994)

ON-LINE RESOURCES

http://americanhistory.si.edu/militaryhistory The Price of Freedom: Americans at War (hosted by Smithsonian National Museum of American History)

http://www.archives.gov/research/ww2 National Archives, World War II Resources, and Finding Aids

http://www.bbc.co.uk/history/worldwars/wwtwo BBC sponsored site on World War II

http://connections.smsd.org/veterans/wwii_sites.htm World War II Sites

http://www.ddaymuseum.org The National World War II Museum, New Orleans

http://www.densho.org The Japanese American Legacy Project (incarceration World War II)

http://www.euronet.nl/users/wilfried/ww2/ww2.htm The World at War, History of World War 1939–1945

http://www.h-net.org/~war/wwtsa World War II Studies Association

http://www.learningcurve.gov.uk/homefront/default.htm The National Archives, Britain

http://www.museumofworldwarii.com Museum of World War II, Boston

http://www.nasm.si.edu/exhibitions/gal103/gal103_former.html The Enola Gay: Former Exhibition National Air and Space Museum

http://www.pbs.org/wgbh/amex/dday D-Day: American Experience

http://www.ushmm.org/wic/en United States Holocaust Memorial Museum, Holocaust Encyclopedia

http://www.wiesenthal.com Simon Wiesenthal Center

http://www.wwiimemorial.com National World War II Memorial, Washington DC

http://www.yadvashem.org Yad Vashem

INDEX

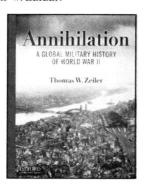
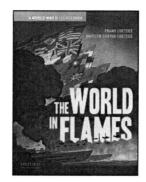

CPSIA information can be obtained at www.ICGtesting.com
Printed in the USA
BVOW06s0544051214

377718BV00004B/13/P

9 780195 174427